NICHOLAS HENRY

Arizona State University

GOVERNING AT THE GRASSROOTS

state
and local
politics

Prentice-Hall, Inc.
Englewood Cliffs, New Jersey 07632

Library of Congress Cataloging in Publication Data

HENRY, NICHOLAS
  Governing at the grassroots.

  Bibliography.
  Includes index.
  1.–State governments. 2.–Local government—United States. I.–Title.
JK2408.H46   320   79-11971
ISBN   0-13-360602-3

To Muriel

Printed in the United States of America

10 9 8 7 6 5 4 3 2 1

Editorial/production supervision
and interior design: Jeanne Hoeting
Cover design: Jerry Pfeifer
Manufacturing buyer: Harry P. Baisley

Selected quotes in Chapter 12 are from "Lindsay of New York" by Larry L. King,
published in *Harper's Magazine*, 237 (No. 1419) and have been reprinted by
permission of The Sterling Lord Agency, Inc. Copyright (c) 1968 by Larry L. King.

PRENTICE-HALL INTERNATIONAL, INC., *London*
PRENTICE-HALL OF AUSTRALIA PTY. LIMITED, *Sydney*
PRENTICE-HALL OF CANADA, LTD., *Toronto*
PRENTICE-HALL OF INDIA PRIVATE LIMITED, *New Delhi*
PRENTICE-HALL OF JAPAN, INC., *Tokyo*
PRENTICE-HALL OF SOUTHEAST ASIA PTE. LTD., *Singapore*
WHITEHALL BOOKS LIMITED, *Wellington, New Zealand*

CONTENTS

Preface, *vii*

PART ONE

PEOPLE, POWER, AND POLITICS

1 The Joy of Politics   3

Political Follies, *4* Americans in an Age of Disillusionment, *7* A Resurrection of State and Local Governments, *8* Americans Slow Down, *9* Two Examples of Grassroots Politics: Sex and Life, *10* Why Study State and Local Politics?, *16* Themes of Governing at the Grassroots, *17*

2 Suburbs, Sunbelt, Snowbelt: The Sweep of   19
   People and Power

The Suburbanization of America, *20* "The Worse Things Get, the Worse Things Get", *22* The Metropolitan Morass, *24* Political Cultures: The Politics of Regionalism, *27*

PART TWO

THE SEMISOVEREIGN STATES

3 Making Governments: Constitutions, Parties,   35
   and the Good Ol' Boys

State Constitutions: Documents of Politics or Principle?, *36* Parties and Politics, *38*

4 Voting: The Ultimate Democratic Act   48

States Stop the Vote, *49* Enfranchising the People: Washington Moves In, *51* The Puzzle of Voting Participation, *53* Who Does Not Vote and Why, *56*

5 Political Pressure   62

Pressure Groups, Power, and Pecking Orders, *63* Power Patterns and Pressure Politics, *66* Politics Without Pressure Groups, *71* The Nitty-Gritty of Legislative Lobbying, *72* Pressure and the Public Interest, *75*

6 The Legislative Drama 77

The Legislative Labyrinth, *78* What Do Legislators Do?, *79* Government by Committee, *79* Electoral Systems, Reapportionment, and Gerrymandering, *82* What Legislators Brawl About, *88* The Realities of Legislative Power, *90* Rules of the Game: Written Ones, *91* Rules of the Game: Unwritten Ones, *92* Breaking the Rules, *93* Who, or What, Uses the Rules?, *95* Who Are Legislators?, *103* The Professionalization of the Legislatures, *107* How Good Are Legislatures? A Problem of Assessment, *109*

7 The Greening of the Governors 115

The Gubernatorial Career, *116* The Governor, the Party, and the Legislature, *119* The Governor and "His" Bureaucracy, *120* Do Governors Govern?, *123* Gubernatorial Style: The Guru of California and the Kingfish of Louisiana, *124*

8 The Politics of Justice 130

The Judicial Scene, *131* The Judicial Style, *135* How and Why Judges Make Public Policy, *136* State Courts as Policy Innovators: The Case of California, *143* Reforming the Courts, *144* Resisting Reform, *149*

PART three

EIGHTY-THOUSAND CREATURES OF THE STATES

9 A Zoo of Governments: Cities, Counties, and Other Oddities 153

Governing Cities, *154* Counties, or the Fading Figure of the Courthouse Gang, *158* Towns and Townships: The Tinier Governments, *165* Multipurpose Districts: Promise V. Practice, *166* Special Districts: Semigovernments of Specialization, *167*

10 The Faces of Federalism 169

Federalism in Turmoil, *170* Of the Constitution and Courts, *173* Governments as Pressure Groups, *175* The Feds and the Revival of Regionalism, *177* The Sates: Sovereignty within Limits, *180* Cities and Other Urban Creatures, *184* Boundaries and Reform: The Problems of Matching People, Policies, and Power, *187* Federalism and the Pyramiding of Power, *195*

11 Power in Communities: Who Plays, Wins, Loses 198

Community: Quarrels Over a Concept, *199* Community Power: Views and Counterviews, *201* The Feds and the "Development" of Community Power, *206* Community Power, Politics, and Participation, *210* Citizens and City Hall, *216* City Councilmembers and City Hall, *218* Conclusion: Paternalism, Power, and Participation, *223*

12 The Urban Executive: Bosses, Mayors, and Managers 224

On Top in the Big City: Boss Rule in City and Suburb, *225* "Hizzoner Da Mare", *227* The Politics of Smooth: The Urban Manager, *237*

PART four

GRASSROOTS BUREAUCRACY

13 Public Administration at the Grassroots — 245

Bureaucrats as Policy Makers, *246* Bureaucracy as Political Technology, *248* The Computer: A Case of Bureaucracy, Technology, and Policy, *250* Public Technology: Science, States, and Cities, *252*

14 Grassroots Bureaucrats — 256

The Civil Service: A Reaction to Patronage, *257* The Power of Public Personnel Administration, *258* How the Merit System Works: The Politics of Complexity, *259* Hiring and (Seldom) Firing Public Bureaucrats, *260* Ol' Lester Versus Rocky: Performance Versus Patronage, *262* The Challenges to "Merit", *264* Public Servants and the Freedom to Be Political: The Challenge of Political Neutrality, *264* Race, Sex, and Jobs: The Challenge of Affirmative Action, *267* Blue-Collar Bureaucrats: The Challenge of Unionism and the Right to Strike, *274* Conclusion: Turmoil in the Public Service, *284*

15 The Public Purse, or Who'll Take Manhattan? — 285

The Growth of Government: The Money Measure, *286* The Intergovernmental Money Game, *288* Purchasing Public Policy: The Local Impact of National Dollars, *294* Problems of the Grant-in-Aid System: Inequity, Distortion, and Confusion, *297* Solutions! Solutions! Revenue Sharing and Bigger Block Grants, *298* Snowbelt Versus Sunbelt: The Grants War, *302* Of Death and Taxes, *304* The Equity Question: Taxes and Fairness, *310* The People's Choice: Taxes and Taxpayers, *316* Revolt!, *318* Paying the Piper: Borrowing and Debt, *319* Who'll Take Manhattan? Hard Times in Fun City, *321* Conclusion, *328*

PART five

POLICIES, CLASS, AND THE GRASSROOTS

16 Policies for the Underclass: The Welfare Mess — 331

Toward a Class Interpretation of Policy, *331* Defining Poverty, *332* Who Is Poor?, *333* Welfare for Whom?, *337* Social Insurance and Public Assistance: The Two Policies for Welfare, *338* Do State and Local Governments Care? The Role of "General Assistance", *342* The Welfare Explosion, *342* Why the Explosion?, *347* Welfare in the States: Chaos or Cynicism?, *349* Has Welfare Worked?, *351* Mismanagement and Welfare: The Big Scandal, *352* Reforming Welfare, *355*

17 Policies for the Underclass: Crime in the Streets — 358

Crime and Poverty, *359* The Poor Protest, *360* The Fear of Crime, *364* The Reality of Crime, *364* What Is Being Done?, *365* Race and the Police, *368* Are the Police Effective?, *369* Alternatives to the Cops, *370* The Courts: Protecting the Accused, *373* The Courts: Protecting Society, *375* Prisons: "Factories of Crime", *378* Crime and Punishment, *380*

18 Policies for the Middle Class: The Education Establishment 384

Paying for Schools: Who Does and Who Should?, *385* Who Runs the Schools?, *392* Do Kids Learn? Not Lately, *395* The Three V's: Violence, Vandalism, and Venality, *396* Collectivizing Teachers, *397* Politicizing Teachers, *399* Race and Schools, *400* Higher Education: Cracks in the Ivory Tower, *406*

19 Policies for the Middle Class: The Planning Ethic 411

The Roots of Urban Planning, *412* The Federal Government and the Power to Plan, *415* Planners, Power, and Politics, *416* The Politics of the Planning Process: Land Use, *419* The Politics of the Planning Process: Transportation, *424*

20 Policies for the Middle Class: Home, Hearth, and Racism 432

Housing: America's Most Racist Policy, *433* The Reasons for Racism, *437* The Federal Role: Making Homes for Middle America, *441* The State and Local Role: Planning Public Housing for Poor People, *443* Home Is Where the House Is: The Future of American Housing, *448*

21 Policies for the Upper Class: Corruption and the Cosa Nostra 451

Corruption, the High Roller of Politics, *452* Kinds of Corruption, *452* "Honest Graft": Examples of Individual Corruption, *454* From Honest Graft to Systemic Corruption: Two Cases of Transition, *455* Systemic Corruption: The Impact of Organized Crime, *458* What Must Be Done?, *467* What Is Being Done?, *469*

Glossary 474

Appendix A. Research Resources in State and Local Government and Politics 485

Appendix B. Major Journals and Periodicals on State and Local Government and Politics and Related Policy Areas 489

Appendix C. Selected Academic, Professional, and Public Interest Organizations, with Addresses 493

Appendix D. How to Address Public Officials 497

Index 499

PREFACE

"Shame! Shame!" The cry is occasionally heard from the back benches of Parliament when a speaker has said something that strikes the opposition party as dreadful. It is a cry that might be echoed after perusing the literature on state and local politics.

This book attempts to rectify at least some of the dullness associated with the study of state and local politics. The better examples of significant research on various facets of state and local politics are put forth, but put forth somewhat differently from standard texts. An emphasis is placed on suburban politics, the politics of bureaucracies, regional politics, politicians as social-psychological actors, and the conflicts between social classes. While some of these themes are present in other books, *Governing at the Grassroots* stresses these facets of state and local government. It covers topics that are either omitted or present only peripherally in other texts—notably the "second civil war" between the Sunbelt and Snowbelt, the politics of a suburbanized America, the grassroots bureaucrats, state and urban planning, public administration, political corruption, and organized crime, among others. Similarly, public finance, while a standard textbook subject, is examined with considerable care, for not since the 1930s has public finance been as important as it currently is. Thus, the financial demise (or, at least, the soaring fiscal fever) of New York City and the California tax revolt are presented in some detail. The women's liberation movement, the relationship between science and government at the grassroots, and the whole approach to public policy (as exemplified in Part Five) as one of conflicts between social classes also are unusual in treatments of state and local politics.

The organization of *Governing at the Grassroots* reflects these emphases. Part One examines some of the dramatic issues confronting state and local politicians and bureaucrats, focusing on the high comedy of politics at the grassroots as well as the underlying despair of the political process. It traces the sweep of people and power across the breadth of this vast nation and shows the political implications of the large-scale demographic shifts this country has experienced during the twentieth century. Part Two approaches the politics of the states, focusing on the politics of making constitutions, political parties, lobbies, legislatures, voting behavior, the politics of justice, and the greening of the governors.

Part Three moves to those eighty thousand creatures of the states—counties, towns, townships, suburbs, cities, special districts, and school districts—and examines the structures of government in the United States, which are many and are constantly evolving. We also consider the increasingly strained relationships between those governments and Washington, D.C.; the complex dimensions of community power (including the role of the federal government in the conscious development of that power); and the urban chief executives, notably political bosses, mayors, and city managers.

Part Four is an unusual one in state and local government books; it discusses public administration at the grassroots. Some of the major political issues of our time are centered within the bureaucracy, and these include affirmative action policies, fiscal federalism, the politicization of the supposedly apolitical civil service, strikes by public employees, tax revolts, and the growing independence of the "fourth branch of government"—bureaucracy itself.

Part Five considers public policies formed and implemented by state and local governments; it approaches these policies from the viewpoint of conflict between social classes. Thus, policies for the poor include welfare policies and policies for crime in the streets. Policies for the middle class include education, state and urban planning efforts (especially planning for land use and transportation), and housing, which is among America's most racist policies.

The book concludes with a chapter on corruption and organized crime as a "policy" benefitting the wealthy. Although everyone knows that corruption is a fact of life in all levels of government—not merely state and local ones—few textbooks talk about it. One reason is that there are little empirical data available on what is usually a highly secretive area of politics, but another reason seems to be the grim determination of political scientists to uphold civic textbook virtues at any expense. This book does not take that approach.

Governing at the Grassroots is designed to be of continuing use to the reader. Thus, a Glossary of terms common to state and local politics follows the final chapter, and a series of useful appendices are included for the student's benefit. There is no reason for the reader to "begin with the wheel" in the event that a research paper is required, and the closing appendices not only should speed library research, but could result in superior term papers. Appendix A is a compilation of major annotated bibliographies and similar research sources in state and local politics; Appendix B lists the major journals that deal with state and local politics; Appendix C is more activist-prone and encourages the student to write to appropriate interest groups and policy makers in the area of subnational politics by providing a description of relevant organizations and their addresses; Appendix D also reflects this activist inclination and instructs the students on how to properly address public officials.

Many people deserve credit for the sucessful completion and production of *Governing at the Grassroots*. No book can be produced without a corps of dedicated typists, and I have been extraordinarily fortunate in having a group of devoted and talented secretaries work on this manuscript. Marian Buckley, Evelyn Hernandez, Cecile Higgins, Karen Neese, Patty Phippeny, and Gwen Weaver all turned out reams of manuscript that, in its original version, numbered more than nine hundred pages. They did this not only with a high degree of professionalism, but with unflagging good will, and for that I am most grateful.

Valari Elardo, my graduate assistant, proved to be a most insightful critic of the manuscript as well as assiduous in her pursuit of the stray footnote and the unclear sentence. Valari is solely responsible for the excellent *Instructor's Manual* that accompanies this book.

On another plane, I am grateful to Professor Richard A. Eribes for his helpful comments on the planning and housing chapters; Professor John Hall for his critique of the education and community power chapters; Professor Al Karnig for his help on the voting chapter; Professor Lawrence Mankin for his constructive assistance with the chapter on grassroots bureaucrats; Professor Elizabethann O'Sullivan for her comments on the chapter dealing with corruption and the Cosa Nostra; and Professor Frank Sackton, who was of great help with the chapter on public finance.

I also am in debt to my editor, Stan Wakefield, for his encouragement in pursuing this project and Prentice-Hall also provided the professional talents of Jeanne Hoeting and her able staff.

Most of all I am grateful to my family; my wife, Muriel, my son, Miles, and my daughter, Adrienne, were most understanding and, indeed, remarkable in letting me write a good portion of this book during the evenings while simultaneously watching the television set. Their support, as always, is deeply appreciated.

N.H.
Tempe

PART

NE

PEOPLE, POWER, AND POLITICS

CHAPTER

1

THE
JOY
OF
POLITICS

State and local politics are high theater. Although it is tempting to assert that politics at the grassroots is either comic or tragic, the line between tragedy and comedy is indeed a fine one.

POLITICAL FOLLIES

Whether the subject is funny or sad, we should approach the study of state and local politics as we would approach going to a movie; and grassroots politics is considerably more entertaining than most movies. Consider some examples. During the late 1960s Georgia had a governor who kept the nation in stitches: Lester Maddox. Governor Maddox was a man of the people, or at least, some of the people. In 1967, Maddox answered a query from *Esquire* magazine about whether he had an eye on Washington when his term expired. He answered, according to *Esquire,* "Naw suh. I jus' wanted to see how fer a li'l feller could go. I wanted to see if this wuz still America . . . . Son, you jus' come on back down here fo' years from now and you gon' fin' me givin' up this here guv'nor stuff and right back to my furniture store, jus' a pickin' and a rickin'."[1] In 1968 Maddox ran for president.

The former governor of Georgia delighted in making a spectacular appearance. One of his favorite stunts was to ride a bicycle backwards, another was to enter political rallies through a large paper hoop while riding on the hood of a car. On one occasion, however, the driver picked up a little too much speed; the governor went through the hoop on the car, but he was spread-eagled over the hood. Some objected that such a posture was less than dignified for a governor.

State politicians often seem to revel in the kind of behavior exemplified by Governor Maddox; sometimes this behavior is intentional and other times not. Consider another example, that of State Senator Fred Berry of Tennessee, who in 1976 came very close to being named the official state fossil. Berry proposed that the state designate an official rock, an official gem, and an official fossil, and he introduced a bill toward this end in the Tennessee legislature. The legislators, full of fun and highjinks at the end of the session, amended the portion concerning the fossil and elected to name Berry the official fossil; the senator hastily withdrew his proposal. On the other hand, Nevada in 1977 actually did consider seriously the adoption of an official fossil for the state. Nevada which is, of course, a desert, gave solemn thought to adopting the Ichthyosaur, a prehistoric reptile that dwelt exclusively in the earth's early oceans, as the state's official fossil.

Nor are fun and games limited to the legislature in grassroots politics.

---

[1] Rex Reed, "Lester Maddox as a Leader of Men." *Esquire* (October, 1976) 172.

4

One of the more entertaining campaigns in recent years was Senator S. I. Hayakawa's upset of Senator John V. Tunney in California. Hayakawa, campaigning in a state that some contend almost invented the Oriental Exclusion Act, is of Japanese descent, sports a tam-o'shanter as a campaign symbol, and is a respected academic in semantics. He amazed his audiences with the absolute candor of his positions. Asked at a fund-raising reception in Orange County, "What is your assessment of the United Nations situation involving the Libyan delegation?", Hayakawa responded, "I'm not terribly informed on this one. What is the Libyan delegation?" When queried about the Panama Canal question, a hot issue at one point in the 1976 campaign for president, Hayakawa replied, "We should hang on to it; we stole it fair and square." When informed by a McDonalds hamburger franchise owner that McDonalds had one hundred outlets in Japan, Hayakawa retorted, "That was too high a price to pay for Pearl Harbor." Hayakawa won handily against an opponent who had achieved a responsible record in Congress.[2]

Of course, part of the reason why Hayakawa won may have been California itself. Politically, California is unpredictable, and culturally it is often where things first happen in America. One sociologist has called California the world's largest outdoor asylum. It has Disneyland; it has both the highest and the lowest point in the contiguous forty-eight states; it has the Hollywood Pet Cemetery, the Golden Yoga Dream Hermitage, and the Golden Gate Bridge; it had the Symbionese Liberation Army, a governor who said "If you've seen one redwood tree, you've seen them all," and a U.S. Senator who rationalized that Mexicans made the best farm workers because they were short and, therefore, closer to the crops. No attempt is made here to single out California; it simply happens to be one of the nation's more spectacular political systems and one endowed with an almost unconscious sense of humor.

A sense of humor pervades most statewide politics. In our Bicentennial Year, the state of Washington put up as a gubernatorial candidate a Mr. Red Kelly, who represented the OWL party. OWL stood for "Out With Logic, On With Lunacy," and, indeed, the party fronted a full slate (which lost) in the Washington election. Kelly promised to abdicate immediately if elected, printed bumper stickers reading "A vote for Red Kelly is two giant steps backward," and maintained that on most issues he was "for everything and against everything else," noting for good measure that "the buck starts here." For lieutenant governor, the OWL party nominated Jack "The Ripoff" Lemon, who campaigned with the slogan: "If you care enough to send the very least, vote for a Lemon and throw the rascals out." "Fast Lucy" Griswold was the nominee for secretary of state, who trumpeted, "I have developed two new recipes, one for welfare rolls and the other for unemployment rolls, using a new special yeast. You can't raise the dough no matter how much you need it."[3]

---

[2]Harold Lavine, *Arizona Republic,* October 7, 1976.
[3]United Press International, October 11, 1976, syndicated nationally.

Oklahoma City was the base of operations for one Larimore Hustle, who qualified for the official ballot in several states during the 1976 presidential election. Candidate Hustle was a 1,000 pound pig who ran on the platform that, according to his agents, was anything but hogwash. Hustle, said his staff, was four-square against swine flu, felt that foreign policy was an area in which we should "bring home the bacon," and that in energy use "one shouldn't be a hog."

Local governments also have their share of color. One of the less known but certainly more entertaining examples of local political color took place in the nation's capitol in 1976, when the Washington Police Department and Federal Bureau of Investigation set up a major fencing operation.[4] The operation, dubbed "The Sting," was designed to net a number of burglars in the District of Columbia, and was eminently successful; "The Sting" involved undercover officers posing as out-of-town Syndicate members; over a period of months they bought more than 3,500 pieces of stolen property estimated at $2.4 million. The fake fence operation paid the alleged thieves $67,000 for television sets, stereos, appliances, cars, guns, and $1.2 million in federal government checks, which apparently had been stolen from a vault during office hours in the Department of Housing and Urban Development. They had business cards printed that identified their fencing operation as "PFF, Inc.," which actually stood for "Police-FBI Fencing, Inc.," although the suspects were told that the initials stood for "Pasquale's Finest Fencing." The operation eventually grew so big that it had to be terminated because the investigation was becoming overwhelmed with administrative tasks, since about two hundred people had made sales to the fencing company, with most becoming regular customers.

All involved thought that the supposed fencing operation was so successful—evidently, it had become the largest one in the city—that its operators (who, of course, were police officers) invited the suspects to a warehouse for a "victory night party" to celebrate the profits of their fencing ring. The police wanted to save thousands of dollars by having the suspects come to them, rather than going to the suspects to arrest them.

The guests arrived at the warehouse in expensive cars, wearing tuxedos, and heavy with jewelry, possibly their own. According to the *Washington Post,* the suspects were asked to check their guns at the door and were told they were going to get to see "the big boss, the don, who is so proud of what you did for us." A Washington policeman, one Carl Mattis, was selected to play the role of "the Don." Mattis, forty-three years old, the father of six, a member of the Elks, the American Legion, and Veterans of Foreign Wars, had no idea what a don was supposed to do, so he sat in a highbacked chair (mainly because he had a back problem) as the host of the supposed party and greeted each incoming arrival with "Bless you, my son." Mattis was

---

[4]Information in the following paragraphs are drawn from: Alfred E. Lewis and Ron Shaffer, *Washington Post,* March 1, 1976; Shaffer, *Washington Post,* March 5, 1976; Timothy S. Robinson, *Washington Post,* March 5, 1976; Sally Quinn, *Washington Post,* March 5, 1976.

introduced as "the boss himself, the man from New York," and gave such a winning performance as the don that more than one guest knelt in front of him and kissed his wedding ring. Hors d'oeuvres, of course, were served. The suspects then were escorted into a back room, where they were met by policemen who advised them of their rights, arrested and handcuffed them, hustled them into rented "U-Haul" trucks parked at the rear of the warehouse, and hauled them off to the police station. One hundred eight suspects were arrested.

The police and FBI had gone into the fencing business with style. Sally Quinn stated in her social column in the *Washington Post,* "It may well be remembered in these unexciting times as THE PARTY of the year."

Pasquale's Finest Fencing operation is just one example of the theatrics of grassroots government. There are others. The town of Brawley, California, passed a resolution forbidding snow within the city limits; Coral Gables, Florida, enacted a law against snoring at night; Atlanta, Georgia, made it unlawful to tie a giraffe to a telephone pole or street lamp within the city limits; and Greenville, South Carolina came out foursquare against selling and buying whiskey unless, of course, the sun was shining.[5]

These examples of state and local politics are cited because it is easy to lose one's sense of humor when viewing the American political scene. The following paragraphs show why this is so.

AMERICANS IN AN AGE OF DISILLUSIONMENT

Seldom have the American people been as disaffected with their governments as they are in this era. A malaise has drenched the political fabric that, conceivably, may result in the gradual unraveling of American democracy; for, hackneyed though the phrase may be, liberty demands vigilance, and the people have turned their backs on government.

Granted, there are significant exceptions to this admittedly sweeping statement. But consider recent events. It has been revealed that our intelligence and law enforcement agencies spy on, extort from, lie to, blackmail, harass, and debase not only foreign citizens but also American citizens. A war in Asia that killed fifty thousand Americans and maimed many more, a war that economists labeled as a primary cause of double-digit inflation in the 1970s was justified to the American people on the basis of half-truths and outright deceptions. Governors and mayors are convicted of corruption and sent to jail. A vice president of the United States is found guilty of accepting bribes from road builders but receives a commuted sentence. A president of the United States cheats on his taxes, lies baldfacedly to his fellow citizens, and resigns in disgrace; the person whom he had appointed as his constitutional successor grants him a readily accepted

---

[5]Dick Hyman, *The Trenton Pickle Ordinance and Other Bonehead Legislation* (Brattleboro, Vt.: Stephen Greene Press, 1975).

presidential pardon, prior to any court action, for all crimes then known or that might surface in the future. It later develops that other presidents may have committed similar violations, but were never charged. In notably sneaky fashion, Congress awards itself a generous pay hike, replete with automatic cost-of-living increases, at the height of one of the nation's most dispiriting recessions and consistently ignores cries for political reforms. In 1976 an administrator of the U.S. Justice Department estimated that federal prosecutors had won convictions of a thousand federal, state, and local officials for corruption in office since 1970. The Justice Department representative felt the figure was conservative.[6] Between 1974 and 1976, a U.S. senator, six congressmen, three governors, two U.S. attorneys, one state supreme court justice, a state treasurer, a state insurance director, fifteen state legislators, seventeen federal housing officials, roughly three dozen city council members, and numerous sheriffs, tax assessors, and purchasing agents were called to the bar of justice. Between 1955 and 1975, sixteen members of Congress were indicted and twelve were convicted or pleaded guilty, usually to charges involving such items as tax evasion and bribes. Judges deal severely with the poor and leniently with the rich; bureaucrats make capricious decisions that affect the courses of countless lives; special interests secretly gouge hidden advantages from "the system" at the expense of its general citizenry; and legislators decry the low state of ethics in everyone but themselves.

The government loses not only its legitimacy but its grip; crime soars, services dwindle, the economy falters, people suffer. A lack of trust and confidence becomes pervasive.

The consequences of this condition are profound. Consider a sampling of recent polls. An extensive national survey found that 60 percent of the Americans queried believed that "most people in government today don't really care about people like me." Other polls reinforce these findings; indeed, surveys conducted in 1974 and 1975 found that politicians ranked near the very bottom of the public's esteem, alternating with used car dealers, between nineteenth and twentieth place.

A RESURRECTION OF STATE AND LOCAL GOVERNMENTS

What are the consequences of such attitudes for American governments? One result, surely, is that our national government seldom has been held in such low repute. And it may be that, if any level of government is going to recapture the respect of the American people in an age of disillusionment, it may be those governments that are closer to them than Washington and that are therefore more accessible to their demands. Such a hopeful notion may sound naive, but there seem to be few, if any, alternatives.

---

[6]United Press International, "U.S. Prosecutors Convict 1,000 for Political Corruption Since '70." August 7, 1976, syndicated nationally.

There is some evidence that the people have more faith in state and local governments than they have in the national government. A 1976 Harris survey found that the public rated state government more worthy of trust than the federal government by a three-to-one margin. State governments legitmately can claim more grassroots support: 65 percent of those polled believed that the state government was closer to the people. By more than three-to-one, they believed that the federal government was more corrupt than state government. Another survey found that 46 percent of the respondents believed that they got "the most for their money" from their state and local governments; only 36 percent thought this to be the case with the federal government. Moreover, this feeling is not new. Similar findings in 1967 indicated that people had more faith in both state and local levels of government than in the federal level.[7]

AMERICANS SLOW DOWN

More concretely, however, definite and very recent demographic trends indicate state and local governments may become more germaine to the politically aware citizen at the potential expense of the national government. Americans are the most mobile people on earth; an average of 20 percent of us have been changing residences every year since 1950; in contrast, comparable mobility rates in Western Europe are roughly 12 percent and in Japan, 8 percent. This mobility, in the eyes of many observers, has resulted in a massive disinterest by Americans with local political issues. If one is changing towns or states, say, every five years or so, then local politics understandably becomes an area of scant concern: Why get involved if there is a high probability of leaving it all behind you in the reasonably foreseeable future? On the other hand, one rarely "leaves" the national political scene; national politics always is with us, a fact that is reinforced by pervasive and nationally oriented news media and an involvement of the federal government in regional, state, and local politics that has been growing steadily since the New Deal.

Recent analyses by the U.S. Census Bureau indicate, however, that the rate of mobility in this country is stabilizing. Between 1970 and 1975, 52.9 percent of Americans five years old and over lived in the same house that they had inhabited five years earlier. During the 1965 to 1970 period, this figure was 51.5 percent, and Bureau demographers consider these statistics as representing a significant slowing of mobility since the 1950s and 1960s.

With more people staying put for longer periods, citizen interest in local politics may well revive. Fewer citizens will view themselves as temporary residents of a locality and will perceive local politics as more relevant to

---

[7]*Congressional Record,* February 15, 1967. See also: *State Government News* (July, 1976), p. 3, and Advisory Commission on Intergovernmental Relations, *Changing Public Attitudes on Governments and Taxes.* Washington: ACIR, 1977, p. 3.

their lives. Increased political participation by more citizens in states and towns could result.

TWO EXAMPLES OF GRASSROOTS POLITICS: SEX AND LIFE

Regardless of the political implications of a stabilized mobility rate, state and local governments are the grassroots governments of our country. It is the statehouses, county court houses, and city halls that lay out democracy raw, that exhibit not only the warts on the nation's body politic, but display the genius of the American political mind.

If there is incompetence, corruption, and graft at these levels of government (and there is), at least we, the people, always have known about it and, to a degree, have even accepted it—in part because the national government offered an alternative and a seemingly more effective mechanism for achieving social goals. With the discovery that incompetence, corruption, and graft flourish in Washington, too, but in a more serious, more secretive, and perhaps more dangerous way, the governments of states and localities may be looking more attractive to the concerned public. These governments are more convenient to the people, often operate more openly, and are more restricted in the potential damage they can wreak. Yet, these governments form policy on and administer the most basic elements of the public's common interests: justice, safety, health, order, education, and welfare. These are the grassroots governments, and they show the American people and the political systems they have devised in their most vivid colors. It is with these governments that each of us has the most likely chance of making and changing public policy.

Despite the fact that state and local governments are closest to each of us, a number of observers contend that the study of state and local governments is dull and boring because what the state and local governments do is dull and boring. Admittedly, many of the texts that have been published constitute less than racy reading, but it does not necessarily follow that the subject itself is dry. Quite the contrary, state and local governments are involved not only in some of the most fundamental kinds of public policies in the nation, but some of the most intellectually intriguing and emotionally laden as well. Consider just two examples: the women's movement and policies for some of the most dangerous scientific research currently being conducted in the world.

STATES AS INSTRUMENTS OF SEXIST SUPPRESSION

Most people have heard of the women's liberation movement, or "women's lib," a major social reality of our time. Although the roots of the women's liberation movement can be traced back for hundreds of years in this country, it is fair to say that much of the turmoil surrounding feminism today is a relatively recent development.

In terms of their attempts to reform fundamental social mores concerning the status of women, the states historically have been the major political target of the women's movement, chiefly because of laws enacted by state legislatures concerning the place of women in American society. For example, an Arizona statute currently provides that a person who "in the presence of or hearing of any woman or child, or in a public place, uses vulgar, abusive, or obscene language is guilty of a misdemeanor," and at least twelve states make it a criminal offense to impugn the chastity of a woman.[8]

There also is evidence of a double standard when the sentences dealt to women by courts for criminal offenses are examined. For example, the New York State Family Court Act provides that youths who are "habitually truant, incorrigible, ungovernable, or habitually disobedient and beyond lawful control of parent or guardian" may be imprisoned. The law applies to boys only up to the the age of sixteen, and a boy may be kept in confinement only until age eighteen; but a girl can be imprisoned until the age of twenty. Deckard cites a study of juvenile delinquents in jails and retention centers across the country in which it was found that more than half of the female delinquents are incarcerated for noncriminal conduct, while only twenty percent of the boys were incarcerated for noncriminal matters; the study concluded that girls served significantly longer terms than boys.[9]

Married women also often are discriminated against in state law, purely on the basis of their marriage. In five states the wife must acquire court approval to engage in an independent business, and in Florida a wife must present a petition giving her name, age, and "her character, habits, education, and mental capacity for business" and she must briefly set out the reasons why such disabilities (to engage in her own business) should be removed."[10] Indeed, it was not until 1921 that women gained the right to practice law in all states, and many states still bar women from such vocations as mining, wrestling, and tending bar.

Such state-legislated prohibitions about the kinds of work women may engage in lead us to the area of protective labor laws that apply to women only (for example, laws stating that women may not lift more than thirty pounds of weight on a job). Protective labor laws generally set out such regulations as maximum hours, minimum wages, and related standards. States vary greatly in the kinds of protective labor laws they have enacted, and a number of these laws use sex as a basis for protection. The effects of these laws, in the view of many, have been to exclude women from job opportunities for which they, in reality, are quite qualified, and it has been

---

[8]Barbara Deckard, *The Women's Movement* (New York: Harper % Row, 1975), p. 143.

[9]Deckard, *The Women's Movement*, p. 149, citing Sally Gold in New York City Commission on Human Rights, *Women's Role in Contemporary Society* (New York: Avon, 1972), pp. 512–513 and 515.

[10]*Ibid.*, 154.

argued that protective labor laws are really designed to protect men's job opportunities at the expense of women's.

In 1963 and 1964, federal legislation designed to eliminate sex discrimination was enacted and quickly came into conflict with a number of state protective laws. This national legislation was the Equal Pay Act of 1963 and Title VII of the Civil Rights Act of 1964. The Equal Pay Act was an amendment to the Fair Labor Standards Act of 1938 and was later extended in 1968. The act has been helpful in eliminating artificial qualifications that prevent women from even being considered for certain jobs.

Title VII of the Civil Rights Act is more significant, stating that it "shall be unlawful employment practice" to, in effect, discriminate on the basis of sex. The act also established the Equal Employment Opportunity Commission (EEOC) to investigate discrimination complaints against companies with twenty-five or more employees. In 1972 the commission was given power to sue an employer in court for violation of the civil rights law, a power that applies to educational institutions and government employers as well as to the private sector.

Title VII states that it is legal to discriminate on the basis of sex, but only where such a discrimination constitutes a "bona fide occupational qualification reasonably necessary to the formal operation of that particular business or enterprise." As a result of this provision, a number of court actions have dealt with what actually should comprise a "bona fide occupational qualification" under Title VII of the Civil Rights Act.

Two major cases occurred in 1968 and 1969. In 1968 the Supreme Court upheld, in *Rosenfeld* v. *Southern Pacific Company,* that certain weight-lifting limitations for women established by California were invalid. In the famous case of *Weeks* v. *Southern Bell Telephone and Telegraph Company* in 1969, the Court of Appeals held that "an employer has the burden of proving that he had reasonable cause to believe . . .that all or substantially all women would be unable to perform safely and efficiently the duties of the job involved," which was the reasoning used to permit Ms. Weeks to become a "switchman," and voided a thirty-pound weight-lifting limit for women established by the state. In effect, the two cases held that certain state protective labor laws cannot be used to deny women a job or promotion and that the burden of proof regarding the fairness of a bona fide occupational qualification is on the employer rather than the employee.[11] In summary, state protective labor laws are increasingly coming under fire by both the courts and the Equal Employment Opportunity Commission as laws that discriminate against women in terms of employment opportunities.

How effective the pressures brought by feminist groups have been in opening more job opportunities to women must be conjectural. It is of note that, by 1977, in nearly half of all marriages in the United States both husband and wife were working, but wives' earnings averaged only about a quarter of family income. Compared to 1955, women have lost ground in

---

[11]*Ibid.,* 165.

earnings compared to men and only 5 percent of the workers earning more than $15,000 a year in 1974 in the U.S. labor force were women. Nevertheless, as state laws continue to come under fire as discriminating against women, the vocational opportunities available to women can only increase over time.

While state protective labor laws and what constitutes a bona fide occupational qualification are under attack in the courts, another route women are taking to eradicate discriminatory practices is the purely political. The most notable example, perhaps, is the Equal Rights Amendment (ERA) passed by Congress in 1972, which required the ratification of thirty-eight states. Equal Rights Amendments were resisted by such powerful groups as the AFL–CIO, which viewed them as a threat to job opportunities for men. By 1974, however, organized labor had reversed its position and was supporting the ERA.

In 1977 the National Organization of Women (NOW), with thirty-three of the necessary thirty-eight states having ratified the amendment, called for the termination of federal aid to all those states that had not ratified the ERA. How strategic this move may have been is a moot point, but it is indicative of the intensity with which women have been lobbying for ERA in the states during the past several years. Those states that have not approved the ERA are largely the same states that did not approve the amendment granting women the vote back in the 1920s.

Perhaps even more effective than the fight to pass the Equal Rights Amendment has been the gradual entrance of increasing numbers of women into grassroots politics.

Women, who make up 53 percent of the voting-age population, occupy little more than 5 percent of the nation's elected offices (as of 1975). Nonetheless, they are making gains, and these gains are particularly in evidence at the state level. By the late 1970s women held two governorships, 10 percent of statewide elected positions, and 9 percent of all legislative seats; locally, five women were elected mayors of big cities.[12] One reason for women's political progress may be the formation of the National Women's Political Caucus (NWPC) in 1971, a multipartisan organization with the basic goal of organizing and asserting the political power of women. The caucus was and is a grassroots movement. By 1973 every state, as well as Washington, D.C., and Puerto Rico, had active caucuses; most NWPC members are middle class women who have had political experience.

In brief and to the point, states are "where the action is" in one of the major social movements of our time. The women's movement is an example of how most major political movements really happen in the states, not in some entity called "the nation." It is state laws that often are the most discriminatory against women, and it is state legislatures that have felt the brunt of feminist activity.

---

[12]Neal R. Peirce, syndicated column, November 18, 1977.

A second example of policies debated and made by state and local governments occurred in 1976 in Cambridge, Massachusetts, when the Cambridge City Council took on Harvard University and the Massachusetts Institute of Technology, both located within its city limits, and voted to terminate temporarily the research underway in their respective biology departments on recombinant DNA.

Before we can appreciate the significance of this vote, we should understand, first, what is involved in biological research in recombinant DNA. To phrase the matter simply (and not especially accurately), the DNA molecule is, in effect, cut into various segments and stuck back together in a new way. DNA is the basic genetic molecule; the molecular basis of heredity in most organisms, including human beings. What biologists have been trying to do—and with increasing success—is to recombine the basic genetic molecule in new formats. Most biologists who are doing recombinant DNA research are inserting animal genes into human intestinal bacteria.

The implications for this kind of research are profound but unknown. In 1974, Paul Berg of the National Academy of Sciences called for a worldwide moratorium on certain experiments involving recombinant DNA. This moratorium was observed for two years by all nations when, after much debate, the National Institutes of Health (NIH) of the federal government developed security guidelines for recombinant DNA research. These guidelines were deemed necessary by many biologists because, when one is creating new forms of life at the bacterial level, one might also be creating new forms of diseases for which there would be no control. As one biologist observed, "What we are doing is almost certainly irreversible. Knowing human frailty, these structures will escape, and there is no way to recapture them. The hazard, if there is a hazard, will not be like DDT or PCBs or aerosols, which you can just stop manufacturing."[13] *Science* magazine remarked that "After the first atomic devices were successfully developed, Robert Oppenheimer remarked that physicists had now known sin. That biologists may be at least moving out of an 'age of innocence' may be heralded by research on recombinant DNA."[14]

Much potential social good, of course, could come from this research, notably new vaccines against viruses. But still, research in recombinant DNA can create new organisms that may spread uncontrollably about the planet, for better or worse. *Science* magazine quoted the head of the Division of Biology at the California Institute of Technology: "Of the potential broader social or ethical implications of initiating this line of research—of its role, as a possible prelude to longer-range, broader-scale genetic engineering of the fauna and flora of the planet, including ultimately, man . . .Do we want to

---

[13]Nicholas Wade, "Recombinant DNA: Guidelines Debated at Public Hearing." *Science* 191 (February 27, 1976) 835.

[14]*Ibid.,* 834.

assume the basic responsibility for life on this planet—to develop new living forms for our own purpose? Shall we take into our own hands our future evolution?"[15]

It was with such issues that the National Institutes of Health grappled, eventually developing guidelines that established four classes of recombinant DNA research, which were designated from P1 (research safe to conduct in virtually any kind of laboratory) to P4 (to be conducted only under conditions of very strict physical surveillance); P4 research, for example, should be conducted only in such places as military fortresses.

In short, recombinant DNA is exciting, but dangerous, involving not only life, but new forms of life. So why would the city council of Cambridge interfere with recombinant DNA research?

On July 7, 1976, the Cambridge City Council, seven men and two women who normally handled such matters as road repairs and taxes, took on what is the most perplexing problem in biology today and debated whether or not recombinant DNA research was safe for Cambridge.

Harvard and MIT wanted to put a P3 class laboratory on the Harvard campus. The faculties of both Harvard and MIT were divided on the wisdom of establishing such a laboratory at Harvard, and the issue centered around security reasons. The meeting of July 7, which lasted until 1:00 in the morning, was described by observers as a "circus." Meanwhile scientists at Harvard and MIT, who had been waiting nearly two years for establishment of NIH guidelines and an end to the worldwide moratorium, suddenly found themselves confronting the Cambridge City Council. The Council was saying, and with authority, that it was an open question as to whether these biologists could conduct such research.

Cambridge is largely a working class town of 100,000 people. That its city council became involved with what is the most sophisticated level of biological research going on in the world today was, to say the least, an interesting policy process. The mayor of Cambridge characterized the DNA researchers as "those people in white coats" who could "build a Frankenstein" or visit upon the populace some deadly organism along the lines of the fictional *Andromeda Strain*. *Science* magazine quoted one city councilman as saying, "The Harvard and MIT people thought that, because Washington had said it was okay to go ahead, that was that. They were flabbergasted to discover that Al Vellucci [the mayor of Cambridge] could have a noose around their neck in just a few days' time. Here's a guy ranting and raving about monsters and germs in the sewers and they have to stop what they want to do because of him. They just didn't understand."[16]

Mayor Vellucci had been approached by a member of the Harvard faculty, who expressed his concern about the proposed lab for recombinant DNA research. Some argued that Vellucci then used this concern as a

---

[15]Nicholas Wade. "Recombinant DNA: The Last Look Before the Leap." *Science* 192 (April 16, 1976) 237.

[16]Barbara J. Culliton, "Recombinant DNA." *Science* 193 (July 23, 1976) 300.

political gambit, since Vellucci already had gained a good deal of political mileage out of the Harvard campus, arguing loudly that Harvard Yard should be converted into a parking lot.

Scientist after scientist appeared before the Cambridge City Council, arguing both for and against the proposed P3 facility and the continuation of recombinant DNA research. Then the biologists made a grievous political error. One of the scientists stated that the health commissioner of Cambridge had been invited to attend meetings of the Harvard Committee on the Regulation of Hazardous Biological Agents. While the city council members may not have known much, if anything, about recombinant DNA, they did know that they did not have a health commissioner. The city had not had a health commissioner for nineteen months and, in one observer's view, it was "something of a sore point with them." Thus, what had started off as a good political gambit for the mayor was not ending well. Ultimately, the city of Cambridge voted that a Cambridge Laboratory Experimentation Review Board comprised of scientists and citizens be established to investigate recombinant DNA and, in the future, other types of dangerous research. They also voted that once a health commissioner was appointed, he or she would have the authority to recommend a course of action for the city council. The city declared a three-month "good faith" moratorium on recombinant DNA research, which Harvard and MIT observed; eventually, the city permitted the two universitites to proceed with its P3 facility at Harvard.

The example provided by the Cambridge City Council's wrestling with one of the most complex, sophisticated, and dangerous biological issues of the twentieth century is a fine example of what local governments do. Although admittedly a more exotic example than most, it highlights the fundamental kinds of issues that governments at the grassroots must grapple with. Consider the opinion of one Cambridge councilman: "I tried to understand the science, but I decided I couldn't make a legitimate assessment of the risk. When I realized I couldn't decide to vote for or against a moratorium on scientific grounds, I shifted to the political."[17] That is probably the way most of the council members felt, but "political" is not used here in a pejorative sense. The council members of Cambridge seemed to want to involve the public in realms where the public had never been involved before, although these decisions could determine the very form of their lives—and not just their lives, but all of ours. Moreover, the Cambridge City Council did this in defiance of federally established guidelines that the global scientific community assumed would end the two-year-old worldwide moratorium. Local government in America is not only fun and vital, it is also powerful.

---

[17]*Ibid.*, 301.

WHY STUDY STATE AND LOCAL POLITICS?

We have seen that state and local governments are important and powerful, and that alone makes the study of subnational politics worthwhile. There is a more practical reason, however, for acquiring a smattering of knowledge about state and local politics: Towns, cities, counties, and states have jobs for college graduates; indeed, they have more jobs than any sector of the national economy. More than three-quarters of all nonmilitary public employees work for state or local governments, and state and local employers have been hiring college graduates at a rate seven times that of the federal government. Of the nation's labor force roughly one employee in six works for one level of government or another, and almost one in five is hired by a government other than the national government. Since the mid-1950s, employment by state and local governments has increased at a rate four times that of the economy as a whole. State and local governments are not only where the power is, they are where the jobs are.

THEMES OF GOVERNING AT THE GRASSROOTS

While the grassroots governments will be seen as powerful and colorful, still other aspects will be developed in the following chapters.

SURBURBAN POLITICS

An emphasis on suburban politics pervades the book. The politics of our last quarter century are taking place in the suburbs, and this reality is changing the composition of state legislatures, bleeding the inner cities, and conservzing the national political mind.

BUREAUCRATIC POLITICS

Bureaucratic politics, will be stressed in Part Four. Increasingly, the bureaucracy makes public policy in America. Some of the most fundamental political debates, covering such topics as affirmative action, taxation policy (and its incumbent revolts), and the panoply of administrative politics, occur in the bureaucratic bowels of government. Yet few, if any, books on state and local governments explain the power of bureaucracy and its implications for democracy.

REGIONAL POLITICS

Regional politics is a third intertwining theme. Ours is an age of "Sunbelt" against "Snowbelt," and this rivalry is becoming the central reality of the entire federal system.

17

POLITICIANS AS PEOPLE

Politicians as people is a recurring thread throughout. While this book, like most, traces the paths of power and influence between political institutions and actors, it places greater emphasis on these political actors as social and psychological human beings. Case histories of chief executives are presented; composites of politicians (including governors, legislators, judges, mayors, urban planners, city councilmembers, political bosses, city managers, and policemen, among others) are examined in some detail; the role of political corruption is discussed as a separate phenomenon.

PUBLIC POLICY AS CLASS CONFLICT

Finally, public policy is viewed as the product of conflict between social classes. The most direct expression of this approach is in Part Five, but it is also a theme of the book, and one unique to the study of state and local politics. Hence, welfare and street crime are analyzed as policies for the underclass; education, planning, land use, transportation, and housing are viewed as policies for the middle class; and corruption is approached as a "policy" of the upper class.

In short, suburban politics, bureaucratic power, regional rivalry, the politician as a person, and policy as class conflict are the continuing threads of *Governing at the Grassroots* that distinguish it from other treatments of American politics. But they remain only threads in the nation's political brocade, whose richness is the result of citizens, groups, governments, and regions contributing their colors, strengths, weaknesses, and tensions to the tangle of yarns that have been woven into a varied political cloth on the loom of the earth's most complex democracy. The warp and weft of American politics—that tensile, underlying strength of the nation's political fabric—are what *Governing at the Grassroots* is about.

CHAPTER

SUBURBS,
SUNBELT,
SNOWBELT:
THE SWEEP
OF PEOPLE
AND POWER

America is a big country. Its people are as different as its regions, its politics as varied as its climates. But where are the people in this nation, and why are they there?

The people are scattered throughout a plethora of political jurisdictions administered by 79,913 governments. Although the numbers of all types of American governments have remained roughly constant (with the exception of school districts, which have declined) since 1900, the number of people and the movements of people have not.

Two major trends emerged in the 1970s that will determine the political realities of our time. One is the *suburbanization* of the nation; for the first time, the historic migrations of Americans to cities is reversing. The other is the rise of the Sunbelt, or those states in the South and Southwest, over the Eastern Establishment and the Snowbelt.

THE SUBURBANIZATION OF AMERICA

To appreciate what *suburbanization* means, a bit of background is necessary. In 1790, when the first census was taken, 95 percent of our people were rural folk and 5 percent city dwellers; by 1970, these figures essentially had been reversed. Related to this migration to the central cities was the black exodus from the South to the North. From 1900 until the 1970s, approximately 10 percent of the South's black populace moved from Dixie every decade, and between 1950 and 1970, some *four million* blacks moved to the North. Most went to the metropolises of Yankeeland, in what amounted to the biggest population migration in world history. There, blacks carved neighborhood enclaves for themselves out of what was usually the cities' cheapest housing and, over time, became entrapped in those same central cities in what we now call "black ghettoes."

Beginning at midcentury, certain countertrends and variational shifts began to emerge. The census of 1970 detected a hefty minority of blacks who were "going home" to the Old South, an area that has changed considerably since 1900. By 1974, for the first time since Emancipation, more blacks were moving south than north. More significant, however, was the emergence of the "white flight" from the cities to the suburbs, starting around 1945. White middle-class families, pressured by competition for housing from blacks, rising property taxes, and other forces, fled from the core cities to the suburban fringe. By the early 1960s the overall rate of population growth in the inner cities had begun to decline, and by the middle of the decade 55 percent of America's black and brown (Hispanic) population lived in the inner cities while only 25 percent of the white population lived there. By 1970, more than a dozen big American cities

21

Suburbs,
sunbelt,
snowbelt: the
sweep of
people and
power

were at least 40 percent black, although the nation's population is less than 11 percent black, and the suburban population (predominantly white) outnumbered the central city population.

Nine of the nation's ten largest cities had lost more people than they had gained by 1973 (Houston was the sole exception), and between 1970 and 1975 major urban centers *lost* 1.6 million people. Contrast this rather startling news with the fact that these same centers *gained* 352,000 *new* residents between 1965 and 1970. The twentieth-century growth of American cities is, for the first time, stopping. By 1977 it was confirmed that fourteen of the nation's twenty largest cities had lost population during the first half of the decade; only Miami and Memphis had gained in populations between 1970 and mid-1975, according to the Census Bureau. Although the overall population of the country rose by nearly 10 million people during the first half of the 1970s, for every 100 people who moved into a metropolitan area, 131 moved out between 1970 and 1975. A 1978 Harris poll indicated that this trend would continue, with half of *all* urbanites expressing an intention to move out of the cities.[1]

At least 76 million Americans live in places like Levittown and Park Forest and, depending on how one defines *suburb,* as many as 90 million people may live in the nation's 20,000 suburbs. Projections indicate that more than 100 million people will be living in America's Levittowns by 1985, and it is estimated that roughly 40 percent of our population now lives in the suburbs. This is a plurality, since about 30 percent of Americans live in cities and another 30 percent in rural areas. Suburbia is where the action is, not only in population growth, but in economic growth as well.

A mini-trend runs counter to this flight from the cities: a small number of middle-class whites is returning to the inner cities, often attracted by cheap, old, and spacious housing. Yet, the overwhelming reality is that money and industry have followed former urban residents to the suburbs, attracted by greater space, superior transportation facilities, improved labor supplies, new external economies, and lower tax rates. As a result, the majority of skilled and professional workers now live on the rims of cities, and 75 percent of union members under the age of forty live there. Nearly 23 percent of those who live on the outer fringes of cities are within the highest status category (as defined by the Census Bureau); fewer than 4 percent are in the lowest status category. (Status categories are determined by the Census Bureau according to social and economic measures based on occupational type, level of education, and amount of income.) When we examine the inner cities, we see that only 14 percent of the people are in the highest category and 9 percent are in the lowest.[2] More to the point, perhaps, about 30 percent, or 8.2 million of the nation's poor as of 1970

---

[1] Harris poll, cited in Ron Hendren, syndicated column, March 29, 1978.

[2] U.S. Bureau of the Census, *Current Population Reports, Technical Studies,* Series P–23, No. 12. Washington: U.S. Government Printing Office, 1974.

lived in the core cities; only 21 percent, or less than 5.2 million, lived in the suburbs.[3]

"THE WORSE THINGS GET, THE WORSE THINGS GET"

In a sophisticated analysis of "urban hardship" in fifty-five major cities, the Brookings Institution ranked the disparities that existed between inner cities and their suburbs on the logic that, "Such disparities often lead to the population movement and economic decline typical of distressed central cities."[4] As the authors observe:

> The picture is familiar. As more residents and businesses move to the suburbs, the the city's tax base is driven down. Property or other tax rates must be raised to compensate, in turn causing more people and industries to leave. A natural law seems to govern these high-disparity cases: "The worse things get, the worse things get." It is a continuous process, feeding on itself.[5]

The Brookings study concluded that forty-three of the cities were worse off economically and socially than their surrounding suburbs, two were about equal, and ten were actually better off than their suburban rings. Table 2–1 lists the fourteen "worst off" cities and the ten "best off" as defined by Brookings' "hardship index" (in the third column from the left). A score of 100 on this index means that a city is roughly equal socially and economically with its suburbs; a score of more than 100 means that the city is worse off, and a score of less than 100 means that the city is better off than its suburbs.

Brookings' fourteen worst-off cities are in bad shape by any measure. They lost, on the average, 4.2 percent of their people between 1960 and 1970. By contrast, Brookings' "Top Ten" gained in population by an average of 18.5 percent during the decade. The "Floundering Fourteen" have almost 10 percent less per capita income than the Top Ten, they have lower median house values and lower tax bases.

The Brookings researchers have uncovered some fascinating patterns of urban hardship and have concluded that the most important differences among big cities were regional. The cities decomposing most rapidly are found largely in those midwestern and northeastern states comprising the northeastern quarter of the country; the more viable metropolises are in the Sunbelt and the West.

The upshot of the black/white, poor/rich imbalance between cities and suburbs is that those local governments with the greatest demand for public

---

[3]John C. Bollens and Henry J. Schmandt, *The Metropolis: Its People, Politics, and Economic Life*, 3rd ed. (New York: Harper and Row, 1975) p. 69.

[4]Richard P Nathan and Paul R. Dommel, "Understanding the Urban Predicament," *The Brookings Bulletin*, 14 (Spring–Summer, 1977) p. 9.

[5]*Ibid.*

TABLE 2–1 CENTRAL CITIES RANKING ABOVE 200 AND BELOW 100 ON AN INDEX OF CITY-SUBURBAN DISPARITY ("HARDSHIP INDEX") IN 1970, WITH SELECTED DATA ON THEIR STANDARD METROPOLITAN STATISTICAL AREAS, 1960–70

Primary Central City of SMSA	Region[1]	Index of City-Suburban Disparity	SMSA POPULATION, 1970		PERCENT CHANGE, 1960–70		PRE-1939 HOUSING IN 1970 (PERCENT)
			Total (Thousands)	Percent in Central City	Population	Land Area	
Central Cities Worse Off than Their Suburbs							
Newark	NE	422	1,857	20.6	−5.7		68.4
Cleveland	NE	331	2,064	36.4	−14.3		73.3
Hartford	NE	317	664	23.8	−2.6		67.0
Baltimore	NE	256	2,071	43.7	−3.5		60.0
Chicago	NC	245	6,975	48.2	−5.1		66.5
St. Louis	NC	231	2,363	26.3	−17.0		73.9
Atlanta	S	226	1,390	35.8	2.0	3.2	30.3
Rochester	NE	215	883	33.6	−7.0		79.5
Gary	NC	213	633	27.7	−1.6		43.7
Dayton	NC	211	850	28.6	−7.4	12.3	52.1
New York	NE	211	11,572	68.2	1.5		62.1
Detroit	NC	210	4,200	36.0	−9.4		61.8
Richmond	S	209	518	48.2	−13.4	60.0	44.8
Philadelphia	NE	205	4,818	40.4	−2.6		69.5
Central Cities Better Off Than Their Suburbs							
Omaha	NC	98	540	64.3	15.0	60.2	46.1
Dallas	S	97	1,556	54.3	24.2	4.7	18.1
Houston	S	93	1,985	62.1	31.4	35.2	17.3
Phoenix	W	85	968	60.1	32.4	32.3	11.2
Norfolk	S	82	681	45.2	1.0	0.5	30.5
Salt Lake City	W	80	558	31.5	−7.2	6.5	52.1
San Diego	W	77	1,358	51.3	21.6	62.8	21.7
Seattle	W	67	1,422	37.3	−4.7	2.2	47.6
Ft. Lauderdale	S	64	620	22.5	66.9	39.0	7.6
Greensboro, N.C.	S	43	604	23.9	20.5	9.7	20.7

Index calculated from data in U.S. Bureau of the Census, *County and City Data Book, 1972* (Government Printing Office, 1972), tables 2, 3, 6; population from Bureau of the Census, *1972 Census of Governments*, vol. 1, *Governmental Organization* (GPO, 1972), table 19; pre- 1939 housing data from *1970 Census of Housing*, Series HC(1)B, *Detailed Housing Characteristics*, table 35.

[1]Northeast (NE): New England states, New York, New Jersey, Pennsylvania.
North Central (NC): Michigan, Ohio, Indiana, Illinois, Wisconsin, Minnesota, Iowa, Missouri, North and South Dakota, Nebraska, Kansas.
South (S): Kentucky, Tennessee, Georgia, Florida, Alabama, Mississippi, Arkansas, Louisiana, Oklahoma, Texas.
West (W): Montana, Wyoming, Colorado, New Mexico, Idaho, Utah, Arizona, Washington, Oregon, Nevada, California.

Source: Richard P. Nathan and Paul R. Dommel, "Understanding the Urban Predicament." *The Brookings Bulletin* 14 (Spring–Summer, 1977):20.

services are least able to afford them because of inordinately weak tax bases. Funds for education, fire protection, police protection, public health, and other basic functions of government are lacking for significant portions of the population.

THE METROPOLITAN MORASS

Compounding the disparities in public service that are inflamed by demographic shifts are the minions of government proliferating in Standard Metropolitan Statistical Areas (SMSAs), or metropolitan areas of fifty thousand people or more. Of the 79,913 governments in the United States nearly a third—25,869 of them—are found in the Standard Metropolitan Statistical Areas of the country. These are independent governments, not agencies or departments. The nation's 272 SMSAs (shown in Figure 2–1) contain nearly three-quarters of the country's people, cover only one-ninth of the nation's land, and average ninety-five governments per metropolis. Despite this median figure, there is considerable variation in the number of governments found in different metropolitan areas. Chicago has the most (a total of 1,214 governments), metropolitan areas in the South are usually leaner. An SMSA's population size seems primarily related to the number of governments that a metropolitan area has. For example, metropolitan areas with a million people or more have, on the average, 293 governments within them, while metropolises between 50,000 and 100,000 people average about twenty-eight governments. Table 2–2 indicates the types and proportions of local governments found inside and outside SMSAs; Table 2–3 shows their growth between 1972 and 1977.

The upshot of this kind of ultralocal arrangement of America's metropolitan governments is that the structure, or lack of it, may add to the public's problems. Consider the evaluation made by the National Research Council:

> Fragmentation rather than correspondence to the scale of metropolitan activity is the rule, not the exception. Administrative disabilities are widespread. Overlapping responsibility is prevalent. Fiscal externalities persist. Control of environmental pollution is impeded. Residents with higher incomes continue their migration to the suburbs. The central city finds it more and more difficult to raise necessary revenues. Differences between city and suburban tax burdens reflect inequitable distribution of metropolitan costs. Efforts to increase metropolitan unity are hampered. The state of metropolitan transportation, water supplies, and waste disposal, for example, remains precarious in many areas. Meanwhile, jurisdictions, like the small enterprises they often resemble, calculate and compete for additional sources of tax revenue. The social problems of the metropolis— crime, inadequate education programs, unemployment, and inadequate housing—slowly spread. Fragmentation of government is only in small

24

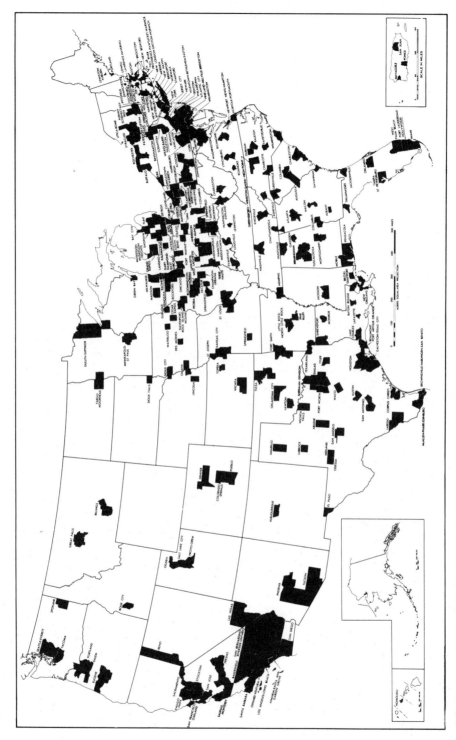

FIGURE 2–1 STANDARD METROPOLITAN STATISTICAL AREAS. AREAS DEFINED BY OFFICE OF MANAGEMENT AND BUDGET, OCTOBER 1975

Source: U.S. Department of Commerce Bureau of the Census

TABLE 2-2 LOCAL GOVERNMENTS INSIDE AND OUTSIDE SMSAs BY TYPE, 1977

TYPE OF GOVERNMENT	UNITED STATES	INSIDE SMSAs	OUTSIDE SMSAs	PERCENT IN SMSAs
All local governments	79,862	25,869	53,993	32.4
School districts	15,174	5,220	9,954	34.4
Other	64,688	20,649	44,039	31.9
Counties	3,042	594	2,448	19.5
Municipalities	18,862	6,444	12,418	34.2
Townships	16,822	4,031	12,791	24.0
Special districts	25,962	9,580	16,382	36.9
Dependent school systems[1]	1,374	601	773	43.7

[1]Not included in count of governments.
Source: U.S. Bureau of the Census.

part a cause of these social problems, but it makes them much more difficult to solve.[6]

Perhaps a more pithy assessment of the human dimension of the problem, as opposed to the governmental dimensions, was made by a mother of two teenage boys: "We live in East Meadow. I work in Garden City. My husband works in Syosset. We shop for clothes in Hempstead. My husband's Pythias Lodge meets in Great Neck. Our temple is in Merrick. The children's doctor is in Westbury. And we pay for our parking tickets in Mineola."[7]

---

[6]National Research Council, *Toward an Understanding of Metropolitan America* (San Francisco: Canfield, 1975) pp. 104–105.

[7]Samuel Kaplan, *The Dream Deferred* (New York: Seabury Press, 1976) p. 9.

TABLE 2-3 GROWTH OF LOCAL GOVERNMENTS INSIDE SMSAs, 1972–1977

TYPE OF LOCAL GOVERNMENT	LOCAL GOVERNMENTS IN THE 272 SMSAs		INCREASE OR DECREASE (−), 1972 TO 1977	
	1977	*1972*	*Number*	*Percent*
Total	25,869	22,185	3,684	16.6
School districts	5,220	4,758	462	9.7
Other local governments	20,649	17,427	3,222	18.5
Counties	594	444	150	33.8
Municipalities	6,444	5,467	977	17.9
Townships	4,031	3,462	569	16.4
Special districts	9,580	8,054	1,526	19.0

Source: U.S. Bureau of the Census.

POLITICAL CULTURES: THE POLITICS OF REGIONALISM

This discussion of the nation's political demography thus far has centered on urban and suburban areas. But the relationships between people and power on a state and regional level are also important and in many ways more interesting.

In his classic study of federalism, Daniel J. Elazar drew a "map" of political cultures for the mainland forty-eight states. He defined three major cultural types: moralism, individualism, and traditionalism.[8] A *moralistic* political culture, in Elazar's view, blankets the West Coast, Midwest, and Northeast. It fosters a high concern for public issues, is directed toward the common man and his search for the good society, views government's place in society positively, disparages partisan politics, is change-oriented, has a high intolerance of political corruption, and is relatively accepting of a professionalized public bureaucracy.

An *individualistic* political culture peppers most of the country, with comparatively high concentrations in the Southwest, Midwest, and Northeast. It stresses the concept that democracy is a marketplace and places a premium on the value of the private sector as opposed to the public sector; It sees the role of the government as one of permitting the growth of prosperity in the private sector. Party affiliation counts for much, issue-orientation is eschewed. It is felt that government should play a passive role in society, and it is deemed relatively legitimate for an officeholder to distribute political rewards, both to himself and to others.

A *traditionalistic* political culture dominates in the South, Southwest, and portions of the Midwest. It is in part a hybrid between the moralistic and individualistic cultures. Although the traditionalistic culture believes in a positive role for government (as does the moralistic culture), its members also assume that a person's first obligation is to oneself and, therefore, it is legitimate to benefit personally from one's political office (as in the individualistic culture). Partisan politics is played down, as with the moralists, and the development of a professional corps of public officials is resisted in very elemental terms. The overriding reality of a traditionalistic culture is the role of a paternalistic political elite, usually comprised of people with "old family" ties. Its mission is the preservation of the status quo. To this end, a widespread citizen disinterest in political issues is the norm.

Aspects of all these political cultures are found in all parts of the nation, but there are particular concentrations in various regions. The population changes that many regions underwent in the 1970s may have farreaching consequences for state and local politics, especially in light of differing political belief-sets among the regions of the country.

---

[8]Daniel Elazar, *Federalism: A View From the States* (New York: Thomas Y. Crowell, 1966) pp. 86–94.

THE POWER SHIFT: ENTER THE SUNBELT

People from the Northeast and Midwest are moving South and West, attracted by lower taxes and more jobs (55 to 60 percent of all new job opportunities are now in the South and West). Between 1970 and 1975, the Northeast and North Central regions lost more Americans than they gained, while the South's net gain nearly tripled from the previous five-year period to 1.9 million persons, and the West's growth rate stayed steady with a gain of another 700,000 people. Census Bureau officials stated in 1975 that 85 percent of the nation's population growth in the 1970s had occurred in the South and West, a much heftier share of the country's growth than those regions had in any other decade for the past fifty years. In the nation's Bicentennial Year it was found that, for the first time, a majority of Americans lived in the South and West. Only six years earlier the South and West had 8 million fewer residents than the North. Five of America's ten largest cities now are in the West and the South: Los Angeles, Houston, Dallas, San Diego, and San Antonio. Kirkpatrick Sale calls these migrations "the power shift."[9] He argues that the nation's economic and political power is shifting from the Eastern Establishment to the "Southern Rim"—that is, those states stretching from Southern California to North Carolina, a region more commonly known as the Sunbelt. As Figures 2–2 and 2–3 illustrate, the "Yanks" are losing control to the "Rebs" and "cowboys."

The evidence supporting Sale's argument is mixed.[10] Economically, the

---

[9]Kirkpatrick Sale, *The Power Shift: The Rise of the Southern Rim and Its Challenge to the Eastern Establishment* (New York: Random House, 1975).

[10]The best analyses to date of regional shifts in power and people are: (1) a series of seven articles in the *New York Times,* beginning with Robert Reinhold, "Sunbelt Region Leads Nation in Growth of Population Section's Cities Top Urban Expansion," (February 8, 1976), pp. 1 and 42; James P. Sterba, "Houston, as Energy Capital, Sets Pace in Sunbelt Boom," (February 9, 1976), pp. 1 and 24; Wayne King, "Federal Funds Pour into Sunbelt States," (February 9, 1976), p. 24; Roy Reed, "Sunbelt Still Stronghold of Conservatism in U.S." (February 10, 1976), pp. 1 and 22; Roy Reed, "Migration Mixes a New Southern Blend," (February 11, 1976), pp. 1 and 30; and B. Drummond Ayres, Jr., "Developing Sunbelt Hopes to Avoid North's Mistakes," (February 12, 1976), pp. 1 and 24. (2) "The Second War Between the States," *Business Week* (May 17, 1976), pp. 92–114. (3) Joel Havemann, Rochelle L. Stanfield, and Neal R. Pierce, "Federal Spending: The North's Loss Is the Sunbelt's Gain," *National Journal* (June 26, 1976), pp. 878–891. (4) John Ross and John Shannon, "Measuring the Fiscal 'Blood Pressure' of the States: Some Warning Signs of Our Federal System and Alternative Prescriptions," paper presented at the Conference on State and Local Finance, University of Oklahoma, 1976. (5) Carol L. Jusenius and Larry C. Ledebur, *A Myth in the Making: The Southern Economic Challenge and Northern Economic Decline.* Economic Development Administration, U.S. Department of Commerce, 1976. (6) Robert W. Rafuse, Jr., *The New Regional Debate: A National Overview.* Washington: National Governors Conference, 1977. There are others.

Because of various factors (such as the fact that the country's regions are never defined in precisely the same way by the studies) different conclusions result. We examine the implications of regional rivalry from the perspective of federal fiscal policy in Chapter 15, but perhaps it is worth recalling here George Washington's concern about "a spirit of jealousy which may become dangerous to the Union, towards the Eastern States." (*Writings,* Vol. 31, p. 28).

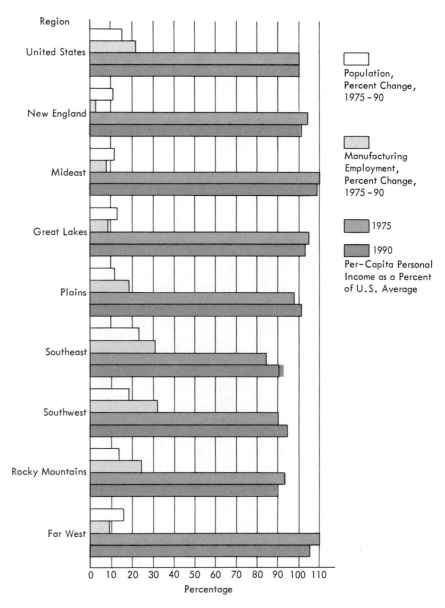

FIGURE 2–2 THE POPULATION POWER SHIFT, 1975 PROJECTED TO 1990

1975 "Fortune 500" list of the country's 500 biggest companies showed that 111 of them had headquarters in the South and West, up from 75 a decade earlier; of the 50 largest corporate giants, 14 were based in the South and West, double the number of ten years ago. New York City's share of these

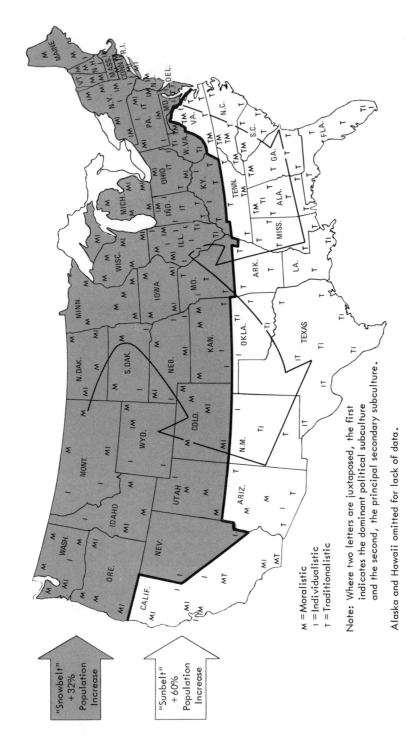

FIGURE 2–3 POLITICAL CULTURES AND THE POPULATION/POWER SHIFT, 1950–1975

Source: Daniel J. Elazar, *American Federalism: A View From the States.* (New York: Crowell, 1966) p. 97.

Note: Where two letters are juxtaposed, the first indicates the dominant political subculture and the second, the principal secondary subculture.

M = Moralistic
I = Individualistic
t = Traditionalistic

Alaska and Hawaii omitted for lack of data.

"Snowbelt" +32% Population Increase

"Sunbelt" +60% Population Increase

31

Suburbs,
sunbelt,
snowbelt: the
sweep of
people and
power

fifty biggest companies dropped from twenty-two in 1965 to ten in 1975. On the other hand, 72 percent of the "Fortune 500" industrial headquarters remain outside the South and West and 78 percent retain their home offices in northeastern or north central states.

Politically, the traditionally strong congressional power of the South and West is declining. In 1965, southerners or westerners chaired fifteen of the Senate's sixteen standing committees, and fifteen of the House's twenty committees; by 1975, however, southerners and westerners headed only eleven of eighteen standing Senate committees, and eleven out of twenty-two House committees.

This clear decline in national legislative power held by the South and West may, in fact, be an offshoot of the demographic power shift. Assuming that Elazar's analysis of political cultures and the Census Bureau's data are basically accurate, we are witnessing a rather precipitous conflict between peoples reared in fundamentally different political environments and holding incompatible political values. The Moralists from the North are invading the western and southern preserves of the Traditionalists. People who believe in widespread political participation, aggressive government programs for social change, and political self-direction suddenly are rubbing shoulders with people who value political apathy, view government as a necessary evil for maintaining the status quo, and accept as only meet and proper the political dominance of paternalistic elites.

The transfer (or diffusion) of people and power from cities to suburbs and from the East and Midwest to the South and West constitutes the primary political reality during the last quarter of this century. These shifts imply that not only will the supposed Eastern Establishment gradually fade as an object of national (or at least regional) resentment, but that Americans may lose some of their preoccupation with politics in Washington and perhaps refocus their attention on their local governments. That refocussing is what this book is about.

PART

THE SEMI-
SOVEREIGN
STATES

CHAPTER

MAKING GOVERNMENTS:
CONSTITUTIONS,
PARTIES, AND THE
GOOD OL' BOYS

"The Sovereign State of . . ." is a sonorous phrase oft heard rolling redolently from the throats of blue-suited gentlemen who call state legislatures into session. A number of southern governors also favor it.

As a statement, it is nonsense. "Sovereignty," according to Webster, means "supreme power" and "freedom from external control"; no American state really has that. Article VI of the United States Constitution lays out in indisputable language that states and the governments within them are subordinate to "the supreme law of the land."

Still, the states have power. They can do anything that the federal Constitution and the laws made by Congress do not prohibit them from doing. This amounts to a big field of play. It encompasses: health, safety, education, commerce, criminal justice, transportation, the courts, taxation—indeed, voting itself. These, and other areas, make up the rights of the states, and between 1861 and 1865 it took the bloodiest war in American history to determine the constitutional limitations of these rights.

STATE CONSTITUTIONS: DOCUMENTS OF POLITICS OR PRINCIPLE?

Within these limitations, however, state constitutions determine how rights, power, laws, and prerogatives are distributed in the states themselves. In very basic terms, state constitutions follow the federal version. A bill of civil rights is included (although, technically, such bills are unnecessary, since state citizens are guaranteed these rights by the Fourteenth Amendment), and an organization of the government is posited. Invariably, three branches of government (legislative, executive, and adjudicative) are specified and their powers and limitations enumerated in a manner similar to the federal checks-and-balances system. A bicameral (two-house) legislative is specified in all but one state, Nebraska, which has a unicameral (one-house) legislature. The fifty state constitutions usually are as inelegant as the state governments themselves. They lack the intellectual brilliance, stylistic grace, and verbal parsimony of the national Constitution of 1789. Most are ponderous tomes that revel in the pretentious. According to their constitutional preambles, Alaskans are "grateful to God," Puerto Ricans are "fully democratic," and Hawaiians not only are "mindful of our Hawaiian heritage," but possess "an understanding heart toward all the people of the earth."

THE POLITICS OF CONSTITUTIONAL CHANGE.

State constitutions are more difficult to change than statutory law, but they are considerably simpler to amend than the United States Constitution. As a result, they do not respond to political change nor provide an anchor of

37

Making
governments:
constitutions,
parties, and the
good ol' boys

social principle. Nevertheless, they can be amended, even rewritten, and states have devised a number of ways of doing so. They include: calling a constitutional convention, appointing constitutional commissions, use of initiative petition, inauguration of legislative action, and other less systematic methods, such as court interpretations and formal elaborations on constitutional clauses by the legislature.

The most fundamental way of changing a constitution is to rewrite it. Traditionally, this entails calling a *constitutional convention*. Often a constitutional convention may be called by putting the proposal to a vote in the legislature. The decision on whether to call a convention may be determined by simple majorities or extraordinary majorities, such as a two-thirds vote. In some states, approval by two separate sessions of the legislature is required for the calling of a constitutional convention.

A variant of the constitutional convention is the *constitutional commission*, a device that is gaining considerable popularity in the states. Almost twice as many states use commissions as use constitutional conventions. Commissions are more easily controlled by legislatures and are considerably less expensive and less public.

A third method of inaugurating constitutional changes is through the *initiative petition* and *referendum vote*, which originated in 1902 in Oregon and is now used in nearly two dozen states. An initiative must bear the signatures of a certain percentage of voters deemed sufficient for calling an election (or referendum) concerning a proposed constitutional change.

Finally, forty-nine of the fifty states (New Hampshire is the exception) permit proposals for constitutional amendments to be *proposed solely by the state legislatures*. Most states require that proposals for changes in their constitutions be subjected to ratification by the voters.

Although changing a constitution is not easy, these methods have produced a proliferation of amendments in a number of states; for example, between 1921 and 1974, the Louisiana Constitution had 494 amendments appended, while California's Constitution of 1879 has been amended 358 times.

In the 1960s and 1970s, the states initiated an unprecedented wave of comprehensive revisions of their constitutions, relying primarily on the constitutional convention and the constitutional commission to do so. In an analysis of why states have so enthusiastically undertaken the revisions of their constitutions, Edward D. Grant has offered three theories: The Renovation-Relearning Model, which contends that states reinforce a tendency to revise their constitutions by interacting among each other; the Federal Factor Model, which holds that the federal government is a central source in stimulating state revisions; and the State System Model, which argues that social, economic, and political variables within the state are the main reasons behind initiating a major constitutional revision. Grant found that the first model, that of Renovation-Relearning, in which neighboring states stimulated each other to revise their constitutions, probably served as the most accurate description of why the states have been renovating their constitutions so prolifically in recent years. Grant also concluded that the states which are the most actively pursuing constitutional revisions tend to have significantly larger populations, be more industrialized, and have higher levels of professionalism in the legislature and the bureaucracy.[1]

State constitutions are indeed "living documents" in the sense that they can be changed and frequently are. Yet, the spate of obsolete clauses present in most constitutions causes one to speculate on whether these supposedly living documents might simply be the Undead.

PARTIES AND POLITICS

If constitutions and how they are changed determine the rules of the political game, political parties are among the major players of the game. The party is one of America's several unique contributions to the world's political workings. As William Nisbet Chambers has observed, "The first modern political parties arose in the United States decades before they appeared in Great Britain and other nations; and this has meant that the first experiments in party politics were made in the American arena."[2] Chambers traces the evolution of the nation's party systems through three stages: (1) when parties were instrumental in "establishing the nation as a going entity" (roughly 1789 to 1815), or the *nation-building stage;* (2) the *establishment of significant form* (1828 to 1860), when parties set up their grassroots organizations, conventions, procedures, and so forth; and (3) the *derivative stage* (1865 to the present), the time when parties became adjustive and reactive to their political environments, rather than innovative and creative in making policy.[3] During the more recent years of this phase, American political parties "have lost the virtual monopoly over nominations, campaigning, and elections which they once enjoyed . . . and the party system has come to play a less significant role than it once did. If party once was king in a democratic polity, it no longer reigns."[4]

Still, political parties perform irreplaceable functions of government. Chambers lists these functions as (1) assisting in the maintenance of the political system's legitimacy; (2) promoting the efficiency of the political system; and (3) rendering the political system more adjustive to social change. Parties have been crucial to the workings of these three interrelated functions, largely because, generally speaking, "the American party systems have been moderate in character and less ideologically oriented than party systems in other nations."[5]

---

[1]Edward D. Grant, III, "State Constitutional Revision and the Forces that Shape It" *State and Local Government Review* 9 (May 1, 1977) 60–64.

[2]William N. Chambers, "Party Development and the American Mainstream," in William N. Chambers and Walter Dean Burnham, *The American Party Systems* (New York: Oxford Press, 1975) p. 4.

[3]*Ibid.,* 23.

[4]*Ibid.,* 15.

[5]*Ibid.,* 4.

REGULATING THE CENTER: PARTIES IN THE STATES

Unlike most democracies, the American states give legal recognition to their political parties. This came about because, following the Civil War, state parties were seedbeds of corruption, and legislatures gradually passed laws designed to stem their influence. In some states, in fact, regulations of parties were written into the state constitutions themselves. In general, these laws limit state parties in a number of ways.[6]

One such way is party finance. Only five states (Alaska, Delaware, Illinois, Nevada, and Rhode Island) do not regulate how parties finance their campaigns and organizations in some fashion. Regulations set limits on campaign financing, say who may and may not contribute to a party, and require reports on party financing.

A second area regulated by the states is the nominating procedures. Parties in the states have very little say on how they will select their candidates for office. Most states require direct primaries (i.e., popular votes on who will be the party's nominee) as opposed to private caucuses, conventions, or any other form of smoke-filled room.

A third area of legislation concerns the organization of the parties themselves. Every state stipulates to a significant degree the legal organizational structure of their state parties.

Finally there is the area of access to the ballot. All states specify how an organization may qualify as a political party and, as such, have its candidates' names and party affiliations listed on the ballot. Their state legislatures view their political parties primarily as organizations for nominating candidates and arguing over issues in elections. As a result, all but five states (Alabama, Arkansas, Georgia, South Carolina, and Virginia) prescribe the structure and duties of committees, conventions, and caucuses of their parties in detail. Alabama, Arkansas, Georgia, and Virginia still have some laws regarding parties, but these laws are considerably looser than they are in the remaining sections of the country. South Carolina abolished all laws regulating parties in order to give the Democratic Party a better chance for evading a court-ordered repeal of the white primary in 1944.

THE CASUAL ORGANIZATION OF POLITICAL PARTIES

The structure of southern political parties reflects the looseness of the laws regulating them, but in most states, the political party serves as a highly unstructured arena where coalitions form and reform over political issues and personalities. The consummate scholar of political parties, V. O. Key, Jr., observed that state parties may be described "as a system of layers . . . . Yet each higher level of organization, to accomplish its ends, must obtain the collaboration of the lower layer . . . ."[7]

[6]National Municipal League, *State Party Structures and Procedures: A State-by-State Compendium* (New York: National Municipal League, 1967).

[7]V. O. Key, Jr., *Southern Politics in State and Nation* (New York: Knopf, 1949), pp. 395–396.

In a few states, notably Wisconsin and California, the legal party organizations as stipulated by the legislature are controlled by what are known
as "political clubs." In both states, the clubs have been spawned as a result
of rebellious factions attempting to wrest political power from entrenched
interests that control the traditional machinery of the party.[8]

All state parties have a central committee, also called an executive
committee, that is influenced in varying degrees by state law. In many
instances, these central committees are large to the point of organizational
unwieldiness, although they can serve useful purposes as a central coordinating agency for election campaigns. The real grassroots organization in
the state political parties, however, is represented by the local committees,
and these organizations are made up of the groups that get out the vote by
serving as poll watchers, campaigners, and doorbell ringers.

WHO'S IN CHARGE HERE?

Who controls these party organizations? Are they run by the methods of
the traditional political machine of the past, or are they more responsive to
the brand of citizen politics that we have seen emerging in recent years? A
partial answer is furnished in a study of six states by John Fenton: He
classified three state party systems as "issue-oriented" or "programatic"
(Michigan, Wisconsin, Minnesota) and another three as "job-oriented" or
"traditional" (Ohio, Indiana, and Illinois).[9] The issue-oriented parties cor-
responded to Daniel Elazar's concept of moralistic political culture (see
Chapter 2); this is a party system that is interested primarily in public issues
in an ideological sense. In contrast, the job-oriented political party system
would correspond to Elazar's notion of traditionalistic political culture.
Fenton argues that a state party system will evolve from a job-oriented to an
issue-oriented system if the following conditions apply:

1. strict civil service systems, which reduce a party's control over the distribution of state offices
2. continued and sustained defeat of one party at the polls, reducing it to a
   shell
3. powerful interest groups that seize control over the party's machinery
4. the existence of an electorate that is issue-oriented along national lines[10]

Whether or not Fenton's analysis is correct, the state political parties are
made up of people who are the political grassroots of this country. In this
light it is of note that a study of how grassroot party officials see themselves

---

[8]See, for example: Frank J. Soranf, "Extra-Legal Parties in Wisconsin." *American Political
Science Review* 48 (1964): 692–704; Hugh A. Bone, "New Party Associations in the West."
American Political Science Review 45 (1941): 1115–1120; and James Q. Wilson, *The American
Democrats* (Chicago: University of Chicago Press, 1962).

[9]John Fenton, *Midwest Politics* (New York: Holt, Rinehart & Winston, 1966), p. 116.

[10]*Ibid.*, 116.

41

Making
governments:
constitutions,
parties, and the
good ol' boys

found that more than three-quarters of them saw their proper role as related primarily to campaigns or party organization. Less than 10 percent saw their most important role as being "ideological"; that is, increasing political information and forming policy. It would appear that, at the grassroots, political parties favor a traditionalistic image of their work.[11]

WHAT DO PARTIES DO?

What, in fact, do parties do? The answers are straightforward. They recruit candidates; they nominate candidates, usually through the device of party primary; and they campaign for those candidates.

Nominating candidates: Caucuses and conventions. Of these functions, perhaps that of nominating candidates for public office is the most vital. Traditionally, the nomination procedure took place in the notorious smoke-filled room, a term that came into use through John Adams, who actually was describing a caucus of political cronies that was held in a smoke-filled attic before a particular election in Boston. Adams was referring to a meeting in 1763 of the Boston Caucus Club. He disapproved, not only because the caucus was entirely extralegal and unpublic, but also because "There they drink flip, I suppose," and determine who will be "selectmen, assessors, collectors, wardens, firewards and representatives" before they ever "are chosen in the town."[12]

Such a method developed naturally enough and was in full bloom by the middle of the eighteenth century, but then caucuses slowly were displaced by party nominating conventions. Delaware, the first state to adopt such a device, inaugurated it during the administration of Thomas Jefferson, and by 1930 most of the northern states had gone over to it.[13]

The proliferating primaries. Although the party convention was a step toward a greater degree of participatory democracy, it was and in most states still is largely controlled by local party committees. Hence, the primary election evolved as an even more democratic method of selecting candidates. The primary is simply a means of making nominations by direct popular election. The first direct primary took place in Crawford County, Pennsylvania, where both Democrats and Republicans adopted the idea prior to the Civil War. It spread to several other states before the turn of the century. In 1903 Wisconsin passed into law the first statewide primary election system, and in 1955 Connecticut became the last state to permit primary elections.[14]

---

[11]Lewis Bowman and Robert Boynton, "Activities and Role Definitions of Grass Roots Party Officials." *Journal of Politics* 28 (February, 1966) 121–143.

[12]Charles Francis Adams, ed., *The Works of John Adams*, Vol. 2. (Boston: Little, Brown, 1850), p. 144. Citation from diary entry of February, 1763.

[13]Daniel R. Grant and H. C. Nixon, *State and Local Government in America* (Boston: Allyn & Bacon, 1975), p. 172.

[14]Malcolm E. Jewell and David M. Olson, *American State Political Parties and Elections* (Homewood, Ill.: Dorsey, 1978) pp. 126–127.

A quick description of the different kinds of primary elections used in the states is worthwhile, since the primary is now the major means of nominating state and local officials. The convention, more often than not, merely ratifies the procedure and makes the nomination official. Moreover, the state primary has developed into the major means for presidential candidates to obtain their parties' nominations. By the nation's Bicentennial, no less than thirty-one states had presidential primary elections. Only twenty-three states had presidential primaries in 1972 and a mere fourteen in 1968. Even so, in the rugged 1976 presidential primaries, which were conducted in a record number of states, only 4.2 percent of the country's voting-age population actually voted in the thirty-one primaries.

Partisan primaries can be closed or open. Most states use the *closed partisan primary:* only Democrats may vote in Democratic primaries, and only Republicans in Republican primaries. In a closed primary, state election officials require a voter to state his or her party preference and even, perhaps, show proof that he or she belongs to the party.

Nevertheless, a secret ballot permits the use of switchover votes in even a closed primary. The stratagem here is that a Democrat will vote for the weakest possible Republican candidate, and the Republican voter will do likewise in the Democratic primary. Only the public loses in such a process, of course. The reverse effect can also hold true—that is, primary voters with normal allegiance to one party will vote for the candidate in another party because he has particular drawing power. This happened dramatically in the 1976 Republican presidential primary in Texas; Democratic voters who favored the candidacy of George Wallace (who, only weeks earlier, had been effectively knocked out of contention by Jimmy Carter's southern victories) elected to switch over to Republican candidate Ronald Reagan, giving him a win of massive proportions.

An even less palatable aspect of the closed party primary is the so-called "white primary," which was popular in the South between 1910 and 1940. This was a device used to prevent black voters from voting in Democratic primaries. The "solid South," of course, was a one-party Democratic region at that time; for the first one hundred years following the Civil War, the tradition was, he who wins the Democratic primary wins the election. The white primary meant that black voters were effectively prohibited from voting at all for public officials. In 1944, the famous case of *Smith* v. *Allwright* was decided by the Supreme Court and, in effect, abolished the white primary in the South. Although this ruling did not really enfranchise black voters, it was a step in the right direction.

A few states have used the *open primary,* notably Michigan, Minnesota, Montana, Texas, Washington, and Wisconsin. The open primary does not accept the notion on which the closed primary is predicated—that is, that competing parties will try to nominate the opposition's weakest candidate or similarly distort the results in their favor. Primary voting is open to all and for all. A variant of the open primary is called *double-filing.* Double-filing is

43

Making
governments:
constitutions,
parties, and the
good ol' boys

a mechanism that permits a candidate to seek the nomination for the same office in two or more parties during the same primary election. California used double-filing until 1959, and it is still employed by New York.

Overall, party primaries tend to favor the large political parties, because many states stipulate that unless a party received a minimum number or a certain portion of the votes cast in the last general election, that party may not enter a primary. Many states use 10 percent as a determinant, although the portion can be as high as 25 percent of the total vote cast for presidential electors, as in Virginia.

The primary is not as democratic a way of nominating candidates for public office as many hoped it might be, and it is expensive. Although it is doubtful that the primary will be displaced by some new method of nominating candidates for public office, the traditional, state-based primary may be due for substantial revision at the national level. The Democrats, at least, are seriously considering restructuring presidential primaries, and a leading prospect may be the consolidation of state primaries into regional ones. In other words, there may be clearly identified Sunbelt candidates battling Eastern Establishment candidates for their party's favor in the foreseeable future.

Do the primaries matter? If by that it is meant, are the primaries the "primary" way to secure the presidential nomination of one of the two major parties, probably not. Such, at least, is the conclusion of a major analysis of party primaries during the forty years between 1936 and 1976.[15] The study found that being considered the "front runner" for roughly three years in advance of the party's national convention counted far more heavily than winning a series of primaries. Thirteen of the fourteen front runners between 1936 and 1976 won the nomination. In short, the contention that primaries are democratic, representative, or needed is highly debatable.

Electing candidates: Is the party over? Regardless of how a party nominates its candidates, the influence of that party on a state's government is determined in large part by the number of officials that may be put up for election. In some states this number is quite low; for example, Maine, New Hampshire, and New Jersey elect only the governor, who appoints everyone else. Alaska, Hawaii, and Tennessee elect the governor and only one other official. Most other states elect a governor, lieutenant governor, and at least ten other executives. Of course, in all states the legislators are elected, but again, the procedure for being nominated and running a campaign devolves to the local party organization at the precinct level.

Although the parties have primary responsibility for conducting campaigns, usually "Candidates are on their own in political campaigns . . . .

---

[15]William R. Keech and Donald R. Matthews, *The Party's Choice* (Washington: Brookings Institution, 1976).

Because of the independence of regular party organizations, no candidate can be sure that they will put forth the effort necessary to elect him. Thus every candidate, to some degree, creates his own campaign organization. . . .[16]

A fascinating variation of the personal campaign organization has emerged for candidates running for Congress. The National Committee for an Effective Congress (NCEC), founded in 1948, was formed to promote what it calls "progressive" candidates for office. (In practice, "progressive" to NCEC generally means Democratic, although it has no formal affiliation with the Democratic party.) In 1973, NCEC implemented a new policy; instead of granting cash contributions to its candidates, it decided to provide them with in-kind services, such as opinion polls, computer services, precinct analysis, professional media advice, and even campaign management. As a result, observers give NCEC credit for the election of thirty-five freshmen congressmen in 1974, all of whom were re-elected in 1976. During that year, in fact, NCEC supported one hundred candidates for Congress, seventy-five of whom were elected.[17]

Campaigns are costly, and money can make the difference. An analysis of campaigns for the U.S. Senate in 1978 found that candidates who outspent their opponents won 85 percent of the contested races.[18] Money, however, is *not* a major factor in winning the campaign, a point that may go against the conventional wisdom of some citizens. Traditional party identification, recent political events, personalities of candidates, and the general level of prosperity count as much in any one election as campaigning expenditures in determining the outcome of the vote.[19]

THE COMPETITION QUESTION

Interparty competition has remained a principal topic of research among political scientists for a number of years, and there are at least three schools of thought about how interparty competition affects the development of public policy in the states. The central question is, which states have parties that more closely reflect state issues: those with highly competitive electoral contests or those dominated by a one-party system?

Ideology equals competition. One school of thought, represented by V. O. Key, Jr., is that states possessing highly competitive party systems are likely to have more ideologically oriented state legislatures and executive

---

[16]Daniel Ogden and Hugh Bone, *Washington Politics* (New York: New York University Press, 1960), p. 47.

[17]James M. Perry, syndicated column, *The National Observer,* November 28, 1976.

[18]Report by Congress Watch, as cited in Associated Press, November 16, 1978. syndicated nationally. But see also: Reports by the Citizen's Research Foundation, Princeton, New Jersey, Herbert E. Alexander, Director. Cited in Austin Ranney, "Parties in State Politics," *Politics in the American States,* 3rd ed. Herbert Jacob and Kenneth N. Vines, eds. (Boston: Little, Brown, 1976), p. 76.

[19]Ranney, *Politics in the American States,* p. 77.

branches.[20] Therefore, different public opinions on policy issues will result in sharp competition between political parties.

The illusion of competition. Another school of thought, represented by Thomas R. Dye, argues just the opposite: interparty competition has at best a minor influence on the form taken by public policies in states.[21] Dye related social welfare expenditures, notably old age assistance, unemployment compensation, and education, to a measurement of interparty competition and found that, statistically, a state's level of welfare expenditures was only weakly related to its degree of interparty competition. On the other hand, the amount spent on such social welfare programs is very strongly related to the level of wealth and resources in the state—a less than surprising conclusion.

The reality of competition. A final variant is represented by Ira Sharkansky and Richard Hofferbert. They argue that high levels of interparty competition do indeed relate to high levels of social welfare expenditures and that correlation between the two is higher than Dye recognizes.[22] Sharkansky and Hofferbert's analysis uses a somewhat more sophisticated set of correlational methods than does Dye's, and their statistics bear out this contention.

The structure of competition. There are four major patterns of interparty competition in the United States.[23] One is the *one-party Democratic system;* that is, states whose politics are dominated completely by the Democratic party. These are entirely in the South. A second is the *modified one-party Democratic system,* states where the Democratic party has a general predominance but can be effectively challenged on occasion. These, with some exceptions, are largely the border states or those on the rim of the old Confederacy. Third are clear *two-party systems,* including virtually all the western and midwestern states and most of the northeastern states. Finally, there are a few states that have a *modified one-party Republican system.* They are North Dakota, Kansas, New Hampshire, Maine, Wyoming, Iowa, and Vermont. Figure 3–1 classifies the fifty states according to the level of interparty competition.

The great majority of states are clear two-party systems and these states share a number of common characteristics. Most notable is the fact that these states are substantially more urbanized than those in the other three categories. All the nation's major cities are located in two-party states, and the populations of these states have higher median incomes, a higher percentage of the labor force engaged in manufacturing and a lower percentage working in agriculture, and higher numbers of immigrants and

---

[20]V. O. Key, Jr., *American State Politics: An Introduction* (New York: Alfred A. Knopf, 1956), p. 201.

[21]Thomas R. Dye, *Politics, Economics and the Public: Policy Outcomes; The American States* (Chicago: Rand McNally, 1966).

[22]Ira Sharkansky and Richard I. Hofferbert, "Dimensions of State Politics, Economics, and Public Policy," *American Political Science Review,* 63 (1969), 867–879.

[23]Ranney, *Politics in the American States,* pp. 59–60.

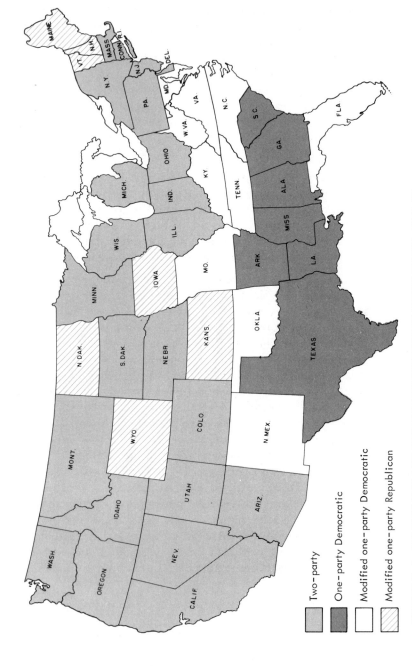

FIGURE 3–1 DEMOCRATIC AND REPUBLICAN SUCCESS IN STATE OFFICE, 1954–75.

Two-party

One-party Democratic

Modified one-party Democratic

Modified one-party Republican

NOTE: Hawaii and Alaska, not shown, are two-party states.

47

Making
governments:
constitutions,
parties, and the
good ol' boys

children of immigrants than do states in any of the other three categories. Two-party states have fewer blacks but more Roman Catholics and immigrants than the one-party Democratic or modified one-party Democratic states. As Ranney notes, however, the predominance of any one particular party system in at least half of the states stems from the fact that the populations of many states are still fighting the Civil War—at least mentally.[24] Traditionally, Southerners have tended not to vote for the party of Lincoln, while Yankees do.

But there is more to voting than region and history. In the following chapter we shall consider state voting patterns in greater detail.

[24]*Ibid.*, 63–65.

4

VOTING:
THE ULTIMATE
DEMOCRATIC ACT

As we learned in the last chapter, the states take a significant hand in regulating the political behavior of large groups of people by enacting laws concerning their political parties. States also take an official interest in determining how individual citizens behave politically, and they do this by putting myriad restrictions and regulations on that ultimate democratic act: voting. Still, the states have come a long way in terms of expanding suffrage. In the 1780s, only about 120,000 of the more than two million people in America were allowed to vote.

STATES STOP THE VOTE

While suffrage has been gradually but steadily extended, over the years the national government probably has been more forceful than the state governments in expanding voting rights. Generally, the state governments have a record of placing obstacles in the way of a citizen trying to exercise his or her right to vote. State political elites generally try to keep the suffrage limited to "their own kind" as a means of keeping "their own kind" in office. Thus, states have a sorry history of discouraging blacks, browns, the poor, women, and the undereducated from voting. What are some of the major impediments the states have erected against voting?

THE REGISTRATION WRANGLE

To be able to vote, first one must register as a voter in the state he or she resides in. The sole exception is North Dakota, which allows its residents to vote without first registering. Most states require a prospective voter to appear in person before a registration board or a voting supervisor to establish his or her qualifications. In some states, these qualifications can be manifold, although some are attempting to simplify registration.

There are two basic kinds of registration for voters. Virtually all the states have some sort of *permanent registration;* a few require *periodic registration.* Vermont requires a voter to register every year; South Carolina, at the other end of the continuum, requires its voters to register every ten years. These voting registration requirements presuppose a stable population, which, of course, is hardly the case in the United States.

Registration was once an effective device for controlling who got to vote in which election. So powerful was the ability to control who got to vote by controlling registration that the federal government began sending general registration officers to areas of the country (notably the South) where it felt registration requirements were being actively used to deter voting by black citizens.

THE RESIDENCE REQUIREMENT

It has been estimated that more than eight million citizens who might otherwise have been eligible to vote in national elections are disenfranchised by residence requirements in the states. Nationally there is a clear trend toward reducing state residence requirements. The United States Supreme Court, in a series of cases from 1969 to 1972, justified a state's right to stipulate that its voters be *bona fide* residents, but denied the validity of lengthy residency requirements as a test of voting qualifications. In 1972, the Court invalidated Tennessee's one-year residency requirement, making it clear that, over time, the judiciary will most likely pressure states to reduce the lengths of their residency requirements.[1]

TAXING VOTERS

Poll taxes were another device used by states, notably in the South, to deny registration of potential voters. The poll tax was introduced around 1890, and by 1910 most of the southern states had adopted the device. The poll tax was designed to reduce the numbers of blacks being registered in the South, which it did effectively. It also reduced the number of poor whites being registered to vote, which was probably not an entirely unforeseen development.

More than half of the states that originally passed poll taxes had abolished them by 1950. By 1962 only five states still had a poll tax, and in 1966 the Supreme Court, in *Harper* v. *Virginia State Board of Elections,* in effect obliterated the last remaining poll taxes in the country. But more will be said about this later.

THE AGE OBSTACLE

Another major obstacle to voting is the age requirement. Traditionally, most states had stipulated that twenty-one be the required age for exercising the right to vote; Georgia, Kentucky, and Alaska were the exceptions. With the passage of the Twenty-sixth Amendment to the United States Constitution in 1970, however, all states were required to let citizens eighteen years of age and over vote in local, state, and national elections.

THE LITERACY LOOPHOLE

Yet another barricade to voting is the so-called literacy test. By 1970 almost a third of the states had some kind of literacy examination. Some of the states allowed an alternative in the form of a property requirement or

---

[1]Robert Thornton, "Election Legislation." *The Book of the States, 1972–73* (Lexington, Ky.: Council of State Governments, 1972) pp. 26–27.

required the potential voter to show an understanding of the "principles of republican government"—whatever that meant. Literacy tests eventually came under fire from the national government. In 1964, Congress passed the Civil Rights Act and in the following year the Voting Rights Act. In 1965, the Supreme Court ruled that the use of "understanding tests," which gave voting registrars discretion to determine who passed or failed the literacy test, was unconstitutional. In 1970, Congress enacted a second Voting Rights Act that suspended all literacy tests, a provision that was upheld by the Supreme Court.

THE PROPERTY PREREQUISITE

A final obstacle to voting is the imposition of property qualifications. Some states permit only owners of property to vote on public bond issues and assessments, a qualification that is favored in the West, and a number of states deny paupers the right to vote.

ENFRANCHISING THE PEOPLE: WASHINGTON MOVES IN

The welter of obstacles erected by the states to prevent potential voters from voting is attributable to the political conservatism often found at the state level. Interestingly, these state hindrances to voting have been increasingly circumscribed by national statute and by amendment to the Constitution. Indeed, the national government has been, by far, the most innovative in permitting citizens to vote and removing restrictions. Consider some of the major enactments in this regard.

THE FIFTEENTH AMENDMENT

In 1870, the Fifteenth Amendment to the United States Constitution was enacted. It states that a person could not be denied the vote because of race. The amendment, enacted by a Reconstruction Congress and a victorious North, also gave Congress the power to enforce black voting rights "by appropriate legislation." In effect, this clause permitted the states to retain their rights to determine voter qualifications, provided that they did not use race as a criterion. This proviso, nonetheless, permitted the states, and particularly the southern states, to practice *de facto,* if not *de jure,* racial discrimination through poll taxes, literacy tests, and so forth. As Thomas R. Dye has written, "it is a tribute to the ingenuity of southern politicians that they were able to defeat the purpose of this amendment for almost a century."[2]

---

[2]Thomas R. Dye, *Politics in States and Communities,* 2nd ed. (Englewood Cliffs, N.J.: Prentice-Hall 1973), p. 88.

THE NINETEENTH AMENDMENT

The next major action by the federal government to enfranchise large numbers of voters came in 1920 with the passage of the Nineteenth Amendment, which enfranchised women by stating that no voters could be disenfranchised because of sex. The federal government thus doubled the number of potential voters with a single amendment.

THE TWENTY-FOURTH AMENDMENT

The Twenty-fourth Amendment, while not making quite so dramatic an expansion of voting rights as the Nineteenth, is perhaps the most significant expression of regional politics that appears in the Constitution. It was (and is) directed primarily at the South; in effect, it prohibited the collection of poll taxes by voter registrars. The Twenty-fourth Amendment was ratified in 1964, the same year in which the Civil Rights Act was passed by Congress. Together, these two statements of public policy represented a dramatic expansion of the franchise for black voters.

THE CIVIL RIGHTS ACT

The Twenty-fourth Amendment affected only the five states that still retained their poll taxes: Alabama, Arkansas, Mississippi, Texas, and Virginia. The Civil Rights Act of 1964 made it illegal for registrars to discriminate on the basis of race in registering voters, or to reject an application for registering to vote on the basis of inconsequential mistakes made by the applicant. The act thus went further than the Twenty-fourth Amendment, which prohibited the poll tax only in national elections.

VOTING RIGHTS ACTS

Neither the Twenty-fourth Amendment, which made poll taxes unconstitutional, nor the Civil Rights Act, which prohibited discrimination by voting registrars, were as successful in enabling blacks to register and to vote as they might have been. In 1965, therefore, Congress passed the first Voting Rights Act. It was designed to make the Fifteenth Amendment more effective in practice. The act applied to any state or county where the literacy test, or some similar test, was enforced and where more than fifty percent of voting-age residents either were not registered or could not cast ballots in the 1964 national election. Where there was evidence of voter discrimination, the U.S. Attorney General could replace local registrars with federal voting registrars. Federal registrars could abolish literacy tests, and they could register voters under federal procedures, which were considerably simpler than those found in some states and localities. In 1966, the

Supreme Court upheld the Voting Rights Act of 1965 as an appropriate piece of legislation with which to combat racial discrimination at the polls.

A second Voting Rights Act was passed in 1970. In this legislation, Congress extended the vote to persons eighteen years old, abolished residency requirements of more than thirty days for voting in national elections, and suspended all literacy tests. The Voting Rights Act of 1970 immediately was challenged in court. In the 1971 case of *Oregon* v. *Mitchell*, the Supreme Court ruled that Congress had the power to extend the vote to eighteen-year-olds in national elections, but not in state or local elections.

THE TWENTY-SIXTH AMENDMENT

Because this court ruling created some constitutional confusion, a drive was initiated to pass the Twenty-sixth Amendment to the Constitution. Ratified in 1971, the amendment prevents denial of voting on the basis of age to citizens eighteen years old and above in national, state, and local elections.

As the foregoing review indicates, the national government has taken an aggressive and affirmative lead in assuring that American citizens have the right to vote and are not hindered by tyrannical voting registrars, unnecessary bureaucratic paraphernalia, or legislators interested in preserving their power base. There is still considerable room for improvement but we evidently cannot expect much initiative from the states, at least if history is any indication. It is the national government that has muscled its way into state and local elections in an effort to assure that residents of those areas may vote. The Fifteenth, Nineteenth, Twenty-fourth, and Twenty-sixth Amendments of the Constitution, the Civil Rights Act of 1964, and the Voting Rights Acts of 1965 and 1970, along with related court cases at the national level, all indicate that the federal government is the leader in expanding the suffrage, not the states or the localities.

This was not always so. Until the midnineteenth century the states were extremely liberal in determining who was allowed to vote; many even allowed foreign nationals to vote in their elections. But around 1850, a wave of nationalism swept the country, and most of these laws were changed. Today, of course, one must be a citizen to vote. Whether or not to expand the right to vote is an important question in a democracy. The record in this country indicates that the rules of the game have, overall, worked in favor of expanding the suffrage to all citizens. But have these rules had any effect? Do people vote?

THE PUZZLE OF VOTING PARTICIPATION

Many factors determine the nature of a potential voter's participation in politics. The kind of election (national, state, or local), the voter's state and region, his or her economic and educational status, race, age, and sex—all help determine how—or if—a potential voter will take part in an election.

First, let us consider the type of election. Presidential elections attract the most voters by far. Almost 60 percent of the registered voters, on the average, vote for a presidential candidate, although this percentage is on a decline, as we shall discuss later in this chapter. Participation in off-year (that is, nonpresidential) elections is considerably lower; between 37 and 45 percent of the voting-age population turned out for these elections between 1962 and 1978, or between 45 and 50 percent of the registered voters. Voting patterns for governors, U.S. senators, and representatives reflect the presidential/off-year dimension. Between 1962 and 1972, the average turnout of registered voters in gubernatorial elections was 62.8 percent in presidential years and 49.6 percent in off years. For U.S. senators, the average turnout was 58.8 percent and 48.5 percent, respectively, and for representatives, 54.8 percent and 45 percent. Voter turnout for these offices is declining.

Perhaps more influential in determining the degree of participation by a voter is where he or she lives. States and regions have very different voting patterns; nevertheless, certain generalizations apply. For example, we know that those states with higher family incomes and relatively well-educated populations tend to have greater voter participation. Higher turnouts are also seen in states where parties are relatively competitive with each other, and also states with fewer laws ruling registration procedures and such items as brief minimum residence requirements, and greater ease of registration and absentee voting. The upshot of these factors seems to be that midwestern, New England, and the Rocky Mountain states rank very high in voter turnout; the deep South and border states are among the lowest. Figure 4–1 ranks the states according to voter turnout.

Of course, certain individual states defy the trends in terms of voter turnout. For example, Utah has a higher turnout in statewide elections than any state in the Union, perhaps because of the influence of the locally powerful Church of Jesus Christ of Latter-Day Saints, or Mormon Church, which encourages a high civic consciousness among its members. Similarly, voting behavior in West Virginia is unique. It is one of the poorest states in the nation, has very low levels of formal education attainments in terms of its overall population, is a border state, and has little competition between parties. Nonetheless, West Virginians go to the polls in large numbers. Apparently this is because the United Mine Workers Union, a major power in West Virginia politics, has long encouraged its membership to vote along organized labor lines and has established a tradition of voting participation in West Virginia.[3]

---

[3]Jae-On Kim, John R. Petrocik, and Stephen N. Enokson, "Voter Turnout in the American States: Systemic and Individual Components." *American Political Science Review* 69 (March 1975), pp. 359–377.

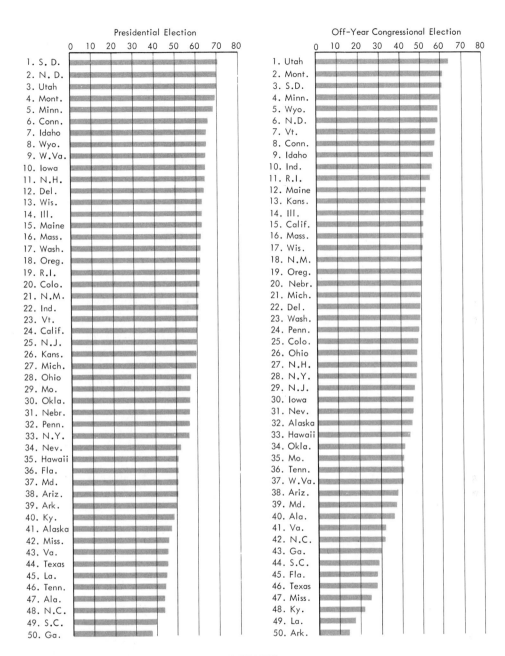

FIGURE 4–1 VOTING TURN-OUT IN THE STATES

Source: Thomas R. Dye, *Politics in States and Communities*, 3rd ed. (Englewood Cliffs, N.J.: Prentice-Hall, 1977) p. 65.

As noted earlier, education, income, and ethnicity (although not necessarily race) also determine the degree of voter participation in the states. The person most likely to vote can be characterized as: having a college education; being in a professional field, managerial occupation or similar white-collar trade; living in a city; being a member of various voluntary associations; being a Catholic or Jew (Protestants vote less frequently); and earning a relatively high income. Those states with populations possessing these characteristics, such as the Upper Plains states, tend to have the highest voter turnout. Voting, in sum, is closely related to social status.

In a 1976 study the U.S. Census Bureau found that voters tended to be college-educated professionals earning $25,000 or more per year. Race does not affect voting turnout. Well educated blacks vote in the same proportions as comparably educated whites.[4] Moreover, the rules of the game were changing in the 1960s and 1970s, and increasing numbers of blacks are voting. Immediately after World War II, no more than an estimated 5 percent of voting-age blacks were registered to vote in the South. By 1952, this proportion had hit 20 percent. Four years later it was 25 percent. In 1960, black registration figures hit 28 percent. In 1964, when the Civil Rights Act passed, black registration zoomed to 39 percent. Still, this figure was little more than half of that for white registration in the South. In 1965, when Congress passed the first Voting Rights Act, the Voter Education Project of the Southern Regional Council was launched. By 1966, nearly 46 percent of the black voting age population were registered and by 1972, the number of new black voters registered to vote in the South surpassed 1.5 million, or more than 55 percent of the eligible blacks, as compared with 70 percent of the eligible southern whites. Increasingly, blacks have elected members of their race to elective office both in the South and in the large northern cities, a phenomenon that will be touched upon in later chapters.

WHO DOES NOT VOTE AND WHY

THE VOTING SLUMP

Although more blacks may be voting than ever before, overall, proportion-ately fewer people are voting. Figure 4–2 indicates the percentage of voter turnouts in presidential and off-year elections from 1954 through 1978.

As can be seen, the proportion of eligible voters who have been turning out to vote in presidential elections, has been declining steadily since 1960. In 1960, 63 percent of the eligible population voted, but in 1976 barely

---

[4]Robert Rheinhold, "American Voters Fall into Elite Category." New York Times syndication, November 3, 1976.

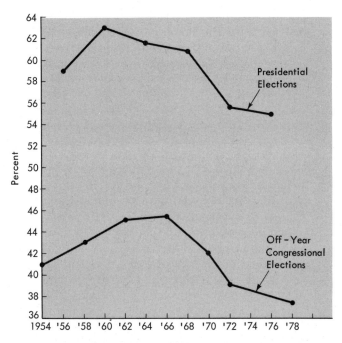

FIGURE 4–2 VOTING TURN OUT AS A PERCENTAGE OF VOTING-AGE POPULATION, 1954–1978

half—54.3 percent—exercised their right to vote. There has been a gain in absolute numbers; in 1972, 77.8 million people voted and in 1976, 80 million people voted. Such an increase, however, is attributed to the growth in the number of eligible voters, not to increases in participation in presidential elections. In fact, the Committee for the American Electorate, after surveying the results of the 1976 elections, concluded that 15 million voters "dropped out." That is, 15 million people who had been registered to vote and who voted in 1968 or 1972 did not vote in 1976. In the view of some pundits, American voters are voting not with their feet, but with their bottoms.

Off-year statewide voting patterns also reflect the overall decline. Participation in off-year elections has been decreasing steadily since 1966, with turnout reaching an all-time low in 1978, when only 37 percent of the eligible voters voted; in three southern states, fewer than a fifth of the voting-age population voted in 1978.

REGISTERING AND VOTING

Of the factors that discourage people from voting, clearly the hassle of registering is a major one. A recent study concluded that state registration laws probably reduced voter turnout in the 1972 presidential election by 10 percent; this means that the national voter turnout could be as high as 60 percent if it were not for state registration requirements.[5] And a Gallup poll found that 38 percent of people who did not vote in the 1976 presidential election stated that they did not do so because they were not registered.[6]

Simplifying registration is among the easiest and most direct policies that states can enact to raise levels of voting, and in recent years some states have moved to make registration more convenient. Among the more notable efforts in this regard are registering voters by mail and permitting voters to register when they vote.

Postcard registration. Registering voters by mail is a new idea. Indeed, prior to 1974, only six states permitted voter registration by mail—Alaska, Kentucky, Maryland, Minnesota, New York, and Texas. Since that time, eight other states, plus the District of Columbia, have permitted voter registration by mail. This device, as of 1976, covered over 40 percent of the nation's more than 141 million eligible voters.

It is too early to determine how well voter registration by mail works in practice. A study conducted for the Council of State Governments concluded that, while mail registration likely adds to the overall convenience of voter

---

[5]Steven J. Rosenstone and Raymond E. Wolfinger, "The Effect of Registration Laws on Voter Turnout." Paper presented at the 1976 meeting of the American Political Science Association, Chicago.

[6]Cited in: Virginia Graham, *Voter Registration (National).* Issue Brief IB74003. Congressional Research Service, Library of Congress, 1977, p. 2.

MACNELLY. Courtesy of Chicago Tribune—New York News Syndicate, Inc.

registration (depending on how well the system is administered), "It seems unlikely that mail registration has an immediate and dramatic impact on registrations and turnout rates."[7] In 1976, only two "postcard" states, Missouri and Minnesota, did not report reduced voting levels. Moreover, there is always the possibility of increased fraud in voter registration schemes when conducted through the mails. For example, one researcher had five hundred nonforwardable voter registration forms sent by first class mail to five hundred totally nonexistent people in Maryland. Had Maryland's fraud protection plan worked, all five hundred forms should have been returned, but about 10 percent of the forms were not returned. Conclusion? "A small conspiracy . . . might be highly successful."[8]

Election-day registration.　The latest suggestion to ease registration requirements proposes that voters be allowed to register on election day. Four states—Oregon, Maine, Minnesota, and Wisconsin—already have adopted election-day registration, and it is likely that the device encourages voting. In 1977, the Carter administration jumped on the election-day registration bandwagon and proposed the establishment of a national voter registration system that would register citizens qualified to vote under the laws of their states on election day at the polling place. All that would be required would be the prospective voter's sworn affidavit that he or she had met the state's requirements and some personal identification. The legislation has yet to be enacted.

THE YOUNG: APATHETIC OR TURNED OFF?

Among the most apathetic voters are the young. By extending the franchise to all citizens eighteen years old and older, the Twenty-sixth Amendment and the Voting Rights Act of 1970 added 8 percent to the eligible voting population. Nevertheless, by 1974, only 36.4 percent of people between eighteen and twenty-one years of age who were questioned in a Census Bureau survey said that they had registered to vote, and only 20.8 percent had voted.[9] A 1976 survey conducted by the Gallup organization found that, while voters between the ages of eighteen and twenty-nine constituted 30 percent of the voting population, only 44 percent had registered to vote, and only 47 percent of this age group had voted in the 1972 election. By contrast, in 1974, 75 percent of the potential voters between fifty-five and sixty-six years of age were registered and 58.3 percent voted. Even so, the older voters, along with youth, also have shown a tendency to opt out of the electoral process in recent years.

---

[7]Jack E. Rossotti and Charles L. Miller, Jr., *State Voter Registration by Mail.* (Lexington, Ky.: Council of State Governments, 1976), p. 9.

[8]Richard G. Smolka. *Registering by Mail: The Maryland and New Jersey Experience* (Washington: The American Enterprise Institute, 1975), pp 78–80.

[9]Rheinhold, "American Voters."

Why the slump? According to a major authority, "What is occurring is a trend for which the term apathy is far too mild a word. There are substantial numbers of Americans who are disenchanted with the political process, disgusted with their leaders, and disillusioned by the failure of government of both political parties to meet their needs."[10] One survey found that 87 percent of the nonvoters it queried believed a lack of courageous leadership to be the nation's major problem.[11]

NONVOTING AS A NEW POLITICS

More information on the nonvoter can be gleaned from a major 1976 study of voting behavior that, as its central object, analyzed the concept of party loyalty.[12] The investigators found (in accordance with recent political polls) that roughly 42 percent of the American electorate identified itself as being with the Democrats, no more than 22 percent (and possibly as few as 18 percent) as Republicans, and 37 percent as independents. In 1952, only 22 percent of the electorate identified itself as independents. Hence, there is a real decline in party affiliation and party loyalty. Most of the abstainers and independents come from the ranks of the eighteen- to thirty-year-olds. Although this group accounts for roughly 30 percent of the electorate, by 1976, only 44 percent of them had registered. The researchers attribute this apathy less to a lack of trust in "the system" than to what they call the impact of the "New Politics" of the 1960s.

The term *New Politics* encompasses the eruption of peace demonstrations, the women's movement, minority politics, student demonstrations, and so forth that occurred during the 1960s and shaped the political attitudes of potential voters who are under thirty years of age. The New Politics created a miasma of unresolved issues of public policy, such as women's liberation, race relations, the generation gap, energy, the environment, foreign policy questions, and others. Thus, the New Politics constitutes a major division in the electorate that has not yet made its impact on the political parties, and neither the Democrats nor the Republicans have shown an ability to cope with the emerging issues of the New Politics. Moreover, this failure on the part of the national political parties may explain the decline of popular trust in government that is clearly a factor in current politics.

In summary, despite the efforts of the national government to expand the suffrage, which on the whole are entirely admirable ones, the nation is still a cradle for large amounts of apathy when it comes to individual participation.

---

[10]Curtis B. Gans, quoted in "Fifteen Million Drop Out as Voters." *Washington Star.* November 21, 1976.

[11]*Ibid.*

[12]Warren Miller and Teresa Levitin, *Leadership and Change* (Ann Arbor, Mich.: Institute of Social Research, 1976).

Groups of people who participate in politics, however, are quite another matter. Indeed, interest groups, lobbyists, organized pressure groups—whatever one may label them—seem to represent, with political parties, quite the opposite side of the coin. In fact, it is the participation of groups that seems to make individual apathy such a critical issue in a democratic context. When individual citizens do not participate in government and in politics, the vacuum they leave permits the relatively unhindered participation of organized pressure groups and special interests. Most political analysts agree that this does not always work to the greatest public interest. In the next chapter we shall consider lobbies and lobbyists and how they play their role in the policy-making process.

CHAPTER

POLITICAL
PRESSURE

Special interests, pressure groups, and lobbies (all of which mean essentially the same thing) are integral to the very idea of democratic government. Indeed, James Madison, writing close to two hundred years ago in *The Federalist*, No. 10, discussed the powers of a "landed interest, a manufacturing interest, a mercantile interest, a monied interest, and many lesser interests" that fought each other for policies favorable to themselves within the confines of the political process.

Madison and his contemporaries saw this situation as quite normal in a democratic polity and, indeed, felt that the workings of such a system resulted in the maximization of the general public's interests. Harmon Zeigler and G. Wayne Peak call Madison's view "the hydraulic theory of politics."[1] The description allows one to visualize a system of forces pushing against each other and emerging with *the* public policy that satisfies all interested parties and in proportion to their relative degrees of power in the system.

A real question has arisen as to whether the "hydraulic theory" still serves as a moral justification of a political process which results in policies that are supposedly in the "best" interests of the public. We shall return to this question at the close of this chapter, but first we should consider some definitions and then discuss how lobbyists play their role in the states.

PRESSURE GROUPS, POWER, AND PECKING ORDERS

An interest group is any collection of people with a common political goal that makes a concerted effort to attain that goal through the normal political channels. One of the favorite methods, and certainly the most notorious, for a group to attain political objectives is lobbying. Lobbying often is performed by professionals who are hired staff members of a particular special interest. Lobbyists normally ply their trade by developing personal contacts among policy makers—both legislators and bureaucrats. Lobbying, of course, is only one technique that interest groups use to affect the policy-making process in their favor; public relations and influencing elections are others.

There is a clear pecking order among the most powerful interest groups in the states. Business heads the list as the lobby generally perceived by policy makers as the "most powerful." In a seminal study, John C. Wahlke and others interviewed in depth state legislators in California, New Jersey, Ohio, and Tennessee. In all four states legislators cited business interests as

---

[1] L. Harmon Zeigler and G. Wayne Peak, *Interest Groups in American Society*, 2nd ed. (Englewood Cliffs, N.J.: Prentice-Hall, 1972) p. 12.

the "most powerful" group more often than any other interest group. Educational interests, such as the California Education Association, ranked second in three of the four states, and were tied for third in the fourth state (Ohio). Labor interests were ranked as the third most powerful in all four states, followed by agricultural interests, public employee associations, ethnic groups, and various religious and civic interests, in that order.

It is quite possible that this rank has changed over the years. Wahlke's study was completed in 1962 and it is likely that such interest groups as associations of public employees, which have become increasingly militant over the years, now would be ranked by legislators as more powerful today than they were then.

Zeigler has confirmed the power of business interests. As Table 5–1 indicates, Zeigler found that business as a category and the single business corporation clearly lead the pack with the highest of legally registered lobbyists in each of the seventeen states he studied. It should not be concluded from Table 5–1, however, that business interests necessarily run the legislatures. For example, farming interests are known to have extraordinary interests and clout in state legislatures, but there are comparatively fewer farming organizations that can be registered in the states as lobbyists.

Moreover, other factors are much more important in determining a lobbyist's influence than numbers registering as official lobbyists. These include (1) the size of the groups, (2) the cohesion of factions within the groups, (3) the geographic distribution of the lobby (for example, statewide versus localized), (4) the social status of the group (the California Education Association probably has more political clout than the Western Nudist Association, for example), (5) the organization and leadership of the lobby, (6) the program that the lobby espouses (for example, the National Association for the Advancement of Colored People probably has a more attractive program to most people than the Ku Klux Klan), and (7) the general political environment in which the interest group must function.

Of these seven sources of interest group strength, perhaps that elusive variable of status is the most important. The term *status* refers to the social standing and economic well being of the members of the interest group. One study concluded that 44 percent of all members of all kinds of groups are described as "upper middle class" by the professional staff directors of their respective associations. Less than 20 percent are seen as working class. "Those who join groups possess disproportionate amounts of such political resources as higher education, occupational status, and the psycho-political resources that typically accompany such properties, including conceptual and forensic skills, an appreciation of one's stake in society, and the political knowledge and interest inspired by this definition of one's situation."[2] In light of this condition, most observers conclude that business and professional groups are the most active lobbies in the state legislatures. Indeed, as

---

[2]Robert Presthus, *Elites in the Policy Process* (Cambridge: Cambridge University Press, 1974), p. 110.

TABLE 5–1 LOBBYISTS BY TYPE IN SELECTED STATES

STATE	BUSINESS	SINGLE BUSINESS CORP.	LABOR	FARM	PROFES- SIONAL	REFORM	PUBLIC AGENCY	RELIGIOUS AND ETHIC	VETERAN	OTHER
California (432)[1]	28.8%	23.1%	10.7%	1.9%	4.7%	4.4%	11.2%	1.1%	0%	14.1%
Florida (439)	18.7	28.2	20.1	2.3	5.7	1.1	10.3	1.0	0	12.6
Iowa (204)	36.3	10.8	8.8	2.9	5.3	6.9	7.4	7.8	1.5	12.3
Kentucky (59)	49.2	6.8	16.8	1.7	10.2	1.7	6.8	0	0	6.8
Maine (165)	40.0	16.4	8.5	3.0	5.4	2.4	14.6	.6	.6	8.5
Michigan (322)	19.9	35.4	8.1	2.1	12.1	5.0	11.2	1.6	1.2	3.4
Montana (180)	27.2	27.2	13.9	4.4	4.4	3.0	8.9	1.0	1.7	8.3
Nebraska (150)	35.3	13.3	4.7	5.3	9.1	4.7	11.3	1.3	1.0	14.0
South Dakota (92)	41.5	21.7	5.4	5.4	8.7	4.3	5.4	0	3.3	4.3
Kansas (41)	9.5	39.4	9.5	2.8	5.2	3.8	13.7	1.9	0	14.2
New York (174)	47.1	27.0	8.1	1.0	7.5	1.0	3.5	1.0	0	3.8
Ohio (173)	35.8	23.9	15.0	1.2	12.1	1.0	4.6	1.0	1.0	4.4
Pennsylvania (243)	32.8	30.8	10.3	1.0	12.4	1.2	7.8	1.6	0	2.1
Virginia (107)	18.7	62.6	8.4	3.7	1.9	0	1.0	0	0	3.7
Connecticut (175)	44.6	26.3	4.6	1.1	6.3	1.7	6.3	1.1	1.1	6.9
Indiana (136)	38.2	11.8	10.3	1.5	7.4	9.4	3.7	2.9	0	14.8
Rhode Island (60)	33.3	21.7	16.7	1.7	8.3	0	0	1.7	5.0	11.6

[1]Numbers in parentheses indicate total number of interest groups registered with the state.

Source: Harmon Zeigler in the first edition of Jacob and Vines, *Politics in the American States* (Boston: Little, Brown, 1965) p.110. Reprinted by permission.

Zeigler and Hendrik Van Dalen note, about 58 percent of the registered lobbyists in the American states represent business, acting either for a single corporation or a combine of corporations in the form of a trade association, as Table 5–1 indicates.[3] Moreover, lobbyists for business interests are clearly the most likely to be perceived as politically powerful by state legislators.[4]

POWER PATTERNS AND PRESSURE POLITICS

Zeigler and Van Dalen have done some provocative work on why some interest groups are more powerful in some states than in others. Basically, their argument is that interest groups have the weakest political impact in the more industrialized and urbanized states with more heterogeneous populations. The logic continues that the more open and competitive the conflict between pressure groups in the states is, then the correspondingly less chance there is of any single group becoming dominant in the making of public policy.

Table 5–2 categorizes types of pressure systems in the states by the social conditions prevailing in those states, and it indicates that pressure group activity, party politics, and the socioeconomic characteristics of states are related. Pressure groups are strongest when there is very little cohesion in the legislature, when there is a low average income per capita, and when there are low levels of education and industrialization.

Obviously, those states that have combative and tough pressure groups should be the most interesting. Zeigler and Van Dalen have forwarded four distinct patterns of interest group conflict in the twenty-four states that they categorize as having strong pressure group politics. These patterns are: (1) an alliance of dominant groups, (2) a single dominant interest group, (3) a conflict between two dominant groups, and (4) what Zeigler and Van Dalen call "the triumph of many interests." We shall consider each of these patterns in turn.

AN ALLIANCE OF DOMINANT GROUPS

A good example of powerful interests working together politically is provided by the state of Maine; "In few American states are the reigns of government more openly or completely in the hands of a few economic interest groups than in Maine."[5] Maine's "Big Three" are the electric power,

---

[3]Harmon Zeigler and Hendrik Van Dalen, "Interest Groups in State Politics." In Herbert Jacob and Kenneth N. Vines (eds.), *Politics in the American States*, 3rd ed. (Boston: Little, Brown, 1976), pp. 110–111.

[4]Wayne L. Francis and Robert Presthus, "Legislator Perceptions of Interest Group Behavior," *Western Political Quarterly* 14 (December, 1971) p. 705.

[5]Duane Lockard, *New England State Politics* (Princeton, N.J.: Princeton University Press, 1959) p. 79.

TABLE 5-2 STRENGTH OF PRESSURE GROUPS IN VARYING POLITICAL AND ECONOMIC SITUATIONS

| Social Conditions | TYPES OF PRESSURE SYSTEMS[1] | | |
	Strong[2] (24 States)	Moderate[3] (14 States)	Weak[4] (7 States)
Party competition			
One-party	29.2	0	0
Modified one-party	25.0	.5	57.1
Two-party	45.8	.5	42.9
Cohesion of parties in legislature			
Weak cohesion	75.0	14.2	0
Moderate cohesion	12.5	35.7	14.2
Strong cohesion	12.5	50.0	85.7
Socioeconomic variables			
Urban population	58.6	65.1	73.3
Per capita income	$1,900	$2,335	$2,450
Industrialization index	88.8	92.8	94.0

[1]Alaska, Hawaii, Idaho, New Hampshire, and North Dakota are not classified or included.
[2]Alabama, Arizona, Arkansas, California, Florida, Georgia, Iowa, Kentucky, Louisiana, Maine, Michigan, Minnesota, Mississippi, Montana, Nebraska, New Mexico, North Carolina, Oklahoma, Oregon, South Carolina, Tennessee, Texas, Washington, and Wisconsin.
[3]Delaware, Illinois, Kansas, Maryland, Massachusetts, Nevada, New York, Ohio, Pennsylvania, South Dakota, Utah, Vermont, Virginia, and West Virginia.
[4]Colorado, Connecticut, Indiana, Missouri, New Jersey, Rhode Island, and Wyoming.

Source: Harmon Zeigler and Hendrik Van Dalen, "Interest Groups in State Politics." In *Politics in the American States*, 3rd ed. Herbert Jacob and Kenneth N. Vines, eds. (Boston: Little, Brown, 1976) p. 35. Reprinted by permission.

timber, and manufacturing industries, which long have been in clear and cohesive alliance with each other. In his study of New England state politics, Lockard points out that when Edmund Muskie was governor, he suffered most of his defeats on those legislative matters that were opposed by the Big Three. For example, Muskie was unable to establish a statewide minimum wage, a state labor relations commission, a state income tax, or a corporate tax. In 1955, the state legislature defeated handily a proposed water pollution law. By the 1969–1970 session, however, there were strong indications that the overwhelming impact of the Big Three was diminishing in Maine. First, new groups of legislators who were consumer-minded, ecology-conscious, and politically active entered the Maine assembly. These legislators were also aware that tourism is Maine's second largest and fastest growing business, bringing more than $500 million a year to the state. Moreover, old interest group patterns were changing. While the Big Three remained a solid block, real estate agents, fishermen, and summer residents in Maine were beginning to form an ecology-conscious conservation coalition. Summer residents would not normally be a particularly powerful force in any state's political system. "However, when the summer residents are named Rockefeller, Cabot, and Du Pont, the picture changes."[6] These and other prominent families maintained vacation homes in Maine and had no desire to see their pleasant summers marred by industrialization.

The more a state urbanizes and industrializes, the more these changes seem to work against formerly dominant economic groups. An example is Alabama, which was dominated by "the big mules," a big-farmer and big-money amalgam. As Alabama industrialized and urbanized, however, organized labor and civil rights interests carved out an increasingly potent role for themselves in Alabama politics.

THE SINGLE DOMINANT INTEREST

The primary example is Montana. Since becoming a state, Montana has been dominated politically by the Anaconda Company, the single largest employer in the state. The Anaconda Company is based on copper mining, but it also owns forests and runs mills, railroads, and similar operations. Politicians in Montana win elections either because of their opposition to or their alliance with "the company," as it is known in Montana.

Anaconda's dominant role in Montana was evident when the state was admitted to the Union. It had in its constitution a clause that mining claims could be taxed only "at the price paid the United States therefor," and that the taxes could be levied only on "net proceeds." This constitutional clause meant, in effect, that oil production, for example, which grossed only 18 percent as much as mines, paid twice as much as the mines in state taxes. Mines contributed less than 9 percent to Montana's revenues, whereas agriculture contributed 32 percent. In 1918, a faculty member of the University of Montana reviewed these inequities in the state's tax system and, as a result, was dismissed by the chancellor. Anaconda's role in the suppression of a book that the professor published on the state's tax system quickly became well known. The professor eventually was reinstated, but only after a considerable controversy. In 1924, the legislature finally revised the tax structure so that each ton of ore produced was taxed and this revision resulted in a substantially more equitable tax structure for the state.

Such setbacks persuaded the company to change its political strategies. Anaconda owned approximately half of the state's newspapers, and one can trace their editorial treatment of political opponents from the 1920s to the 1950s as waning steadily less vitriolic. In the late 1950s the company sold its newspapers, and since then Anaconda has become a quiet but still highly influential political force. Anaconda has changed its strategy rather than its position, and now works directly through the legislative process.

---

[6]Zeigler and Van Dalen, "Interest Groups in American Politics," p. 97.

More recently, Anaconda has been challenged by a growing coalition of environmentalists and smaller business interests in Montana. They have been spurred to more intense political action by the knowledge that, since 1961, Anaconda actually has had the right of eminent domain. Eminent domain is an authority usually reserved to governmental bodies; it allows then to condemn private properties if such condemnation is in the public interest—for example, buying land for a road. To give such governmental authority to a private interest is an entirely different matter; it gives the company the legal authority to level an entire city and dig an open pit mine on the location. The rise of environmental interests, however, reflects a pattern of political resistance similar to that seen in Maine, where these and other interests coalesced against the Big Three.

Like Anaconda's growing mellowness in the political frays of Montana, other dominant economic interests in other states have found it expeditious to keep the cap on vitriol in policy disputes. Oil interests in Texas have become increasingly less overt in their tactics; business interests in Delaware have tried to establish a "good guy" image in that state's politics. Big economic interests in state politics, in spite of their money and influence, can lose and lose consistently when public opinion is mobilized.

CONFLICT BETWEEN TWO DOMINANT GROUPS

Maine, Alabama, and Montana are similar in that they all have rather underdeveloped economies that have contributed to a bipolarization of political infighting. We have yet to consider a state with competitive political parties, with strong grassroots organizations, which is industrial, urban, and has relatively high educational and income levels. Michigan provides an example of this kind of economy and social structure. Although its economy may be even less diversified than Montana's, it is dominated by the automobile industry, which constitutes the largest single employer in Michigan. Hence, two dominant groups have emerged in Michigan, the automobile industry and organized labor. But they differ from dominant groups in the previous examples in that they work through two strong and cohesive political parties. The United Automobile Workers uses the Democratic party to attain its political ends; the automobile manufacturers are deeply involved in the Republican party. Neither of these two interest groups controls its respective parties, but both are extremely powerful and influential within those parties' inner workings.

One national ranking placed Michigan sixth among the states in the degree of partisan conflict, as perceived by a sample of legislators, and fourth in the amount of pressure group conflict, as perceived by Michigan's representatives to the state assembly. Unlike interest groups in the preceding two categories, interest groups in states like Michigan, which have two dominant groups competing for influence, work through the political parties rather than relying on their own political organizations.[7] They are the "junior partner" in their alliance with political parties.[8]

THE TRIUMPH OF MANY INTERESTS

The example here is an obvious one—California. Early in its history, California developed as the railroads developed, and the Southern Pacific Railroad clearly dominated California politics. Around the turn of the century, however, a wave of political reform rolled over California, weakening the parties and clearing the way (quite unintentionally) for the rise of extraordinarily powerful pressure groups. These pressure groups emerged in large part because California actively discouraged the development of political parties; from 1917 until 1954, California laws stated that a person could enter both the Democratic and Republican primaries (known as crossfiling), then enter the general election without his or her party affiliation appearing on either ballot. After 1954, party labels were required on the ballot, but until 1959 cross-filing was retained. These requirements seriously weakened the development of any political party within the state; candidates for the state legislature and other elective offices were virtually on their own and were forced to develop their own personal organizations if they wished to run for office effectively. Organized interest groups were more than willing to help a candidate gain office if he or she was sympathetic to their needs. This situation is reflected by Wahlke's finding that 9 percent of all legislators in California referred to interest groups as the chief sponsors of their political careers, in contrast to only 1 percent in New Jersey and 2 percent in Ohio. In Tennessee 16 percent of the legislators referred to interest groups as the primary sponsors of their legislative careers, a higher portion than in California, but it is noteworthy that parties in Tennessee are even less competitive than those in California.[9] Thus, the notion seems to be validated that weak political parties in a state tend to pave the way for the emergence of powerful interest groups that function very similarly to parties.

From 1942 to 1953 public policy formulation in California was a product of interest groups. It was during this period that the notorious lobbyist Artie Samish arose as king pin in the California pressure group system. Samish began his career in the 1930s working for the bus companies in California, but soon he represented other interests as well, including brewers, railroads, horse racing and gambling interests, the motion picture industry, and a

---

[7]Wayne L. Francis, *Legislative Issues in the Fifty States: A Comparative Analysis* (Chicago: Rand, McNally, 1967) p. 44–45.

[8]V. O. Key, Jr., *Public Opinion and American Democracy* (New York: Knopf, 1961) p. 524.

[9]John C. Wahlke, Heinz Eulau, William Buchanan, and LeRoy C. Ferguson, *The Legislative System* (New York: John Wiley, 1962) p. 100.

number of others. Samish's influence was not so much a product of "filthy lucre" being poured into California's legislature by the interest groups that he represented, but rather of his organizational talents in welding the many interests he represented into an organization that worked as a political party would have worked. Samish's primary drive was to prevent the industries he represented from being taxed.[10] It was ironic that in 1959, the same year in which cross-filing was abolished in California, the legislature passed the first significant hike in beer taxes. In the 1960s and 1970s, other interest groups became politically active in California and, as in Maine and Montana, the environmental issue provided the main rallying point for a number of diverse groups. In the early 1970s a coalition of California oil companies, utilities, and organized labor was influential in preventing the formulation of a statewide antipollution agency, but in 1974, when the environmentalists were joined by the sixty-five thousand member California chapter of Common Cause, the Political Reform Act was enacted, much against the wishes of the oil, labor, and utilities combine. Among other reforms, the act prevented lobbyists from spending more than ten dollars per month (including campaign contributions) in a manner designed to influence state officials. The Political Reform Act (also known as Proposition 9) in California may spell the end of the traditional pressure group system in that state—as, indeed, it was designed to do.

POLITICS WITHOUT PRESSURE GROUPS

The four categories considered in the foregoing passage all apply to states with high levels of pressure group activity. In those states where there is not a symbiotic relationship between political parties and pressure groups, the interest groups take the place of political parties and actually function as political parties.

Missouri, however, presents an example of a state without a dominant pressure system. Missouri has a pressure system of temporary alliances rather than permanent and on-going ones. This shifting pattern is attributable to a high issue orientation among competing economic interests in Missouri that is unable to offset the very stable and competitive party system. Interest groups do not work closely with parties, nor do they function as parties, and the existence of this typically weak interest group situation is due principally to the fact that there are no major economic interests that dominate the state.[11]

---

[10]William Buchanan, *Legislative Partisanship: The Deviant Case of California*, University of California Publications in Political Science, Vol. 13 (Berkeley, Calif.: University of California Press, 1963).

[11]Nicholas A. Masters, Robert H. Salisbury and Thomas H. Eliot, *State Politics and the Public Schools* (New York: Knopf, 1964) pp. 37–38.

Zeigler and Van Dalen have shown by their study of pressure group patterns in the states that, even in those states where there is a concentrated economic and political influence structure, the situation is hardly monolithic. Challenges can arise to even the most established economic and political powers in these states through the mobilization of contrary interests. Recognizing this fact, how do lobbyists, who represent special interests in a state, work? How do lobbyists have their way with legislators?

Lobbying, in its essence, is a communications process. Lobbying is conducted quite differently in the state capitals than in Washington. Both the lobbyists and legislators in our nation's capital consider state-level lobbying to be substantially more corrupt, blatant, and crass. According to one analyst, "Lobbying is very different before state legislators; it is much more individualistic. Maybe this is the reason they have more bribery in state legislatures than in Congress. . . . In the state legislatures, lobbying is definitely on a lower plane. The lobbyists are loose and hand out money and favors quite freely. . . . Lobbying at the state level is cruder, more basic and more obvious. . . . Lobbying at the state level is faster and more free wheeling and less visible; that is why it is more open to corruption."[12]

Lobbying is a subtle process even at the state level, involving sophisticated interplay between raw political clout and strategic finesse. An adroit lobbyist quickly learns that it can be counterproductive to threaten a legislator. For example, if the Anaconda Company in Montana threatened to "punish" legislators who voted the "wrong" way, certain representatives would feel it necessary to vote against Anaconda simply for the sake of showing the public that they were independent.

Figure 5–1 indicates this tendency among legislators. For example, in

---

[12]Lester Milbrath, *The Washington Lobbyists* (Chicago: Rand McNally, 1963) pp. 241–243.

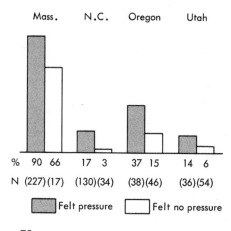

Mass.   N.C.   Oregon   Utah

| % | 90 | 66 | 17 | 3 | 37 | 15 | 14 | 6 |
| N | (227) | (17) | (130) | (34) | (38) | (46) | (36) | (54) |

☐ Felt pressure   ☐ Felt no pressure

FIGURE 5–1 RELATION BETWEEN LEGISLATORS' BELIEF THAT THEY WERE "PRESSURED" BY EDUCATION LOBBYISTS AND THEIR ATTITUDE TOWARD EDUCATION GOALS: PERCENTAGE FAVORING INCREASED EDUCATION BUDGET

Source: L. Harmon Zeigler and Michael A. Baer, *Lobbying: Interaction and Influence in American State Legislatures* (Belmont, Calif.: Duxbury Press, Div. of Wadsworth, 1969). 118.

Massachusetts, one of four states studied by Zeigler and Michael A. Baer, only 66 percent of the legislators who felt that they were being pressured by organized education lobbyists favored an increase in the state education budget, whereas 90 percent of those who felt no pressure from education were predisposed to favor an increase.

Lobbyists in the states often seem to be wiser and more experienced in the workings of their legislatures than the legislators themselves. Zeigler and Baer found that in three of the four states they studied intensively, the lobbyists had longer experience in their positions than the legislators did in theirs and there were fewer "freshmen" among lobbyists than among legislators.

On the other hand, lobbyists do not appear to visit legislative chambers very frequently. In a study of lobbying in Oklahoma, it was found that more than 60 percent of lobbyists in that state spent half their time or less engaged in actual lobbying.[13] In Zeigler and Baer's study, only in Oregon (which is a weak party–strong lobby state) did the time spent in actually lobbying by lobbyists approach anything close to an eight-hour day on a regular basis.

Interestingly, few state lobbyists are lawyers, although nationally a majority are. The largest single category of employment for state lobbyists is that of full-time executive. In short, most state lobbyists also are paid administrators for the interest that they represent.

Also, unlike Washington lobbyists, very few state lobbyists have previous experience as legislators. Significantly, few lobbyists show a pattern of consciously wanting to enter a lobbying career at some point in their lives; instead, they tend to "drift" into this field. In contrast, legislators as a group tend to recall an early childhood desire to enter politics.

As was mentioned earlier, lobbying at the state level seems to be cruder in style and form than lobbying at the national level. One reason is that state legislatures convene less often and for shorter periods of time than Congress does, thereby preventing the evolution of a set of rules of conduct (both formal and informal) such as those adopted by the U.S. House and Senate. Such rules, at least in theory, should discourage legislators from the kind of unethical behavior that has contributed to an image of political corruption.

The turnover rate is also much higher among state legislators than among members of Congress. About half of the legislators in the Zeigler and Baer study were first-term members of their respective houses and, as a consequence, not only were unfamiliar with the mores and norms of the state legislature but frequently had to rely on lobbyists for information about how their state assemblies worked. State legislators are, in short, less likely to be professionals and more likely to regard a stint in the legislature an an interesting, but secondary, avocation. Finally, state legislators often

---

[13]Samuel C. Patterson, "The Role of the Lobbyist: The Case of Oklahoma." *Journal of Politics* 25 (1963) p.79.

DUNAGIN'S PEOPLE

"A SPECIAL INTEREST GROUP IS SIMPLY ONE THAT CONTRIBUTES TO THE OTHER GUY'S CAMPAIGN."

DUNAGINS PEOPLE by Ralph Dunagin. Courtesy of Field Newspaper Syndicates.

are not well paid and, as a result, incur more expenses stemming from their legislative duties relative to their income than do members of Congress. This situation, of course, can increase the temptations when dealing with lobbyists. Fortunately, the lobbying process is not as corrupt as one might infer; both lobbyists and legislators in the Zeigler and Baer study ranked bribery as the least effective lobbying method.

Legislators, like most people, tend to communicate with and listen to people who support their views. This certainly happens in the lobbying process. Zeigler and Baer found that lobbyists are most effective with those legislators who are predisposed to agree with them on ideological grounds.[14]

Legislators, for their part, use lobbyists as sources of influence with other legislators. They ask lobbyists to influence other legislators by mobilizing public opinion in favor of the legislator's position, by including lobbyists in strategy sessions on how to move legislation through the assembly, and in negotiating their bills through the legislature. In this fashion, money assumes a renewed importance. Entertainment, for example, evidently is used with greater success at the state level than at the national level. Parties

---

[14]L. Harmon Ziegler and Michael A. Baer, *Lobbying: Interaction and Influence in American State Legislatures* (Belmont, Calif.: Duxbury Press, Div. of Wadsworth, 1969) p. 82.

(social ones, not political parties) play an important role in state legislative politics, and campaign contributions (not quite the same as bribes) have a greater importance at the state level than at the national level.

In summary, the techniques of lobbying, while admittedly more crass at the state level than at the national, have gravitated toward a subtle interchange between lobbyists and legislator and away from the more brutal power-play mode that often dominated state legislative politics in the past. Contacts, access, and who knows whom (as opposed to what) are more important variables in swinging legislation in one's favor than is pure political clout.

PRESSURE AND THE PUBLIC INTEREST

Irrespective of the style of pressure group lobbying in the states, the question first asked at the beginning of this chapter on interest groups still must be addressed: Does the conflict between pressure groups in the political system result in a public policy that is in the "best" public interest? In other words, does Zeigler's "hydraulic theory of politics" work most effectively toward the public interest?

The standard answer forthcoming from political scientists is, Yes, it does. Those with more power in the political system have that power because they represent more people; therefore, if a policy tends to favor the more powerful groups, then it is necessarily closer to being in the public interest. Competitive interest groups, in effect, offset any policy that would tend to run over minority rights. It is a classic world view of political science.

Perhaps Zeigler's hydraulic theory still "works," and interest group compromises really are in the public interest in those areas of public policy that are made largely by legislatures or by the courts. But to work, the hydraulic theory must rest on at least three basic assumptions concerning the American policy-making process:

1. That all people affected by any one particular policy question (for example, public transit) are aware that the resolution of the question actually will affect them and the way they live
2. That all people affected will have a reasonable understanding of the issues in question and how their resolution will impact on the way they live
3. That if the people affected are not aware of the policy question, then it is only a matter of time before they find out about it and join in the policy-making battles simply to protect their own self interests

These assumptions of the hydraulic theory of policy making have provided a well-accepted and not entirely unreasonable explanation of the policy-making process in our democracy—at least until recently. But in the late twentieth century, there are new forces at work that have not been dealt with satisfactorally by political thinkers. Primarily, these forces are (1) the emergence of a bureaucracy employing many millions of government workers and (2) the simultaneous development of an advanced technology. Indeed, America is the archtype of technological society in the world today. Both technology and bureaucracy deny the basic assumptions underlying the hydraulic theory of politics.

Bureaucracy denies the first and third assumptions. Bureaucrats, as has been amply documented, have a penchant for secrecy, and there is mounting evidence that neither bureaucrats nor the citizenry always act in their most rational self-interest; these facts undercut the basic premises that people are informed of what matters to them, and that they will act on what matters to them.

Technology denies the second assumption. Technology is very complicated; because of its complexity it is difficult for most people to understand the political problems that are brought about by technology. How many people, for example, really understand the technical and political issues behind nuclear energy? Therefore, it would seem that the classic view of interest groups, in which they are viewed as battling out the most beneficial public policy to all the people, must come under increasing scrutiny by citizens who are interested in a just society. Interest groups only rarely, if at all, represent anything close to all the people. More often they represent elites. These elites have control of knowledge about the issues in question. Consequently, they are extremely influential in making policies that affect all the people in our increasingly interrelated society. Hence, when we discuss interest groups from the traditional perspective of political science, one should be aware that pressure politics may be how the policy-making process works. But is special interest pressure in the best interest of all the people in a complex, technological, and increasingly bureaucratized society?

CHAPTER

THE
LEGISLATIVE
DRAMA

Perhaps more than any other political institution, state legislatures are the object of Americans' love and hate. On the love side, we can visualize an image of concerned citizens working for the good of their people, grappling with problems that perhaps they are ill-equipped to understand, given the complexity of twentieth-century America, but nonetheless trying to do the right thing under difficult circumstances.

On the hate side, quotable observations are more plentiful. For example, John Gardner has stated of legislatures, "Most of them are riddled with conflict of interest, riddled with corruption and are wholly inadequate instruments of self-government. The conflict of interest in the state legislatures is the worst evil they have. There are men making laws who most of the time are in the employ of the interest they are making the laws about."[1]

THE LEGISLATIVE LABYRINTH

Outwardly at least, state legislatures are rather simple structures—indeed, perhaps too simple. As Herbert Jacob has suggested, "State legislatures may be our most extreme example of institutional lag."[2]

All state legislatures have a bicameral, or a two-house, structure made up of the house and the senate. The exception, of course, is Nebraska, which became a one-house, or unicameral, legislature in 1934.

The arguments for and against unicameralism, as opposed to bicameralism, can be quickly stated. Those in favor of bicameral legislatures argue that they serve as checks on each other, bringing together the relative intellectual sophistication of the senate with the popular preferences represented by the house. The melding of the two value systems produces legislation that is in the best possible public interest. Those who argue for the unicameral system claim that it is relatively inexpensive and that it furnishes more responsible government because it discourages buck-passing between the two houses and delay in the policy-making process.

Size is an important consideration. Nebraska's unicameral legislature has varied, roughly, from thirty to fifty members. Normally, however, the upper house, or senate, in most states oscillates between twenty members, as in Alaska and Nevada, and sixty-seven members, as in Minnesota. The lower house can range from forty members, as in Alaska and Nevada, to the enormous New Hampshire House of Representatives with its four hundred

---

[1] John Gardner, as quoted by United Press International, January 3, 1972. reprinted in Daniel R. Grant and H. C. Nixon, *State and Local Government in America,* 3rd ed. (Boston: Allyn and Bacon, 1975) p. 206.

[2] Herbert Jacob, "Dimensions of State Politics." *State Legislatures in American Politics,* Alexander Heard, ed. (Englewood Cliffs, N.J.: Prentice-Hall, 1966) p. 3.

members. The average size of the lower house in the states is about one hundred members; the average size of the senate, thirty-eight members.

Each house of a state legislature is comprised of numerous functional committees, most notably finance, taxation, education, judiciary, and rules committees. The lower house elects a speaker to preside over its sessions; the lieutenant governor presides over the senate in most states. A few states that do not have a lieutenant governor elect a president pro tempore to preside over the senate. In states with a lieutenant governor, the president pro tempore presides in the absence of the lieutenant governor.

Traditionally, state legislatures have met only every two years, or biennially. The national trend, however, has been toward yearly sessions. By 1978 forty-three states had annual sessions. More than half the states limit sessions to seventy-five days or less. It seems likely that the average length of time for the legislative session will increase. During the 1960s, a total of 257 special legislative sessions were held simply because the business at hand could not be concluded during the normal sessions. Holding special sessions often are extremely expensive for a state and bring howls of anguish from local newspaper editors over the resultant "waste" of public dollars.

WHAT DO LEGISLATORS DO?

What do legislatures do? While they act as a constitutional check to the judiciary and executive branches, conduct impeachments, and investigate public issues, their chief duty is to make laws. In the mid-1970s, each state legislature processed on the average more than 4,000 bills and resolutions; the average state enacted more than 1,000. The larger states were shouldered with huge work loads. In New York, for example, almost 35,000 bills and resolutions were introduced during the 1975–1976 biennial session, and more than 2,500 were enacted. In the early 1950s all the nation's legislatures combined considered only about 25,000 bills a year; by the mid 1970s the figure had grown in excess of 150,000. During that same twenty-year period, the total number of bills and resolutions enacted burgeoned from roughly 15,000 per year in the 1950s to more than 50,000 in the 1970s. Table 6–1 summarizes the typical state legislative procedure and what is involved in getting each bill passed. Of course, a bill may be defeated at any point along the way.

The cost of this complicated process, as well as the enormous increase in legislation considered and enacted, has been all too measurable. Since the early 1960s, the cost of legisative operations in all fifty states soared by almost three hundred percent.

GOVERNMENT BY COMMITTEE

The concept of the committee is central not only to the organization of the legislature, but to the enactment of legislation in the states as well. "The committee hearing is generally the most important source of information

TABLE 6-1 GETTING A BILL THROUGH

1. INTRODUCTION OF BILL	One or more members file bill with clerk or presiding officer who gives it a number and refers it to a committee. This is the first reading.
2. COMMITTEE HEARINGS	Important bills may be given public hearings at which all interested persons or groups may testify.
3. COMMITTEE REPORT	Committee meets in executive (closed) session. Bills may be amended or pigeonholed or reported favorably or unfavorably.
4. BILL PLACED ON CALENDAR	Bills reported by committee are placed on calendar for floor consideration. Urgent or favorite bills may get priority by unanimous consent or informal maneuvering; other bills may be delayed, sometimes indefinitely.
5. FLOOR DEBATE, AMENDMENT, VOTE	The second reading of the bill before the entire chamber is usually accompanied by debate and perhaps amendments from the floor. Often the crucial vote is on an amendment or on second reading.
6. THIRD READING AND PASSAGE	Usually a bill is delayed one day before it is brought to the floor for third reading. On third reading debate is not customary and amendments usually require unanimous consent. After final vote, bill is certified by presiding officer and sent to second house.
7. REFERRAL TO SECOND CHAMBER	Bill is sent to second chamber where steps 1 through 6 must be repeated. Bills must pass both chambers in identical form before going to governor.
8. CONFERENCE COMMITTEE	If there are differences in wording in the bills passed by each house, one or the other house must accept the wording of the other house or request a conference committee. This committee is made up of members of both houses and it arrives at a single wording for the bill.
9. VOTE ON CONFERENCE COMMITTEE REPORT	Both houses must vote to approve conference committee wording of bill. Bills may be shuttled back and forth and eventually die for lack of agreement between both houses.

TABLE 6-1 continued

10. GOVERNOR'S SIGNATURE OR VETO	An identical bill passed by both houses becomes law with the governor's signature. It may also become law without his signature after a certain lapse of time (e.g., 10 days) if the legislature is still in session. If the legislature has adjourned during this time, the governor's failure to sign is the same as a veto. A governor may formally veto a bill and return it to the house of origin for reconsideration. An unusual majority is generally required to override a veto.

for legislators and lobbyists tend to flock to the committee rooms as the focal point of their contact with legislators."[3]

The committee system is simply a division of labor into certain functional areas that the legislature must consider. The more important areas—appropriations, welfare, education, and labor—generally are consigned to *standing committees*, which are permanent committees of the legislature. *Special* or *select committees* are appointed to investigate passing problems that may or may not surface again—civil disorders, political scandals, and so on. There are also *interim committees*, which conduct studies between sessions of the legislature and, of course, there are *joint conference committees*, composed of members from both houses and designated to reconcile differences between each house over particular pieces of legislation. Maine, Massachusetts, and Connecticut are among the states that make the most use of the joint committee device as a means of minimizing deadlocks between the two chambers.

The typical legislature has between twenty and thirty standing committees, and the trend since 1946 has been to reduce the number of such committees in the legislature. By 1975, the average state house of representatives had seventeen committees; the average senate had twelve.

An important but difficult-to-answer question is: How influential are committees in the legislative process? Some argue that state legislative committees actually have relatively little influence on legislation, particularly in comparison with committees in the United States Congress, because (1) most legislatures meet relatively infrequently, thereby giving committees relatively scant time for meaningful review of bills; (2) state legislative committees seldom have adequate staff assistance; (3) legislatures lack a prevalent seniority system comparable to that of Congress; and (4) there are high levels of legislative turnover.[4] Indeed, a study conducted of

---

[3]Harmon Zeigler and Michael Baer, *Lobbying: Interaction and Influence in American State Legislatures.* (Belmont, Calif.: Wadsworth, 1969,) p. 126.

[4]Malcolm Jewell, *The State Legislature.* (New York: Random House, 1962) p. 93.

committee service by legislators in twelve state legislatures showed that, in not a single one of these legislatures did more than half of the legislators who served on a particular committee in one session serve on the same committee in any subsequent session.[5] As a result committee members in the state legislatures rarely acquire the experience and expertise of their counterparts in Congress, often causing a wide variation in the importance that committees assume in various state legislatures.

Nevertheless, if the multitude of studies on state legislatures indicate anything, it is that committees have less influence, as committees, over legislation in two-party states where there is a high degree of party discipline, and in two-party states where the governor and the legislative majority are of the same party. Committees, by contrast, are more likely to be influential in one-party states where the governor is not a particularly strong leader, where he or she has little legal authority, or where the government is divided along some other line, such as ideology or class.[6] Thus, we can perceive certain patterns: In the Texas senate, a state dominated by the Democrats, 70 percent of all bills reported from its twenty-three standing committees during the 1969–1970 session either were amended on the floor or rejected outright. During the same approximate time frame (1968–1971) in New Jersey, a state with a relatively high level of party competition, more than 90 percent of the committee-reported bills passed on the floor without significant change.

ELECTORAL SYSTEMS, REAPPORTIONMENT, AND GERRYMANDERING

It is a truism that the kinds of people who become legislators are put there more often than not by the kinds of people whom they nominally represent. How legislators get to represent particular kinds of people depends on the electoral system used in any particular state.

ELECTORAL FORMULAS: THOSE WHO HAVE, GET

Most American states use an electoral formula known as the *plurality vote*, which is associated with the *single member district* system. Under this formula, each electoral district in a state may elect one representative to the legislature by plurality (in contrast to majority) vote. The arrangement is called the

---

[5]H. Owen Porter and David A. Leuthold, "Acquiring Legislative Expertise: Appointment to Standing Committees in the States." Paper presented at the 1974 Annual Meeting of the American Political Science Association and cited in Samuel C. Patterson, "American State Legislatures and Public Policy," *Politics in the American States*, 3rd ed., Herbert Jacob and Kenneth N. Vines, eds. (Boston: Little, Brown, 1976) p. 184.

[6]Alan Rosenthal, "Legislative Committee Systems." *Western Political Quarterly* 26 (June, 1973) pp. 252–262.

single member district, plurality vote system. About 75 percent of the state senates and about 50 percent of the state houses rely on a single member district system.

The remaining chambers use a *multimember district system*: the number of votes won by any particular political party is proportioned out accordingly to that party in terms of seats in the legislature. For example, if the Democrats won 75 percent of the votes and the Republicans 25 percent of the votes in a district-wide election, and if four seats were available in the legislature from such a district, then the Democrats would get three seats and the Republicans one—at least in theory. During the last decade, the number of states relying on the use of multimember districts has declined for the lower houses and has stayed relatively steady for the senates. A major reason for this situation is the fact that the judiciary, since the early 1960s, has been adamant in forcing states to enforce a "one-person, one-vote" principle in their legislative apportionment plans.

What are the political effects of these various electoral formulas? The single member district, plurality vote system tends to result in a situation in which the political party that accumulates the largest slices of a district's vote will garner an even larger proportion of the district's legislative seats, while parties with relatively smaller percentages of the vote tend to acquire even fewer legislative seats. This condition is known as the "Matthew effect," named after the passage in Matthew 13:12 that says, "To him who has will more be given, and he will have abundance; but from him who has not, even what he has will be taken away." When partisan gerrymandering is combined with the plurality vote formula, the Matthew effect is even more emphatic. Hence a party that may win between 55 to 60 percent of the popular votes in a state will in reality win between 65 to 70 percent of the legislative seats. On the other hand, the party that may win only 40 to 45 percent of that statewide vote will be allocated only 35 percent or less of the seats available in the legislature.

REAPPORTIONMENT: REDISTRICTING FOR "PEOPLE, NOT TREES"

The Matthew effect was considerably worse before the courts became involved in reapportioning legislative districts in the states. Because a number of state legislatures simply refused to reapportion on the basis of national censuses, rural interests dominated urban interests in many states. In Maryland, for example, a state senator from a rural county in 1961 represented 15,481 citizens, whereas a senator from urban Baltimore County represented 492,428 people. Although almost 80 percent of Maryland's population in 1960 lived in four counties, they elected only a third of the members of the Maryland senate.

But Maryland was only one example among many, and those legislators who were in power before court-ordered reapportionment began were determined to keep things as they were.[7] In the face of such determination, only another branch of government, such as the courts, could effectively change legislative malapportionment in the state.

This is precisely what happened in 1962 in the case of *Baker* v. *Carr*. This famous decision concerned the contention of urban residents in Tennessee that the largest district in the state's house of representatives was twenty-three times larger than the smallest district. They argued that such malapportionment denied them "equal protection of the law" as guaranteed by the Fourteenth Amendment of the Constitution. In response to this argument, the Supreme Court decided: (1) that despite that fact apportionment is a legislative concern, the federal courts can and should accept jurisdiction where a constitutional question is at issue; (2) that voters in underrepresented areas are entitled to judicial relief if apportionment laws have violated their constitutional rights; and (3) that arbitrary state apportionment laws violate the Fourteenth Amendment's prohibition against laws that deny citizens equal protection.

As a result of *Baker* v. *Carr*, citizens throughout the country started taking their legislatures to court, suing for reapportionment. The courts were responsive. In 1964, the case of *Westberry* v. *Sanders* was resolved; the presiding justice stated, "As nearly as practicable, one man's vote should be equal to another's."[8] This was the one-person, one-vote principle.

Two years after *Baker* v. *Carr*, the Supreme Court decided a second major case known as *Reynolds* v. *Sims*. This case involved an attempt by Alabama to base representation in its upper house on counties. The Supreme Court decided that both houses of the state legislature had to be apportioned fairly and according to population. This was a second revolutionary decision, in that it went against the deep-running concept in mainstream American legislative thinking of bicameralism, which traditionally has one house based on political units (such as states or counties), rather than on population. It was in this decision that Mr. Chief Justice Earl Warren wrote, "Legislators represent people, not trees or acres. . . . The complexions of societies and civilizations change, often with amazing rapidity. A nation once primarily rural in character becomes predominately urban. Representation schemes once fair and equitable become archaic and dated."[9]

The impact of the Supreme Court's decisions was immediate and profound, as Figure 6–1 indicates. By 1967, all states had been reapportioned and only minor inequalities remained.

Redistricting continued throughout the 1970s, but the impact of the Court was made. For example, during the 1972–1973 legislative year, reapportions occurred in 28 states for at least one house. In fact by 1973 in

---

[7]For an excellent case study of this resistance, see: Gilbert Y. Steiner and Samuel K. Gove, *The Legislature Redistricts Illinois*. (Urbana: University of Illinois, Institute of Government and Public Affairs, 1956).

[8]Westberry v. Sanders, 84 U.S. 526 (1964).

[9]Reynolds v. Sims, 84 U.S. 1362 (1964).

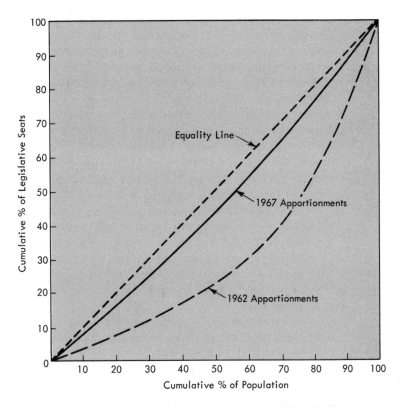

FIGURE 6–1 INEQUALITY IN STATE LEGISLATIVE APPORTIONMENTS

Source: These Lorenz curves are based on Gini Indices calculated by H. George Frederickson, See also Samuel C. Patterson, " Political Representation and Public Policy," unpublished paper presented at the Social Science Research Council Conference on the Impacts of Public Policies, St. Thomas, Virgin Islands, December 1971, pp. 10–11.

the case of *Mahan* v. *Howell*, the Court evidently felt that a strict mathematical reapportionment mandated by the courts no longer was necessary, and it permitted the Virginia House of Delegates to reapportion on the basis of what it called a "rational approach," rather than requiring rigid mathematical formulae to be implemented. In any case, it is clear that state legislatures, purely because of the judiciary, now reflect a one-person, one-vote philosophy.

GERRYMANDERING FOR PARTY, NOT FOR RACE

Race, an issue of apportionment in the states, was not addressed by the Supreme Court in either the *Baker* v. *Carr* or *Reynolds* v. *Sims* cases. It was addressed, however, in 1960 in the case of *Gomillion* v. *Lightfoot*, when the Supreme Court eliminated gerrymandering based on race by holding that the Alabama legislature could not redraw the city limits of Tuskegee so as to exclude virtually all black residents. This Court decision, more than any other single decision, has probably opened the way for black representation in state legislatures.

Nevertheless, the issue of partisan gerrymandering (as opposed to racial gerrymandering) has never been resolved by the judiciary—an issue that has increased the inequitable Matthew effect in those legislatures that are based on single member district, plurality vote electoral systems. Partly because gerrymandering along partisan lines has not been rectified, the main electoral effect of the plurality vote formula under court-ordered reapportionment has accrued to the advantage of the majority party in a state.

In the 1970s partisan gerrymandering resulted in advantages for the Democrats, since they, more often than not, were in a position to redistrict electoral districts according to the 1970 Census. The Democrats were not recalcitrant in redistricting for their own benefit, and it has been estimated that anywhere from nine to forty-three Congressional seats were "bonus" seats for the Democrats as a direct consequence of their partisan gerrymandering.

State legislatures have been moving to compensate for the courts' evident disinterest in eliminating gerrymandering for the benefit of a particular party. In 1978 the Florida Constitution Revision Commission recommended that a constitutional amendment be enacted to remove redistricting from the hands of incumbent politicos and to make it the responsibility of a bipartisan reapportionment commission.[10] Colorado, Hawaii, and Montana currently have similar plans, but apparently it will be some time before many politicians relinquish their tight grasp of the gerrymandering power— even within the one-person, one-vote edict.

THE RESULTS OF REAPPORTIONMENT

Samuel C. Patterson has summarized the most important consequences of reapportionment in the states.[11] First and most obviously, the number of state legislators from urban and suburban areas has increased, while the number of legislators from rural areas has decreased. Among the states where this has happened dramatically are Georgia, New York, California, and Florida. Second, reapportionments probably have worked more to the advantage of the Democratic party than the Republican party. In this light they seem to have stimulated party competition for seats in the legislature and more highly partisan voting behavior by legislators once they are in office. Partisanship seems to have increased most dramatically where mal-

---

[10]David S. Broder, syndicated column, February 15, 1978.
[11]Samuel Patterson, "American State Legislatures and Public Policy." In *Politics in the American States*, pp. 155–156.

apportionment was the most serious. Finally, in Patterson's view, reapportionments may have contributed to the greater responsiveness of state legislatures. One reason for this is that in some states (notably New York, California, and Florida) the turnover of membership in the legislature that has been induced by reapportionment seems to have produced a higher proportion of younger, better-educated representatives and, in the South, a marked increase in the representation of minorities, particularly blacks.

What effects, if any, has reapportionment had on the public policies emanating from the state legislatures? There are of number of views on this issue. The most common opinion is that the urban interests have pushed aside the rural interests in the state assemblies and, as a result, the nation is getting more education- and welfare-oriented policies. This conventional wisdom, however, has been challenged by such scholars as Thomas Dye, Richard I. Hofferbert, and Malcolm Jewell.

Dye contends that the malapportionment/reapportionment variable has very little to do with the kinds of policies emanating from state legislatures, and that the causal variable is in fact the state's economic status. Dye addressed the major issues of education, health and welfare, highways, taxation, and what he called the "regulation of public morality." Of these, only education policy seemed to bear any kind of a relationship with reapportionment; after reapportionment, expenditures for educational programs in the states often went up.[12]

On the other hand Hofferbert's study, conducted at about the same time, concluded that a state's predisposition toward welfare programs is less a result of reapportionment and more of a reflection of the level of financial support for various educational and welfare programs and the level of direct state aid to the two largest cities in the state. Hofferbert, in fact, found no relationship whatever between policy and reapportionment.[13]

By contrast, Jewell and others argue that reapportionment does indeed make a difference in the kinds of policies adopted by a state legislature. To quote Jewell, "The effects of malapportionment on policy outputs can be best evaluated not by measuring differences among states with different degrees of malapportionment, but by studying the response of state legislatures as a whole to the challenges of the metropolis."[14]

If reapportionment has had an impact on the kinds of policies made by legislatures, the effect has already been felt, if not measured, in the state

[12]Thomas R. Dye, *Politics, Economics and the Public: Policy Outcomes in the American States.* (Chicago: Rand McNally, 1966) p. 294.

[13]Richard I. Hofferbert, "The Relation Between Public Policy and Some Structural and Environmental Variables in the American States." *American Political Science Review* 60 (March, 1966) pp. 73–82.

[14]Malcolm Jewell, "Will *Baker v. Carr* Save the States?" Paper delivered at the National Conference of the Southern Political Science Association, 1966. Cited in Grant and Nixon, *State and Local Government*, p. 261. See also Yong Hyo Cho and H. George Frederickson, "The Effects of Reapportionment: Subtle, Selective, Limited." *National Civic Review* 63 (July, 1974) pp. 357–362.

legislative systems. In any case, one-person, one-vote representation is here to stay.

WHAT LEGISLATORS BRAWL ABOUT

How and why people fight is a source of endless fascination to virtually everyone, and studies of state legislators have delved fairly deeply into the causes of legislative conflict. A major study of the legislatures in California, New Jersey, Ohio, and Tennessee found six major sources of legislative conflict. Table 6–2 ranks these sources of conflict in the order assigned to them by legislators in the four states, and it is clear that the rural/urban dimension was the most salient as a source of conflict.

THE QUESTIONABLE VALIDITY OF THE URBAN/RURAL SPLIT

No doubt the urban/rural conflict was an important one in 1962 (when the study was conducted) and still is. Nevertheless, there is reason to believe that as a source of conflict this dimension may be waning in significance. One study of all state legislatures concluded that the variable of political party was perhaps the major source of conflict in legislatures.[15] Table 6–3, derived from the study, arranges the legislative issues confronting state legislators by the types of conflicts that they generate. For instance, an issue related to political party would be that of elections; an issue related to regional representation (the urban/rural dimension) would be that of apportionment. The research was published well after the effects of court-

---

[15]Wayne L. Francis, *Legislative Issues in the Fifty States.* (Chicago: Rand McNally, 1967).

TABLE 6–2 LEGISLATIVE ISSUES ARRANGED BY TYPES OF CONFLICT BEFORE COURT-ORDERED REAPPORTIONMENTS

TYPE OF CONFLICT	CALIFORNIA	PERCENT DECLARED NEW JERSEY	"IMPORTANT"* OHIO	TENNESSEE
Urban-Rural	65%	53%	79%	91%
Party	26	96	49	23
Governor	18	76	36	89
Liberal-Conservative	58	22	52	29
Labor	65	18	61	54
Regional	69	18	17	13

*Figures are for members of lower house only, in each state.

Source: Adapted from John C. Wahlke, Heinz Eulau, William Buchanan, and Leroy C. Ferguson, *The Legislative System: Explorations in Legislative Behavior,* p. 425. Copyright © 1962 by John Wiley & Sons. Reprinted by permission of John Wiley & Sons, Inc.

TABLE 6-3   LEGISLATIVE ISSUES ARRANGED BY TYPES OF CONFLICT AFTER COURT-ORDERED REAPPORTIONMENTS

		TYPES OF CONFLICT			
Ranking	*Party*	*Factional*	*Regional*	*Interest Group*	*Issue "Importance"*
1	Elections	Liquor	Apportionment	Labor	Taxation
2	Labor	Constitutional revision	Local government	Liquor	Apportionment
3	Land	Agriculture	Constitutional revision	Business	Education
4	Finance	Civil rights	Social welfare	Civil rights	Finance
5	Administration	Business	Civil rights	Gambling	Labor
6	Apportionment	Apportionment	Gambling	Natural resources	Health
7	Taxation	Gambling		Agriculture	Business
8	Social welfare	Taxation		Taxation	Civil rights

Source: Derived from Wayne L. Francis, *Legislative Issues in the Fifty States* (Chicago: Rand McNally & Co., 1967).

ordered reapportionment were being felt in the state legislatures, and it implies that regional conflict, conflict between "country folks" and "city slickers," may be on the wane, and conflicts between economic and social interest groups and political parties may be on the rise.

THE URBAN/SUBURBAN SPLIT

There is additional reason to doubt the continuing validity of the urban/rural split as a source of conflict in the state legislatures. Although there is obviously a degree of tension between city and country, simply because interest groups and parties tend to split along the urban/rural dimension, such a division nonetheless is better understood as a conflict of inner city versus surrounding suburb. It is the suburbs that have made the greatest gains in state legislatures since court-ordered reapportionment. Rural interests (and by that is meant farming interests) have lost representation. The inner cities have gained to some extent, but not as dramatically as the suburbs have. Therefore, we may predict that regionalism will be reflected in the state legislatures as suburbs (that is, white, middle-class interests) versus the core city (that is, predominately black and other minority groups of lower income level). The suburbs will battle for such middle-class issues as education; the central cities may find the salient issues to be welfare measures and urban rejuvenation projects. If this inner city/outer suburb dimension should wax into a major division among state legislators, the suburbs will probably win. It is the suburbs that are gaining legislative representation, and it is the middle class (which is found most frequently in the suburbs) that has always been the most politically active in this country. As one observer has noted, "The United States is an urban nation, but not a big city nation. The suburbs own the future."[16]

THE REALITIES OF LEGISLATIVE POWER

Recognizing that there are a number of sources of political conflict in society, what are the means of resolving conflict in state legislatures? Conflict in the political process is resolved through the use of power. To be tagged as a "nice guy" in politics is not a compliment. Duane Lockard has provided us with a cogent overview of the sources of legislative power.[17]

One major power base is the *use of legislative rules and structure*. Those who understand the rules of the game and the terrain of the playing field

---

[16]William J. D. Boyd, "Suburbia Takes Over." *National Civic Review* 54 (June, 1966) pp. 294–298.

[17]Duane Lockard, *The Politics of State and Local Governments*, 2nd ed. (New York: Macmillan, 1969) pp. 274–277.

have a natural power base. (We shall return to this point in our discussion of "Rules of the Game" in the legislatures.)

A secondary source of power is *campaign contributions, patronage, and political support*. Money, access, and votes always help a legislator get his or her way; we already have considered these power sources in our reviews of political parties, interest groups, and voting behavior.

Finally, there is the *state bureaucracy* as a base of power. The symbiotic relationship between legislators and bureaucrats is complex and this book has devoted several upcoming chapters to it.

RULES OF THE GAME: WRITTEN ONES

As mentioned, a major method of reconciling conflicts between legislators is simply the use of rules. Rules are both formal and informal, and political scientists tend to stress the use of informal sanctions in legislative strategies and in the legislative process generally. Nevertheless, the formal rules should not be overlooked. The formal rules, as Lockard has noted, often provide a major and effective power base for blocking or enacting public policy. At the national level, such eminent legislators as the late Lyndon Baines Johnson, the late Sam Rayburn, and former Representative Wayne Hayes come readily to mind; they understood and used the formal rules of the legislative branch in extraordinarily effective ways. Legislators at the state level can also use formal rules effectively. As Lockard observes, the formal rules of the legislature are "utterly incomprehensible to many a fledgling legislator, and indeed some of those who stay on and gain legislative experience never learn the rules in detail."[18] Indeed, most legislators are not meant to. The "needless" complexity is there for reasons of power, and those who understand the parliamentary procedures gain some additional power as a result. It is the old saw revisited, "Knowledge is power." Because of the enormous work load of some state legislatures, and because state legislatures are made up more of amateurs than professionals, such knowledge can give a legislator a power source of considerable significance.

Consider some major formal rules of the game in state legislatures: One such rule concerns the *quorum*—that is, the specific proportion of the total membership that must be present for any official action to be taken. This proportion varies from legislature to legislature, but normally it requires at least a majority of the membership.

Quorum calls furnish another vehicle of political strategy in a legislature. For example, members of the legislature in Tennessee have been known to break a quorum and delay legislation by crossing over the state border into Kentucky, a device that also renders them immune from arrest for noncriminal conduct, since it is against Tennessee law to deliberately stall legislation while remaining in the state.

---

[18]*Ibid.*, p. 275.

Another major rule concerns the powers given to the officers of the legislature, notably the speaker of the house and the president pro tempore of the senate. The speaker of the house usually has more power than his senate counterpart, primarily because the house in most states has far more rules to work with than the senate; a larger membership results in longer lists of regulations and rules.

RULES OF THE GAME: UNWRITTEN ONES

Patterson has observed that informal rules may be viewed either as "inside" influences on the legislature or "outside" influences on the legislature. Notable among the inside influences are basic rules of human behavior, including the roles played by friendship and expertise in swaying legislation one way or another.[19] Studies of the Michigan legislature, for example, found that when sources of expertise were relied upon in making policy, 59 percent of the responding legislators indicated that their "experts" on a subject were other legislators rather than outside sources.[20]

John C. Wahlke and his colleagues, in a study of four state legislatures, conducted a more systematic review of the internal, unofficial rules of the game.[21] These rules, they found, serve six functions:

1. Rules that are *intended to promote group cohesion and solidarity*. Such sanctions protect other members' "legislative rights" (for example, "support another member's local bill if it doesn't affect you or your district"; "don't steal another member's bill"). Some rules promote impersonality ("oppose the bill, not the man"; "don't criticize the moral behavior of members"); some govern personal behavior ("don't be a prima donna"; "don't talk for the press or the galleries"); some emphasize respecting other members' political rights ("don't embarrass him in his district"). Finally there's the all-important rule, the rule of institutional patriotism—a legislator defends the institution and its members against outsiders.
2. Rules that *promote the predictability of legislative behavior*. This is perhaps the most important of the informal rules and involves the concept of keeping one's word. Quotations from legislators that illustrate this concept include "abide by your agreements," "be frank in explaining bills," and "don't conceal your opposition."
3. Rules that *channel and restrain conflict*. Rules in this area encourage a willingness to compromise and respect for the seniority system (for example, "accept half a loaf"; "don't try to accomplish too much too soon").
4. Rules that *expedite legislative business*. These rules center primarily around the value of self-restraint in debate ("don't talk too much").

---

[19]Patterson, *American State Legislatures,* p. 183.

[20]H. Owen Porter, "Legislative Experts and Outsiders: The Two Step Flow of Communication." *Journal of Politics* 36 (August, 1974) pp. 703–730.

[21]John C. Wahlke, Heinz Eulau, William Buchanan, and LeRoy C. Ferguson, *The Legislative System.* (New York: John Wiley, 1962) pp. 146–161.

5. Rules that *give tactical advantages to individual members*. In other words, it is expeditious for an individual legislator to recognize the tenets of courtesy, gracefulness in defeat, negotiation, and caution in making commitments, simply because such politeness will accrue to his personal advantage in the long run.

6. Finally, rules that revolve around the development of *desirable personal qualities*. Legislators responding to these kinds of rules mention such characteristics as integrity, virtue, objectivity, and intelligence.

BREAKING THE RULES

Do legislators break these rules? What can legislators do to get their colleagues really "ticked off"? One study found at least nine areas of highly undesirable legislative behavior.[22] Of these, the most important is never concealing the real purpose of a bill or misrepresenting it to assure its passage. No one likes to be "snuckered," least of all legislators. Others, including dealing in personalities in debates on the floor, refusing unanimous consent when the legislative leadership desires it, leaking confidential knowledge to the press, and being overly committed to a special interest group, also rank high among informal legislative norms. A glance of Table 6–4 indicates the substance of the study.

---

[22]F. Ted Hebert and Lelan E. McLemore, "Character and Structure of Legislative Norms," *American Journal of Political Science* 17 (August, 1973) pp. 506–27.

TABLE 6–4 INFORMAL LEGISLATIVE NORMS[1]

"HIGHLY UNDESIRABLE" LEGISLATIVE BEHAVIOR
1. Concealing the real purpose(s) of a bill or purposefully overlooking some portion of it in order to assure its passage.
2. Dealing in personalities in debate or in other remarks made on the floor of the chamber.
3. Being a thorn to the majority by refusing unanimous consent, etc.
4. Talking about decisions which have been reached in private to the press or anyone else.
5. Seeking as much publicity as possible from the press back home.
6. Being generally known as a spokesman for some special-interest group.
7. Introducing as many bills and amendments as possible during any legislative session.
8. Talking on a subject coming before the legislature about which you are not completely informed.
9. Giving first priority to your re-election in all of your actions as a legislator.

[1]Items that at least 40 percent of Iowa house and senate members checked as "highly undesirable." See F. Ted Hebert and Lelan E. McLemore, "Character and Structure of Legislative Norms," *American Journal of Political Science* 17 (August, 1973): 506–527.

When in the opinion of most legislators, enough of these rules are broken, a number of sanctions can be invoked, such as ostracism, loss of political perquisites, denial of certain privileges, and, most frequently, the obstruction of the personal bills of the legislator being disciplined. Table 6–5 indicates in greater detail the sanctions used by legislators against each other.

TABLE 6–5 SANCTIONS FOR ENFORCING RULES OF THE GAME PERCEIVED BY LEGISLATORS IN FOUR STATES

Sanction	PROPORTION OF LEGISLATORS NAMING EACH SANCTION IN			
	Calif.	*N.J.*	*Ohio*	*Tenn.*
Obstruction of His Bills: abstain or vote against him; bottle up his bills in committee; amend his bills; pass them only if of major importance to general welfare.	55%	42%	57%	72%
Ostracism: give him the "silent treatment"; subtly reject him personally.	24	14	31	29
Mistrust: cross-examine him on floor, in committee; don't put any trust in him.	34	14	25	12
Loss of Political Perquisites, Inducements, and Rewards: take away patronage, good committee assignments; report to constituents, local party organization.	15	9	19	4
Denial of Special Legislative Privileges: denial of unanimous consent; otherwise delaying bills.	9	8	4	2
Reprimand: in caucus, in private.	—	12	*	1
Overt Demonstrations of Displeasure: ridicule, hissing, laughter, etc.	3	1	2	3
Miscellaneous Other Sanctions	5	12	*	3
No Sanctions Perceived	7	14	11	10

*Less than 1%

Source: John C. Wahlke, Heinz Eulau, William Buchanan, and Leroy C. Ferguson, *The Legislative System: Explorations in Legislative Behavior*, p. 154. Copyright © 1962 by John Wiley & Sons. Reprinted by permission of John Wiley & Sons, Inc.

WHO, OR WHAT, USES THE RULES?

Three major sources of influence on the internal workings of legislatures through extensive use of the informal rules of the policy-making process are *political parties, pressure groups,* and *constituents*. We shall consider each of these manipulators separately.

THE PARTY AS AN INFLUENCE

The political party's role in influencing the legislative process is difficult, if not impossible, to determine precisely. Wahlke and his coauthors concluded in their study of legislative behavior that "ambivalence and uncertainty about the meaning of 'party' is a fact of political life, felt by the legislators themselves; it is not just a reflection of the state of political research."[23] It was with this viewpoint in mind that Wahlke constructed Table 6–6, which is the ranking of evaluations of party influence on legislative behavior by state legislators. Researchers have found that the state in which a legislature operates determines to a large degree the influence of party on the legislative process. Ninety-six legislative chambers in the United States are elected on a partisan basis; only in Nebraska and Minnesota are legislators elected on nonpartisan ballot. Although party influence in the legislatures is hardly a uniform phenomenon, nonetheless, certain patterns emerge. It is obvious, for example, that parties in one-party states are not able to enforce any high degree of party discipline and lack a strong ability to bring their legislators "into line" on political issues. Wahlke, in fact, quotes a Democratic legislator from Tennessee (a one-party state) as saying, "You never thought about the Democratic party unless the Republicans were trying something—for example reapportionment."[24]

Legislatures in which parties have high degrees of influence seem to develop most easily and completely in the urbanized and industrialized states. The memberships of political parties are relatively homogeneous in these states: Democratic legislators are from urban areas, are labor-oriented, and are relatively more representative of various minorities and low-income groups; Republican legislators come from the higher-income suburbs and smaller communities. Such homogeneity of membership makes party discipline easier to enforce; people who tend to think alike, act alike. Increasingly, legislators may be thinking and acting like Democrats. In every election from 1966 through 1976, the Republicans lost legislative seats; the Grand Old Party in 1976 controlled less than a third of the nation's legislative seats, and dominated both houses of the legislatures in only five small states.

---

[23]Wahlke et al., *Legislative System*, p. 376.
[24]*Ibid.,* p. 359.

TABLE 6-6 EVALUATIONS OF PARTY INFLUENCE ON LEGISLATIVE BEHAVIOR BY STATE

EVALUATION[1]	NEW JERSEY	OHIO	CALIFORNIA	TENNESSEE
Much/considerable influence				
Republicans have	37%	34%	1%	16%
Democrats have	22	1	5	3
Both parties have	33	16	—	1
Some/increasing influence				
Republicans have	—	7	5	16
Democrats have	1	6	15	4
Both parties have	—	5	34	3
Little/no influence				
Republicans have	1	2	8	2
Democrats have	—	17	—	4
Both parties have	6	12	32	51

[1]The percentages refer to the proportion of all interviewees making a specified evaluation of a particular party's influence on legislative behavior. The percentages do not refer to the proportion of legislators belonging to one party or the other, nor to the normal voting strength of each party in the legislature.

Source: John C. Wahlke, Heinz Eulau, William Buchanan, and Leroy C. Ferguson, *The Legislative System: Explorations in Legislative Behavior*, p. 355. Copyright © 1962 by John Wiley & Sons. Reprinted by permission of John Wiley & Sons, Inc.

In 1978, however, the GOP gained 300 legislative seats, for a national total of about 2,700, and control of thirteen legislatures.

In rural states, parties have more diverse constituencies; therefore, party influence on individual legislators is relatively weak. As Dye has concluded, "The weight of evidence seems to support the hypothesis that party influence is most effective where the parties represent separate and distinct socioeconomic coalitions,[25] which generally means the more urbanized states. Consider, for example, studies of relatively urban Ohio and relatively agrarian Iowa. It was found that only one-third of Ohio legislators interviewed disagreed with the precept of supporting their party's position on a policy issue in the legislature if the party's position conflicted with the views held by the legislator's constituency. In Iowa, however, more than half of the legislators interviewed felt this way—that is, they would not follow the party line if it was at odds with the overall opinion of their constituencies.[26]

The type of political issue involved also affects the relative influence of a legislator's party affiliation on how he or she will vote on a bill. The issues where a party is most apt to influence a legislator's thinking concerning a particular bill are those that pertain to elections, proposed legislative reorganizations that might directly affect the party, local government, state administration, and so forth. Issues that concretely affect the party's status or the organization are likely to cause the party to behave like a normal interest group.

Finally, a third major variable should never be underestimated in assessing the party's influence on a legislator's behavior. That is the respective roles of the leaderships of the legislature and of the party. The more "professional" legislatures—in other words, those that pay their members relatively high salaries and maintain large professional research staffs—tend to have less turnover of party leadership, longer periods of waiting for leadership positions by other legislators, established patterns of succession, and fewer brawls over who would succeed to leadership positions. In these legislatures, which normally are found in urban and industrialized states, legislative leaders tend to be relatively powerful and to think in terms of party ideologies.[27]

THE PRESSURE GROUP AS AN INFLUENCE

Pressure groups, or lobbyists, constitute the second major influence on legislators when they are making policy. Of the three sources of influence under consideration—parties, pressure groups, and constituents—pressure

---

[25]Thomas R. Dye, *Politics in States and Communities,* 3rd ed. (Englewood Cliffs, N.J.: Prentice-Hall, 1977) p. 149.

[26]Patterson, *American State Legislatures,* p. 178.

[27]Douglas Camp Chaffey and Malcolm Jewell, "Party Opposition in the Legislature: The Ecology of Legislative Institutionalization." *Polity* 4 (Fall, 1972) 744–66.

groups are probably the most stereotyped; they supposedly have irresistible influence that they are able to exercise on state legislators. No doubt this image of relative omnipotency stems from the last century when certain interest groups, notably railroads, were able to literally buy whole legislatures—lock, stock, and senator.

The phenomenon of interest groups is discussed in the preceding chapter, but let us consider here some of the specific ways in which lobbyists interact with legislators.

Probably the most succinct statement of the real influence lobbyists have on state legislators was made by a legislator: "Lobbyists do affect the vote. Maybe they don't change your vote—lobbyists are only effective with those that are undecided—but they can sure make you bleed."[28] Lobbyists probably cannot "buy" legislators, but they can make life uncomfortable for them.

In their study of Massachusetts, North Carolina, Oregon, and Utah, Harmon Zeigler and Michael Baer found that legislators were more free to respond to the pleas of interest groups on relatively specific topics than on those bills dealing with major issues affecting the general public interest.[29] Beyond that relationship, however, there was a considerable difference of cause and effect between lobbyists and legislators. In Massachusetts and North Carolina, only about 20 percent of the respondents confessed that lobbying on an issue changed their position frequently, or at least occasionally. But in Oregon and Utah, almost 50 percent of the legislators agreed that this was the case. Of course, the more that legislators and lobbyists interact, the greater the degree of influence held by lobbyists over legislators. This is particularly so when both groups tend to share the same social and economic status and have similar professional backgrounds. Table 6–7 indicates the findings from the Zeigler and Baer study.

Other researchers have found different patterns of relationships between kinds of legislatures and the influence of lobbyists. Wahlke and his coauthors found that even in the absence of strong party competition, such as in Tennessee, lobbyists had relatively little influence.[30] Yet in Massachusetts, where the legislature is highly partisan, there were also relatively low levels of influence exercised by lobbyists.[31] In theory, one would surmise that when there is a power vacuum created by a lack of party competition, lobbyists would enter that vacuum and exercise increasing degrees of influence. But this does not seem to be so.

The degree of legislative professionalism also affects the power of pressure groups in a legislature. Information from California indicates that the more staff assistants provided to legislators, the less likely legislators are to rely solely on information provided by interest groups. Lobbyists are

---

[28]Quoted in: Wahlke et al., *Legislative Systems*, p. 340.

[29]Zeigler and Baer, *op. cit.*.

[30]Wahlke et al., *Legislative Systems*, p. 323.

[31]Zeigler and Baer, *Lobbying*, pp. 155–160.

TABLE 6-7 PERCEIVED EFFECT OF LOBBYING BY LEGISLATORS IN FOUR STATES

	MASS.	NO. CAR.	ORE.	UTAH
Persuasion				
Percentage of legislators believing they have been influenced to the extent of:				
Changing from one position to another	20%	18%	51%	42%
Leaning more to the news of lobbyist	31	20	42	38
Questioning a previously held opinion	34	22	45	32
Information				
Percentage of legislators indicating they:				
Depend upon information from lobbyists	50	41	83	80
Have confidence in information from lobbyists	55	56	88	70
Find information from lobbyists helpful	41	28	61	43

Source: Derived from data supplied in Harmon Zeigler and Michael Baer, *Lobbying: Interaction and Influence in American State Legislatures* (Belmont Calif.: Duxbury Press, Div. of Wadsworth, 1969).

more likely to have power in those legislatures that have relatively limited professional staffs. Of course, it also holds that the larger the membership of the interest group (notably teachers' associations), the more likely that it is going to have higher degrees of influence on the legislative process.[32]

Individual legislators assume certain roles when interacting with lobbyists. Some act as *facilitators*; they tend to have a friendly attitude toward lobbyists and are relatively well informed about the groups the lobbyists represent. Others take the role of *resisters*; they are relatively hostile toward lobbyists although, like facilitators, they also possess a fair amount of knowledge about the groups that lobbyists represent. Still others are *neutrals*; they have no particular attitude concerning an interest group, regardless of their level of knowledge about it, or they simply have very little knowledge about the group. Wahlke found an almost equal number of facilitators and neutrals (nearly 37 percent of each) in his four-state study; close to 27 percent were classified as resisters.[33]

The group Wahlke categorizes as resisters is probably the group that has been primarily responsible for various laws enacted against lobbying activity, especially since resisters as a category most frequently express the opinion that pressure group activity "is a wholly disruptive force which ought to be eliminated."[34] Examples of these antilobbying laws abound, and more than thirty states have various laws designed to resist lobbying efforts.

Still, recognizing that lobbying is less than a wholly pure activity, it is worth observing what happens when a legislature tries to enact bills without any organized group support (or resistance). Consider the following example: During the 1955 session a Republican member of the Connecticut House of Representatives had singlehandedly and relentlessly attempted to get a bill enacted that advocated a more sensible psychiatric treatment of sexual deviates in prisons and mental hospitals. So unmitigating and so personal was her campaign that her colleagues had begun "to duck behind a pillar when she approached." She eventually made her views known to Governor Abraham Ribicoff during the last days of the session; the governor sent a messenger to the Democratic senate caucus room with the message that he had decided to support the bill, and he requested the support of the caucus. Given Connecticut's considerable partisanship in legislative voting, there would normally have been no dissent, but on this occasion the senators "blew the roof off and ranted and raved at the messenger . . . . and almost bodily threw him out of the caucus room." The reason? There was no or very little organized support for the bill, and the governor had done for the bill's sponsor what he had not done for other individual members of the

---

[32]William Buchanan, *Legislative Partisanship: The Deviant Case of California*, (Berkeley Calif.: University of California Press, 1963) pp. 101–107; see also Joel M. Fisher, Charles M. Price, and Charles G. Bell, *The Legislative Process in California*. (Washington, D.C.: American Political Science Assn., 1973) pp. 65–70.

[33]Wahlke et al., *Legislative Systems*, p. 325.

[34] *Ibid.*

assembly—that is, he had given his support for a personal bill. Without organized support, the frustrations of a group of tired and aggravated legislators got the better of the suggested legislation, and the bill never made it to the floor for a vote.[35]

The moral of the story is that pressure groups do serve a purpose. They push legislation, for better or for worse, that might otherwise not even be considered.

THE PEOPLE AS AN INFLUENCE

Still a third source of influence is the people who vote for the legislator—that is, his or her constituency. Of the three major sources of influence, the constituency is no doubt the most important.[36] Indeed, it can be argued that even in strong two-party states the constituency is the primary influence on the political party, which acts only as an intermediary in applying pressure to a legislator. When the party represents an effective coalition of social and economic groups, it usually is the result of constituencies that already happen to fall along these economic and social lines; the nature and make-up of a constituency is more responsible than any other factor for party cohesion.

The elusive comfort of voting on principle. Legislators tend to vote for or against bills on the basis of how they think their constituents may vote for them as a consequence of their stand, and thus the constituency has more influence on legislators than either the party or pressure group. Interestingly, research indicates that legislators are loathe to admit to this fact. Nearly two-thirds of the legislators Wahlke studied identified themselves with the "Burkean position," as opposed to the populist position. By this, Wahlke meant that most legislators seemed to agree with the statement by the "founder of conservatism," Edmund Burke, that the elected representative should be guided not by "local purposes and prejudices," but by "his unbiased opinion, his mature judgment, his enlightened conscience." Legislators' cries that they are independent of their constituencies (or, for that matter, of political parties and pressure groups) should be taken with a grain of salt. Everyone, legislators included, likes to proclaim his or her independence of social institutions and to tell the world that they make their own decisions. But, conventional wisdom indicates that we can agree with the legislator who noted, "Basically you represent the thinking of the people who have gone through what you have gone through and who are

---

[35]Lockard, *Politics,* pp. 271–272.

[36]See, for example: Hugh L. LeBlanc, "Voting in State Senates: Party and Constituency Influences." *Midwest Journal of Political Science* 13 (February, 1969) 33–57; Malcolm Jewell, "Party Voting in American State Legislatures," *American Political Science Review* 49 (September, 1955) 773–791; Thomas A. Flinn, "Party Responsibility in the States: Some Causal Factors." *American Political Science Review* 58 (March, 1964) 60–71.

what you are. You vote according to that. In other words, if you come from a suburb, you reflect the thinking of the people in the suburbs; if you are of a depressed people, you reflect that. You represent the sum total of your background."[37]

The bliss of political ignorance. Yet, it is a moot question as to whether legislators really know their constituents, whether they do vote as their constituents would have voted on particular issues. In studies of the Iowa and Florida legislatures, it was found that legislators could predict only in a very mixed way how their own districts would vote on certain proposed constitutional amendments and referenda. On highly salient and politically charged issues, such as home rule, reapportionment, and busing, the legislators accurately forecast their constituents' votes by as much as 90 percent and no less than 70 percent. The less salient issues had a considerably lower percentage of legislators accurately predicting their constituents subsequent voting.[38]

The irony of legislative anonymity. The other side of the coin, of course, is not how well legislators know their constituents, but how well their constituents know them. In a national survey conducted by the Gallup organization, only 28 percent of those polled could name their state senator and only 24 percent knew who their representative was. Interestingly, people in small towns and in rural areas were much more likely to know their state representatives than were those living in big cities.[39]

The next question that arises is if the constituents of a state care what their legislature is doing. In a poll conducted in Minnesota during the middle of the legislative session, about one-third of the citizens of Minnesota indicated no interest whatever in what their own legislature was doing,[40] and a similar study completed in Iowa found that nearly 50 percent of those polled said they paid very little or no attention to the legislature.[41] Yet, both Iowa and Minnesota have reputations for politically active and interested citizenries. It may be that if such polls were conducted in other states, they would find even lower percentages of citizens expressing an interest in what their legislatures did or were doing.

If, indeed, most constituents neither know who their legislators are nor care what their legislatures are doing, then legislators can afford to be "Burkean." They can tell their constituents that they "vote their own mind"

---

[37]Quoted in: Wahlke et al., *Legislative Systems,* pp. 267–286.

[38]See: Ronald Hedlund and H. Paul Friesma, "Representatives Perceptions on Constituency Opinion," *Journal of Politics* 34 (August, 1972) 730–752. Robert S. Erikson, Norman R. Luttbeg, and William V. Holloway, "Knowing One's District: How Legislators Predict Referendum Voting." *American Journal of Political Science* 19 (May, 1975) 231–234.

[39]Gallup Opinion Index, *Report Number 20* (February, 1967) 17.

[40]Press release of the Minnesota poll, *Tribune,* July 11, 1965. As cited in: Samuel C. Patterson, *American State Legislatures,* 163.

[41]Independent Research Associates, Inc., "A Study of Voters' Opinions of State Legislatures: Iowa," prepared for Legis 50/The Center for Legislative Improvement formerly The Citizens' Conference on State Legislatures (June, 1968) 6–7.

with impunity because the evidence indicates that few people are paying much attention to them anyway.

WHO ARE LEGISLATORS?

The 7,800 state legislators are an upwardly mobile group. In general, they enjoy higher social, economic, and professional status than their parents did, and they tend not to be from old-line, established families in their states. Politicians emanating from statewide "aristocracies" tend to enter gubernatorial and congressional elections and rarely, if ever, run for the state legislature.

LEGISLATORS AS A SEMIELITE

One's profession or occupation, of course, is closely related to one's upward mobility or lack of it. Among state legislators, a plurality are lawyers, although the proportion who are lawyers has been declining—from a fourth in 1967 to a fifth in 1977. Businessmen are the next most represented profession (15 percent in 1977), and many of them are retirees. Farmers, long an interest group with a particular concern over state politics, also are heavily represented in legislatures. State employees are also represented, having made remarkable inroads in recent years. Educators in particular are moving on to the statehouses, tripling their representation from 1967 to 1977; in four states educators are the largest single occupational block. Still other types of government employees control 4 percent of the nation's legislative seats. Working people occupy a mere 1 percent of legislative seats, an apparent decrease from 2 percent twenty-five years ago.[42] Table 6–8 lists the occupations of state legislators in greater detail.

Few legislators are women, and rarely do women constitute more than 10 percent of a typical state's legislature. There are more women legislators in the rural New England and the western states. Women appear to be slowly gaining ground in legislatures, but they still occupy only 9 percent of the country's legislative seats. Interestingly, the less "professional" a legislature is, the more likely it is to have more women, regardless of regional consideration.[43] Table 6–8 also indicates the percentage of women legislators by region.

Minorities also are underrepresented relative to their percentage in the population. Of the 7,800 legislators in the country, less than two hundred

---

[42]Insurance Information Institute Survey as reported in *U.S. News & World Report* (January 9, 1978) p. 69. Also Belle Zeller, ed., *American State Legislatures.* Report of the Committee on American Legislatures, American Political Science Association (New York: Thomas Y. Crowell, 1954) p. 71.

[43]Insurance Information Institute Survey. Also Emmy F. Werner, "Women in State Legislatures." *Western Political Quarterly* 21 (March, 1968) 40–50.

TABLE 6–8 OCCUPATION AND SEX OF STATE LEGISLATORS BY REGION, 1977

BREAKDOWN BY OCCUPATION	North-east	North Central	South	West	TOTAL U.S.
Lawyers	18%	17%	31%	13%	21%
Other professionals	6%	6%	6%	8%	6%
Owners, self-employed	14%	12%	18%	15%	15%
Agriculture	2%	16%	7%	13%	9%
Executives, managers	6%	7%	6%	7%	6%
Real estate, construction	5%	5%	7%	5%	6%
Insurance	5%	4%	6%	4%	5%
Communications, arts	2%	3%	3%	4%	3%
Other business jobs	6%	5%	4%	6%	5%
Education	9%	9%	7%	12%	9%
Government employes	5%	4%	2%	4%	4%
Homemakers, students	6%	4%	2%	3%	3%
Labor, nonprofit-organization officials	1%	1%	*	1%	1%
Information not available	15%	7%	1%	5%	7%
BREAKDOWN BY SEX					
Women	13%	8%	6%	10%	9%
Men	87%	92%	94%	90%	91%

*Less than 1/2 of 1%

Source: Insurance Information Institute.

are black. If blacks were represented in the legislatures proportionately to their percentage in the national population (11 percent), the number would be closer to eight hundred. Blacks are relatively well represented in the legislatures of northern urban industrial states, and generally tend to come from the inner cities in those states. They are seriously underrepresented in the South and in the border states, largely because of the residency patterns and the nature of legislative districting in those states. In the South and rural border states, blacks are more or less spread around the countryside. In the North blacks tend to be concentrated in the inner city, where they make up larger portions of these districts' populations and are therefore more likely to be voted into office.[44]

In keeping with their upward mobility, legislators have substantially more formal education than the population at large. Indeed, approximately 75 percent of state legislators in the country have had some college education. Legislators also tend to be "home country boys," who enter the legislature in their early forties; most of them lived all or most of their lives in the district that they represent in the legislature.[45] They are not at all geograph-

---

[44]Frank Sorauf, *Party and Representation* (New York: Atherton Press, 1963) pp. 89–94.
[45]Wahlke et al., *Legislative Systems*, p. 488.

ically mobile compared to the population generally. Along with having deep roots in his or her district, legislators also seem to reflect their district in social, economic, and religious characteristics as well. For example, a study of the Pennsylvania legislature found that Protestant candidates came from Protestant districts and Catholics from Catholic districts. These religious differences paralleled ethnic and economic differences as well.[46]

ROLES OUR REPRESENTATIVES PLAY

What kind of psychological factors do legislators bring to the business of representing the people? To aid in answering this question, a political scientist was somehow able to pursuade a number of South Carolina legislators a number of years ago to undergo some rather thorough psychological testing. He found that the legislators from South Carolina were relatively self-sufficient, self-confident, extroverted, somewhat more domineering, less neurotic, and less authoritarian than the average American.[47] A considerably more recent study of Iowa state legislators determined that this group also was generally more tolerant of others and more sympathetic toward minority groups than was a corresponding sample of Iowa voters.[48] These findings are not surprising. It would be an odd person in politics, for example, who was less than gregarious, self-confident, and flexible, which seems to be the typical mental make-up of state legislators.

Once a budding legislator runs for office and wins, what happens then? What roles do legislators assume in working with their colleagues? Although the number of roles a legislator can play is almost infinite, some political scientists have taken pains to describe a few of them.

James David Barber has categorized state legislators as *spectators, advertisers, reluctants,* and *lawmakers.*[49] *Spectators* are largely passive people who enjoy watching the circus of the legislative process, would like to stay on, and seem to have been attracted to the legislature by the social prestige of the office. Spectators are "compensating for feelings of social inferiority."

Advertisers, on the other hand, are quite active but not especially keen on returning to the legislature because their primary purpose is to attain some personal publicity, usually for business reasons. Advertisers "show occupational insecurity and marked inner conflicts."

The *reluctants* are just that. They did not want to get into the legislature in the first place, but feel that they must do their civic duty for their friends

---

[46]Sorauf, *Party and Representation*, pp. 89–94.

[47]John C. McConaughy, "Some Personality Factors of State Legislators," In, *Legislative Behavior: Reader in Theory and Research,* John C. Wahlke and Heinz Eulau, eds. (Glencoe, Ill.:Free Press, 1959).

[48]Ronald W. Hedlund, "Psychological Predispositions: Political Representatives and the Public." *American Journal of Political Science* 19 (August, 1973) 489–505.

[49]James David Barber. *The Lawmakers: Recruitment and Adaptation to Legislative Life.* (New Haven:Yale University Press, 1965) p. 163.

and neighbors. They have difficulty in "adapting to a strange, fast-moving situation."

Finally, the *lawmakers* are about as close as legislators come to being inner-motivated professionals. They probably plan to stay in the legislature for some length of time, and they concentrate on the major issues of public policy because they are "freed for this by personal strength and powerful adjustive techniques."

Wahlke came up with quite a different set of roles, which he described as encompassing "the legislature as decision maker"; these were the *ritualist, tribune, inventor,* and *broker.*[50] The *ritualist* prefers the mechanics of the job. He or she is fascinated by procedures and rules and purposefully sets out to master this admittedly complex topic. Often ritualists can become rather powerful individuals in the legislature simply because they understand the rules of the game.

The *tribune,* to put the matter bluntly, is a blow-hard. He is close to being a modern-day populist and is primarily concerned with knowing the needs and feelings of the people and becoming their spokesman.

The *inventor* is a frustrated person. But he is also a perceptive one, because he recognizes that in the twentieth century the center for public policy formulation and execution resides in the executive branch of government. He sees himself as thoughtful and far-sighted, possessed of imagination, and eager to devise new ways of solving current problems. He maintains that the legislator should "be in the front of things" but recognizes that it is not.

Lastly, the *broker* is a legislator who provides the grease between the wheels. He sees his function as balancing competing interests, achieving compromise, and coordinating and integrating groups that are at loggerheads. The sophisticated broker perceives conflicting groups in terms of power potentiality and the "moral worth" of the groups in contention, whereas the naive broker tends to believe that a compromise can be achieved if he merely listens to the competing group (he might say for example, "Isn't this just a communications problem?").

A third unified theory of the roles that legislators play has been offered by Frank Sorauf.[51] Sorauf categorizes legislators as *trustees, delegates,* and *partisans.* A *trustee* is one who votes his conscience; a *delegate* tends to follow the instructions (at least as he perceives them) of his constituents; the *partisan,* or *politico,* follows the orders of party leadership. Of course, as with all the other theories concerning legislative role-playing, these categories overlap considerably when applied to an individual legislator.

THE TURNOVER TRAUMA

Regardless of the kinds of roles that legislators play, political scientists who have studied these peculiar creatures have concluded that it takes at least three terms before a legislator can become genuinely effective and have an

---

[50]Wahlke, et al., *Legislative Systems,* pp. 249–257.
[51]Sorauf, *Party and Representation,* pp. 121–146.

impact on the formulation of public policy.[52] Yet, generally about a third of all legislators in any given session are new to the job. Legislative turnover is extraordinarily high, in part because of the impact of reapportionment. During the years of unprecedented legislative reapportionment (1963–1971), for example, the overall turnover rate for the fifty state senates was 30.4 percent, for the forty-nine lower chambers 36.1 percent.[53] By contrast, national congressional turnover during the same period was 10 percent for the Senate and 15 percent for the House. Reapportionments resulting from the 1970 census resulted in even higher state legislative turnover rates for 1971–1972; 43 percent in the senates and 38 percent in the houses. Turnover rates were declining by the mid-1970s.[54]

Neither reapportionment nor losing at the polls can completely account for the high legislative turnover in the states. Rather, many legislators voluntarily leave the legislature; they are defeated for reelection far less frequently than they "opt out."

Large states that have longer legislative sessions and more professionalized legislatures show a pattern of lower turnover rates. The declining turnover rate in state legislatures seems related to the fact that legislatures are professionalizing; bigger staffs, higher pay, increasing prestige, and the normal perquisites of political office seem to be slowly reducing legislative turnover. Ironically, as legislative turnover rates slacken, congressional turnover is increasing. Between 1974 and 1978, legislative turnover was about 25 percent, while congressional turnover was almost 50 percent[55]—an increase that could be attributable to a "post-Watergate morality" by voters.

THE PROFESSIONALIZATION OF THE LEGISLATURES

Professionalism implies working at one's job on a relatively full-time basis and trying to do the job well, as defined by standards that relate directly to the job. Just as a lawyer is supposedly a "professional," so is a legislator, at least in some of the states.

MAKING LAWS AND MAKING MONEY

One clear indication of the degree of professionalism possessed by a legislature is how much the legislators are paid. The average biennial wage of legislators has grown dramatically in the states—from about $4,000 in the early 1960s to more than $18,000 in the mid-1970s. California legislators are the highest paid, receiving a biennial compensation of more than

---

[52]Charles S. Hyneman, "Tenure and Turnover of Legislative Personnel." *The Annals of the American Academy of Political and Social Science* 195 (January, 1938) 30–31.

[53]Alan Rosenthal, "Turnover in State Legislatures," *American Journal of Political Science* 18 (August, 1974) 609–616.

[54]William Pound and Carl Tubbesing, *Book of the States, 1978–79.* (Lexington Ky.: Council of State Governments, 1978) p. 7.

[55]*Ibid.,* and "The Penny Wise 98th" *Newsweek* (November 20, 1978)p. 56.

$64,000, and three additional states pay their legislators more than $40,000 a year. The low end of the continuum is represented by New Hampshire, whose constitution prohibits the state from paying its legislators more than $200 for the two-year session.[56]

THE BUREAUCRATIZATION OF THE LEGISLATURES

Another criterion indicating the professionalization of state legislatures is the growth of the professional staffs attached to the legislature. These staffs provide at least three major functions to a legislature: the legislative reference service, the bill drafting service, and the legislative council.

The *legislative reference service* is found in virtually all states. It was inaugurated in 1901 in Wisconsin, and has since been adopted elsewhere. Usually located in the state archives, legislative reference services provide research on upcoming legislation.

Often the legislative reference service is integrated with the *bill drafting service*. Together they draft bills that articulate (in lawyer-like fashion) the public policy that legislators really wish to accomplish. Normally both the legislative reference and bill drafting services are directly responsible to the legislature rather than to the executive branch of government.

A third type of professional staff is the *legislative council*, which got its start in 1932 in Kansas. Virtually all state legislatures now have a council whose purpose is to provide a continuous and ongoing research staff for the legislature, whether or not that body is in session. The average council has fifteen members, but individual councils range in size from five in South Carolina to more than two hundred fifty in Pennsylvania. Frequently the legislative council functions as a liaison between the chief executive and the legislature in the development of public policy.[57]

There has been a recent trend to abolish legislative councils and replace them with *legislative management committees*, as Connecticut, Florida, and Utah have done. The intent is to consolidate the administration of legislatures within a single organization. A related development is the recent establishment of permanent research *staffs specializing in technical and scientific areas*, such as energy. About a dozen legislatures have such staffs. Finally, all legislatures have *budget review staffs*, whose sole function is to analyze budgetary and fiscal matters. Almost all also have some sort of *auditing staffs*. Each legislator also has a *personal staff* of some kind, with the legislative leadership normally having a larger personal staff.

Professional staffs have burgeoned in size since mid-century. California and New York provide the most illustrative examples. In 1974, the California

---

[56]William Pound and Carl Tubbesing, "The State Legislatures." *Book of the States, 1978–79.* (Lexington, Ky.: Council of State Governments, 1978) p. 7.

[57]William J. Siffin, *The Legislative Council in American States* (Bloomington, Ind.: Indiana University Press, 1959).

assembly paid $22 million to employ nearly two thousand clerks and professional staff members for its legislature. Of these, more than seven hundred were professional staff members, an increase from approximately fifty in 1950. Similarly, the legislative staff in New York totaled almost fifteen hundred in the early 1970s, including clerical help.

Despite the growth of both salaries and staffs in the state legislatures, legislatures are not organized hierarchically, as is the executive branch and even the judiciary. Thus, legislatures have difficulty grappling with the problems of administration and expertise. It can be argued that the only reason legislatures have even bothered to professionalize at all is simply because professionalization provides the surest method for countering information "fed" to them by the executive branch of government. Legislators have felt a need to develop their own sources of expert information, and staffs provide this means.

SHOULD LEGISLATURES PROFESSIONALIZE? THE CASE FOR THE CITIZEN LEGISLATOR

The original concept of legislatures was that of the citizens' assembly. According to this view, legislators ought to be full-time citizens and part-time policy makers. They should have jobs to earn their daily bread and should contribute to the formulation of public policy only as a civic duty. New Hampshire has adopted this view perhaps more completely than has any other state, and it is not a bad view.

The counterargument runs that the more the legislator is paid and the more professional staff support that he or she receives, the more responsive the legislature will be and the better public policy will be for the state. The argument continues that social, economic, and political realities in the states have become far too complex; that America is in the throes of a technological revolution that has resulted in new relationships among traditional elements of society. A part-time legislature may result in legislation that is only partially responsive and responsible. California and New York, two states that are among the most complex socially of any states in the Union, have adopted this view most completely. In short, among the more interesting aspects of state politics are the structural alternatives that the states use to make public policy and nowhere is this contrast more evident than in the "citizens' legislature" versus the "professional legislature."

HOW GOOD ARE LEGISLATURES? A PROBLEM OF ASSESSMENT

Some one once very wisely observed that the making of laws, like sausage, should not be watched. Nevertheless, we still must ask: How well do legislatures perform in making public policy for their states? Virtually every citizen of every state has asked the question at one time or another, but the answer is elusive.

DO LEGISLATURES MATTER?

How much impact do legislatures actually have on the formulation of policies in their own states? Dye argues that legislatures are merely incidental in the policy processes of the states. The central realities, he claims, are such factors as wealth, education levels, degree of urbanization and industrialization, and related social and economic variables. Dye goes on to contend that most state legislatures are arbiters of public policy rather than initiators. Dye states that "policy initiation is the function of the governor, the bureaucrat, and the interest group," but not the legislature. He adds that legislatures "inject into public decision making a parochial influence" in that they represent local interests rather than the statewide interest.[58]

William L. Shade and Frank J. Munger take issue with Dye, arguing that the variables of legislative professionalism, levels of information available to legislators, and interparty competition are the strongest determinants of responsive state policies.[59]

ASSESSING LEGISLATURES

It is admittedly difficult to determine how important legislatures are in making public policies in the states. Still the question remains: How well do they make public policy? We can measure and evaluate the quality of their performance in a number of ways.

The yarkstick of professionalism. One way is to employ the criteria of professionalism. The Citizens' Conference on State Legislatures evaluated the fifty state legislatures using five criteria: functionality (administrative quality), accountability, information-handling capability, independence, and representativeness.[60] California ranked highest; Alabama ranked fiftieth. Table 6–9 gives the ranking of the states as rated by the Citizens' Conference on State Legislatures.

The yardstick of public opinion. A second major method of evaluating state legislatures is simply finding out what the citizens of the states think of their legislatures. We already noted that most citizens (at least in selected states) do not know who their legislators are nor what their legislature is doing. Even so, Americans have definite opinions about the performance of their legislatures. Table 6–10 shows how citizens in thirteen states evaluated their legislatures' performance from 1968 through 1974. It is apparent that many Americans are critical of the performance of their state legislatures. Never-

[58]Dye, *Politics in States and Communities,* pp. 160–161.

[59]William L. Shade and Frank J. Munger, "Consensus, Conflict, and Congruence: Policy-Making in the American States." A paper delivered at the American Political Science Association, New Orleans, September 4–8, 1973.

[60]Legis 50/The Center for Legislative Improvement formerly The Citizens' Conference on State Legislatures. *Report on an Evaluation of the 50 State Legislatures* (Denver, November 1971) 29.

TABLE 6–9 STATE LEGISLATIVE PERFORMANCE AS MEASURED BY SELECTED PROFESSIONAL STANDARDS

OVERALL RANK	STATE	FUNCTIONAL	ACCOUNTABLE	INFORMED	INDEPENDENT	REPRESENTATIVE
1	California	1	3	2	3	2
2	New York	4	13	1	8	1
3	Illinois	17	4	6	2	13
4	Florida	5	8	4	1	30
5	Wisconsin	7	21	3	4	10
6	Iowa	6	6	5	11	25
7	Hawaii	2	11	20	7	16
8	Michigan	15	22	9	12	3
9	Nebraska	35	1	16	30	18
10	Minnesota	27	7	13	23	12
11	New Mexico	3	16	28	39	4
12	Alaska	8	29	12	6	40
13	Nevada	13	10	19	14	32
14	Oklahoma	9	27	24	22	8
15	Utah	38	5	8	29	24
16	Ohio	18	24	7	40	9
17	South Dakota	23	12	15	16	37
18	Idaho	20	9	29	27	21
19	Washington	12	17	25	19	39
20	Maryland	16	31	10	15	45
21	Pennsylvania	37	23	23	5	36
22	North Dakota	22	18	17	37	31
23	Kansas	31	15	14	32	34
24	Connecticut	39	26	26	25	6
25	West Virginia	10	32	37	24	15
26	Tennessee	30	44	11	9	26
27	Oregon	28	14	35	35	19
28	Colorado	21	25	21	28	27
29	Massachusetts	32	35	22	21	23
30	Maine	29	34	32	18	22
31	Kentucky	49	2	48	44	7
32	New Jersey	14	42	18	31	35
33	Louisiana	47	39	33	13	14
34	Virginia	25	19	27	26	48
35	Missouri	36	30	40	49	5
36	Rhode Island	33	46	30	41	11

TABLE 6-9 continued.

OVERALL RANK	STATE	FUNCTIONAL	ACCOUNTABLE	INFORMED	INDEPENDENT	REPRESENTATIVE
37	Vermont	19	20	34	42	47
38	Texas	45	36	43	45	17
39	New Hampshire	34	33	42	36	43
40	Indiana	44	38	41	43	20
41	Montana	26	28	31	46	49
42	Mississippi	46	43	45	20	28
43	Arizona	11	47	38	17	50
44	South Carolina	50	45	39	10	46
45	Georgia	40	49	36	33	38
46	Arkansas	41	40	46	34	33
47	North Carolina	24	37	44	47	44
48	Delaware	43	48	47	38	29
49	Wyoming	42	41	50	48	42
50	Alabama	48	50	49	50	41

Source: Report on an Evaluation of the 50 SState Legislatures (Denver, Co.: Legis 50/The Center for Legislative Improvement formerly The Citizens Conference of State Legislatures, 1971) p.29.

TABLE 6–10 LEGISLATIVE PERFORMANCE IN SELECTED STATES AS MEASURED BY PUBLIC OPINION

State	Year	PERFORMANCE EVALUATION[1] Percent who approve	Percent who disapprove	Percent who have no opinion
Massachusetts	1968	32	57	12
New York	1968	29	56	15
Pennsylvania	1968	40	50	11
Illinois	1968	44	46	9
Minnesota	1965	26	44	30
	1968	49	41	10
	1971	19	56	25
	1973	37	51	12
	1974	35	48	17
Iowa	1959	28	48	24
	1963	25	60	15
	1965	28	53	19
	1966	51	42	7
	1967	20	64	16
	1968	48	33	19
	1969	22	53	25
	1972	29	29	42
Ohio	1968	55	34	12
South Dakota	1968	49	43	8
California	1968	33	51	16
Florida	1968	37	50	13
North Carolina	1968	51	36	13
Texas	1968	46	42	12
Alabama	1968	52	31	14
Louisiana	1968	47	43	11
National U.S. sample	1968	41	41	18

[1]The usual question asked is: "In general, how would you rate the job the state legislature has done: excellent, pretty good, only fair, or poor?" In this table, "approve" includes excellent and pretty good ratings; "disapprove" includes fair and poor.
Except for Iowa, the 1968 percentages are from Merle Black, David M. Kovenock, and William C. Reynolds, *Political Attitudes in the Nation and the States* (Chapel Hill, N.C.: Institute for Research in Social Science, University of North Carolina, 1974), 186: Iowa data come from surveys conducted by the Iowa Poll, reported in news releases for the *Des Moines Register and Tribune:* Minnesota data are from news releases of the Minnesota Poll for the *Minneapolis Tribune.*

Source: Samuel C. Patterson, "American State Legislatures and Public Policy. "In *Politics in the American States*, 3rd ed., Herbert Jacob and Kenneth N. Vines, eds. (Boston: Little, Brown, 1976) p. 164. Reprinted by permission.

theless, though Americans may not always like what their state legislatures do, they clearly support the *concept* of the legislature; Americans appreciate the legislatures as a keystone in the arch of democracy.

The yardstick of responsiveness. A third way to evaluate legislative performance is to measure the legislatures' responsiveness to public demands. A comprehensive analysis of all fifty states found a reasonably high degree of close agreement between popular preferences in the states and the actual policies enacted by their legislatures—at least on such issues as civil rights, welfare policies, liquor and gambling laws, and unionization of public employees. There was considerably less congruence between the people's opinions and the policies legislated by their representatives on such issues as right-to-work laws, election legislation, firearms regulation, motor vehicle registration, and aid to parochial schools.[61]

The yardstick of illusion. All these efforts in evaluating the performance of legislatures and their worth in society are perhaps best summed up by philosopher T. V. Smith, who not only was a university professor of philosophy but served in the Illinois Senate and the U. S. House of Representatives. He noted that legislators have

> a magnificent protection against external hostility in the friendly bosom of
> a "we group," nonetheless dependable because achieved *ad hoc* and
> perennially shifting in membership. By making it possible for representa-
> tives amiably to stand the gaf, this "we group" bulwark gives opportunity
> for a great many good citizens to do a great deal of criticizing harmlessly.
> Legislators become scapegoats. . . . What, for instance, would most editors
> have to work themselves into decent form upon were it not for the "ex-
> travagance," the "waste," the "inefficiency," the "stupidity," the "venality"
> and, in general "the never ending audacity of elected persons"? Nor are
> editors alone in this need. . . it is safe to say that no other institution today
> has half the effectiveness of the legislature in soaking up and sterilizing
> the wastage produced in society when the will to perfection meets the will
> power in the lives of good men and women. To have a "show" that every
> citizen can "show up" without fear of retaliation (since he supports it)
> maximizes the fun and minimizes the fury of the social process.[62]

---

[61]Ronald E. Webber and William R. Shaffer, "Public Opinion and American State Policy-Making." *Midwest Journal of Political Science* 16 (November, 1972) 683–691.

[62]T.V. Smith, "Two Functions of the American State Legislature." *Annals of the American Academy of Political and Social Science* 195 (January, 1938) 187. See also T.V. Smith, *The Legislative Way of Life* (Chicago: University of Chicago Press, 1940).

THE
GREENING
OF THE
GOVERNORS

With new developments in federalism, and one of their own in the White House, the 1980s are witnessing a political revival of the governorship. In this chapter we review some of these developments as they affect the greening of the governors.

In discussing governors, I shall use the term "he" for convenience, although "he" is not meant to imply that all governors and other political leaders at the state and local levels are men, as an increasing number of political leaders are women who have established electoral careers of consequence in their own right.

THE GUBERNATORIAL CAREER

Governors generally have been in state politics for some time before they ever considered trying for the office. Roughly half of the nation's governors were state legislators or public attorneys when they ran for the governorship, and a plurality held some statewide elected office prior to running. The majority hold law degrees, and an even greater majority have practiced law or been in business. The median age for governors at inauguration is the late forties; most are married and have served in the military.[1] Governors also are accomplished grassroots politicians who understand the inner workings of their party. If a governor is to be effective, it is essential that he avoid factionalizing his own political party in the process of gaining his party's nomination, and most governors, or would-be governors, realize this.

Once in office, governors can serve terms of varying length. Nineteen states have a four-year term with no restrictions on reelections, and these states are located primarily in the West and Midwest. Another twenty states have four-year gubernatorial terms, but the governors are restricted to serving only two terms; these states are scattered fairly evenly throughout the country. A half-dozen states allow a single four-year term; consecutive reelection is prohibited. These states are found almost entirely in the South. Finally, four states—Arkansas, New Hampshire, Rhode Island, and Vermont—have a two-year term with no restrictions on reelection. Table 7–1 indicates which tenure systems are the most likely to accord the greatest potential power to the incumbent governor. Obviously, a four-year term with no restrictions on reelection is most advantageous to the governor; a two-year term is least advantageous. As Table 7–1 indicates, the trend over

---

[1]Samuel R. Solomon, "Governors: 1960–1970." *National Civic Review* 60 (March, 1971), 128–131.

TABLE 7–1 CHANGES IN GOVERNORS' TENURE
POTENTIAL, 1960–1978

	1960	1978
Four-year term		
No restraint on reelection	12	19
One reelection permitted[1]	7	20
No reelection permitted	15	6
Total	34	46
Two-year term		
No restraint on reelection	14	4
One reelection permitted	2	0
Total	16	4

[1]Includes two states with absolute two-term limitation (Delaware and Missouri).

Source: Book of the States, 1960–1961; ibid., 1978–79 (Lexington, Ky.: Council of State Governments).

time has been to extend the tenure of the governor; the reasoning behind this trend is that some executive stability is needed for the efficient administration of the state.

WHAT HAPPENS TO GOVERNORS?

A conventional wisdom is that the governorship is a dead-end job in American politics; there is no place to go afterward except to the political graveyard. As with most conventional wisdoms, this one has only elements of truth. Almost two-thirds of the governors retire to private life, but nearly 20 percent are appointed to significant federal jobs in Washington, or to what Joseph Schlesinger calls "the presidential office complex."[2] Another 12 to 15 percent are elected to the United States Senate, and 5 to 6 percent become judges.[3] And, of course, in 1976 when Jimmy Carter of Georgia was elected president, he became the first governor since Franklin Delano Roosevelt to win the highest office in the land.

In the 1960s and 1970s, more governors were Democrats than Republicans; the exceptions were 1966 and 1968, when the Republicans held the majority of governors' offices in the nation. But by 1976 only twelve

---

[2]Joseph A. Schlesinger, *Ambition and Politics: Political Careers in the United States* (Chicago:Rand-McNally, 1966).

[3]Joseph A. Schlesinger, "The Politics of the Executive." In *Politics in the American States,* 2nd ed. Herbert Jacob and Kenneth N. Vines, eds. (Boston: Little, Brown, 1972), p. 213.

governors belonged to the Grand Old Party, the lowest proportion the Republicans had ever reached; with the 1978 elections, the Republicans were in eighteen of the statehouses.

IS THE GOVERNOR POWERFUL?

Granting the premise that there can be a distinguished political future for governors in the United States, the question still stands: Is the office worth it? In other words, is the governor powerful? He probably is. He has, as Sarah McCally Morehouse notes, at least six major political bases: patronage, publicity, the promise (or threat) of campaign support (or opposition) to other politicians, control over information, influence over the scheduling of local legislation, and promise of advancement within the governor's party or his faction within the legislature.[4]

Others, notably Thomas R. Dye and Ira Sharkansky, argue (or come close to arguing) that "determinism" is the major form of public policy in the states; economic and social factors, not the influence of individual personalities or political leadership, are what really determine policy outcomes.[5] In a cogent argument against this deterministic thesis as it pertains to governors, Morehouse contends that the personality and ability of the governor can determine policy outcomes significantly. When a governor's abilities are combined with favorable tenure policies (four-year terms with unlimited succession being the most favorable), a high level of professionalism in the legislature, a competitive party system, and a high level of participation by the citizens in the state's political system, then the governor can have real policy-making powers. Morehouse's argument is a powerful one. It appeals not only to common sense but to a sense of hope for the future. As she observes, "The role of political leadership has been minimized in recent years as a result of studies that stressed the influence of socioeconomic variables over policy outcomes. In much of the literature in state policy output, the deterministic view of what leadership in the state can accomplish is a counsel of despair."[6]

If we accept Morehouse's conclusion—that the governor can indeed be powerful and have a major influence on how policy is made—then we should examine in some detail why he is powerful. In making this examination, we shall consider both the governor's relationship with his party and the legislature and his relationships with his own bureaucracy, focusing particularly on administrative organization, his appointive powers, and his role in the budgetary process.

---

[4]Sarah McCally Morehouse, "The Governor as Political Leader." In *Politics in the American States*, 3rd ed. Herbert Jacob and Kenneth N. Vines, eds. (Boston: Little, Brown, 1976), pp. 221–222.

[5]See the discussion of interparty competition in Chapter 4.

[6]Morehouse, "Governor as Political Leader," p. 239.

THE GOVERNOR, THE PARTY, AND THE LEGISLATURE

A governor must keep his political fences mended if he is to be an effective policy maker. His relationships with his own party, both inside and outside the legislature are critical. No governor enjoys complete control over his party; power is always a two-way street.

Morehouse, after analyzing the working relationships between governors and legislators in twelve western and northern states, found that governors garnered the greatest support from legislators (1) who were elected from districts that had voted heavily for the governor, and (2) who belonged to the same party as the governor and perceived his party's organization as pivotal in getting him nominated and elected. On the other hand, the degree of competition between political parties in a legislator's own district did not affect the legislator's support for the governor one way or the other.[7] The governor has the best chances for effectiveness in making policy when his party has a comfortable but not an overwhelming majority in the legislature. "The Governor can handle a modest majority, but when his party has an overwhelming majority, coalitions form against him, which he cannot undermine with his traditional stock of rewards and punishments. The optimum legislative contingent, then, would appear to be a comfortable majority—say about 55 percent in both houses of the legislature."[8]

Under these conditions, the governor, with the support of his bureaucracy can function most effectively as a lobbyist. The governor as lobbyist is a normal political reality in all states. As "Big Daddy" Jesse Unruh of California once observed, "The Governor is the biggest lobbyist in the state, and these [referring to the state bureaucracy] are his troops."[9]

Of course, the governor's greatest single source of authority in his dealings with the legislature is his *veto power*. The formal power of the veto varies among the states. In forty-four of the states, the governor has the *item veto* (that is, he can veto certain portions of a bill if he so wishes), and at least a majority of the legislature is required to override his item veto. Only in North Carolina does the governor have no veto power whatever. Table 7–2 ranks the states according to power of the veto. For example, the governor has a very strong veto power in Alaska, which requires three-quarters of the legislature to override. Actually, governors very rarely use the veto power; the threat of it often is adequate for a governor to have his way with the legislature. Governors on the whole, however, probably do not relish the use of the veto: It creates conflict within their own party, and the governor's relationships with his party likely are paramount to his political

---

[7]Sarah McCally Morehouse, "The State Political Party and the Policy-Making Process," *American Political Science Review* 67 (March, 1973), 55–72.

[8]Morehouse, "The Governor as Political Leader," p. 231.

[9]Bruce Keppel, "The State's Biggest Lobbyist: Executive Agencies." *California Journal* (December, 1972). Reprinted in Eugene C. Lee and Larry L. Berg, *The Challenge of California: Text and Readings,* 2nd ed. (Boston: Little, Brown, 1976), p. 175.

effectiveness. "The governor's outside party organization generates discipline within the legislative party" and that, therefore, "a model of gubernatorial influence would give the most weight to the ability of the governor to form winning coalitions both within and outside the legislature."[10]

THE GOVERNOR AND "HIS" BUREAUCRACY

The governor must deal with another major political force: the bureaucracy he has inherited from previous administrations. The bureaucracy, like the legislature, can make or break its own chief executive. One major reason why this is so is because a majority of offices, agencies, boards, bureaus, and commissions that constitute the state bureaucracy are not formally under the control of the governor. More agencies are under the direct control of the legislature than the governor, and this organizational reality does not bode well for the degree of effective control that the governor can exercise over his own executive branch.

BUREAUCRACY AND THE MYTH
OF GUBERNATORIAL AUTHORITY

There are a number of states using a decentralized administrative system, and presumably they encounter some of the same kinds of problems. As administrative efficiency continues to emerge as a public value in the twentieth century, it seems likely that the national trend will continue to be

---

[10]Morehouse, "The Governor as Political Leader," pp. 232–233.

TABLE 7–2 THE GOVERNORS' VETO POWERS

VERY STRONG		STRONG	MEDIUM	WEAK
Alaska	Minnesota	Alabama	Florida	Indiana
Arizona	Mississippi	Arkansas	Idaho	Maine
California	Missouri	Kentucky	Massachusetts	Nevada
Colorado	Nebraska	Tennessee	Montana	New Hampshire
Connecticut	New Jersey	West Virginia	New Mexico	North Carolina
Delaware	New York		Oregon	Rhode Island
Georgia	North Dakota		South Carolina	Vermont
Hawaii	Ohio		Texas	
Illinois	Oklahoma		Virginia	
Iowa	Pennsylvania		Washington	
Kansas	South Dakota		Wisconsin	
Louisiana	Utah			
Maryland	Wyoming			
Michigan				

Source: Book of the States, 1978–1979 (Lexington, Ky.: Council of State Governments).

the gradual elimination of independent boards, agencies, and commissions, slowly decimating a legion of public officials who are elected separately from the governor.

Certainly the governors would prefer to have control over their own bureaucracy. More than 46 percent of the governors responding to one study listed the lack of the power to reorganize their agencies as among their chief frustrations. They ranked this second only to the lack of appointive power as their major administrative problem.[11] Not all agency administrators agree with their governors in this regard. Another study of top administrators in fifty states found that only 42 percent wanted to be under the primary control of the governor. A plurality of those agency heads who were under the direct control of the legislature would prefer to shift to an independent status; less than a quarter wished to shift to direct gubernatorial control. Given his druthers, the director of an agency or commission would prefer, first, to be the head of an independent board; second, to be under the control of the governor; and, third, to report directly to the legislature.[12]

Moreover, public administrators appear to view any reorganization plans with a jaundiced eye. As the head of a public agency in Mississippi rationalized, in responding to how he felt about consolidating functions in that state's government,

> I think this is one of the very best things that has ever been done in the state of Mississippi and I long have been of the opinion that this work should have been accomplished in the past. However, my department is of a type, character and kind that cannot be consolidated with any other agency, as its duties and functions are unique, and a reduction of personnel or a transfer of any duties of this department would work a hardship and prevent certain citizens from receiving benefits to which they are entitled.[13]

Thus, it is not unreasonable to sum up the views of state administrators in the phrase, "Reorganization for everyone but me."

Closely related to the governor's powers to reorganize the executive branch are his powers to appoint and remove his own officials. Indeed, this may be his most important administrative power. One study found that governors felt their appointive powers to be more important than any other formal power, with two-thirds stressing the absence of the appointive power in certain areas as the most critical weakness in their power as chief

---

[11]Thad L. Beyle, "The Governors' Formal Powers: A View from the Governor's Chair." *Public Administration Review* 28 (November–December, 1968), 543.

[12]Diel S. Wright, "Executive Leadership in State Administration." *Midwestern Political Science Review* 11 (February, 1967), 1–26.

[13]Karl Bosworth, "The Politics of Management Improvement in the States." *American Political Science Review* 47 (March, 1953), 90.

executive.[14] Table 7–3 indicates the states that give the governors either very strong or very weak appointive powers.

A variant of the appointive power of the governors is the patronage power. While patronage is obviously a form of appointment, it is normally associated with the lower levels of the state bureaucracy rather than the upper ones. Patronage, as it is normally understood, is in decline in the American states. Because patronage is offensive to the growing middle class in America, it "is also losing its respectability. Its ethic—the naked political quid pro quo—no longer seems to many a natural and reasonable ingredient in politics. . . ."[15] A related major reason why patronage is declining in America is the rise of the civil servant, or merit, systems in state and local governments. We consider this aspect more thoroughly in Chapter 14.

GOVERNORS BATTLE THE BUDGETEERS

The final principal area of power that the governor has in relation to his bureaucracy is that of the budget, and the governor has less flexibility in allocating funds to various programs in his state than might generally be realized. Governors serve, on the average, less than five years in office and the budget is a complex document that takes time to master. As a result, the real control over budgetary matters often devolves to the bureaucracy. As Allen Schick discovered in his study of the budgetary process in fifty states, "as the budget has increased in size and developed into a tool of executive leadership, the legislature has suffered a decline in its budget power . . . it

---

[14]Beyle, "The Governors' Formal Powers," pp. 540–545.

[15]Frank J. Sorauf, "State Patronage in the Rural County." *American Political Science Review* 50 (March, 1956), 155.

TABLE 7–3 APPOINTIVE POWERS OF GOVERNORS

VERY STRONG	STRONG	MODERATE	WEAK	VERY WEAK
Hawaii	Arkansas	Alabama	Kansas	Arizona
Illinois	California	Alaska	Maine	Colorado
Indiana	Connecticut	Iowa	Nevada	Florida
Maryland	Delaware	Louisiana	New Hampshire	Georgia
Massachusetts	Idaho	Missouri	North Carolina	Mississippi
New Jersey	Kentucky	Montana	Wisconsin	New Mexico
New York	Michigan	Nebraska	Wyoming	North Dakota
Pennsylvania	Minnesota	Rhode Island		Oklahoma
Tennessee	Ohio	Utah		South Carolina
Virginia	Oregon	Washington		Texas
	South Dakota	West Virginia		
	Vermont			

Source: Book of the States, 1978–1979. (Lexington, Ky.: Council of State Governments).

no longer can play an effective role as 'watchdog of the treasury' and its oversight of administrative actions is confined to a few areas on a hit or miss basis."[16] Unlike legislators, the governors appear to realize that budgetary allocations represent policy outcomes, and their battles with the budgeteers can become intense.

Another investigation found that agency heads tended consistently to request more funds, and that governors or legislative reviewers were predictable in their propensity for reducing these requests. Governors had an overriding desire to balance their budgets, but usually at a higher level of expenditure, thus providing more services. Legislatures tended to approve higher appropriations while simultaneously disputing with the governor over which sources of revenue to tax.[17] In other words, state agencies tend to overestimate their needs because they anticipate a cut from the governor and his staff, and possibly from the legislature as well. A financial compromise usually results, but, even so, all parties are constrained in this process of fiscal negotiation.

State constitutions and legislation often earmark revenue from certain sources for particular purposes (such as the tax on gasoline for highway construction) and more than 50 percent of state revenues are earmarked for particular purposes. A good portion of the remaining revenues are called "general fund expenditures," which often are committed to programs that are difficult to alter, such as welfare and education.

Nevertheless, the general tendency over time has been to give the governor in most states increasing control over the budget. In thirty-four states, the governor has the entire responsibility for preparing the budget and, in a dozen others, he divides this function with an appointee of the civil service or a professional bureaucrat. Governors, while constrained in the influence that they have in some areas of the budget, nonetheless seem to feel that their control over the process is generally adequate. One study found that only 8 percent of the governors mentioned the lack of budgetary power as a problem in their duties as manager of the state.[18]

DO GOVERNORS GOVERN?

The organization of the executive branch, as exemplified by such processes as management, appointive powers, and the budgetary process, does make a difference in what kind of policies a state gets. Dye has argued that it does not. He states that there is very little evidence to support the idea that

---

[16]Allen Schick, *Budget Innovation in the States* (Washington, D.C.: Brookings Institution, 1971), p. 167.

[17]Thomas J. Anton, "Roles and Symbols and the Determination of State Expenditures." *Midwest Journal of Political Science* 11 (February, 1967), 27–43.

[18]Beyle, "The Governors' Formal Powers," p. 543.

fragmentation in the executive branch in itself affects the content of state public policy; Dye, in keeping with his overall view of the public policy process, contends that it is the social and economic variables that have the real impact on how policy is made.[19] Nevertheless, common sense and observable data would indicate that, in Morehouse's words, "It takes organization to put forward and pass a sustained program in behalf of the needy. Disorganization can obstruct such a program. A fragmented executive may be holding operation, a bastion of the status quo. A governor who can appoint those who share his views can develop programs to present to the legislature and can use the resources which are his to build a coalition to pass the proposals."[20]

It is such variables that led Schlesinger to compile his index of the formal powers of governors. The index was comprised of the governors' tenure provisions, appointive powers, responsibilites for preparing the budget, and veto powers. He found that the governors of South Carolina, Mississippi, and Texas occupied the weakest power position relative to the politics of their states, while the governors of New York, Illinois, and Hawaii had the most formal powers with which to enact their policies. The more urban states tend to accord their governors more formal powers; the rural and poorer states give their governors fewer formal powers.[21]

Regardless of formal powers, few can argue that personal abilities do make a difference in the effectiveness of a governor. To consider this aspect in more detail, let us examine how two of the more spectacular American governors built their power bases, then used their power.

GUBERNATORIAL STYLE: THE GURU OF CALIFORNIA AND THE KINGFISH OF LOUISIANA

THE GOVERNOR AS POLITICAL MYSTIC: EDMUND G. BROWN, JR., OF CALIFORNIA

"Jerry" Brown entered politics in 1969 when he ran for the Board of Trustees of the Los Angeles Community College District.[22] Son of Edmund G. (Pat) Brown, Sr., Governor of California from 1959 through 1966, Jerry Brown already possessed high name identification in California politics. In

---

[19]Thomas Dye, "Executive Power and Public Policy in the States." *Western Political Quarterly* 27 (December, 1969), 926–929.

[20]Morehouse, "The Governor as Political Leader," p. 225.

[21]Schlesinger, "The Politics of the Executive," pp. 220–234.

[22]The following paragraphs on Jerry Brown are drawn from: Winston W. Crouch, John C. Bollens, and Stanley Scott, *California Government and Politics,* 6th ed. (Englewood Cliffs, N.J.: Prentice-Hall, 1977), pp. 156–160.

1970, Brown ran for secretary of state. Despite his unlikely prospects for winning, he won that election and subsequently brought some recognition to himself by attempting to bring about substantial campaign law reforms.

In 1974, at the age of thirty-six, he ran for governor on the Democratic ticket. His Republican opposition was Houston Flournoy, who at that time was the state's comptroller. The Republicans launched an aggressive campaign, charging that Brown was too young and inexperienced; moreover, Brown, as a bachelor, did not have the image of a sedate family man. Beyond that, however, there were allegations that Brown was simply far too "mystical" for the average electorate. Brown had spent four years in a Jesuit seminary studying to be a priest and maintained a peculiar lifestyle (at least by some standards): He lived a very spartan existence, drove a Plymouth, practiced Transcendental Meditation, and breakfasted on Granola. Nevertheless, Flournoy was fighting the Watergate scandals and, as a Republican, was tainted by them; he seems to have compounded this problem by asking President Gerald Ford to campaign for him, which Ford did. Brown won by the narrow margin of 2.9 percent.

As governor Brown had to deal with the California Assembly. The assembly had a two-thirds Democratic majority and the leadership of both houses supported his budget bills. Brown presented unusual policy packages to the legislature. In one sense he emulated his predecessor's policy of "cut, squeeze, and trim" as a budgetary approach, justifying this position on the grounds of reducing an inflationary economy and dwindling state revenues. But he also promulgated some major social reforms within the state, notably regulating farm labor-employer relations, extending collective bargaining to public employees, applying tougher air pollution standards to automobile plants, and reforming the public schools. Not all of these programs met with success in the legislature, but Governor Brown's style helped to enact most of them. Brown would deliver extremely brief oral presentations to the legislature outlining his programs. He would follow these up with more ample written messages. Then he would personally participate in marathon conferences with key legislators and key interest group representatives. Among his major accomplishments, he instituted an innovative medical malpractice insurance system for the state; in a close working relationship with C´sar Chavez's United Farm Workers Association, he helped establish a secret ballot election system for farm workers who were voting on union representation; and he made an aggressive effort to employ more minorities and women in state government at high levels (under his predecessor's administration, less than 1 percent of the state's top administrative officials were women). In 1978, Brown was reelected by a wide margin.

Brown's unique political style has had a national impact. In 1976, despite a very late start in the Democratic presidential primaries, he received a surprisingly large share of the votes. Brown's austere lifestyle likely was attractive to many voters, both nationally and in California. He eschewed the governor's mansion, preferring to live in a modest apartment in Sacramento and, like the present occupant of the White House, he has made a point of living simply despite his high office.

THE GOVERNOR AS POLITICAL MEGALOMANIAC: HUEY LONG OF LOUISIANA

A man who represents the antithesis of Brown in virtually every respect (or at least one would hope so) is Huey P. Long, Jr., the "Kingfish." He was born in 1893, the eighth of nine children, in an agricultural area of Louisiana "characterized by a large number of hogs and children."[23] Huey completed a three-year program at the Tulane Law School in less than one year, and quickly passed the bar examination. At twenty-six he ran for his first public office, that of the representative from the Third District for the state's Railway Commission; this was the only office open under the state constitution for one of his age, since it had no age limitation whatever. He won. When the new state constitution of 1921 converted the Railway Commission to the Public Service Commission, Huey had his opportunity to build a political base. After a tilt with the Cumberland Telephone and Telegraph Company, Long managed to push through a retroactive refund to all telephone users, thus becoming a state hero overnight. For good measure, he also lowered rates for gas and electricity for Shreveport's street cars and all of the state's intrastate railroads. In 1924, when he was thirty, the minimum legal age for a gubernatorial candidate, Long made his first bid for the governorship. He lost his campaign for the Democratic nomination (which was the only election that really counted in Louisiana), but used the next four years to mend his political fences. In 1928, he entered the campaign for governor with substantially more press and popular support than he had enjoyed during his first attempt.

Long's 1928 campaign can be summed up as "the redneck as reformer." He came out strongly and self-righteously against the notorious Choctaw Club of New Orleans, which was the controlling political machine of that city, mainly because it would not support him. On the positive side, he argued for free textbooks, free bridges, better roads, improved schools, repeal of the tobacco tax, and more taxes on Standard Oil, Inc., the state's major industry. He won, and he won largely with a class-based campaign; the poor and dispossessed consistently voted Long into office. The big planter parishes (counties) of Louisiana and the small dirt farmers traditionally voted against each other and, after Long's victory in 1928, the plantation interests joined with the major urban political machines in an effort to defeat Long. In 1929 these interests combined in an unsuccessful attempt to impeach Long. The impeachment process was conducted with

---

[23]Allen P. Sindler, *Huey Long's Louisiana: State Politics, 1920–52* (Baltimore:Johns Hopkins,1956), p. 45.

incredible sloppiness, and Long was able to defeat it. But he remembered the attempt, saying, "I used to try to get things done by saying 'please.' That didn't work and I'm a dynamiter. I'll dynamite 'em outta my path."[24]

After only two years in office, Long announced that he was going to run for the U.S. Senate on the curious understanding with the people of the state that he would not leave the governorship for two more years, and on a platform advocating a state "good roads" program. Long rationalized this situation by stating that Louisiana's representation in the U.S. Senate would not decline by Long's staying in Baton Rouge to complete his gubernatorial term for two more years because, with the incumbent Senator Ransdell in office, "the seat was vacant anyway."[25] Long won the Democratic primary of 1930, thus assuring himself a seat in the Senate. Under the state's constitution, the lieutenant governor should have moved into office after Long's election, and the lieutenant governor immediately had himself duly sworn into office by a Shreveport notary. The lieutenant governor was a political rival of Long's, so Long responded to this act by having the president pro tempore of the senate, one of his own men, take the oath as governor. He then informed the lieutenant governor that his oath was illegal and that he had forfeited his position as lieutenant governor by virtue of his illegal assumption of the governorship. This position was upheld by the Louisiana Supreme Court, which was under Long's dominance by that time, on the grounds that it "lacked jurisdiction." Thus, the Kingfish not only put his own man into the governor's office, but eliminated an irritating political rival.

In 1932, Long worked tirelessly for the nomination of Franklin Delano Roosevelt as president at the National Democratic Convention but, during the same year, he introduced his "Share Our Wealth" program, which promised to make "every man a king, but let no man wear the crown." This program, which was in direct competition with FDR, by 1935 had more than twenty-seven thousand clubs located in every state and claimed more than 7,500,000 members. "Huey, along with the rude, plain-spoken agitators of the new South, was founding a personal dictatorship."[26] President Roosevelt, concerned about the rise of the Kingfish on the national scene, started working to undermine his Louisiana political base. Roosevelt had more than $10 million of federal public works projects curtailed in Louisiana and had Long and his aides investigated by the Internal Revenue Service for tax evasion charges.

These actions, plus other internal statewide factors in Louisiana, had an effect and, by 1934, Long was in some trouble. Still, he controlled the legislature absolutely, and in 1934 he had the Louisiana assembly pass

---

[24]Quoted in *Ibid.*, 67.

[25]*Ibid.*, 70.

[26]*Ibid.*, 83.

measures very favorable to lower-class interests, he declared war on the "corrupt" Choctaw Club of New Orleans, and he "erected, through laws, the most thorough state dictatorship known to twentieth-century America."[27] By way of example, Long had his newly installed governor—with neither a proper warrant, nor by invitation of the civil authorities, nor by proclamation of marshal law—order the National Guard to enter New Orleans and seize the voter registration offices. With the National Guard present, Long supervised the nomination of his candidates for Congress, the Public Service Commission, and the State Supreme Court from the city of New Orleans. Only then did he retire the National Guard from the city.

Later, Long had the state legislature enact a series of laws which allowed him to take supervisory control of New Orleans's finances, and had the city officials in Baton Rouge and Alexandria replaced by gubernatorial appointments. He also established authority over nonelective municipal fire and police chiefs, and later this authority was extended to virtually every appointive municipal and parish employee in the state, including teachers, school-bus drivers, and janitors. Long also pushed through legislation that enabled the governor to call out the militia at any time, without challenge from the courts, and empowered the governor to increase without limit the personnel of the State Bureau of Identification, which soon became known throughout Louisiana as "Huey's Cossacks." "Long had taken advantage of every inadequacy of the state constitution and every exigency of the Depression to centralize power and to suppress opposition. In terms of the controls he possessed, the Kingfish had swallowed the Pelican State. They tuk Sah Huey."[28] In 1935 there was a popular riot of anti-Longs, protesting his ruthless control over the state.

In September of that year, the Kingfish was in Baton Rouge to supervise the successor to his appointed governor. As he left the capitol, surrounded by bodyguards, he was assassinated by a medical specialist whose family members had been prominent anti-Longs; the assassin was killed immediately by Long's guards.

Long made an impact on Louisiana and may have made a larger impact on the nation had he lived long enough. There is no question that he was a tyrant, and a very shrewd one, capitalizing on the class biases of southern politics. Indeed, he was idolized in Louisiana after his death. The state presented a statue of the Kingfish, as one of its two great sons, to be recognized in statuary hall in Washington; it purchased his New Oreleans home as a museum; and it made Long's birthday a legal holiday. For many years after Long's death, the personal columns in the New Orleans *Times-Picayune* frequently included such items as "Thanks to St. Peter, St. Joseph, St. Huey."

---

[27]*Ibid.*, 83.
[28]*Ibid.*, 99.

While it is difficult to conceive of two governors more dissimilar than Jerry Brown and Huey Long, they share two things in common: Both built power bases without regard for the formal authorities granted them, and both had style.

Quite a different power base and political style are evidenced in the institution we consider in the next chapter: the courts.

THE
POLITICS
OF JUSTICE

As formulators of public policy, the courts use the murkiest of processes. Even so, "State courts are not less political than state legislatures or state executive agencies, but they are usually less openly partisan. They are more the captive of a single profession than any other major institution of government, but they nevertheless participate in almost all major conflicts that occur within the state political arena."[1]

THE JUDICIAL SCENE

That "single profession" is law. In an extensive analysis of all fifty states, it was found that the legal profession indeed has a major policy impact on the workings of the court system.[2] Although the depth of judicial professionalism in any one state varied, the large industrial urban states had higher levels of court professionalism. The southern states tended to have less professional court systems. The only major exception was Indiana, which, although it is a large industrial urban state, ranked low in judicial professionalism. Table 8–1 indicates the level of judicial professionalism in the American states. As we shall see, any public institution whose behavior is formed by a single profession has characteristics that relate peculiarly to that profession, particularly in the institution's decision-making process.

Decisions, of course, are what courts are all about, and the courts in the states make an enormous number of decisions. State and local courts try roughly three million cases every year; in comparison, the federal courts handle about 140,000 cases per year.

Despite this onerous work load, the states do not spend much of their revenue on justice. In 1971 all fifty states spent a total of $2.6 billion on criminal justice activities—a mere 3 percent of their total expenditures. For courts alone, a rather paltry $328 million was expended, or only $2.20 per capita. Some of the major dilemmas in the criminal justice system of the United States, which certainly garners a great deal of publicity in terms of its manifold problems, may be simply the result of low levels of expenditure.[3]

The courts are organized along the lines sketched in Table 8–2. As the table shows, all courts within a state, including city courts, traffic courts, and justices of the peace, are part of the same system. The courts are generally organized in three tiers: *state appellate courts,* whose primary function is to

---

[1]Kenneth N. Vines and Herbert Jacob, "State Courts and Public Policy." In *Politics in the American States,* 3rd ed. Herbert Jacob and Kenneth M. Vines, eds. (Boston: Little, Brown, 1976), p.265.

[2]Henry Robert Glick and Kenneth N. Vines, *State Court Systems* (Englewood Cliffs, N.J.: Prentice-Hall,1973), p.60.

[3]Vines and Jacob, "State Courts and Public Policy," pp. 256–257.

TABLE 8−1 JUDICIAL PROFESSIONALISM IN THE AMERICAN STATES

RANK OF STATES	COMPOSITE SCORE
1. California	21.7
2. New Jersey	18.0
3. Illinois	17.7
4–5. Massachusetts, New York	16.7
6–7. Alaska, Michigan	16.3
8–9. Maryland, Hawaii	15.3
10. Pennsylvania	15.0
11–13. Colorado, Washington, Wisconsin	14.3
14. Ohio	14.0
15. North Carolina	13.7
16. New Hampshire	13.4
17–19. Arizona, Oregon, Rhode Island	13.3
20. Nevada	13.0
21. Connecticut	12.6
22–24. Idaho, Minnesots, Oklahoma	12.0
25. North Dakota	11.3
26. Kentucky	11.0
27. Iowa	10.9
28–29. Maine, Wyoming	10.7
30. Vermont	10.3
31–33. Florida, Montana, Virginia	10.0
34–36. Delaware, Louisiana, Missouri	9.6
37–38. New Mexico, Utah	9.3
39–40. Nebraska, South Dakota	9.0
41. South Carolina	8.7
42–45. Georgia, Kansas, Tennessee, Texas	8.0
46. Indiana	7.6
47. West Virginia	7.3
48. Alabama	6.0
49. Arkansas	5.3
50. Mississippi	3.4

Source: Henry Robert Glick and Kenneth N. Vines, *State Court Systems* (Englewood Cliffs, N.J.: Prentice-Hall, 1973) p. 12.

review the decision of lower courts; *state trial courts,* which have general jurisdiction and the broadest authority; and a number of *specialized local trial courts* of relatively limited jurisdiction, primarily over minor cases. Of course, the structure of each state's court system varies to a significant degree, ranging from the simple and modern to the complicated and traditional. Table 8–3 indicates these differences by state.

Certainly the most famous (or infamous) segment of the state court structure is the lowest level, referred to in Table 8–2 as the *trial courts of limited jurisdiction.* Frequently, judges in these courts have little or no legal training, but they have a great deal of political experience. The most exemplary in this dubious regard are those judges who are known as justices of the peace. Consider, for example, the following description of "Jeddart

TABLE 8–2 STRUCTURE OF STATE COURT SYSTEMS

SUPREME COURT

All states have one supreme court. In some states this court is termed the Supreme Judicial Court or Court of Appeals.

INTERMEDIATE APPELLATE COURTS

23 states have intermediate courts of appeals. Oklahoma, Tennessee, and Texas have 2 intermediate courts of appeals, 1 each for civil and criminal cases. Intermediate appellate courts have various names: Superior Court, Court of Appeals, Appellate Division of Supreme Court or Superior Court, Superior Court.

TRIAL COURTS OF GENERAL JURISDICTION

38 states have 1 type of trial court of general jurisdiction, 9 states have 2, 2 states have 3, and 1 state has 4. The names of these courts vary widely: Circuit Court, Superior Court, District Court, Common Pleas, and in New York, the Supreme Court.

TRIAL COURTS OF LIMITED JURISDICTION

8 states have only 1 or 2 of these kinds of trial courts; 10 states have different kinds; 20 states have 4 or 5; 12 states have 6 or more different kinds. The names and functions of these courts vary widely. They include: Probate Courts, Justice Courts, Police Courts, Small Claims Courts, City and Town Courts, Juvenile Courts, Orphan's Courts, Courts of Oyer and Terminer, and Courts of Chancery.

Sources: State Court Systems (Chicago: The Council of State Governments, 1966); *Martindale-Hubbell Law Dictionary, 1970; Intermediate Appellate Courts* (Chicago: American Judicature Society, 1967), as derived by Henry Robert Glick and Kenneth N. Vines, *State Court Systems* (Englewood Cliffs, N.J.: Prentice-Hall, 1973), p. 28.

Justice" (or what Andy Griffith used to mete out as the sheriff in "Mayberry, R.F.D.").

I had often heard of the "Jeddart Justice" doled out by rural magistrates to motorists, of the iniquities of paying magistrates on a commission basis, of the insult to the law and its majesty which these methods involved. My host, whose car was moving rapidly down the great highway to the warm sun and true spring of Central Illinois after the rain, fog, and cold of the shores of Lake Michigan, had written on the subject. He had been the pupil and the collaborator of one of the greatest of American constitutional lawyers. His opinion was worth having. A car was backed off the road and a policeman signalled us in. . . . We were pinched for speeding. The traffic cop's not very smart uniform bore the words "Special Police." He had cartridges on his belt; they were of different colours and may have been dummies, but he was in complete command of the situation. He demanded the license which was fortunately available. He gave instructions. "Turn round and stop at the grocery store." "Can I make a U-turn?" asked my host ironically. "Sure." We entered the grocery store, and there was American justice at the receipt of custom.

The magistrate was a bronzed jurist in a shabby shirt. He had one arm and no badge of office. This was not the Old Bailey. The representative of the "Senatus Populusque Illinoisensis" required no fasces, no mace to impress his customers. He duly pointed out that the accused could claim a jury trial, but that if he didn't, and pleaded guilty, the whole thing could be expedited.

TABLE 8–3 DIFFERENCES IN STATE COURT ORGANIZATION[1]

| SIMPLE AND MODERN | | COMPLEX AND TRADITIONAL | |
Group 1 N = 6	Group 2 N = 20	Group 3 N = 20	Group 4 N = 4
*Arizona	*Alabama	Connecticut	*Arkansas
*California	*Alaska	Idaho	Delaware
*Illinois	*Colorado	Iowa	Mississippi
*North Carolina	*Florida	Kansas	Virginia
*Oklahoma	*Georgia	Kentucky	
*Washington	Hawaii	Maine	
	*Indiana	Massachusetts	
	*Louisiana	Minnesota	
	*Maryland	Montana	
	*Michigan	Nebraska	
	*Missouri	New Hampshire	
	Nevada	North Dakota	
	*New Jersey	Rhode Island	
	*New Mexico	South Carolina	
	*New York	South Dakota	
	*Ohio	*Tennessee	
	*Oregon	Utah	
	*Pennsylvania	Vermont	
	*Texas	West Virginia	
	Wyoming	Wisconsin	

*States marked with an asterisk have intermediate appellate courts.
[1]In order to place the states in one of the four groups distributed along the continuum, they were given a weighted score according to the specific characteristics of the court system. The higher the score, the more simplified and modern the court system. The score was computed as follows:

A. A court system is considered simplified and modern if it has one intermediate appellate court, but more complex if it has two or more types of intermediate appellate courts. It is considered much less modern, however, if it has no intermediate appellate court. Therefore, each state received:

4 points for having one intermediate appellate court
3 points for having two or more types of intermediate appellate courts
0 points for having no intermediate appellate court

B. The fewer types of trial courts of general jurisdiction which a state has, the more modern and simplified its court system is considered to be. Therefore, each state received:

2 points for having one trial court of general jurisdiction
1 point for having two types of trial courts of general jurisdiction
0 points for having more than two types of trial courts of general jurisdiction

C. The fewer types of trial courts of limited jurisdiction which a state has, the more modern and simplified its court system is considered to be. Therefore, each state received:

3 points for having one trial court of limited jurisdiction
2 points for having two types of trial courts of limited jurisdiction
1 point for having three types of trial courts of limited jurisdiction
0 points for having more than three types of trial courts of limited jurisdiction

The score for each state is the sum of its scores in sections A, B, and C. Scores ranged from 1 to 9. The scores included in each group are: Group 1–7, 8, 9; Group 2–4, 5, 6; Group 3–2,3; Group 4–1.

Source: Henry Robert Glick and Kenneth N. Vines, *State Court Systems* (Englewood Cliffs, N.J.: Prentice-Hall, 1973), p. 30.

The policeman's complaint-sheet was produced; a conviction for speeding was duly entered in it; a receipt (a flimsy piece of paper) was issued. Ten dollars fine, $4 costs (which we believed went to the jurist). In two minutes it was all over. After all, there were other customers. My friend had "a record," for the first time in his life he had been in an American police court.

In a famous opinion Mr. Justice Frankfurter had laid it down that a court of the American system was not to be compared to the court of a Cadi sitting down under a tree. There was no tree, simply a third-rate village store. I recalled Mr. Frankfurter's dictum to my friend. He was not consoled.[4]

In the next tier of the court structure are the major *trial courts of general jurisdiction,* which deal with criminal felonies (serious crimes) and civil cases (noncriminal offenses). Normally their scope of jurisdiction is the county or city. There are about fifteen hundred major trial courts in the country. Juries usually decide cases at this level.

Every state has a court of last resort, generally called the *supreme court.* These courts range in size from three to nine justices and hear cases on appeal from the major trial courts. In a few states, however, the supreme courts have the right of *original jurisdiction* in certain types of cases (that is, they may try a case before it is heard by another court). They do not rely upon a jury for rendering judgments, since they are considering questions of law rather than questions of fact.

Finally, many states have *special courts* and, as their title indicates, they handle such special problems as wills, small claims, and juvenile delinquency. These courts are usually found in the more urban and industrialized states with large populations.

THE JUDICIAL STYLE

The courts determine and resolve issues of public policy differently from the other two branches of government. These differences are ones of style, access, procedures specificity, and apparent objectivity.[5]

In *style* the courts are passive; they hardly ever initiate policy decisions. Decorum, dignity, and unanimity are highly valued styles of judicial decision making.

Access to the courts is also established by peculiar procedures. Courts must agree that they have proper jurisdiction in particular cases, and litigants must have a fair amount of cash available to acquire a ruling from the courts. People also must be able to demonstrate to the court's satisfaction that they have a real case to argue. In other words, a litigant must show

---

[4]W.D. Brogan, "Down from the Ivory Tower." *Manchester Guardian Weekly* (May 31, 1956), p.11.

[5]Thomas R. Dye, *Politics in States and Communities,* 3rd ed. (Englewood Cliffs, N.J.: Prentice-Hall, 1977), pp.187–188.

personal damage; he or she cannot bring a suit solely as a matter of principle.

Procedures in the courts also differ from procedures in other branches of government. Communication between all parties involved in litigation is extremely formalized, and propriety is the rule of the day in all courtroom proceedings.

Courts also must direct themselves to *specific cases*. Normally, courts refrain from addressing themselves to general policy issues, and almost always have opted instead to deal only with a particular situation. For example, the U. S. Supreme Court in *Topeka* v. *Brown* said in effect that the Topeka school system ought to be desegregated. It did not say that *all* school systems ought to be desegregated, although such was the actual impact of that "specific" decision.

Finally, the *appearance of objectivity* in the courts is highly valued; partisanship and compromises are eschewed in all judicial decision making. An objective appearance in courtroom decision making is enhanced by the judiciary's reliance on the technique of *stare decisis,* or precedent. What was done previously often forms a basis for current decision.

These distinctive aspects of policy making accord the courts an unusual amount of legitimacy in the political sphere, particularly in contrast to the legislature and the bureaucracy. Their unique stature aids the courts in achieving popular acceptance of their decisions.

HOW AND WHY JUDGES MAKE PUBLIC POLICY

Each one of the three million cases considered by the state and local courts every year represents a public policy decision. In state supreme courts criminal appeals make up nearly one-third of the work load; civil liberty issues are involved in only 2 percent of the cases, because such cases are often shifted to the federal courts. Most state supreme court decision making concerns contentions between economic interests.

What factors influence the judges as they make decisions about these important issues? There are a number of significant variables, most of which are included in Figure 8–1. They include the socioeconomic status of the states in which the courts must function, the personal backgrounds of judges, the unique roles of dissent and conflict in judicial decision making, the influence of political parties, the role of ethnic identification among judges, ideological considerations, and the way judges view their own roles and place in the policy-making process. We consider these in turn.

THE POLITY OF THE STATE

There is a relationship between the kinds of economic litigation (which is the largest single kind of case considered by state courts) and the social and economic characteristics of the state. Supreme courts in rural, southern,

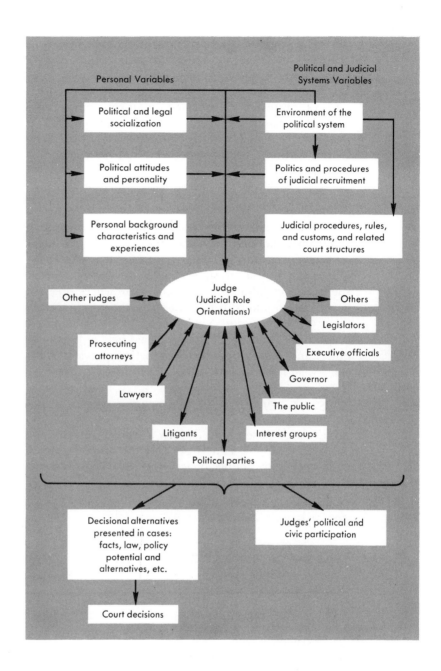

FIGURE 8–1 VARIABLES AFFECTING JUDICIAL ROLE ORIENTATIONS AND A DESCRIPTION OF JUDGES' ROLE RELATIONSHIPS.

Source: Henry Robert Glick and Kenneth N. Vines, *State Court Systems* (Englewood Cliffs, N.J.: Prentice-Hall, 1973) p. 55.

and relatively poor states spend considerably more time on the litigation of private economic disputes (such as wills, estates, contracts, titles, and trusts) while courts in the more urban, industrial, and northern states are more involved with issues of governmental regulation of big economic interests and corporate law.[6] Such a finding, of course, appeals to common sense. A poor state has fewer large economic interests with which the courts are going to be concerned; court-resolved economic conflicts would center instead around disputes between individuals and relatively small-scale matters.

WHO ARE THE JUDGES?

A second consideration is the shared experiences the judiciary had before its members donned the black robes of justice. In an extensive study of 306 state supreme court judges, it was found that they shared certain characteristics to an almost awesome degree. Nearly 90 percent of this population spent their childhoods in the same state where they were appointed to the bench, an additional 6 percent spent their childhoods in the same region, if not the same state. Ninety-two percent had a law degree (not terribly surprising), but almost 73 percent had held at least one nonjudicial political office, and only 31 percent had held a previous state or local judgeship (somewhat less expected). Table 8–4 indicates these characteristics.

DISSENT, CONFLICT, AND SUPPRESSION

The role of dissent and conflict in courtroom decision making is another important variable and is perhaps the most distinctive aspect of how the judiciary resolves public policy issues. The suppression of dissent is a byword

---

[6]Burton M. Atkins and Henry Glick, "Determinants of Issues in State Courts of Last Resort." *American Journal of Political Science* 20 (February, 1976), pp. 27–74.

TABLE 8–4 SELECTED BACKGROUND CHARACTERISTICS OF STATE SUPREME COURT JUDGES

CHARACTERISTICS	PERCENT OF JUDGES ($N = 306$)
Spent childhood in same state as court	89.0
Spent childhood in same region but not state as court	6.1
Attended law school in same state as court	60.4
Attended law school in same region but not state as court	20.5
Had law degree	92.4
Held previous state or local judgeship	31.2
Held at least one nonjudicial political office	72.5

Source: Various volumes of *Who's Who* and other state publications, as derived by: Henry Robert Glick and Kenneth N. Vines, *State Court Systems* (Englewood Cliffs, N.J.: Prentice-Hall, 1973), p. 48.

in terms of the courts' role in society and, even more importantly, in many respects is vital to its carefully cultivated image in society. As Table 8–5 indicates, the number of dissenting opinions in the state supreme courts is moderate at best, and unanimous decisions are the rule. "No where else in the American political process (not even in the federal courts) is conflict so well suppressed or disguised."[7] The rate of dissent in the state supreme courts is less than 10 percent in more than half the states, and in only a handful of states (California, New York, Ohio, Michigan, and Pennsylvania) is the dissent rate more than 20 percent on any regular basis.[8]

---

[7]Vines and Jacob, "State Courts and Public Policy," p.261.

[8]Council of State Governments, *Workload of State Courts of Last Resort* (Chicago: Council of State Governments, 1962).

TABLE 8–5 PERCENTAGE OF DISSENTING OPINIONS IN STATE SUPREME COURTS, 1966 AND 1972

STATE	1966	1972
Highest-dissent courts		
(in 1966)		
Michigan	46.5	56.2
Pennsylvania	41.0	29.7
New York	41.0	38.4
Ohio	34.9	29.7
California	32.3	37.5
Florida	28.2	39.9
Oklahoma	26.5	26.2
South Dakota	24.3	22.9
Lowest-dissent courts		
(in 1966)		
Massachusetts	1.2	5.1
Rhode Island	1.4	2.1
North Carolina	2.4	10.7
South Carolina	3.4	11.6
Maryland	5.4	3.4
Arizona	6.1	3.2
Minnesota	6.8	4.4
New Jersey	7.1	11.0
Illinois	7.2	17.6
Alabama	7.4	17.0
Average dissent rate for all 50 states	12.6	15.1

Source: State reporters, 1966 and 1972, as compiled by Kenneth N. Vines and Herbert Jacob, "State Courts and Public Policy." In Herbert Jacob and Kenneth N. Vines, eds. *Politics in the American States: A Comparative Analysis,* 3rd ed. (Boston: Little, Brown, 1976), p. 261. Reprinted by permission.

This relative lack of open disagreement among the members of one of the nation's foremost political institutions can be attributed to several factors. One is *legal tradition*, which long has placed a strong stress on erudite unanimity and on judicial decisions that are not confused by opposing opinions. Another is the *heavy case load* of the state supreme courts. This situation has resulted in the assigning of cases to only one judge, who becomes responsible for both researching and writing the ensuing opinion that ultimately is endorsed by the court at large. Because the other judges are busy writing their own opinions on other cases assigned to them, they seldom bother to check the opinions of their colleagues.

There also is considerably *less diversity among the personalities* that constitute supreme courts than among other branches of government, such as the legislature and the bureaucracy. People of similar backgrounds, as we have noted, often tend to agree on policy issues.

Beyond these factors that work to suppress overt conflict in state supreme courts, there are techniques that are used to settle disputes and reduce dissent. These techniques include persuasion, compromise, and a judicial form of logrolling among justices. Social and economic characteristics of the states do not seem important as determinants of dissent rates among the state supreme courts.[9]

THE OMNIPRESENT PARTY

Political party also has considerable influence on how judges make decisions. Although people do not like to think of judges as making decisions on the basis of partisan affiliation, at least a couple of studies have found that, nonetheless, judges tend to do so. For example, in competitive party states judges are more apt to air their disagreements and dissents with each other in public; judges in states without competitive party systems are less apt to.[10] This generalization holds, of course, only when judges of both parties are represented on the court.

Republicans are far more successful than Democrats in capturing judge-ships; they outnumber Democrats almost two to one in judical positions. Although this varies with the type of state (for example, Republicans do not fare as well in seeking judgeships in states controlled by the Democrats), they are very competitive in winning judgeships in two-party states and do considerably better than Republican candidates for the legislature or governorship in such states.[11]

Although a judge's party affiliation has little importance in the decision-

[9]Vines and Jacob, "State Courts and Public Policy," p.263.

[10]Dye, *Politics in States and Communities,* p.195.

[11]Stuart Nagel, "Unequal Party Representation in State Supreme Courts." *Journal of the American Judicature Society* 44 (1961), 62–65.

making process on the lower trial court level (a level that has little to do with public policy making), political party membership does seem to be a factor in the upper echelons of the court hierarchy. Stuart Nagel found that Democratic judges were different from their Republican counterparts in that they decided for the defense measurably more frequently in criminal cases, for the administrative agency in business regulation cases, for the claimant in unemployment-compensation cases, for finding a constitutional violation in criminal cases, for the government in tax cases, for the tenant in landlord-tenant cases, for the consumer in sales-of-goods cases, for the injured party in motor vehicle cases, and for the employee in employee-injury cases. Nagel concluded that Democratic judges basically were more in sympathy with the working man, the defendant (at least in criminal cases), and the consumer. Democratic judges were less sympathetic with utilities and businesses.[12]

RACE AND RELIGION

Ethnicity and religion also play vital parts in the decision-making process of judges. Judges generally come from higher income groups, and White Anglo-Saxon Protestants (WASPs) are overrepresented among state judges. In contrast to judges who were WASPs, Nagel found that judges from minority groups were prone to decide for the defense in criminal cases, for finding a constitutional violation in criminal cases, and for the wife in divorce cases. Catholic judges tended to decide for the defense in criminal cases, for the administrative agency in business regulation cases, for the wife in divorce settlement cases, for the debtor in cases between debtors and creditors, and for the employee in employee injury cases.[13]

WORLD VIEWS AND IDEOLOGIES

The ideology of judges is also important when judges make decisions and is closely related to that of political party affiliation. One clear conclusion may be drawn: the bench is conservative, although there are liberal and conservative dimensions within this framework. Judges with more liberal attitudes decide more frequently for the defense in criminal cases, for the administrative agency in business regulation cases, for the injured person in automobile accident cases, and for the employee in employee injury cases. The more conservative judges exhibit a propensity to find in favor of the

---

[12]Stuart Nagel, "Political Party Affiliation and Judges' Decisions." *American Political Science Review* 55 (June, 1961), 843–851.

[13]Stuart Nagel, "Ethnic Affiliation and Judicial Propensities." *Journal of Politics,* 24 (February, 1962), 92–110.

state prosecutor in criminal cases, against the state in business regulation cases, and in favor of insurance companies and employers.[14]

In an interesting analysis of the Louisiana Supreme Court under Governor Huey Long in the 1930s, political ideology of the judges appears to be the central determinant of how cases were decided. In the Louisiana instance, ideology meant a judge's personal allegiance to Huey Long; from 1928 to 1935 the state supreme court was crucial in maintaining the "Kingfish" in office. Similarly, another investigation found that between 1954 and 1960 judges in New Orleans sentenced blacks with considerably more harshness than whites. As racial tensions grew during those six years, the severity of sentencing for blacks by white judges increased as well.[15]

ROLES JUDGES PLAY

A final source of important influence on how judges make decisions is how judges view their role in the judicial process, and indeed, in the policy-making process itself. A study of supreme court justices in four states found that judges define their duties according to five distinct roles: the ritualist, the adjudicator, the lawmaker, the administrator, and the constitutional defender.

The *ritualist* focuses on the clerical and day-to-day routines of the judge's job, such as supervising secretaries and law clerks. A majority of the justices were ritualists.

The *adjudicator* centers his activities around the weighing of arguments among attorneys, focusing on the imperativeness of deciding cases, or concerning himself primarily with whether the decisions made in the lower courts should be reversed or upheld.

The *lawmaker* sees the overriding orientation of his role as one of literally "making law." He realizes that "Judges make decisions which have the potential of substantially altering the interpretation of state law and its application to numerous economic, social, and political relationships."[16]

The *administrator* focuses on two forms of control that state supreme courts can wield over the lower courts. One is that the supreme court can review the decisions of lower courts and, in effect, change the procedures of the lower courts in certain cases if it so wishes. The other function is that the supreme court can also regulate the personal conduct of personnel in the lower courts and of lawyers practicing throughout the state.

Finally, the *constitutional defender* sees himself as a guardian of "the

---

[14]Stuart Nagel, "Off the Bench Judicial Attitudes." In *Judicial Decision-Making*, Glendon Schubert, ed. (Glencoe, Ill: The Free Press, 1963).

[15]Both studies are in: Herbert Jacob and Kenneth N. Vines, *Studies in Judicial Politics* (New Orleans: Tulane Studies in Political Science, Vol. XIII, 1963).

[16]Glick and Vines, *State Court Systems*, p. 60.

American form of government by protecting the Constitution against various political enemies."[17]

The clear majority of judges viewed their role as one of ritualism and adjudication. This is less than astounding, since both roles are vital to the basic functions of the courts in society. Most of those few judges who saw themselves as lawmakers opted for a conservative interpretation of that role; the administrator and constitutional defender roles were not especially important to most judges.

STATE COURTS AS POLICY INNOVATORS: THE CASE OF CALIFORNIA

Although judges tend to take the more conservative view of their role in society as policy makers, a significant proportion of them are quite willing to act as a full and vibrant third branch of government and make new and innovative public policies through their judicial decision making. Moreover, it is important to realize that the social impact of the decisions made by judges are not confined to the cases they decide: "Although court decisions are usually directed only at litigants directly involved, they generally have a ripple effect. . . . Thus, although in form court actions are particular, their effect is general."[18] An example is provided by the U.S. Supreme Court's ruling on abortions; as a result of that decision, it was not necessary for every patient to file her own court action in order to have an abortion.

This ripple effect is amplified when the courts are innovative, and courts are more innovative as policy makers than often is realized. A study of state supreme court cases found that the courts were most innovative as policy makers in the areas of constitutional rights of defendants and criminals, civil rights, taxation, governmental regulation of business, elections, legislative apportionment, and other types of suits against the government. Table 8–6 indicates the results of the analysis.

The California Supreme Court perhaps is the most innovative of all the state supreme courts and, indeed, has recently shown itself to be more innovative than the U.S. Supreme Court. For example, it was the California supreme court that ruled in the famous case of *Serrano* v. *Priest* that discrimination on the basis of wealth was not constitutional. This ruling had and is having a major impact on the distribution of education budgets in the states, because the California court ruled that students from less wealthy school districts were being denied a civil right by not acquiring an education comparable to that received by students from wealthier districts. Twenty other state courts soon were hearing similar cases after *Serrano* v. *Priest* was decided by the California supreme court.

---

[17]*Ibid.*, p. 60.

[18]Vines and Jacob, "State Courts and Public Policy," p.243.

TABLE 8–6 INNOVATIVE POLICIES IN STATE SUPREME
COURTS, 1964–1969

Constitutional rights of defendants and criminals ($N = 16$)
Civil rights ($N = 7$)
Taxation ($N = 7$)
Governmental regulation of business ($N = 5$)
Elections ($N = 5$)
Legislative apportionment ($N = 4$)
Other suits against government ($N = 8$)

Source: Henry Robert Glick and Kenneth N. Vines, *State Court Systems* (Englewood Cliffs N.J.: Prentice Hall, 1973) p. 95, as derived from *State Government News,* 1964–1969. Glick and Vines borrowed Walker's concept of policy innovation in constructing Table 8–6. See: Jack L. Walker, "The Diffusion of Innovations Among the American States." *American Political Science Review.* 63 (December, 1969) pp. 880–889.

Another area of policy innovation is that of class action suits and, again, California has expanded the concept significantly. In the 1970s the California supreme court ruled that consumers may bring a class action suit against a company, even though each consumer was treated as an individual, rather than as a "class," when he or she did business with that company. Prior to California's state supreme court ruling to this effect, consumers were treated by the law as individuals, not as a class that could take action. The expansion of class action to incorporate this concept is a great boon to consumer protection.

Finally, the California supreme court has led the way in confronting the death penalty and calling for its elimination on the grounds that the death penalty is cruel and unusual punishment, an act prohibited by the U.S. Constitution.

In short, although the innovativeness of the state courts often is obscured by the legalistic and unemotional language that the courts use in announcing their decisions, the policies nonetheless are creative and have a major impact on the social fabric of the country. In the examples just listed, for instance, the supreme court of the nation's most populous state has redistributed educational opportunity among all income groups, has given consumer interests a major new tool for defending themselves against unscrupulous corporations, and has eliminated the ultimate penalty for crime. These are not minor public policies.[19]

REFORMING THE COURTS

Because they are such basic makers of policy and, relatively, are so removed from popular control, the courts are especially prone to reformist pressures. Chief among the proposals for reform are acquiring and retiring judges,

---

[19]*Ibid.,* 244–46.

court administration, and revamping the criminal code, which we shall consider in turn.

GETTING JUDGES

One of the great dilemmas of the American judiciary is how to select judges. How judges have been and are chosen in the American states has varied with modes of social thinking throughout our history. For a time the original thirteen states continued the method used by their colonial governors, which was simply gubernatorial appointment. Election by the legislators was favored by some states immediately following the Revolution and, to a degree, still is. Other states recruit by partisan elections, particularly in the East and the South—areas that "were most affected by the Jacksonian movement."[20] Western and midwestern states, on the other hand, tend to favor nonpartisan election of judges. These states perhaps were the most affected by the Progressive Reform Movement and related nonpartisan movements in politics at the time of their admission to the Union.

The newest method for the selection of judges, called the Missouri Plan, is gaining widespread popularity. During the past twenty-five years, in fact, no state has changed to any method other than the Missouri Plan. Missouri and California adopted the Missouri Plan in 1940, and currently nine states have switched to it. The Missouri Plan, which boasts the trappings of reform in judicial selection, states that the governor may appoint all (or the more important) judges, but that after a two-year interim in office the judges are put up for popular election. Voters may cast a vote, "Yes" or "No," for each judge's retention after his or her performance is on the record. The idea is to acquire both judicial expertise and popular responsiveness in judges through this combination of appointive selection and voter ratification.

What are the consequences of these various selection plans? What impact will they have on public policy? Insofar as most studies can determine, not much. For example, gubernatorial appointment of judges does not actually seem to remove the judge from politics, as some people contend it should. In one significant study, it was concluded that "governors have used their appointments to reward friends or past political supporters and have implemented the plan very largely from a personal and political view-point."[21]

Nonpartisan, or for that matter, partisan election of judges does not seem to make the judiciary more responsive to the popular will, which is the argument generally trotted out in its support. Perhaps this is the case in part because governors in the states often have found ways to bypass the election of judges. In one investigation, for example, it was found that 242

---

[20]Glick and Vines, *State Court Systems*, p.40.
[21]Richard A. Watson and Rondal G. Downing, *The Politics of Bench and the Bar: Judicial Selection Under the Missouri Nonpartisan Court Plan* (New York: John Wiley, 1969), pp.338–339.

judges, who were supposed to win their initial appointment to the bench by popular election, actually received interim appointments from the governor. Only 192 judges in the sample had actually entered office through election.[22] In another study it was found that "merit-plan" judges (gubernatorial appointees) did not have noticeably better legal qualifications or other attributes of consequence than judges who were elected to office.[23] In fact, the majority of judges who seek reelection are generally unopposed, and less than 10 percent of the judges seeking reelection are ever defeated.[24]

Use of the Missouri Plan has not changed these kinds of patterns. In a study of the Missouri Plan, it was found that only one judge out of 179 appointed under the plan had ever been defeated by election of the people. This seems to be the case because it is quite easy to win an election when you are running against no one.[25]

In summary, it appears that whatever method of selecting judges is used—popular nonpartisan election, partisan election, gubernatorial appointment, legislative appointment, or the Missouri Plan—there is little difference in results. How judges are placed on the bench appears to be more a result of passing social fancy than of matching a selection process with preferred judicial behavior.

GETTING RID OF JUDGES

Another area of concern to judicial reformers is how long judges may stay in office and how the people can rid themselves of incompetent judges. As Table 8–7 indicates, judges, as compared to legislators and governors stay in office for quite some time. In most states governors hold office for four years, state representatives are elected to two-year terms, and state senators are elected to four-year terms. But judges serve for periods ranging from a minimum of two years to the remainder of their life, up to the age of 70. The reason given for lengthy tenure is that many states have adopted the view that if a judge's job cannot be threatened by outside political pressures, then he or she is more likely to exercise independence and good conscience in making decisions. It also can be argued, of course, that the judge is just as likely to exercise bad judgment or dependence on particular sources of power. Recall, in this respect, the courts of the 1930s in Louisiana, in which the primary criteria for decisions made by the Louisiana judiciary seemed to be the Kingfish's political needs or simple racism.

---

[22]James Herndon, "Appointment as a Means of Initial Accession to Elective State Courts of Last Resort." *North Dakota Law Review* 38 (1962), 60–73.

[23]Council of State Governments, *State Court Systems* (Lexington, Ky.: Council of State Governments, 1974), pp.53–68.

[24]Jack Ladinsky and Alan Silver, "Popular Democracy and Judicial Independence." *Wisconsin Law Review* (1966), 132–133.

[25]Watson and Downing, *Politics of Bench and the Bar.*

TABLE 8-7 LENGTH OF TERMS OF STATE JUDGES

TERMS *(Number of Years)*	COURTS OF LAST RESORT *(Number of States)*	INTERMEDIATE APPELLATE COURTS *(Number of States)*	MAJOR TRIAL COURTS *(Number of States)*
Life (or to age 70)	4	1	3
14–15	3	1	3
10–12	15	6	4
5–8	27	15	26
4	0	0	16
2	1	0	0
Total	50	23	52[1]

[1]The total is greater than 50 because some states have several major trial courts with different lengths of terms in each.

Source: Book of the States, 1974–1975 (Lexington, Ky.: Council of State Governments) pp. 122–123.

This takes us to another area of concern to reformers, that of the removal of judges. In comparison with other state officeholders, judges are generally subject to broader and less defined criteria for removal. For example, judges have been removed from office for showing lascivious movies at a social gathering, consorting with criminals, or not cooperating with other state officials. In thirty-two states, judges are removed by impeachment or by vote of the legislature. A few states are empowered to use the recall; a few permit removal by the state supreme court. Forty-eight states have adopted clearly reformist ideas on how to remove judges. Many states have *judicial tenure commissions* that hold hearings and make recommendations (for the most part, directly to the state supreme court) for the removal or retention of lower-court judges, while the other states use *judicial courts* and, in instances where these courts find for judicial misconduct, they may remove the judges.

Despite a spate of devices for doing so, precious few judges are removed for reasons of incompetence, and those who are have often diminished the dignity of the courts by making public spectacles of themselves. Consider some examples:[26] One William Perry, who was relieved of his position as judge in the Long Island traffic court in 1975 for ordering a coffee vendor arrested and hauled into his courtroom in manicles, where he was berated by Perry over the quality of the coffee that the vendor had sold him. Or the

---

[26]The following examples are drawn from: New York Times Syndicate, "Tirade About Bad Coffee Costs Judge His Job and a Small Fortune," July 21, 1977; Associated Press, March 28, 1977 and January 8, 1977; and New York Times Syndicate, "Independent Women Lawyer Trounces Recalled Judge," September 12, 1977.

eighty-two year old justice of the California Supreme Court who was fired in 1977 by that state's Commission on Judicial Performance on grounds of senility—the venerable justice would occasionally doze off while presiding over trials, then reinvigorate himself by doing exercises in the courtroom. Or, in perhaps the most notorious instance of judicial incompetence, the popular recall in 1977 (Wisconsin's first) of County Judge Archie Simonson, who released into custody two teen-aged rapists on the interesting logic that women in Madison were guilty of wearing "provocative" clothing. (Evidently, the judge considered sweatshirts and jeans to be seductive, since those were what the victim had been wearing.) Judge Simonson was challenged by no less than five candidates for his seat, which was won by a young woman running as an independent, who became the first woman elected to that office in Dane County (Madison).

MANAGING THE COURTS

A third area of interest to judicial reformers is that of administration. Courts, like the other branches of government, have bureaucrats, too, and it is becoming increasingly evident that all branches of government, including the courts, could use higher-quality administrators than currently seem to be available. Indeed, efficient administration is particularly important in the courts, since justice itself is defined by the speed with which it is executed. A major reform of this facet of the judiciary has been the establishment of the office of *court administrator.* By 1977, all states had created such an office (in 1965, only half the states had one) to assist the chief justice of the state supreme court in his management of the overall court system in his state.

Related suggestions for administrative reform focus on the need for reorganizing the court structure. Reformers generally feel that all court systems should be unified under the supervision of the chief justice of the state supreme court and that judges should be subject to assignment throughout the state by the chief justice.

THE LAW ITSELF

A final area of reform concerns the criminal code itself. It is argued that certain kinds of cases, such as victimless crimes, automobile accidents, and traffic violations should be handled by some means other than that of a full-blown jury trial. In this light, "no-fault" insurance programs can be interpreted as a step toward the modernization of the court systems in that they reduce the pressure on the courts to handle a burgeoning case load of insurance claims stemming from automobile accidents. Similarly, half the people in prison and half the trials in the states involve people accused of victimless crimes. Decriminalizing certain crimes (such as public drunkenness, as has already been done in six states) could substantially reduce the case load of the courts.[27]

RESISTING REFORM

Reforming the courts has not been and will not be an easy task. Although a number of "heavies" support the kinds of court reforms just reviewed, notably the National Center for State Courts, the American Bar Association, the Conference of Chief Justices, the Institution for Judicial Administration, and the American Judicator Society, the system itself often works against reform.

Courts are major dispensers of political patronage as well as makers of public policy. Both political parties and economic interests will fight to preserve the existing structure of the courts if the proposed reform seems threatening. By way of example, in Chicago the Democrats succeeded in forcing the acceptance of a compromise state court reform proposal that did not affect the selection procedures in Cook County. Although the proposals did not win voter approval in a statewide referendum, the proposal itself was designed to preserve Democratic dominance in recruiting judges in Chicago. Similarly, minority groups and labor unions have been known to oppose the appointment of judges through a commission system because they feel that they will be excluded from more judgeships than they would be if judges were elected by the populace at large. Rural interests occasionally block reform and often for sensible reasons; county court dockets are often not as loaded as urban court dockets. Indeed, those states that have been most influenced by proposals for reform uniformally have a high degree of urbanization and industrialization. California, New Jersey, Illinois, Massachusetts, and Michigan are perhaps among the most responsive to professional calls for modernization of the court system. The three lowest ranking states in this regard are Alabama, Arkansas, and Mississippi; indeed, most of the southern states are resistant to changing their courts.[28] Finally, even as legal professional groups vociferously propose court reforms, lawyers are among those who are the most vocal in opposing selected reforms, because lawyers may feel that the existing system works to their best economic advantage.

Nevertheless, when all is said and done, the states are generally responsive to proposals for court reform. A survey of reform efforts conducted over a decade indicated that of ten major proposals for court change in ten

---

[27]Alan V. Sokolow, "The State of the Judiciary." *Book of the States, 1974–75* (Lexington, Ky.: Council of State Governments, 1974), pp. 115–119.

[28]Kenneth N. Vines and Judson B. Fisher, "Legal Professionalism in the American States." Mimeographed paper, State University of New York at Buffalo, 1971, as cited in Vines and Jacob, "State Courts and Public Policy," p.256.

states, eight were adopted. Seven of these reforms concerned structural changes in the courts and three established a commission form of selection for certain kinds of judges. The people, it seems, are interested in the politics of justice and, in spite of the arcane aspects of courtroom procedures, participate in judicial politics and wish to make it better.

EIGHTY-THOUSAND CREATURES OF THE STATES

A ZOO
OF GOVERNMENTS:
CITIES, COUNTIES,
AND OTHER
ODDITIES

In Part Three we consider the politics of the 79,862 creatures of the states: cities, counties, special districts, towns, townships, suburbs, and other communities. It is these species that make up America's governmental zoo, and we begin with the biggest: cities.

GOVERNING CITIES

Municipalities use two major kinds of government, the "weak executive" model and the "strong executive" model. Within these two categories are various forms of municipal government, notably the mayor-council form, which may rely on either a "weak mayor" or a "strong mayor" system, the commission form, and the council-manager plan.

THE "WEAK EXECUTIVE" FORM OF URBAN GOVERNANCE

The two principal models of the "weak executive" form of municipal administration are the "weak mayor" government and the commission plan. Both are characterized by their integration of the executive and legislative functions.

The *weak mayor form of government* is usually associated with a *mayor-and-council* arrangement in city hall. The mayor has inconsequential powers, and most of the managerial perquisites are parcelled out to the many elected officials or are already vested in the members of the city council. Council members are generally elected by ward. The long ballot of municipal elections, characteristic of weak mayor governments, assures that administrative powers are splintered among council members and other elected officers. The mayor is little more than a chairperson of the city council.

The problems of a weak mayor form of government are the classic problems of any overly decentralized administrative system. Comprehensive planning, especially comprehensive financial planning, becomes virtually impossible. Compounding this is the areal decentralization prevalent in most Standard Metropolitan Statistical Areas—a plethora of districts and jurisdictions, each with its own powers and administrative responsibilities.

It is often difficult to adjudge whether or not a city government uses a weak mayor or strong mayor form (although clearly Los Angeles and Minneapolis are examples of the former). Perhaps the classic example is the late Richard Daley's Chicago. Mayor Daley inherited a weak mayor form of

155

A zoo of
governments:
cities,
counties, and
other oddities

municipal government and, at least on paper, that remains the structure of Chicago's government. Daley "reported" to a city council of fifty members; the city had numerous independent boards (including those that dealt with such important areas as education and housing) and had other features that make a weak mayor form of government. Nevertheless, there is no question that Mayor Daley was a strong mayor and that he implemented, in practice if not on paper, a strong mayor form of government.

The *commission plan,* initially created as a reaction against the weak mayor form of government, ironically shares many of its underlying disadvantages. It came about because of a local disaster. In 1900, Galveston, Texas, was flooded by a raging Gulf of Mexico. Within twenty-four hours, one-sixth of the population was dead or injured, fresh water supplies were gone, food was dwindling, sanitation nonexistent, and looting rampant. The mayor called together Galveston's leading citizens—the city's "real" leaders—and from their ranks formed a Central Relief Committee, which became Galveston's operational government. Each member of the committee was "commissioned" to accomplish a particular task and to make policy on how that task was to be accomplished. Thus, the committee possessed both an executive and a legislative function and, in terms of restoring order out of chaos, the committee worked.

Galvestonians were convinced that they had discovered a revolutionary form of municipal government; they petitioned the Texas legislature to legitimate it, which it did, and the commission form of government was inaugurated.

Under the commission plan city commissioners are generally elected at large in an attempt to reduce parochialism, and the short ballot (i.e., comparatively few office holders are elected) predominates. Each member of the council is formally both a legislator and administrator. Policy is set collectively and executed individually, and the mayor is little more than an important commissioner. Indeed, in some cities commissioners rotate the office of mayor among themselves. The initiative, referendum, and recall generally are features of the commission plan, and the value of nonpartisan elections are the norm. Unfortunately, because each commissioner is both legislator and administrator, he is often predisposed to protect his individual "barony," and to do so he must "go along to get along" with his fellow commissioners. Were he to do otherwise, he would be singled out and his power base would necessarily be undercut. He would become a minority player in a game that can be won only by a majority.

Ten years after the Galveston flood the commission plan was in use in 108 cities, but by 1970 only 37 cities of more than fifty thousand people, plus a number of smaller towns, mostly in the South, were using it. Currently, only about 5 percent of the nation's cities use the form; the lack of administrative integration and the belief of many citizens that the commission plan amounted to government by amateurs has led to its decline.

THE "STRONG EXECUTIVE" FORM
OF URBAN GOVERNANCE

While the mayor-and-council form of urban governance can employ a weak mayor variant, more frequently the form favors the use of the *strong mayor-and-council form*. Nine of the ten largest cities in the United States have a strong mayor form of government and, in fact, all American cities of more than one million people have a mayor-council form of government. Only five of the nation's twenty-six largest cities—Dallas, San Antonio, Kansas City, San Diego, and Phoenix—use the alternative council-manager system. That big cities would choose a strong mayor form of government is predictable: The media tend to focus on the mayor as the representative of power in city hall; the size and complexity of big cities mandate a political executive who is more than a figurehead; and, because of the city's legal subservience to the state, a strong mayor option helps attract able persons to municipal service, persons who can deal effectively with the governor and state.

Political patterns in strong mayor cities are similar to the basic patterns of the national and state governments. Under a strong mayor form a skilled mayor can become both chief legislator and chief executive just as an adept president or governor can. The city council usually is small, elected by wards, and relatively "pure" in its legislative function. The partisan short ballot is common; often only the mayor, council members, and auditor are subject to election. The mayor has the sole power to form budgets, administer municipal departments, and make most of the policy decisions. The council, of course, must approve budgets, appointments, and policies, and it has the power to launch potentially embarassing investigations of the mayor's administration.

Besides being associated with big cities, strong mayor-city council forms of government are also associated with cities that have relatively older citizens, more blue-collar workers, a less well educated population, and slower economic growth rates. The obverse of these characteristics in a city tends to be associated with council–manager and commission forms of government. Mayor–council governments are also clearly associated with the eastern and midwestern cities.[1]

The last remaining major form of urban government is the *council –manager form*. Like the commission form, it has an unusual history. In 1908, the city council members of Staunton, Virginia, became frustrated with the welter of "administrivia" of city government that tends to crop up under any weak executive model. They decided to hire a professional manager— the council would decide policy, the city manager would execute it. Although the commission plan was then the national rage, Staunton's idea gradually began taking root. In 1913, the influential National Municipal League

---

[1]Leo Schnore and Robert Alford, "Forms of Government and Socioeconomic Characteristics of Suburbs." *Administrative Science Quarterly* (June, 1963), pp. 1–17.

157

A zoo of
governments:
cities,
counties, and
other oddities

approved the plan in its model city charter. But the decision in 1914 of Dayton, Ohio (which, like Galveston, had been badly damaged by flood), to alter its governmental form and switch to a council–manager system provided the real impetus for the novel plan. With its new city manager, Dayton centralized, economized, and enlarged a number of municipal functions, rebuilding and improving a largely destroyed town in record time.

The essence of the council–manager form is that while legislative (city council) and executive (city manager) powers are clearly separate, administrative powers are highly unified under the aegis of a professional city manager. The council controls only the manager—it hires and may fire him—while the manager controls the administrative apparatus of the city. Elections in council–manager municipalities usually are nonpartisan (unlike strong mayor governments), have a short ballot, and the electorate has the initiative, referendum, and recall.

Since 1914 the council–manager plan has been growing in popularity among municipalities. More than half of American cities of more than ten thousand population have city managers, nearly half of towns with less than five thousand people use the plan, and it is encroaching on big cities, which traditionally have favored a strong mayor form of government. The most notable example is Dallas, eighth largest city in the nation. Just as the mayor–city council form of government is associated with big cities in the East and Midwest having heterogeneous and working-class populations and declining or stable growth rates, the council–manager form of government is associated with medium-sized cities, usually with populations of 25,000 to 250,000 people, in the Sunbelt. The use of the council–manager form also is related to cities that have middle-class, white-collar workers, relatively low proportions of foreign-born residents, and people with comparatively high educational attainment. In other words, council–manager government normally walks hand-in-hand with middle-class values, while mayor–council forms are associated with working-class values. Hence, council–manager forms of government are found mostly in the suburbs. Politically, council–manager governments usually rule in cities with nonpartisan elections, with one dominant party, or with weak political parties. Mayor–council forms of government tend to be associated with competitive party systems.

The form of government in the cities also reflects its state's political system. Mayor–city council plans are found most frequently in states with competitive two-party systems; council–manager forms are found most frequently in states with either one dominant party or with relatively weak party organizations. To quote one observer, "Whatever the case, manager government appears incompatible with strong partisan politics in a community."[2]

In some ways the council–manager and the mayor–council variants of

---

[2]Thomas R. Dye, *Politics in States and Communities*, 3rd ed. (Englewood Cliffs, N.J.: Prentice-Hall, 1977), p. 240.

urban government appear to be blending into a new office, the *chief administrative officer*, which is rising in popularity in the cities. It is held by a professional administrator (such as a city manager) who is accountable only to the mayor, rather than responsible to the city council. Figure 9–1 illustrates the forms of urban government that have been discussed.

COUNTIES, OR THE FADING FIGURE OF THE COURTHOUSE GANG

Counties govern close to 190 million Americans directly. As of 1977, there were 3,042 counties plus 22 city-county consolidations and 36 independent cities located beyond any county area, which performed functions similar to

"Weak Executive" Forms

1. Weak Mayor–Council Form

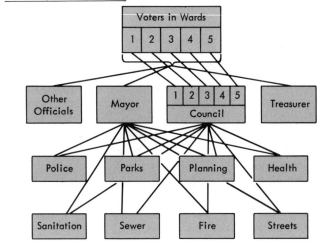

2. Commission Form

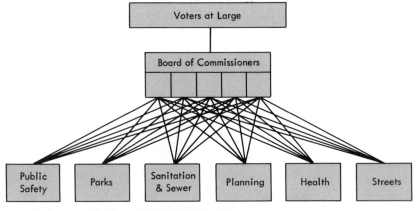

FIGURE 9–1 FORMS OF URBAN GOVERMENT

159

A zoo of
governments:
cities,
counties, and
other oddities

that of county governments. In sum, there are 3,100 "county-type" governments and an average of 65 counties per state. Although each county serves slightly more than 62,000 people on the average, county populations vary widely, as Table 9–1 indicates.

With the exception of Connecticut and Rhode Island, all states have county governments, and they are among the oldest form of government in the country. Those readers who saw the television series *Roots*, which dealt with the black experience in the United States, could draw the conclusion from that series alone that the counties were the most viable of all forms of governments, at least in the early days of our nationhood. And,

"Strong Executive" Forms

1. Strong Mayor–Council Form

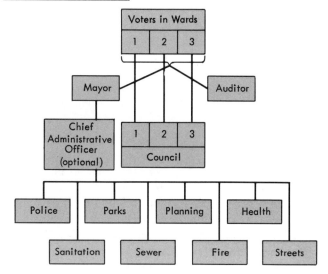

2. Council–Manager Form

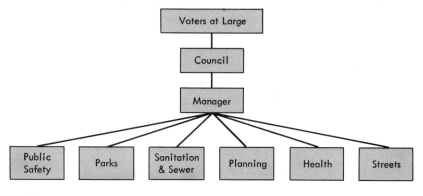

FIGURE 9–1 continued

TABLE 9-1 COUNTIES BY POPULATION SIZE

POPULATION-SIZE GROUP	COUNTY GOVERNMENTS		POPULATION SERVED BY COUNTY GOVERNMENTS, 1975 (ESTIMATED)	
	Number	Percent	Number (1,000)	Percent
United States	3,042	100.0	189,691	100.0
250,000 or more	137	4.5	92,392	48.7
100,000 to 249,999	206	6.8	32,085	16.9
50,000 to 99,999	336	11.1	23,503	12.4
25,000 to 49,999	596	19.6	20,976	11.1
10,000 to 24,999	980	32.2	16,079	8.5
5,000 to 9,999	496	16.3	3,758	2.0
Less than 5,000	291	9.6	897	0.5

Note: Because of rounding, population detail may not add to total.

Source: U.S. Bureau of the Census, 1977.

indeed, counties have been governing in the United States for more than 330 years.

THE COMMISSION PLAN

During most of this period, the mode of government in the counties has traditionally been the *commission plan,* also known as the *plural executive plan.* Indeed, more than 2,500 of the 3,101 county-type governments still use the commission form of government, and the majority of boards consist of three to five members who are elected for two- to four-year terms.[3] These county boards of commissioners are responsible for appointing advisory boards and commissions, adopting the county budget, and enacting various ordinances. But, "With no single person recognized as overall county administrator in this form, the governing board shares the administrative responsibilities with officials elected to perform specific county operations."[4] Traditionally, however, the chairman of the county board is often in effect the chief executive officer for the county.

There are advantages to the traditional commissioner form of county government: It brings government closer to the people and is, in that sense, democratic. It promotes a unified system of administration and policy making, since this form of government does not distinguish between politics

---

[3]U.S. Department of Commerce, Bureau of the Census, *Governing Boards of County Governments* (Washington, D.C.: U.S. Government Printing Office, 1973), p. 4.

[4]Florence Zeller, "Forms of County Government." *1975 County Yearbook* (Washington, D.C.: National Association of Counties and International City Management Association, 1975), p. 28.

1. Commission Form

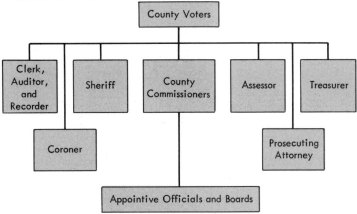

2. Council–Administrator Form

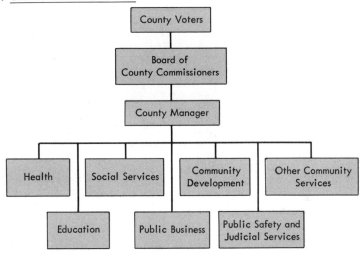

FIGURE 9–2 FORMS OF COUNTY GOVERNMENT

As derived from: Florence Zeller, "Forms of County Government." *1975 County Yearbook*. (Washington, D.C.: National Association of Counties and International City Management Association, 1975), pp. 27, 30, and 32.

and administration. It has a widespread system of checks and balances that results from the individual election of officials. The disadvantages are perhaps more obvious: It is an antiquated form of government that predates the American Revolution and may no longer be suitable for the twentieth century. The lack of a chief executive officer can lead to inefficiency in delivering services to county residents. Administration by the "citizen-legislator" no longer is feasible in a society as highly technological as ours. Voters are seldom sufficiently familiar with the labyrinth of officials that they must

3. Council-Elected Executive Form

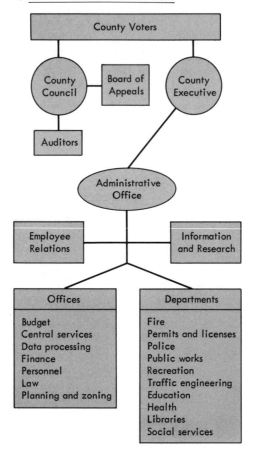

FIGURE 9–2 continued

elect—such officials as auditors, treasurers, coroners, recorders, clerks, engineers, and sheriffs—which can give certain county officials a concentration of power, since no one really knows who they are nor what they do.[5]

THE COUNCIL–ADMINISTRATOR PLAN

In many respects, the commission plan, which is favored by the vast majority of the counties, is analogous to the commission plan used by cities and shares many of its deficiencies. As a consequence, one of the trends in county government is the adoption of the *council–administrator form* of government. This is the counties' counterpart to the council–manager plan

---

[5]*Ibid.*

162

163

A zoo of
governments:
cities,
counties, and
other oddities

used by cities. The first county to adopt this plan was Iredell County in
North Carolina in 1927.

Like the council–manager plan for cities, the council–administrator plan
for counties gives a county administrator chief administrative responsibility
and policy-making responsibility in a county board. The plan is clearly the
coming trend in county administration; between 1972 and 1974, almost
two-hundred counties adopted the plan. The advantage of the council
–administrator plan is that it separates policy making and administration,
supposedly removing the administrator from political influence. Appointed
administrators often are recruited on a national basis, unlike locally elected
county officials, and thus are likelier to provide professional management
skills. Criticisms brought against the council–administrator plan include the
argument that because the administrator is appointed he cannot be responsive to the needs of the people and is at the mercy of the county board,
particularly when the board is politically split.

THE COUNCIL–ELECTED EXECUTIVE PLAN

The third type of county government is used in fifty-one counties that
govern more than 26 million people and also is perhaps the most complex
of all governmental versions. The *council–elected executive plan* provides
legislative and executive branches. The executive branch is headed by a
strong elected administrator who is the formal executive officer of the
county and often has a veto power similar to that of a state governor. The
power of the county administrative officer under the council–elected executive form is greater than that of the other forms of county government,
although the relationship between the county council and the county
executive are similar to that of the council–administrator form. The disadvantages of the council–elected executive form center around the possibility
of political bossism emerging in the form of the elected administrative
officer. There are talent problems, since the position does require at least
as much political skill as administrative abilities. Other disadvantages include
risks of fostering a legislative conflict and high cost, since this represents a
relatively professional form of county government. The advantages of the
elected executive form of government include: the visibility of the policy-
making process in the community; the development of strong political
leadership, which is particularly advantageous in large urban areas; political
responsiveness, since the elected executive is responsible to the public;
greater public visibility of the county government; and a desirable system of
checks and balances provided by the separation of powers.

Trends in county government have favored the council–elected executive
plan and, during the past fifteen years, counties have opted for hiring full-
time, professionally qualified administrators. Very few counties have voluntarily chosen the commission plan in recent times.

Perhaps, in some ways, counties represent the most significant but least recognized innovation in American government. Counties have been with us longer than our portion of the continent has been a nation, yet their very traditionalism permits counties to be more innovative than other governments, simply because governmental innovation in counties is not as noticeable. To quote the National Research Council, "Already in existence, the county does not raise the fear of a new unit of government. Recognition of the fact that counties can provide services over a wider area has led to efforts to modernize county governments, which in many places are archaic. . . . Recently, county responsibilities have been increased in such states as Mississippi, Pennsylvania, New York, and North Carolina. . . . In a few cases, states have cooperated in city-county consolidations."[6]

THE URBAN COUNTY: L.A.!

It is this condition—a unique amalgam of administrative traditionalism, a low political profile, and potential governmental innovation—that has led to the rise of "the urban county." Perhaps the most spectacular example of what the urban county entails is Los Angeles County, the nation's most populous, with 7 million inhabitants. Los Angeles County has increased the number and level of urban services that it provides to unincorporated areas; it has transferred functions from city government to county government for the sake of furnishing services to citizens on a county-wide scale; it has intensified on a county-wide basis such programs as recreation, parks, and libraries; and it has expanded cooperative agreements within its boundaries between municipalities.

Much of this has come about in Los Angeles County because of what is known as the Lakewood Plan, so named because in 1954 the newly incorporated city of Lakewood contracted with Los Angeles County to have its municipal services provided by the county. The Lakewood Plan is now an extensive network of contract service agreements between thirty-two municipalities in Los Angeles County. Under the system, a local government within Los Angeles County receives a considerable package of municipal services (in some instances, virtually all of them) from the county government by contract. The state of California has supported this arrangement, which is a major factor in its adoption. The Lakewood Plan is different in many respects from earlier city-county service arrangements in that it entails contracting for a package of services, such as police and fire protection and sanitation, instead of arranging separate services on a piecemeal basis.

The political impact of such arrangements as the Lakewood Plan, which is the archetype of the urban county in terms of an administrative arrangement, often includes the loss of local control to a central authority—in this case, county government. Indeed, at least three municipalities have termi-

---

[6]National Research Council, *Toward an Understanding of Metropolitan America.* (San Francisco: Canfield, 1975), pp. 110–117.

165

A zoo of
governments:
cities,
counties, and
other oddities

nated their service contract with the county for police protection, largely on the grounds that the centralized nature of Los Angeles County police protection was not deemed suitable for local requirements. These municipalities wished to have a larger say in policy making for public safety, and membership in the Lakewood Plan denied them this say.[7]

In short, county government, a political system often overlooked in political circles, may be on the verge of a significant resurrection that will have a large influence over the kinds and quality of governmental services that people receive.

TOWNS AND TOWNSHIPS: THE TINIER GOVERNMENTS

Closely related to both the notion and the reality of county government in the United States are the New England towns and townships, the "two important regional exceptions to the commonly established system of local government. . . ." [8] Both can trace their origins, as can counties, to prerevolutionary America; both have deep roots in the American tradition of self-government; and, it is in the town or township where the original "town meeting," a device so praised in texts on democracy, got its start.

About 48 million people, or 20 percent of the American population, are directly governed by the 16,882 towns or townships, although fewer than half the states (only twenty) have towns or townships as entities of government. Most towns are found in New England; townships are generally found in the Middle Atlantic States and the Midwest. The New England town clearly is the more viable and dynamic of the two forms. In colonial times, the townspeople "selected" selectmen at their town meetings to run the day-to-day affairs of government between meetings. This tradition carries on today, although it has evolved in many New England areas from a direct democratic form of government to a representative form, as the New England towns have grown in size from hundreds to thousands of people. More important, New England towns function as counties, and virtually all of New England (the exceptions are largely in Maine) is governed by towns. There are no areas that are governed by counties when the territory is not covered by a municipal government, as in other parts of the country.

Townships, however, are quite different governmentally and clearly are on the decline politically. The township, like counties or some small villages, is governed by a board of supervisors or trustees that is elected directly by the people. But the township shares powers with county governments and other types of governments, so it does not have the independent status or the dynamism of the New England town. Indeed, it is often seen more as

---

[7]John C. Bollens and Henry J. Schmandt, *The Metropolis,* 3rd ed. (New York: Harper and Row, 1975), p. 303.

[8]*Ibid.,* p. 48.

an anachronistic hindrance than a facilitator of the policies of the people. Table 9–2 indicates the regional distribution of townships and New England towns and their populations.

MULTIPURPOSE DISTRICTS: PROMISE V. PRACTICE

In considering municipalities, counties, towns, and townships, we have been talking about political and administrative units that share at least one commonality: They usually have relatively comprehensive political and administrative authority over a particular geographic area. For example, a county has control over a number of public functions, such as transportation, health, and road maintenance, not just one special function, such as road maintenance. Although the concept of multipurpose functions of a governmental unit is a good one, a problem is that no matter how many functions a government is empowered to perform, frequently the problems go beyond that government's territorial boundaries. To counteract this condition, a number of governments have cooperated in what is known as the multipurpose district. What a multipurpose district does depends upon the nature of the district itself, but through these districts local governments have tried to match governmental power with the public's problems on an area-wide scale.

Multipurpose districts are a fairly new idea. They are authorized to make policy and administer it within a considerable range of different governmental functions. The multipurpose district is a government unto itself, virtually like a county or a municipality. It can be created in one of three ways: by giving existing metropolitan districts more functions; by consolidating those functions in existence; by passing broad new state legislation that basically forms whole new agencies or permits their formation in the future. Although there has been some progress in forming multipurpose

TABLE 9–2 NEW ENGLAND TOWNS AND TOWNSHIPS BY REGION AND POPULATION

AREA	NUMBER OF TOWNSHIP GOVERNMENTS	ESTIMATED 1975 POPULATION (1,000)
Total	16,822	48,344
6 New England States (*i.e.* New England Towns)	1,425	6,700
3 Middle Atlantic States (New Jersey, New York, Pennsylvania)	2,711	16,044
11 Other States	12,686	25,600

Note: Because of rounding, population detail may not add to total.

Source: U.S. Bureau of the Census, 1977.

districts, their adoption has been quite limited. Of the nation's 25,962 special districts, only 1,720 are responsible for more than one function.

SPECIAL DISTRICTS: SEMIGOVERNMENTS OF SPECIALIZATION

Far more common units of government are the special districts. If we count school districts as special districts (which they are), as of 1977 there were 41,136 special districts in the country. America's 15,174 school districts are considered more thoroughly in an upcoming chapter, but other kinds of special districts warrant a description here.

Special districts continued to increase during the 1970s, although not as rapidly as in the 1950s and 1960s. Special districts are favored in the Standard Metropolitan Statistical Areas, and make up about one-third of all types of governments found in the SMSAs. Between 1964 and 1974, the number of special districts increased 45 percent in the SMSAs, compared to only 24 percent in nonmetropolitan areas.

The 25,962 special districts (9,580 of which are in the SMSAs) concern themselves with a wide variety of functions. For example, forty-one states

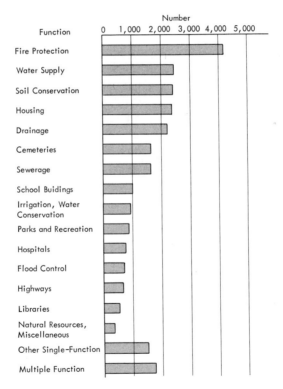

FIGURE 9–3 SPECIAL DISTRICTS, BY FUNCTION: 1977
Source: U.S. Bureau of the Census, 1977.

have special districts responsible solely for housing; thirty-four have sewer and water districts; twenty-nine have fire protection districts. Special districts are also assigned responsibility for such functions as airports, sewage disposal, bridges, housing, public transportation, tunnels, terminals, water supplies, parks, and recreation, and most are single-function districts. Figure 9–3 indicates the kinds of services that special districts provide. The National Research Council concluded that the proliferation of special districts is a political byproduct of the fact that metropolitan areas have been unable to obtain voter approval of proposed reorganization plans, but that the public's needs these plans are designed to meet nonetheless remain. Hence, politically expeditious special districts continue to multiply because local governments seem unable to create more administratively rational multipurpose districts.[9]

---

[9]National Research Council, *Toward an Understanding of Metropolitan America*, pp.115–116.

CHAPTER

THE
FACES
OF FEDERALISM

Because of the multiplicity and variety of governments, the relationships that those governments maintain with each other are worth exploring. Political science calls these relationships *intergovernmental relations,* or *federalism.* Federalism is the relations among governments; intergovernmental relations is more formally defined as the series of legal, political, and administrative relationships established among units of government, which possess varying degrees of authority and jurisdictional autonomy.

FEDERALISM IN TURMOIL

The concept, structure, and practice of federal relations in the United States have been in turmoil for the last decade. Authorities differ on the effects of new forms of federalism on the public and its interests. Theodore J. Lowi has attacked new variations of federalism, particularly those of the Johnson administration, as overly decentralized, inducing a "crisis of public authority" antithetical to the national interest, and indicative of "the end of liberalism."[1] Lowi's attack is devastating, particularly in his real-life account of urban renewal in "Iron City," where federal administrations knowingly permitted and financed what amounted to a "Negro removal" program by local officials. On the other hand, Vincent Ostrom has applauded the decentralizing overtones of new ventures in federal relations as beneficial to the assurance of a "compound republic"—that is, one where multiple and jurisidictionally overlapping administrative units are most responsive to the needs of the individual citizen.[2]

Considering how opinions differ among both politicians and political scientists on the nature of intergovernmental relations, it is not surprising to learn that we are dealing with an extraordinarily complex system. Figure 10–1, showing forces affecting the complexity of the intergovernmental system, is a simplified version of this reality.

Given the complexity of the federal system, the crises of federalism, not surprisingly, are many. These crises are administrative, jurisdictional, political, and financial. Political and financial problems are of such importance that they are considered in separate chapters. In this chapter we will concentrate instead on the administrative and jurisdictional problems of intergovernmental relations. Table 10–1 shows the 79,913 governments in the United States by type, and indicates their fluctuations between 1967 and 1977. Figure 10–2 gives these figures by state.

---

[1] Theodore J. Lowi, *The End of Liberalism* (New York: Norton, 1969), pp. 250–266.

[2] Vincent Ostrom, *The Intellectual Crisis in American Public Administration* (University, Ala.: University of Alabama Press, 1973), pp. 10–11.

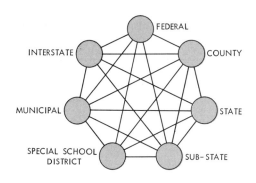

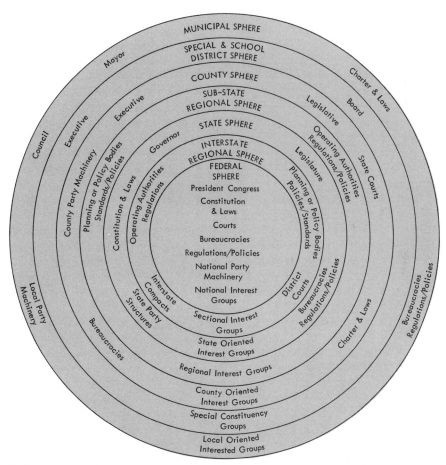

FIGURE 10–1 FORCES AFFECTING THE COMPLEXITY OF THE INTERGOVERNMENTAL SYSTEM

Source: James L. Garnett, "Bureaucratic and Party Politics in an Intergovernmental Context." In *Intergovernmental Administration: 1976*, James D. Carroll and Richard W. Campbell, eds. (Syracuse, N.Y.: Department of Public Administration, Syracuse University 1976), p. 85.

TABLE 10–1 AMERICAN GOVERNMENTS BY TYPE, 1967, 1972, AND 1977

TYPE OF GOVERNMENT	1977	1972	1967
Total	79,913	78,269	81,299
U.S. Government	1	1	1
State governments	50	50	50
Local governments	79,862	78,218	81,248
Counties	3,042	3,044	3,049
Municipalities	18,862	18,517	18,048
Townships	16,822	16,991	17,105
School districts	15,174	15,781	21,782
Special districts	25,962	23,885	21,264

Source: U.S. Bureau of the Census, 1977.

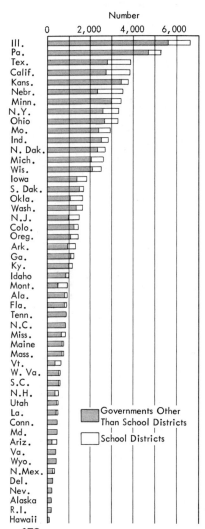

FIGURE 10–2 LOCAL GOVERNMENTS, BY STATES: 1977

Source: U.S. Bureau of the Census.

Figure 10–2 and Table 10–1 indicate that American governmental units are many. The U.S. Task Force on Land Use and Urban Growth in its report on the *Use of Land* noted that much of this fragmentation goes back to "a long American tradition of localism in land use control, dating at least to the issuance of the Standard State Zoning Enabling Act of 1924, an act which most states copied and which viewed land use controls as a matter of local rather than state control."[3] Much of the proliferation of units of local government occurred in the years following World War II, particularly around the fringes of big cities. It was largely due to white flight from the inner cities and unplanned metropolitan growth. The lack of prior planning for urban regions is particularly noticeable when we consider these examples of growth: Forty-four new suburban governments were created between 1945 and 1950 around St. Louis by builders desirous of escaping strict municipal building codes. New towns were formed around Minneapolis solely as a means of taxing a newly arrived industry, and one village was incorporated for the single purpose of issuing a liquor license. Bryan City, California, was created so that a circus owner could zone for animal populations as he saw fit. The town of New Square, New York, was established so that a kosher slaughterhouse could be operated. Gardenia, California, was incorporated so that its residents might play poker legally.[4] Yet, eager as Americans appear to be to set up small towns, they are wary of creating large ones. Community efforts to merge urban and suburban governments (considered later in this chapter) have generally failed, despite frequently intensive efforts by urban political elites. With the exceptions of school districts, which have been diminishing in number since the 1930s, and special districts, which have been slowly multiplying, the numbers of governmental units in all categories have remained essentially the same since 1900.

Jurisdictional crises of federalism are real and severe, yet at most levels governments have been making genuine strides during the last twenty years to reduce the adverse effects of governmental fragmentation. We shall consider some of these efforts in turn, first approaching the federal government's role in intergovernmental relations, then moving to the states' role, then considering some aspects of interlocal cooperation.

OF THE CONSTITUTION AND COURTS

The federal government interacts in major ways with both state and local governments. We shall consider federal interaction first with states, then with localities.

---

[3] Task Force on Land Use and Urban Growth, *The Use of Land* (New York: Thomas Y. Crowell, 1973), p. 16.

[4] Henry S. Reuss, *Revenue Sharing: Crutch or Catalyst for State and Local Governments?* (New York: Praeger, 1970), pp. 53–56.

Much of the federal government's cooperation with state governments is specified by the Constitution, which organized the federal system around three basic ideas: (1) drawing of boundaries between governmental activities of the states and the nation; (2) establishing and maintaining the identity of state and national governments; and (3) politically integrating the nation and the states.[5]

Section 8 of Article I of the Constitution was instrumental in making distinctions between state and national functions. It delegated seventeen specific powers to the national government, including defense, general welfare, and commerce, and left the remaining powers to the states. These remaining powers are now known as "reserved powers," a phrase taken from the Tenth Amendment, which was added rather hastily by the founders in response to such populist rabble-rousers as Patrick Henry. The Tenth Amendment was designed to grant the states a more visible and defined territory for exercising their powers. Section 9 of Article I also dealt with states' boundaries by preventing the national government from doing certain things, such as suspending the writ of *habeus corpus,* and also forbidding the states from doing certain things, such as entering into treaties with foreign nations and coining money.

The second area of constitutional federalism deals with establishing and maintaining the identities between state and nation. The most important clause here is Section 2, Article IV, which stipulates that "no new States shall be Formed or Erected within the jurisdiction of any other State; nor any State be formed by the junction of two or more States, or Parts of States, without the Consent of the Legislature of the States concerned."

Finally, the Constitution dealt with the integration of national and state governments, primarily by providing for cooperation among them in the performance of certain functions. For example, the states and the nation cooperate in amending the Constitution and electing a president. As Kenneth Vines observes, "Perhaps the most important factor in making possible political integration between the two levels is the scarcity of officials with a clearly defined identification with the states, resulting in the creation of a group of national officeholders who also have links to the states."[6] This arrangement, of course, was designed by the founders. As Madison noted in the *Federalist* papers, "a local spirit will infallibly prevail much more in the members of Congress than a national spirit will prevail in the Legislatures of the particular states."[7]

These three major features of the relations between the state governments and the national government—boundary settlement, separate identities, and national and state integration—were refined by the courts over

---

[5] Kenneth N. Vines, "The Federal Setting of State Politics." In *Politics in the American States,* 3rd ed. Herbert Jacob and Kenneth N. Vines, eds. (Boston: Little, Brown, 1976), p. 4.

[6] *Ibid.*, p. 7.

[7] Alexander Hamilton, John Jay, and James Madison, *The Federalist* (New York: Random House, 1937), p. 347.

time. Without question, the most influential single case in this process of refinement was *McCulloch* v. *Maryland,* which was settled by the Supreme Court under Chief Justice John Marshall in 1819. Marshall and his colleagues supported the expansion of national powers under the commerce clause of the Constitution, which gave the national government a powerful ability to interpret what was necessary and proper in the way of policy under the Constitution. The case involved the state of Maryland's attempt to tax the second United States Bank, which was located in Maryland. Alexander Hamilton, as secretary of the treasury, had proposed a national bank and argued that it could be established under a strong national government, which could and should adopt such measures because they were "implied powers" under the Constitution, even though the Constitution did not specifically authorize such policies as the establishment of the bank. The Marshall Court agreed with Hamilton's argument, stating that, although a bank was not explicitly authorized as a power granted to Congress under the Constitution, it nonetheless was implied under Congress' abilities to establish and collect taxes, regulate commerce, raise and support armies, and so on. Hence, Congress had the ability to adopt appropriate measures for the realization of the powers granted to it by the Constitution to do whatever is "necessary and proper to implement its specified functions." This notion of implied powers as an interpretation of the necessary and proper clause of the Constitution is with us today, and (with the exception of the Civil War) remains the strongest statement of national power as opposed to state power.

GOVERNMENTS AS PRESSURE GROUPS

THE STATES AS SPECIAL INTERESTS

Operating within the formal rules of the game established by the Constitution and by subsequent judicial interpretation, the states have become increasingly active lobbyists to the national government. Much of their lobbying stems from the states' interest in acquiring more money from the national government to pursue their own policies, a point which we shall consider in greater detail in Chapter 15. Suffice it to note for now that national aid contributes from 20 to 40 percent of the states' budgets, and how this money is granted means a great deal to the states.

Also, in recent years the national government has taken some unprecedented steps in intervening with policies made by the states. Although none of this intervention approaches the magnitude of the Civil War in terms of the national government establishing its supremacy over state political systems, various public problems have involved the national governments in the management of state governments in new and different ways. The action of the governor of Arkansas in the 1950s to block school desegregation in Little Rock, the efforts of the governor of Mississippi to block desegregation of the University of Mississippi, when the governor of

Alabama "stood in the school house door" to stop the representative of the U.S. Attorney General, Nicholas Katzenbach, from enrolling a black student in his state's major university—all represent major interventions by the national government in state governments. Hence, the states have assumed an increasingly active role as lobbyists in Washington for both financial and political reasons. It is not too surprising that, while only one state had a Washington liaison office in 1960, twenty-seven states had such offices by 1972.[8]

The major lobbying organization for the states is the National Governors Association (NGA), formerly called the National Governors Conference. Ironically, the NGA was initiated by President Theodore Roosevelt in 1908 as a device for pressuring Congress to pass more legislation dealing with natural resources. The NGA had fallen into dormancy until, in 1966, it established a full-time Washington office called the National Governors Conference for Federal-State Relations. Ten years later the significance of the NGA was even greater when, for the first time, one of its own occupied the White House. The National Governors Association has increasingly taken outspoken policy positions on various issues. Perhaps most notable has been the NGA's consistent position that the national government should take over all social welfare policies in the United States, rather than letting these policies reside with the states.

The NGA's lobbying function is bolstered through such related state lobbies as the National Association of State Budget Officials, the American Association of State Highway Officials, the National Association of Housing and Redevelopment Officials, and the National Association of Attornies General. These are more specific lobbies, but nevertheless they work in conjunction with the NGA on state-related national legislation.

URBAN LOBBYING

Just as the National Governors Association has evolved into a powerful tool for states lobbying the federal government, the major urban areas have also become increasingly active in pressuring the federal government for relief. The major lobbying organizations for cities are the United States Conference of Mayors and the National League of Cities. They often are joined by such groups as the Urban Coalition, the National Housing Conference, the National Association for Housing and Redevelopment Officials, and similar groups. The United States Conference of Mayors brings together the chief executives of the 435 largest cities in the country, and "is the fulcrum of collective urban lobbying"; smaller cities tend to work through the National League of Cities.[9]

---

[8] Vines, "Federal Setting of State Politics," p. 38.

[9] Suzanne Farkas, *Urban Lobbying* (New York: City University of New York Press, 1971), p. 67.

The Conference of Mayors was quite successful during the 1930s in its national lobbying efforts. Its success was attributable to the desperation of the Depression and shrewd tactics, but primarily to Franklin Delano Roosevelt's need for political support, which was based in the big cities. The League of Cities has had good relationships with the Republicans, and the Conference of Mayors with the Democrats; together they work as an effective coalition for urban interests.

The states' lobbying organizations and the cities' lobbying organizations can often be in conflict when presenting their cases to the national government. A recent example of this is the dispute between "dirty cities" and "clean states" in the effort to renew the nation's clean air laws. Representatives from the less industrialized states have tended to resist clean air legislation on the grounds that such laws discourage industrial development of less developed states. Senator Jake Garn of Utah, for example, killed a compromise clean air bill in 1976 with a personal filibuster because he felt it would hamper industrialization in his state. The nonindustrialized states often have congressional allies with industrial interests. It is the representatives from the "dirty cities" that are pushing clean air legislation, because they can feel and see the effects of air pollution on the health of their citizens more readily than the representatives of the less industrialized states. Clean air legislation is but one example among several at the federal level where the tensions between states and cities is evident when lobbying is at its sharpest.

THE FEDS AND THE REVIVAL OF REGIONALISM

Since the late 1950s the federal government has made a concerted effort to strengthen coordination between the national government and state and local agencies. In 1959, the Advisory Commission on Intergovernmental Relations was established. It is made up of representatives of national, state, and local governments and the public. This increasingly influential commission studies common intergovernmental problems and makes recommendations. In 1969 former President Nixon set up under the vice president the Office of Intergovernmental Relations, which combined into a single staff the various people who had been working in the area of intergovernmental relations.

Since 1967 the federal government has required that a federally approved, area-wide agency must "review and comment" on every grant proposal submitted by localities in terms of its comprehensive planning for the metropolitan area in question. Perhaps the best known result of this authority granted to area-wide planning units by the federal government are the Councils of Governments (COGs). Although they originated in 1954 in Detroit, by 1965 only nine were in operation. Since 1965, however, and largely as the result of several pieces of federal legislation, the number of COGs has expanded dramatically. There are more than 300 COGs, and every one of the nation's SMSAs has its own Council of Government.

At least three pieces of federal legislation have contributed to the development of Councils of Governments: the Demonstration Cities and Metropolitan Development Act of 1966; the Intergovernmental Cooperation Act of 1968; and the National Environmental Policy Act of 1969. These acts, combined with federal planning grants to state and local governments administered by the Department of Housing and Urban Development (HUD) under its "701" program and, more significantly, Circular A–95 of the Office of Management and Budget (OMB), are the cornerstones of Councils of Governments.

Section 204 of the Demonstration Cities and Metropolitan Development Act facilitated the growth of COGs. It required that applications for federal grants and loans under the act be submitted "for review to any area-wide agency which is designated to perform metropolitan or regional planning for the area within which the assistance is to be used . . . ." The applicant must show that the comments of the review agency have been considered before the grant or loan can be granted.

Title IV of the Intergovernmental Cooperation Act also boosted COGs' development by specifying that the president may establish rules for the evaluation and review of federal programs that have an impact on area and community development. All viewpoints—"national, regional, state and local"—must be considered in planning federal or federally aided development projects. In the words of the act, "to the maximum extent possible, consistent with national objectives, all federal aid for development purposes shall be consistent with and further the objectives of state, regional, and local comprehensive planning."

Section 102 of the National Environmental Policy Act established the requirement of written "environmental impact statements" for all federally assisted projects. An environmental impact statement reviews the ecological costs and benefits of any project that uses federal money, and any project may be stopped (or, more precisely, denied federal funds) by any citizen because of an inadequate impact statement or because too much environmental degradation will result from the project.

All these acts and programs, along with Section 701 of the Urban Planning Assistance Act of 1954, which allocates grants to local planning agencies for coordination, were drawn upon when the Office of Management and Budget wrote its Circular A–95 in 1969, then broadened its scope significantly in 1971. OMB Circular A–95 encourages a process of review and comment by promoting intergovernmental planning for a variety of federal development programs; it provides a means of coordinating federal development projects with state and local planning agencies; it furnishes methods for securing environmental impact statements for federal or federally funded projects. It accomplishes all this intergovernmental planning and policy coordination through the establishment of "clearinghouses," to use the term employed in Circular A–95: state clearinghouses designated by the governor or by state legislation; metropolitan clearinghouses or planning agencies recognized by OMB; and nonmetropolitan regional clearinghouses inaugurated by the governor, by state legislation, or through interstate agreements. A–95, however, has had its major impact on the metropolises. Virtually all metropolitan clearinghouses either are COGs or regional planning commissions and, as Melvin B. Mogulof has observed, the policies coordinated by Circular A–95 have "almost overnight established the potential for evolving 'a new level of government.'"[10]

COGs are designed to rationalize particular kinds of metropolitan governmental activities according to administrative criteria for an area. These include: those activities that involve large numbers of people and many political boundaries (such as transportation planning); those activities in which action (or lack of action) by one jurisdiction may undercut the effectiveness of programs in another jurisdiction (such as antipollution programs); and those activities involving economies of scale (such as time-sharing arrangements between governments on a single computer, or area water supplies).

Some observers contend that the COG "is the mildest of all approaches" to these interjurisdictional dilemmas, "building on the status quo without disturbing its formal organization."[11] Still, the funding patterns that stem from the newly designated review-and-comment authority of COGs certainly bode ill for the forces of ultralocalism and splintered autonomies. Mogulof concluded that the "differences it has made as a new institution of government are real and important"; COGs have created regional senses of community, sharpened the interdependencies of governments, questioned the utility of establishing more single-purpose government agencies in regions, and effectively coordinated governmental programs.[12]

Even so, the central problem now confronting all COGs is that of willingness to be authoritative on regional issues. If COGs are to gain greater authority over the member governments, they will have to show some changes of attitude, greater coordination between HUD (which controls "701" planning funds) and OMB (which administers the funding process through Circular A–95), increased popular representation at local levels, and more staff members in all levels of government. Overall, the Councils of Governments "are generally forms in which local officials protect the autonomy of their jurisidictions."[13] If that is the case, then COGs are unlikely to evolve into a "new level of government." Nevertheless, it can be argued that COGs have facilitated the intergovernmental process more than they have hindered it.

---

[10] Melvin B. Mogulof, *Governing Metropolitan Areas: A Critical Review of Councils of Governments and the Federal Role* (Washington, D.C.: Urban Institute, 1971), p. 1.

[11] Stanley Scott and John C. Bollens, *Governing a Metropolitan Region: The San Francisco Bay Area* (Berkeley, Calif.: Institute of Governmental Studies, 1968), p.2.

[12] Mogulof, *Governing Metropolitan Areas*, p. 1.

[13] National Research Council, *Toward an Understanding of Metropolitan America* (San Francisco: Canfield, 1975), pp. 124–125.

THE STATES: SOVEREIGNTY WITHIN LIMITS

So far we have been discussing federalism from the viewpoint of the government in Washington. But the states also have active governments. In this section we review the states' relations with each other and their involvement (or lack of it) in the business of their cities, counties, and towns.

INTERSTATE COOPERATION—AND CONFLICT

States have been known to cooperate and not cooperate with each other, although the Constitution requires that "full faith and credit shall be given in each state to the public acts, records, and judicial proceedings of every state." Since the clause applies only to civil matters and not necessarily to criminal violations, we occasionally witness states harboring fugitives from other states if public officials feel that the fugitive has been treated unjustly in the state from which he or she fled. States also cooperate to create interstate compacts and interstate agencies. There are 169 interstate compacts in operation, and 47 of these were adopted in the 1960s. Their popularity is rising; between 1789 and 1900, only 24 such compacts were made. Interstate compacts normally require congressional approval to be set into motion. Many such compacts have evolved into ongoing interstate agencies, and in 1976 there were sixty-one such agencies dealing with educational concerns, river basin management, transportation, waterfronts, fisheries, and energy. Perhaps the most notable example of an interstate agency is the Port Authority of New York and New Jersey. Established in 1921 and headed by six commissioners appointed by the governor of each member state, the Port Authority is in charge of virtually all transportation in the New York and New Jersey areas. It has eight thousand employees, more employees than any other interstate agency (few interstate agencies exceed fifty employees and a number have none).

THE WATER WAR

Most textbooks on state and local government delineate the kinds of cooperative activity between states, but few discuss the kinds of conflict that states engage in. The most obvious example occurred in 1861 when the nation went to war with itself, an event that in the North is called the Civil War, but in the South it is still referred to as the War Between the States. A more recent example, and one which may well affect all of us, concerns the current shortage of water in the nation. Although this shortage is more pronounced in the West than in other parts of the country, nonetheless, some researchers have estimated that by the year 2000 only three of the nation's nineteen water regions will be able to live even close to comfortably within their water supplies. (The three exceptions are New England, the Ohio Basin, and the South Atlantic–Eastern Gulf areas.)

This possible serious shortage in the nation's water is already straining relationships among states. Montana and Idaho in 1977 threatened to sue the state of Washington if that state seeded clouds over the Pacific Ocean, thereby "stealing" water that might have fallen as rain inland. Oregon and Washington are seriously resisting attempts to divert water to areas in the western Sunbelt states. Boston has embarked on a program to divert water from the Connecticut River, and Connecticut is currently resisting these plans, because it does not wish to give up water rights that it may need in the future. As the nation's water crisis deepens, if indeed it does, we can expect the states to grow increasingly antagonistic with each other as their politicians battle for this scarce resource.

THE STATES TAME THEIR "CREATURES"

The states can cooperate with each other as equals, but their relationships with their own local governments are quite different. Indeed, the title of Part Three of this book, "Creatures of the States," is drawn from a statement made by Judge John F. Dillon in 1868 that is now known as "Dillon's rule." "Creatures of the state," a concept upheld by the U.S. Supreme Court in 1923, simply means that such units of government as counties, towns, townships, special districts, multipurpose districts, cities, and villages have no independence beyond what the state grants them. The state government determines the areas of political and administrative discretion its subunits of government may or may not have. "This means that a city cannot operate a peanut stand at the city zoo without first getting the state legislature to pass an enabling law, unless, perchance, the city's charter or some previously enacted law unmistakably covers the sale of peanuts."[14]

State legislatures achieve this kind of control through the type of charter that they grant a city. Most city charters are quite long (New York City's, for example, fills several hundred pages) because the states often want to retain minute degrees of control. There are four general types of charters: special act charters, general act charters, optional charter laws, and home rule charters.

The *special act charters* are charters that have been drawn specifically for a particular city. Such cities remain completely under state legislative control; often these charters help state legislatures to pass laws that are written specifically for a particular city. Edward Banfield and James Q. Wilson quote by way of example an ordinance stating that "Fall River be authorized to appropriate money for the purchase of uniforms for the park police and watershed guards of said city."[15]

General act charters tend to categorize cities by population, then apply state

---

[14] Edward C. Banfield and James Q. Wilson, *City Politics* (Cambridge: Harvard University Press, 1963), p. 65.
[15] *Ibid.*, p. 66.

legislation to all cities in each size category. Usual divisions are cities with less than ten thousand people, with ten thousand to twenty-five thousand people, and so on.

Optional charter laws give city governments relatively more free choice. They offer optional forms of government that a city may wish to adopt, such as council-manager, commission, or whatever.

Finally, *home rule charters* provide cities with the greatest degree of self-governance. Still, home rule charters are furnished by the state legislature or the state constitution and may be taken away as easily as they are granted. Home rule got its start in 1875 in Missouri; today more than half of the states have constitutional clauses that provide for home rule charters. Roughly two-thirds of the cities in this country with populations of more than 200,000 people have some form of home rule. Political battles over acquiring urban home rule often are bloody, with good government groups, city mayors, and city managers usually pitted against rural legislators and large municipal taxpayer groups.

Regardless of the type of charter a city may have, the point remains that these charters are granted according to the discretion of the state polity; Judge Dillon's rule stands in that all cities and other units of government remain the creatures of the state.

THE "MIXED BAG" OF STATE URBAN POLICY

As the foregoing review of city charters implies, states can treat their creatures with severity or laxity. Joseph Zimmerman has observed that states may play the role of inhibitor, facilitator, or initiator in their relations with their own local governments, and the role the most frequently played in Zimmerman's view is, unfortunately, the first.[16] Nonetheless, the states have made some limited strides in contributing constructively to urban government. For example, forty states have more than five hundred regional planning and development districts that are designed to aid metropolitan areas. Such districts represent a growing perception by state governments of the need to handle certain kinds of public problems on a regional basis.

Virtually all states have established offices specifically endowed with responsibilities pertaining to local affairs, although only five existed prior to 1966.[17] These offices provide advisory services and assist the state in coordinating local administrative functions. Most are concerned primarily with regional planning; relatively few have responsibility for specific programs such as urban renewal, housing, and poverty.

In a few states these and related offices are beginning to take on a

---

[16] Joseph F. Zimmerman, "The Role of the States in Metropolitan Governance." Paper presented at Conference at Temple University, Philadelphia, Penna., August 27, 1973. Cited in John C. Bollens and Henry J. Schmandt, *The Metropolis*, 3rd ed. (New York: Harper and Row, 1975), p. 58.

[17] National Research Council, *Toward an Understanding of Metropolitan America*, p. 109.

genuine policy-making role for their urban and local governments. Texas, for example, has been active in discouraging the separate incorporation of satellite cities, as have Indiana and Minnesota, although to lesser degrees. In 1968 Connecticut abolished counties as a unit of government and, as a result, "state government may in effect become the metropolitan government unit in Connecticut, since Connecticut transferred county functions to the state."[18]

What of the larger panorama of relationships between the states and their local governments? Is the role of the states declining? The view most often expressed is that the states are more of a hindrance than a help to their local governments. In Colorado, for example, suburban and rural state legislators combined forces against big-city interests, notably Denver, to block legislation that would have have been beneficial to that city.[19] More broadly, "despite the increasing amount of effort that they have devoted to urban affairs, the states have continued to evidence little desire to intervene in metropolitan governmental reorganization—with the important exception of school districts."[20] And, as a major study concluded, "Although states have increased their aid to local governments, such aid generally has not gone to the areas of greatest need."[21] It is not surprising in this light that a survey of local officials of cities with populations of more than 100,000 found that approximately two-thirds of those officials believe the national government to be more responsive to their problems than the governments of their own states! As Victor Jones has observed, "the most startling and far-reaching change in American federalism is the emergence of the national government as a focus for discussion of urban and metropolitan affairs."[22] And Daniel R. Grant has noted that "if one were to use the past as the basis of forecasting the future role of the state and local government reorganization, the prospects for a new, affirmative role would be exceedingly dim."[23]   Grant's assessment is probably accurate: the future place of the state in its relations with its own local governments will be "a highly mixed bag with contents varying all the way from states which continue the present position of grudging involvement and passive indifference, to a small and select group of states which takes the bull by the horns and restructures metropolitan area government."[24]

---

[18] *Ibid., p. 109.*

[19] Susan W. Furniss, "The Response of the Colorado General Assembly to Proposals for Metropolitan Reform." *Western Political Quarterly* 26 (December, 1973), 765.

[20] Bollens and Schmandt, *The Metropolis,* p. 58.

[21] National Research Council, *Understanding of Metropolitan America,* p. 108.

[22] Victor Jones, "Representative Local Government: From Neighborhood to Region." *Public Affairs Report* (Berkeley: University of California, April 1970), p. 15.

[23] Daniel R. Grant, "Urban Needs and State Response: Local Government Reorganization," in Alan K. Campbell, ed; *The States and the Urban Crisis* (Englewood Cliffs, N.J.: Prentice-Hall, 1970), pp. 59–84.

[24] *Ibid.*

CITIES AND OTHER URBAN CREATURES

DIRECT FEDERALISM: THE FEDS AND CITIES

If anything, the federal government has a greater political impact on localities than on states. The formal linkage between local and national government often has been called "direct federalism," indicating that state governments are frequently bypassed. Nevertheless, the major impact of the federal government on local governments is more accidental than planned. For example, Rand Corporation studies have shown that federal officials may often have more control than local officeholders over the shape of the economy in a particular locality. The Rand studies indicated: in St. Louis federal housing and highway policies attracted many central city residents to the suburbs; in San Jose, federal military procurement procedures accelerated the local growth rate; in Seattle, Federal Civil Aviation policies were probably detrimental to the area's major employer.[25] There is, in fact, substantial evidence to warrant the conclusion that "federal stimulation produced independent housing authorities, a type of special district, and federal encouragement of the growth of suburbia through underwriting liberal mortgage arrangements indirectly led to the creation of many new suburban governments," and that the creation of the federal Department of Housing and Urban Development and Department of Transportation are "both institutional examples of recognition by the national government of its deep involvement in metropolitan affairs."[26]

Both departments are beneficial in that they at least are sensitive to the needs of coordinating metropolitan policies and reducing political fragmentation. However, as Samuel Kaplan and others have argued, "The federal government could help stimulate regionalism, if it wanted to, by enforcing Title IV of the Intergovernmental Cooperation Act of 1968 which requires all federal aid for development purposes shall be consistent with and further the objectives of state, regional and local comprehensive planning."[27] It is Kaplan's contention that the federal government has not enforced this and related legislation in any adequate way.

Still, it is clear that the federal government probably has more impact on local policies than the governments of the localities' own states. Housing, planning, and revenues are among the major examples of this impact, and we shall return to these in later chapters. A less well known instance is the federal government's involvement in the basic political structure of urban areas.

A revealing example is San Antonio, Texas. In 1977 San Antonians voted

---

[25] R. B. Rainey, *et al.*, *Seattle: Adaptation to Recession;* Barbara R. Williams, *St. Louis: A City and Its Suburbs;* Daniel Atesch and Robert Arvine, *Growth in San Jose: A Summary Policy Statement* (all published in Santa Monica: Rand Corporation, 1973).

[26] Bollens and Schmandt, *The Metropolis,* p. 60.

[27] Samuel Kaplan, *The Dream Deferred* (New York: Seabury, 1976), p. 160.

to stop electing their city councilmembers at large and instead to elect them by a ward system. This in itself is not unusual; what is unique is that the U.S. Justice Department pressured for this basic change in the political structure of the city. The Justice Department contended that the city's land annexations, which were completed in 1972, effectively reduced the voting power of the city's Mexican-American population from 53.1 percent to 51.1 per-cent. As a consequence, the city had to change its electoral procedures along lines mandated by the Department. The Voting Right Act Extension of 1975 enables the Justice Department to disallow certain types of municipal policies, including changing a city's boundaries. In San Antonio's case, the Department said it would disallow the 1972 annexations unless the city dropped its at-large electoral system. The city fathers were concerned that, if they attempted to challenge the Justice Department's position in court, the city would be forbidden to hold its scheduled City Council elections, to annex land, or to float bond issues until the suit was settled. In any event, the San Antonio example illustrates the impact that the federal government has on a city's basic political system.[28]

INTERLOCAL AGREEMENTS: CITIES, COMPANIES, AND OTHER CITIES

If there is tension between Washington and cities, the cities themselves seem to be getting on famously with each other. A major survey of all munici-palities with populations over twenty-five hundred asked about intergovern-mental agreements involving seventy-six different services. Of the 2,375 cities responding, 63 percent had entered into a variety of formal or informal agreements for the provision of services by other units of govern-ment or by private firms. The survey also found that the more people a city has, the more likely it is to enter into agreements with other units of government. Most of the service agreements are among local governments only, but a considerable number also involved state governments or private firms. Fifty percent of those cities and towns that "farmed out" their personnel administration services (such as police training) through inter-governmental agreements received those services from the state.

The private sector plays a big role in "intergovernmental" agreements. Of the municipalities responding 88 percent had contracted to private firms for refuse collection; 85 percent had contracted with private companies for engineering services; 84 percent for legal services; 79 percent for street lighting; and 67 percent for public relations services.[29] When it comes to local agreements, the line between the private and public sphere is indeed a fine one.

---

[28] "San Antonio Under the Gun." *Wall Street Journal*, January 20, 1977.

[29] National Research Council, *Understanding of Metropolitan America*, p. 121.

Cooperative agreements between local governments share certain characteristics. First, most are agreements between two governments over a single activity, such as police services. Second, the agreements pertain to services rather than to facilities; although cities prefer to build their own buildings, they will frequently enter into service arrangements with other governments. Third, these agreements are not always permanent ones, and often contain provisos for the future renegotiation or termination of the agreement by either party. Fourth, many agreements are of a stand-by nature and come into effect only when certain conditions arise; this "mutual aid pact" becomes operative when some disturbance, such as a fire or a riot, occurs. Finally, most interlocal agreements are permitted by specific state legislation that authorizes cooperation among local governments in one particular field. States usually specify that their local governments may cooperate only in the areas that they stipulate; they limit interlocal agreements to special functions. However, states are gradually moving away from this concept and are permitting interlocal cooperation along a broad variety of fronts.

GETTING IT TOGETHER: PHILADELPHIA AND DETROIT

Many metropolitan areas have moved forthrightly and extensively into interlocal cooperation. We reviewed in Chapter 9 the extensive interlocal cooperation seen in the Lakewood Plan in Los Angeles County. Philadelphia and Detroit also warrant some attention.

Studies conducted in Philadelphia found that cooperative arrangements between school districts and particular schools tend to develop between districts and schools that are very similar in social rank and level of financial resources. A similar pattern emerges in agreements between localities over sewage—that is, sewage agreements tend to occur more frequently between governments representing people of comparable status, and this aspect appears to be more important than any other. Yet, in other functional areas no particular pattern appears; for example, in police radio agreements, social and economic distance between localities appear to have no effect on contractual patterns. When the social and economic disparaties between municipalities are not the overriding factor, the next most significant variable is that of comparable economic and fiscal resources between each government.[30]

The Detroit findings concerned different kinds of intraurban patterns, although investigations in Detroit generally support the Philadelphia con-

---

[30] The three Philadelphia studies are: Jephtha J. Carrell, "Learning to Work Together." *National Municipal Review* 44 (November, 1954), 526–533. George S. Blair, *Interjurisdictional Agreements in Southeastern Pennsylvania* (Philadelphia: University of Pennsylvania Institute of Local and State Government, 1960). Oliver P. Williams, Harold Herman, Charles S. Liebman, and Thomas R. Dye, *Suburban Differences and Metropolitan Policies: A Philadelphia Story* (Philadelphia: University of Pennsylvania Press, 1965).

clusions. The Detroit investigations discerned an association between the type of government structure and the level of cooperative activity. Council–manager cities, regardless of differing social and economic characteristics, participated in joint arrangements to a measurably greater degree than did mayor–council governments. Professional contacts between city managers provided a basis for establishing cooperation between municipalities.[31]

In summary, then, it seems likely that comparable social status, financial resources, and type of government are significant in the predisposition of cities to enter into cooperative arrangements with each other.

BOUNDARIES AND REFORM:
THE PROBLEMS OF MATCHING PEOPLE, POLICIES, AND POWER

Matching people, politics, and political boundaries to best meet the needs of the citizens is one of the overriding dilemmas of American government. Reorganizing the structure of local governments and redrawing jurisdictions are not easy tasks. Political boundaries can be matched with the needs of the citizenry in many ways. Which ways political scientists would choose to bring boundaries and people together depend very much on the values the particular political scientists hold. There are at least three different approaches to the boundary question in metropolitan affairs: (1) ultralocalism; (2) gargantua; and (3) compromise.

ULTRALOCALISM:
THE STATUS QUO AND THE STATUS QUO ANTE

A large and growing circle of political scientists argue that what really is needed is the current state of fragmentation of local governments—or perhaps even more fragmentation of local governments. This school of thought is called "public choice" or "political economy." Not too long ago it was called the "no-name school of public administration" because its main theorists, who are associated largely with public administration, had not fully defined what they were doing. Since then, these theorists have formed the Public Choice Society.

Perhaps the classic expression of public choice as it is applied to urban affairs is an article that appeared some years ago entitled "The Organization of Government in Metropolitan Areas: A Theoretical Inquiry," by Vincent Ostrom, Charles M. Tiebout, and Robert Warren. The authors argued for what they termed "polycentric or multinucleated political systems" as the most responsive to the citizenry's needs. The view is that many units of

---

[31] Vincent L. Marando, "Inter-Local Cooperation in a Metropolitan Area." *Urban Affairs Quarterly* 4 (December, 1968), 185–200.

government, units that often overlap jurisdictionally and are perhaps inefficient economically, will be most responsive to a citizen's demands.

To offer a hypothetical example, suppose you were a resident of an urban area and your house was being broken into be a very mean looking burglar. Your first inclination would be to lock the bedroom door and call the police. The public choice theorists would say that, under the normal system of government, you would have only one option: to call your metropolitan police. Your city's finest might not respond because they would have an effective monopoly on the delivery of the services to you as a citizen. Or a squad car might be at your door in thirty seconds. Or the sergeant answering your call might chuckle at your plight. Under public choice theory, however, you could call (a) your metropolitan police, (b) the county sheriff's office, (c) the state troopers, or (d) perhaps even a private firm offering security protection against burglars. Under the public choice school, all of these crime prevention agencies and perhaps even others not yet conceived would have overlapping jurisdictions. Hence, if one police department was not up to snuff or was unresponsive, another police department could fill that gap. Free market competition thus equals governmental responsiveness. To quote Ostrom, Tiebout, and Warren:

> By analogy, the formal units of government in a metropolitan area might be viewed as organizations similar to individual firms in an industry. Individual firms may constitute the basic legal entities in an industry, but their conduct in relation to one another may be conceived as having a particular structure and behavior as an industry. Collaboration among the separate units of local government may be such that their activities supplement or complement each other, as in the automobile industry's patent pool. Competition among them may produce desirable self-regulating tendencies similar in effect to the "invisible hand" of the market.[32]

Perhaps it is because of this kind of analogy that critics of the public choice school argue that it is a highly conservative political theory that can work against the dispossessed. Members of the political economy camp argue that it is just the opposite. Many proponents of public choice seem to come from Los Angeles and its environs, where interlocal cooperation perhaps works better than in most major metropolitan areas.

Regardless of criticism, however, it seems apparent that "minigovs" are required for urban governance for much the same reasons as are "unigovs." In 1968, the National Commission on Urban Problems reported that "the psychological distance from the neighborhood to City Hall has grown from blocks, to miles, to light-years. With decreasing communication and sense of identification by the low-income resident with his government have come

---

[32] Vincent Ostrom, Charles M. Tiebout, and Robert Warren, "The Organization of Government in Metropolitan Areas: Theoretical Inquiry." *American Political Science Review* 55 (December, 1961), 831–842, as reprinted in Jay S. Goodman, *Perspectives on Urban Politics* (Boston: Allyn & Bacon, 1970), pp. 100–101.

first apathy, then disaffection, and now—insurrection."[33] Similarly, middle-class residents of "bedroom" suburban communities have become disaffected with town councils controlled by local construction interests that zone the town for their maximal profit and ensure that questions of public concern are placed on the agenda of council meetings for consideration during the wee hours on weekdays. It is an unusual town meeting that is attended by a significant portion of the town's people.

From a practical viewpoint, the adoption of a public choice concept in the real governance of metropolises probably is best expressed in the movement begun in the mid-1960s toward neighborhood governments. Much of this movement is a reaction against what is perceived as the condescension of "professional managers" in the urban bureaucracy, and the very existence of the movement—which advocates a limited disannexa-tion of neighborhood communities rather than outright secession from city hall—does not do credit to public officials in big cities.[34]

Two practical consequences of the neighborhood government movement have been the rise of "neighborhood corporations" and the now dormant drive for community control of public schools in municipalities. Neighbor-hood corporations are nonprofit organizations, chartered by the state, and managed for the public benefit of specified urban areas by its residents. Many received their initial funding in 1966 under the provisions of the Economic Opportunity Act of 1964, and later under the Model Cities program. An analysis of these groups concluded that, although their record of success had been spotty, neighborhood corporations had established a genuine rapport with residents. Nevertheless, just how representative the corporations are is open to question when it is realized that resident turnout to elect the directors of these organizations has been less than 5 percent of the eligible voters.[35]

GARGANTUA

The term *gargantua* is used in the same sense that Robert C. Wood used it several years ago: "the invention of a single metropolitan government or at least the establishment of a regional superstructure which points in that direction."[36] A number of political scientists, in complete contrast to the

---

[33] National Commission on Urban Problems, *Building the American City* (Washington, D.C.: U.S. Government Printing Office, 1968), p. 11.

[34] See: Joseph F. Zimmerman, *The Federated City: Community Control in Large Cities* (New York: St. Martin's, 1972). Milton Kotler, *Neighborhood Government* (Indianapolis: Bobbs-Merrill, 1969). Alan A. Altshuer, *Commmunity Control: The Black Demand for Participation in Large American Cities* (New York: Pegasus, 1970).

[35] Howard W. Hallman, "Guidelines for Neighborhood Management." *Public Management* (January, 1971), 3–5.

[36] Robert C. Wood, "The New Metropolis: Greenbelt, Grass Roots versus Gargantua." *American Political Science Review* 52 (March, 1958), 108–122.

public choice school, argue that the many splinters of metropolitan government must be consolidated if the public is to acquire effective and efficient public services. The emphasis is not on "responsiveness"; it is on "efficiency." Often, of course, responsiveness and efficiency are synonymous—most taxpayers prefer getting the biggest bang for their buck—but they are not always the same. For example, if your house is being burglarized, getting a police car there quickly may be very important to you at the time of the burglary. But when you are filling out your local income tax form you may object vociferously to the "waste" engendered by many overlapping units of government, even though this so-called waste may have facilitated that police car speeding to your house when you needed it.

It is efficiency that has been valued by such groups as the Committee for Economic Development, a business-dominated organization that in 1966 recommended reducing the number of the nation's local governments by a whopping 80 percent (to sixteen thousand), and consolidating the country's twenty-seven hundred nonmetropolitan counties into no more than five hundred. Four years later, however, the committee modified its view and recommended what amounted to a compromise reorganization of metropolitan governments.[37] Similarly, in 1968 the National Commission on Urban Problems urged governmental consolidation, but less for the sake of fiscal economies and more to encourage the construction of new housing and greater responsiveness to other kinds of urban crises.

Consolidation for efficiency. Economic waste is commonplace and unavoidable in overly small governments.[38] For example, in the opinion of a study team in Illinois, the liquidation of *all* town governments in the state and consolidation of its 102 counties into 24 would save Illinois taxpayers as much as 40 percent. The 80,000 governments in the United States, many of which are of Lilliputian dimensions, support some 500,000 elected and appointed officials. Consider, for instance, Blue Earth County, Minnesota, whose 44,000 residents were governed a few years ago by 155 units of local government, 105 state bureaus, and 38 federal agencies. Or consider Allegheny County, Pennsylvania, with 129 municipalities, 78 boroughs, 23 first-class townships, 24 second-class townships, 116 school districts, as well as the governments of the city of Pittsburgh and Allegheny County. Then there is the awesomely bureaucratized community of Wilton, New Hampshire, whose 60 officials administered a total of 1,724 citizens in 1960. Bayfield County, Wisconsin, had fewer than 12,000 people in 1964 but was governed by 100 elected legislators in various legislatures, assemblies, and councils and nearly 200 additional elected officials, including 29 treasurers,

---

[37] Committee for Economic Development, *Modernizing Local Government* (New York: Committee for Economic Development, 1966); Committee for Economic Development, *Reshaping Government in Metropolitan Areas* (New York: Committee for Economic Development, 1970).

[38] The following examples of governmental fragmentation at the local level are drawn from Reuss, *Revenue Sharing.* While the statistics are somewhat dated, the facts of fragmentation still remain.

29 assessors, and 29 tax collectors. More than 85 percent of all local governments in the United States have less than 5,000 people, and less than 50 percent even contain 1,000 constituents.

Delivering public services to the citizenry can be obstructed to the point of absurdity in jurisdictionally fragmented regions. For example, a few years ago there was a fire in a house less than three blocks from a fire station in Las Vegas, but just beyond the city limits. The Las Vegas firemen watched the house burn until county fire engines arrived. The city firemen had been instructed by their superior to prevent the fire from reaching city property. Angry neighborhood residents hurled rocks at the immobile city fire engines, causing substantial damage. To take another example: the 40,000 independent police jurisdictions in the United States render coordinated law enforcement action difficult. In 1965 St. Louis County plainclothes detectives conducting a gambling raid were arrested by police from the town of Wellston, who were staging their own raid. Coordinated and effective programs in air and water pollution control, public health, and highways also are impeded or prevented by the irresponsibility, diseconomies, and buck-passing brought about by a plethora of tiny governments.

It has been contended that the argument for governmental consolidation is the product of an "efficiency mentality," which prefers dictatorial efficiency to democratic due process, participation, and representativeness. But making certain government services more effective and less costly through administratively rational consolidation does not necessarily mandate the establishment of a supercentralized bureaucracy unhindered by popular preferences and insensitive to the subtleties of neighborhood values. Nor is the implicit argument of the defenders of ultralocalism adequate—that is, that the status quo assures governmental responsiveness to local needs. In fact, Americans are still apathetic about local politics (an average of only 30 percent of the eligible voters vote in local elections; in contrast, 50 to 60 percent vote in presidential elections). The long ballot used in many localities is also of questionable value to democratic ideals because it diverts voter attention from the policy-making offices. For example, a woman obtained the nomination for the coroner's office in a New Jersey primary by persuading nine of her friends to write in her name on the ballot. Although she publicly proclaimed herself totally unfit for the office, she won the election by 80,000 votes because she was the candidate of the dominant party. The voters of Milton, Washington, elected (to their subsequent embarrassment) a mule to the Town Board. No doubt this lack of popular concern over local governance is at least in part attributable to a belief by Americans that their local governments are incapable of responding to their needs.

The argument for gargantua is not as unsophisticated as it might appear at first glance. One review of much of the research on economies and diseconomies of scale concluded that only in the smaller cities, those with less than 25,000 people, could economies of scale be attained by broadening the scope of government. (Economy of scale means that some functions, such as garbage collection, are more efficient when conducted by a single organization over a large region rather than by many small agencies over the same area.) Size was not a factor in cities between 25,000 to 250,000 people. In cities with more than 250,000 people expanding the scope of government further seemed to produce *dis*economy of scale and lower levels of service to the public when calculated on a per capita basis.[39] Although it's doubtful that such findings will hold true for every city, the point is aptly made that economies of scale can work two ways.

Consolidation by annexation. In practice, the cities have attempted to swallow their surrounding local governments politically. The efforts of major metropolises to annex their environs can be seen as having three historical phases. Phase one occurred before the turn of this century and had three major characteristics. Municipalities absorbed great hunks of territory, the land they annexed was largely rural when the cities grabbed it, and often with annexation came a reorganization of government, such as the separation of a city from a county. Phase two occurred after 1900. The character of municipal annexation changed dramatically and, until World War II, annexation was very seldom used by cities.

After the war, however, Phase three was initiated. In 1945, 152 cities with populations of 5,000 or more annexed outlying territory. The total exceeded by substantial margins the number of annexations that had been accomplished during the 1930s and this trend has yet to be stopped; between 1970 and 1976, more than 1,000 cities with more than 25,000 people conducted more than 28,000 separate annexations and consolidations, adding nearly 9,000 square miles and almost 2,500,000 people to themselves in the process.[40]

This resurgence in annexation can be traced to two factors. One is continued metropolitan growth; the second is the almost universal reluctance of the public to accept comprehensive governmental reorganization. Usually this reluctance emerges politically in the form of outlying suburbs resisting annexation; it is the tax-hungry central cities that generally want it. Small suburban governments tend to resist annexations most strongly when the metropolitan area is older, as are areas in the East or the South; when there are wide status differences between the inner city and the outer suburb; and when the form of city government is something other than the council–manager system.[41]

A major variant of annexation, and one that may represent a break-

[39] Elinor Ostrom, "Metropolitan Reform: Propositions Denied from Two Traditions." *Social Science Quarterly* 53 (December, 1972), 474–493.

[40] Richard L. Forstall and Joel C. Miller, "Annexations and Corporate Changes: 1970–76." *1978 Municipal Yearbook* (Washington, D.C.: International City Management Association, 1978), as derived from Table 3–1.

[41] Thomas R. Dye, "Urban Political Integration: Conditions Associated with Annexations in American Cities" *Midwest Journal of Political Science* 8 (November, 1964), 446.

through in comprehensive governmental services, is that of *city–county consolidation*. Prior to 1900, all city–county consolidations were brought about by state legislation, not by the approval by local voters, and usually a vestigial county government was permitted to remain in some fashion. Between 1900 and 1945, only three city–county consolidation proposals even made it to the voters. Most consolidation proposals were unable to hurdle the chief obstacle of consolidation, which was achieving a state constitutional amendment, or at least enacting enabling legislation.

After World War II, however, a spate of city–county consolidations took place. The city of Baton Rouge merged with East Baton Rouge Parish in 1947; Nashville merged in 1962 with Davidson County; Jacksonville merged in 1967 with Duval County; and Indianapolis joined with Marion County. These four are the major city-county consolidations that have occurred since World War II, although a total of eleven city-county consolidations of consequence had taken place as of 1977. It seems probable that annexation will continue as a technique of making metropolitan government more rational, but it is dubious that city-county consolidations will occur as rapidly as they have in the last few years.

It also seems likely that school districts will continue their remarkable consolidation, and in this respect they too can be included in the gargantuan tradition of political reform. School districts have been reduced from roughly 127,000 (or nearly 75 percent of all governmental units) in the 1930s to a little more than 15,000 in 1977, and we will consider this trend more thoroughly in an upcoming chapter. Suffice it to note, however, that the garagantuan "approach to area-wide problems has in general seen its heyday [and] with some exceptions will almost certainly be bypassed in favor of other techniques."[42]

THE COMPROMISE APPROACH

The third and final approach to questions of boundaries and power is the compromise approach, which is of course the classic one of the American polity. This accommodation recognizes that efficiency and responsiveness are both beneficial values. On the one hand, responsiveness can be obtained in areas where it ought to be retained, such as planning, community/police relations, complaint systems, recreational activities, schools, public health clinics, building and housing code inspections, and other operations that call for quick, responsive, and personal reactions by governments. On the other hand, certain other kinds of functions that governments perform can be centralized for greater economy. These functions that belong in the gargantuan category of metropolitan government include, at least potentially, environmental planning, pollution control, tax collection, sanitation,

---

[42] Bollens and Schmandt, *The Metropolis,* p. 264.

fire protection, computer services, crime control, and a variety of operations that are subject to economies of scale, that can be standardized, and that require coordination. Hence, both fragmentation and gargantua are reconciled in the compromise approach.

In practice, the compromise approach to urban governance has taken two major tacks: metropolitan districts and comprehensive urban county plans. Let us consider them in turn.

The metropolitan district. Metropolitan districts are certainly the less controversial version of the compromise approach. A metropolitan district generally encompasses the entire metropolitan region, or at least a major portion of it; some, in fact, have waxed into regional governments. We have reviewed a number of their variations in the discussion of special districts in Chapter 9 and, as noted, most metropolitan districts are relegated to a single service or to a very limited area of activities. Roughly 125 metropolitan districts are now functioning in more than a quarter of the Standard Metropolitan Statistical Areas, and they are particularly popular in cities of more than 500,000 people. They administer such services as port facilities, transportation, parks, public housing, and water supplies. The Port Authority of New York and New Jersey and the Bay Area Rapid Transit (BART) District in San Francisco are among the better known examples of metropolitan districts. State legal provisions permit them to flourish, at least in comparison to other forms of metropolitan governmental innovation, but they have been criticized as not being politically accountable to the citizenry, and thus not responsive to the people. When one realizes that we are talking about a governmental form that generally is responsible for only a single function of government, and one that often requires a good deal of expertise, the problem of popular representation in metropolitan districts becomes a particularly difficult one. Metropolitan districts have also been criticized because of their single-purpose organization and the ensuing lack of policy and administrative coordination that often results.

The comprehensive urban county plan. A second variation of the compromise approach is the *comprehensive urban county plan.* The only metropolitan area in the nation that uses this is Miami and Dade County. This fact need not detract from its potential utility, particularly when it is realized that a number of artificial barriers prevent its widespread use. Cleveland, Dayton, Houston, and Pittsburgh, for example, have all tried to establish such a plan and have failed because of these barriers. The barriers include the lack of legal authorization by states to use this concept; entrenched local officials who may resist what they often regard as a sweeping renovation of local government; the difficulty in selecting criteria for structuring the new governmental body of the county; the new duties to be assigned to county government; and inadequate funds to finance the new authority of county governments under such a plan.

That comprehensive urban county plans are useful has been testified to by the Miami–Dade County experience. In that metropolitan region a county-wide land use plan that includes tough regulations on air and water pollution control has been adopted. Such functions as traffic laws and traffic courts, tax assessment and collection, zoning regulations and enforcement, youth services, and mass transit all have been coordinated and standardized throughout the region.

EFFICIENCY OR RESPONSIVENESS? A PROBLEM OF BALANCE

Matching political boundaries with political functions has always been difficult for American government. Ultralocalism brings with it inefficiencies and ineffectiveness, but the American populace has tolerated these fiscal and administrative inefficiencies as the price of responsiveness. Indeed, it can be argued that the American people prefer these inefficiencies in that the governmental fragmentation that spawns them is the price of the most effective defense possible against tyranny.

Yet, when the price of ultralocalist government soars too high, the citizens respond accordingly. We have witnessed this response in taxpayer revolts against school bond issues. Indeed, as school district consolidations have increased dramatically, the number of taxpayer revolts against school bond elections also has gone up; in the 1970s more than 90 percent of the school bond issues went down in defeat, despite the radical consolidations for the sake of economy and efficiency. There are exceptions to this rule—some citizens revolt against school districts on political rather than economic grounds—but it is the exception that proves the rule. An example is Kanawha County, West Virginia, whose citizens banned certain books from the school system because they felt these books were depraved, anti-Christ, and immoral. But if the data are to be read dispassionately, it seems that most Americans will let their children read anything the school assigns and will let the school bureaucracy distance itself from accountability to parents, so long as educational costs can be kept down. Only in the schools (which consume nearly half of state and local budgets) do Americans seem to prefer efficiency over responsiveness; this preference has not yet made itself felt in the counties, cities, and towns.

FEDERALISM AND THE PYRAMIDING OF POWER

A final summing up on the nature of relations between governments in the United States points to one conclusion: that governmental power in this country is centralizing despite Americans' ultralocalist leanings.

Perhaps the clearest indication of this can be seen by examining the measures of financial resources, services, and manpower. The nation's nearly nineteen thousand municipalities raise less money today than the nation's fifty state governments and considerably fewer dollars than the national government. Although money is paid the national government and part of it is sent back to the state and local governments through revenue sharing and block grants, this practice connotes, at least in the view of some, a centralization of governmental power at the national level. But such centralization also may be happening at the state level. By ranking the local proportions of financial resources, services, and manpower by state, G. Ross Stephens found that certain states were quite centralized in relation to their local governments, while others were relatively decentralized. Stephens concluded that larger states tend to be decentralized governmentally, smaller states are more centralized.[43]

There is additional evidence that governments are centralizing. A comprehensive study commissioned by the Advisory Commission on Intergovernmental Relations (ACIR), which covered 3,319 municipalities, concluded that functional and political responsibilities in all governments were shifting, and principally upward.[44] Nearly a third of the municipalities responding had permanently transferred responsibility, either voluntarily or involuntarily, for a particular function to another governmental unit. Normally, the functions transferred dealt with solid waste collection and disposal, law enforcement, public health, sewage treatment, taxation and assessment of property, building and safety inspections, planning, and the broadly generic area entitled social services. Larger cities and towns generally shift their governmental responsibilities more frequently than smaller ones; indeed, more than a third of the responding local governments with populations of more than 500,000 people had transferred responsibilities for five or more major functions during the past ten years, and these city functions normally went to counties and special districts. Counties, in particular, received transferences of solid waste collection and disposal, law enforcement, and public health. Special districts generally took over transportation and sewage collection and treatment. States took over social services. The reasons usually cited for these transfers by government officials related to the "gargantuan" model: the elimination of duplication, sharing of facilities and equipment, and the easing of fiscal restraints. The states rarely initiated the transfers; most local governments transferred functions to other governments through cooperative arrangements, not because of state mandates.

The major trends in these transferences were the shifting of urban responsibilities for services to the county and to the state. The states received 14 percent of the functions that were shifted by local governments; counties took on 56 percent of the services transferred by municipal governments.

The survey also indicated that municipalities have taken over a number of services previously managed by private firms. Almost half of the functions assumed by municipalities previously had been performed by private corporations, and this was especially true of the big cities; two-thirds of the

---

[43] G. Ross Stephens, "State Centralization and the Erosion of Local Autonomy." *Journal of Politics* 36 (February, 1974), 67.

[44] Advisory Commission on Intergovernmental Relations, *Pragmatic Federalism: The Reassignment of Functional Responsibility* (Washington, D.C. ACIR, 1976).

cities with more than 50,000 people had transferred some services to private corporations. A number of functions had been transferred to special districts and such transfers constituted nearly a fifth of all the transfers of powers between governments. The county, of all units of government, is most preferred by urban officials as the government to which powers should be transferred. The Advisory Commission on Intergovernmental Relations predicts that in the future the county and the "urban state" are going to become increasingly important units of local government.

In short, the "bottom line" of intergovernmental relations in the 1980s is that governmental power will centralize in this country. This centralization has many ramifications and not the least of them is the implication that this aggrandizement of political power has for the whole concept of "community" in America, a concern that we take up in the following chapter.

11

POWER
IN COMMUNITIES:
WHO PLAYS,
WINS, LOSES

"Community power" long has been an object of research. In this chapter, we sample the traditional literature on community power, but with a difference. Instead of dwelling on elitist versus pluralist interpretations of community power, we emphasize the role of Washington and its intervention in the local politics of cities and suburbs; further, we shall review how the feds have, in the 1980s, withdrawn their support of activist local groups and the subsequent patterns of political participation at the grassroots.

To accomplish this, we shall (1) consider what *community* means to policy makers (an important consideration, since the definition of community has determined national policies for communities); (2) review some selected literature on elitist and pluralist conceptions of community power; (3) examine the impact of Washington on the distribution of that power in localities; and (4) conclude with a discussion of how local citizens participate in the distribution of community power—from voting, to lobbying, to legislating.

COMMUNITY: QUARRELS OVER A CONCEPT

Before getting to the nitty-gritty of grassroots politics and power, we first must define *community*. John C. Bollens and Henry J. Schmandt observe that "two core definitions" emerge from the literature on communities: "One refers to the modes of relationships in which the individuals and families involved share common values and objectives and closely identify themselves with the aggregate population; the other indicates a spatially defined social unit that has functional significance and relates to the interdependence of individuals and groups."[1] The first definition is the classic one, and it applies to such groupings as a village, neighborhood, or New England town. The second definition refers to the interdependence that arises among groups as a result of large scale specialization, or professionalization. "The strong interest of communion and shared values characteristic of the first meaning [*i.e.*, the village] may no longer be present, but the high degree of interdependence in daily activities that the urban system imposes on the aggregation creates a social group with strong ties of mutual interest and concern." The community, in this sense then, is a "mosaic of subareas whose inhabitants are highly interdependent on a daily basis in terms of needs, communication, and commutation to and from work."[2]

---

[1]John C. Bollens and Henry J. Schmandt, *The Metropolis* 3rd ed., (New York: Harper and Row, 1975), p. 7.

[2]*Ibid.*

The National Research Council perhaps puts the foregoing—and rather arcane—concepts into perspective when it notes that, if the ideal of "community" is to be attained, then "metropolitan people and their leaders must somehow gain a clearer appreciation of their actual interdependence and their potential common interest. This is what community in the most useful sense means."[3]

In this book, we accept the proposition that *community* refers to economic, social, and political interdependence among people who fall into broad social categories, as opposed to the "village" idea. This is a fairly important point—we are saying that the traditional definition of community no longer applies. We are contending that not only is "the melting pot" (that is, ethnic groups intermarrying, homogenizing, and "Americanizing" over time) a fallacy, but that the ethnic neighborhood increasingly is becoming a memory rather than a reality. For example, although there is a "Little Italy" in Chicago, about half of the Italian immigrants did not settle in Italian neighborhoods, but dispersed themselves throughout the metropolitan area. In arguing against the "community-as-village" thesis, research repeatedly finds that as urban units increase in size, their populations become less traditional and less conservative. "This is true for various aspects of life, including race relations, sexual behavior, the family, religion, and law and politics . . . consequently, cities historically have been the scenes of scientific, economic, social and political innovation as well as turbulence and dislocation."[4]

Another conventional wisdom concerning the idea of community is the image of neighbors talking to neighbors, residents knowing each other (and keeping tabs on each other), and the whole *Gestalt* of folksy neighborliness. Nevertheless, little if any of this exists in metropolitan areas. One study found that in six metropolitan areas only one-third of suburban residents had any contact at all with their immediate neighbors, and in the inner cities the percentage was even less.[5] It seems that people do not really interact with other people in the suburbs and cities on a neighborhood basis; they interact instead on a social and economic basis. That is, lawyers talk to lawyers, the poor talk to the poor, but neighbors rarely talk to neighbors.

Like most of the findings in social science, this conclusion is not without its exceptions, but it does seem that the local neighborhood has become substantially less significant either as a "community" or as a force in forming individual personality. The neighborhood survives primarily as a means of control over the immediate physical environment, and people in it tend to work together only when challenged by some outside force.

---

[3]National Research Council, *Toward an Understanding of Metropolitan America* (San Francisco: Canfield, 1975), p. 45.

[4]*Ibid.*

[5]A. H. Hawley and B. B. Zimmer, *The Metropolitan Community: Its People and Government* (Beverly Hills, Calif.: Sage, 1970).

COMMUNITY POWER: VIEWS AND COUNTERVIEWS

Both the "village" and the "class/professional" definitions of *community* have held sway over researchers in their attempts to discern how power politics is played in cities and towns. Some scholars appear to accept implicitly the "village" definition by engaging in *reputational analyses* of community power: they simply ask notable people in a community who they think has power, and proceed from that point. Those who have local reputations for "getting things moving" are seen as powerful in this kind of an analysis. The classic example of reputational analysis is Floyd Hunter's 1954 study, *Community Power Structure*, in which he concluded that Atlanta, Georgia, was ruled by a handful of powerful men.

At the other end of the continuum is what is known as *event analysis*, which appears more suited to a "class/professional" definition of community. Event analysis traces patterns of interaction among policy makers rather than the opinions of community residents about who is powerful. The best known exponent of event analysis is Robert Dahl. His work, *Who Governs*, used event analysis to examine how sixteen decisions were made on urban redevelopment, public education, and mayoral nominations in both political parties for a period that extended through seven elections in New Haven, Connecticut.

POWER: PLURALIST OR ELITIST?

Regardless of the methods used to study community power, at least two major points of view have emerged in the literature over time: the pluralist view and the elitist view.

Pluralism assumes that while a community may have some powerful individuals, power nonetheless in accessible to virtually anyone who becomes interested in acquiring it. Power is dispersed. Elites are not monolithic power elites that can start or stop any project at anytime, anywhere, but rather there are many elites that specialize in many issues. Although these elites may be powerful in terms of a particular issue, they are not powerful on all issues. Dahl, who represents the pluralist view, states that no one elite is a "ruling group, but are simply one of many groups out of which individuals sporadically emerge to influence the politics and acts of city officials."[6]

The elitist model, on the other hand, assumes that there is indeed an all-powerful ruling elite in a community, and change can be accomplished only with the consent of this power elite. Without that consent, change is not accomplished. Moreover, this elite is commercial rather than political—that is, it is economically powerful, but not elected or appointed to office.

Of course, it should be noted that *pluralist* and *elitist* are highly relative

---

[6]Robert Dahl, *Who Governs?* (New Haven, Conn.: Yale University Press, 1961), p. 72.

terms: "No matter what methodology is employed and no matter what the type or size of town examined, the results invariably show that only a small minority of the citizen body, actually less than 1 percent, are active and direct participants in the community decision-making process (other than voting on referenda)."[7]

Another major factor in community power studies is the physical size of the community to be analyzed. Researchers have studied cities from the size of Atlanta and New York to cities the size of Muncie, Indiana, which at the time of the study had a population of 35,000. Taken together, size of the community and elitist or pluralist conclusions about the type of power structure found in those communities are perhaps the two most significant variables pertaining to all the community power literature. We consider some of these studies in turn.

THE POWER ELITE IN BIG CITIES

Hunter found that a small elite of businessmen pretty much ran Atlanta in the early 1950s.[8] Peter B. Clark, however, approached the same idea from quite a different point of view.[9] He studied businessmen rather than communities and found America's men of commerce to be extraordinarily uncreative in suggesting new civic policies. Generally businessmen were used as prestigious front men for ideas that were thought up by professional staffs of civic organizations or the city government itself. Once a well-thought-out innovation for a community had received the public backing of prestigious businessmen, the innovation almost always became a city policy.

Edward C. Banfield came up with a variation on the same idea.[10] In the early 1960s Banfield found that the ruling elite of Chicago, while not a ruling elite in the classical sense, nevertheless tended to be concentrated in the city government itself, principally in the form of the late Mayor Daley's political machine. Although there was no economic or business-oriented ruling elite of Chicago, wealthy individuals played prominent political roles. Nevertheless, because business leaders do not always agree on all issues, because they do not communicate effectively among themselves, and because they do not have their own political organization, they in effect had to defer to the Daley machine to implement any kind of policy, and even to reconcile their own differences. Therefore, the Chicago power elite was clearly political, not economic.

---

[7]Bollens and Schmandt, *The Metropolis*, p. 112.

[8]Floyd Hunter, *Community Power Structure* (Chapel Hill, N.C.: University of North Carolina Press, 1953).

[9]Peter B. Clark, *The Businessman as a Civic Leader* (New York: Glencoe, 1964).

[10]Edward Banfield, *Political Influence* (New York: Glencoe, Free Press, 1961), p. 263.

THE POWER ELITE IN SMALL TOWNS

A classic study of community power was conducted by Robert Lynd and Helen Lynd. Known as the "Middletown" studies, they were conducted over a period beginning with the mid-1920s and continuing through the mid-1930s. The Lynds used an anthropological approach and focused on one "Family X," which, in their view controlled the destiny of most "Middletowners" (actually, residents of Muncie, Indiana). The Lynds concluded, "The lines of leadership and the related controls are highly concentrated today in Middletown"; they added that they felt the control had centralized over time.[11]

A fascinating variation on the Lynds' conclusions about Muncie is contained in Robert O. Schultze's study of "Cibola," which was actually Ypsilanti, Michigan. Schultze found that as Ypsilanti's local commerce integrated with the national economy, the "old families" of Ypsilanti gave way to a new management class—that is, highly paid employees who worked for absentee corporate landlords.[12] He found that the new managerial elite did not have the same interest in local issues and in the local community as the traditional, locally based industrialists. The managers were mainly concerned with what those in their national company headquarters were thinking, although the headquarters were often located several thousand miles away.

THE BIG CITY AS A PLURALIST SYSTEM

Quite the opposite of the elitist model is the pluralist model. Pluralism accepts the idea that all organized groups can become actively involved in the community's political process. As we observed in Chapter 4 this view represents "the hydraulic theory of power," in which countervailing interest groups are at loggerheads with each other. Those groups with the greater skill or power tend to garner policies from "the system" that are more favorable to them than do others.[13] The conventional wisdom in political science circles is that this system represents a good and just policy. Pluralism sees an interest in politics and a willingness to be involved in a piece of the action as the keys to influence, whereas the elitist concept puts mere economic wealth as the cornerstone of community power.

Frank J. Munger studied patterns of political power in Syracuse, New York, and came up with a pluralist conclusion about how politics was

---

[11]Robert S. Lynd and Helen M. Lynd, *Middletown in Transition* (New York: Harcourt Brace Jovanovich, 1927 and 1965). Reprinted in *The Search for Community Power*, Willis D. Hawley and Frederick M. Wirt, eds. (Englewood Cliffs, N.J.: Prentice-Hall, 1974), p. 50.

[12]Robert D. Schultze, "The Role of Economic Dominants in a Community Power Structure." *American Sociological Review* 23 (February, 1958), 3–9. See also Robert O. Schultze, in *The Bifurcation of Power in a Satellite Community*, Morris Janowitz, ed. (New York: Glencoe, 1961).

[13]L. Harmon Zeigler and G. Wayne Peak, *Interest Groups in American Society*, 2nd ed. (Englewood Cliffs, N.J.: Prentice-Hall, 1972).

structured in that city. Munger's conclusion was that "in reality, there appear to be many kinds of community power with one differing from another in so many fundamental ways as to make virtually impossible a meaningful comparison." He goes on to note that there were "as many decision centers as there are important decision areas, which means that the decision-making power is fragmented among institutions, agencies and individuals."[14]

Similarly, Wallace B. Sayre and Herbert Kaufman in their enormous work, *Governing New York City*, concluded that "no single ruling elite dominates the political and governmental system of New York City," and added that "New York was governed by ceaseless bargaining and fluctuating alliances among the major categories of participants in each center, and in which the centers are partially but strikingly isolated from one another."[15] Thus, in Sayre and Kaufman's view, New York is run through a process that they call "decisions as accommodation." In this light "building temporary or lasting alliances, working out immediate or enduring settlements between allies or competitors, and bargaining for an improved position in the decision centers are the continuing preoccupations of all leaders—whether party leaders, public officials, leaders of organized bureaucracies, or leaders of nongovernmental groups."[16]

PLURALISM IN SMALL TOWNS

The final category in this discussion of community power structure concerns those small towns that have been seen by some analysts as pluralist systems. Overall, the literature tends to regard big cities as composites of many competing forces (in other words, a pluralist system) and small towns as dominated by powerful economic elites. Of course, there are exceptions to this rule. Perhaps the best known exception to the conventional wisdom that small towns are dominated by powerful rich folks was conducted by Aaron Wildavsky of Oberlin, Ohio. He found a number of different power bases and all kinds of controversies. Although Wildavsky's investigations do not disprove the findings of those many analysts who have found significant economic elites dominating small towns in America, they do indicate that there is no preset pattern of political power that necessarily will dominate in a small town setting. As Wildavsky concluded, "the roads to influence . . .are more than one; elites and nonelites can travel them, and the toll can be paid with energy and initiative as well as wealth."[17]

---

[14]Frank J. Munger, *Decisions in Syracuse* (Bloomington, Ind.: Indiana University Press, 1962), p. 119.

[15]Wallace Sayer and Herbert Kaufman, *Governing New York City* (New York: Norton, 1975), 710 and 716.

[16]*Ibid.*

[17]Aaron Wildavsky, *Leadership in a Small Town* (Totowa, N.J.: Bedminister Press, 1964), p. 214.

CONCLUSIONS ABOUT COMMUNITY POWER

The findings of the literature on community power are considerably more sophisticated than the preceding overview indicates. Thomas R. Dye, in a useful summarization, notes the following conclusions, or hypotheses, on community power that have been drawn from this voluminous body of writing:[18]

1. Communities without substantial class or racial cleavages have more concentrated power structures; social differences and community conflicts tend to be associated with a pluralist political system.
2. An upswing in many different kinds of industrialization tends to increase political pluralism, whereas elite power structures tend to be found in communities with a single dominant industry.
3. Metropolitan central cities tend to be pluralist in nature; suburbs in those same metropolitan areas are usually more elitist.
4. The bigger the city, the greater the likelihood of a pluralist power structure.
5. The older a community, the greater the likelihood of an elitist structure.
6. Southern cities tend to be more elitist than northern cities.
7. Cities with nonpartisan elections, council-manager governments, and highly professional bureaucracies (a fairly common combination in suburbs) tend to be associated with elitist power structures, whereas cities with partisan elections, a mayor-council form of government, and relatively more patronage positions available in city government normally are associated with pluralism.
8. Community power tends to destabilize over time, so that communities with elitist power structures tend to evolve into pluralist systems.

The bulk of research indicates that although power in small towns often is held by business leaders who are not formally elected or appointed to office or by alliances of economic interest groups and formal officeholders, in big cities, at least, the power largely is where it is supposed to be. In other words, political power in major cities is held by those who are formally elected or appointed to office, and these officials serve as brokers between competing interest groups in the community.

In support of this contention, Claire Gilbert, in her review of 167 studies of community power, found that in towns with twenty thousand to fifty thousand people, business leaders who did not hold public office did indeed tend to dominate the local power structure. But the studies also indicated that in the big cities there was no covert power elite that manipulated the formal officeholders. The power was held by those who were elected or appointed to public office;[19] indeed, Banfield's study of Chicago, Sayre and

---

[18]Thomas R. Dye, *Politics in States and Communities*, 3rd ed. (Englewood Cliffs, N.J.: Prentice-Hall, 1977), pp. 58–59.

[19]Claire Gilbert, "Community Power and Decision-Making: A Quantitative Examination of Previous Research." In *Community Structure and Decision-Making: Comparative Analyses*, Terry N. Clark, ed. (San Francisco: Chandler, 1968), pp. 139–158.

Kaufman's study of New York, and Munger's study of Syracuse all confirmed this. Hence, it seems to follow that the larger a community is, the
more likely it is that the people who are in a position to control and filter
information that they receive from various interest groups become the
effective decision makers in communities. In large cities, power is less in the
hands of a privileged elite and increasingly in the hands of the "brokers,"
whether elected or appointed, who can bring together the various components of decision making in the community. Nevertheless, this conclusion is
less valid for the smaller towns, where a local elite can indeed dominate the
elected and appointed officials of the community—at least most of the time.

THE FEDS AND THE "DEVELOPMENT" OF COMMUNITY POWER

Brokers, local elites, and even pluralistic systems of interest groups headed
by their own elites, somehow do not strike us as "democratic." And it
appears in retrospect that particularly in the 1960s the federal government
made an effort to reach down to the grassroots of local polities, nourish
those roots, and thereby change and "democratize" community power
structures. In some ways, this federal effort (supplemented, to be sure, by
spontaneous, home-grown organizations) represented a somewhat nostalgic
attempt to reinstate the "village" concept of community at the expense of
the "class/professional" model.

As Frank X. Steggert has observed in his excellent empirical study,
Community Action Groups and City Government, there has been a new federal
emphasis on citizen participation in the policy-making process of local
government and "a broad range of attempts to institutionalize new channels
for such citizen expression. The thrust of this new movement toward
institutionalization has derived from action at the federal level."[20] The
federal government has called for neighborhood action task forces, more
effective methods for processing citizen grievances, and hearings by local
legislative bodies on inner city problems. It has encouraged the setting up
of neighborhood city halls to act as informal channels for complaints and
grievances and called for more effective community participation through
neighborhood self-determination or control by the community.

The principal rationale that federal policy makers and politically liberal
local elites have used to justify this activity is usually called *community
development*. Community development assumes that, while there is enough
indigenous leadership in communities, some help from the outside nonetheless is needed. Conflict between the power elite in a city and the
grassroots is discouraged; instead, learning to "work with" the power elite
is promoted. Occasionally, this emphasis of the community development
approach alienates local citizens. For example, "Even organizations such as

---

[20]Frank X. Steggert, *Community Action Groups and City Government* (Cambridge, Mass.: Ballinger, 1975), pp. 1–2.

the Urban League that have long worked within the established structure were compelled to assume more militant stands to avoid losing the support of blacks altogether." This occurred when blacks felt that they were not being accorded their full rights in local government; thus, "the community development model is more compatible with the American myth of 'pulling oneself up by his own bootstraps,' and this arouses less hostility."[21]

What does community development mean precisely? At the federal level it is seen as a particular kind of public policy through which government improves the living conditions of its people. This is how Richard M. Nixon defined it as president in 1971, when he proposed to Congress the creation of a new Department of Community Development. The federal government has at least four basic concerns relating to community development: (1) the physical improvement of the urban environment; (2) the improvement of the social aspects of urban areas; (3) the improvement of the performance of local governmental institutions; and (4) the increased participation by local citizens in making decisions that affect their own communities. This will serve as our working definition of community development for this book.

THE ROOTS OF COMMUNITY DEVELOPMENT

Congress first became concerned with community development in 1892 when it appropriated $20,000 for a study of slum conditions. In 1908 President Theodore Roosevelt established a commission to survey slums. Neither study resulted in any federal action that benefited cities.[22] It was not until Theodore's cousin, Franklin, became president in the 1930s that the federal government again took an interest in community development. During FDR's New Deal, federal ventures into such areas as slum clearance established a precedent for the Housing Act of 1949. This act declared as a goal for all Americans the creation of a suitable living environment and inaugurated the nation's Urban Renewal program, which served as the feds' primary articulation of community development in the 1950s.

MAKING WAR ON POVERTY:
COMMUNITY ACTION VERSUS MODEL CITIES

The 1960s saw a resurgence of federal interest in community development, largely through President Lyndon Johnson's "War on Poverty." The two major community development programs initiated by Johnson were (1) the Economic Opportunity Act of 1964, which set up the U.S. Office of Economic Opportunity (OEO) and Community Action Agencies in most of

---

[21]Bollens and Schmandt, *The Metropolis*, pp. 122–123.
[22]National Research Council, *Toward an Understanding of Metropolitan America*, pp. 81–82.

the nation's cities, and (2) the Demonstration Cities and Metropolitan Development Act of 1966, which established City Demonstration Agencies in sixty-six cities to administer the Model Cities Program.

The Economic Opportunity Act was designed to ultimately redistribute urban political power through a broadly based antipoverty program. Although Community Action Agencies could be set up to operate within city hall, most (70 to 80 percent) chose to remain outside. Significantly in this respect, the act mandated "maximum feasible participation" by the poor in any programs conducted through Community Action agencies.

Big city mayors in particular were not at all happy with the Community Action Agencies. They viewed the agencies as being staffed by "radicals" and often felt that the agencies constituted a threat to their own political machines. As a result of pressure from big city mayors, in 1966 Congress passed the Demonstration Cities and Metropolitan Development Act. Rather than requiring "maximum feasible participation" by the poor, this act simply remarked that "widespread citizen participation" would be nice. Consequently, City Demonstration Agencies were set squarely within city hall, and often became hemmed in politically by the urban bureaucracy. A "technical board" was required to review all programs proposed by City Demonstration Agencies; a citizen's board was also required. Many observers objected that the required technical boards gave effective veto power to the urban bureaucracy, but, beyond that, final approval of all programs developed by City Demonstration Agencies lay with the mayor or the city council, or both, not with neighborhood citizen groups.

If the 1966 act was not adequately discouraging to the development of citizen action groups, in 1967 Congress passed the "Green Amendment" to the Economic Opportunity Act of 1964. Named in honor of Representative Edith Green of Oregon, the amendment was enacted at the behest of a number of big city mayors. It deleted the clause calling for "maximum feasible participation" of the poor and prohibited Community Action Agency personnel from clashing with city hall through protest marches, voter registration drives, and similar activities. Congress also broadened the Political Activities Act of 1939 (the Hatch Act), which prohibits political activity by federal employees in the civil service, to cover state and local employees working in federally funded projects and personnel in private organizations working in Community Action Programs. This extension of the Hatch Act also effectively dampened conflicts between neighborhood organizations and city hall.

By the late 1960s Community Action Agencies had evolved into an "outside," contention-oriented program, but their budgets and programs had already been seriously slashed as a result of congressional reaction to pressure from the big cities. Meanwhile, City Demonstration Agencies had developed into "inside," work-within-the-system groups that were restricted in their political clout by administrative and political checks brought on by being located within city hall itself. In 1975 OEO became the Community Services Administration, and its future looked less than certain. Nevertheless, the two programs—the more liberal Community Action Agencies and the more conservative City Demonstration Agencies—have provided excellent examples of official involvement in "developing" communities. Indeed, some urban observers argue that the programs' real goals—that of raising the political consciousness of the poor and the dispossessed—have effectively been achieved and that official instigation of community development no longer is necessary.

CONSERVATIZING COMMUNITY DEVELOPMENT: THE HOUSING AND COMMUNITY DEVELOPMENT ACTS

The most recent major pieces of federal legislation dealing with community development are the Housing and Community Development Acts of 1974 and 1977. The 1974 act authorized $8.3 billion to be distributed over a three-year period by the Department of Housing and Urban Development (HUD). These payments were to be in the form of broad, flexible block grants to local governments. Included within these community development block grants were the programs of urban renewal, model cities, water and sewer facilities, open spaces, neighborhood facilities, rehabilitation loans, and public facility loans. Localities were required to give priority to programs that benefit urban families with low or moderate incomes, and the secretary of HUD could disapprove an application if he or she felt the proposed local use would be plainly inappropriate. Thus, the main features of the Housing and Community Development Act are that it (1) supplants the seven existing grants-in-aid programs just listed; (2) introduces a very simplified application procedure requiring HUD to act speedily on applications from large cities; (3) establishes a statutory formula for allocating community development funds instead of relying on competitive, "grantsmanship" procedures; (4) sets up a direct linkage between community development and housing policies; and finally, (5) contains no requirement that a locality has to match any funds received from the feds. The act is a truly innovative community development policy.

Congress was sufficiently pleased with the Housing and Community Development Act that it enacted a second one three years later. This act continued the innovations of the 1974 legislation, increased funding levels for community development, and initiated an innovative, $1.2 billion, three-year Urban Development Action Grant Program targeted at 2,100 decaying cities, largely in the Snowbelt. The Action Grant Program, designed primarily to upgrade cities physically and economically by "leveraging in" the private sector, is central to the Carter Administration's efforts to develop a comprehensive urban policy; in some respects it represents a return to the business-oriented tenets of Urban Renewal.

The trend of federal involvement in community development is increasingly conservative, particularly during the last fifteen years. When we look at the Economic Opportunity Act of 1964, an act which originally required the "maximum feasible participation" by the local citizens in all federally sponsored community development programs, we can perceive quite a change. Although the Housing and Community Development Act of ten years later was flexible and innovative, it nonetheless was directed more toward the needs of public bureaucrats and local politicians, rather than the citizenry. This is not to say that local public administrators are not able to meet the needs of their citizenries more readily than federal administrators, but rather that federal public policy for community development is increasingly aimed at the public official rather than the citizen. Whether or not this change will benefit local citizens more than past federal policies have remains a moot point, but the relationship between the federal government and American communities is increasingly one between Washington and city hall, rather than between Washington and individual citizens.

COMMUNITY POWER, POLITICS, AND PARTICIPATION

For the most part we have been discussing local elite policy makers and Washington's efforts to get local citizens to participate more actively in their own local politics. Initially this effort by the feds was noble, then it turned paternal, and now it seems to verge on the cynical. But do not the people participate in their own politics without help (or hindrance) from federal bureaucrats? Obviously, they do, and this participation can range from lethargic to fanatic. In this concluding section of the chapter, therefore, we consider the major forms of political participation in cities, suburbs, and towns: voting, lobbying, and legislating.

VOTING IN CITIES AND TOWNS? NOT LIKELY

The most obvious way of participating in politics is voting, and we have considered voting as "the ultimate democratic act" in Chapter 4. But because that discussion did not address voting in municipal elections, a word of elaboration is in order. Most notably, voter turnout is lowest in local elections; substantially fewer people turn out to vote in municipal elections than in state or national elections. We can expect from 50 percent to 65 percent of the nation's eligible voters to vote in a presidential election, but only between 25 to 50 percent to vote in a local election, and sometimes even fewer vote. Studies of voters in St. Louis and Dayton concluded that more than 25 percent of those eligible to vote in local elections have never voted at all. The studies also indicate that although those who do vote in local elections also are likely to vote in state and national elections, the reverse seldom holds true. In other words, a voter who votes for national and state officeholders does not necessarily vote for local ones.[23]

---

[23]John C. Bollens, ed., *Exploring the Metropolitan Community* (Berkeley, Calif.: University of California Press, 1961), p. 82; *Metropolitan Challenge* (Dayton: Metropolitan Community Studies, 1959), p. 231.

America's cities, as a rule, tend to favor nonpartisan elections (that is, elections with the candidate's party not listed on the ballot) over partisan elections. In cities with partisan elections about 50 percent of the eligible voters usually turn out, but in cities with nonpartisan elections 30 percent generally turn out. Table 11–1 indicates the mean percentage of voting adults by type of election, form of government, and city population. As it shows, most cities still hold their elections independently of all other races except elections for mayor and city council, and this probably reduces potential voter turnout. Table 11–2 shows that overall voter turnout in municipal elections had declined somewhat since 1962, but has especially declined in those cities that hold nonpartisan elections or that have a mayor–council form of government. That voter turnout in partisan elections is almost double that in nonpartisan ones is no doubt a product of higher popular interest in partisan political campaigns and the greater likelihood of a dedicated core of party workers getting out the vote.

TABLE 11–1 INDEPENDENT AND CONCURRENT MUNICIPAL ELECTIONS, 1962 AND 1975

			METHOD OF HOLDING LAST ELECTION					
	No. of cities reporting		*Independent (%)*		*With other local elections[1] (%)*		*With state or national election[2] (%)*	
Classification	*1962*	*1975*	*1962*	*1975*	*1962*	*1975*	*1962*	*1975*
Total, all cities	529	782	66	60	20	23	14	17
Population group								
Over 500,000	15	23	40	48	47	35	13	17
250,000–500,000	25	29	64	28	20	41	16	31
100,000–249,999	69	90	64	61	17	25	19	14
50,000– 99,999	142	211	66	61	20	29	14	10
25,000– 49,999	278	429	67	62	19	17	14	21
Form of government								
Mayor-council	170	289	59	59	20	20	21	21
Council-manager	306	439	68	60	20	25	12	15
Commission	53	54	72	66	19	18	9	16
Form of election								
Partisan	137	216	51	50	22	23	27	27
Nonpartisan	391	566	71	64	19	22	10	14
Unknown	1		...		...		...	

Leaders (...) indicate data are unknown.
[1]Excludes cities which also held elections concurrent with state or national elections.
[2]Includes cities which held elections concurrent with state or national and with other local races.

Source: Albert K. Karnig and B. Oliver Walter, "Municipal Elections: Registration, Incumbent Success, and Voter Participation," *1977 Municipal Yearbook* (Washington, D.C.: International City Management Association, 1977), p. 69. Reproduced by permission of the publisher.

TABLE 11-2 PERCENT OF ADULTS VOTING BY TYPE OF MUNICIPAL ELECTION: 1962 AND 1975

Classification	ALL CITY ELECTIONS				CITY ELECTIONS HELD WITH STATE OR NATIONAL RACES				CITY ELECTIONS HELD WITH OTHER LOCAL RACES[1]				CITY ELECTIONS HELD INDEPENDENT OF ALL OTHER ELECTIONS			
	No. of Cities Reporting		Median Voter Turnout (%)		No. of Cities Reporting		Median Voter Turnout (%)		No. of Cities Reporting		Median Voter Turnout (%)		No. of Cities Reporting		Median Voter Turnout (%)	
	1962	1975	1962	1975	1962	1975	1962	1975	1962	1975	1962	1975	1962	1975	1962	1975
Total, all cities	461	739	33	29	63	125	50	38	87	173	44	30	303	441	29	27
Population group																
Over 500,000	15	23	39	31	2	4	...	38	7	8	39	30	5	11	20	27
250,000–500,000	25	27	37	32	4	7	56	39	5	12	35	27	16	8	34	31
100,000–249,000	54	83	32	30	9	11	50	42	9	23	46	29	36	49	29	30
50,000– 99,999	124	200	33	27	17	20	51	36	24	59	51	31	82	121	29	24
25,000– 49,999	243	406	33	30	31	83	47	38	42	71	41	30	164	252	29	27
Form of government																
Mayor-council	137	271	50	38	31	54	51	38	28	59	50	35	78	158	44	39
Council-manager	281	419	27	24	29	64	43	38	54	105	35	26	193	250	23	22
Commission	41	49	38	34	3	7	33	38	5	9	57	43	32	33	38	31
Unknown[2]	2		...													
Form of election																
Partisan	109	201	50	36	31	52	51	40	22	48	53	37	56	101	41	34
Nonpartisan	350	538	30	27	32	73	43	38	65	125	35	27	246	340	27	25
Unknown	2		...										1		...	

[1]Excludes cities also holding elections concurrent with state or national elections.

Source: Albert K. Karnig and B. Oliver Walters, "Municipal Elections: Registration., Incumbent Success, and Voter Participation," *1977 Municipal Year Book* (Washington, D.C.: International City Management Association, 1977), p. 70. Reproduced by permission of the publisher.

This pattern of partisan/nonpartisan city elections parallels that of big city versus small city. Big cities in America are more apt to use partisan elections than small cities, and voter turnout in the larger cities for municipal elections is higher than that of small cities.

Overall, we may expect a *lower voter turnout* in cities that are located in the Midwest, West, and South; that have middle-class and homogeneous populations; that are small or medium-large in size; that hold their elections separately from state or national elections; and that have a council-manager form of government and nonpartisan electoral systems. *Higher voter turnout* can be expected in the East in cities that include many different kinds of ethnic and economic groups; in the big cities; in elections that are held simultaneously with state and national elections; in cities with a strong mayor form of government; and in cities with partisan elections and competitive party systems.[24] In contrast to national and state elections, the number of citizens registered to vote in local elections does not relate to percentage of voter turnout; there can be many potential voters registered in a city, but few real voters in a municipal election.[25]

VOTING IN SUBURBS: THE SMUGNESS FACTOR

The number of suburbanites who vote in their own suburban elections probably represents the bleakest tribute to democracy in the nation. The smaller, more homogeneous, richer, and more smugly self-satisfied a suburb is, the less likely its residents will vote. While the findings supporting this contention are mixed, a major investigation concluded that suburbs have the lowest overall participation rates of any six types of urban areas studied. Sidney Verba and Norman Nie held social status constant and categorized urban areas according to (1) villages or rural areas, (2) isolated towns, (3) isolated larger towns and non-metropolitan cities over 10,000 people, (4) small suburbs, (5) large suburbs and, of course, (6) central cities.[26] Participation was lowest in the small suburbs, a fact which Verba and Nie attributed to the absence of strong local ties. The authors argue that their data confirmed that "community" is declining as the nation urbanizes.

Additionally, as cities "reform"—as they adopt nonpartisan, at-large elections, eliminating the ward system—voting turnout declines. One investigation concluded that such reform movements discouraged political participation in American cities with more than 50,000 people.[27] Since suburbs

---

[24]Dye, *Politics in States and Communities*, pp. 272–273.

[25]Albert K. Karnig, "Registration and Municipal Voting: Putting First Things Second." *Social Science Quarterly* 55 (April, 1974), 159–166.

[26]Sidney Verba and Norman Nie, *Participation in America: Political Democracy and Social Equality* (New York: Harper & Row, 1972).

[27]Robert Lineberry and Edmund Fowler, "Reformism and Public Policies in American Cities." *American Political Science Review* 61 (September, 1967), 165–166.

often favor nonpartisan, at-large-elections, this "reform" factor may contribute to low voter turnout there as well. Hence, suburbanites are satisfied, and this very satisfaction may be attributed to the fact that they feel less of a need to get out into the political arena and brawl over policy issues. As a consequence, "suburbs are not beehives of political activity."[28]

SUBURBIA: GLORY HOLE OF THE GRAND OLD PARTY

If the metaphor about beehives and politics is accurate, one reason why is because about three-quarters of the nation's cities use the nonpartisan ballot, and most of them are suburbs with council–manager governments. Table 11–3 indicates that 71 percent of 1,884 suburbs responding to a national survey taken in the mid-1970s used a nonpartisan ballot.

Political scientists argue that the nonpartisan ballot increases the clout of the Republican party, and they point to the suburbs as their example in supporting this contention. Suburbs not only favor the nonpartisan ballot but have tended to vote Republican more heavily than Democratic. But the blade cuts two ways. In partisan elections, the Democrats have the edge: "Nonpartisan elections more often than not facilitate the elections of Republicans in cities which usually vote Democratic in partisan races."[29] Why this is so is unclear, although some have argued that Republicans are more adept in working behind the scenes through various "good government" committees that have no overt party affiliation.

In any event, "There is little question that suburbia has remained a major problem for the Democrats . . . just as it has remained a bastion for the Republicans except when they occasionally slip."[30] For an example of this occasional slip, consider one Robert Dill, who ran as a Republican for the County Executive of Nassau County in New York. Among other slips, Dill characterized the Democrats as "greasy, slimy pigs," and despite a two-to-one Republican registration ratio in Nassau county, Dill's Democratic opponent won the election. But such a win for the Democrats certainly was an exception in suburban, middle-class, largely white Nassau County.[31]

WHY ARE SUBURBS REPUBLICAN? TWO VIEWS

While it is by no means clear that the suburbs tend consistently to vote Republican in municipal elections, it nonetheless seems to be the case. Political scientists have evolved two theories as to why this may be true: the

---

[28]John Rehfuss, "Suburban Development and Governance." *Public Administration Review* 37 (January/February, 1977), 116.

[29]Willis D. Hawley, *Nonpartisan Elections and the Case for Party Politics* (New York: Wiley Interscience, 1973), pp. 165–166.

[30]Samuel Kaplan, *The Dream Deferred* (New York: Seabury, 1976), p. 140.

[31]*Ibid.*, pp. 144–145.

TABLE 11-3 NONPARTISAN OR PARTISAN ELECTORAL SYSTEMS IN CITIES, SUBURBS, AND TOWNS

Classification	No. of cities reporting (A)	NONPARTISAN		PARTISAN	
		No.	% of (A)	No.	% of (A)
Total, all cities	3,885	2,935	76	950	24
Population group					
Over 500,000	19	15	79	4	21
250,000–500,000	24	19	79	5	21
100,000–249,999	79	59	75	20	25
50,000–99,999	203	153	75	50	25
25,000–49,999	397	306	77	91	23
10,000–24,999	871	614	70	257	30
5,000–9,999	947	685	72	262	28
2,500–4,999	1,160	909	78	251	22
Under 2,500	185	175	95	10	5
Geographic region					
Northeast	906	347	38	559	62
North Central	1,222	996	82	226	18
South	1,106	964	87	142	13
West	651	628	96	23	4
Metro/city type					
Central	282	214	76	68	24
Suburban	1,884	1,341	71	543	29
Independent	1,719	1,380	80	339	20
Form of government					
Mayor-council	1,790	1,149	64	641	36
Council-manager	1,842	1,606	87	236	13
Commission	121	100	83	21	17
Town meeting	97	57	59	40	41
Rep. town meeting	35	23	66	12	34

Source: Robert P. Boynton, "City Councils: Their Role in the Legislative System," *1976 Municipal Year Book* (Washington, D.C.: International City Management Association, 1976), p. 69. Reproduced by permission of the publisher.

conversion theory and the transplantation theory. The *conversion theory*, as espoused by Robert C. Wood, argues that when inner city residents move "up" to suburbia, their desires to be accepted by the community overwhelm their traditional voting preferences. "Green grass, fresh air and new social status work their magic; class and ethnic appeals lose their potency . . . .The ownership of land, the symbol of community, these provide the sources for suburban loyalty and interest."[32] This becomes particularly true when the

---

[32]Robert C. Wood, *Suburbia: Its People and Their Politics* (Boston: Houghton Mifflin, 1959).

new suburbanite receives his or her property tax bill, or when the new suburbanite learns that the community may somehow be rezoned.

The other theory, that of *transplantation*, holds that those voters who move to the suburbs have always in fact been conservative, which is one reason why they moved to suburbia in the first place. When these "transplants" get to suburbia, they simply come out of the closet and vote Republican. In support of the transplantation theory, it does seem that, as migration from the central cities to the suburbs has increased, so the proportion of Republican votes has increased in the suburbs while declining in the central cities. In any case, the literature on the subject seems to indicate that, although the notion of "pure Republican suburbs" in contrast to "pure Democratic cities" has been overstated, the "typical suburb" (whatever that is) tends to vote Republican while the "typical central city" (ditto) tends to vote Democratic. Whether or not this inclination can be attributed to a conversion or transplantation theory is a moot point, but the tendency nonetheless is there.

CITIZENS AND CITY HALL

Regardless of how, why—and if—citizens vote in local elections, some of those citizens participate far more intensively in the local political scene than merely voting, and the most common form of participation beyond voting is confronting city hall and demanding change—in short, lobbying.

Perhaps the single best analysis of citizen involvement in local lobbying comes from the Urban Observatories studies of Albuquerque, Atlanta, Baltimore, Boston, Cleveland, Denver, Kansas City (Kansas), Kansas City (Missouri), Milwaukee, Nashville, and San Diego.

These surveys found that the membership figures for groups concerned with local problems ranged between 6 and 19 percent of the adult urban population. The major social factors that seem to explain membership in community action groups include social class, race, age, and length of residence in the community. High-income citizens were the most likely to belong to organized groups with an interest in city problems. Interestingly, the studies as a whole found that whether a person was white or black was negligible in accounting for participation in community action groups. However, upper-class blacks were much more likely than upper-class whites to belong to these kinds of organizations. People older than thirty-four were much more likely to belong to groups concerned with city problems; people between eighteen and thirty-four were considerably less likely to be members. People who had lived in the ten study cities for more than twenty years were found more frequently in such groups than were relative newcomers.[33]

---

[33]Steggert, *Community Action Groups*, pp. 4–8.

Whether a citizen was trustful or distrustful of city government had very little to do with whether or not he or she joined a community action group. On the other hand, a feeling of personal political effectiveness (which is quite different from level of political trust) played a very definite role in whether or not a citizen joined a group. If the citizen felt that he or she actually could change the government, or be effective in influencing government, then such a citizen was likely to join a community action group. People with no sense of political efficacy were much less likley to belong to a group concerned with city problems.

The urban interest groups were not simply paper tigers. Once formed, they did in fact play a powerful role when relevant issues arose. In one city studied it was found that, of the roughly two hundred groups with an expressed interest in influencing local government, all of them were politically active during the year. "A city's community action grouping may represent a minimum potential for organized political action. Most community organizations—including many that may appear to be only peripherally related to local government—can be politicized when the occasion requires."[34]

It was found that most of these groups concerned themselves with the issues of planning and development, usually involving housing, freeway construction, race relations, taxation and revenue, and education. The issue of race relations appeared to be paramount in the minds of citizens and opinion leaders alike. Generally speaking, the larger the minority population, the more race relations became a major theme in the politics of all issues.

How do the people in power feel about community action groups? Most elected representatives and appointed bureaucrats paid lip service to the concept of community involvement in the policy-making process, but expressed reservations about the ability of central city residents to run their own programs and usually insisted that elected officials had to have final decision responsibility. A few bureaucrats and politicians argued that most community action groups were dominated by a willful power elite who raised emotional issues merely to justify their own existence in their organizations. Those groups with which elected and appointed officials did choose to work generally represented a higher than average income level in the community and were perceived as being more conservative than other segments of the local population. "City officials did develop expectations about how citizen groups should act. To a degree, this involved the absence of conflict . . . .Group effectiveness may depend to a considerable degree on the ability to meet expectations of local government officials . . . . 'Successful' community action groups are cooperative rather than conflict oriented . . . .Such successful groups used their problem related information

---

[34]*Ibid.*, p. 6.

in simple and forthright ways, they made the kind of demands that could be politically acceded to."[35] In brief, those who go along, get along.

Even more pointed insofar as the impact of local lobbies is concerned is Betty A. Zisk's research on pressure group politics in the Bay Area. Zisk found that only 16 percent of 115 council members whom she interviewed did not perceive any groups whatever as "influential" in their city; 68 percent identified at least two groups as influential and some 17 percent were able to name five or more as influential.[36] The recognition of the roles that interest groups play is considerably higher among city council persons than among state legislators—indeed, more than twice as high.[37]

Both the California and Urban Observatories investigations imply that interest groups at the local level have a very different style than at the state level. Most lobbies in communities take such forms as citizen groups and improvement associations, rather than groups with economic interests. In Zisk's California study, 94 percent of the council members saw interest groups as largely a civic association phenomenon; only 28 percent identified economic interests as major pressure groups in their cities. This is not because economic interests are not concerned with local government, but because interest groups assume a different form at the local level than at the state and national level.[38]

Viewed as a whole, research indicates that the effective community action groups have made a dedicated effort to learn how "the system" of local government works and, indeed, this effort may be the major reason for their success. The reverse, however, is not necessarily true; local officials have made little effort to learn how community action groups work or what their concerns are. Given recent federal policies concerning community development, it is unlikely that local officials will be forced to learn much about their own local groups, since the national government is giving the money to the city halls and not to the neighborhoods.

CITY COUNCILMEMBERS AND CITY HALL

If it is true that certain kinds of community action groups know more about policy makers than vice versa, then it is also true that researchers know more about local policy makers than they know about local lobbyists.

Among the more significant kinds of policy makers at the local level are city councilmembers. Most American cities, almost 60 percent, elect councilmembers "at large." Roughly a quarter of all cities use a ward, or district, system, and 14 percent combine both systems. About half of all cities elect

[35]*Ibid.*, pp. 7–8.

[36]Betty A. Zisk, Heinz Eulau, and Kenneth Prewitt, "City Councilmen and the Group Struggle." *Journal of Politics* 27 (August, 1965), 633.

[37] Dye, *Politics in States and Communities,* p. 300.

[38]Zisk, Eulau, and Prewitt, "City Councilmen and the Group Struggle."

their councilmembers for four-year terms and most of the remaining cities elect councilmembers for two-year terms.

An unusual number of councilmembers are appointed to office. A major study undertaken of Bay Area cities found that almost 25 percent of the councilmembers interviewed were initially appointed to office, rather than elected.[39]

COUNCILMEMBERS, INCUMBENCY, AND AUTONOMY

Once in office, incumbency (or being an elected officeholder) is a major advantage in running for city councils. As Table 11–4 shows, 78 percent of the council incumbents in 1975 who ran for reelection won. Moreover, more incumbents are campaigning for reelection and winning than ever before. In 1962, 61 percent of the incumbent city councilmembers decided to run for reelection; by 1975 this proportion had risen to 72 percent.

---

[39]Kenneth Prewitt, *The Recruitment of Political Leaders: A Study of Citizen-Politicians* (Indianapolis: Bobbs-Merrill, 1970), p. 148.

TABLE 11–4 COUNCIL INCUMBENCY AND TURNOVER, 1962 and 1975

Classification	NO. OF CITIES REPORTING		INCUMBENTS SEEKING REELECTION (%)		INCUMBENTS REELECTED (%)		OFFICES FILLED BY INCUMBENTS (%)	
	1962	1975	1962	1975	1962	1975	1962	1975
Total, all cities	574	778	61	72	76	78	46	58
Population group								
Over 500,000	19	23	77	76	88	88	67	68
250,000–500,000	26	29	66	71	76	78	50	55
100,000–249,999	72	91	59	70	78	82	46	58
50,000– 99,999	150	205	60	70	71	82	43	57
25,000– 49,999	307	430	61	73	76	75	46	54
Form of government								
Mayor-council	186	280	63	73	78	80	49	59
Council-manager	322	446	63	69	73	77	46	53
Commission	58	52	71	81	74	70	52	57
Unknown	8		...		...		...	
Form of election								
Partisan	157	210	62	73	76	82	47	59
Nonpartisan	414	568	61	72	75	76	46	55
Unknown	3		...		...		...	

Source: Albert K. Karnig and B. Oliver Walter, "Municipal Elections: Registration, Incumbent Success, and Voter Participation," *1977 Municipal Yearbook* (Washington, D.C.: International City Management Association, 1977), p. 66. Reproduced by permission of the publisher.

Consequently, the percentage of council seats filled by reelected incumbents rose, too, from 46 percent in 1962 to 56 percent thirteen years later. Only in cities with a commission form of government did incumbents' election victories decline, and incumbents in partisan elections stood a better chance for reelection than their counterparts in nonpartisan elections. With the exception of the very biggest cities, incumbents tended to be retained in office "regardless of population size, governmental form, and electoral form."[40]

Of all elected lawmakers—members of Congress, state legislators, city commissioners, and councilmembers—the councilmembers are the most autonomous. When we realize that perhaps a quarter of all councilmembers are appointed rather than elected to their first term in office, that nearly three-fourths of incumbent councilmembers stand for reelection and that almost eight in ten of these win, that the median number of citizens voting for their councilmembers is less than 30 percent and falling, and, finally, that most councilmembers are never thrown out of office by a disaffected electorate but simply retire voluntarily[41]—then real questions about democratic accountability must be asked. City councilmembers, like their constituents, appear to have relatively little interest in their own political futures, and such a condition gives councilmembers considerable political leeway.

WHO ARE THE COUNCILMEMBERS?

A major study of local lawmakers conducted in 1971 surveyed all cities with more than five thousand people.[42] The study found that the average councilmember was likely to be a white male in his midforties who probably had not completed college, was middle-class, and had served four years or less on the city council. The more politically oriented mayor–council cities have fewer new members than the council–manager governments. Women clearly are underrepresented; only about 20 percent of all the cities surveyed reported one or more women as members of the city council. Women were particularly underrepresented in the smaller cities and in the South. Minority representation on the councils also was relatively low. The smaller the city (that is, the more "suburban" it was) the less likely it would be to have a nonwhite councilmember. In fact, of the 1,882 cities that responded to the survey, only 318 reported one or more nonwhite councilmembers, and only 550 councilmembers were from minority groups.

The data derived from massive studies of the Bay Area largely support the findings of the national study, but with some interesting variations. Bay

---

[40]Albert K. Karnig and B. Oliver Walter, "Municipal Elections: Registration, Incumbent Success, and Voter Participation." *1977 Municipal Yearbook.* (Washington, D.C.: International City Management Association, 1977), p. 66.

[41]Prewitt, *Recruitment of Political Leaders*, p. 148.

[42]Allan Klevit, "City Councils and Their Function in Local Government." *1972 Municipal Yearbook* (Washington, D.C.: International City Management Association, 1972), pp. 15–19.

Area councilmembers were likely to represent such economic interests as manufacturing and utilities (22 percent); banking, insurance, and accounting (21 percent); business and real estate (13 percent); law (10 percent); construction and trucking (16 percent); civil service and public administration (a somewhat surprisingly high 14 percent); and agriculture (4 percent). A number of members of city councils in the area were retired or were housewives. In the cities with nonpartisan elections, Republican councilmembers outnumbered Democrats by an 11 percent margin, even in the relatively liberal Bay Area; in recent years, the party registration rates for the Bay Area electorate have favored the Democratic party by almost a three-to-two ratio.[43] Such data correspond to other findings concerning the edge that Republicans seem to have when campaigning in nonpartisan elections.

GAMES COUNCILMEMBERS PLAY

City councilmembers are remarkably similar—they are middle-aged, middle-class, and have mid-level educations—but the roles that they play once they enter the city council can be quite varied. Zisk has given us a particularly useful categorization of these roles. She observes that there are the *pluralists*, or those who value interest groups, who perceive many groups, and who are "relatively sophisticated in regard to the group universe."[44] Then there are the *tolerants*, who may be one of three types: those who are neutral toward groups; those who have strong feelings one way or the other about groups, but demonstrate both low levels of perception of how many groups exist and low levels of sophistication about how they work; and third, those who esteem groups but are either unsophisticated in their views or perceive relatively few groups. Finally, there are the *antagonists*, who are sophisticated in their view of groups and demonstrate a high perception of how many groups there are, but who reject groups as not being legitimate.

These types of roles also correspond to how councilmembers interact with each other and their colleagues in city hall, notably the mayor or city manager. Pluralists, like those in the other roles, seek out city officials as their main source of advice when making policy, but they are less likely than other types of councilmembers to depend on the expertise of the city manager and his or her staff. The pluralist prefers to interact with representatives of interest groups. Antagonists are relatively oblivious to requests or contacts from groups, and they rarely seek advice from groups. Antagonists get their advice in making policy from city officials and "influential individuals." Tolerants, as might be expected, are in a midway position; they are less likely than the pluralists but more likely than the

---

[43]Heinz Eulau and Kenneth Prewitt, *Labyrinths of Democracy* (Indianapolis: Bobbs-Merrill, 1973), pp. 626–628.

[44]Betty A. Zisk, *Local Interest Politics: A One-Way Street* (Indianapolis: Bobbs-Merrill, 1973), p. 19.

TABLE 11–5 RELATION BETWEEN INTEREST GROUP ROLE ORIENTATION OF CITY COUNCILMEMBERS AND SEEKING OF GROUP SUPPORT*

	INTEREST GROUP ROLE ORIENTATION		
	Pluralist (N=100)	*Tolerant* (N=252)	*Antagonist* (N=30)
Percentage of Councilmen Who Seek Group Support	57	27	10
Type of Groups from Whom Support Is Sought:		Percentage of Total Responses (N=196)	
Chamber of Commerce, Jaycees	21%	25%	—†
Homeowners groups, taxpayers	25	23	
Service clubs	17	8	
Merchants groups	7	8	
Women's groups	5	5	
All other, including *ad hoc* organizations (no category was mentioned by more than 4% of the respondents)	25	31	
	100%	100%	
Kinds of Support Sought:		(N=131)	
Help at hearings or in trying to sell councilman's position to others	61%	55%	—†
Information on public attitudes, on potential impact of proposal on groups	19	12	
Facts, expertise, background information	6	9	
Effort to convince group of correctness of councilman's position	14	24	
	100%	100%	

*The question: "Before a Council decision is made, do you ever actively seek support from any of the groups you have mentioned? (IF YES): What kind of support do you seek? May I ask from which groups you have sought support?"

†We have not computed percentages for the responses of the three Antagonists who seek support, since figures computed on such a small base are misleading and meaningless.

Source: Betty H. Zisk, *Local Interest Politics: A One-Way Street* (Indianapolis: Bobbs-Merrill, 1973), p. 57.

antagonists to look for help or advice from groups. Interestingly, tolerants are the least likely of all councilmembers to identify representatives of special economic interests as influential people when they are making their decisions, and they are the most likely to base their decisions on advice from the public and the city staff. Zisk concludes that while tolerants "believe in general terms of accessibility to the public, their conception of local politics appears the very antithesis of an interest based bargaining process or 'group struggle.'"[45]

Table 11–5 summarizes Zisk's findings in terms of how councilmembers perceive pressures at city hall. Steggert's feeling that city officials should learn more about community action groups, while well taken, would seem to be most welcomed by the pluralist type of city councilmember. Antagonists and tolerants, according to Zisk's research, would not be particularly receptive to learning anything about community action groups (or, for that matter, any other kind of groups) in their own communities. Thus, while the ways of democracy, at least in urban areas, are labyrinthian, the essence of urban democracy is simple power.

CONCLUSION: PATERNALISM, POWER, AND PARTICIPATION

"Simple power?" Hardly. The exercise of power, though on occasion raw and brutal, is never simple, and nowhere is the complexity of political power more in evidence than in America's local governments. The complexity of community politics takes many forms, and in this chapter we have sketched only the more obvious ones: the concept of community in political terms, the traditional research on elitist and pluralist patterns of community power, the feds' involvement in "developing" community power, and how people participate politically in their own communities.

It appears from our review that community power is temporary and held by precious few for any length of time. Controlled wholly by no single group, power at the grassroots is elusive, rolling to and from politicians, pressure groups, and even voters. Still, political power on occasion can be directed, and we consider next the persons most likely to provide that direction: the political "bosses," mayors, and city managers.

---

[45]*Ibid.*, p. 58.

CHAPTER

THE URBAN
EXECUTIVE:
BOSSES, MAYORS,
AND MANAGERS

Urban politicians are among the most colorful in the country, and in this chapter we sample some of the more vivid varieties of local politicos, as well as describing the political patterns and styles of the urban chief executive.

ON TOP IN THE BIG CITY: BOSS RULE IN CITY AND SUBURB
BIG CITY BOSSES

Few topics are more entertaining in American politics than political bosses. Often they carry nicknames in the style of organized crime. Around the turn of the century, many such figures were well-known nationally: "Czar" Martin Lomasney of Boston, "Big Tim" Sullivan of the Bowery, the "Honorable" William M. Tweed of New York, "Honest John" Kelley also of New York, the "Genial Doctor" Albert A. Ames of Minneapolis, "Judge" Israel W. Durham of Philadelphia, "Duke" Edwin H. Vare also of Philadelphia, "Old Boy" George B. Cox of Cincinnati, "Old Man" Hugh McLaughlin of Brooklyn, "King" James McManes of Philadelphia, and "the Mystery Man of Chicago," a pseudonym for one Frederick Lundin, also known as "the Silent Boss" or "the Poor Swede."

In his fascinating study, *City Bosses*, Harold Zink analyzed extensively twenty of the most significant bosses in the United States around the turn of the century. Half were of Irish stock; five, in fact, had been born in Ireland. Most rose from abject poverty or extreme hardship, thirteen did not get beyond grammar school, and seven had been leaders of juvenile gangs. When they made it to the top, many lived in high style. The Honorable Tweed maintained a small palace on Fifth Avenue, went sailing in his own steam yacht, and kept his horses in a mahogany stable inlaid with silver. Two city bosses, in fact, made the *Social Register* and Tweed "even shared the hospitality of [Tycoon James] Fisk's mistress."[1] Such communalism was not always such fun; Tweed had also shared a prison with his fellow inmates at one period in his life.

The bosses got into politics in different ways. A quarter of them entered politics through their service in volunteer fire departments, a couple entered as young lawyers looking for a practice, and some simply wanted to protect other business interests. They generally took about twenty years to attain the singular status of a Big City Boss, and most were well into their forties by that time. An ability to brawl in bars played a major role in their rise to prominence, and connections with major corporations and the criminal underworld were helpful in retaining their power. Most of the bosses stayed

---

[1] Harold Zink, *City Bosses in the United States* (New York: Duke University Press, 1968), p. 29. Initially published in 1930.

in office until they died, "Reform movements [did] not seem to play much of a part in breaking city bosses, in spite of the fact that such movements have dogged the footsteps of almost all of them."[2]

On the whole, the city bosses were known for their "generosity to the poor, loyalty to obedient henchmen, reasonable emphasis on high standards of personal morals, and interest in religion. A large proportion labored with persistence, displayed more than ordinary courage, and possessed intensely practical minds." Many "found it necessary as mere children to assume a burden as bread winner because of the premature death of a father or because of his general shiftlessness."[3]

BOSSISM IN DECLINE

In short, big city bosses were products of their times. It also seems that they are a declining breed. The big influxes of new immigrants to the big cities no longer arrive; state and federal welfare agencies supply many of the services that the old precinct captains used to provide; patronage jobs are no longer as attractive as the country becomes increasingly middle class and as the civil service undercuts many patronage positions. The "good government" movement is the new political machine of the middle class, and it has displaced (and is displacing) the traditional "ward heeler."

A MINI-RESURRECTION: BOSSISM IN SUBURBIA

Although the big city political boss and his machine seem to be in decline, the elements of boss rule and the machine are still present in America, if on a vastly more decentralized plane. Counties, small towns, and suburbs often seem to still retain the elements of boss rule.

A present-day example is that of Joseph M. Margiotta, Republican County Chairman of Nassau County, New York. Margiotta acquired his position as a result of peculiar political circumstances in Nassau County and of the national Republican presidential debacle in 1964. While the Democrats fought over issues, Margiotta tightened his reins on the Republican workers, virtually all of whom were there by dint of patronage, ultimately rebuilding the Republican machine in Nassau County. By 1970, the Republicans were well ensconced in Nassau's driver's seat, and their regained power position derived as much from Margiotta's shrewd use of patronage as from any other factor. The old ways can still work.

By the mid-1970s, Margiotta raised and spent at least $1 million every year (in contrast to about $50,000 by the Democratic county organization), and some of this money was devoted to his own $40,000 salary and a

---

[2]*Ibid.*, p. 59.

[3]*Ibid.*, pp. 63–64.

227

The urban
executive:
bosses,
mayors, and
managers

chauffeured Cadillac. In addition to his salary and expense account as Republican County Chairman, Magiotta garnered well over $50,000 in salary alone in New York as a state legislator, plus his fees from a law practice. Nassau's 17,000 county and town employees contributed roughly 1 percent of their salaries to Margiotta's organization, the 971 election districts contributed an average of $400 each, and each Republican leader contributed about $6,000. Republican leaders in Nassau County also supported a $500-a-plate dinner, a $125 per guest cocktail party, and a $125 per person "Joseph M. Margiotta Invitational Golf Tournament." Of course, Margiotta gave as well as he got. Approximately 75 percent of the 1,800 Republican committeemen were on the state, county, or town payroll. Also on it were Margiotta's sister, mother-in-law, and sister-in-law. This is a sizable political army, and Margiotta was able to mobilize it. The Republicans, sustained major losses in 1974 in Nassau County but they were able to stage a comeback of no mean proportions in the 1975 off-year local elections, because the average Nassau voter was not that interested in politics and the Republicans were well organized.[4]

"HIZZONER DA MARE"

Interestingly, political bosses rarely are mayors. Zink's study of almost fifty years ago confirmed this: Although all twenty big city bosses had held some sort or elective office, relatively few were mayors.

THE MAYOR AND THE POLITICS OF PROSCRIBED POWER

Political bosses may avoid this job because mayors often are limited in their formal powers—indeed, they are more limited than most governors. More than a quarter of the nation's mayors, for example, are not elected directly by the voters of their cities; they are elected instead by members of the city's council or commission. The average American city limits its mayor to a two-year tenure. In 8 percent of all cities, the mayor has no voting power whatever; he may not even break ties among his own commissioners or councilmembers. In 43 percent of the cities, the mayor may vote only to break a tie, and in more than a third of the cities, the mayor has no veto power whatever.

Generally speaking, mayor–council cities tend to give their mayors more formal powers than do commission or council–manager cities. Almost 60 percent of mayor–council cities, for example, permit the mayor to veto all measures *in toto*, to item veto, or to veto selected portions of an ordinance.[5]

---

[4]Samuel Kaplan, *The Dream Deferred* (New York: Seabury, 1975), pp. 141–147.

[5]Robert P. Boynton, "City Councils: Their Role in the Legislative System." *Municipal Yearbook, 1976* (Washington D.C.: International City Management Association, 1978), pp. 71–73.

Tables 12–1 and 12–2 delineate mayoral terms of office and veto power by city size, region, urban type, and form of government.

MAYORAL STYLE: "KING RICHARD" AND "THE WHITE KNIGHT"

When all is said and done, relatively few cities in America give their chief executive significant formal powers. Consequently, the question arises as to whether or not a talented mayor really needs formal powers to have his way in a city.

"Boss:" the mayor as machine manager. As we noted in Chapter 9, the late Mayor Richard Daley of Chicago assumed "power" under a weak executive form of government, yet from 1953 when he was elected chairman of the Cook County Democratic Party (he was not elected mayor of Chicago until 1955) until his death in 1976, no one questioned his virtually absolute authority in Chicago.[6] Many have said that Daley was a "throwback" and, indeed, he paralleled remarkably the characteristics of the turn-of-the-century big city bosses analyzed by Zink. He was born of first-generation Irish parents, was a Roman Catholic, went to work in the stockyards, and only twenty years later took over the Chicago City Council.

"King Richard," as he was called in Chicago, often played political kingmaker. In 1960, Daley scrounged enough votes from his machine-dominated "river wards" to deliver Illinois and the presidency to John Kennedy. In the mid-1960s, the Reverend Martin Luther King, Jr., called Chicago "the most segregated city in the North," and roused the boss's ire. When King was murdered, and riots by blacks erupted in Chicago as a result, Daley ordered police to kill arsonists and to shoot "to maim or cripple" looters. As one black noted about Richard Daley, "I think that one of the real problems he has with Negroes is understanding that the Irish are no longer the out-ethnic group," and this assessment certainly seemed to apply on occasion.[7] During the infamous 1968 National Convention of the Democratic Party held in Chicago, Daley, fighting both liberal Democrats and "Yippies" in his home city, stood up in the convention hall, shook his fist at Connecticut Senator Abraham Ribicoff, and ordered all power cut off to the delegates' microphones. He then turned his police on the antiwar demonstrators in the streets, and staged what appeared to be one of the least spontaneous political demonstrations in American political history—which was, of course, pro-Daley, with neatly printed placards stating "I Love Mayor Daley" being carried around the convention hall by members of his organization.

Daley also had some endearing qualities, the most notable being his

---

[6]Unless noted otherwise, the discussion of Daley is drawn from: David Halberstam, "Daley of Chicago." *Harper's Magazine* 237 (No. 1419), 25–36.

[7]Associated Press, December 21, 1976, syndicated nationally.

TABLE 12–1 MAYORS' TERMS OF OFFICE

| Classification | LIMITATIONS ON NUMBER OF CONSECUTIVE TERMS MAYOR MAY SERVE | | | TERM OF OFFICE FOR MAYOR, IN YEARS | |
	No. of cities reporting (A)	Yes No.	% of (A)	No. of cities reporting	Mean
Total, all cities	3,713	109	3	3,587	2
Population group					
Over 500,000	18	2	11	19	3
250,000–500,000	24	4	17	23	3
100,000–249,999	79	6	8	79	2
50,000–99,999	199	14	7	193	2
25,000–49,999	385	19	5	377	2
10,000–24,999	818	32	4	792	2
5,000–9,999	907	12	1	878	2
2,500–4,999	1,118	14	1	1,079	2
Under 2,500	165	6	4	147	2
Geographic region					
Northeast	769	12	2	699	3
North Central	1,205	26	2	1,186	2
South	1,104	35	3	1,095	2
West	635	36	6	607	2
Metro/city type					
Central	279	26	9	275	2
Suburban	1,790	56	3	1,736	2
Independent	1,644	27	2	1,576	2
Form of government					
Mayor-council	1,783	36	2	1,773	3
Council-manager	1,756	71	4	1,654	2
Commission	120	1	1	117	3
Town meeting	42	0	...	36	2
Rep. town meeting	12	1	8	7	2

Note: Leaders (...) indicate not applicable.

Source: Robert P. Boynton, "City Councils: Their Role in the Legislative System," *Municipal Yearbook, 1976* (Washington, D.C.: International City Management Association, 1976), p. 71. Reproduced by permission of the publisher.

almost uncanny ability to mangle the English language. For example: "We will reach greater and greater platitudes of achievment"; or "They have vilified me, they have crucified me, yes, they have even criticized me!" or "The policeman is here to preserve disorder"; or "I resent these insinuendos." The press loved it.[8]

_____

[8]United Press International, December 21, 1976, syndicated nationally.

TABLE 12-2 MAYOR'S VETO POWER

Classification	MAYOR HAS AUTHORITY TO VETO COUNCIL PASSED MEASURES			WHEN MAYOR MAY EXERCISE VETO[1]											
	No. of cities reporting (A)	Yes No. (B)	% of (A)	All actions of council No.	% of (B)	Ordinances only No.	% of (B)	Specific sections of ordinances No.	% of (B)	Appropriations only No.	% of (B)	Specific sections of appropriations No.	% of (B)	Resolutions and other No.	% of (B)
Total, all cities	3,592	1,254	35	592	47	540	43	50	4	63	5	40	3	114	9
Population group															
Over 500,000	19	14	74	3	21	8	57	3	21	4	29	1	7	4	29
250,000–500,000	24	13	54	5	38	5	38	0	...	0	...	2	15	3	23
100,000–249,999	79	36	46	21	58	13	36	2	6	2	6	3	8	4	11
50,000–99,999	196	65	33	29	45	26	40	3	5	1	2	0	...	10	15
25,000–49,999	385	110	29	56	51	46	42	4	4	7	6	7	6	8	7
10,000–24,999	806	273	34	120	44	126	46	16	6	21	8	12	4	29	11
5,000–9,999	887	350	39	148	42	168	48	12	3	14	4	4	1	30	9
2,500–4,999	1,044	369	35	196	53	140	38	9	2	13	4	10	3	26	7
Under 2,500	152	24	16	14	58	8	33	1	4	1	4	1	4	0	...
Geographic region															
Northeast	719	339	47	115	34	198	58	12	4	18	5	4	1	17	5
North Central	1,163	549	47	288	52	206	38	30	5	31	6	29	5	61	11
South	1,073	264	25	148	56	86	33	6	2	10	4	6	2	29	11
West	637	102	16	41	40	50	49	2	2	4	4	1	1	7	7

Metro/city type															
Central	281	114	41	49	43	50	44	8	7	7	6	7	6	22	19
Suburban	1,747	597	34	261	44	285	48	26	4	30	5	18	3	47	8
Independent	1,564	543	35	282	52	205	38	16	3	26	5	15	3	45	8
Form of government															
Mayor-council	1,714	1,010	59	506	50	412	41	45	4	53	5	33	3	91	9
Council-manager	1,723	223	13	76	34	118	53	5	2	10	4	6	3	23	10
Commission	114	18	16	10	56	8	44	0	...	0	...	1	6	0	...
Town meeting	32	2	6	0	...	1	50	0	...	0	...	0	...	0	...
Rep. town meeting	9	1	11	0	...	1	100	0	...	0	...	0	...	0	...

Note: Leaders (...) indicate not applicable or less than 0.5%.
1Percentages do not add to 100% owing to multiple responses allowed.

Source: Robert P. Boynton, "City Councils: Their Role in the Legislative System." *Municipal Yearbook, 1976* (Washington, D.C.: International City Management Association, 1976), p. 73. Reproduced by permission of the publisher.

Was Daley "good" or "bad" for Chicago? That question, perhaps, will never be answered. He does not seem to have been personally corrupt, and lived modestly in the neighborhood where he grew up. Although many of his close aides were convicted of corruption, Daley never was. When pressed by reporters on such improprieties, Daley replied that his mother once told him that, in such situations, he should "pin the mistletoe on my coattails."[9]

Some have argued that Daley was successful where social reformers may have failed, that he made Chicago "work." And no doubt Daley had a hand, and a creative one, in his extensive urban renewal of Chicago, which resulted in some of the most magnificent architecture in the country today. Although Chicago unlike New York was in relatively sound fiscal shape, Chicago in fact paid no welfare bills, supported no schools, and paid only a small portion of the cost of its own mass transit system; the Transit Authority and the Board of Education of Chicago, both controlled by the Daley machine, were always under severe fiscal restraints.

King Richard was a pragmatist who understood power and man's corruptability. He was unique as a mayor, boss, and party chairman. His fifty-member city council, which occasionally had a political spread of forty-nine Democrats and one Republican, was "frequently described as a trained dog act" and Daley was not above turning off an alderman's microphone when he disagreed with his statement during city council meetings. "In sharing the power that fueled his political organization, he resembled a shark with a chunk of meat."[10] But even Daley recognized that the day of the big city boss was gone or going fast.

"Mr. Clean:" the mayor as broadway. Representing quite the opposite of Boss Daley in virtually every conceivable way was Mayor John V. Lindsay of New York.[11] While Daley was a Democrat and a machine politician who was less than elegant in his appearance and manner, Lindsay was a Republican, a reformer, and, above all, a sophisticate. As a resident of Chicago who was a transplanted New Yorker once observed, "We think of reform as being an effete Easterner idea."[12]

John Lindsay as mayor was a reformer to his very soles. The son of a wealthy lawyer, an Episcopalian educated at Yale, he was pure WASP. He grew up as a great admirer of Mayor Fiorello LaGuardia, one of New York's most vigorous reform mayors.

Between 1958 and 1966, Lindsay was a Congressman from Manhattan's "silk stocking" district, and in his last congressional race in 1964, he received an incredible 71 percent of the vote, despite the presence of Barry Goldwater on the ballot as the national candidate for president, whom his

---

[9]Associated Press, December 21, 1976, syndicated nationally.

[10]*Ibid.*

[11]Unless noted otherwise, the discussion of Lindsay is drawn from: Larry L. King, "Lindsay of New York." *Harper's Magazine* 237 (No. 1419), 37–44.

[12]Quoted in: Halberstam, "Daley of Chicago," p. 27.

233

The urban
executive:
bosses,
mayors, and
managers

district voted against. As a Republican reform mayor in a city where at the time of his election, registered Democrats outnumbered Republicans 2,-400,000 to 700,000, he was known as "Pretty Boy," "The White Knight," "Destiny's Tot," or "Mr. Clean"—perhaps fitting appellations for one who called New York "Fun City."

Fun City was never that much fun. As Lindsay testified in 1966 before a congressional subcommittee, 2 million white residents, mostly in middle- and high-income groups, had moved away from New York during the twenty years prior to his administration. And 750,000 blacks and Puerto Ricans, who for the most part were very poor people, had moved in, expanding their ratios in the city's population from 10 percent in 1945 to 25 percent two decades later. Almost 15 percent of the entire city budget was devoted to welfare alone, excluding hospital, health services, and poverty costs; 2 million people in New York were living below the poverty line when Lindsay became mayor.

Lindsay's outstanding characteristics as mayor were his style and his desire to get out in the streets and mingle with the people, particularly poor people. "More than any other New York Mayor (including the chesty LaGuardia) he has gone into the streets to seek out his constituency. In so doing, he has disdained protection and exposed himself to as many dangers as the late Robert Kennedy . . . .Lindsay is the only metropolitan mayor credited with almost single-handedly cooling the black ghettos through what Bill Buckley, the conservative icon, disdains as street walking." As a leader of a militant black organization called the Harlem Mau-Maus stated, "Lindsay helps. He'll leave Gracie Mansion on five minutes' notice and he'll talk to the bottom of the barrel."

In contrast to Boss Daley of Chicago, Lindsay argued that "We are not going to shoot children in New York City," but also was aware that "New York or Chicago or any other big city could ignite tomorrow. There are incidents that could act as a trigger every day. If New York blows first, the press will charge that my 'soft' policies failed. If it happens in Chicago first, they'll write Daley's 'hard line' tactics were at fault. In either case, it will be an over-simplification and unfair."

Lindsay did have some successful accomplishments. He reduced fifty-one departments to ten in the city of New York. He broke up what was known as the "Irish Mafia"that had long ruled police precinct houses, and he increased the police force substantially at the same time. He enacted the nation's strongest air pollution law up to that time, closed Central Park to Sunday traffic, and initiated tough towing programs for illegally parked vehicles. He established "Little City Halls" in various neighborhoods, a program that got him into some trouble with his own city council, since it was seen as a ploy to establish his own personal political organization; unlike his counterpart in Chicago, Lindsay had to deal with a recalcitrant city council that was predominantly controlled by the opposition party.

Given Lindsay's genuine concern for the poor and dispossessed in New York, he may have been an ideal mayor for the tumultuous 1960s, just as one of his predecessors, Jimmy Walker, was fitting for the Depression-racked 1930s. While the infamous "Beau James" was no reform mayor, the style that he brought to the mayor's office in New York was certainly similar to Lindsay's. Consider the following incident, when Jimmy Walker greeted his first crowned head to the city:

Queen Marie of Romania was the first "crowned head" greeted by Walker. Whether or not Her Majesty was charmed by Walker's speech of welcome or by two incidents which happened more or less off the record, the still beautiful Queen did not say. One of these occurred while Jim was attempting to pin a medal upon her coat. The lady from the Balkans owned a splendid, although somewhat buxom figure, and the place where the medal properly belonged—high up, and a bit to the left—suggested, among other things, a delicate target for a carelessly directed pin.

"Your Majesty," Jim said, "I've never stuck a queen, and I hesitate to do so now."

"Proceed, Your Honor," replied the Queen. "The risk is mine."

"And such a beautiful risk it is, Your Majesty," Jim said in a low voice.

The Queen and her royal party left New York for Washington at the conclusion of the City Hall ceremonies. Although it was a raw October day, Marie was seated in an open-top automobile so that citizens along the way from City Hall to Pennsylvania Station might look upon a reigning monarch.

Jim sat at Her Majesty's left in the touring car. As the royal automobile was passing a newly begun skyscraper on Seventh Avenue, her lap robe slipped from her knees. Walker leaned over to adjust the robe. At this, one of the riveters perched on a girder of the partly completed steel framework of the building cupped his hands and called out, "Hey, Jimmy! Have you made her yet?"

Just how much slang Queen Marie understood I am not prepared to say. She turned an inquiring glance upon her host and said sweetly, "You Americans are quite droll, don't you think?"

"When you travel across our great country," Jim hedged, "you will come upon many interesting evidences of our democracy."

"Everyone seems to know you in this great city," she observed.

"Yes, Madam," Walker replied, "and some of them know me very well indeed."[13]

While all mayors have style, few mayors have style like New York mayors.

---

[13]Gene Fowler, *Beau James: The Life and Times of Jimmy Walker* (New York: Viking Penguin, 1949), pp. 184–186.

MAYORS AND THE POLITICS OF URBAN RACISM:
THE OFAY OF L.A.

Racism, like reform, has its own politics, and while the examples of racial politics at the state and local levels are numerous, one of the more illustrative examples of racial politics occurred in Los Angeles in 1969 and 1973.

"Mayor Sam." Mayor Sam Yorty, known to most Angelinos as "the Little Giant" and self-proclaimed as "America's Greatest Mayor," had served as mayor of Los Angeles since 1961. Born in Lincoln, Nebraska, into a family of strong Populist leanings, "Mayor Sam" moved to L.A. at the age of eighteen in 1927. His initial politics were ultraliberal and he espoused a number of share-the-wealth plans that were popular in the 1930s. But, by 1939, his tune had changed substantially and, by the time he was mayor, a favorite device of his was to call everyone in sight a communist. Municipal-level communism is a ridiculous charge on its face and, when one probes deeper, it is still ridiculous. Nevertheless, it seemed to work for Mayor Sam, at least most of the time. "Sam Yorty's favorite campaign issue has been anti-communism . . . .If an opponent is more liberal than he is, Yorty can credibly paint him as backed by radicals. If the opponent is more conservative, then Yorty responds that he is a victim of a communist smear attack."[14] Yorty also established a reputation for launching personal attacks during a campaign, calling former governor Pat Brown first, "minor league" then a "machine" politician. Ronald Reagan became an "amateur," and George McGovern was "anti-American" and he "spoke like Hanoi."[15]

The black challenge: "Bradley power?" These kinds of campaign tactics reached full flower in the mayoral campaigns of 1969 and 1973 in Los Angeles, when one Tom Bradley, a black, ran for mayor. Bradley had emigrated to California in the 1920s and had served as an officer in the Los Angeles Police Department for twenty-one years before he ran for mayor. By studying at night he received a law degree from Southwestern University and, in 1963, with Yorty's endorsement, Bradley ran for the Los Angeles City Council and won easily in his largely black district. He and two others were the first black men in Los Angeles's history to be elected to serve on that city's council.

In 1969, Yorty ran an insipid campaign for mayor and, much to everyone's surprise, Bradley garnered nearly 42 percent of the vote (Yorty received 26 percent, the other votes were divided among some minor contenders). A run-off election was required, and Yorty, seeing these results, stiffened his resolve and his organization for the second try. Bradley was

---

[14]John C. Bollens and Grant B. Geyer, *Yorty: Politics of a Constant Candidate* (Pacific Palisades, Calif.: Palisades, 1973), p. 214.
[15]*Ibid.,* p. 138.

235

and is a moderate who had stated that "I believe the way that you change the system is from the inside. Separatism won't work."[16] Nevertheless, Yorty launched a consciously racist campaign, stating that Bradley was backed by "extremist militants." Ludicrously, but effectively, Yorty charged that Bradley, despite his twenty-one years on the L.A. police force, was "anti-police" because he favored citizen review of police actions. In spite of the fact that Yorty was a Democrat, he based most of his campaign organization on talented campaign managers furnished by conservative Republican Ronald Reagan, then governor of California. Bumper stickers mysteriously appeared during the campaign printed with the upraised black fist, and proclaiming "Bradley power"; pamphlets were distributed in largely white neighborhoods urging voters to make Los Angeles "a black city."[17] Bradley evidently had no connection with any of these distributions and Yorty took no public credit for them. Yorty did take credit, however, for putting up posters inquiring, "Will your family be safe?" and "Will your city be safe with this man?" "Sam wanted to make sure that whites were universally aware of Bradley's blackness."[18]

Yorty won—in part because of his smear tactics, but also because of a seasoned and tough campaign organization. Also Bradley unwisely dwelt on such issues as corruption in city hall and environmental pollution, when the "real" issues in Los Angeles that year were, according to the polls, street crime and school-related issues such as busing. And one must recall that the late 1960s were a period of racial disturbances across the country. This fact could not have been lost on the white voters of Los Angeles, who were being exhorted by Yorty troops not to vote for an "extremist group that put up a black man for the purpose of polarizing the community."[19] Still, Bradley did all right, winning nearly 47 percent of the vote to Yorty's 53 percent.

In 1973, Bradley tried for the mayor's office again, but Bradley had spent the four intevening years softening up the L.A. voters, emphasizing his moderate racial position and his experience in fighting crime. While he still spoke about smog and mass transit, crime and his law-and-order position became a major theme. Yorty resurrected his smear tactics, but this time Bradley was both better organized and better financed, with money coming in from national contributors. Bradley trounced Yorty in 1973 with 56 percent of the vote. Most estimates claim that he won almost one-half of the white vote and virtually all of the black vote in the city.

Since becoming mayor, Bradley has established himself as a competent and low-key chief executive. In 1974 he was elected president of the National League of Cities.

---

[16]*Ibid.*, p. 165.
[17]*Ibid.*
[18]*Ibid.*, p. 166.
[19]*Ibid.*, p. 167.

Reform and race, as exemplified by Daley, Lindsay, Yorty, and Bradley, always have been central themes in American urban politics. They are dramatic and emotional themes and are not often present in any overt way in discussions of our final type of urban chief executive, the city manager. The city manager exemplifies the politics of administration. It is a subtle and quiet form of politics, with its own way of getting things done.

THE POLITICS OF SMOOTH: THE URBAN MANAGER

Because city managers, or chief administrative officers, in cities and towns are appointed rather than elected, they have a relatively unusual way to achieve policy goals. City management is a quiet profession in a chaotic urban world, and only comparatively recently have political scientists begun to appreciate the policy impact that the city manager has. Indeed, it has been argued that city managers and their bureaucracies are the real policy makers in urban areas and the magnitude of the manager's purview is impressive, with more than half of all American cities, including some of the nation's largest, using the council–manager plan exclusively.

A PROFESSIONALIZATION OF POLITICS?

Traditionally, city managers were drawn from the engineering disciplines, but now a substantial majority have degrees in the social sciences and mostly in political science or public administration. The trends indicate that the field of city management is professionalizing as never before and that academic qualifications in the area are increasingly going to be a prerequisite for entry.

During the 1960s, the role of the professional city manager came under fire. When cities exploded in race riots, the thrust of the criticism was, and still is, that the profession of city management is overly technical, and in its intellectual thrust it has defined out vital political variables. "Technocrats," as exemplified by city managers, have little sensitivity to the human problems of cities and little understanding of the plight of minority groups, unlike such mayors as John Lindsay of New York. The National Advisory Commission on Civil Disorders stated in the late 1960s that "city manager government has eliminated an important political link between city government and low-income residents."[20] The argument continues that city managers are more likely than a life-long "pol" to have a technocratic "engineering mentality" and that, if true, this mental set could exacerbate political tensions in cities.

This line of thinking assumes that administrators do only "administration" and politicians do only "politics." Such an assumption is rarely accurate.

---

[20] *The National Advisory Commission on Civil Disorders* (New York: Bantam Books, 1968), p. 287.

The field of public administration long ago recognized that it is difficult if not impossible to distinguish what is administration and what is politics. It accepts as legitimate the concept that public administrators do political things and make political decisions.

Empirical investigation seems to indicate that although city managers are certainly involved in both politics and administration, their political style is very different from that of an elected chief executive. A study of Florida city managers found that in cities where politics maintained a relatively low profile and low levels of conflict, city managers lasted longer in their jobs; where political conflict was high and factions were obvious, city managers lasted less long. A major reason for this was that members of city councils tended to use city managers as their scapegoats when their own policies proved to be unpopular.[21]

MAKING CITIES WORK: "POLITICS" OR "ADMINISTRATION"?

City managers have always been aware that politics is necessary to survive, and in fact, more recent investigations indicate that the city manager is evolving into a conscious political force in metropolises.

A comprehensive study of San Francisco Bay Area city managers found that a high portion of the city managers responding in that study perceived clear political roles for themselves. Interestingly, education appeared to affect whether city managers saw themselves as "politicians" or as "administrators." Those managers who saw themselves in a highly political role tended to have majored in the social sciences or public administration. Those who viewed themselves as relatively managerial in nature were less likely to have a college degree and displayed career patterns that often started with such jobs as Director of Public Works, Building Inspector, City Engineer, and so on, and from these jobs they moved to the top position after several years of working for the city. Nevertheless, all managers believed that they should participate in the initiation, formulation, and presentation of policy proposals to their councils. By contrast, city councilmembers tend to perceive the city manager as no more than a staff administrator, a servant to the council, and they thought this only proper.[22] Table 12–3 indicates this quiet conflict between managers and councilmembers. For example, 53 percent of the city managers agree with the proposition that the city manager functions as a political leader, but only 12 percent of the city councilmembers responding agree with that notion.

Most studies consistently indicate that city managers generally tend to see

---

[21]Gladys M. Kammerer and John M. DeGrove, *Florida City Managers: Profile in Tenure* (Gainesville, Fla: Public Administration Clearing Service, University of Florida, 1961), pp. 34–35.

[22]Ronald A. Loveridge, *The City Manager and Legislative Policy* (Indianapolis: Bobbs-Merrill, 1971).

TABLE 12-3 CITY COUNCILMEMBER EXPECTATIONS FOR THE CITY
MANAGER'S POLICY ROLE

1. *City manager as policy administrator*
   (The city manager should act as an administrator and leave policy matters to
   the council.)

	Agree			Disagree	
A	TA*	%	%	TD*	D
205	54	87	13	32	7

2. *City manager as political leader*
   (The city manager should work through the most powerful members of the
   community to achieve his policy goals.)

	Agree			Disagree	
A	TA	%	%	TD	D
9	26	12	88	85	176

3. *City manager as political campaigner*
   (The city manager should give a helping hand to good councilmen who are
   coming up for re-election.)

	Agree			Disagree	
A	TA	%	%	TD	D
21	33	18	82	48	195

4. *City manager as policy adviser*
   (The city manager should work informally with councilmen to prepare
   important policy proposals.)

	Agree			Disagree	
A	TA	%	%	TD	D
141	95	80	20	27	33

5. *City manager as political recruiter*
   (The city manager should encourage people whom he respects to run for the
   council.)

	Agree			Disagree	
A	TA	%	%	TD	D
31	36	23	77	63	165

6. *City manager as policy neutral*
   (The city manager should maintain a neutral stand on any issues which may
   divide the community.)

	Agree			Disagree	
A	TA	%	%	TD	D
121	68	64	36	45	61

7. *City manager as policy innovator*
   (The city manager should assume leadership in shaping municipal policies.)

	Agree			Disagree	
A	TA	%	%	TD	D
48	77	42	58	59	112

8. *City manager as political advocate*
   (The city manager should advocate policies even if important parts of the
   community seem hostile to them.)

	Agree			Disagree	
A	TA	%	%	TD	D
80	57	46	54	72	86

TABLE 12–3   continued

9. *City manager as budget consultant*
(The city manager should consult with the Council before drafting his own budget proposal.)

Agree			Disagree		
A	TA	%	%	TD	D
91	53	49	51	60	92

*TA and TD mean "Totally Agree" and "Totally Disagree"

Source: Ronald. O. Loveridge, "The City Manager in Legislative Politics." *Polity* I (Winter, 1968): p. 230.

their roles as more political than administrative; city councils tend to view the managers more administrative than political. Shrewd city managers can deal with this difference in viewpoint and avoid conflict while still getting their way. A major study of 1,744 responding cities found that almost 90 percent of the city managers and chief administrative officers in cities indicated that they always, or nearly always, participate in formulating municipal policy; the percentage was even higher in the larger cities. More than 60 percent of the managers responding felt they always, or nearly always, played a leading role in making policy, and more than 94 percent took some responsibility for setting the policy agenda of cities. Interestingly, more than 12 percent reported that they always, or nearly always, gave political help to incumbent candidates for the city council; under most city charters, this would be in clear violation of the nominal role that the city manager is expected to play.[23]

URBAN POLITICS AND THE CONTROL OF INFORMATION

Some other fascinating gleanings from the study: The most consistent finding was that in cities of all types more than 60 percent of the managers voiced strong opposition to a full-time paid city council, and the study noted that "this item evoked the strongest expression of opinion in the entire series of questions."[24] Moreover, a majority of city managers in the study opposed the provision of a full-time separate staff for the mayor, and 77 percent of the respondents reported that they always, or nearly always, resisted council involvement in management issues. These opinions on the part of city managers indicate that the appointed urban chief executive officer is well aware that one of his major political bases is the control of

---

[23]Robert J. Huntley and Robert J. McDonald, "Urban Managers: Managerial Styles and Social Roles." In *Municipal Yearbook, 1975* (Washington, D.C.: International City Management Association, 1975), pp. 149–159.

[24]*Ibid.*, p. 150.

241

The urban
executive:
bosses,
mayors, and
managers

information. A full-time professional staff for the mayor and a full-time, hard-working city council that is interested in management issues are anathema to the typical city manager. His is an example of the politics of expertise, an area that provides the city manager with an ability to have his policies adopted by the city council primarily because he controls a major source of information, the city bureaucracy itself.

A similar study conducted of 645 city managers concluded that the more professional and the more highly educated the manager was, the more the manager tended to resist public participation in city decision making, particularly in fiscal matters. Additionally, the more professionally oriented city manager tended to see himself in a more positive policy-making role than the more locally oriented city manager.[25]

The implications of the more recent studies on city managers have an intriguing corollary for higher education. The studies taken whole indicated that the more educated and professional a city manager is, the more likely he is to assume a greater personal policy-making role in cities. Moreover, education in the social sciences and public administration seems to correlate more heavily with city managers who are oriented toward the political sphere than does an education in engineering, or simply less education. Education may, after all, have an impact on the way people see themselves, at least if the surveys on city managers are an indication.

The data also indicate that city managers are experts in the politics of being smooth. While they often seem to get their way in forming urban policies, they do so by maintaining a low profile, by using finesse rather than clout, and anonymity instead of notoriety. In this regard they are very different from governors, mayors, or other elected officials. They play the same games quietly, sometimes safely, and above all effectively.

City managers also are responsible for hiring, firing, and using the vast urban bureaucracy; we consider the state and local bureaucracy, and public policies concerning it, in the following chapters.

---

[25]Timothy A. Almy, "City Managers: Public Avoidance and Revenue Sharing." *Public Administration Review* 37 (January-February, 1977), 19–27.

GRASSROOTS BUREAUCRACY

CHAPTER

PUBLIC
ADMINISTRATION
AT THE
GRASSROOTS

Big bureaucracy is a reality of twentieth-century America. That reality is no less real in state and local governments, as anyone who has attempted to acquire a driver's license can attest.

BUREAUCRATS AS POLICY MAKERS

A number of analysts argue that the "bureaucracy" (meaning the executive branch), not the legislatures or judiciary, is the real maker and former of public policy in this country. For better or worse, this view has much to support it.

Despite its power, however, the public bureaucracy remains the "black box" of the policy-making process: in the bureaucracy policy inputs are somehow converted into policy outputs. As such, the bureaucracy is the least understood of all political institutions.

Increasingly, however, public policy analysts are taking an interest in how the bureaucracy makes policy and how the bureaucracy relates to the policy-making process in other political spheres. Theodore J. Lowi, Randall B. Ripley, Robert Salisbury, John Heinz, and Dean Schooler, Jr., number among the major contributors to this focus, and they attempt to categorize public policies according to policy-making subsystems.[1] For example, Lowi classifies public policies according to four "arenas of power": redistributive, regulative, distributive, and constituent. In a redistributive arena, for example, power is "redistributed" throughout the polity in a fundamental way. Redistributive policies tend to be highly ideological and emotionally charged for particular groups, involving a fight between "haves" and "have-nots" but possessing low partisan visibility; usually, redistributive politics is centered in the bureaucracy. Lowi, in fact, considers redistributive policies to be concerned with "not use of property but property itself, not equal treatment but equal possession, not behavior but being."[2] He believes that, because of the bureaucratic secrecy and shrouding, the redistributive policy

---

[1] See, for example: Theodore J. Lowi, "Decision-Making versus Policy-Making: Towards an Antidote for Technocracy." *Public Administration Review* 30 (May–June, 1970), 134–139; Randall B. Ripley, "Introduction: The Politics of Public Policy." in *Public Policies and Their Politics: An Introduction to the Techniques of Government Control*, Randall B. Ripley, ed. (New York: W.W. Norton, 1966) pp. i–xv; Robert Salisbury and John Heinz, "A Theory of Policy Analysis and Some Preliminary Applications." In *Policy Analysis in Political Science*, Ira Sharkansky, ed. (Chicago: Markham, 1970), pp. 39–60; Dean Schooler, Jr., *Science, Scientists, and Public Policy* (New York: Free Press, 1971).

[2] Theodore J. Lowi, "American Business, Public Policy, Case Studies, and Political Science." *World Politics* 16 (July, 1964), 691. But see also: Theodore J. Lowi, "Population Policies and the American Political System." In *Political Science and Population Studies*, Richard L. Clinton, William S. Flash, and R. Kenneth Godwin, eds. (Lexington, Mass.: D.C. Heath, 1972), pp. 25–53.

process not only has received the least study by social scientists, but also is likely the most basic of all policy types.

Adding to the irony of academic ignorance about bureaucracy (at least relative to the other branches) is its comparative size. The bureaucracy is enormous.

In 1975, there were 14,971,000 full-time and part-time government employees. Of these, 12,854,000 were full-time employees (or the equivalent thereof). Of the almost 13 million full-time employees, 2,742,000, or more than 21 percent, were federal civilian (nonmilitary) employees. An almost equal number, 2,742, 000, were state employees. Another 16.7 percent of the total were employed by cities. Yet another 1,408,000, or 11 percent, were employed by counties. These figures do not include school district employees, who make up more than 25 percent of the total (3,243,000) and who comprise almost half (44 percent) of all local government workers, nor does it include 561,000 employees who are employed by townships and special district units of government.[3] The total government payroll for these nearly 15 million government employees in 1975 was $13.2 billion, and salaries were increasing apparently at a rate higher than that of the private sector.[4]

The recent growth in government employees, particularly at the state and local levels, is staggering. In the fifteen-year period from 1960 through 1975, local governmental employment went up 87 percent, while state governmental employment shot up 99 percent.[5] By contrast, federal employment increased by on 17 percent. Figure 13–1 indicates the rate of growth in state and local public employment, in contrast to federal employment, from 1950 and projected through 1985. The figures speak for themselves.

When we place the bureaucracy's size in perspective, the disparity between it and the other branches of government is stark. Contrast the nearly 12 million state and local employees (of whom perhaps some 2 million can be reasonably categorized as public executives) with the numbers of officeholders in the other branches of government; there are about 30,000 state and municipal judges, 7,800 legislators, roughly 16,000 county supervisors, less than 40,000 city councilmembers, about 7,000 mayors, fifty governors, and about 150 additional state elected officials. By dint of sheer numbers, the bureaucracy—what some have called the "fourth branch of government"—overwhelms the legislative, judicial, and elected executive branches.

Can its awesome size be reduced? What research that has been conducted on this problem has not produced comforting answers. Herbert Kaufman, for example, wanted to find out whether or not government organizations,

---

[3]U.S. Bureau of the Census, *Public Employment in 1975, Ge-75 No. 1* (Washington, D.C.: U.S. Government Printing Office, 1976).

[4]Marianne Stein Rah, "City Employment and Payrolls: 1975." In *The 1977 Municipal Yearbook* (Washington D.C.: International City Management Association, 1977), p. 173.

[5]U.S. Bureau of the Census, *Public Employment in 1975*, p. 1.

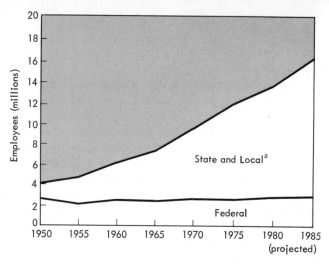

FIGURE 13–1 HOW GOVERN-
MENT EMPLOYMENT HAS
GROWN

Source: U.S. Department of Labor,
Bureau of Labor Statistics, *Government Occupations,* Bulletin 1955-42
(Washington, D.C.:U.S. Government Printing Office, 1978), p. 2.
ªIncludes public education

in effect "lived forever." While his study focused on the federal government, his findings nonetheless have pertinence for state and city governments as well.

Kaufman wanted to see how many U.S. government agencies "died" (were actually phased out, not just changed in name) between 1923 and 1973. He found 175 identifiably separate agencies within the U.S. government in 1923. By 1973, 109 of these same agencies still were going strong, and the government agency "population" had exploded to 394 separate agencies. Only 15 percent of the original 175 agencies had disappeared, and "the chances that an organization in 1923 would not only be alive in 1973 but in virtually the same status were quite good."[6]

Kaufman also compared the "death rate" of government agencies with the rate of business failures over the fifty-year period. He found that in any given year the rate of business failures exceeded the agency death rate. In fact, when the figures were averaged, the annual rate of business failure was more than twice the annual rate of government agency deaths.

Kaufman's study is the first of its kind and has not been repeated at the state or local levels. Nevertheless, its findings suggest what many Americans already believe: that government bureaucratic agencies are indeed "immortal," and that their growth cannot be stopped. While Kaufman's research indicates that this contention is not without its exceptions, government organizations do endure a relatively long time. The question that Kaufman did not address was whether they in fact outlive their usefulness.

BUREAUCRACY AS POLITICAL TECHNOLOGY

Quite aside from its importance, enormity, and endurance, the bureaucracy is politically unique in a democracy, and its uniqueness accounts for much of its power. The bureaucracy represents a different set of values than other

---

[6]Herbert Kaufman, *Are Government Organizations Immortal?* (Washington: Brookings Institution, 1976), p. 34.

branches of government. The American bureaucrat interprets "technology" (defined in very broad terms) to the public and reconciles the human needs of the people with the requirements of a technological state. Bureaucracy is the inescapable political expression of technology.

And ours is indeed a technological society. Computers, automation, and advanced modes of transportation and communication are developed in America first. The rest of the world adopts our technologies as experiments after they have become commonplace here. But technology brings with it new and interesting political problems. ("May you live in interesting times" is a curse in China.)

Consider a simple example—highways. Most people can understand highway technology. The Romans, indeed, understood highways as a technology supremely well 2,500 years ago. Yet American society has grown so complex that highways have taken on new meanings as a technology. For example, in the late 1960s the U.S. Department of Housing and Urban Development found that large and disproportionate numbers of urban rioters, notably in Watts and Newark, were people who had lived in their areas for a year or less. Moreover, these people came to the riot-torn areas because they had been displaced from their original homes by such projects as urban renewal and highway construction. As a result, neighborhood "fabrics" were torn and former residents scattered—they became *new* residents in other areas, they had nothing to lose and no neighborhood to protect. Hence, the building of large highways through large urban areas, according to federal officials, may have affected the intensity of the urban riots of the late 1960s.

Similarly, the United States highway program has spawned a major national debate over what is known as a "balanced" transportation policy. The central question in this debate is: Do we want the automobile to remain the central mode of transportation in America at the expense of such alternative forms of transit as buses, trains, and subways?

In sum, the highway, which most of us consider a relatively simple technology, brought complicated social and political problems that ultimately must be settled by the public at large.

How is the public to understand the more complex aspects of technological problems? Highways provide only one example; there are many others. Consider the environment and its relationship with the energy dilemma. Where does full employment end and the potential degradation of the earth begin? Or consider the population explosion. Where does the right to life end and the rights of the individual woman begin? Of course, these are not merely technological questions; they are deeply moral and ethical ones. But technology has injected new layers of complexity that are only beginning to be understood by "experts" in their respective fields. Yet the political questions and the public problems that these technologies and others raise require that policies concerning them be formulated in the most broadly public sense conceivable. So the question is posed: How is the public in a democracy to understand such issues as they pertain to these extraordinarily complex and technical questions?

The answer that has emerged in fact is the public bureaucracy. Bureaucrats are hired to be specialists. They are, in a sense, experts in their particular fields. Because technology requires expertise, bureaucrats have been saddled with the responsibility of interpreting complex technological and political problems so that as many Americans as possible might understand the issues involved. Whether or not the bureaucrats do a particularly good job of this chore is another question altogether. But their abilities as specialists are one reason why they are there.

THE COMPUTER:
A CASE OF BUREAUCRACY, TECHNOLOGY, AND POLICY

Few instances better illustrate the dilemmas surrounding technology's impact on democratic politics nor are more symbolic of the bureaucracy itself than the computer. It has had a major impact on the conduct of state and local government, particularly in planning, demographic analysis, financial management, public safety, and other areas of considerable importance. All fifty states have some sort of comprehensive information system, and there are about five hundred computer systems humming their electronic tunes for state governments. The computer has had an even larger impact on urban public administrators. According to a survey taken in 1974 of all cities with a population greater than fifty thousand people, the major interest expressed by local officials in terms of improving urban planning and management was to develop information gathering and analysis capabilities and establish better utilization of the data processing facility.[7]

What are the political implications of computers in state and local governments? Some critics have contended that the computer, by its very nature, is "dehumanizing" and alienating to the populace; others have argued that it assures responsive and responsible government. No doubt the computer can assume some Buck Rogerish qualities in the minds of many people. For example, John Kemeny, writing in 1967, predicted that the city of 1990 will be using computers extensively: to predict the impact of policies five years hence in a matter of seconds and to choose the correct policy accordingly; to control traffic; to fight against pollution; to plan schools, parks, recreation areas, youth centers, and centers for the aged; to fight organized crime; and to eliminate traffic jams. Moreover, every home would have its own computer, which would have an impact on the very structure of the city itself. "I see the city of 1990 as a gigantic depository of information, as a major mode in the computer-communication network, and as a source of education and entertainment."[8]

---

[7]Thomas Thorwood, "The Planning and Management Process in City Government." In *1975 Municipal Yearbook* (Lexington, Ky.: Council of State Governments, 1975).

[8]John Kemeney, "The City and the Computer Revolution." In Stephen B. Sweeney and James C. Charlesworth, eds., *Governing Urban Society: New Scientific Approaches* (Philadelphia: Annals of the American Academy of Political and Social Science, 1967), p. 62.

Heady stuff. More realistically, the computer can assist in the making of public policy by arranging and sorting data collected about people in ways that clarify policy choices. And policy makers always want information, and the more refined the information the better.

This pressure for more data, however, could possibly result in bureaucrats violating the privacy of citizens on whom information is collected. Security systems for computer data banks are not secure, particularly at the state and local levels. In theory, an unscrupulous person could gain access to the data bank, use information in it to blackmail an individual, or simply to sell the information to the highest bidder.

In reality such a break-in is not even necessary, since computer systems exchange data with other computer systems. Not too long ago a private mortgage lender could purchase a person's confidential file (which included information on the applicant's "marital stability") from the Federal Housing Administration for $1.50. Similarly, the FBI's National Crime Information Center, which centralizes the dossiers on individuals from local police departments all over the country, has been known to include the fact of a person's arrest or indictment and omit the fact that he or she was later found innocent.[9]

Some argue that data-sharing between computer networks is even more irresponsible and pervasive at the state and local levels than at the national level. Electronic data processing and federal program requirements for local coordination in federally financed projects have spurred the sharing of confidential data among local agencies but, unlike federal data-sharing activities, which affect people of all social classes, local information-sharing programs tend to single out the dispossessed, such as the poor and various social deviates.[10] Under these circumstances, the opportunities for misusing confidential information are magnified.

The executive director of the National Association for State Information Systems has stated that the lack of significant state legislation governing security and privacy for information systems could "represent potential catastrophies of great dimensions."[11] In 1974, only one state indicated that it had sufficient legislation and policies protecting the confidentiality and privacy of computer-based data on individual citizens.[12]

The proliferating use of information storage-and-retrieval systems in state and local governments brings with it new problems of public policy. As we learn more about out citizenry we can develop more responsive and effective public policies—but where should the line be drawn? At what point does the collection, storage, retrieval, and sharing of social information

---

[9]Nicholas Henry, *Copyright/Information Technology/Public Policy*, Volume I (New York: Marcel Dekker, 1975), pp. 12–13.

[10]Albert Mindlin, "Confidentiality and Local Information Systems." *Public Administration Review* 28 (November–December, 1968), pp. 509–518.

[11]Charles Trigg, "State Information Systems." *Book of the States, 1976–77* (Lexington Ky.: Council of State Governments, 1976), p. 148.

[12]*Ibid.*, p. 148.

become an invasion of the citizen's privacy? How much information is needed to form sensitive and responsive policies?

Emerging from this fundamental dilemma of how state and local governments should use computers are such delicate political issues as: Who will control this new technological capacity? Will new knowledge of old problems inspire new problems in society? Where does the expertise and planning enabled by the computer end, and where does democratic participation by the public in public policy making begin?

PUBLIC TECHNOLOGY: SCIENCE, STATES, AND CITIES

The expanding role of the computer in state and local administration leads us into the larger consideration of the role that science and technology are playing in state and local politics and government. While bureaucracy represents the political expression of technology, a more formal relationship exists between the spheres of science and the spheres of politics at the state and local levels.

SCIENCE IN STATES

In an analysis of how "public technology" is being used by state governments, it was found that most scientific and technical capacities are located in the executive branches of state government. This scientific input usually is coordinated in one of two ways: Either scientific advice is built into the agency itself, particularly in the growing energy agencies at the state level, or it is institutionalized as a separate unit in the governor's office.[13]

There are, of course, other ways of incorporating scientific advice into the executive branch of state government. According to one survey, the major sources of scientific advice for state administrative units were simply other state administrative units. For example, if a state administrator felt that he or she needed a certain type of technical advice, then the administrator was most likely to consult with other administrators; after that, private consultants or the state universities were looked to for advice.[14] Still, more than a third of the states have a centralized scientific and technology advisory agency.[15]

Legislatures also are increasing their use of scientific and technical advice. In 1977, Alabama, California, Hawaii, Illinois, Iowa, Kentucky, Maryland, Massachusetts, New York, Utah, and Wisconsin either had created offices of technical assistance or had integrated scientists into the legislative council.

---

[13]Edward L. Helminski, "Public Technology." *Book of the States, 1976–77* (Lexington, Ky.: Council of State Governments, 1976), pp. 138–144.

[14]Nicholas Henry, "State Agencies and Academia." *State Government,* 49 (Spring, 1976), pp. 99–104.

[15]J. Robert Havlic, "Science, the States, and Change." *1972 Municipal Yearbook* (Washington, D.C.: International City Management Association, 1972), p. 113.

TECHNOLOGY IN TOWNS

Cities and other local governments also are interested in public technology, and in 1971, Public Technology, Inc., was created under the sponsorship of a number of urban interest groups and with funding from the Ford Foundation. Cities do not use a centralized scientific advisory board in the same sense that the states use them. While some cities, notably Chicago, Los Angeles, Oakland, New York, and Seattle, have tried such devices in the past, such boards tend to come and go with elections. Nevertheless, local governments have made substantial use of technological innovations in the administration of public programs. Much of this innovation in recent years has been encouraged by Public Technology, Inc., but a number of local governments have brought about technological innovations of their own. Savings that result can often be substantial; for example, the cost of fire protection services, which averaged $12.00 per capita nationally in 1971, was reduced in one community to $2.30 per capita through relatively simple improvements in technology and organization.[16]

Technology in city government is not particularly glamorous. It deals with such subjects as trash collection and traffic control. One of the more remarkable examples of a successful technological innovation brought about almost entirely by the city's own initiative occurred in Scottsdale, Arizona. After much struggle, the city secured a $100,000 matching federal grant to develop a new type of refuse collection truck. This truck extended a mechanical arm that picked up standardized trash containers, emptied the trash into the truck, and replaced the container where it found it. The driver never had to leave his cab. To develop this system, city officials investigated various types of plastics for use in the trash containers and according to its manager "Finally ended up with a guy that built plastic pickle vats in his backyard."[17] The city built the actual truck itself; the first model was named "Godzilla," and the second one, with refinements, was labeled "Son of Godzilla." With its $200,000 investment, Scottsdale reduced its work force and cut monthly trash pick-up costs by 40 percent.

Of course, not all such technological innovations are as successful as Scottsdale's. A considerably more ambitious project was undertaken in the late 1960s in New York City. Systems analysis was to be applied to a renovation of the black Bedford-Stuyvesant ghetto. The late Senator Robert Kennedy mobilized the distinguished architect I.M. Pei, Boston's talented development administrator Edward J. Logue, the U.S. Department of Labor, the Ford Foundation, neighborhood political organizations, the government of the city of New York, local businessmen, and others to, in effect, rebuild Bedford-Stuyvesant. At the end of a year and a half the only

---

[16]The Urban Institute, *The Struggle to Bring Technology to Cities* (Washington, D.C.: The Urban Institute, 1971), p. 18.

[17]*Ibid.*, p. 27.

visible results were a handful of newly repainted houses and pronounced community discord. Despite this impressive array of intellectual talent, the project came to its untimely demise primarily because of a municipal judge who successfully accused the project's administration of being dominated by women, an accusation that did not go over well with the male residents of Bedford-Stuyvesant.[18] Science does not always win in the realm of politics, and these two value systems are not always easily reconciled.

OBSTACLES TO "URBAN SCIENCE"

The obstacles to applying innovative technological solutions to public problems are formidable. Institutional factors, political risks, budget constraints, job security requirements, distrust of "the experts" from industry, absence of an accepted performance standard and of cost data, and the lack of technical evaluation capability all have stood in the way of cities implementing new technological innovations. Similarly, industry has not been brought in—at least, not in any significant fashion—to solve urban problems through technology.[19]

Not all writers in the area of public technology think of science as a panacea to all urban and social ills. In terms of local governments particularly, one scenario holds that urban problems will intensify and multiply and that many of these problems, such as pollution, deterioration, and sprawl, will require extensive—and expensive— system-wide solutions based on science and technology. Urban governments will grow increasingly less able to provide solutions to their own problems, at least in part because of a declining tax base on which to support local technical talent. Even so, this local technical talent may become more necessary if local governments are to qualify for federal funds with which to solve their problems. On the other hand, federal urban research, notably in the Departments of Housing and Urban Development, Transportation, and Justice, and in the National Science Foundation, already have very high technical capacities. It seems possible that federal standards for planning, management, and similar areas that require technological sophistication to prepare local applications for funds will rise as local ability to meet those standards declines. As a result, informal working accommodations between local, state, and national agencies may be established over time (and seem to be being established) so that cities might receive both money and "urban science" at maximum levels. This practice could work to raise local decision making to state and national levels. In this sense, we may be witnessing the rise of "territorial government" as a means of controlling "the decerebrate frog" of urban government and

---

[18] James Bailey, "RFK's Favorite Ghetto." *Architectural Forum* 138 (April, 1968), 46–52.
[19] The Urban Institute, *The Struggle to Bring Technology to Cities,* pp. 52–54.

its proliferating problems.[20] The study by the U.S. Advisory Commission on Intergovernmental Relations, cited in Chapter 10, suggests that the functions of government are centralizing to higher and higher levels. The political and managerial sophistication required in applying science and technology to urban problems may be a component in this apparent centralization of decision making in state and local governments.

Of course, the foregoing scenario assumes that state and local public officials are somehow less able or less sophisticated than national public administrators. This is a major assumption, and quite possibly an inaccurate one. In the next chapter, we examine the more important public administrators of state and local governments. We shall find them to be, for the most part, dynamic and capable.

---

[20]John W. Gardner, "The Keynote." In *Science, Technology, and the Cities.* Committee on Science and Astronautics, U.S. House of Representatives (Washington: U.S. Government Printing Office, 1969), p. 7. For an elaboration of the scenario described in this paragraph, see: Nicholas Henry, "Science and the City: Some Political Implications," in *South Atlantic Urban Studies,* Vol. 1. Jack R. Censer, N. Steven Steinert, and Amy M. McCandless, eds. (Columbia: University of South Carolina Press, 1977), pp. 137–169.

14

GRASSROOTS
BUREAUCRATS

The major challenge to machine politics and boss rule in American state and local governments has been the introduction of the "merit principle" in public personnel administration. At least, such is the conventional wisdom. In this chapter, we examine what the merit system has done—and what it has not done—in the quest for efficient and responsible government. *Merit* is a very broad term and we are using it in its traditional sense to mean the hiring, promotion, demotion, and firing of public employees as determined by their ability to "do a job" (which is to say, to complete a task efficiently and effectively).

The merit system is close to an article of faith in the civil service, which is comprised of white-collar workers and is administered according to long-standing practices. The overriding characteristic of the civil service is the emphasis that is placed on the *position*: its description of duties, responsibilities, requirements, qualifications, standards, and so forth. Above all, the public personnel system of the civil service values such concepts as neutrality, impersonality, merit, and being insulated from politics. By contrast, the patronage system has its own definition of *merit*. In this context, merit means the ability to please one's political boss.

How has the merit system developed? How does it work, or not work? What is its power in politics? What are the challenges to the merit system?

THE CIVIL SERVICE: A REACTION TO PATRONAGE

The federal government has had a major impact on how civil service systems have evolved in state and local governments. The single law that has had the most influence is the Civil Service Act of 1883; known as the Pendleton Act it was designed to make government administration a profession. This was the operative public personnel policy at the national level until 1978, when the Civil Service Reform Act was passed. Over time, state and local governments slowly began adopting the basic principle (at least on paper) set forth in the Civil Service Act. By 1975, thirty-four states had statewide merit systems and another seventeen had partial merit systems. Today all cities of more than 250,000 people have some sort of provision for an urban civil service system, and only 12 percent of cities with populations of more than fifty thousand have no merit system at all. Virtually all the larger cities and states have merit systems today.

The reasons behind the expanding adoption of state and local merit systems are reasonably clear. With state and public employment growing by leaps and bounds, it is not surprising that patronage slowly would be displaced by people demanding "fairer" access to government jobs. Technical credentials for employment also have proliferated as society and its governments become more complex.

Regardless of why the merit system has burgeoned in state and local governments, one should realize that:

> all statistics concerning merit system coverage are inherently deceptive. While such figures may be numerically accurate, they merely indicate that merit systems are "on the books," not that they exist in practice.... Consequently, while the arithmetic of these surveys [on state and local merit systems] may be impeccable the resulting summaries frequently belie the true extent of merit systems coverage. Remember, the City of Chicago has an excellent merit system on the books, yet it manages to retain its well-earned reputation as the large American city most famous for its patronage abuses.[1]

THE POWER OF PUBLIC PERSONNEL ADMINISTRATION

"Merit," as a concept, is quintessentially middle class. It is designed to displace the machine bosses whose primary constituency were the poor, the immigrants, and the dispossessed. Given this premise, does the merit system work as it is supposed to? Does it assure more responsive government? Probably not. Although the merit system may assure "cleaner" government, at least by middle-class standards, a major criticism of the whole concept of merit is that it establishes a vast bureaucracy over which no one has control. "Political" appointees are indeed inept on occasion, but it does not necessarily follow that appointments made according to civil service criteria are necessarily any better. Many politicians believe that the "civil service thwarts government progress. Civil servants, considered by some to be human paperweights, can sabotage an administration through laziness, inefficiency, or by being just plain ornery. Unaccountable to anyone, they can easily thwart those who are accountable to the electorate."[2]

If this generalization is false at the state and local levels, it may be false only because state and local bureaucrats have managed to fudge the system. On paper, the merit system is in effect everywhere, or at least virtually everywhere (counties generally are a stalwart exception), but in practice, such systems can and are being bypassed. Frank J. Thompson, in his excellent study of personnel policy and politics traces how this shortcircuiting of merit systems can be and is being accomplished in Oakland, California, one of the most "reformed" of city governments. Council –manager, or reformed, governments tend to shift the center of personnel decision making to the urban bureaucracy: "Reformed government strips power resources from elected officials and emphasizes that professionally

---

[1] Jay M. Shafritz, Walter L. Balk, Albert C. Hyde, and David H. Rosenbloom, *Personnel Management in Government: Politics and Process* (New York, Marcel Dekker, 1978), p. 45.

[2] Martin Tolchin and Susan Tolchin, *To the Victor . . .Political Patronage from the Clubhouse to the White House* (New York: Vintage, 1971), p. 102.

trained experts should conduct much of government's business."[3] Hence, the person with the real power in Oakland's personnel decisions was the personnel director. With more than 98 percent of the city's personnel classified under civil service, the personnel director has far-reaching power. Moreover, having "imbibed the good government, anti-party culture so much a part of Oakland's local government tradition, [the mayor and his council] have little desire to influence bureaucratic appointments and removals."[4] This means, in effect, that bureaucrats control the bureaucracy.

HOW THE MERIT SYSTEM WORKS: THE POLITICS OF COMPLEXITY

If public bureaucrats were to manage by the rules and regulations set down by their civil service commissions, it is unlikely that they could accomplish anything of consequence in terms of transferring, hiring, and firing of public personnel. Frequently, finding ways to get around the regulations of their own system becomes the objective of civil servants. Whether this bypassing is intended to maintain the spirit of good government or is designed to further political patronage depends upon the situation. But, in any event, "The perversion of most civil service merit systems for private, administrative, and especially partisan ends is one of the worst kept, yet least written about, secrets in government."[5]

In council–manager cities where the impact of the merit principle in public personnel administration thinking is the most profound, the city manager ultimately reigns supreme in personnel decisions. Contrary to conventional wisdom, the city manager is not an empire builder—indeed, quite the reverse. "The manager naturally casts a jaundiced eye on any request which will further drain the city treasury. For him, the basic concern is not whether a proposal will enhance organizational efficiency . . . . In his unrelenting war against greater costs, the manager believes that it is particularly important to resist work force expansion."[6] This stands to reason: the manager must report to the council and the council, in turn, must report to taxpayers. Therefore, it behooves the manager to keep government costs down.

In contrast to the city manager, the heads of municipal agencies usually want to expand the number of people and the areas of authority that they control. But they are seldom able to accomplish this without the approval of the city manager. While Thompson found that most of the Oakland's top bureaucrats were "at least latent manpower imperialists," these bureau-

---

[3] Frank J. Thompson, *Personnel Policy in the City: The Politics of Jobs in Oakland* (Berkeley, Calif.: University of California Press, 1975), pp. 15–16.

[4] *Ibid.*, p. 76.

[5] Shafritz *et al.*, *Personnel Management in Government*, p. 52.

[6] Thompson, *Personnel Policy in the City*, pp. 21–22.

crats found it difficult to actually act on such an expansionist disposition without the approval of the city manager.

HIRING AND (SELDOM) FIRING PUBLIC BUREAUCRATS

CONNING THE GOVERNMENT: GETTING A JOB

How does one get a job in government? According to merit principles, all one should need is the "right" educational and professional credentials and a high score on a test. But more is involved, particularly when a personal interview is required. Employers in government (and presumably in private enterprise as well) would rather hire somone who is less able according to technical criteria and more amiable according to personal criteria. Consider the following passage from Thompson's Oakland study:

> The attitudes of the statistical service officer show how important amiability can be. He would rather hire a mediocre programmer who is easygoing and pleasant , than a very able one who is abrasive—who "makes waves and stirs up trouble." On one occasion, he served on an oral board which was interviewing a young lady. In terms of the applicant's computer knowledge, she was clearly superior to all the other applicants. But he and the other board members felt that she was too "aggressive and dynamic." There was too much "hostility" in her replies and, consequently, they flunked her.[7]

So much for merit principles in hiring.

There is some evidence to suggest that the test-based merit system does not work even when judged by its own standards. In a study conducted in 1970 of the New York City civil service, which had roughly 250,000 out of a total of 400,000 employees who were considered "competitive class" employees (that is, they were hired and advanced on the basis of competitive tests), it was found that the "merit system discriminated *against those applicants who are most qualified according to its own standards.* Candidates with low passing grades are actually *more* likely to be hired than those with high passing grades! Furthermore, this perverse result seems to hold true for all skill levels."[8]

How so? The investigators found that the city had a lengthy waiting period between the date that an applicant took the examination and the date of hire—a median of seven months—and that, during this period, the best qualified were skimmed off by other employers. Conclusion: *"New York City's civil service system functions as an inverse merit system* (something the public at large has cynically assumed for years)."[9]

---

[7] *Ibid.,* p. 106.

[8] E.S. Savas and Sigmund G. Ginsburg, "The Civil Service: A Meritless System?" *The Public Interest* 32 (Summer, 1973), 76. Emphasis is original.

[9] *Ibid.,* p. 77.

One of the major arguments against civil service systems is that it provides a sinecure for life to public bureaucrats. Consequently, they are responsible and responsive to no one since their jobs cannot be threatened. Nevertheless, it is unclear how firmly ensconced in their positions public bureaucrats really are. Although it is difficult to compare the proportionate number of dismissals between the public and private sectors, it nonetheless appears that, "There is every reason to believe that the annual rate of removal, ranging from a little less than one to about one and a half percent of public jurisdictions in the United States as a whole, is exceeded, if at all, in certain categories of private employment, such as a few areas of manufacturing."[10] In other words, the proportionate numbers of people fired in both private enterprise and in government are about the same.

If these figures are accurate, then it is surprising that the rate of dismissal in the public sector is as high as it is. It is inordinately difficult to fire a public employee. In California, for example, a teacher may demand a hearing upon receiving notice of dismissal and, unless it rescinds its action, the school board must file a complaint in Superior Court requesting the court to make an inquiry and to determine if the basis of dismissal is supportable. Then court-appointed referees hold hearings and report back to the court, a trial is held by the court itself, and a decision is made on whether the board may, in fact, dismiss the teacher. In effect, any contested dismissal of a California teacher brings the judiciary into the act.[11]

But even getting to the point of firing a public employee is difficult, and it is much more difficult to adjudge an employee's performance in some types of jobs than in others. In local government, the standards used to evaluate performance can themselves be unclear, and the visibility of a subordinate to his or her supervisor can vary from agency to agency. For example, it is relatively clear whether or not a secretary is turning out typing (the usual standard of performance for a secretary), and a secretary is relatively visible to his or her supervisor. But in such agencies as police departments, patrolmen are not very visible to their supervisors, nor is their standard of performance particularly clear.[12]

To compensate for these problems of assessing personnel in agencies where employees are relatively on their own, supervisors develop complicated performance forms and rating systems. These forms seldom follow function, and the presumption that the form is actually evaluating the performance of an employee is to likely be wrong. Nevertheless, bureaucrats are not spending their time ritualistically filling out useless pieces of paper;

---

[10] O. Glen Stahl, *Public Personnel Administration*, 7th ed. (New York: Harper and Row, 1976), p. 309.

[11] *Ibid.*, p. 390.

[12] Thompson, *Personnel Policy in the City*, pp. 142–143.

the forms actually are used to prevent problems from arising and to justify to outsiders a disciplinary action or decision to remove an employee.[13]

Public administrators using past personnel records as a political defense is not as cautionary as it may seem. Employees who are fired often attempt to bring in outsiders and apply public pressure to be reinstated. The ploy of expanding the scope of conflict between the employee and the employer, either in the courts or with the public, is a classic one in public employment circles. For example, while dismissals of the Oakland work force averaged less than 1 percent a year, almost two-thirds of those fired were on probation and therefore had no right of appeal to the city's civil service commission, but at least one-third of those persons who were dismissed as regular, non-probationary employees appealed their dismissal to the commission.[14] In short, a supervisor can expect problems if he or she fires someone in the public bureaucracy.

Although state and local civil service systems may be both perverse and perverted by bureaucrats and elected officials alike, the presence of the system makes a difference in terms of how the politics of patronage is conducted. For example, in Oakland, a city that is virtually the archetype of reformed governments and council–manager rule, we have seen that the city manager and various appointed bureaucrats conduct the politics of personnel, but in boss-rule cities the mayor takes over. For instance, the late Mayor Daley of Chicago was known to review the applications for even the lowest-level positions throughout the city.[15] Daley's chief concern was loyalty to himself and the Democratic party, but even he could not totally ignore minimal professional competence as a requisite for an appointment. Similarly, we may expect state legislators and city council members to be much more interested in public appointments in states and cities where civil service traditions are not strong than in states and cities where a civil service system has been entrenched for some years.

OL' LESTER VERSUS ROCKY: PERFORMANCE VERSUS PATRONAGE

How the patronage power is used by an elected chief executive is often surprising. Consider the difference in how Lester G. Maddox, as the governor of Georgia, conducted patronage, and how the late Nelson A. Rockefeller, as governor of New York, used his patronage powers. Conventional wisdom would lead us to believe that Maddox indulged in the worst excesses of political patronage, while Rockefeller would have put "performance above politics" in making his political appointments. Yet nothing could be further from the truth.

Maddox stated that, "If you want to put politics first, then patronage is

---

[13] Herbert Kaufman, *The Forest Ranger* (Baltimore: Johns Hopkins, 1960), p. 158.

[14] Thompson, *Personnel Policy in the City*, p. 156.

[15] Mike Royko, *Boss* (New York: Signet, 1971), pp. 22–23.

necessary. If you want to put government and efficiency first, it isn't."[16] Moreover, he meant it. As governor of Georgia from 1968 to 1972, Maddox substantially reduced the discretionary favors provided by the Georgia state government. Maddox did away with purchasing gasoline for state vehicles from friends of the governor and placed gasoline purchasing on a competitive basis, saving $500,000 a year; he did the same with the state's computers. He initiated reforms in the state's parole system, noting that formerly, "the most influential, meanest crooks could get attention, now all people, not just influential people, are given the same consideration."[17] And, despite his reputation for wielding pick handles at blacks, Maddox appointed more blacks to state patronage jobs than any of his predecessors, including some sensitive appointments in the Georgia Bureau of Investigation. Said Maddox, "I told all departments to hire whoever they could get as long as they were qualified."[18]

As a political maverick without his own organization, Maddox had scant use for Georgia's patronage traditions. Maddox was among the last of the true populists, so Maddox

> wedded his policies to the welfare of everyone—which he believes to be the essence of democratic government. What Maddox has shown, by combining antipatronage rhetoric with the new populism, is how antithetical patronage and pure democracy really are. For patronage is a selective way of governing, with special groups and persons chosen arbitrarily to receive the rewards of government. Maddox and populism, theoretically at least, stand for the opposite view—dispensing government rewards on an equitable basis, for the good and benefit of all.[19]

In stark contrast to Governor Maddox's patronage policy stood Governor Rockefeller's policy. During the 1968 session of the New York legislature, Rockefeller rammed through his $6 billion slum clearance bill by twisting the arms of thirty-four legislators and arranging for them to change their original votes; Rockefeller noted that, "he would be unable to do their personal favors . . . such as signing bills and appointments."[20] Rockefeller's patronage dealings were so flagrant in 1969, when he traded two votes on his proposed state budget for appointments on the Civil Service Commission and on the State Harness Racing Commission (both paying at the time more than $20,000 a year), that a law suit was brought charging a violation in the Public Offices Law. (Under this law it was a felony to accept or promise a reward in return for a vote.) Rockefeller denied any deals but stated, "Let me say that what they did on the budget doesn't make me feel punitive toward these individuals."[21]

---

[16] Quoted in: Tolchin and Tolchin, *To the Victor*, p. 92.

[17] *Ibid.*

[18] *Ibid.*

[19] *Ibid.*

[20] *Ibid.*, pp. 93–94.

[21] *Ibid.*, p. 94.

By the end of his third term, Rockefeller had placed most of the Republican county leaders on his state payroll. Rockefeller's patronage powers permitted him to distribute almost thirty thousand state jobs that were excluded from the civil service, many of which had no fixed job requirements. Rockefeller, by all accounts, used this power to the hilt.

THE CHALLENGES TO "MERIT"

We have seen in the preceding pages that the politics of public personnel administration, whether conducted according to the principles of merit or the boodle of patronage, can be complicated and arcane. Public personnel administration is a political phenomenon, and none the less so because of the rise of the civil service. In recent years, the civil service personnel system has received a series of major challenges to its principle of merit. These challenges are: (1) the question of political freedom for public employees, notably freedom of political expression and assembly; (2) the question of hiring and promoting greater numbers of citizens from deprived groups such as minorities, women, and the physically handicapped; and finally, (3) the rise of unionism, collective bargaining, and strikes among public employees. These issues constitute the major challenges to the concept of merit in public employment.

PUBLIC SERVANTS AND THE FREEDOM TO BE POLITICAL: THE CHALLENGE OF POLITICAL NEUTRALITY

Being "value neutral" is a central concept of the merit system, and, of course, when one is value neutral, one also must be, by definition, "politically neutral." Personnel specialists at the national, state, and local levels of government have taken this admonition very much to heart and, in 1939, much of this thinking was formalized at the federal level with the passage of the Political Activities Act, known as the Hatch Act.

PROHIBITING POLITICS: THE FEDERAL IMPACT

The Hatch Act, and subsequent legislation at all levels of government, essentially prohibited the following kinds of political activity by public servants: running for public office; campaigning for others who are running for public office; soliciting contributions to political parties; and holding an office in a political party. In 1940, a "Second Hatch Act" was enacted, which extended the same prohibitions to state and local government employees whose principal employment was connected with projects that were federally financed in whole or part and, as noted in Chapter 11, this coverage was extended even further in 1967 to employees of community development agencies.

During the 1940s and 1950s, state and local governments, following the lead provided by the federal government, began enacting their own "little Hatch Acts." In 1947, the constitutionality of the Hatch Act was tested in the U.S. Supreme Court *(United Public Workers of America (CIO)* v. *Mitchell)* and the act was upheld as constitutional by a four-to-three decision

During the years following the passing of the Hatch Act, the U.S. Civil Service Commission was especially zealous in insulating public servants from politics. For example, in its crusade to purge politics from the public service, the commission ruled over the years that federal employees may be punished for disparaging the president during private conversations, failing to discourage the political actions of a spouse, and criticizing the government's handling of veterans during a closed session of the American Legion. This was political insulation with a vengance.

During this period, a number of litigations challenged the constitutionality of the Hatch Act. In 1973, the Supreme Court again heard a case concerning the act *(U.S. Civil Service Commission* v. *Letter Carriers)* and again, the Court stated that the act was constitutional, thus throwing the ball back to Congress. In 1974, the first and only national liberalization of restrictions on political activity that affected state and local employees was passed by Congress, although it applied only to those state and local public workers who were engaged in programs receiving federal financing. This was a clause in the Federal Election Campaign Act Amendments of 1974, which continued many basic political prohibitions on state and local employees, but did extend permissible political activities in the states. It authorized the free expression of opinions on political issues and candidates, permitted the solicitation and collection of party contributions without coercion or pressure, permitted active participation in political parties (short of holding an office in the party), and finally, allowed the active campaigning by state and local workers on behalf of partisan candidates. In 1976, Congress really moved and repealed the Hatch Act. But when it was sent to then-President Gerald Ford, he promptly vetoed the repeal measure.

The Hatch Act affects a lot of people. The act has discouraged more than 5 million federal and federally related civilian employees from political participation beyond voting in elections. This is roughly 2.5 percent of the nation's population, about 7 percent of the voting population, and about 16 percent of the civilian work force.[22] In some jurisdictions, the Hatch Act means that large proportions of voters are barred from political activity. Alaska's 17,000 federal workers, for example, make up 21 percent of the state's voting population.[23]

---

[22] Philip L. Martin, "The Hatch Act: The Current Move for Reform." *Public Personnel Management* 3 (May–June, 1974), 180–184.

[23] Philip L. Martin, "The Hatch Act in Court: Some Recent Developments." *Public Administration Review* 33 (September–October, 1973), 443–447.

PUBLIC SERVANTS AND POLITICAL PARTICIPATION: PORTENTS FOR THE FUTURE

Proponents of prohibitions on political activity by government workers argue that, without such legislation, it would be possible to subvert the public bureaucracy for political purposes because employees could be pressured, threatened, or fired for refusal to cooperate in partisan politics. Patronage unchecked could destroy the merit system as we understand it. The arguments that may eventually sweep away such laws revolve around the fact that the government employee is denied all independent political rights other than voting, and that he or she has been left unprotected and at the mercy of the legislature and various civil service commissions. Their vagueness and ambiguity permit wide latitudes of discretion on the part of personnel specialists in determining whether or not a public employee has violated prohibitions against political activities.

Would abandonment of the Hatch Act and "little Hatch Acts" have an impact on the levels of political participation by government employees? It is an impossible question to answer but, judging by a study of federal employees, the political activities of government workers probably would not increase as state and local governments reduced their restrictions on political activity. The survey indicated that only 8 percent of the respondents said they would be "a lot more active" if they were permitted a greater degree of political freedom. Moreover, 71 percent maintained that they didn't take part in certain kinds of political activities because they had never wanted to; they didn't refrain from doing so because they were civil servants.[24] It is not unreasonable to surmise that state and local employees have the same attitudes regarding political activity.

Nevertheless, though public employees as individuals may not suddenly wax political as soon as the ban on partisan activities is lifted, public employees as union members may feel differently. Some 4.7 million state and local government employees are organized in some fashion. If they were freed of restrictions on their political activities, their union leaders and professional associations could channel this vast political resource toward raising salaries and benefits at the taxpayers' expense. What ambitious legislator would spurn the campaign money and manpower that a well-heeled union could offer? And what union of public employees would not expect the legislator it backed to come through with hefty wage increases at appropriations time? Such are the dilemmas surrounding the proposed rescinding of limitations on the political freedom of public employees.

---

[24] Jeffrey C. Rinehart and Lee E. Bernick, "Political Attitudes and Behavior Patterns of Federal Civil Servants." *Public Administration Review 35* (November–December, 1975), 603–611.

RACE, SEX, AND JOBS:
THE CHALLENGE OF AFFIRMATIVE ACTION

One of the myths of American democracy is that jobs, especially public jobs, are open to all. They are not. Prejudice is still with us, and it works against both women and members of minority groups. As a result, the public bureaucracy has witnessed the rise of "affirmative action." Affirmative action is a policy that argues for the hiring of members of disadvantaged groups on the grounds that government positions should be open to as many people as possible.

AFFIRMATIVE ACTION: PRO AND CON

Affirmative action is a highly sensitive issue in state and local public administration today. Those who favor affirmative action argue that government should make special efforts, including the reduction of entrance standards, to hire members of those segments of American society that have endured various forms of racial, religious, ethnic, or sexual discrimination. They reason that, because of cultural bias in testing, lack of educational opportunity, and general social prejudice, government owes those people who have suffered these injustices a special chance to get ahead. If this issue entails some bending of the civil service regulations, as often is done for veterans, so be it. Such rule-bending will, after all, only balance the social equities for those applicants who have had to suffer bigotry in the past. This is as it should be, since government is the single institution most responsible for assuring equality of opportunity in society.

Those who argue against affirmative action claim that no "lowering of standards" should be tolerated, regardless of the applicant's past tribulations. The logic for this viewpoint is that government owes the best possible governance to all the governed. To hire applicants who do not score as well on tests as other applicants, or who do not have comparable educational attainments, or who are just somehow less qualified, irrespective of the tough breaks in their backgrounds, is to do a disservice to the populace generally, deprived groups included. The economy, efficiency, effectiveness, and responsiveness of government will deteriorate to the detriment of all, unless only the top applicants are hired and promoted.

THE FEDERAL IMPACT

The federal government has adopted the first position. It favors hiring members of deprived groups, and consequently, it has implemented affirmative action policies that have had and are having a profound effect on state and local governments. The major legislation in this regard is the Civil Rights Act of 1964, which paved the way in a general fashion for the more specific efforts that followed. These included: tougher executive orders by the president; prohibition of discrimination in federal agencies and by private contractors on the federal payroll; and some significant court decisions.

An especially important new law in this light is the Equal Employment Opportunity Act of 1972. This brought state and local governments under the provisions of the Civil Rights Act for the first time. It also provided the first statutory grounds for the federal government's equal employment opportunity programs. The act prohibits discrimination based on race, religion, sex, and national origin, and directly affects roughly 13 million state and local government employees. The U.S. Equal Employment Opportunity Commission (EEOC), which the act established, may investigate charges of employment discrimination in state and local governments and, if no conciliation is achieved, the U.S. Department of Justice may bring suit against the alleged offender. On top of that, the person in question may also initiate his or her own private litigation. It is this kind of federal legislation, plus significant court cases, that have made state and local governments extremely aware of the demands of minority groups and women.

QUOTAS OR "QUALITY"?

These realities in national policy bring us quickly to the question of quotas. The term *quota* refers to the argument that the traditional entry and promotion qualifications of the civil service should be reduced or waived for women and minority group members until their numbers in government, at all ranks, equal their proportion of the population at large. In brief, each group would have a quota, or a percentage, of the public jobs allotted to it and that percentage would be equal to the group's percentage in the state's or city's population. If a city had 10 percent blacks in its population, then blacks would be allocated 10 percent of the city's jobs.

Pressure to establish quota systems in state and local governments has met with some success. In 1972, for example, a federal district court ordered that one black be hired for every newly hired white until the all white Alabama state police force was 25 percent black, a figure corresponding to the percentage of blacks in Alabama according to the 1970 census. Although in another 1972 decision the federal court denied the legitimacy of an outright quota system, it nonetheless ordered the Minneapolis Fire Department to hire at least one minority applicant for every two whites in its next sixty openings. In 1973, the federal court ordered the San Francisco Civil Service Department to establish two separate lists of candidates for entry-level positions and promotions, one list for minorities and one for nonminorities, and to hire three minority candidates for every two nonminority candidates until the number of minority police patrolmen was brought up to at least 30 percent of the total. The court also ordered the department to promote one minority and one nonminority candidate until the total number of minority sergeants in the department also equalled at least 30 percent of the total number of sergeants. Similarly, openings in the Chicago police force were ordered to be filled in groups of two hundred, with one hundred positions to be filled by blacks and Spanish-surnamed males, thirty-three to be filled by women, and sixty-seven to be filled by other men.[25] Victor A. Thompson contends that the Chicago police department had more than six hundred vacancies in 1974 "as a result" of such court orders.[26]

THE "REVERSE DISCRIMINATION" DILEMMA

Such court orders and public policies have resulted in the accusation of "reverse discrimination," a charge usually levelled by organizations made up largely of white males. White policemen in Dayton, Ohio, for example, sued that city in 1973 charging racial discrimination in promotions. The most famous reverse discrimination case is *Regents of the University of California* v. *Bakke*, in which one Allan Bakke, a white male, was denied admission to the University of California's Medical School at Davis because that institution had set aside a portion (16 percent) of each entering class for blacks and other "approved minorities." In 1977, the California Supreme Court upheld a lower court's ruling, and with it Bakke's position, by refusing to endorse racial quotas, arguing that doing so "would call for the sacrifice of principle for the sake of dubious expediency," going on to note that people should "be judged on the basis of individual merit alone." Both the lower court and the California Supreme Court, in deciding against the university, had ruled that the university had violated the Civil Rights Act of 1964 and, significantly, the Fourteenth Amendment of the Constitution, which forbids states to "deny to any person . . . the equal protection of the laws." The University of California appealed to the U. S. Supreme Court, which agreed to hear the case.

In 1978, the Supreme Court, in a five-to-four decision, ruled against the university, thus upholding the California Supreme Court. But the Court's ruling was not clear cut. Justice Lewis Powell, Jr., writing the Courts main opinion, stated that the medical school had gone too far in considering race as a criterion for admission, but Powell also said (if rather vaguely) that affirmative action programs could properly be a factor in admitting students. Powell stated, "Preferring members of any one group for no reason other than race or ethnic origin is discrimination for its own sake," holding that such discrimination, as expressed by rigid racial quotas, was in violation of the Fourteenth Amendment and thus was unconstitutional.

Importantly, each of the remaining four justices in the majority wrote his

[25] Charles S. Rhyne, "The Letter of the Law." *Public Management* 57 (November, 1975), 9–11.
[26] Victor A. Thompson. *Without Sympathy or Enthusiasm: The Problem of Administrative Compassion* (University, Ala.: The University of Alabama Press, 1975), p.79.

own separate opinion, and none of them took Powell's position that quotas were unconstitutional. Instead, they held that Bakke should have been admitted to the University of California Medical School on the basis of the Civil Rights Act of 1964; Justice John Paul Stevens opined, in words reflecting this tack, that the act prohibited "in unmistakable terms . . . the exclusion of individuals from federally funded programs because of their race."

The distinction between ruling racial quotas unconstitutional (as Powell did) or illegal (as the other four justices did) is significant. If the majority had held that the University of California had violated the Constitution, then affirmative action programs across the country would probably have faced dismantling. Fortunately for these programs, however, all the nine justices agreed that affirmative action programs per se were neither unconstitutional nor illegal, and that being from a minority group could "be deemed a 'plus' in a particular applicant's file," to quote Justice Powell, although it would "not insulate the individual from comparison with all other candidates . . . ."

Justice Thurgood Marshall, the Court's only black, wrote the dissenting opinion, stating, "If we are ever to become a fully integrated society, one in which the color of a person's skin will not determine the opportunities available to him or her, we must be willing to open those doors" that have been shut to blacks in the past.

The *Bakke* decision, while limited to education admissions policies, had obvious ramifications for affirmative action programs in all sectors, and for that reason was greeted with demonstrations across the country calling for its overturn. Clearly, the judiciary's wrestling with the dilemma of reverse discrimination is far from over.

Regardless of how reverse discrimination suits will be decided in the courtroom, it is clear that the problem is both real and divisive not only for public administrators but for the citizenry. A review of public opinion polls on the topic concluded that "Americans are sensitive to the distinction between *compensatory action* and *preferential treatment*" in the hiring and promotion of minorities and women.[27] In other words, vast majorities of whites in various surveys conducted from 1972 on respond that they approve of such actions as government job-training programs for minorities, but draw the line in suspending normal merit standards as a means of hiring and promoting minorities. Indeed, blacks and women also respond in this way; in a 1977 Gallup poll, for example, blacks endorsed promoting minorities on the basis of "ability" over "preferential treatment" by 64 to 27 percent, and 71 percent of the women respondents favored the same distinction.[28]

Nevertheless, whose ox is gored remains a valid political principle, and the discrimination issue is no exception. College faculty members, for

---

[27] Seymour Martin Lipset and William Schneider, "An Emerging National Consensus." *The New Republic* (October 15, 1977), 8. Emphasis is original.

[28] *Ibid.*, p. 9.

example, heavily favor using affirmative action criteria in deciding the admission of undergraduates to college (62 percent in 1975), but when it comes to deciding their own careers, they are not nearly so positively disposed toward the notion: less than 35 percent of the nation's professors favor giving preferential treatment to women and minority applicants for faculty positions.[29]

In responding to the dilemma of reverse discrimination, some state and local governments seem to have gone overboard—perhaps in part because of the wilyness of their employees. Consider these examples.[30] In 1977 fifty-three San Francisco police officers claiming that they were American Indians were hauled before the Equal Opportunity Commission and all were officially reclassified as white.

In Los Angeles, a city long under federal pressure to desegregate its schools, the school board was attempting to attain faculties in each school that were at least 30 percent minorities. Both white and minority teachers began claiming they were of a different race to avoid being sent to another school district. To counter this ploy, Los Angeles established "ethnic review committees" that investigated "ethnic discrepancies" among teachers.

In New York, both teachers and pupils are "visually confirmed" by the board of education for racial identification purposes—and the subsequent assignment to a school.

If all this sounds a bit like springtime in Hitler's Germany, it is. Racial certification, regardless of motivation, is unpalatable to most Americans. Nevertheless, racial review boards may become a standard component in the state and local governments of the future as public employees of all races try to "pass" for the sake of enhancing their work location and promotion prospects.

Perhaps the best single hope for meeting both the demands of disadvantaged groups and the demands of those who are qualified but not disadvantaged is the almost incredibly rapid growth of employment in state and local governments. As a consequence, there is a fair amount of slack in the system. This growth is put in perspective when we realize that for nearly thirty years, state and local employment has been increasing at more than twice the rate of employment in the private sector. With some 13 million people employed in the state and local governments work forces, there may be room to accommodate both sets of seemingly irreconcilable demands pertaining to "discrimination" and "reverse discrimination."

THE POLITICS OF AFFIRMATIVE ACTION: THE OAKLAND EXPERIENCE

How local governments respond to the question of affirmative action has been detailed in Thompson's case study of Oakland. In 1969, spokespersons for minority job hunters challenged Oakland's personnel director over his

---

[29] *Ibid.*

[30] The examples of "reverse passing" are in: "Disadvantaged Groups, Individual Rights." *The New Republic* (October 15, 1977), 7 and Eliot Marshall, "Race Certification." *Ibid.,* p. 19.

affirmative action policies. The challenge came as the result of a report issued by the U.S. Commission on Civil Rights, which observed that Oakland was the only major jurisdiction among seven metropolitan areas studied in which the three main minority groups were substantially underrepresented in the city's job rosters. With a minority population of almost 50 percent in Oakland, only 15.3 percent of its city hall's employees were black, 1.5 percent had Spanish surnames, and 1.6 percent were Oriental.

Oakland's minority leaders focused on two strategies. They attempted to "bang Oakland officials over the head" with the city's dismal record of minority employment, and they also tried to involve themselves in the recruitment structures of the city. A major target of the minorities was the police force; minority leaders felt that its written tests were culturally biased, and a suit was duly filed. Minorities also pressured for a Citizens' Advisory Committee for the force; the police chief and the personnel director resisted, seeing it as a front for a community control board.

Oakland city officials were quick to construct their own version of a domino theory on affirmative action: if one department "fell" to minority pressure, then all the departments would become more susceptible to affirmative action demands. Although Oakland officials had the legal and actual power to flatly deny the demands of minorities, they chose not to be so direct and thus avoided an image of unresponsiveness. Delay was a major tactic in this strategy. Because recruitment authority in Oakland's city hall was widely dispersed, officials had a great deal of opportunity to pass the buck. One frustrated minority spokesman compared the bureaucracy of Oakland to a "monolithic multi-headed hydra—when we approach one head, it always tells us that the other head is responsible." Or, as another minority member stated, "In Oakland the buck never stops."[31]

Meanwhile, city officials marshalled a variety of tactics designed to justify their own positions and throw the blame on the minorities. For example, the personnel director warned, "The city is responsible to the taxpayer and can't afford to hire people not capable of doing their jobs."

Not all of Oakland's officials were so recalcitrant on the issue. Some procedures were changed to encourage minority applicants, and the use of oral examinations was expanded to facilitate the entrance of minorities into city government. As Thompson observes, "Orals make favoritism feasible both in structuring the mechanism and scoring applicant responses. Furthermore, racial preference in the oral is not as visible within the bureaucracy as other adjustments aimed at helping minorities (for example, lowering credential requirements). Consequently, manipulation of the oral is less likely to precipitate organized opposition."[32] Thompson concludes that, in the face of demands from minorities to expand minority representation in the city, a personnel director generally will put more pressure on those city

---

[31] Quoted in Thompson, *Personnel Policy in the City,* p. 120.
[32] *Ibid.,* p. 136.

departments that have hired few minorities, have made little effort to recruit them, and that have a substantial number of open slots.

THE EFFECTS OF THE EFFORTS

The city of Oakland is a microcosm of the problem of representation of deprived groups in state and local governments across the country. In 1969, the last year for which data are available, both minorities and women were underrepresented and underpaid in state and local governments.[33] Of the more than 3 million employees, excluding teachers, who were working in local governments in 1969, fewer than 500,000 were blacks. Of these, less than 5 percent of the black males were among the highest-paid managerial and administrative categories. By contrast, more than 12 percent of the white males were in these classes, and more than 6 percent of the white women. Slightly more than 113,000 city employees during that year were of Spanish origin, and less than 5 percent of the Spanish males were categorized as managers and administrators, and less than 3 percent of the Spanish women were so classified.

When we look at the status of women in state and local governments, quite aside from race, we find that their salaries are substantially lower than those of males for the same kinds of jobs, although, even here, black women and women of Spanish origin earn substantially less than white women.

A 1973 survey of more than two thousand city managers found that even less progress had been made in the upper echelons of local government. Ninety-eight percent of the city managers responding were white, and 99 percent were male. Fifty-four percent of the city managers responding said that no action plans had been taken by their jurisdictions concerning affirmative action plans for women and, of the 46 percent of those cities that had taken such action, the action was initiated by the city manager himself in 84 percent of the cases; in only 52 percent of the cases did the manager have the support of his own city council.

In terms of initiating affirmative action plans for minorities, the percentages were a little higher; 55 percent of the cities surveyed had initiated an affirmative action plan for minorities, a substantially higher proportion than that for women. In 84 percent of those cities the initiative had been taken by the city manager, and in 56 percent of those cases the manager had the support of his city council. "While managers and chief administrators exhibit no strong personal commitment to such [equal opportunity] goals, they are far and away the principal initiators of affirmative action in their governments."[34] Indeed, of all the cities surveyed, council–manager cities tended

---

[33] Bureau of the Census, *1970 Census of Population: Government Workers*, PC(2)-7D. (Washington, D.C.:U.S. Bureau of the Census, 1973, pp. 171–173.

[34] Robert J. Huntley and Robert J. McDonald, "Urban Managers: Organizational Preferences, Managerial Styles, and Social Policy Roles." *The Municipal Yearbook: 1975* (Washington, D.C.: International City Management Association, 1975), p. 157.

to be the most positive in establishing employment goals and objectives for minorities and women and in relaxing temporarily civil service requirements to increase minority employment.

The picture of minority employment in the public service is bleak, but a glimmer of change is on the horizon. A 1977 study found that 51 percent of all black male college graduates are employed by governments; this compares to about 25 percent of white male college graduates. Black professionals now occupy proportionately more governmental positions than white professionals in such fields as law, personnel, labor relations, and administration. During the 1960s, black managerial workers employed by government nearly tripled. For the first time in the nation's history, "young highly educated black men and all black women are beginning their careers on rough parity with comparable whites." [35] If this conclusion is accurate, then it is largely because of government affirmative action programs.

Affirmative action or, more properly defined, the giving of an even break to people who have been disadvantaged in society because of their race or sex, is one of the knottier problems of state and local governments. Judging by the available data, state and local governments have been less than forthcoming in the hiring of members of disadvantaged groups, especially in the areas of public safety, such as police and firefighters. But the pressure is on, and it is growing increasingly intense. If government—the institution in society most responsible for according people an equal chance regardless of race, religion, or sex—is not responsive, then what social institution will be?

BLUE-COLLAR BUREAUCRATS: THE CHALLENGE OF UNIONISM AND THE RIGHT TO STRIKE

THE BIG GROWTH IN BIG LABOR

That unionization and collective bargaining are burgeoning realities in state and local governments is evident from Figure 14–1, which shows the growth of unionism in state and local governments from 1962 through 1974, the last year for which official figures are available. It shows that unionism across the board in state and local governments essentially tripled within that twelve-year time frame.

The major associations and unions of state and local government employees are the American Federation of State, County, and Municipal Employees (AFSCME) with more than 750,000 members, the American Federation of Teachers (AFT) with 475,000 members, the recently militant National Education Association (NEA) with 1.8 million teachers in its ranks

---

[35] Richard B. Freeman, Carnegie Commission on Higher Education, cited in: Lawrence Feinberg, "Blacks Scoring Employment Gains." *Washington Post,* reprinted in *The Arizona Republic,* May 17, 1977.

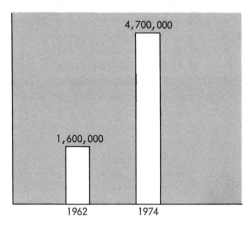

FIGURE 14–1 GROWTH OF ORGANIZED LABOR IN STATE AND LOCAL GOVERNMENTS, 1962–1974

Source: Derived from Eugene C. Hagburg and Marvin J. Levine, *Labor Relations: An Integrated Perspective.* (New York: West, 1978), p. 133.

(making it the nation's second biggest union), and the International Association of Fire Fighters with 175,000 members. Both the AFSCME (now the sixth largest union in the country) and the AFT tripled their membership rosters between 1964 and 1976 and, overall, it is in public employment that Big Labor sees its real growth opportunities for the future. In fact, organized labor's share of employees in the private sector has declined sharply in recent years, while its share of public employees has jumped dramatically. More than half of all state and local employees (4.7 million as of 1974) are organized.

Although union membership does not exceed more than a third of the state and local employees in any one state (excluding teachers), state and local governments nevertheless are the fields worth tilling insofar as organized labor is concerned. If we include the one million state and local government workers who belong to professional associations (again excluding teachers) that bargain on behalf of employees (but which technically are not considered unions), the number of "unionized" public workers amounts to 20 percent of all the people who work for state and local governments. When teachers are included in the calculations, we find that, in 1974, 56 percent of the nation's full-time local employees and nearly 21 percent of the country's state employees were organized. Table 14–1 breaks down these figures on union membership by the major kinds of public employment and type of government. As it indicates, nationally the most heavily organized government workers at the state and local levels were firefighters, with nearly 77 percent of their members organized, teachers, with almost 70 percent, and police, with almost 56 percent.[36]

---

[36] The figures on union growth in the public sector are drawn from: *LMRS Newsletter*, Vol 3, #1 (January, 1972), 5; H. Conany and L. Dewey, "Union Membership Among Government Employees." *Monthly Labor Review* 93 (July, 1970), 15–20; Robert E. Walsh, "Sorry, No Government Today." In *Union vs. City Hall* (Boston, Beacon Press, 1969), Chapter 4; Carl W. Stenberg, "Labor Management Relations in State and Local Governments." *Public Administration Review* 32 (March–April, 1972), 102–107; U.S. Department of Commerce, Bureau of the Census, *Labor Management Relations in State and Local Governments: 1974.* Special Studies No. 75 (February, 1976), p. 9.

TABLE 14-1 STATE AND LOCAL GOVERNMENT ORGANIZED EMPLOYEES, BY SELECTED FUNCTIONS, BY TYPE OF GOVERNMENT

SELECTED FUNCTIONS

Item	All functional	EDUCATION			High-ways	Public welfare	Hospi-tals	Police protec-tion	Fire Protec-tion	Sanitation other than sewerage
		Total	Teachers	Other						
UNITED STATES										
Number of Full-Time Employees										
Employees	8 578 162	4 113 716	2 718 563	1 395 153	551 364	283 409	856 120	473 293	194 185	116 953
State Governments	2 312 410	738 689	266 080	472 609	283 021	112 102	437 348	61 932	–	–
Local Governments	6 265 752	3 375 018	2 453 531	921 487	268 343	171 307	418 772	411 361	194 185	116 953
Counties	1 176 569	235 668	168 219	67 449	121 448	128 378	194 075	81 863	9 514	4 447
Municipalities	1 920 226	338 901	252 445	86 456	116 327	42 349	122 040	309 654	172 059	107 524
Townships	191 115	90 148	70 863	19 285	26 515	580	1 478	19 844	7 272	4 695
School Districts	2 710 301	2 710 301	1 962 004	748 297	–	–	–	–	–	–
Special Districts	267 541	–	–	–	4 053	–	101 179	–	5 340	287
Number of Full-Time Organized Employees										
Organized Employees	4 319 941	2 327 711	1 889 380	438 331	253 748	127 714	356 970	262 943	148 511	58 630
State Governments	942 532	197 087	82 107	114 980	163 882	49 787	228 244	33 551	–	–
Local Governments	3 377 409	2 130 624	1 807 273	323 351	89 866	77 927	128 726	229 392	148 511	58 630
Counties	458 504	148 400	133 266	15 134	34 108	46 315	60 754	31 474	5 964	1 192
Municipalities	1 047 346	238 122	185 642	52 480	47 277	31 604	56 447	186 872	137 873	54 562
Townships	98 570	59 889	51 087	8 802	7 229	8	201	11 046	4 674	2 783
School Districts	1 684 213	1 684 213	1 437 278	246 935	–	–	–	–	–	–
Special Districts	88 776	–	–	–	1 252	–	11 324	–	–	93
Percent of Full-Time										
Employees Organized	50.4	56.6	69.5	31.4	46.0	45.1	41.7	55.6	76.5	50.1
State Governments	40.8	26.7	30.9	24.3	57.9	44.4	52.2	54.2	–	–
Local Governments	53.9	63.1	73.7	35.0	33.4	45.5	30.7	55.7	76.4	50.1
Counties	39.0	63.0	79.3	22.4	28.1	36.1	31.3	38.4	62.7	26.8
Municipalities	54.5	70.3	73.5	60.7	40.6	74.6	46.3	60.3	80.1	50.7
Townships	51.6	66.4	72.1	45.6	27.3	1.4	13.6	55.7	64.3	59.3
School Districts	62.1	62.1	73.3	33.0	–	–	–	–	–	–
Special Districts	33.1	–	–	–	30.9	–	11.2	–	–	32.4

Source: Department of Commerce, Bureau of the Census, *1972 Census of Governments, Volume 3: Public Employment.* (Washington, D. C.: U.S. Government Printing Office) p. 8.

Efforts to organize public employees are not new, and attempts to organize government workers goes back to the 1830s.[37] And, in the 1800s, there was much reason for public employees to organize. Police and firefighters, for example, who are among the most heavily unionized public employees today, have traditionally tolerated among the worst working conditions. In 1907, the New York Health Department condemned thirty of the city's eighty-five police stations as uninhabitable, and the police worked from seventy-three to ninety-eight hours a week. Firefighters, who commonly were paid low salaries, worked twenty-one hours *a day* and had only one day off in eight! Still, despite such conditions, there was considerable resistance to the unionization of public employees. The reasons were mostly ideological, but also economic. As merit systems developed in state and local governments, job security became more assured and working conditions did improve. There were (and are) also a spate of state and local laws forbidding or discouraging any kind of union activity by government workers (the constitutionality of which is at least questionable). White-collar workers, as a class, had never really identified with unionization and, finally, there was a considerable weight of public opinion against the notion of government workers being allowed to disrupt vital public services by resorting to the strike.

BIG LABOR AND PUBLIC MANAGEMENT

The initial indications that attitudes on the issue of organizing public workers were shifting came at the state and local levels. In 1959, Wisconsin passed the first law requiring its local governments to bargain collectively, and by 1974 thirty-five states had similar statutes, and only seven states prohibited strikes by their workers. However, a special study of local governments conducted during the same year by the U.S. Census Bureau found that only 15 percent of America's eighty thousand local governments had any kind of labor relations policy that addressed organized public employees.[38]

State and local governments are only beginning to become sophisticated in their collective bargaining with organized employees. Generally, state and local policies on government negotiations with organized employees are of two types. The *collective bargaining* approach permits decisions on salaries, hours, and working conditions to be made jointly between employees and employer representatives. The *meet-and-confer* tack says only that both sides

---

[37] This paragraph is drawn from: Sterling Spero and John M. Capozolla, *The Urban Community and Its Unionized Bureaucracies* (New York: Dunellen, 1973), p. 15; Hugh O'Neill, "The Growth of Municipal Employee Unions." In Robert H. Connery and William Farr, *Unionization of Municipal Employees* (New York: The Academy of Political Science, 1970), pp. 3–4; and Lawrence D. Mankin, "Public Employee Organizations: The Quest for Legitimacy." *Public Personnel Management* 6 (September–October, 1977), 334–340.

[38] U.S. Department of Commerce, Bureau of the Census, *Labor Management Relations*, p. 9.

must meet and confer over these issues, but that management has the final decision. Judging by their written policies, the great majority of states and localities prefer the collective bargaining approach.

State and local governments are becoming increasingly innovative in bargaining with their employees. Englewood, Colorado, for example, has passed a city ordinance stipulating that an impartial fact-finders' recommendation will be put on the ballot with the best last offer of the union and management alongside it; then Englewood lets the voters decide the issues. Englewood reflects the increasing use of "goldfish bowl bargaining," in which the public is being brought increasingly into the negotiation process, a process that traditionally, particularly in the private sector, has gone on behind closed doors. This protects the public's right to know and opens up the bargaining at a time when the public's knowledge can affect the outcome of the negotiation process. Goldfish bowl bargaining is now a fact of public life in a number of states and cities.[39]

COLLECTIVE BARGAINING: THE RECORD IN DOLLARS

The basic dilemma of collective bargaining in the public sector is the fact that, unlike the private sector, neither side is bargaining with its own money. Public labor is demanding tax monies that may or may not be in the public till, and public management is negotiating with tax money that likewise may not be in the public till. The person who pays is the taxpayer. With this reality in mind, it is not too surprising that public labor unions have made considerable gains financially in their negotiations with public management. Currently, personnel costs account for between 50 to 80 percent of a typical city budget, and much of it stems from the gains that workers have won in collective bargaining. From 1962 to 1967, the number of city employees grew by only 19 percent, but municipal payrolls burgeoned by 46 percent. Major gainers during this period were the heavily unionized employees.[40]

An important negotiating area between public employers and employees is that of pensions. In police departments, for example, the national tendency has been to permit retirement at half-pay after twenty years' service. Such arrangements, of course, aggravate urban financial problems, as happened in New York City. In New York, transit workers, police, firefighters, and other workers are allowed early retirement with generous benefits, and "the pension specialist" of the American Federation of State, County, and Municipal Employees has been quoted as saying that its "members are just beginning to realize that pensions can be negotiated." When queried where the money for higher pensions is coming from, the pension specialist for AFSME replied, "That's government's problem. Just

---

[39] Sam Zagoria, "Attitudes Harden in Governmental Labor Relations." *ASPA News and Views* 26 (December, 1976), 1, 21, and 22.

[40] Spero and Capozolla, *The Urban Community*, p. 218.

because there is a pinch for money, it's no excuse to make the employees do without."[41]

Collective bargaining has given public employees a relatively good deal compared with workers in the private sector, and evidence of this is provided by a study conducted by the U.S. Bureau of Labor Statistics in twenty-two large and middle-sized representative cities. In a report that covered eleven large cities (Atlanta, Boston, Buffalo, Chicago, Houston, Kansas City, Los Angeles, New Orleans, Newark, New York, and Philadelphia), it was stated that in nine of these cities government workers in clerical jobs were paid more than their counterparts in either private industry or federal government. Most of these cities also showed higher pay scales for computer-related jobs and janitorial jobs. Employees in skilled and semi-skilled blue-collar jobs earned more than their counterparts in industry, mainly because their jobs were steadier than those in the private sphere.[42]

The Bureau of Labor Statistics did not address the issue of whether or not collective bargaining was a reason behind these kinds of increases relative to the private sector, but a study by the Institute of Labor Relations of twelve Michigan school districts concluded that collective bargaining appeared to have given teachers 10 percent to 20 percent more in wage increases than unilateral school board action would have furnished.[43]

THE PUBLIC STRIKE: THE PUBLIC RECORD

Because of the potential fiscal impacts that collective bargaining can have on state and local governments, states and cities often are reluctant to "come across" to union demands. The result of such reluctance can be, and occasionally is, a strike. At one time sanitation workers were the most frequent public employees to walk picket lines; more recently it has been teachers who are most inclined to strike. In 1973, there were 117 teacher strikes involving 51,400 workers, and the next year the number soared to 133 strikes of teachers involving 60,100 people. In 1974, there were 384 strikes by public employees. Of these, 348 occurred at the local level, 34 at the state level, and 2 at the national level; 106,700 workers were involved and 1,404,200 days lay idle during the year. Compare these figures with 1956, when there were only 27 such strikes involving only 3,460 people and 11,100 days idle.[44] Table 14–2 indicates the types of work stoppages in

---

[41] *Ibid.*, p. 219.

[42] Stephen H. Perloff, "Comparing Municipal Salaries with Industry and Federal Pay." *Monthly Labor Review* 94 (October, 1971), 46–50: and Spero and Capozolla, *The Urban Community*, pp. 219–220.

[43] Charles N. Rehmus and Evan Wilner, *The Economic Results of Teacher Bargaining: Michigan's First Two Years* (Ann Arbor, Mich.: Institute of Labor and Industrial Relations, 1968).

[44] U.S. Department of Labor, Bureau of Labor Statistics, *Analysis of Work Stoppages: 1973* (Washington, D.C.: U.S. Government Printing Office, 1975), p. 31; *Ibid: 1974*, pp. 5–6; U.S. Department of Labor, Bureau of Labor Statistics, *Handbook of Labor Statistics* (Washington, D.C.: U.S. Government Printing Office, 1975), p. 407.

TABLE 14–2 TYPES OF WORK STOPPAGES IN GOVERNMENT BY ISSUE

ITEM *Total*	1973 NUMBER OF STOPPAGES *387*	WORKERS INVOLVED *196.4*	DAYS IDLE *2303.9*	1974 NUMBER OF STOPPAGES *384*	WORKERS INVOLVED *160.7*	DAYS IDLE *1404.2*
Issue:						
Wages	235	159.0	2005.1	255	131.3	1207.9
Supplementary benefits	4	.6	2.7	5	1.2	2.6
Wage adjustments	5	.4	2.4	10	1.6	5.3
Hours of work	3	.4	1.7	3	.7	3.9
Other contractual matters	5	1.8	23.7	7	1.0	2.4
Union organization & security	42	10.7	123.7	41	5.8	56.1
Job security	26	13.1	91.9	25	10.2	92.2
Plant administration	52	8.2	37.8	33	8.1	22.7
Other working conditions	7	1.0	6.9	3	.4	10.2
Interunion or intraunion matters	4	.9	7.5	—	—	—
Not reported	4	.4	.6	2	.3	.8

Source: U. S. Department of Labor, Bureau of Labor Statistics, *Work Stoppages in Government, 1974* (Washington, D. C.: Government Printing Office, 1976), p. 6.

government by the issues involved. It is clear from the table that wages are the paramount issue in strikes of public employees, followed closely by supplementary benefits such as pensions.

Regardless of whether or not there are laws permitting or prohibiting strikes in the public sector, strikes are realities. The emotional issue of the public employees' right to strike nonetheless runs deep. One viewpoint holds that a strike by public employees amounts to an act of insurrection because such strikes are directed against the people themselves. The opposing view contends that the right of government workers to strike is a basic freedom protected under the Constitution. To deny public employees a right granted to workers in private corporations is to treat public personnel as second-class citizens. The courts thus far have held that there is no Constitutional right of public workers to strike, but neither has the judiciary prohibited the enactment of laws permitting government employees to strike.

THE PUBLIC STRIKE: THE COPS AND "COOL CAL"

In any case, it is increasingly apparent that strikes are here to stay and, while it may be difficult to believe, over the years strikes by public employees have become more moderate (if also more frequent). Consider, for example, the Boston police strike of 1919, which was the nation's first true taste of a public employee labor dispute. Boston's police had extensive and legitimate gripes, and a precipitating issue of the strike was whether or not Boston's Finest could affiliate with the American Federation of Labor. For a period of six years, Boston's police had received no increases in their starvation salaries, despite the fact that the cost of living had soared 86 percent during the period. Politics was rife in the police personnel system, and a patrolman had to be on the good side of the commissioner to be promoted. Most of Boston's police staged a walkout in September of that year, and Boston's crooks had a field day. When mob rule started to get out of hand, the governor sent the entire Massachusetts State Guard, with himself in complete control, to Boston and summarily dismissed the strikers. Samuel Gompers, head of the American Federation of Labor, protested Boston's refusal to allow its police to affiliate with his union. The governor replied, "There is no right to strike against the public safety by anybody, anywhere, any time." This hard line stand against "anarchy" was politically beneficial to the governor of Massachusetts. In the following year, he was elected vice president of the United States and, when the president died in 1923, he became president. His name was Calvin Coolidge.[45]

THE PUBLIC STRIKE: "IRON MIKE" AND THE "WHITE KNIGHT"

Strikes by public employees, of course, are replete with politics in the present day, just as they were in 1919. Consider the example of New York City, particularly in its dealings with the city's Transit Workers Union. New York became effectively involved in labor negotiations in 1954, when Robert Wagner became mayor. Wagner, a Democrat and son of the author of the National Labor Relations Act of 1935, liked organized labor and needed its support to win in New York politics. Michael Quill, known as Iron Mike to his followers, was the leader of the Transit Workers Union, and the relationship between the mayor and Iron Mike was a cozy one.

The scenario went as follows:

> The transit workers' contract would require renewal on December 31. Quill would begin his display in November making demand after demand, threat after threat, with great flair and publicity. As the hour for the obligatorily threatened New Year's Day subway strike drew near, Quill entered into a private session with Wagner. Ultimately, they emerged, Quill smiling; Wagner, frowning, would mutter something along the lines of how costly the settlement would be to the City. New Year's Day, the trains ran."[46]

Quill did not bother with such trivia as announcing the content of the proposed contract in detail to his transit workers, but would run for reelection in February and garner overwhelming victories.

---

[45] Shafritz *et al.*, *Personnel Management in Government*, pp. 213–214.

[46] *Ibid.*, pp. 221–224.

In point of fact, Quill's contracts with Wagner were paragons of fiscal responsibility, enabling the city to raise standards of operating efficiency by allowing thousands of jobs to be squeezed out over time in New York's deficit-ridden transit authority; on occasion, the transit system was seriously undermanned.

Then John Vliet Lindsay was elected. Lindsay, a silk-stocking Republican with few ties to organized labor, would have difficulty with Iron Mike.

In 1966 the "White Knight" rode into city hall on a reformist Republican ticket. "The Yalie," as Iron Mike called him, had a limited understanding of the white working man, maintaining that "the plight of the cities is on the bargaining table," and intimating that he would not succumb to the likes of Quill. After five days in office, Lindsay was greeted with a twelve-day bus and subway strike. Quill, a master of publicity, tore up the court order enjoining him against striking before the television cameras, and promptly was jailed for contempt after tactfully stating: "Let the judge drop dead in his black robes!" Having said that, Quill was admitted to Bellevue Hospital with a heart attack. Iron Mike eventually ended up with a contract that doubled any previous settlement. The Yalie had been taught a lesson (in subsequent elections Lindsay received the backing of the city's unions), but the lesson was administered at the expense of the New York taxpayers.

THE PUBLIC STRIKE:
PUBLIC WORKERS AND POPULAR RESISTANCE

Taxpayers can be mean when aroused, as a large-scale strike in San Francisco indicated. In 1975, San Francisco's police and firefighters went on strike in what quickly became a bitter struggle with the city. Then-Mayor Joseph Alioto, long sympathetic to labor, in the view of many caved in completely to the strikers' demands. More importantly, however, the strikers succeeded in offending the public. Police had packed pistols on their hips in their picket lines, and some were evidently drunk and would jostle passers-by. Out-going Mayor Alioto's generous agreement with the police and firefighters was roundly criticized by San Franciscans and in the following year, when the city's craft workers struck, organized labor was faced with a considerably tougher attitude by the city's citizens.

San Francisco's craft workers had struck to protest plans to restructure the city's pay scales. The restructuring would have cut the wages of street cleaners from $17,353 a year to $16,178, and of plumbers from $23,843 annually (for a thirty-five hour week) to $20,143. They were quickly joined by other city workers, notably the city's 2,000 transit workers, thus shutting down San Francisco's trollies and buses. The water and electricity departments were especially hard-hit in the strike, which lasted thirty-nine days. The attitudes of the citizens of San Francisco were clear and unambiguous—they already had voted out several supervisors of San Francisco who had supported the police and firefighters—and they rejected the unions' latest demands by a margin of three-to-one. Organized labor itself was divided, with the teamsters, longshoremen, and workers in the city's main museum supporting the supervisors. Citizens voluntarily swept the streets, cleaned the city's swimming pools, and did not hassle the supervisors about the massive transit slowdown, despite the fact that almost a quarter of a million San Franciscans regularly relied on the public transit system.

Californians generally expressed resistance to the demands of public unions during this period. Voters in Santa Barbara repealed an ordinance giving municipal workers automatic wage increases based on the cost-of-living index. Voters in San Diego gave city management the power to fire employees who struck. Voters in San Rafael gave their approval to a measure that required the firing of police and firefighters who struck, and cut the salaries of those who came down with "the blue flu"—that is, engaged in deliberate work slow downs. Voters in Oakland repealed a law granting automatic pay increases to police and firefighters and reduced pensions. San Francisco was not alone in its resistance.

UNIONS VERSUS "MERIT": THE BASIC DIFFERENCES

The future of collective bargaining, unionization, and the right to strike bodes ill for the traditional merit standards of the civil service personnel system. At root, the differences between the "collective system" and the "civil service system" are two. One difference concerns the notion of *sovereignty.* The civil service system holds that a public position is a privilege, not a right, and that each public servant is obliged to uphold the public trust accorded to him or her by a paternalistic government. Conversely, the union system holds that employees are on an equal footing with employers, and that they have a right to use their collective powers as a means of improving their conditions of employment. The civil service system, by contrast, sees this contention as a threat to the sovereignty of the state, while the union system views the traditions of the civil service as redolent of worker exploitation.

The second difference concerns the concept of *individualism.* The American civil service system long has valued the ideal that the individual worker be judged for a position on the basis of his or her unique merits for performing the duties of a particular job. The union system, on the other hand, argues that the identity of the individual should be absorbed in a collective effort to better the conditions of all workers. Hence, the relations of the individual with his or her government employer are replaced by a new set of relations that exist between the government employer and a collective "class" of employees. Among the conflicts that result from these fundamental differences between the two systems over sovereignty and individualism are: disputes over employee participation and rights (equal treatment versus union shop); recruitment (competitive tests versus union membership); promotion (performance versus seniority); position classification and pay (objective analysis versus negotiation); working conditions (determination by legislatures and managements versus settlement by negotiations); and grievances (determination by civil service commissioners versus union representation to third-party arbitrators).

CONCLUSION: TURMOIL IN THE PUBLIC SERVICE

The problems that we have reviewed here dealing with "the administrative class" in state and local governments are complex and massive. Public personnel administration, like any other form of public administration, has large dollops of politics as part and parcel of it. The historic efforts of "good government" reformers to rid public personnel systems of "politics" traditionally have been based on the introduction of "merit principles" in the management of the public bureaucracy. Merit principles, as they normally have been understood, are now under considerable attack. The efforts to include more minorities and women in government, the attempts to expand freedom of political expression for government employees, and the reality of strikes, unionism, and collective bargaining, all lead one to wonder what "merit" in public personnel administration really means. Of these developments, perhaps that of union pressure is the most pertinent to our upcoming chapter on public finance.

15

THE PUBLIC PURSE, OR WHO'LL TAKE MANHATTAN?

Only one thing is more important to government than the people's trust, and that is money. Money, it is said, makes the world go round, and governments are very much a part of that world.

THE GROWTH OF GOVERNMENT: THE MONEY MEASURE

In 1978, government expenditures at all levels exceeded $757.2 billion, a phenomenal sum by any reckoning. Even more phenomenal is the fact that government spending had increased ten times since 1950. State and local governments spent their shares of that money (or $278.3 billion in 1978) on the basic human needs of their citizens. As the late James A. Maxwell and J. Richard Aaronson observe in their excellent volume on the topic, "State and local governments together spend three times as much as the federal government to provide civilian services for citizens. Education, roads, welfare, public health, hospitals, police, sanitation—these are state and local responsibilities, and their cost falls mainly on state and local sources of revenue . . .." [1]

The increase of state and local expenditures on these basic human needs has been particularly startling. As Table 15–1 indicates, though the U.S. population increased by only 16 percent in the fifteen years between 1961 and 1975, state and local government expenditures combined increased by 229 percent, and national government expenditures by 232 percent. To be fair, however, we should adjust these figures for inflation. The 1961 dollar had lost 46 percent of its value during this fifteen year period or, to put it another way, what cost fifty-four cents in 1961 cost a buck in 1975. When we take inflation into account, real state and local expenditures across the nation went up by 77 percent and real federal expenditures went up by 79 percent. These are considerable raises in levels of public expenditure and, moreover, the raises are real; they are not tilted by inflationary factors. Table 15–2 breaks down the same data by state *and* local expenditures.

Total government expenditures amounted to a per-person spending equivalent of $859 in 1961 and $2,444 in 1975; when adjusted for inflation, the 1975 figure becomes $1,320. Nevertheless, the actual growth in per capita governmental expenditures for the fifteen-year period was 53.7 percent. Then too, American governments absorbed 26.5 percent of the Gross National Product (GNP) in 1954, but by 1975 their expenditures accounted for an astounding 35 percent of the GNP—a jump from $97 billion to $525 billion. Most of this money was consumed by the federal

---

[1] James A. Maxwell and J. Richard Aaronson, *Financing State and Local Governments*, 3rd ed. (Washington, Brookings Institution, 1977) p. 1.

TABLE 15–1 FEDERAL AND COMBINED STATE/LOCAL GOVERNMENT EXPENDITURES, 1961–1975

ITEM	PERCENTAGE CHANGE 1961–1975	PERCENTAGE CHANGE 1961–1975 AFTER ADJUSTING FOR INFLATION
U. S. Population	+ 16	—
Federal Expenditures	+232	+79
State/Local Expenditures	+229	+77

government (from 19.1 percent in 1954 to nearly 24 percent in 1975), but the *rate* of increase was faster at the state and local levels, which used 7.4 percent of the GNP in 1954 and 11.7 percent in 1975.

Revenues, of course, also went up but not as rapidly as expenditures. Table 15–3 indicates this increase in the money that governments got from their citizens between 1961 and 1975. Revenues for state and local governments increased by 335 percent between 1961 and 1975, although the per capita increases went up only by 274 percent. Federal contributions to state and local governments increased substantially—by 560 percent.

The point of showing these dramatic increases in both expenditures and revenues of America's state and local governments, as well as of the federal government, is to demonstrate the growing importance of governments in the nation's economy. Governments account for an increasingly larger chunk of the nation's commerce and, in gobbling larger and larger slices of the country's economic pie, the public sector constitutes roughly one-third of the Gross National Product in today's economy. Table 15–3 also indicates how the federal government increasingly is helping state and local governments meet their obligations to their citizens.

In this chapter we shall consider, first, the impact that the federal government has on state and local finances, focusing especially on the grants-in-aid system, revenue-sharing, and the policy implications of federal decisions on transferring money to states and localities. We also shall examine the many types of taxes and other sources of revenue that state

TABLE 15–2 FEDERAL, STATE, AND LOCAL GOVERNMENT EXPENDITURES, 1961–1975

ITEM	PERCENTAGE CHANGE 1961–1975	PERCENTAGE CHANGE 1961–1975 AFTER ADJUSTING FOR INFLATION
U. S. Population	+ 16	—
Federal Expenditures	+232	+ 79
State Expenditures	+282	+106
Local Expenditures	+182	+ 52

TABLE 15–3 STATE AND LOCAL GOVERNMENTS GENERAL
REVENUE INCREASES, 1961–1975

Item	ALL STATE AND LOCAL GOVERNMENTS Total	Per Capita
Population		
1961	183,691,000	—
1975	213,466,000	—
% change	+16%	—
Total General Revenue from all Sources		
1961	$ 64,592.6 Million	$ 351.64
1975	$280,942.5 Million	1316.10
% change	+335%	+274%
Federal Contribution Portion of Above		
1961	$ 7,130.7 Million	$ 38.82
1975	$47,053.8 Million	220.43
% change	+560%	+468%

and local governments depend on and the issues of borrowing and debt in
state and local governments, zeroing in on that paragon of fiscal virtue,
New York City.

THE INTERGOVERNMENTAL MONEY GAME

Governments in America give each other money. All governments give this
money back to some of their citizens, and all citizens give some of their
money to government. The federal government gives money directly to
both state and local governments. More often than not, the federal government will give money to states with the understanding that these funds will
be channeled to the states' local governments, but states also grant money
to local governments on their own. We shall consider first the area of
federal transfer of money to state governments, then federal transfers to
local governments, and finally state grants to local governments.

A lot of money is involved in these transfers.[2] In 1977, payments by the
federal government to state and local governments totalled more than $70

---

[2]The following figures on intergovernmental transfers of money are taken from: Thomas
H. Kiefer, *The Political Impact of Federal Aid to State and Local Governments.* (Morristown:
General Learning Press, 1974) p. 9; and Advisory Commission on Intergovernmental
Relations, *Significant Features of Fiscal Federalism, 1976–77, Volume II.* (Washington: U.S.
Government Printing Office, 1977) Table 38.

billion, and state payments to local governments totalled more than $50 billion. These kinds of intergovernmental transfers of money have been proliferating for the past forty years, and the probability is that their scope will be enlarged in the future.

The increasing reliance of state and local governments on federal aid is both dramatic and disquieting. In 1902, the first year for which such figures were kept, federal aid to state and local governments amounted to only 2.6 percent of all federal domestic expenditures; by 1977, this proportion had attained nearly a quarter of all domestic, nondefense expenditures. In 1902, all federal aid amounted to only 0.7 percent of state and local general revenues; by 1977 the percentage was almost 28 percent. Most of this money (more than 70 percent) was used for welfare programs. Figure 15–1 indicates the growing dependence by state and local governments on the feds for money.

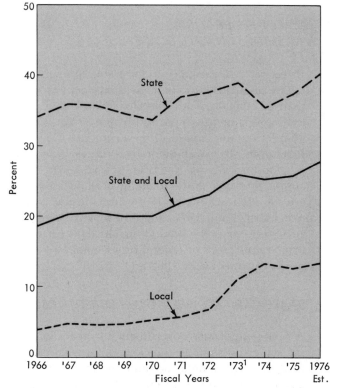

¹ Beginning in 1973, includes federal general revenue sharing.

FIGURE 15–1 FEDERAL AID IN RELATION TO STATE AND LOCAL GENERAL REVENUE FROM OWN SOURCES, 1966 THROUGH 1976

Source: Advisory Commission on Intergovernmental Relations, *Significant Features of Fiscal Federalism*, 1976–1977, 2:43.

FISCAL FEDERALISM: WASHINGTON, THE STATES, AND BIG MONEY

The 1930s was a period of great expansion in federal grants to state governments, and this expansion became an explosion in the 1960s and 1970s. In 1963, there were 181 federal grants to states; ten years later there were more than 500. The cost of these 181 grants in 1963 was $8.324 billion, or $44 per person; by 1973, this amount had grown to $43.121 billion, or $204 per capita. Table 15–4 indicates the shifts in federal grant policies toward state governments and their purposes from the postwar years to 1973. In that year, more than 80 percent of total federal intergovernmental transfers were in the form of grants-in-aid.[3] Federal grants were used largely for public assistance—programs for the blind, the disabled, the old, children, and the generally needy—followed by public health (notably Medicaid), education, and highways.

DIRECT FEDERALISM: WASHINGTON, CITIES, AND SUBURBS

Direct federal assistance to local governments, as opposed to state governments, also constitutes a major component of fiscal transfers. In 1973, more than $11 billion was channeled from the federal government directly to local governments. It made up more than 25 percent of total federal aid going to state and local governments. This increasing use of "direct federalism" by Washington constitutes an innovative approach to fiscal relationships among American governments. The major federal legislation authorizing this short-circuiting of state governments in fiscal federalism are the Housing Act of 1949, the Housing and Community Development Acts of 1974 and 1977, and a number of pieces of legislation dealing with air and water pollution and airport construction. Table 15–5 indicates the primary purposes of federal funds going directly to local governments and their growth between 1968 and 1973.

STATE CAPITALS FEED THEIR "CREATURES"

A final type of intergovernmental transfer of money deals with funds that the states distribute to their own local governments. Money that states give to their own localities account for more than a third of the typical local government's annual revenues. State money is given to local governments in two ways: straight grants, which almost always are tied to some specific purpose, and shared taxes. A *shared tax* refers to taxes that state and local governments divide up between themselves; one level of government, either state or local, collects the tax and shares it with the other level. The norm

---

[3]Maxwell and Aaronson, *Financing State and Local Governments*, p. 47.

TABLE 15–4 FEDERAL GRANTS, 1948, 1963, AND 1973

Purpose	TOTAL, IN MILLIONS OF DOLLARS			PERCENTAGE DISTRIBUTION		
	1948	1963	1973	1948	1963	1973
Public assistance	$718	$2,580	$7,296	45.4	31.0	20.0
Health	55	442	5,668	3.5	5.3	15.5
Education	120	558	4,348	7.6	6.7	11.9
Economic opportunity	...	334	3,635	...	4.0	10.0
Miscellaneous social welfare	335	912	5,635	21.2	11.0	15.4
Highways	318	3,023	4,724	20.1	36.3	12.9
Other	33	477	5,179	2.1	5.7	14.2
Total	1,581	8,324	36,486[1]	100.0	100.0	100.0
General revenue sharing	...	...	6,636			
Total	1,581	8,324	43,121			
	Per capita, in dollars					
All purposes	11.01	44.39	204.04			

[1]In 1973, grants-in-aid accounted for over 80 percent of total federal intergovernmental transfers. Small amounts are in the form of shared revenues (most of which go to the states with large federal acreage), and net loans and repayable advances.

Source: Maxwell and Aronson, *Financing State and Local Governments*, p. 48.

TABLE 15–5 FEDERAL INTERGOVERNMENTAL TRANSFERS TO LOCAL GOVERNMENTS, 1968 AND 1973, IN MILLIONS OF DOLLARS

PURPOSE	1968	1973
Education(school operation and construction in federally affected areas)	$ 694	$1,400
Housing and community development	784	2,025
Model cities	...	653
Airport construction	57	232
Waste treatment and water facilities	284	837
Urban mass transit	...	275
Other	453	1,221
Total	2,272	6,643
General revenue sharing	...	4,424
Total	2,272	11,067

Source: U.S. Bureau of the Census, *Governmental Finances in 1967–68*. (Washington, D.C.: Government Printing Office), Table 6; *Governmental Finances in 1972–73, Table 6.*

is for the state to collect the tax and share portions of it with its local governments.

Until the mid-1960s, state and local governments collected the same proportion of taxes between them, but around 1965 or so this relationship changed and states began collecting proportionately more taxes from their citizens than did local governments. Figure 15–2 indicates this trend, which is likely to continue and grow. On the other hand, local governments always

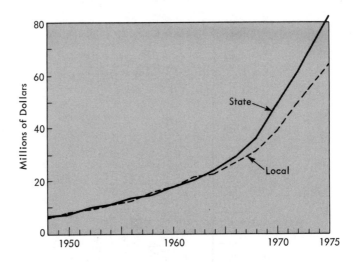

FIGURE 15–2 TAX COLLECTIONS OF STATE AND LOCAL GOVERNMENTS, 1948–1975

Source: U.S. Bureau of the Census, *Historical Statistics of the United States: Colonial Times to 1957* (Washington, D.C.: U.S. Government Printing Office, 1960), pp. 727 and 729; and Census Bureau, *Governmental Finances,* annual issues.

have spent more than state governments and this trend also seems to be accelerating over time, although less dramatically. Figure 15–3 indicates this relationship. The conclusion that we can draw from both charts is that states are reallocating their tax revenues increasingly to localities.[4]

And facts support such a conclusion. The most obvious feature of state aid to cities and towns is its incredible growth—up from $52 *million* in 1902 to $52 *billion* in 1975. Most of this growth has occurred during the last quarter century; a $5 billion level was achieved only in 1952.

Relatedly, local governments have become increasingly hooked on their annual fiscal fixes from the states. In 1913, localities received less than 6 percent of their budgets from their state governments, but in 1975 cities and towns were depending on nearly six times that figure—almost 36 percent—as the state contribution to their budgets. Currently, however, the state-aid component of local budgets appears to be stabilizing at about one-third of local revenue sources.

Most state aid is used by local governments for education—more than half of the states' money has gone to local education since 1952. This use

[4]*Ibid.*, pp. 82–84.

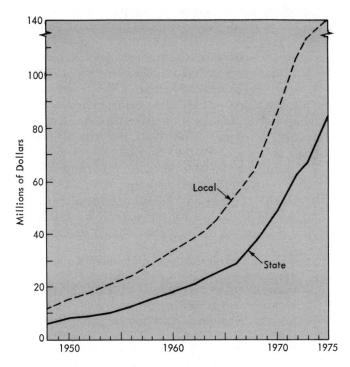

FIGURE 15–3 GENERAL EXPENDITURE OF STATE AND LOCAL GOVERNMENTS, 1948–1975

Source: U.S. Bureau of the Census, *Historical Statistics*, pp. 728 and 730; and *Governmental Finances*, annual issues.

has been declining in recent years, however, just as local use of state aid for building highways has been diminishing over a much longer period. The resulting slack has been taken up by public welfare; the localities now use more than 15 percent of state aid for public welfare. California and New York, however, take up much of this percentage—two-thirds of all state aid used for welfare payments by local officials is accounted for by these two states alone! Table 15–6 traces the growth of state aid to local governments (excluding shared taxes) during this century and shows how these grants were used by local officials.

PURCHASING PUBLIC POLICY:
THE LOCAL IMPACT OF NATIONAL DOLLARS

It is obvious from the foregoing overview that "big bucks" are involved in transfers of money among American governments, and the largest portion of these transfers is in the form of federal money going to state and local governments. What is federal policy toward the allocation of dollars to state and local governments? Does federal policy affect the formulation of state and local public policies? With federal grants to state and local governments accounting for more than a quarter of all state and local revenues, federal policy in fiscal transfers clearly has a major impact on state and local public policy.

As we have noted, the grants-in-aid system has burgeoned in recent years but, since 1960, it has also changed in ways that have had a major impact on the very nature of state and local governments. First, 1960 marks the point at which the federal government began shouldering a more substantial share of the state and local financial burden. In most of the grants-in-aid programs enacted after 1960, the federal government began picking up half or more of the tab. Second, after 1960 federal grants-in-aid became forthrightly national in purpose; prior to that year, grants-in-aid were used chiefly as a means of achieving state and local objectives.[5] The federal grants-in-aid program, therefore, is used for considerably more purposes than that of alleviating the state and local financial burden. The major purposes of the national grants-in-aid system are:

1. The establishment of minimum national standards and certain programs for all states;
2. the equalization of resources among states (or "the Robin Hood principle");
3. improvement of state programs;
4. the establishment of "critical mass" programs in certain states to circumvent duplicate efforts (*e.g.*, air pollution research grants);
5. the stimulation of program experimentation and testing;
6. the improvement of state and local public administration;

---

[5]James L. Sundquist and David W. Davis, *Making Federalism Work.* (Washington: Brookings Institution, 1969).

TABLE 15–6 COMPOSITION OF STATE AID, 1902–1975 (IN MILLIONS OF DOLLARS)

YEAR	TOTAL		GENERAL LOCAL GOVERNMENT SUPPORT		EDUCATION		HIGHWAYS		PUBLIC WELFARE		ALL OTHER		HEALTH AND HOSPITALS ONLY	
1975	$51,978	100.0%	$5,129	9.9%	$31,110	59.9%	$3,225	6.2%	$8,101	15.6%	$4,412	8.5%	N.A.	N.A.
1974	45,941	100.0	4,803	10.4	27,107	59.0	3,211	7.0	7,369	16.0	3,451	7.5	N.A.	N.A.
1973	40,822	100.0	4,280	10.5	23,316	57.1	2,953	7.2	7,532	18.5	2,741	6.7	N.A.	N.A.
1972	36,759	100.0	3,752	10.2	21,195	57.7	2,633	7.2	6,944	18.9	2,235	6.1	$955	2.6%
1971	32,640	100.0	3,258	10.0	19,292	59.1	2,507	7.7	5,760	17.6	1,823	5.6	751	2.3
1970	28,892	100.0	2,958	10.2	17,085	59.1	2,439	8.4	5,003	17.3	1,407	4.9	567	2.0
1969	24,779	100.0	2,135	8.6	14,858	60.0	2,109	8.5	4,402	17.8	1,275	5.1	446	1.8
1968	21,950	100.0	1,993	9.1	13,321	60.7	2,029	9.2	3,527	16.1	1,080	4.9	371	1.7
1967	19,056	100.0	1,585	8.3	11,845	62.2	1,861	9.8	2,897	15.2	868	4.5	301	1.6
1966	16,848	100.0	1,281	7.6	10,177	60.4	1,725	10.2	2,882	17.1	783	4.6	275	1.6
1964	12,968	100.0	1,053	8.1	7,664	59.1	1,524	11.8	2,108	16.3	619	4.8	235	1.8
1962	10,906	100.0	839	7.7	6,474	59.4	1,327	12.2	1,777	16.3	489	4.4	189	1.7
1960	9,443	100.0	806	8.5	5,461	57.8	1,247	13.2	1,483	15.7	446	4.7	176	1.9
1958	8,089	100.0	687	8.5	4,598	56.8	1,167	14.4	1,247	15.4	390	4.8	150	1.9
1957	7,439	100.0	668	9.0	4,212	56.6	1,083	14.6	1,136	15.3	340	4.6	142	1.9
1956	6,538	100.0	631	9.7	3,541	54.1	984	15.0	1,069	16.4	313	4.8	132	2.0
1954	5,679	100.0	600	10.6	2,930	51.6	871	15.3	1,004	17.6	274	4.8	N.A.	N.A.
1952	5,044	100.0	549	10.9	2,523	50.0	728	14.4	976	19.3	268	5.3	N.A.	N.A.
1950	4,217	100.0	482	11.4	2,054	48.7	610	14.5	792	18.8	279	6.6	N.A.	N.A.
1948	3,283	100.0	428	13.0	1,554	47.3	507	15.4	648	19.7	146	4.5	N.A.	N.A.
1946	2,092	100.0	357	17.1	953	45.6	339	16.2	376	18.0	67	3.2	N.A.	N.A.
1944	1,842	100.0	274	14.9	861	46.7	298	16.2	368	20.0	41	2.2	N.A.	N.A.
1942	1,780	100.0	224	12.6	790	44.4	344	19.3	390	21.9	32	1.8	N.A.	N.A.
1940	1,654	100.0	181	10.9	700	42.3	332	20.1	420	25.4	21	1.3	N.A.	N.A.
1932	801	100.0	140	17.5	398	49.7	229	28.6	28	3.5	6	0.7	N.A.	N.A.
1927	596	100.0	98	16.4	292	49.0	197	33.1	6	1.0	3	0.5	N.A.	N.A.
1922	312	100.0	35	11.2	202	64.7	70	22.4	4	1.3	1	0.3	N.A.	N.A.
1913	91	100.0	5	5.5	82	90.1	4	4.4	–	–	–	–	N.A.	N.A.
1902	52	100.0	5	9.6	45	86.5	2	3.8	–	–	–	–	N.A.	N.A.

N.A.–Not available.

Source: U.S. Bureau of the Census, *Census of Governments, 1972,* Vol. 6, No. 3, *State Payments to Local Governments.* (Washington, D. C.: Government Printing Office, 1974); *State Government Finances in 1973–74.*

7. the promotion of unrelated social missions, such as the standard anti-discrim-
ination clause present in all grants to states and localities; and

8. the minimization of the federal government's role in the implementation of
programs.

Of this final goal, "Perhaps the most important political achievement of
the grants system is to have solved the apparent dilemma arising from the
American electorate's contradictory desires, (a) to attack problems that the
state and local governments lacked the resources to handle while, (b) not
enlarging the federal government."[6]

The federal government transfers money to state and local governments
on the basis of two principles. One is that of *recipient autonomy.* The amount
of latitude and discretion permitted the government that is receiving money
from the feds becomes the crucial question. When the federal government
does not want a state or local government to have very much latitude in
deciding how to spend the money that it is giving it, then it issues *categorical
grants.* A categorical grant is highly specific in its purpose, and permits
extremely little discretionary action by the receiving government; an example would be the types of grants administered by the U.S. Environmental
Protection Agency relating to sewage treatment facilities. In 1978 there
were 492 separate categorical grants-in-aid programs being conducted by
the federal government.

When the feds feel that it would be expeditious for a recipient to have
more freedom in determining how money is spent, it issues *block grants.*
Block grants are tied to a general area of concern, such as health or
community development, and federal money may not be used for purposes
beyond that stated area. Nevertheless, considerably more discretionary
authority is yielded to the recipient than with categorical grants. The federal
government conducts five block grant programs in addition to general
revenue sharing: Partnership for Health, Law Enforcement Assistance,
Comprehensive Employment and Training (CETA), Community Development, and Social Services.

The other criterion that the federal government uses in determining how
a grant should be issued is that of *how funds should be distributed*, whether on
the basis of some formula or a specific project. A *formula grant* distributes
money among all eligible recipients by some prearranged method. There is
virtually no discretionary authority, either by the granting government or
by the recipient government. An example of the formula grant is provided
by the program of public assistance for the blind, in which the national
government matches state payments to blind citizens on the basis of the
number of persons whom the state certifies as eligible; the payments are
distributed equally to all those persons on the roster as a "right." A formula

---

[6]Michael D. Reagan, *The New Federalism.* (New York: Oxford University Press, 1972) p. 75.

grant is a form of categorical grant, and about one-third of all categorical grants use a formula-based distribution of funds.

At the other end of the continuum are *project grants*. A project grant is designed to alleviate some particular problem, and the money is distributed in no fixed proportions, or by no formula. Under a project grant system, federal administrators are in a substantially more advantageous position to decide which state and local problems need federal money to solve them than when they are under a formula grant arrangement; traditionally the federal government has favored the use of project grants. A project grant is a type of categorical grant, and about two-thirds of all categorical grants are project grants.

PROBLEMS OF THE GRANT-IN-AID SYSTEM: INEQUITY, DISTORTION, AND CONFUSION

A major difficulty of the grants-in-aid system as administered by the federal government (and very likely as administered by state governments as well) is that project grants and categorical grants tend to undermine the objective of equitably distributing federal resources among state and local jurisdictions. Those governments with professional staffs that are adept at grantsmanship and with the tax bases to support them are more likely to get the project grant, and even the categorical grant.

A second, and related problem is that grants-in-aid, especially formula grants, tend to warp state and local budgets. Budgetary decision makers will favor those public programs that are eligible for "free" federal funds, rather than developing budgets that more accurately reflect their own local needs.

By way of indication, a study of all cities and counties found that 73 percent of the cities and 81 percent of the counties said that they had received a grant from the federal government during the year. About two-thirds of these cities, and roughly 80 percent of the counties, indicated that they would have made different budgetary allocations had the categorical grants they received from the federal government permitted them to do so. Interestingly, more than two-thirds of the city officials and 77 percent of the county officials thought that their governments would shift local funds to other efforts if federal categorical grants suddenly were cut off.[7] Such a finding implies that local officials are to a large extent making policy decisions based on what federal money is available, rather than on what their real local needs are.

A third problem of the grants system is that the proliferation of categorical grants for specific programs has created administrative confusion

---

[7]Albert J. Richter, "Federal Grants Management: The City and County View." *The Municipal Yearbook, 1977*. (Washington: International City Management Association, 1977) pp. 183–184.

in states and localities; the classic example is the town that ended up with a freeway *and* an urban renewal project planned for the same neighborhood.

Fourth, grants-in-aid of all types do not help states and localities in resolving public problems beyond the scopes of their stated purposes.

Fifth, a lot of red tape is involved in applying for a grant, and state and local public administrators have become increasingly resentful of it. By way of example, the appropriately named town of Lazy Lakes, Florida, a community of fifty residents, turned back (or at least tried to turn back) the check for $1,198 that it received in federal revenue-sharing funds on the grounds that it neither needed nor wanted the money, nor did it want the added cost and paperwork created by revenue sharing—a fiscal transference, it should be noted, that probably is simpler than virtually any other insofar as state and local administrators are concerned. The mayor of Lazy Lakes, incidentally, found that it was much more difficult to return revenue-sharing money than to accept it.[8]

SOLUTIONS! SOLUTIONS!
REVENUE SHARING AND BIGGER BLOCK GRANTS

THE SAGA OF REVENUE SHARING

Because of these problems in the grants system, in 1972 Congress passed the State and Local Fiscal Assistance Act, better known as revenue sharing. It provided $3.2 billion to be distributed to states and localities over a five-year period and, by 1977, the Office of Revenue Sharing in the Treasury Department had distributed more than $23 billion to more than thirty-nine thousand state and local governments.

Public support for revenue sharing was pronounced when it was enacted. A Gallup Poll conducted in 1971 reported that 77 percent of the public endorsed revenue sharing, and that this support transcended party lines.[9]

What is revenue sharing? Revenue-sharing funds are distributed according to the proportion of federal personal income tax funds provided by state and local units of government; thus, richer units of governments, as defined by their tax bases, tend to be favored. New York, California, Pennsylvania, Illinois, Texas, Michigan, and Ohio generally are the leading recipients of revenue-sharing funds in any given year. Roughly one-third of revenue-sharing funds go to the states; the other two-thirds go to county commissions, city halls, and Indian tribal councils. More politics than fiscal rationality went into the complex formula that Congress devised to disburse revenue-sharing funds, and full consideration was given to whose district would get what. As a result, financially marginal units of government are

---

[8]Associated Press, July 3, 1977, syndicated nationally.

[9]Parris N. Glendening and Mavis Mann Reeves, "Federal Actions Affecting Local Government." *The Municipal Yearbook, 1977* p. 50.

supported, and more viable governments that are in desperate need of additional cash, notably the big cities, often are underfunded.

This situation came about because of two basic and opposing themes within Congress. One group of congressmen insisted that revenue sharing be computed on the basis of need. Only a reading of the poverty levels and the number of people at or below the poverty level would be necessary to develop the formula. But another large group within Congress believed revenue sharing should be an incentive to state and local governments to do more for themselves. This group reasoned that those governments that did more for themselves, by deriving greater revenues from their people, should be rewarded by receiving federal money through general revenue sharing. Obviously, the two points of view were contradictory. The final result was a compromise. Consequently, the formula finally adopted, though very complex, nevertheless did resolve the problem by accommodating both the "need" and the "incentive" factors. In other words, the formula considered "need" by determining the number of families at or below the poverty level, but it also recognized that state and local governments that taxed more and did more for themselves would be rewarded.

State and local governments may use revenue-sharing dollars for capital expenditures, maintenance, and operating costs in areas including public safety, environmental protection, transportation, health, recreation, libraries, social services for the old and the poor, and financial administration. Figure 15–4 illustrates how state and local governments spent their revenue-sharing money in the mid-1970s.

The chart, however, does not tell the whole story. Analyses of revenue sharing by the Brookings Institution that have been conducted since 1972[10] conclude that, while small cities and towns use about three-quarters of their revenue-sharing funds for new spending programs (mostly for capital projects), bigger urban areas with 100,000 people or more use only half of the money for spending programs; the remaining half goes to keep taxes down or to avoid borrowing. Among the states, only a third of shared revenues is used for new programs, and the tendency of both state and local governments to use shared revenues for keeping a muzzle on the tax bite rather than initiating new spending programs appears to be increasing. One reason for this trend is that inflation slashed the real purchasing power of revenue-sharing dollars by 17 percent between 1972 and 1979; thus, state and local governments must use the money mainly to keep their fiscal heads above water by maintaining existing services without raising taxes.

In 1976 revenue sharing came up for renewal in Congress and the issue quickly turned into a political brawl. Many members of Congress had strong misgivings about the program, arguing that it eventually would prove to be

---

[10]Richard P. Nathan, Allen C. Manvel, Susannah E. Calkins, and Associates, *Monitoring Revenue Sharing.* (Washington D.C.: Brookings Institution, 1975); and Richard P. Nathan and Charles F. Adams, Jr., and Associates, *Revenue Sharing: The Second Round.* (Washington: The Brookings Institution, 1977).

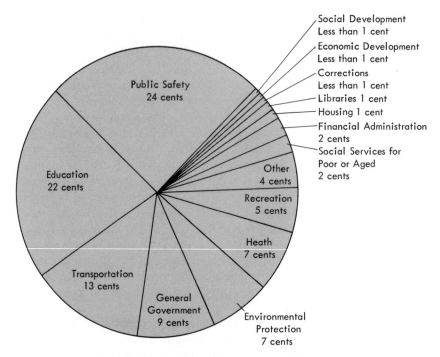

FIGURE 15–4 HOW THE AVERAGE GENERAL REVENUE SHARING DOLLAR WAS SPENT
JULY 1, 1974–JUNE 30, 1975

Source: Office of Revenue Sharing, Department of the Treasury, *Reported Uses of General Revenue Sharing Funds 1974–75*. (Washington, D.C.: U.S. Government Printing Office, 1976), p. 7.

a drain on the treasury; that minorities and other deprived groups received a better shake under the categorical grants system than under revenue sharing, simply because the grant approach was more likely to embody national, as opposed to local, values; and that revenue sharing did not press for the administrative reform of local governments for purposes of more efficient and responsive public management. In 1975, the Advisory Commission on Intergovernmental Relations reported that only 55 percent of the public supported the program[11] (contrast this to the 77 percent who supported the program in 1971). The Brookings studies lend credence to some of these congressional concerns in that they found that fiscally hard-pressed governments were likely to merge revenue-sharing funds with other revenue sources, thus reducing the political visibility of revenue sharing; that traditional patterns of political power were retained in most cities despite revenue-sharing and, if anything, the clout of entrenched special interests increased; and that, contrary to widespread speculation, revenue

---

[11]Advisory Commission on Intergovernmental Relations, *Changing Public Attitudes on Governments and Taxes.* (Washington D.C.: ACIR, July 1977), p. 2.

sharing had not forced changes in the structure of state and local governments, in fact, it seemed to reinforce those often inefficient structures.[12]

Proponents for continuing revenue sharing in 1976 largely were Republicans, and the vanguard of the lobby to maintain the program consisted of a coalition of the National Governors Association, the National Conference of State Legislatures, the National League of Cities, the U.S. Conference of Mayors, and the National Association of Counties. Democrats represented a looser amalgam of resisters to revenue sharing, and ultimately the program was retained and extended through 1980.

THE BIAS OF BLOCK GRANTS

We have seen how the traditional grant approach permits national policy makers to maintain greater control over state and local public programs, while the newer revenue-sharing and expanded block grant approaches permit the states and localities greater discretion in determining and implementing their own policies.

Real policy differences result, and to summarize these differences crudely, but effectively, national officials, using the traditional grant approach, tend to be more attuned to the needy, while state and local officials tend to be more sensitive to the middle class. For example, when seven basic national programs were consolidated under the Housing and Community Development Act of 1974, essentially converting them from categorical to block grants, thereby giving local leaders more control over how the funds underwriting these programs were used, the Brookings Institution found that poverty neighborhoods had fared better under the old Model Cities Program, initiated during the 1960s, than under the new Community Development Programs. (Model Cities, of course, was one of those programs subsumed by the Housing and Community Development Act.) There had been a shift, both in funding and decision making, away from the poorest people in neighborhoods to more mixed patterns, and programs had changed from an emphasis on social services, such as health and education, to short-term capital spending for projects such as parking lots and downtown renewal. Social services spending was found to be low under the Community Development Program.[13]

On the other hand, when national officials do retain control they tend to opt for the needy, when possible. This is true even with block grants, which give greater control to local administrators. For example, while the Housing and Community Development Act (a block grant program) did delegate more authority to state and local officials than previous programs, it

---

[12]Nathan and Adams, *Revenue Sharing*.

[13]Paul R. Dommel, Richard P. Nathan, Sarah F. Liebschutz, Margaret T. Wrightson, and Associates, *Decentralizing Community Development: Second Report on the Brookings Institution Monitoring Study of the Community Development Block Grant Program.* (Washington, D.C.: Brookings Institution, 1978).

nonetheless had built into it a formula that favored, and still favors, "needy" cities in the North and Midwest over the relatively vibrant cities in the South and West. This favoritism was accomplished by distributing the $3.2 billion in community block grant funds on a formula that favored housing age, defined as the number of houses built before 1939, and "population lag," or the population dips that fall short of the national growth rate. Since the cities in the North and Midwest are older than those in the South and West and are losing people to those regions, the "needier" cities are favored. Similarly, the Department of Housing and Urban Development (HUD) allocated $400 million to be distributed at the discretion of the secretary for economic development specifically in large eastern and midwestern cities.

SNOWBELT VERSUS SUNBELT: THE GRANTS WAR

As a result of these kinds of national policies sharp words were exchanged during the 1977 national meeting of the U.S. Conference of Mayors. The mayor of Albuquerque was quoted as stating that HUD's policies were "blatant efforts in the so-called war between the frostbelt and the sunbelt," and a number of mayors of major western cities opposed a resolution endorsed during that conference giving special consideration to the needs of cities in sixteen northern states.[14]

The tensions between Snowbelt and Sunbelt cities over who should get federal goodies are tightening in Congress as well. Nearly half of the members of the House of Representatives have joined the Northeast-Midwest Economic Advancement Coalition, which is a congressional group designed to promote the flow of federal funds to those regions of the country; Sunbelt representatives complain that the coalition has successfully rigged federal funding formulas to its own advantage.

Various analyses (cited in Chapter 2) of the regional distribution of federal money have drawn varying conclusions about who gets more than whom. A recent Library of Congress study was essentially accurate, however, when it stated that most defense and public works dollars go to the Sunbelt (with 83 percent of all defense personnel, 63 percent of all defense procurements, and 80 percent of all defense installations), while most antipoverty and economic development grants go to the Snowbelt.[15]

In terms of all federal grants-in-aid, the Northeast receives the largest overall share, but if welfare grants are excluded, then the Northeast drops to third place, after the West and South. When regions are ranked according to grants per person, grants per $1,000 of personal income, and the percentage of state and local revenues that are obtained from Washington, the Northeast leads, followed by the South, West, and Midwest, in that order. Figure 15–5 shows how much federal grant money per capita that

---

[14]Jana Bommersbach, "Sunbelt Mayors Tired of U.S. Fund Rules." *Arizona Republic*, June 13, 1977.

[15]Library of Congress Report, 1977. Cited in Ellen Hume, syndicated column, *Los Angeles Times*, November 23, 1977.

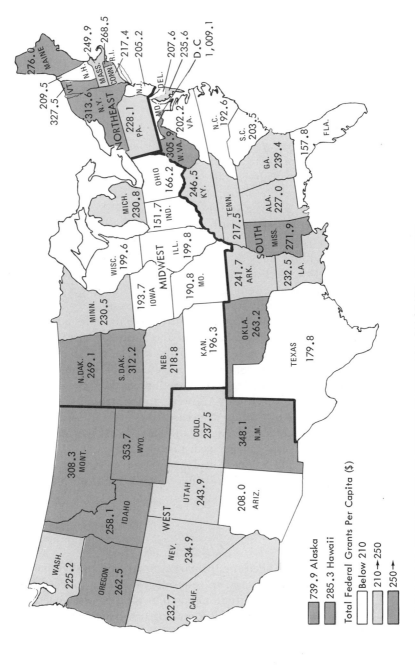

FIGURE 15–5 TOTAL FEDERAL GRANTS PER PERSON BY STATE, 1970–1975

Source: Charles L. Vehorn, *The Regional Distribution of Federal Grants-in-Aid.* (Columbus: Academy for Contemporary Problems, 1977), p. 2.

each state got during the first half of the 1970s. In the 1970s, however, the average dollar differences between regions narrowed, which suggests a fairer regional distribution of grant money by Washington.[16]

In brief, the ways that governments, and especially the federal government, distributes money to other governments not only has an impact on what public policy is and becomes in states and localities, but can be a divisive or unifying force for the nation as a whole.

OF DEATH AND TAXES

Thus far we have been discussing how the federal government helps state and local governments off the proverbial fiscal hook to the tune of almost 27 percent of their annual budgets through grants and revenue sharing. Now we turn to how state and local governments help themselves, which they do largely by taxing their citizens. Forty-five cents of each tax dollar paid by Americans go to their state and local governments, and more than half of that amount (which is nearing $200 billion a year) went to the states.

Perhaps no single policy reflects the differences in state and local political cultures more than their tax systems. Obviously, we cannot consider here the tax structures of all fifty states, but it is worth observing that some states prefer taxing the poor and other states (though precious few) prefer taxing the rich. Moreover, some states favor taxing everyone less and other states favor taxing everyone more. Figure 15–6 provides a handy reference of the tax rates and related charges in the various states per $1,000 of personal income. As it indicates, most of the states that have very low tax rates are found in the South; states that tax at a medium rate tend to concentrate in the West and Midwest; and states that tax their citizens the most tend to be located in the Southwest, Midwest, and Northeast.

Regardless of the tax structure, all state and local governments acquire their revenues from essentially the same sources, primarily property, income, and sales taxes. States rely disproportionately on the income tax and the sales tax; localities have developed the property tax as their major revenue source. Figure 15–7 illustrates the primary sources of state and local revenues.

THE INCOME TAX

The states have been the primary users of both individual income taxes and sales taxes.[17] States, and to some degree, major cities, got into the income tax business shortly after a national income tax was enacted as the Sixteenth Amendment to the Constitution in 1913. By the late 1970s forty-one states

---

[16]Charles L. Vehorn, *The Regional Distribution of Federal Grants-in-Aid.* (Washington, D.C.: Academy for Contemporary Problems, 1978).

[17]The foregoing discussion is drawn largely from Maxwell and Aaronson, *Financing State and Local Governments,* pp 92–96.

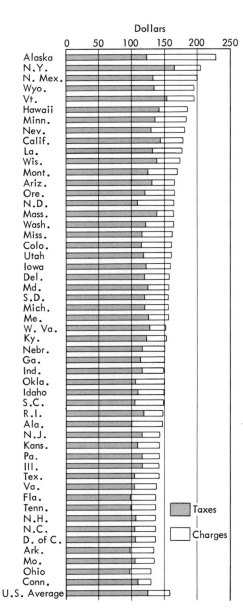

FIGURE 15-6 STATE AND LOCAL TAXES AND CHARGES PER $1,000 OF PERSONAL INCOME, BY STATE (RANKED FROM HIGH TO LOW—TAXES AND CHARGES)

Source: Advisory Commission on Intergovernmental Relations.

plus the District of Columbia had income taxes, and only nine had no such tax: Connecticut, Florida, Nevada, New Hampshire, South Dakota, Tennessee, Texas, Washington, and Wyoming.

The state income tax has been a steadily rising source of state revenues. It produces about one-quarter of all state tax collections, although the amount collected varies widely among the states; Oregon, at one extreme, collects 50 percent of its revenues through its income tax; Louisiana collected only 9 percent of its revenues through this tax. City income taxes are used in ten states and generated about $2.5 billion in the mid-1970s.

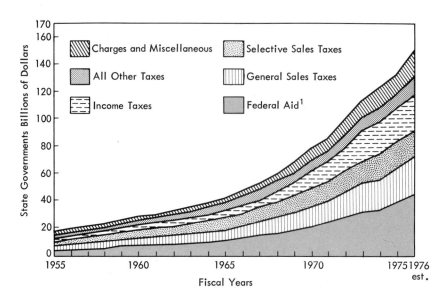

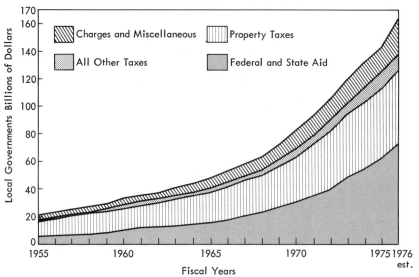

¹Includes minor amounts of local transfers.

FIGURE 15–7 MAJOR SOURCES OF STATE AND LOCAL GENERAL REVENUE, 1955 TO 1976 EST.

THE SALES TAX

Another major source of revenues favored by state governments is the sales tax.[18] The most common types of sales or excise taxes are those on gasoline, liquor, tobacco, and parimutuels, though there are others. Taxes on gasoline

---

[18]The foregoing discussion is drawn largely from *ibid.*, pp. 98–106.

and related products are the cornerstone sales tax for all the states, accounting for almost half of all sales tax collections. Oregon passed the first gasoline tax in 1919, and every state in the Union had one within a decade. The next largest source of sales tax revenues for a specific item is that on tobacco; it accounts for 18 percent of all sales tax revenues. Iowa, in 1921, enacted the first cigarette tax, and by 1961 all the states and the District of Columbia taxed tobacco in some form.

The biggest sales tax of all, however, is the general retail sales tax. With the stock market crash of 1929, states saw virtually all their sources of income drying up, and turned to the sales tax as a means of financial salvation. Mississippi was the first state to adopt such a tax in 1932, and by 1944 the general retail sales tax became the most important tax source of all for state governments. In 1977, forty-seven states plus the District of Columbia had a sales tax, and it accounted for nearly a third of all tax collections by the states.

Local governments also initiated the general sales tax, following the example set by New York City in 1934. Nearly 5,000 local governments in twenty-six states (but particularly in California, Illinois, Texas, and Washington) use a general retail sales tax garnering, on the average, about 6 percent of local tax revenues. The big cities, however, rely on the general sales tax to the tune of about 20 to 30 percent of their total tax collections; in the medium-sized cities, the general sales tax accounts for 40 to 60 percent of urban revenues.

THE PROPERTY TAX

The property tax is most used by local governments as a source of income. Generally, it is by far the most important source of state and local income across the board and has been during most of the nation's history.[19] In 1902 it provided more than half of total federal, state, and local tax collections, but with the rise of taxes on income and sales its position quickly slipped. Today the property tax provides less than 15 percent of total tax collections in the nation. Nevertheless, the property tax remains a fiscal cornerstone for local governments and provides a third of all their revenues (tax *and* non-tax).

In the 1930s state governments began moving away from the property tax (largely because the Depression had raised the spectre of mass tax defaults by property owners), leaving it to the purview of local governments, and by the mid-1970s the general property tax provided less than 5 percent of state tax revenues in forty-five states. Today, the general property tax has become virtually the only local tax of consequence, and in the mid-1970s it provided about 83 percent of local tax revenues; only large cities have generated other sources of revenue that are of any import.

Still, local governments have other sources of revenue—largely state and

---

[19]The foregoing discussion is drawn largely from *ibid.*, pp. 134–165.

federal aid and some miscellaneous sources. When we put the local property tax into the context of *all* local revenues, tax and nontax alike, we find that the significance of the property tax for local governments has decreased in recent years, chiefly because state and federal aid has displaced the need to rely on it. In terms of *all* urban revenues in the mid-1970s, the property tax accounted for 37 percent of city income, while state and federal aid accounted for more than 40 percent. In 1927, however, the property tax accounted for almost 74 percent of total local revenues.

Still, the property tax remains extremely important to local governments, and the reason is clear: local governments have very few other options. Levying local taxes on personal income, sales, or businesses could potentially reduce the local tax base, and it often does. People and businesses can and do move out of the city; land cannot.

The property tax has an enormous administrative problem associated with it, that of assessment. By *assessment* is meant how governments evaluate the worth of the property to be taxed, and the rule of thumb is to assess property well below its true market value. If all property is assessed at the same percentage of true value, this practice is, of itself, not necessarily unfair, but such uniform assessment is rare, and assessments vary widely from jurisdiction to jurisdiction.

In the mid-1970s, property owners shelled out $45 in property taxes per every $1,000 of personal income, on the average. Table 15–7 lists each state's property tax per $1,000 of personal income and compares it with the national average; thus, the New England states, for example, pay a higher property tax than the national average–33 percent more, in fact.

OTHER SOURCES OF STATE AND LOCAL REVENUES

Other than transfers of funds between governments themselves, taxes on income, sales, and property are the major sources of revenues for state and local governments. Nevertheless, there are other sources and a brief review of them is in order.[20]

One of the more significant sources used by states is the *corporation income tax,* which started in Wisconsin in 1911. By 1976, forty-five states, fifteen major cities, and the District of Columbia had a corporation income tax and, on the average, these taxes contributed about 8 percent of state revenue.

Death and gift taxes provide slightly more than 2 percent of total state tax collections. All the states levy inheritance and estate taxes, and sixteen levy taxes on gifts.

Localities and states also generate revenues that rely on taxing users of particular services, notably levying charges for water, electric power, and highway tolls. These kinds of *use taxes* appear to be growing in their

---

[20]This discussion is drawn largely from *ibid.,* pp. 166–168.

TABLE 15–7 STATE–LOCAL PROPERTY TAXES PER $1,000 OF STATE PERSONAL INCOME, BY STATE, 1975

STATE AND REGION	AMOUNT	AS % OF U.S. AVERAGE	STATE AND REGION	AMOUNT	AS % OF U.S. AVERAGE
United States	$45	100			
			Southeast	(25)	(56)
New England	(60)	(133)	Virginia	30	67
Maine	51	113	West Virginia	23	51
New Hampshire	65	144	Kentucky	22	49
Vermont	66	147	Tennessee	26	58
Massachusetts	75	167	North Carolina	26	58
Rhode Island	50	111	South Carolina	24	53
Connecticut	55	122	Georgia	34	76
			Florida	31	69
Mideast	(40)	(89)	Alabama	13	29
New York	60	133	Mississippi	26	58
New Jersey	66	147	Louisiana	20	44
Pennsylvania	30	67	Arkansas	22	49
Delaware	20	44			
Maryland	36	80	Southwest	(34)	(76)
District of Columbia	28	62	Oklahoma	26	58
			Texas	39	87
Great Lakes	(46)	(102)	New Mexico	24	53
Michigan	50	111	Arizona	47	104
Ohio	37	82			
Indiana	44	98	Rocky Mountain	(45)	(100)
Illinois	45	100	Montana	62	138
Wisconsin	52	116	Idaho	33	73
			Wyoming	55	122
Plains	(46)	(102)	Colorado	39	87
Minnesota	43	96	Utah	35	78
Iowa	50	111			
Missouri	36	80	Far West[1]	(50)	(111)
North Dakota	34	76	Washington	41	91
South Dakota	57	127	Oregon	53	118
Nebraska	53	118	Nevada	44	98
Kansas	46	102	California	63	140
			Alaska	32	71
			Hawaii	25	56

Note: Regional dollar amounts are unweighted averages.
[1] Excluding Alaska and Hawaii.

importance to state and local revenue collections. Local charges to users of specific services, such as hospitals, parks, sewerage, and education, also constitute important nonproperty tax sources of revenue. In 1973 user charges accounted for more than 17 percent of locally generated revenues and almost 11 percent of state generated revenues; twenty years earlier these figures were less than 13 percent and 9 percent respectively.

Public lotteries are one of the newer and more exotic sources of state and local revenues. Introduced in 1964 in New Hampshire, these games of chance were offered to their citizens by thirteen states by 1976. Lotteries have proven to be neither good deals for the state nor the gambler. Few states ever have succeeded in generating more than 1 percent of their total revenues with lotteries, and prizes as a proportion of gross receipts are much lower in state-run lotteries than for casino gambling or even in the numbers racket.

THE EQUITY QUESTION: TAXES AND FAIRNESS

Before continuing our discussion of the public purse, let us address here the question of fairness and tax policy. *Fairness,* or *equity,* means that a tax system does not cut more deeply into the incomes of poor people than rich people in terms of real purchasing power. In this light, taxes may be progressive, regressive, and proportional. Taxes are *progressive* when the ratio of tax-to-income rises as income rises; they are *regressive* when the ratio of tax-to-income falls as income rises; and taxes are *proportional* when the ratio of taxes to income is the same for all classes of income.

It is generally believed that a progressive income tax is fairest to all taxpayers. The federal income tax, for example, does not tax the very poor at all, and it taxes the very rich beyond 90 percent. At the state and local levels, however, taxes are not always necessarily progressive.

Stephen E. Lile found that, while a state may have a stiff overall tax rate, it still may be a good place to live for the relatively affluent. Connecticut, for example, has the second highest tax rate in the nation for people with $5,000 incomes, but it ranks only twenty-seventh in terms of the tax rates that it levies on the top income brackets. New York, right next door, soaks its rich more than any state, but is ranked only twenty-first at the $5,000 level. Only two states in the nation, Oregon and New York, have genuinely progressive tax rates. Washington has the most regressive tax system; in that state, the lowest income group pays 10.4 percent of its income out to taxes, and the top income group pays only 3.5 percent.[21] Table 15–8 summarizes Lile's unique research on state and local tax equity.

Both state and local tax policies are regressive in comparison to national policies. Regardless of which theory of economics is applied to the data, federal taxes are progressive tax policies, but state and local taxes clearly

---

[21]Stephen E. Lile, "Tax Report," *Wall Street Journal,* January 21, 1976.

are regressive for virtually all income groups.[22] Perhaps the major causes for inequitable state and local tax systems is the predominance of the sales and property taxes at these levels, both of which are highly regressive. Let us examine these in greater detail.

THE SALES TAX:
UNFAIR, BUT NOT AS BAD AS IT MIGHT BE

A tax on sales taxes what people consume and since, by definition, poor people must consume the necessities of life (such as food and shelter) approximately as much as rich people, they pay an unfair share of the sales tax relative to their incomes. Table 15–9 indicates clearly the regressive aspects of the state and local general sales tax for a family of four by income. For example, a family of four with an annual income of $5,000 is going to pay 1.8 percent of that $5,000 in sales taxes; by contrast, a family earning $50,000, or ten times as much, is going to pay only 0.7 percent of its income in sales taxes. Given the nature of the sales tax, this regressivity cannot be avoided and this fact of tax life is one of the main arguments against relying on the sales tax for state and local revenues.

It is quite unlikely, however, that states which rely primarily on both the

[22]Joseph A. Pechman and Benjamin A. Okner, *Who Bears the Tax Burden* (Washington: The Brookings Institution, 1974), pp. 61–64.

"DELIVER US, THY TAX-EXEMPT SUBJECTS, FROM THE WRATH OF THY AMENDMENT THIRTEEN CALIFORNIA QUAKE, O, LORD!"

Source: OLIPHANT, © 1978, *The Washington Star*. Reprinted with permission, Los Angeles Times Syndicate.

TABLE 15–8 DISTRIBUTION OF MAJOR STATE-LOCAL TAX BURDENS RELATIVE TO FAMILY INCOME SIZE, BY STATE, 1974[1]

(TAX BURDENS AS PERCENTAGES OF INCOME)

State	ADJUSTED GROSS INCOME, FAMILY OF FOUR, 1974					
	$5,000	$7,500	$10,000	$17,500	$25,000	$50,000
All States[2]	11.3	10.0	8.9	8.5	8.1	7.8
Alabama	9.8	8.7	8.2	7.6	7.2	6.4
Arizona	9.9	8.7	7.7	7.3	7.1	6.9
Arkansas	8.5	7.8	7.0	6.8	6.8	7.4
California	11.8	9.9	8.8	9.2	9.1	10.8
Colorado	11.8	10.6	9.5	9.2	8.9	8.4
Connecticut	18.4	15.1	12.3	11.9	9.8	7.6
Delaware	9.8	8.9	8.3	9.0	9.5	8.6
Florida	7.5	6.0	4.9	4.2	3.5	2.6
Georgia	10.6	8.9	7.8	8.1	8.1	8.0
Idaho	9.7	8.3	7.8	8.3	8.6	9.0
Illinois	14.3	12.5	10.7	10.1	8.9	7.6
Indiana	13.0	11.3	9.6	9.3	8.1	6.8
Iowa	14.5	13.4	12.1	11.3	10.6	9.5
Kansas	14.3	12.2	10.5	10.3	9.3	8.5
Kentucky	9.5	9.6	9.0	8.6	8.4	7.7
Louisiana	6.1	5.0	4.6	4.1	3.7	3.6
Maine	13.6	11.5	9.7	9.2	8.3	7.8
Maryland	13.9	13.6	12.8	12.4	11.9	11.7
Massachusetts	16.0	15.8	13.9	14.3	13.0	11.6
Michigan	10.9	9.8	8.8	9.3	8.6	8.7
Minnesota	12.7	12.7	12.1	11.9	12.0	11.8
Mississippi	6.8	5.2	6.6	4.9	4.7	4.5
Missouri	12.0	10.5	9.3	8.8	8.5	7.9
Montana	11.2	10.0	9.2	9.1	8.8	8.8
Nebraska	12.2	10.5	9.0	8.8	7.8	7.4

Nevada	8.4	6.8	5.5	4.9	4.0	3.1
New Hampshire	12.3	10.2	8.2	7.5	6.4	5.1
New Jersey	20.5	16.6	14.4	13.5	11.6	9.6
New Mexico	9.9	8.5	7.4	7.0	6.8	7.6
New York	11.6	11.2	10.6	10.7	11.5	15.0
North Carolina	10.3	9.6	9.0	8.9	8.8	8.8
North Dakota	10.1	9.0	7.8	8.1	8.5	8.5
Ohio	10.5	9.0	7.9	7.7	7.3	7.1
Oklahoma	9.0	7.5	6.4	6.4	6.4	6.8
Oregon	6.6	8.3	8.4	9.0	9.4	10.6
Pennsylvania	12.5	12.9	11.5	10.8	9.9	8.9
Rhode Island	14.3	12.2	10.5	10.4	9.3	8.8
South Carolina	9.1	7.9	7.3	7.6	7.7	8.0
South Dakota	12.7	10.6	8.8	7.8	6.6	5.2
Tennessee	10.5	8.7	7.2	6.2	5.2	4.0
Texas	9.3	7.5	6.1	5.6	4.6	3.5
Utah	10.3	9.2	8.2	8.4	8.1	7.4
Vermont	11.9	11.5	10.4	10.3	10.0	11.0
Virginia	10.0	8.6	7.9	8.2	7.8	7.5
Washington	10.4	8.3	6.8	5.8	4.7	3.5
West Virginia	7.7	6.4	5.6	5.2	4.9	5.1
Wisconsin	16.3	16.1	14.8	14.7	14.7	14.6
Wyoming	8.8	7.1	5.8	5.2	4.3	3.3

[1]All income is assumed to come from wages and salaries and earned by one spouse in the city of residence. Families are assumed to reside in the largest city in each state. Includes the following state and local taxes: state individual income, state general sales, local individual income, local sales, property tax on residence, cigarette excise, motor vehicle and gasoline excise.

[2]Excluding Alaska and Hawaii.

Source: Family Tax Burdens compared among States and among Cities located within Kentucky and Neighboring States. A study prepared for the Kentucky Department of Revenue by Stephen E. Lile, Associate Professor, Western Kentucky University, December 15, 1975.

TABLE 15–9 ESTIMATED BURDEN OF
STATE AND LOCAL GENERAL
SALES TAXES FOR A FAMILY
OF FOUR, BY INCOME GROUP,
1972

FAMILY INCOME, IN DOLLARS	RATE, PERCENT
5,000	1.8
7,500	1.6
10,000	1.4
20,000	1.1
25,000	0.9
50,000	0.7

Source: Advisory Commission on Intergovernmental Relations, *Significant Features of Fiscal Federalism, 1973–74*, table 38, p. 53.

income tax *and* the sales tax as their sources of revenue will abandon the sales tax, or use one in favor of the other. Because the sales tax is relatively "hidden," at least in comparison to the income tax, raising it is less likely to result in voter opposition. Moreover, if state income taxes were truly progressive and cut relatively deeply into the incomes of high earners, the rich might move from the state, thereby further diminishing the state's tax base.

Trends also indicate that the states will rely on both taxes in the future. By the late 1970s, only New Hampshire had neither a general retail sales tax nor an individual income tax; nine states had no individual income tax but did rely on a general sales tax, while four states (Alaska, Hawaii, Montana, and Oregon) have gone the opposite way, using only the income tax. But overall, the states probably will continue to favor sales taxes, if for no other reason than the federal government has left it available for their use. Thirty-seven state governments have both income and sales taxes, and it is likely more states will join this list.

THE PROPERTY TAX: UNFAIR OR MISUNDERSTOOD?

Most people believe that the property tax is the most regressive and unfair tax in America. In 1970 a family of four with an income of $2,000 or less paid almost 17 percent of its income in residential property taxes, but a family with an income of $25,000 or more paid only 2 percent of its income in residential property taxes.[23] Moreover, the property tax seldom adjusts to the changing fortunes of the individual. For example, if a family

---

[23]Advisory Commission on Intergovernmental Relations, *Financing Schools and Property Tax Relief: A State Responsibility.* (Washington, D.C.: ACIR, 1973), p. 36.

purchased and paid for a house in their thirties, and retired in the same house in their late sixties, the property tax would not adjust to their declining income; indeed, it would probably go up as the value of the property went up.

In this light, it also has been charged that the property tax actually promotes the deterioration of cities. If a homeowner improves his or her residence and makes it worth more in the open market, the property is consequently assessed at a higher value and the homeowner must pay a higher property tax, despite the money and effort that he or she may have poured into the house. Thus, in a peculiar kind of way, it "pays" to let one's house fall into disrepair, at least insofar as the property tax system is concerned.

Finally, large tracts of land in cities and states are not taxed at all—for example, land belonging to another government, such as the state or national government, to churches, and to various kinds of charitable institutions. These exemptions have increasingly become sore points with people who pay residential property taxes, and the logic justifying them is that such institutions work for the public welfare and therefore should not be subject to tax. Nevertheless, exempting them from the property tax has contributed to the erosion of the local tax base. Although the total value of all such excluded property nationally is not known, it appears to be substantial. Table 15–10 indicates that the value of totally tax exempt property in seventeen states and the District of Columbia in 1976 amounted to more than $121 billion. Most of the exemptions, nearly 60 percent, applied to government buildings.

There are still other types of property tax exemptions. In many localities, industries are exempted, at least for a period of time, in order to lure these employers to the locality. Eleven states permit exemptions from the local property tax to farmers, and many states also grant exemption of some sort to veterans.

The circuit breaker on the property tax also reduces revenues to state and local governments. A *circuit breaker* goes into effect when the property tax exceeds a predetermined percentage of the personal income of an

TABLE 15–10 VALUE REPORTED FOR EXCLUDED (TOTALLY EXEMPT) PROPERTY, BY TYPE OF EXEMPTION, FOR SELECTED STATES: 1976

(MILLION DOLLARS)

17 States[1] *and District of Columbia*	*Total*	*Govern- mental*	*Educa- tional*	*Religious*	*Charitable*	*Other or unallocable*
Total	121,643	70,188	18,885	8,158	3,759	20,651

[1]The states are: Arizona, California, Colorado, Florida, Hawaii, Indiana, Iowa, Kansas, Maryland, Minnesota, Nevada, New Jersey, New Mexico, New York, Ohio, Oregon, and Rhode Island.

Source: U.S. Bureau of the Census, *Census of Governments, 1977*, No. 2. (Washington, D.C.: U.S. Government Printing Office, 1978) Table E, p. 6. Figures are rounded.

individual. It relieves the excess financial pressure by reducing or eliminating the homeowner's property tax. This device is intended to make the property tax somewhat more equitable, and by 1974 twenty-four states and the District of Columbia had circuit-breaker programs.

Although most people would agree with the intention of rendering the property tax more progressive, not everyone agrees that circuit breakers work as they are supposed to. Henry J. Aaron, for example, contends that circuit-breaker laws are unfair because they give the most tax relief to those in each income class who possess the greatest net worth in the first place—that is, those who own a house and property, as opposed to those who have never been wealthy enough to purchase a house and property. Aaron argues that the real problem is not the nature of the property tax itself, but the administration of it that causes inequities.[24] In this contention, Aaron is at least partially correct, and among the administrative reforms that should be undertaken are the reorganization of local assessment districts and state supervision of the administration of local property assessment and taxation.

THE PEOPLE'S CHOICE: TAXES AND TAXPAYERS

We have seen how state and local tax systems work and what some of the experts think about how they should work. But how do the taxpayers themselves view the tax system and the kinds of taxes that they pay?

Several public opinion polls conducted during the 1970s have attempted to assess how people feel about what types of taxes.[25] Generally, people loathe the local property tax; a full third of one survey's respondents believed it to be the "least fair" tax, while a majority felt the federal income tax to be the "fairest." Sales taxes tend to register somewhere between income and property taxes on the fairness scale. Respondents who are rich, white homeowners are more likely to favor the continuance of a sales tax; blacks who live in the Northeast are least likely to favor a sales tax.

What if a community needs to raise more money? Which taxes are the least likely to cause public outcry if they are raised? Could the tax system be altered to better accommodate the people's wishes? Respondents believed for the most part that at least some of the services and facilities that were usually supported from general city taxes could be put on a break-even, fee-for-service basis (in other words, a user charge). A majority of the respondents in nine of ten major cities surveyed in one poll were willing to

---

[24]Henry J. Aaron, *Who Pays the Property Tax? The New View.* (Washington, D.C.: Brookings Institution, 1975).

[25]The following discussion is drawn from: Advisory Commission on Intergovernmental Relations, *Public Opinion and Taxes.* (Washington D.C.: U.S. Government Printing Office, 1972) p. 16; Advisory Commission on Intergovernmental Relations, *Changing Public Attitudes on Governments and Taxes.* (Washington, D.C.: U.S. Government Printing Office, 1977); and Floyd J. Fowler, Jr., *Citizens' Attitudes Toward Local Government Services and Taxes,* (Cambridge, Mass.: Ballinger, 1974), pp. 57–86.

start taxing private schools as a new means of raising revenues, and in seven cities most people were willing to start taxing church property.

The sales tax is by far the most popular way of raising revenues, the income tax is next, and the property tax is clearly the least popular method of taxation among all respondents. Of course, there are some variations; the wealthier respondents are more likely to favor increasing the sales tax than are the poor respondents, although even among these low income groups there is a clear preference to raise the sales tax relative to any other form of taxation. People who rent their residences are more likely to favor a hike in the property tax than those who own their own homes, but none of these variations really affect the basic ordering.

Although not all respondents feel local taxes are too high, many feel that people are not getting their money's worth out of their tax dollar; a 1977 survey found that 46 percent of those surveyed felt that they were getting the most for their state or local tax money, but only 36 percent felt this way about their federal tax money. If additional taxes are needed, most of those surveyed felt the money should come from tax-exempt property and the sales tax.

DUNAGIN'S PEOPLE

"A TAXPAYERS' REVOLT COULD BE SERIOUS... THERE'S A LOT OF THEM OUT THERE, YOU KNOW."

Source: DUNAGIN'S PEOPLE by Ralph Dunagin. Reproduced through the courtesy of Field Newspaper Syndicate.

REVOLT!

In the late 1970s, the often-touted but seldom substantive "taxpayers' revolt" began gaining momentum. In 1978, no less than seventeen tax limitation initiatives were voted in by the people; across-the-board tax cuts were enacted in four states, but rejected in three others. It appears that the tax revolt will continue, but probably in the form of linking tax rates to the states' economies.

In 1978 Tennessee voters became the nation's first to approve a constitutional amendment placing a ceiling on the dollars that their officials could spend, but the more spectacular property tax reduction battle was waged in California during the same year. The Jarvis-Gann initiative, after gathering more than 1.5 million signatures, became Proposition 13 in a state wide referendum. It called for a draconian slash of all residential and commercial property taxes to 1 percent of the property's 1975–76 market value, and prohibited tax increases of more than 2 percent a year until the property was resold. This amounted to a 57 percent relief of property taxes and would reduce property tax revenues from $12 billion annually to $5 billion.

The California governor promptly labelled Proposition 13 a "meat-ax approach" to public finance and introduced Proposition 8, which would have provided "only" a 30 percent tax relief in contrast to Proposition 13's 57 percent. More importantly, Proposition 8 gave homeowners a better break than Proposition 13, which did not discriminate between homeowners and commercial interests.

Proposition 13 passed by a landslide. A record number of Californians voted nearly two-to-one (66 percent to 34 percent) in favor of it, while the countermeasure, Proposition 8, was defeated handily. Most of the voters in favor of Proposition 13 were homeowners.

Proposition 13 was the fourth attempt of its kind in California during the past decade. It was also the most radical. What was its appeal?

Clearly, Californians were victims of a madly speculative real estate market (at one point, house values in some areas were increasing at the rate of 10 percent a month!) and an inflexible property assessment system. As a result "horror stories" were rife of homeowners witnessing their property tax bills shoot to double and even ten times the tab they were paying only one to three years earlier.

It appears that many states may vote in their own versions of Proposition 13 in the future, and this urge apparently is the result of a combination of skyrocketing inflation, a larger tax bite (the total tax rate rose from less than 24 percent of the Gross National Product in 1956 to more than 30 percent in 1976), and a popular resentment toward state and local tax policies in particular. Figure 15–8 indicates the burgeoning tax bite on the middle and upper classes between 1965 and 1975; note that state and local taxes increased the most dramatically, although they still amount to less than the national tax. Indeed, as Figure 15–9 shows, the national tax burden has been declining as a proportion of the GNP, while state and local taxes have been increasing. These relationships obviously have not been lost on the

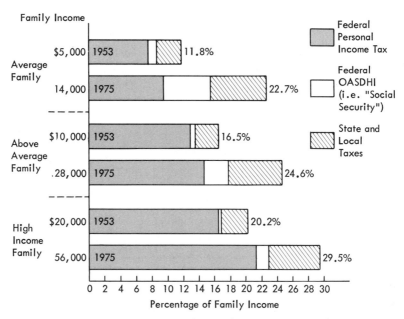

Family Income

FIGURE 15-8 THE NARROWING OF THE GAP IN DIRECT TAX BURDENS BORNE BY AVERAGE AND UPPER INCOME FAMILIES, 1953 and 1975*[1]

*These estimates assume a family of four and include only: Federal personal income, Federal OASDHI, state and local personal income and general sales taxes, and local residential property taxes.

†Average family income in 1953 was $5,000; in 1975 $14,000.

Source: Advisory Commission on Intergovernmental Relations, *Significant Features of Fiscal Federalism, 1976–77*, 2:43.

average taxpayer, who no doubt is aware, at least viscerally, that the states collect more than $100 billion every year from their citizens and that many often end the fiscal year with substantial surpluses. (California, for example, had at least a $5 billion surplus when Proposition 13 was enacted.)

Perhaps the mood of the rebellious taxpayers of the 1980s is best summed up by Grayce, a lady in a novel by P.G. Wodehouse. When explaining why Grayce is trying to smuggle a necklace through customs, an acquaintance states, "Grayce doesn't like the idea of paying duty. She says it's such a waste, she says the government has got more money than is good for it already and would only spend it."

PAYING THE PIPER: BORROWING AND DEBT

Despite unprecedented revenues, virtually all governments in America are in hock. They have borrowed money to finance projects of various kinds and, occasionally, to pay for day-to-day operations. Governments borrow this money from the people. The interest on municipal bonds, for example, is tax exempt and such bonds normally pay at a higher than usual rate.

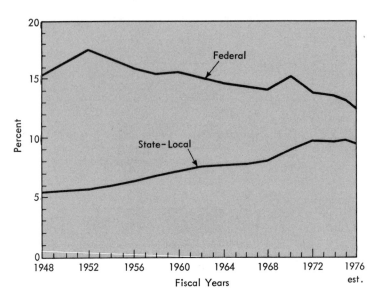

FIGURE 15–9 THE RELATIVE GROWTH IN FEDERAL TAXES LAGS THE STATE-LOCAL SECTOR, SELECTED YEARS 1948–1976 (FEDERAL, STATE AND LOCAL TAXES AS A PERCENT OF GNP)

Source: Advisory Commission on Intergovernmental Relations, *Significant Features of Fiscal Federalism, 1976–77*, 2:7.

While this indebtedness is not necessarily dangerous in and of itself, the peril in borrowing by government occurs when it borrows to meet current expenses or to finance programs that are not of an emergency nature. Mortgaging future revenues in this way creates a mounting debt, which ultimately requires additional borrowing to make up the old debt, and it takes from the money marketplace capital that is needed for the development of private industry.

STATE AND LOCAL INDEBTEDNESS IS RISING FAST

Between 1938 and 1973, local debt increased by more than a factor of eight and state debt increased by a factor of almost eighteen. Combined state and local debts in 1973 were almost ten times that of 1938. Table 15–11 summarizes governmental outstanding debt in the United States between 1961 and 1975. During that relatively short fifteen-year period, state debt increased by 261 percent, local debt by 171 percent. Most of this state and local borrowing has been undertaken to finance capital expenditures, such as roads, buildings, and public services, although education has cut out an increasingly large portion of the debt for itself, relative to past years, rising from 4 percent of the debt in 1941 to 26 percent of it in 1973.

Have state and local governments overextended themselves? That is a

TABLE 15–11 PAYING FOR IT: PUBLIC DEBT BY LEVEL OF GOVERNMENT, 1961–1975

LEVEL OF GOVERNMENT	1961	1975	% CHANGE 1961–1975
Federal	$292,900.0	$544,100.0	+ 86%
All State-level	19,993.2	72,127.4	+261
All Local-level	55,030.0	149,096.4	+171

Source: Census Bureau, *Governmental Finances in 1960–61*, Table 16; *Governmental Finances in 1974–75*, Table 19.

difficult question to answer. Between 1966 and 1973, the state and local debt per person rose by about 65 percent, but the "debt service payments" (or interest) in relation to state and local revenues have remained constant at about 20 percent. Similarly, the percentage of total debt outstanding to the total personal income in states and localities also has remained at about 20 percent.[26] Experts generally think that these figures indicate an ability by most state and local governments to pay their debts without going under, but there are exceptions. In late 1978, Cleveland defaulted on $15.5 million in short-term bank notes but, although it never defaulted, a far more serious fiscal situation occurred in New York.

WHO'LL TAKE MANHATTAN?[27] HARD TIMES IN FUN CITY

In early 1975 New York City discovered that it no longer could borrow money in the municipal bond market. Investors no longer believed in the city's ability to pay back the bonds, and thereby began a long saga.[28]

In March of 1975 the first of a series of stopgap measures was enacted when the state advanced the city some $800 million. In June the Municipal Assistance Corporation, known as "Big Mac," was established to serve as a borrowing agency for the city. Despite the fact that Big Mac was backed by the state of New York and was offering an unprecedented tax-exampt interest rate of up to 9.5 percent, Big Mac still could not sell the bonds, and eventually tax-free interest rates were forced up to 11 percent. By September 1975 New York was unable to find a syndicate that would underwrite its borrowing, a situation that led to the next stop-gap measure, the enactment

---

[26]Maxwell and Aaronson, *Financing State and Local Governments,* p. 196.

[27]The subtitle is an outright steal from Theodore J. Lowi's paper presented at the 1976 National Conference of the American Political Science Association.

[28]The following discussion is drawn largely from: Congressional Budget Office, *New York City's Fiscal Problem: Its Origins, Potential Repercussions, and Some Alternative Policy Responses.* Background Paper No. 1, October 10, 1975. (Washington, D.C.: U.S. Government Printing Office, 1975).

by the New York legislature of the Financial Emergency Act, which provided the City with $2.3 billion—enough to meet its most pressing cash requirements. The act also set up the Emergency Financial Control Board, which was dominated by state officials; in effect, the city was being managed by the state on an increasingly wide scale.

Still, this was not enough. Standard and Poor's, which rates the risk associated with various municipal bond issues, warned the state that it would be jeopardizing its own finances if it poured much more money into the city, and Moody's Investor Service, which also rates bonds, reduced the state's bond rating from "A" to "B," thereby further discouraging investment in the city. In November 1975 then-President Gerald R. Ford agreed to back the city with federal money, although for two months he had been stridently maintaining that New York was not the nation's responsibility. (The New York *Daily News* had headlined the president's position with its now notorious headline: "Ford to City: Drop Dead.") Ford offered New York short-term loans up to $2.3 billion, terminating in 1978, and to be channeled through the Emergency Financial Control Board of the State of New York. The offer was accepted readily.

New York City, of course, had to do its share, and the budgetary slashing became savage at points. Within the first year of the fiscal emergency, $500 million in taxes were imposed on what were already the most heavily taxed citizens in the country. The city income tax for New Yorkers was increased an average of 25 percent, and taxes on corporations, property, and cigarettes were raised. The city's work force was reduced by 55,000 people to 239,000, the lowest level in more than a decade. Wages of most remaining workers were frozen, and wages previously promised were deferred for a year. The illustrious 129-year-old policy of free tuition at the City Colleges was ended abruptly. The transit fare was hiked; seventy-seven day care centers were closed, affecting about 5,000 children who had relied on them; the number of city hospitals was reduced, and thirty-two public schools were closed.

WHY NEW YORK WENT BROKE: THE "COMPASSION" FACTOR

How did "Fun City" get in such sad shape? Certain short-term factors clearly were a problem, notably the immediate crisis in investor confidence, the recession of 1974, which reduced city revenues sharply, and the severe inflation of the same period. The long-term factors were of greater consequence, however; the poor are, and for sometime had been, moving into New York City, particularly from the rural South and Puerto Rico. There is an out-migration of the middle class to the suburbs, and the city's population is growing both older and poorer. Between 1950 and 1970, the portion of the city's population over sixty-five years of age grew from 8 percent to more than 12 percent, and the proportion of the city's families with incomes below the nation's average income level rose from 36 to 49 percent. While New York's population has remained relatively constant,

New York lost jobs rapidly between 1970 and 1975. Meanwhile, taxes went up. A glance at Table 15–12 indicates the steep rise in New York City taxes and their relationship to the personal income of New Yorkers between 1969 and 1975.

Beyond these relatively uncontrollable events, however, New York suffered from mismanagement, and among the most notable aspects of this mismanagement was the city's relationship with public unions. U.S. Treasury officials estimate that it costs New York City an average of $30,000 every year to pay and provide fringe benefits for each municipal employee; this compares with an average of $13,000 to $14,000 for each federal civil service employee. New York City's payroll in 1976 exceeded $7 billion, and $2 billion of this went to civil service pensions alone, which ranged from $12,000 to $30,000. In 1976 New York paid more than $35,000 for the average firefighter, and almost $19,000 for the average senior clerk.

Moreover, the fringe benefits were phenomenal. A good portion of the city's employees had contracts which, in effect, permitted them to work only half a year for a full year's pay.[29] In 1976, police officers in New York had twenty-seven days' vacation, eighteen days off in return for a fifteen-minute early arrival for briefings, three days off for giving blood, three days off for "good arrests," an average of ten days of sick leave, eleven annual holidays, and two regular days off on the seven-day swing shift. Employees in the Sanitation Department had the same type of arrangement, and both calculated out to about six months off every year. Teachers, with summer holidays, the Easter and Christmas weeks off, school closure days, sick leaves, sabbaticals, "short-days," early breaks, and election days off, received what amounted to five to six months off annually. One hundred percent of each employee's health insurance was paid for by the city, in some cases including free dental care and eyeglasses for retired workers.

---

[29]The following discussion of New York City's retirement pensions is drawn from Victor Riesel, "Year's Pay, Six Months' Work, The Fun City Way." Syndicated column, October 15, 1976.

TABLE 15–12   THE NEW YORK CITY TAX BURDEN, 1969–1975

FISCAL YEAR	PERSONAL INCOME ($ BILLIONS)	TAXES[1] ($ BILLIONS)	TAXES AS % OF PERSONAL INCOME
1969–70	39	2.958	7.5
1970–71	41	3.178	7.7
1971–72	43	3.736	8.7
1972–73	45	4.017	8.9
1973–74	48	4.506	9.4
1974–75	50	5.111	10.2

[1]Excludes fees and charges, stock transfer taxes, and nonresident income taxes.

Source: New York City Finance Administration

TABLE 15–13 MAJOR U.S. CITIES BY WELFARE RECIPIENTS, PER CAPITA EXPENDITURES, PUBLIC EMPLOYMENT, EMPLOYEE SALARIES, AND PER CAPITA DEBT, 1975

(1) CITY	(2) FRACTION OF POPULATION RECEIVING WELFARE PAYMENTS[1]	(3) PER CAPITA EXPENDITURES 1972–1973	(4) LOCAL GOVERNMENT EMPLOYMENT PER 10,000 POPULATION 1974	(5) PUBLIC EMPLOYEE AVERAGE SALARIES 1974				(6) DEBT OUTSTANDING PER CAPITA 1972–73[1]	
				(a) Teacher	(b) Police	(c) Fire	(d) Sanitation	(a) Total	(b) Short-term
New York City[2]	12.4	$1,224	517.1	$17,018	$14,666	$16,964	$15,924	$1,676	$352
Boston	16.9	858	378.0	13,938	14,352	13,844	10,666	1,385	334
Chicago	11.1	267	140.0	17,409	14,146	15,525	11,956	733	169
Newark	14.4	692	391.1	13,720	13,282	13,282	8,473	616	112
Los Angeles	8.0	242	162.2	13,058	15,833	21,180	13,168	650	14
Philadelphia[2]	16.2	415	163.8	12,800	14,354	13,869	13,337	1,015	101
San Francisco[2]	9.1	751	312.5	14,855	15,529	17,765	13,023	1,225	151
New Orleans[2]	11.4	241	177.3	8,715	10,746	10,645	4,170	770	39
St. Louis[2]	15.8	310	241.9	14,894	11,748	13,185	9,593	731	49
Denver[2]	7.2	473	237.0	13,505	12,907	14,198	10,258	786	52
Baltimore[2]	16.3	806	434.1	10,488	10,098	10,980	8,126	609	45
Detroit	11.1	357	194.8	18,836	15,636	16,107	13,814	658	63

[1]Central County.
[2]Boundaries of the city are coterminous with those of the central county.

Source: Derived from Congressional Budget Office, *New York City's Fiscal Problem*, Background Paper No. 1, October 10, 1975. (Washington, D.C. U.S. Government Printing Office, 1975), pp. 16, 17, and errata sheet.

A married employee in New York who retired at sixty-five with twenty-five years' service received an after-tax retirement income equal to 125 percent of his or her take-home pay during the last year on the job. By comparison, the retirement rate in Atlanta was 43 percent of the last year's salary; in Chicago, 47 percent; in Dallas, 53 percent; and in Los Angeles, 54 percent.

By 1975, New York City workers were earning consistently higher salaries than their counterparts in virtually every major city in the country. A major reason why New York's benefits are so high is that the city employees and their families cast about a half million votes in city elections, and Fun City's politicians have been duly responsive. In the 1960s, city employees' salary and fringe benefits increased by 15.7 percent and 19.4 percent respectively in each of the city's two election years. Table 15–13 indicates the salaries of New York's employees and also itemizes the percentage of the city's population receiving welfare payments, per capita expenditures of city government, local government employment per 10,000 population, and debt outstanding per capita, and compares these data with other major central cities in the nation. With a debt of more than $14 billion, New York's outstanding debt per capita in 1972–1973 was almost $1,700; the next largest was Boston with a debt of almost $1,400 per person.

NEW YORK AND THE WONDERS OF "CREATIVE ACCOUNTING"

Other than bad bargaining with unions, New York also relied extensively on another system of mismanagement, known in some circles as "creative accounting." New York became a "fiscal junkie" by relying on the "expense fix," the "revenue fix," the "capital fix," and the "outright deficit fix."[30] Basically, these "fixes" amounted to treating current costs as next year's costs, treating anticipated revenues as current revenues, diverting capital expenditures to day-to-day operating costs, and simply borrowing against anticipated revenues for daily operating expenses. Of these, the revenue fix, which had been initiated very quietly by Mayor Robert Wagner in 1965 as a means of financing a $100 million deficit that the city then had, was ultimately perhaps the most damaging.

In 1977, the U.S. Securities and Exchange Commission (SEC) charged that the city's financial practices had gone beyond the bounds of creative accounting and that Mayor Abraham Beame and six major banks had arranged the sale of $4 billion in municipal bonds to an unsuspecting public in 1975, knowing full well that the city was about to go down the fiscal tubes. While some of these banks were pushing the sale of New York bonds, they simultaneously were dumping their own holdings on the marketplace

---

[30]Steven R. Weisman, "How New York Became a Fiscal Junkie." *New York Times*, August 17, 1975.

before the financial roof caved in. Duped investors lost 45 percent of their bonds' face value when New York's monetary plight was exposed later that year.

Democrat Beame called the SEC's 1,000 pages of charges "a shameless, vicious political document," since it was released shortly before New York's Democratic mayoral primary. The banks also denied any impropriety. Nevertheless, the SEC maintained that New York "employed budgetary, accounting and financial practices which it knew distorted its true financial condition"—such as listing city-owned property on tax rolls, even though no city taxes its own property.

Beame, who had been New York's chief financial officer for eight years before he was elected mayor in 1973, was defeated by relatively conservative Edward Koch in 1977. During Beame's tenure, the city had managed to repay all its emergency loans from the federal treasury on time or before they were due, although the city's debt actually was slightly higher when Koch became mayor than it was at the height of the fiscal crisis in 1975— chiefly because of the city's annual debt service charge of an almost unbelievable $2 billion. Still, New York's financial *chutzpah* persists; in 1978 Mayor Koch asked Washington for more emergency funding (the city still was frozen out of the municipal bond market), just as he announced that he was raising the salaries of 2,100 city executives by between $3,000 to $7,000 a year![31] Congress came through with a guarantee to back New York bond issues with another $1.65 billion to stave off municipal bankruptcy.

WHAT IF? THE IMPACT OF BANKRUPTCY

New York City is the second biggest government in the country; it is surpassed in size only by the national government. Therefore, when a government of its magnitude runs into financial snags, the effects may not be limited to the municipal boundaries. If the city had been, or ultimately were, forced to default on its obligations, a number of investors could be hurt. The Congressional Budget Office observed, "While it is possible that the collapse of New York would precipitate a storm of bankruptcies in the private sector, and a wave of municipal defaults, it is also possible that the default by the city would generate but a ripple on the nation's financial waters."[32]

In 1975 the large New York banks held roughly $2 billion of the $14.6 billion in outstanding debt, which amounted to only 5 percent of their total assets. Approximately 60 percent of the nation's 9,000 banks that do not belong to the Federal Reserve System have more than half of their capital in New York City securities, and a similar number of city securities are held by the 5,000 banks that are members of the Federal Reserve System.

---

[31]Andy Logan, "Around City Hall." *The New Yorker* (January 23, 1978): pp. 98–103.
[32]Congressional Budget Office, *New York City's Fiscal Problems*, p. 19.

Nevertheless, the Federal Reserve has agreed to back these nonmember banks in the event of a New York default, thereby lessening the economic impact.

Ultimately, however, the impact of New York City going bankrupt would depend on the psychology of the bond market. This is something no one really can predict, although there are indications that investors are getting nervous over New York. In 1975, bonds were rejected in three states— Ohio, New Jersey, and New York—by large margins at the polls, and these defeats were linked by experts to the New York City financial crisis. Larger, older cities, particularly those in the North Central area and in the East, already have been forced to pay unusually high rates of interest, and the Congressional Budget Office has linked this situation to their "superficial fiscal resemblance to New York."[33] The interest rates paid by Philadelphia, Detroit, and New York State, for example, were all forced up substantially in 1975, largely because of the fiscal albatross of New York City.

Just as the investment community is concerned about New York City, so is the public at large. A sampling of public opinion polls taken in 1975 indicated that between 18 and 35 percent of Americans really did not want to do anything for New York City; between 24 and 42 percent definitely favored an effective cash aid to help New York.[34] By 1977, however, 44 percent of the nation opposed aid to major cities in fiscal trouble, while 43 percent favored it; in the Northeast, not surprisingly, 58 percent favored such aid.[35]

IS NEW YORK UNIQUE? NOT LIKELY

American cities have gone bankrupt in the past. In 1838 Mobile, Alabama, became the first to hold that dubious distinction. Most municipal defaults on obligations occurred right after the Civil War and then during the Depression of the 1930s. After World War II 431 American cities defaulted on obligations, but at least 306 of these were technical and temporary defaults. Defaults totalled less than one-half of 1 percent of all municipal debts outstanding in 1970.

Other cities are facing Cleveland's and New York's experiences, if in less traumatic terms and considerably less precipitously. Chicago, Boston, and even Washington, D.C. eventually may be in similar straits, according to some experts. In 1978, the Advisory Commission on Intergovernmental Relations released startling data indicating that ten of America's most depressed big cities (not including New York) had become dramatically more dependent on Washington to make ends meet than they were only

---

[33]*Ibid.*, pp. 20–21.

[34]Kevin Phillips, "New York Bail Out, Polls Only Confuse Issue." Syndicated column, November 27, 1975.

[35]ACIR, *Changing Public Attitudes on Government and Taxes.* 1977.

two years earlier. The cities, on the average, received 31 cents from the feds for every dollar they raised from their own sources in 1976, but only two years later were receiving more than 54 cents for each local tax dollar. The cities were Atlanta, Baltimore, Boston, Buffalo, Chicago, Cleveland, Detroit, Newark, Philadelphia, and St. Louis.[36]

There are exceptions to such dismal statistics. Seattle provides a fine example of a city that has maintained fiscal control despite some tough economic sledding. Seattle underwent terrific economic disruptions as a result of massive cutbacks in aircraft production by Boeing Corporation in the early 1970s. Seattle countered by raising taxes and reducing its workforce. Moreover, the city's unions, in the view of many, have become a conservative force for fiscal responsibility and this attitude has been of considerable help in keeping Seattle financially viable, which it largely is today.

Less well known than the urban financial crisis is the fact that many states may be in precarious fiscal circumstances. If true, some states may be in severe budgetary straights largely because of unrealistic pension plans for their retired employees. Sixteen states, for example, offer retirement plans to their school teachers that (when combined with Social Security payments) result in an actual increase in after-tax income.[37] It may turn out that some states will be forced to renege on their pension plans for retiring employees, and Massachusetts and Delaware have already begun to limit their employee retirement plans.

CONCLUSION

As we have seen, public finance is not simple and in this chapter we have examined only one side of the fiscal coin: getting the money. In Part Five we look at the other: how state and local governments spend their money.

---

[36]Advisory Commission on Intergovernmental Relations, cited in Associated Press, April 2, 1978, syndicated nationally.

[37]Neal R. Pierce, "Pensions: Capital Punishment of Taxpayers." Syndicated column, September 2, 1977.

PART I

POLICIES, CLASS, AND THE GRASSROOTS

POLICIES
FOR THE
UNDERCLASS:
THE
WELFARE MESS

In Part Five we consider the major political issues that state and local governments must face: welfare, crime, education, planning, land use, transportation, housing, and corruption.

TOWARD A CLASS INTERPRETATION OF POLICY

This book's approach to state and local public policy issues is frankly class-based. The issues of poverty, welfare, and crime are all interrelated and affect predominantly society's underdogs; these are public policies designed largely for the poor and the deviant. On the other hand, planning, housing, transportation, and education policies are designed primarily for the middle class, which always has taken a peculiar interest in these problems. The issue of political corruption, one not normally covered in books on state and local governments, approaches political corruption as the politics of the rich. Political corruption can, of course, occur at all levels of society, but the people who reap the greatest benefits from it are often among the wealthier classes.

A class-based approach to the study of public policy is hardly new (Karl Marx, for one, was vaguely aware of it), but class is often overlooked as a central variable in understanding how and why public policies are made. It is worth recalling that public policies are made for groups (and classes) of people at least as much as they are formed for "all the people." Charles Reich has castigated public policy in America as an "inhuman medium" largely on the grounds that, since the New Deal of the 1930s, laws have been written for groups and categories of people (for example, farmers, old people, young people, the poor, students, veterans, and so forth) and not for the individual citizens, who once stood as equals before the law simply as persons, rather than as "farmers" or "students." By addressing groups rather than individuals, public policy has waxed into something that the lone citizen no longer can understand, but that groups of citizens *must* understand if they are to be a part of the larger society.[1]

Whether or not Reich's analysis is correct, it is provocative enough to warrant approaching public policy issues as class issues in this and the succeeding chapters of this book.

We begin at the bottom, with the poor.

DEFINING POVERTY

The poor always will be with us. One reason is because *poverty* must be defined in relative terms. Poverty, by definition, means that someone is getting much less money than someone else, and when the discrepancy

---

[1]Charles Reich, *The Greening of America,* (New York: Random House, 1970).

333

Policies for
the
underclass:
the welfare
mess

between income levels becomes intense, the lower portion of the scale becomes the impoverished.

In 1955 the federal government defined *poverty* in more quantitative terms; a federal survey of that year revealed that the poor spent 30 percent of their after-tax income for food. Using this finding, the "poverty line" was invented and established by federal statisticians at a point slightly more than three times the price of an "adequate" diet. How realistic this kind of "poverty line" is is a matter of conjecture but, in any case, the poverty line uses a grim measure of indigence: eating or starving.

WHO IS POOR?

Using this official statistic, there are approximately 24 million poor people in this country, or slightly more than 11 percent of the population. This meant in the late 1970s that an average poor family of four was earning less than $6,400 per year. Table 16–1 indicates the precentage of the American population below the poverty level. A poor person is likelier to be black or brown, to live in the central cities or rural areas rather than the suburbs (although only 27 percent of all Americans live in rural areas, 40 percent of the nation's poor reside there), to be either very young or very old, to be

TABLE 16–1 PERCENTAGE OF POPULATION BELOW POVERTY LEVEL

Total	11.6
White	8.9
Black	31.4
Central Cities	14.4
Suburbs	7.1
Rural	14.4
Under 25	16.1
25–65	8.5
Over 65	15.7
Families with male head	7.1
Families with female head	34.4
Less than 8 years school	21.3
8 years school	11.4
High school graduate	8.1
College graduate	3.1

Source: U.S. Bureau of the Census, *Current Population Reports*, Series P-60, "Money Income and Poverty Status" (Washington, D.C.: U.S. Government Printing Office, 1975).

part of a family headed by a woman, and to have had no more than eight years of formal schooling.

THE RACISM OF POVERTY

Among the poorest in the land are the blacks.[2] Almost a third of *all* black families in the nation earn incomes below the official poverty line for an urban family of four; less than 9 percent of all white families are in comparable straits. During the past twenty years the average family income for all black families has been from 33 to more than 40 percent lower than the income for all white families; while this gap has narrowed slightly since 1950, the difference between black and white average incomes remains broad. As Figure 16–1 shows, 55 percent of the country's blacks live in the most depressed central cities and (as we shall see in Chapter 20) cannot get out.

Unemployment patterns reveal a similar disparity. In the late 1970s, 10 to 15 percent of the adult black labor force was jobless; only 4 to 6 percent of adult white workers were without jobs. Among teen-agers, the figures become astounding; unemployment among black teen-agers rose from 35 percent in 1972 to nearly 40 percent in 1978; white teen-aged unemployment in 1978 was a relatively mild 14 percent. Perhaps even worse, blacks tend to lose their jobs more rapidly than whites when hard times strike;

---

[2]The material concerning the racial aspects of poverty that follows is drawn from "The American Underclass." *Time* (August 29, 1977), pp. 14–27; and Don Bacon, "Young Blacks Out of Work: Time Bomb for U.S.," *U.S. News & World Report* (December 5, 1977), pp. 22–25.

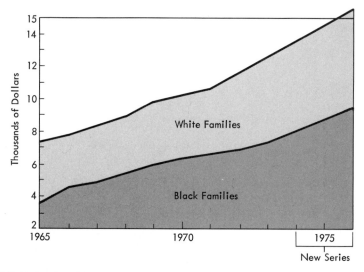

FIGURE 16–1 MEDIAN INCOMES, BLACK AND WHITE FAMILIES, 1965–1976

TABLE 16–2 PERCENTAGE DISTRIBUTION OF OCCUPATIONS OF EMPLOYED
URBANITES, BY RACE, 1970

OCCUPATIONAL CATEGORY	WHITE	BLACK	SPANISH HERITAGE
Professional and technical	17	9	9
Managers and administrators	9	3	5
Sales workers	9	3	5
Clerical workers	20	16	16
Craftsmen	14	9	14
Operatives	15	23	27
Laborers	4	9	9
Service workers	11	20	14
Private household workers	1	8	1
Total	100	100	100

Source: U.S. Bureau of the Census, *Census of Population: 1970, General Social and Economic Characteristics: United States Summary* (June 1972), Table 92.

during the economic recession of 1973–1975, blacks were laid off at almost twice the rate of whites.

People of Spanish origin are also poorer than whites and have higher rates of unemployment, but they are perhaps better off than blacks. Forty-nine percent of Hispanics live in central cities (less, proportionately, than blacks); they have have slightly lower unemployment rates, earn somewhat higher incomes, and tend to hold better jobs than blacks. Still, Latinos are substantially worse off than whites; in the late 1970s, brown families averaged only three-quarters of the average annual income of white families. Table 16–2 indicates the kinds of jobs that white, black, and brown people tend to have. Clearly, whites occupy the more enviable positions.

We should stress that the statistics just cited are "official" ones furnished by the federal government. But some (including the National Urban League) believe that Washington's numbers—especially in the area of unemployment—are inaccurate, and that the reality of poverty is substantially worse. For example, government statisticians do not count in their unemployment calculations "discouraged" job-seekers—those more than one million potential workers who in any given year have looked for jobs but have grown discouraged and quit trying. If these people are taken into account, more than half of the nation's black teen-agers may be unemployed.

THE UNDERCLASS: POVERTY'S HARDCORE

These discouraged job-seekers lead us to the toughest problem of poverty: those people who cannot escape and who appear to be on the road to becoming a permanent underclass festering in the heart of the earth's richest nation. This underclass includes not only people who have opted out of the nation's labor supply, but also about 2.5 million "permanent" welfare mothers (those who have been on the rolls for a year or longer), the chronically unemployed eighteen- to twenty-one-year-olds, and a large segment of the handicapped. Mostly black, but with many browns and whites, the nation's underclass is estimated to range from 7 million to as many as 10 million people. How to lift up the underclass is among the most vexing dilemmas of American politics, especially in light of the fact that the underclass appears to be growing; for example, the black birthrate is 51 percent higher than the white birthrate, and it is even higher among poor blacks.

The underclass also is destructive, both to itself and to other economic classes. During the 1977 blackout in New York City, for instance, 55 percent of the arrested looters were unemployed. One official of the Department of Housing and Urban Development (HUD) has observed that "The underclass presents our most dangerous crisis, more dangerous than the Depression of 1929, and more complex."[3]

THE REALITY OF POVERTY

Even in material terms poverty is relative, and even America's poorest are relatively well off. Nevertheless, it behooves us to remember that, of the 24 million Americans living under the official poverty line, less than half own cars, less than half own their own homes, almost 50 percent have no savings, and approximately 25 percent have no refrigerators, hot water, access to a telephone, a kitchen, or indoor plumbing. Virtually all our poor suffer from malnutrition of some kind.[4] About one-fourth of all recipients of Aid to Families with Dependent Children (AFDC) or "welfare" live in California or New York, and more than a fifth live in New York City, Los Angeles, Chicago, Philadelphia, or Detroit. About 90 percent of welfare recipients are old, disabled, or women with small children.

Numbers, of course, do not tell the whole story. Thomas Gladwin, an anthropologist, states in succinct terms that poverty in America means being not only poor but also powerless, incompetent (insofar as the employer is concerned), and despised. Significantly, being despised does not necessarily associate with being a member of a minority race, but being poor does:

> It is obvious that poverty and discrimination are closely and complexly interrelated. For example, putting the relationship the other way around, it is hard to think of any large group of really poor people about whom stereotypes and prejudices have *not* developed. In the 1930s numbers of small independent farmers, in other times idealized as staunch repositories of the American pioneering spirit, were stripped of their farms and their money. They became almost overnight the most stigmatized population

---

[3]Monsignor Geno Baroni, quoted in "The American Underclass," p. 15.

[4]Herman T. Miller, "The Dimensions of Poverty." In *Poverty as a Public Issue.* Ben B. Seligman, ed. (New York: The Free Press, 1965), pp. 153–176.

337

Policies for
the
underclass:
the welfare
mess

of the Depression years, the Okies. Similarly, the purest descendents of the early days of White Anglo-Saxon Protestants have now become in their poverty the Appalachian hillbillies, probably as ruthlessly plundered of their property and power as any of our minorities, except the decimated Indians, and the butts of a special school of American belittling humor which extends back over several generations. The little child in eastern Kentucky, hiding and peeking out in wide-eyed fright at the stranger, knows as well as any child in an urban ghetto that he is powerless to protect himself against a world which has judged him worthless. Under these circumstances, what good would it do him to be told that he is a blond blue-eyed Anglo-Saxon and therefore potentially heir to all the privileges of the land?"[5]

WELFARE FOR WHOM?

It should be stated early and clearly that welfare in America is not something provided only to the poor. Farm price supports, "corporate welfare" (such as is occasionally supplied to giant aircraft corporations), subsidies to the railroads, tax deductions for interest incurred on home mortgages, and tax preferences for families and people over sixty-five—all are forms of welfare, and most of the time such welfare provides benefits to people who are not poor at all. About one-fifth of all American households receive some kind of public assistance, and the nearly $192 billion annual public assistance budget accounts for approximately one-seventh of all personal income in the nation; almost $90 billion of this money is paid out in social security checks.

Nevertheless, welfare as normally understood is a policy for the poor and, as Robert Albritton has cogently observed, welfare "is a system replete with anomalies—intended to reduce dependency, it requires dependency as a condition of receiving welfare benefits; encouraging recipients to find gainful employment, it penalizes their success by withdrawing benefits so that a former client is often in worse straits while employed than while receiving welfare."[6] Facts support Albritton's statement. In Oregon and New York, for example, the cash payments available to a family of four under just two welfare programs—Aid to Families with Dependent Children and food stamps—exceed the earnings of a full-time worker at the minimum wage in twenty-two states![7] In the opinion of most Americans, former President Richard M. Nixon was correct when he spoke of welfare as a "monstrous, consuming, outrage."[8]

---

[5]Thomas Gladwin, *Poverty U.S.A.* (Boston: Little, Brown, 1967), pp. 83–84.

[6]Robert Albritton, "Welfare Policy." In *Politics in the American States*: A Comparative Analysis, 3rd ed., Herbert Jacob and Kenneth N. Vines, eds. (Boston: Little, Brown, 1976), pp. 349–350. Reprinted by permission.

[7]Donald C. Bacon, "Another Go at the Welfare Mess: Will It Work?" *U.S. News & World Report* (August 8, 1977), p. 47.

[8]Richard M. Nixon, State of the Union Address, 1971, quoted in Albritton, "Welfare Policy," p. 350.

SOCIAL INSURANCE AND PUBLIC ASSISTANCE: THE TWO POLICIES FOR WELFARE

THE SOCIAL SECURITY ACT OF 1935: WELFARE'S CORNERSTONE

If there is a single act of legislation that is the rockbed of welfare policy in the United States, it is the Social Security Act of 1935, enacted as a major response to the Great Depression, and its subsequent amendments. "Social security" as a policy has two broad thrusts; one is social insurance and the other is public assistance.

Social insurance benefits are paid for by compulsory payroll taxes; the category entitled FICA (Federal Insurance Contributions Act) on a paycheck stub notes how much of one's check is deducted for "social security." *Public assistance* spending for "welfare" is funded from general tax revenues and, unlike social insurance, this money is not earmarked. Thus, when money is spent for welfare policies, it is being spent at the potential expense of some other policy. Social insurance is a national policy which covers the vast majority of all Americans, and it is uniform in its distribution of benefits throughout the states. By contrast, public assistance is a decentralized system predicated on the premise that state governments can better judge the needs of their people and the resources of their taxpayers than Washington bureaucrats can, and is administered on the basis of federal grants to state governments. Public assistance is handled in one of two ways, either by direct formula grants to states, based on certain categories of need, or by categorical grants to the states, which permit the states to retain greater discretion on how those federal funds are used.

SOCIAL INSURANCE: "SOCIAL SECURITY"

Within these two broad thrusts of social insurance and public welfare are a number of specific programs. The first, pertaining only to social insurance, is Old Age, Survivors, Disability, and Health Insurance, or OASDHI. This program, commonly known as social security, is designed to reduce the loss of a person's income because of unemployment resulting from old age, disability, or death of the head of the family. A major component of OASDHI is Medicare, and we consider Medicare later. In 1977, OASDHI paid out nearly $90 billion to 33 million people, or one-seventh of the population. It is no small domestic welfare program.

SOCIAL INSURANCE: UNEMPLOYMENT BENEFITS

A second program initiated by the Social Security Act is unemployment insurance. Although benefits are actually provided by the federal government through a tax on all employers who employ four employees or more,

339

Policies for
the
underclass:
the welfare
mess

states have a greater say in determining how unemployment benefits should be paid.

In the late 1970s, almost eight million people were unemployed in America. Unemployment tends to hit all skill levels in the work force, but it concentrates on particular age groups and women. Those who are forty-five to fifty-four and the young, particularly teen-agers, are statistically the hardest hit by unemployment and, as we have noted, black teen-agers are especially hard hit. This tendency for the young to be unemployed more frequently than most other age groups strikes blacks especially hard, since nearly half of all black Americans are under twenty-five. In other words, although unemployment insurance as a welfare policy is applicable to all groups in society, it tends to focus on women, minority groups, the young, the middle-aged, and people who have little or no work experience.

To encourage state and local governments to grapple with their own unemployment problems Congress enacted the Comprehensive Employment and Training Act of 1973 (CETA) and the Youth Employment and Demonstration Projects Act of 1977. CETA, as expanded in 1977, is the biggest public employment program since the New Deal, and provides state and local governments with nearly $13 billion to hire some 5.6 million Americans (1.8 of whom are young minorities) and put them on their public payrolls. States and cities however, have not been forthcoming in hiring the very poor, but evidently opt instead to hire those who are only temporarily out of work. Moreover, critics contend that CETA money is not being used to hire additional personnel by state and local governments, but instead to fund positions that normally would be paid out of state and local budgets.

The Youth Employment and Demonstration Projects Act allocates $1 billion for several experimental programs designed to prepare almost one-half million young people—more than half of whom are from minority groups—for permanent entry into the work force. Critics have contended that the program often does little more than bribe youths to stay off the streets between school years.

SOCIAL INSURANCE: GENERAL HEALTH CARE AND MEDICARE

A third component is health insurance. Health care is the nation's third largest industry, and in 1975 health spending accounted for 8.3 percent of the Gross National Product, a percentage that is higher than that of any other country in the world. The figure amounts to an astounding $118.5 billion, or $547 per person. Of course, these kinds of sums are not all spent by the government; most, in fact, are expended within the private sphere. All government spending for health (federal, state, and local combined) accounts for slightly more than 42 percent of the nation's health expenditures, and in 1975 government health spending increased at a rate two and one-half times faster than private health spending.

Federal health expenditures account for most of the public spending on health (70 percent). The states spent about 11 percent of their total budgets, on the average, for health in the mid-1970s, while the federal government spent roughly 7.5 percent of its budget on health care, excluding health-related outlays for defense, veterans' benefits, and international affairs. Among the states, Rhode Island leads the list by spending more than 19 percent of its total budget on health care, and Alaska ranks last, spending slightly more than 4 percent.[9]

In 1965 Congress enacted two important pieces of legislation designed to enhance health in America: Medicare and Medicaid. Medicare provides comprehensive medical care for people over sixty-five and is part of the Social Security Insurance program. Medicare also provides low-cost voluntary medical insurance for the aged, and it is financed through payroll taxes collected under FICA.

PUBLIC ASSISTANCE: MEDICAID

Unlike Medicare, which is a social insurance program, Medicaid is clearly a public assistance program designed for the needy, and its beneficiaries generally are welfare recipients. The cost of Medicaid has surpassed all expectations—in the mid-1970s, an average of almost half of *all* state spending for health purposes was allocated solely to Medicaid. Almost 25 million people receive Medicaid benefits; nearly half of them are children. Medicaid is jointly financed by federal and state governments, but it is principally a state responsiblity and about 5.5 percent of the typical state budget is spent on it.

PUBLIC ASSISTANCE:
SUPPLEMENTAL SECURITY INCOME ASSISTANCE

Federal formula grants to states for welfare are used to assist three categories of the needy: the aged, the blind, and the disabled. Old Age Assistance, Aid to the Blind, and Aid to Permanently and Totally Disabled have remained relatively stable in terms of their cost to the states since the 1960s, although Aid to the Permanently and Totally Disabled has increased, largely as a result of a more flexible application of eligibility requirements.

In 1974 a new national program called Supplemental Security Income Assistance, or SSI, went into effect. Before the enactment of SSI, each state could calculate its own minimum income standards for its poor, and the determination of cash assistance levels and eligibility were entirely matters of state policy. Under SSI, however, national minimum standards for eligibility and for cash assistance were established. It was further stipulated

---

[9]Gary J. Clarke, "State Health and Mental Health Programs," *Book of the States, 1976–77.* (Lexington, Ky.: Council of State Governments, 1976), pp. 367–368.

341

Policies for
the
underclass:
the welfare
mess

that, if one category of need was receiving higher monthly benefits than another (for instance, the blind have traditionally received more than the elderly), then the other two categories had to be brought up to the same level. Thus the Supplemental Security Income Programs have had two effects. First, all categories of "the needy" have been equalized in terms of level of cash assistance; the blind, for example, are not receiving more money than the elderly simply because they are blind. Second, state policy makers have been displaced by national policy makers in the degree of discretion that they may wield over these areas of welfare. Unless states elect to go beyond federal cash assistance levels (which for the most part is not likely), the states have lost a great deal of their influence over how the blind, the old, and the disabled may be assisted as a result of SSI. In 1976, 4.3 million Americans received benefits of about $6 billion under the SSI program and three-quarters of this sum was paid by the federal government, with the states adding supplementary payments.

PUBLIC ASSISTANCE: AID TO FAMILIES WITH DEPENDENT CHILDREN AND FOOD STAMPS

Finally, there are two forms of public welfare that have grown extremely controversial in recent years: the Aid to Families with Dependent Children Program and the Food Stamp Program. Both programs are administered almost entirely by state governments, but in some states local governments are also involved.

AFDC is the largest federally assisted program for state public welfare. Originally it was meant to provide a minimum standard of existence for orphans, children cared for by a widowed mother, or families where the father was unavoidably absent. Over time the kinds of family units receiving AFDC payments has changed. Since 1962, for example, AFDC payments can go to two parents in the same home if one parent is incapacitated or unemployed. Under AFDC the federal government pays from a relatively small 50 percent of the cost in eleven states to as much as 78 percent of the expenses in the remainder. Thirty-eight state governments bear the entire nonfederal share of AFDC payments; twelve states require their local governments to pay up to half this amount. More than eleven million people (nearly 45 percent of whom are blacks) receive AFDC funds, with current payments nearing $12 billion every year.

Supplementing AFDC payments are food stamps. The Food Stamp Program was enacted in 1964 with the passage of the Food Stamp Act, which is intended to improve nutrition in low-income families. The federal government administers the program through the U.S. Department of Agriculture's Food and Nutrition Service, but state and local welfare agencies are empowered to establish eligibility for the program, issue the stamps, and maintain quality control. The program has been operating nationwide only since 1974 and, like AFDC, the expenses are burgeoning. Between

1965 and 1976 food stamp outlays ballooned from $35 million to $5.6 *billion,* and almost 18 million people were receiving food stamps. The program allows a family of four to pay about 25 to 30 percent of its net income for a specified dollar value in food stamps. The food stamps are redeemed at a grocery store for a fraction of the true value of the food that food stamp recipients purchase and, in this fashion, the needy have their diets supplemented.

DO STATE AND LOCAL GOVERNMENTS CARE? THE ROLE OF "GENERAL ASSISTANCE"

Welfare policy is a highly intergovernmental process in which state and local governments play a peculiar role; for example, twenty-two states share the expenses of AFDC payments with their local governments, and Table 16–3 indicates the percentage of AFDC cash assistance and Medicaid payments borne by local governments in these states. In some cases, this sharing can place a substantial burden on the local governments, as it does in New York, Minnesota, and Wyoming.

In addition to administering certain portions of the national welfare program, the states have also implemented their own *general assistance programs* for their citizens. General assistance is entirely a state and local responsibility, and about one million people receive roughly $1.2 billion in general assistance from their state and local governments each year, although the total welfare costs to all state and local governments exceeds $7.5 billion annually.[10] Monthly general assistance payments per recipient vary even more widely than do AFDC payments—from $12 to $144. Most states count on their local governments to provide general assistance, and less than half the states make a significant contribution to support local general assistance programs. Recall, in this regard, that federal welfare accounts for only four categories of people: the blind, the old, the disabled, and impoverished families with children. It is up to state and local governments—and primarily local governments—to care take care of other kinds of needy people.

THE WELFARE EXPLOSION

Certainly the most obvious feature of the welfare system is its explosively growing cost. Total welfare costs nearly doubled from $146 billion a year in 1970 to $287 billion a year in 1975. In 1960 the combined federal, state, and local social welfare expenditure was a relatively insignificant $52 billion and accounted for 10.3 percent of the Gross National Product.[11] By 1975

---

[10]Committee for Economic Development, *Welfare Reform and Its Financing.* (New York: Committee for Economic Development, 1976), p. 13.

[11]Tax Foundation, *Facts and Figures on Government Finance.* (New York: Tax Foundation, 1977), pp. 7–8.

TABLE 16–3 FRACTION OF AFDC CASH ASSISTANCE AND MEDICAID PAYMENTS BORNE BY LOCAL GOVERNMENTS (FISCAL YEAR 1974)

STATE[1]	PERCENT
New York	23.0
Minnesota	21.8
Wyoming	18.5
California	14.5
Kansas	11.3
Colorado	9.4
Nebraska	8.8
Nevada	8.3
No. Carolina	8.3
Indiana	6.9
New Jersey	6.5
Iowa	4.8
No. Dakota	4.6
Maryland	4.2
Montana	2.8
Virginia	0.6
Utah	0.6
Louisiana	0.2
Oregon	0.1
New Hampshire	*
Mississippi	*

[1]States not listed do not require any local contribution.
*Less than 0.1 percent.

Source: Congressional Budget Office, *New York City's Fiscal Problem*. (Washington, D.C.: Government Printing Office, 1975), p. 13.

welfare expenditures constituted 19.1 percent of the GNP, although government outlays for direct cash benefits (that is, SSI and AFDC), food stamps, and medical care for the poor accounted for only 3 percent of the GNP. As Figure 16–2 illustrates, in 1970 state government expenditures for public welfare exceeded expenditures for highways for the first time, and the welfare-cost curve is rapidly approaching the state expenditure level for education, which has traditionally been the states' greatest expense.

The major categories of welfare most responsible for the rise in expenditure are Medicaid and the Aid to Families with Dependent Children Program. Table 16–4 indicates the increases the states have borne in welfare costs. Between 1965 and 1973, total state spending on welfare increased by almost 300 percent; nonwelfare-related spending increased by only 142 percent. Medical assistance, however, increased by an incredible 1,380

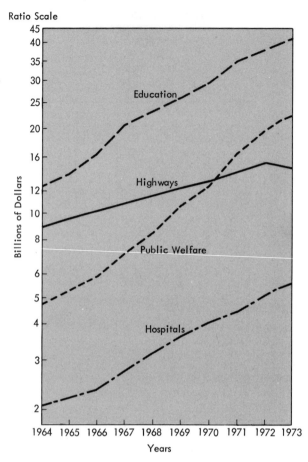

FIGURE 16–2 TRENDS IN STATE GENERAL EXPENDITURE FOR SELECTED FUNCTIONS, 1964–1973

Source: U.S. Department of Commerce, *State Government Finances*. (Washington, D.C.: U.S. Government Printing Office, 1973).

TABLE 16–4 CHANGES IN STATE WELFARE SPENDING AND SPENDING FOR ALL PURPOSES, 1965–1973 (BILLIONS)

	1965	1973	INCREASE	% INCREASE
Total state spending	$45.639	$118.836	$73.197	160
Welfare spending	5.505	21.678	16.173	293
Non-welfare-related spending	40.134	97.158	57.024	142
Nonmedical welfare spending	4.917	11.972	7.054	141
Medical assistance	.588	9.706	8.118	1380

Computations are based on data from U.S. Department of Commerce, *State Government Finances* (Washington, D.C.: U.S. Government Printing Office, 1965, 1973); Department of Health, Education and Welfare, *Social Security Bulletin*, 1965, 1973).

Source: Robert Albritton, "Welfare Policy." In *Politics in the American States*, 3 ed. Herbert Jacob and Kenneth N. Vines, eds. (Boston: Little, Brown, 1976), p. 361.

344

345

Policies for
the
underclass:
the welfare
mess

percent within that eight-year period. Medicaid expenditures have increased by an average of 15 percent every year since it began, escalating from $362 million in 1966 to $17 billion in 1977.

AFDC is the other major area to show an increase. Figure 16–3 indicates the rise in the number receiving Aid to Families with Dependent Children compared to those receiving aid under the other public assistance programs—that is, Supplemental Security Income Assistance and general assistance programs administered by the states. The reasons for these increases in costs, notably in the areas of Medicaid and AFDC, are simple: The programs are serving more people. Between 1965 and 1975 the number of welfare recipients doubled, and the cost of serving them quadrupled.

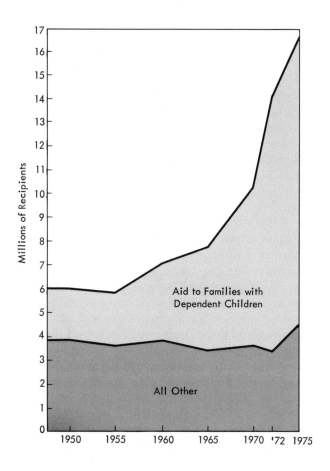

FIGURE 16–3 THE WELFARE EXPLOSION: AFDC PAYMENTS VERSUS OTHER KINDS OF PAYMENTS

AFDC: THE CORE OF WELFARE POLICY

In the 1970s approximately three-quarters of all people receiving welfare assistance were affiliated in some fashion with the AFDC program. Thus, AFDC becomes central in our understanding of the whys and wherefores of welfare policy in the states.

Another reason why AFDC is central to any discussion of welfare policy is that once a family in enrolled in AFDC it automatically becomes eligible to receive food stamps, Medicaid, free or low-rent public housing, free lunches for the children in public schools, and, depending upon the state in which the family resides, a variety of other services. These benefits can often be considerable. A federal government study reported that in the early 1970s a family of four New Yorkers could receive benefits amounting to the equivalent of $7,000 per year just by receiving four basic kinds of aid—public assistance, food stamps, school lunches, and Medicaid—and the General Accounting Office has placed the total value of all social services available to an urban family of four at more than $11,000 a year.

AMERICANS DIVIDED: THE BITTERNESS OF WELFARE

These kinds of policies may have fostered a popular stereotype of welfare recipients as shiftless "bums" who live off the hard-working taxpayer. Food stamps have probably heightened this popular image more than the other welfare policies. Who has not heard at least one story of the well-dressed woman who pays for her groceries in food stamps and drives away in a Cadillac? This stereotype is inaccurate, although there are those receiving welfare who, somehow, do not look as if they "ought" to be receiving it (and who perhaps should not be receiving it), and they will always be highly visible as "welfare cheats" to the average citizen.

The facts are that most welfare recipients have some physical disability, small children in the home, or no marketable skills, and consequently they have an inordinately difficult time finding work. But racism also may be a factor in the popular rising antipathy that many lower- and middle-class working-class whites have toward "welfare bums." Although whites still make up a majority of welfare recipients, the proportion of nonwhites on the welfare rolls has increased dramatically, apparently because for the first time federal court decisions have forced southern states to admit blacks to their welfare programs. Albritton contends that, as the proportion of blacks receiving AFDC assistance has increased, popular support for this form of welfare has declined. (In 1961, for example, 14 percent of all black children received AFDC payments, but in 1977, 38 percent of all black children were receiving AFDC payments.) Court orders have forced many states to abandon their traditional requirements that a woman with children receiving welfare be married, and this abandonment also may have promoted some hostility toward welfare recipients among the middle class.[12]

---

[12]Albritton, "Welfare Policy," p. 357.

346

347

Policies for
the
underclass:
the welfare
mess

As a program, AFDC has not only brought about resentment of many Americans toward the dispossessed, but it has also reduced the self-respect of the poor. State welfare bureaucrats have been inclined to admit fatherless families to their welfare rolls more readily than families with fathers (in fact, roughly four-fifths of the AFDC population are families headed by women), on the logic that, because there is no breadwinner in the household, their need is greater. The effect of this practice is to encourage the break-up of family units, at least in the view of some observers, because fatherless families may receive welfare more readily.

An example of the growing disgust with welfare policy and its attendant inequities is provided by the mayor of Hondo, Texas, who wrote President Carter in 1977 requesting a list of 181 "loafers" he could import to Hondo to increase the city's unemployment rate and thereby qualify it for federal funds. The mayor argued that, because 24 percent of Hondo's 8,000 residents earned salaries below the national poverty level, he needed 181 people who would not work to raise Hondo's unemployment from 3 percent to 6 percent. Federal administrators treated the mayor's request as a joke, which it evidently was not.[13]

In short, a dramatic expansion of welfare rolls, an increase in the number of minority recipients of welfare, and popular stereotypes of welfare "bums" have gone far to divide American society against itself.

WHY THE EXPLOSION?

Of these factors, perhaps the most significant is the startling numerical increase of welfare case loads in the 1960s and 1970s, and that increase is also among the most difficult to explain.[14]

MOVING NORTH?

One rationale for the rise in welfare rolls argues that poor blacks have moved from the states in the Deep South which grant low welfare payments to more generous states in the North. Facts deny this interpretation. Black migration from the South into the northern industrial states peaked during the 1950s, yet AFDC case loads increased only moderately during this period. In the 1960s, when black migration rates to the north actually declined, AFDC case loads were increasing by a factor of three to seven times in the large urban states. "By far the largest portion of AFDC increases occurred as a result of persons already resident in the state moving on to the welfare rolls."[15]

---

[13]United Press International, July 3, 1977, syndicated nationally.

[14]The following discussion of the welfare explosion is drawn largely from Albritton, "Welfare Policy," pp. 378–385.

[15]*Ibid.*, p. 379.

[16]See, for example, Daniel Moynihan, *The Negro Family: The Case for National Action.* (Washington, D.C.: U.S. Department of Labor, 1965).

THE "MOYNIHAN THESIS"?

A second explanation for the increase in welfare rolls has been expounded by Patrick Moynihan.[16] Moynihan argued, first, that discrimination against blacks throughout society amounted to a major reason for the disproportionate dependency of blacks on welfare (not especially a surprising thesis in itself). But then Moynihan extended this view, arguing that the black family was essentially matriarchal (*i.e.,* mother-dominated), and the black males did not play a large role in keeping the family together; indeed, black males frequently did not remain with the family. Hence, matriarchal black families were increasingly dependent upon welfare and this "cultural" factor explained the increasing numbers of blacks on the welfare rolls even in times of prosperity.

Empirical data deny the Moynihan thesis (and since he entered politics, Moynihan himself has denied it). Between 1959 and 1966 neither the desertion by males of either black or white families nor illigitimacy rates were factors in the increasing number of families receiving AFDC assistance.[17] Similarly, surveys conducted in 1961 and 1967 found, "While the absolute number of deserted families increased during this period, they actually represented a slightly smaller percentage of the national regular AFDC case load in 1967 than in 1961."[18] Thus, while more families headed by women (both black and white) are receiving AFDC, their proportionate representation on the welfare rolls seems to be declining.

UNEMPLOYMENT EQUALS WELFARE?

A third explanation for the increase in welfare recipients is that as unemployment increases, welfare rolls go up. This is, of course, true up to a point. But unemployment does not seem to explain adequately the increase in AFDC case loads. For example, among the states that have adopted an "unemployed parent" component in their AFDC policies (a national program optional for the states) the recipients under this program accounted for less than 5 percent of all AFDC recipients. Consequently, unemployment is "hardly a significant factor in explaining sharp rises in welfare spending or case loads, even in participating states."[19]

BLACK POWER?

A fourth, and one of the more romantic explanations for the rise in welfare case loads, contends that state and local governments did become more

---

[17]Irene Lurie, *An Economic Evaluation of Aid to Families with Dependent Children.* (Washington, D.C.: The Brookings Institution, 1968).

[18]Gilbert Steiner, *Social Insecurity: The Politics of Welfare.* (Chicago: Rand-McNally, 1966), p. 30.

[19]Albritton, "Welfare Policy," p. 381.

348

349

Policies for
the
underclass:
the welfare
mess

generous during the 1960s to the poor, but purely in response to governmental confrontations with blacks and other minorities in the form of race riots and greater voting participation by minorities. Nervous state and local officials, the argument continues, "bought off" the poor by expanding their welfare rolls as a means of preventing a social revolution.[20]

The facts do not support this thesis, either. The obvious test of the "keep-the-lid-on-the-revolution" hypothesis is whether or not a rise in welfare rolls in particular cities coincides with large urban riots in those same localities. Welfare case loads did increase in most of the large urban areas that experienced racial disturbances during the 1960s, but case loads increased at a *declining rate,* which would seem to argue against the black power theory. Moreover, when real spending power is measured, the relative economic condition of the poor actually declined during the 1960s, because welfare payments did not keep up with the rise in the cost of living.[21]

THE IMPACT OF WASHINGTON

Since none of these theses adequately explains the rise in welfare rolls, what is the answer? It appears that the impact of the federal government on state welfare policies is the single greatest factor explaining the rise in welfare costs and case loads. In 1965 Congress adopted a series of amendments to the Social Security Act, notably Medicaid, which rapidly rose to become the largest single item in state public assistance budgets. The degree to which the federal government matched categorical assistance programs was increased. These federal incentives to the states to increase their welfare rolls succeeded beyond the expectations of a number of policy makers. The rise in case loads clearly correlates with these innovations in federal welfare policy. As Albritton concludes

> The pattern of welfare spending for medical care is clearly consistent with an explanation of the general rise in state welfare spending as a response to innovations in legislation at the federal level. . . . . Interpreted in this light, the course of welfare activity does not warrant characterization as an explosion; rather it simply records the abrupt change in the welfare policy system due to federal legislation and returns it to normal growth patterns or even lesser levels of growth, albeit at a notably higher level.[22]

WELFARE IN THE STATES: CHAOS OR CYNICISM?

While the federal government has had a substantial influence in expanding state welfare rolls through its revisions of welfare policies in 1965, the states

---

[20]Frances Fox Piven and Richard Cloward, *Regulating the Poor: The Functions of Public Welfare.* (New York: Random House, 1971).

[21]Albritton, "Welfare Policy," pp. 381–383.

[22]*Ibid.,* p. 385.

themselves have considerable latitude in forming welfare policies for their poor, notably those receiving Aid to Families with Dependent Children. This is primarily because with the implementation of the Supplemental Security Income Program in 1974, states necessarily must focus their political and fiscal attentions on AFDC, food stamps, and Medicaid.

At first glance, state policies for the poor are chaotic—a perception that does not change with a second glance. Consider some examples.[23] In Washington State, no welfare recipient can possess a car that is worth more than $1,500; in Arkansas the figure is $300; and in Georgia the rule is that the car cannot be less than four years old. In New York, a family of two was eligible for welfare with a monthly income of $309 in 1977, but in Texas the same family with an income over $115 was not eligible. In many states possessing life insurance renders people ineligible for welfare, and it is possible for a divorced woman with two children and a home or car worth more than is allowed by the state to be ineligible for welfare assistance even though she has no income whatever. Thirty-eight states have done away with placing a maximum value on a home as a condition for receiving welfare, so that a family does not have to dispossess itself to be eligible. But some states still retain such a rule. In Alabama, for example, a person with more than $2,500 equity in a house cannot qualify for aid. Hawaii, with a higher cost of living, stipulates that the tax-appraised value of a home cannot exceed $25,000 to be eligible for welfare. In Minnesota, a family may have no more than $500 cash value in life insurance to qualify for welfare, but in Delaware the cash value per person of life insurance can be as high as $1,500. Delaware and New Jersey both insist that a potential welfare recipient have too little cash to provide groceries and shelter for one month. For a child to qualify for public aid in twenty-nine states, his or her father must be unemployed. There may be a trend toward a uniform welfare policy for the poor in America but it is by no means the rule.

The degree to which states are concerned with their needy can be measured in a variety of ways. One such measure is the amount a state spends on welfare per $1,000 of personal income. On such a scale, Massachusetts normally leads the pack contributing more than $35 per $1,000 of personal income toward welfare. Another measure is welfare expenditures as a percentage of general state expenditures. On this scale, California usually ranks highest, with more than 35 percent of its total budget allocated to welfare. There are other measures, but the only conclusion one can draw from all of them is that welfare as a policy is not favored in any one geographical area; states that are relatively generous to their poor and states that are relatively parsimonious are located everywhere. The only variable that does correlate positively with a high level of welfare spending by states is the amount of money a state gets from the federal

---

[23]The following examples are drawn from Myra McPherson, "The Crazy Quilt Called Welfare," syndicated column of July 21, 1977, *Arizona Republic*, as reprinted from the *Washington Post.*.

351

Policies for
the
underclass:
the welfare
mess

government to be used for welfare, and here there is a very strong relationship. The more a state gets from the federal government for welfare, the more it is going to spend on welfare. "Poverty is not simply a condition of poor persons in a society; to some degree it is a condition of poor governments as well."[24] The decentralization of policy making for welfare in the United States means that the plight of the poor is, to a considerable degree, related to the poverty of the states. Economic resources, then, are the primary determinant of level of welfare expenditures by states. Research has indicated, for instance, that neither voting turnout nor party competition particularly influences the formulation of welfare policies.

HAS WELFARE WORKED?

Assessing welfare's effectiveness is relatively simple: Are there more or are there fewer poor in America after the inauguration of welfare policies?

Measured by historical time, it is apparent that the middle class is expanding, while the upper and lower classes are shrinking. In 1929 the poorest 20 percent of the country accounted for a mere 3.5 percent of all personal family income; by 1974 the poorest 20 percent had increased its percentage of personal family income to 5.4 percent. By contrast, the top 20 percent received almost 55 percent of all personal family income in 1929; by 1974 the amount they received had declined to 41 percent.[25] Also heartening is the fact that the percentage of families earning less than $6,400 a year declined between 1970 and 1975 by almost 12 percent.

Such data, of course, reflect some very broad economic trends that may or may not be particularly influenced by welfare policies, and when we evaluate specific welfare policies we find they have not "cured" poverty, although they may have alleviated it. Despite the fact that there were 24 million poor people in the mid-1970s, *most of the nation's poor do not receive public assistance!* Yet, ironically, more than 16.5 million people are on the welfare rolls. Obviously, not all these welfare recipients could be "officially poor." A major reason why most of the nation's poor do not receive public assistance is because they work for a living. They are ineligible for welfare assistance simply because they hold jobs, despite the fact that these jobs pay very little. The average welfare payment to families on AFDC is less than 60 percent of the poverty level, and the average food stamp benefits account for only another 9 percent, bringing the national average of welfare assistance to less than 70 percent of the poverty level. In thirty states, however, AFDC families receive even less than the national average monthly payment, and to bring all states up to a minimum of two-thirds of the subsistence level (or the national average) would cost about $1.4 billion

---

[24]Albritton, "Welfare Policy," p. 368.

[25]Thomas R. Dye, *Politics in States and Communities,* 3rd ed. (Englewood Cliffs, N.J.: Prentice-Hall, 1977), p. 444.

more.[26] Overall, then, welfare policy in America has not alleviated poverty to the degree it might have.

MISMANAGEMENT AND WELFARE: THE BIG SCANDAL

A final aspect of the "welfare mess" is the management—or lack of it—of the system generally. There is little question that welfare has been mismanaged at both the state and local levels, and the welfare policies most mismanaged are those conducted largely by state and local governments, notably Aid to Families with Dependent Children, the Food Stamp Program, and Medicaid, although these programs are hardly unique in their mismanagement.

With 381,000 bureaucrats—one for every sixty-one welfare recipients—and a $40 billion public assistance budget, the prospects for mismanagement (and outright fraud) are manifest.[27] Most of these welfare employees work for state and local governments: more than half work for local governments, more than 42 percent for state governments, and less than 8 percent for the federal government. Paperwork seems to reign in administering these programs. New York State processes some three billion sheets of paper in its welfare bureaucracy each year, and some states require as many as sixty forms be completed for a single application.

The dimensions of welfare's mismanagement become clearer when we realize that, according to its own calculations, in 1977 alone the Department of Health, Education and Welfare "lost" from $6.3 billion to $7.4 billion to bad management or fraud. The loss amounted to about 5 percent of HEW's total budget of $147 billion, which is equivalent to three times the budget of the U.S. Department of Justice! Moreover, HEW's figures did not include the Food Stamp Program; it included only Medicare, Medicaid, Social Security, and AFDC.

Certainly one way of reducing the billions wasted is to assure that those who receive welfare checks are qualified to do so—and those deserving people who are not receiving welfare be placed on the rolls. Those in the first category are the more notorious and are represented by such "welfare queens" as Chicago's Linda Taylor who, by using aliases, collected about $150,000 a year in benefits; or by the venture of eight wealthy women in Alameda County, California, who posed as welfare mothers and were given assistance. Verifying the applicant's identity and economic condition is done inordinately rarely, although as we shall see, welfare management is slowly improving. First, however, let us review the administrative problems associated with each kind of welfare program.

---

[26]Committee for Economic Development, *Welfare Reform*, p. 12.
[27]The data contained in this and the following paragraphs are drawn from Don Bacon, "Mess in Welfare–The Inside Story," *U.S. News & World Report* (February 20, 1978), p. 23, and "The $7 Billion that Vanished at HEW," *U.S. News & World Report* (April 24, 1978), p. 25.

352

SCANDALS IN THE STATES: THE CASE OF AFDC

In the Aid to Families with Dependent Children Program, overpayments and underpayments abound. In 1974 the Department of Health, Education and Welfare decided to "get tough" with states in their administration of the AFDC program, and states were told they had to reduce their error rates. By 1976 HEW reported to Congress, that, nationally, payments to ineligible people had been reduced from 10 to 6 percent, overpayments from 23 percent to 15 percent, and underpayments from 8 to less than 6 percent. Only five states had met HEW goals, although erroneous payments, accounting for 16.5 percent of the total AFDC payments in 1973, had been reduced to less than 9 percent by 1977.[28] Nevertheless, in that year, HEW still lost more than half a billion dollars of its AFDC expenditures (11 percent of its budget) to mismanagement and fraud.

An innovative program designed to reduce what the government pays out in welfare were amendments to the Social Security Act concerning child support and establishment of paternity. Enacted in 1975, the Child Support Enforcement Program is designed to assist states in locating and obtaining support payments from parents who had moved; it applied to 1.3 million absent parents. HEW estimated the cost of these payments to the AFDC program to be in excess of $1 billion. The new program relies on state welfare agencies cooperating with each other to locate parents through computer searches. How effective it will be in reducing AFDC payments is speculative, but the early auguries for the program seem to be good, with 325,000 people removed from the welfare rolls within its first year of operations.[29]

Similarly, in 1977, Congress quietly enacted a controversial program to compare computer tapes on 110 million workers who pay taxes to Social Security with the names listed on state welfare rolls. The object: Match who is paying Social Security taxes with who is collecting welfare, particularly AFDC payments. Almost immediately, a computer run of welfare rolls in twenty-four states and Washington, D. C. found more than 13,500 people who were receiving welfare benefits in two or more jurisdictions, costing taxpayers at least $20 million! Earlier versions of HEW's "Project Match" found more than 26,000 *federal* workers who were collecting welfare checks.

FOOD STAMPS: WHO'S EATING AT THE PUBLIC TROUGH?

Another major area scandal is the Food Stamp Program. As noted earlier, food stamps, perhaps more than any other program, account for the popular hostility against welfare "bums," although less than half of all AFDC recipients receive food stamps. Conversely, not much more than half of the

---

[28]United Press International, May 4, 1977, syndicated nationally.

[29]R. Douglas Roederer, "State Public Assistance and Related Programs." *Book of the States, 1976–77.* (Lexington, Ky.: Council of State Governments, 1976), p. 382.

353

nineteen million people using food stamps are on any other kind of public assistance. Still, there appears to be some fraud in the program; in 1976, nearly 20 percent of Food Stamp payments went to ineligible recipients, and a 1977 investigation conducted by the U.S. General Accounting Office concluded that $590 million was overpaid in food stamps during the year. Nevertheless, more than 72 percent of the recipients in 1974 earned less than $6,000, which is approximately the official poverty line. Moreover, it is legally possible, under current policy, to qualify for food stamps with a high income if one has many children, say six or eight, and unusually heavy expenses. In any event, it is clear the Food Stamp Program could benefit from better management, and perhaps $1 billion a year or more could be saved by tightening it up.[30]

THE MAW OF MEDICAID

Perhaps the most scandalous welfare program of all in terms not only of mismanagement but outright fraud is that of Medicaid and, to a lesser degree, Medicare. We consider the more fraudulent aspects of Medicaid and Medicare in Chapter 21, but we should note here that health care programs for the indigent cost more than programs giving cash payments directly to the needy. In 1975, AFDC payments, SSI payments, and general assistance, excluding food stamps, cost taxpayers $16 billion in state money. Medicare and Medicaid cost $22 billion in federal money alone, and another $5.6 billion in state money. One reason for this, according to HEW, is that there is little, if any, incentive to keep down hospital costs. Instead, the higher the billings and the more services provided, the higher the money garnered by the physician. Thus, the health care system itself contributed spiraling costs, quite aside from the problem of outright fraud. The quality-control study launched by the Social and Rehabilitation Service of HEW found a more than 41 percent error rate, amounting to some $10 billion a year in the Medicaid program, although within eighteen months this was reduced to a 32 percent error rate.

Despite HEW's threat in 1977 to cut off Medicaid funds in twenty-two states because of their administrative incompetence, the General Accounting Office charged the following year that there was still "virtually no monitoring" of some Medicaid contracts by either federal or state officials.[31] Perhaps as a result of this managerial lassitude, HEW lost about $2.5 billion of Medicaid dollars in 1977 to maladministration and fraud, or roughly a quarter of the entire Medicaid budget. Overall, in fact, health care programs suffered from the worst mismanagement of any of the welfare policies. Between $4.5 and $5 billion were lost in 1977 because of administrative ineptness in the country's health care programs and $2 billion of this was

---

[30]Committee for Economic Development, *Welfare Reform*, p. 14.
[31]Quoted in United Press International, January 30, 1978, syndicated nationally.

misspent in the nation's hospitals; outright fraud accounted for more than $1 billion of the loss.[32]

REFORMING WELFARE

THE CARTER PACKAGE

In light of these problems of mismanagement, fraud, welfare "cheaters," and the like, it is not surprising that welfare as a public policy has been a prime candidate for significant reform. In 1977 the Carter Administration undertook a study of welfare reform, largely at the urging of the National Governors Association. States generally have urged the national government to take over all forms of welfare, although some estimate such a takeover would cost an additional $2.5 to $15 billion. Nevertheless, President Carter announced his intention to enact reforms that would involve "no higher annual cost than the present system."[33]

Carter's package for welfare reform proposed abolishing the three basic welfare programs—Aid to Families with Dependent Children, Supplemental Security Income, and food stamps—and eliminating the Public Services Job Program, which is part of the Comprehensive Employment and Training Act. These welfare programs would be replaced with a single system. Under the system, the old, the disabled, children under eighteen, and the parents of small children would not be expected to work and would receive a single standard monthly cash payment. Adults without small children would be provided public jobs at the minimum wage. Their cash benefits would be cut sharply if they rejected work, but if they did work, their earned income would be supplemented by welfare payments. Perhaps the single most innovative aspect of the Carter proposal is that it would make more poor people, and especially the working poor, eligible for benefits.

A study undertaken by the *New York Times,* using HEW data, calculated the program as originally proposed by Carter could have some substantial effects on which states got what in welfare funds. According to the *Times's* calculations, rural states in the South and West would fare far better than the industrialized states in the East and Midwest. This was true for two reasons: first, the Public Services Jobs Program, which would be eliminated under the Carter proposal, was designed to benefit communities with exceptionally high unemployment. Second, the wage level is higher in the industrialized states than in the rural states; therefore, the minimum wage job offered under the new system would be less attractive to workers in industrial states. The result would be that some states might have to spend

---

[32]Bacon, "The $7 Billion that Vanished at HEW," p. 25.
[33]President Jimmy Carter, as quoted in George F. Will, "Welfare Reform to Be Incremental." Syndicated column, May 21, 1977.

more than they currently spend to supplement federal welfare payments merely to maintain welfare benefits at the current levels.[34]

THE STATE AND LOCAL EFFORTS

If the more grandiose welfare reforms proposed at the national level are not readily attainable, more limited improvements being undertaken by state and local governments nonetheless have had dramatic effects. When Philadelphia changed over to a photo-identification system for cashing welfare checks, for instance, the number of checks reported stolen per month fell from 20,000 to 2,000. Going beyond the federal Project Match, some states have gained access to the payrolls of private employers (Michigan, for example, checks its welfare rolls against Ford's and General Motors' payrolls) to locate employed people on welfare. Many states and localities have found that investing in training welfare workers better pays off by reducing overall expenses.[35]

REORGANIZING FOR REFORM: THE FLORIDA CASE

State governments have made efforts to improve the administration and effectiveness not only of their own general assistance welfare programs but also of federal welfare programs. Since 1965 more than half the states have reorganized those programs known as *human services*, a term that generally includes social services, health, mental health and retardation, corrections, youth services, vocational rehabilitation, and employment. They have consolidated these functions into single departments, and no doubt this effort has gone far in making state welfare programs more effective.[36]

The reorganizations and centralization of such state programs under a single state superagency are neither as easy to accomplish or as "unpolitical" as they first may appear. Professional associations, such as physicians' organizations, for example, may object to a loss of professional identity that can accompany the absorption of "their own" health department into a larger human resources agency. This, in fact, happened in 1969 when Florida adopted a new constitution that consolidated about two hundred boards and commissions into twenty-one departments, including a new human resources department. The new department centralized most of Florida's social service programs that rely on the federal government for funding and brought together thirty thousand state officials to service more

---

[34]"South and West Reportedly Would Gain Most Under Carter Welfare Plan," *New York Times* as reprinted in the *Arizona Republic,* June 24, 1977.

[35]Bacon, "Mess in Welfare—The Inside Story," pp. 23–24.

[36]Roederer, "State Public Assistance," p. 381.

357

Policies for
the
underclass:
the welfare
mess

National Academy of Public Administration praised it as a "pioneering venture" that had placed the state "in a position of national leadership."

Pioneering or not, the special interests who were affected did not like being melded into a superagency. In 1973 Congress, largely as the result of than a million clients.[37] So innovative was Florida's experiment that the pressure from the National Rehabilitation Association, required that vocational rehabilitation services be conducted solely by a single vocational rehabilitation agency, and in 1978 the Florida Medical Association pressured the state's constitutional revision commission to remove health services from the new department. Florida challenged the new federal law in court, and the head of the state's human resources department charged that the Florida Medical Association represented a "small group of rich and powerful people trying to buy government to suit their tastes and pocketbooks." Florida's experience makes the point that reorganizing the administration of welfare programs for economy and efficiency can be intensely political and may or may not be achievable.

All the same, these efforts to improve the cost effectiveness of welfare administration by state and local governments seem to be paying off. The total national rate of all welfare errors, overpayments, underpayments, and payments to ineligible people had been reduced from more than 41 percent in 1974 to less than 27 percent in 1976; roughly $950 million had been saved. While a 27 percent error rate is less than admirable on most efficiency scales, it is a clear improvement, expecially since the effort by public administrators to improve welfare management has only recently begun in earnest.

In short, the "welfare mess" is precisely that and, though a basic reform of its structure is unlikely to render welfare to a spic-and-span condition, it could make it less messy.

Welfare is designed to alleviate poverty and, as such, it obviously applies to the poor. Other major public policies that affect the poor more directly than any other social class are various policies against crime. This is not to argue that these policies were designed specifically for the poor or that only the poor are criminals. But statistics clearly indicate it is the poor who are found most frequently in prisons for robbery and acts of violence—in other words, "street crime." We consider this area next.

---

[37]The information concerning the Florida reorganization attempt is drawn from Neal R. Peirce, "In Florida, Efficiency Under Attack." Syndicated column, February 9, 1978.

CHAPTER

17

POLICIES
FOR THE
UNDERCLASS:
CRIME
IN THE STREETS

CRIME AND POVERTY

Like public welfare, policies concerning street crime do not apply only to the poor, but there is, in fact, a high degree of correlation between people who are in prison for committing street crimes and people who come from poverty-stricken backgrounds. No less a personage than President Carter recognized this grim fact of life when he stated to a western audience, "I have inspected many prisons, and I know that nearly all inmates are drawn from the ranks of the powerless and poor. A child of privilege frequently receives the benefit of the doubt; a child of poverty seldom does."[1]

The poor have fewer resources and less ability to defend themselves in court, therefore, they are more subject to arrest. Historically societies have always hassled those less able to defend themselves, and American society is no exception. For example, the President's Commission on Law Enforcement and Administration of Justice observed some years ago that a survey of several hundred skid-row residents in Philadelphia concluded that 71 percent had been arrested sometime during their lifetime; one does not find these kinds of proportions in the more affluent areas of cities, and one reason why this is so is that, according to the same survey, skid-row residents showed a low verbal facility, thus making them "extremely vulnerable to dubious police and magistrate practices."[2]

Data reinforcing the common view that policies for criminal justice generally affect the poor more than other classes were found in an analysis of distribution patterns of crime in big cities. A study of the nation's thirty-two largest cities concluded that patterns of metropolitan suburbanization are linked to rapidly increasing rates of reported crime in the central cities. In other words, the central cities are populated by lower-class whites, blacks, and browns who cannot get out of the inner city, while the middle class has fled to the suburbs. Thus, in this thesis, the poor feed upon themselves and victimize each other; therefore, the more extensive the suburbanization around the central city, the higher the crime rates within the central city.[3]

Also in keeping with the vulnerability-of-the-poor theory, it is relatively easy for police to arrest the poor, because the impoverished have fewer means of defending themselves. To quote the President's Commission on Law Enforcement and Administration of Justice, "Dubious police practices

---

[1] President Jimmy Carter, address, May, 1978. Quoted in R. Stanton Evans, syndicated column, May 17, 1978.

[2] President's Commission on Law Enforcement and Administration of Justice. *Task Force Report: The Courts.* (Washington, D.C.: U.S. Government Printing Office, 1967), p. 139.

[3] Wesley G. Skogan, "Public Policy and the Fear of Crime in Large American Cities." *Public Law and Public Policy*, John A. Gardiner, ed. (New York: Praeger, 1976), pp. 13–14.

like the investigative arrest fall heaviest in the slums. Slum residents bring few suits for false arrest, and the police are aware of this. A New York City newspaper reported the case of two young Puerto Ricans, picked up by the police on their 119th Street stoop and held eight months in jail for murder before a ballistics test, in another case, implicated a different suspect."[4]

Similarly, access to legal resources can make a great difference in how cases are decided in court. In March 1965, for example, 1,590 homeless men were arraigned in New York City's criminal court for disorderly conduct. Of these, 1,259 pleaded guilty, 325 were acquitted, and 6 were convicted after trial. One year later, after legal aid representation had been introduced into the court, 1,326 were arraigned, 1,280 were acquitted, 45 pleaded guilty, and one was convicted after trial.[5]

On the other hand, it can be well argued that such provisions for the poor are less than adequate. In 1977 the U.S. assistant attorney general stated that trial judges, criminal lawyers, and society have combined to prevent America's poor from obtaining "even adequate legal justice," noting that while the rich have their own attorneys, the poor must depend on public defenders, whom she called "warm bodies with law degrees." With an average case load of 173 clients per public defender in 1976, the easiest road for public defenders to follow was to undertake plea bargaining on behalf of their clients, a topic to which we shall return later. The assistant attorney general also noted that "too often the courthouse lawyers who will represent the poor are simply walking violations of the Sixth Amendment."[6]

In short, policies against street crime clearly are policies designed primarily for the poor in society, because it is the poor who are most often accused of and victimized by street crimes.

THE POOR PROTEST

The most dramatic form of violent crime is the riot. The 1960s were a decade of riots, and these riots were race riots. One reason why the riots were *race* riots is that the poor and uneducated also are more likely to be black and brown.

THE RACE RIOTS OF THE 1960s

Most of the race riots of the 1960s occurred in the big cities of the North. In the five years between 1963 and 1968 there were 283 racial disturbances of varying degrees of intensity in cities of more than 25,000 people while during the fifty years between 1913 and 1963 there were only 76 major

[4]President's Commission on Law Enforcement and Administration of Justice, *Task Force Report*, p. 140.
[5]*Ibid*, p. 144.
[6]Barbara Babcock, address before the 24th Annual National Institute on Crime and Delinquency, as quoted by United Press International, June 20, 1977, syndicated nationally.

361

Policies for
the
underclass:
crime in the
streets

racial disorders. Among the major ones were these: The Watts riot of 1965 in Los Angeles scorched an area of more than forty-five square miles, killing thirty-four people, of whom thirty-one were black, and damaging or destroying more than 600 buildings. Newark, New Jersey, erupted in 1967, requiring more than 4,000 legal officers to restore order and killing twenty-three people, of whom twenty-one were black. Detroit, the worst, blew up in the same year with five days of concentrated rioting, killing forty-three people, of whom thirty-nine were black, levelling more than 1,300 buildings, looting more than 2,700 businesses, and deploying 15,000 peace officers and soldiers to quell the riot. In 1967 alone, the most explosive year of the riots of the sixties, 139 riots or serious racial incidents in 114 cities and towns erupted in virtually every section of the country, killing 95 people, maiming more than 1,700, and resulting in more than 12,000 arrests. The National Guard and Army paratroopers were brought in to restore order in fifteen cities in 1967, and property damage in eight communities alone that year totalled more than $250 million.[7]

Virtually all the disturbances in the 1960s occurred in black neighborhoods. They were usually directed against symbols of white authority. In most cases, no single incident precipitated the riots; rather they were preceded by a series of tension-heightening occurrences culminated by a final incident (usually police-related) that led to violence. Riots occurred, however, only in those cities with large black populations, and particularly in cities with high population density that had experienced recent upsurges in the size of their black population. The "typical" rioter was a young black male, a life-long resident of the city in which he rioted, underemployed or working in a menial job, hostile to whites and middle-class blacks alike, racially proud, politically informed, alienated, and better educated than blacks in his neighborhood who did not riot.[8]

Why did they riot? A survey taken by the National Advisory Commission on Civil Disorders of twenty riot-torn cities of the 1960s indicates that at least a dozen reasons could be listed, but the three major "causes" of the riots were, first and foremost, police practices, followed by unemployment or underemployment, and inadequate housing.[9]

DID THE RIOTS WORK?

Did the riots of the sixties accomplish anything for blacks? During the 1960s, Benjamin L. Hooks, now National Director of the National Association for the Advancement of Colored People, told a white audience that,

---

[7]David L. Langford, "Black Plight Changed Little Since Turbulent '67 Summer." United Press International, *Arizona Republic*, July 10, 1977.

[8]Seymour Spilerman, "The Causes of Racial Disturbances." *American Sociological Review* 35 (August, 1970) 617–649.

[9]National Advisory Commission on Civil Disorders, *Report*. (Washington, D.C.: U.S. Government Printing Office, 1968).

"Pragmatically, riots work"[10] and, to be sure, during the decade between 1967, the peak year of black rioting, and 1977, blacks made substantial political gains. In 1967 there were only 400 blacks in the whole country who held an elected political office (although this was four times the number of only three years earlier); by 1977 there were 4,311. In 1967 there were no black mayors; by 1977 there were 130. The number of blacks in Congress increased from 3 in 1967 to 16 in 1977. Most political scientists feel that blacks were responsible more than any single group for electing President Carter in 1976.[11]

Blacks also made significant overall strides economically and educationally during the decade following the riots. The average income of black families was less than $5,000 in 1967 and more than $9,000 in 1975; the proportions of blacks eighteen to twenty-one years old who were in colleges more than doubled from a modest 10 percent in 1966 to 23 percent in 1976.[12]

But what have these gains meant to blacks on the streets, the poor blacks? Blacks still do not earn nearly as much money as whites, they are not educated as well as whites, and they are disproportionately represented on the welfare rolls. Employment levels fell off precipitously for nonwhites between 1967 and 1977 with nonwhite unemployment rising from more

---

[10]Quoted in Langford, "Black Plight Changed Little."

[11]*Ibid.*

[12]"Those Riot Torn Cities: A Look at Progress Ten Years Later." *U.S. News & World Report* (August 29, 1977), p. 51.

MACNELLY. Courtesy of Chicago Tribune—New York News Syndicate, Inc.

363

Policies for
the
underclass:
crime in the
streets

than 7 percent in 1967 to nearly 14 percent ten years later. These layoffs have hit the poor black and brown people far more forcefully than middle- and upper-class minorities.

In the riot areas the ruins of destruction persisted ten years later. Although the riots brought federal, state, and local aid to the Twelfth Street neighborhood in Detroit, to the Fourteenth and Seventh Street corridors in Washington D.C., and to Watts in Los Angeles, these and other riot centers of the sixties clearly are worse off than they were in 1967. Of the 200,000 people who left Detroit between 1967 and 1977, 12,000 were from the Twelfth Street area alone and vacant lots that once supported small businesses abound. Only ten stores that were in operation before 1967 were still doing business along Washington's Fourteenth Street, and the percent- age of poor people in the neighborhood has increased since the rioting. Blacks have fled Watts since the devastation, leaving behind the poorest families, and unemployment is estimated at more than 25 percent—consid- erably higher than it was in the mid-1960s.[13]

Moreover, blacks may be in even worse shape emotionally than they were in the 1960s. The National President of Operation PUSH, the Reverend Jessie Jackson, has stated, "As opposed to the politics of confrontation, right now we are in the politics of escapism. Blacks today are doing something that's more destructive than external riots, they are beginning to self-inflict riots upon their bodies with extreme alcoholism, heroin, cocaine, marijuana, and premature pregnancy."[14] The United Nations Fund for Drug Abuse estimates that there are more than 620,000 drug addicts in the United States, most of whom live in big city ghettoes and who commit more than half of the nation's street crimes—not surprising, since a heroin habit now costs more than $50 a day; one thousand addicts are *born* every year in New York City alone, and about two thousand people across the country die each year from heroin overdoses.[15]

While blacks have made some major political gains, and some less dramatic social and economic advances, the problem of the black poor is little changed and may have become worse since the 1960s. In sum, Hooks may have been wrong; rioting did not work, at least not for the very poorest members of society. To quote one Willie Alexander of Rochester, New York " . . .I threw a few stones, but I don't think it did no good, though. I didn't have a job then and I'm still not workin' . . ." Or, as another participant noted, "In some ways it might have been better then. At least then we had decent places to shop. What's there now? A big hole in the ground."[16]

This frustration exploded in 1977 when New York City experienced a major power failure. During the blackout, hundreds of stores were sacked

---

[13]*Ibid*., pp. 50–51.
[14]Quoted in Langford, "Black Plight Changed Little."
[15]United Press International, November 2, 1977, syndicated nationally.
[16]Quoted in Langford, "Black Plight Changed Little."

by residents of their own neighborhoods, an action in stark contrast to the city's power failure of 1965; in 1977 roughly 3,500 people were arrested for looting during the power failure, in 1965 only around one hundred were arrested on similar charges. A conclusion one might draw from this contrast is that, as frustration in the ghetto mounts, the poor have turned on themselves.

THE FEAR OF CRIME

The urban race riots of the 1960s and the massive looting of 1977 in New York are instances of spectacular crimes. Far more pervasive and insidious is the "normal" street crime—robbery, burglary, murder, and rape. Such crimes have had a far greater impact on the American psyche than the occasional, if more violent and spectacular, riot.[17]

Moreover, the fear of crime in America is intensifying. In 1949 Gallup found that only 4 percent of big city residents saw crime as their community's worst problem; by 1965 crime had emerged as a vital issue, and by 1975 Gallup found that nearly half of Americans—a record 45 percent—were afraid to walk in their own neighborhoods at night, and in the nation's largest cities, those of half a million people or more, the figure was 56 percent. Among women in large urban areas, 77 percent were afraid of going out at night, and 19 percent were afraid of household intruders.

The overall fear of crime as measured by such polls has remained essentially constant since 1972, but there have been some radical attitude changes among segments of the population. Poor people are more afraid of crime than those with higher incomes, blacks are more frightened of violent crimes than whites, women are more afraid than men, and the old are more fearful than the young. Quite aside from the reality of crime, the point stands that all people, and particularly poor people and black people, are afraid of it.

THE REALITY OF CRIME

Fears of the citizenry over crime against their persons and their property, especially among the poor and minorities, are well founded. The United States has more crime, according to its own statistics, then any other Western industrialized nation. More people are murdered (more than 10,000 a year) in America than in any other country in the world. According to the Federal Bureau of Investigation's Uniform Crime Reports, crimes have been increas-

---

[17]The following data concerning polls on the fear of crime are drawn from: Gene A. Fowler, *Citizen Attitudes Toward Local Government, Services and Taxes.* (Lexington, Mass.: Ballinger, 1974), pp. 147–150; George Gallup, Associated Press, July 28, 1975, syndicated nationally; and "Crime Scene Top Problem for Cities." *The Washington Post*, July 27, 1975, for the Harris Survey.

365

Policies for
the
underclass:
crime in the
streets

ing almost exponentially between 1960, when Uniform Crime Reports first were maintained, and 1975. During that fifteen-year period (in which the U.S. population went up by only 16 percent), the number of murders and manslaughters doubled, forceable rapes tripled, robberies more than tripled, and assaults, burglaries, larcenies, and car thefts all more than doubled by substantial margins. The total crimes against persons (by which is meant murder, manslaughters, rapes, and assaults) soared from 160 per 100,000 population in 1960 to 459 per 100,000 in 1975. The total crimes against property (by which is meant burglary, larceny, robbery, and auto theft) shot up from 1,716 per 100,000 people in 1960 to 4,363 per 100,000 in 1975.[18]

These are only the "official" statistics; the "unofficial" statistics reveal a far bleaker picture of crime in America. In recent years, criminal victims have been surveyed in several cities and states, and they indicate that the FBI Uniform Crime Reports tell only half, or even only a third, of the crime actually committed in the seven standard categories just listed. According to one such poll one household in every four was hit by some crime at least once during the twelve months between 1974 and 1975. In the big cities, those with more than 500,000 people, the ratio is even more staggering, with one household in three being struck by some criminal act.[19]

There are some important local deviations from the national picture. For example, the highest crime rates are found in states and cities that are both rich and urbanized. Thus, California and New York usually rank among the states with the highest reported crime rates, while North Dakota and Mississippi usually have the lowest rates. Recently, crime has been expanding more rapidly in suburbs and rural areas than in cities, and especially in the suburbs. Even so, the greatest volume of crime is found in that heartland of middle America, the average-sized towns and cities.

Particular groups show an alarming propensity both for committing crimes and being the victims of crimes. The President's Commission on Crime found that those most prone to commit crimes are young people, particularly the fifteen- to seventeen-year-old age group. Although this group constitutes less than 6 percent of the population it has the highest arrest rate and accounts for almost 13 percent of all arrests. Projections by the commission forecast that approximatly 40 percent of all male children in our nation eventually will be arrested for a nontraffic offense sometime during their lives.[20] The President's Commission on Law Enforcement and Administration of Justice sketched the "typical" perpetrator of urban robberies, rapes, and murders in America as under twenty-five, poorly educated, extremely deprived economically, likely unemployed, unmarried, reared

---

[18]Federal Bureau of Investigation, *Uniform Crime Reports 1960–1975*, (Washington, D.C.: U.S. Government Printing Office, 1976).

[19]Gallup Poll, quoted in Associated Press, July 3, 1975, syndicated nationally.

[20]President's Commission on Crime, *Report of the President's Commission on Crime.* (Washington, D.C.: U.S. Government Printing Office, 1967).

in a broken home, and probably having a prior criminal record.[21] Between 1960 and 1975, arrests of youths for crimes increased 246 percent, twice the rate for adults. Overall, young people between ten and seventeen years old, who accounted for only 16 percent of the population, made up nearly 50 percent of *all* arrests for thefts and criminal violence between 1960 and 1975.[22] Given the facts that roughly half of American blacks are under twenty-five, about 14 percent of blacks of all ages are unemployed or underemployed, and nearly 40 percent of black teen-agers are in similar straits, it follows that a disproportionate share of street crimes are committed by blacks against blacks.

WHAT IS BEING DONE?

Maintaining law and order is, by definition, essential to the very concept of government. What has government done about both the rise in the fear of crime and the rise of real crime? The evidence indicates, given the increases in crime, government has not done much. Part of the reason is that the police still rely on very traditional methods of crime control.

THE SHERIFF, OR "YOU' IN A HEAP OF TROUBLE, BOY"

Certainly the most traditional of these defenses that society has erected against crime is the office of county sheriff. Analyst after analyst, for more than fifty years, has argued for the abolition of the office of county sheriff as an anachronism in modern society. Alfred Millspaugh wrote more then forty years ago that, "What the sheriff's office has caused society in terms of criminality, insecurity, and highway accidents cannot be computed."[23]

The county sheriff typically is untrained and frequently has no previous law enforcement experience; in every state except Rhode Island he is elected to office. In many states the sheriff is permitted to collect a fee for every warrant, arrest, or order that he dispenses. And it is the county sheriff, perhaps more than any other officer, who conjures up in the American mind an image of potbellied, sauntering, sunglassed officialdom, who drawls, "You' in a heap of trouble, boy."

THE LOCAL CONSTABULARY: WHO ARE THE COPS?

The towns and cities of America, with their more sophisticated police departments, have been relatively responsive to the dynamic of social change and its relationship to the rise in crime. There are 17,464 local police

---

[21]President's Commission on Law Enforcement and the Administration of Justice, *The Challenge of Crime in a Free Society*. (New York: Avon, 1969).

[22] Associated Press, May 23, 1976, syndicated nationally.

[23]Alfred Millspaugh, *Local Democracy and Crime Control*. (Washington, D.C.: Brookings Institution, 1936), p. 35.

367

Policies for
the
underclass:
crime in the
streets

agencies in America, and most of these are very small—in fact, more than half have fewer than five full-time employees. About one-half of the country's more than 38,000 local jurisdictions have law enforcement agencies, and almost 70 percent of these departments have fewer than ten sworn officers.[24] The National Advisory Council on Criminal Justice Standards and Goals recommended in 1975 that police departments with less than ten employees be consolidated as a major means of upgrading the war against criminals.[25]

What kinds of people inhabit these almost 17,500 police departments across the country? The typical police officer is from a working class background; very few hail from the middle class. Ninety percent of the nation's police departments require no more education than a high school diploma or the equivalent; only a tenth of 1 percent require a bachelor's degree, and 2 percent of the localities do not have formal education requirements. Nevertheless, the National Advisory Commission on Criminal Justice Standards and Goals recommended that all police departments require four years of college by 1982, and roughly 23 percent of American cities do provide incentive programs for their officers to further their educations.[26]

Of course, cities and towns get what they pay for, and in the early 1970s the U.S. Bureau of Labor Statistics concluded that the cities did not pay much for their policemen. The average patrolman's pay in major cities was 33 percent less than what was needed to support a family of four in urban areas, and it appears that the situation may since have worsened.[27] Fifty years ago, policemen earned higher salaries than nearly all other trades and there were more qualified applicants than positions. Some experts estimate that from a third to a half of all metropolitan policemen moonlight; 97 percent of American cities permit their police to take on outside employment.[28] It would appear that cities recognize the fact that they themselves underpay their police officers, and that the police officers often have to support a family.

Similarly, training programs for the police are minimal at best, quite aside from formal educational attainment. In terms of the average minimum training hours required by state governments, physicians must put in 11,000 hours, embalmers 5,000 hours, barbers 4,000 hours, beauticians, 1,200 hours, and policemen an almost paltry 200 hours.[29] Yet, these are the

---

[24]S. Emphany McCann, "Law Enforcement Agencies in Urban Counties." *County Yearbook, 1975.* (Washington, D.C.: National Association of Counties and the International City Management Association, 1975), pp. 110–113.

[25]As quoted in *ibid.* p. 112.

[26]As cited in James R. Mandish and Laurie S. Frankel, "Personnel Practices in the Municipal Police Service: 1976." In *Municipal Yearbook, 1977.* (Washington, D.C.: International City Management Association, 1977), pp. 160–161.

[27]Cited in Nicholas Henry, *Public Administration and Public Affairs.* (Englewood Cliffs, N.J.: Prentice-Hall, 1975), p. 254.

[28]Mandish and Frankel, "Personnel Practices," pp. 160–161.

[29]Cited in Henry, *Public Administration*, p. 254.

people on whom society straps a pistol and expects, at least officially, to react to dangerous and disorienting human situations as if they were combinations of Sherlock Holmes, Sigmund Freud, Perry Mason, and Sergeant Preston of the Mounties.

Perhaps it is not too surprising, then, that across the country police are increasingly adopting a siege mentality relative to their own communities. In a poll of the attitudes of experienced policemen in 286 state and local departments across the country, 83 percent of the policemen felt that most people looked upon a policeman as an "impersonal machine" rather than as a fellow human being. Only half of the officers felt that public support of the police was improving, and almost 75 percent felt they were not receiving enough support from city hall.[30] In fact, studies have revealed that some policemen hide their occupations from their neighbors because they think that many people do not like to be friendly with policemen!

RACE AND THE POLICE

If the police do indeed feel that they are under seige in their own communities, then this condition may be at least the partial result of their own attitudes. Survey after survey has shown that blacks are far more distrustful of the police than whites. A 1969 Harris poll found that almost one-fifth of the whites and four-fifths of the blacks felt that police discriminated against minority groups. A 1971 Harris survey found that nearly two-thirds of the white respondents were "deeply skeptical" about the dangers of alleged police brutality, but that more than 50 percent of the blacks felt that accusations of police brutality were more likely than not to be true. The same poll found that whites, in contrast to blacks, tended to accept the idea of a conspiracy afoot to kill policemen.[31] Another survey of citizen attitudes toward police found that black's feelings were negative primarily because blacks felt that police did not respond adequately to calls for help.[32]

Traditionally, and regrettably, black perceptions of the police have been largely accurate, although this factor may be changing with the relatively rapid influx of blacks into the nation's police forces. Interviews with policemen in the cities that experienced the major riots of 1967 indicated that policemen accurately perceived the hostility that was directed toward them by blacks.[33] Policemen felt that very few blacks saw them as friends,

---

[30]Nelson A. Watson and James W. Sterling, *Police and Their Opinions.* (Washington, D.C.: International Association of Chiefs of Police, 1969), p. 55.

[31]The surveys are cited in: Advisory Commission on Intergovernmental Relations, *State and Local Relations and the Criminal Justice System.* (Washington, D.C.: U.S. Government Printing Office, 1971). Reprinted in *Perspectives on State and Local Governments* W.P. Collins, ed. (Englewood Cliffs, N.J.: Prentice-Hall, 1974), pp. 120–121

[32]Fowler, *Citizen Attitudes Toward Local Government*, p. 170.

[33]National Advisory Commission on Civil Disorders, *Supplemental Studies.* (Washington, D.C.: U.S. Government Printing Office, 1968), p. 44.

but that the great majority of whites did. The survey found that the hostility toward blacks among white policemen was fairly pronounced, with 49 percent of the police not approving of "socializing" between blacks and whites in residential neighborhoods.[34]

ARE THE POLICE EFFECTIVE?

In the light of soaring crime rates, a burgeoning popular paranoia over crime, and hostility between the police and the community (at least insofar as the poor and minority races often are concerned), how well have the police fared in their war against crime? Consider an example: the Forty-first Precinct in the South Bronx of New York City between 1970 and 1976. In the 1960s the fifty miles of the precinct's streets were occupied by sedate Irish, Italian, and Jewish residents who were stalwartly middle class. In the early 1970s the area literally exploded in crime for reasons that are not entirely clear, and ninety thousand people—half of the area's population—left, leaving behind eighty thousand who could not. One-third of the apartments and business premises were destroyed during the six-year period, turning the area into what one writer called "a moonscape." The Forty-first Precinct was known nationally in police circles as "Fort Apache," although now it is called the "Little House on the Prairie" because the intense crime has moved elsewhere.[35]

For understandable reasons, the police of "Fort Apache" were ill equipped to deal with such sustained and prolonged violence against people and property. But when the police are provided with adequate resources, what is the result?

Two studies of consequence have concluded that greater levels of police activity do not result in less crime. E. Terrance Jones studied crime rates and related them to police manpower levels and expenditures in 155 cities from 1958 through 1970 and was unable to find any evidence to support the thesis that more and better equipped police result in less crime.[36] Similarly, a behavioral study that is in many ways more intriguing was the famous Kansas City Patrol experiment, which was conducted with a particularly rigorous methodology between 1972 and 1973. In this study, the Kansas City Police Department, with assistance from the Police Foundation, divided certain of its beats into three categories. In one area, no patrols were sent out; police responded only to specific calls for help. In the second area, patrols were strengthened substantially, often to the point of being doubled or tripled. In the third area, the control group, the patrols were maintained at previous levels. The results indicated that there were no

---

[34]*Ibid*.

[35]Peter Arnett, "Peace in Crime-Devastated South Bronx Would Look Like Chaos Anywhere Else." Associated Press, July 3, 1977, syndicated nationally.

[36]E. Terrence Jones, "Evaluating Everyday Policies: Police Activity and Crime Incidents." *Urban Affairs Quarterly* 8 (March, 1973) 267–279.

statistically significant differences in crime rates among the three types of beats. There also were no differences in citizen attitudes, the number of reports of crimes, citizen behavior, or even in the rate of traffic accidents.[37]

In short, it may be that no matter what the police do, and no matter what society does to support its police, crime may continue unabated.

ALTERNATIVES TO THE COPS

This dismal, if tentative, conclusion leads us to ask the question: What can society do to prevent crime other then relying on the police?

A MASS MOVEMENT: CONTROLLING GUNS

Certainly the single most massive popular movement extant in America today to prevent crime is the gun control movement. A Harris poll conducted in late 1975 indicated that 73 percent of Americans favored the registration of all gun purchases.[38] (A similar survey conducted only eight years earlier, showed that 66 percent of Americans favored such a policy.) Harris found that gun registration was favored by all kinds of citizens, including those who owned firearms, city and rural dwellers, and people in all regions of the country. Forty-nine percent of all Americans, according to Harris, believed that easy access to guns was a major contributor to criminal violence. And the people should know. An astounding 47 percent of the nation's households own at least one gun, and the average gun ownership per American household is 1.3. In other words, statistically speaking, all American households own more than one gun, and the fear-of-crime surveys indicate that perhaps a third of Americans have bought a gun specifically to protect themselves against criminals. When we realize that 86 percent of murders are committed with a firearm, the potential for violence represented by the gun is significant.

Nevertheless, whether or not gun registration actually would reduce crimes is a moot point. Douglas R. Murray compared gun control policies in all fifty states with their crime statistics, and found no relationship. There was little difference between states with stiff gun controls and those with few or no controls in the levels of homicide, assault, suicide, or robbery.[39] Almost half of the people in America have relatively easy access to a gun, and therefore registering those firearms may not make much of a difference in terms of reducing crime rates.

CITIZENS: ADVISING (AND CONTROLLING?) THE POLICE

Another way in which citizens are trying to become more involved with crime and the police is the effort to establish "police–community relations

---

[37]George Kelling *et al.*, *The Kansas City Preventive Patrol Experiment: Summary Report.* (Washington, D.C.: The Police Foundation, 1974), pp. v–vi.
[38]Associated Press, October 25, 1975, syndicated nationally.
[39]Douglas R. Murray, as cited in Kevin Phillips, syndicated column, July 10, 1976.

371

Policies for
the
underclass:
crime in the
streets

organizations" and "community review boards." As the Advisory Commission on Intergovernmental Relations concluded, "Not only is crime prevention rendered ineffective by the absence of cooperative citizen action, but bad feeling toward the police actually stimulates crime for a number of reasons," going on to note "that suspicious incidents or persons are not reported to the police, witnesses refuse to testify, actions against the police occur, and the police become reluctant to enforce the law in hostile neighborhoods."[40]

Police–community relations programs can significantly reduce tensions between people (especially minorities) and the police. Moreover, both the people and the police like the idea. One poll found that 69 percent of the police felt that community relations programs were important as a means of opening up lines of communication, building respect, and gaining cooperation from citizens; 68 percent of the white civilians and 82 percent of black civilians favored this idea.[41]

The use of police–community relation programs is on the rise. In 1967 20 percent of the cities responding in a national poll had a police–community relations program; three years later 44 percent had such a program.[42] Larger cities favored such programs more than the smaller ones.

Civilian review boards, which are empowered to review the behavior of police and to check brutality, are quite another matter. The public generally favors establishing civilian review boards of police action. One poll found that 69 percent of the white respondents and 74 percent of the black respondents felt that "the public has a right to pass judgment on the way the police are doing their jobs." By contrast, 62 percent of the policemen polled opposed establishing such boards.[43] Nevertheless, Chicago, Washington, Philadelphia, Minneapolis, Rochester, and New York City, among others, had established such boards by the early 1970s, although many of them were later abolished or ignored. Civilian review boards are perhaps the thorniest point of contention between police departments and their communities today.

WASHINGTON: THE NEGLIGIBLE IMPACT OF BILLIONS

A third movement of significance to help the police has been provided by the federal government. Traditionally, Washington has maintained a "hands-off" policy toward state and local law enforcement; under the Constitution, crime is not a national problem but a state and local one. This is still relatively true, with the federal government employing fewer than 50,000

[40]Advisory Commission on Intergovernmental Relations, *State and Local Relations*, p. 119.
[41]*Ibid.*, p. 122.
[42]International City Management Association, "Recent Trends in Police-Community Relations." *Urban Data Service* 2 (March, 1970) 10–11.
[43]Advisory Commission on Intergovernmental Relations, *State and Local Relations*, p. 122.

people in all of its law enforcement agencies, compared with more than 500,000 state and local law enforcement officials. But, nevertheless, Washington pays a greater proportion of the costs for local law enforcement than it does for local primary and secondary education costs and, by 1980, the Law Enforcement Assistance Administration had disbursed nearly $6 billion to communities to fight crime.

The federal government got into the crime control business in 1965, when Congress passed the Law Enforcement Assistance Act. The act established the Office of Law Enforcement Assistance, an ill-begotten agency designed to collect, evaluate, and disseminate information about crime and to make direct grants to states and communities for training in the criminal justice professions. The office was not successful; Congress did not fund it at the levels that were needed, and it was seen as a potential competitor with the Federal Bureau of Investigation at a time when the late J. Edgar Hoover was still "king" of that agency.

In 1968 the Omnibus Crime Control and Safe Streets Act was enacted, setting up the Law Enforcement Assistance Adminstration, which replaced the Office of Law Enforcement Assistance. LEAA was designed to distribute billions of dollars in block grants to state and local governments to help these governments fight their respective wars against crime. By the 1970s, the agency was funded at about $800 million every year. Even so, LEAA was coming under increasing fire, with an article in *Time* magazine stating, "The handling of the programs has been extraordinarily inept. The history of the LEAA has been one of waste and mismanagement".[44] Eighty-five percent of the billions distributed under LEAA was given directly to the states, yet the states also were inept in using the money to effectively combat crime. Studies by the Brookings Institution and the General Accounting Office concluded that even by 1975 there was not a single model LEAA state operation.[45] In a notorious program designed to reduce crime by 20 percent in eight "high impact" cities (Atlanta, Baltimore, Cleveland, Dallas, Denver, Newark, Portland, and St. Louis), LEAA spent $160 million. In seven out of the eight cities crime rose, even against the national trend, and in Atlanta crime rates actually went up 25 percent. By 1976 Senator Edward Kennedy had introduced new legislation designed to overhaul the agency in a major fashion, dubbing LEAA "one of the most poorly organized and mismanaged agencies of the federal government."[46] In short, the billions funnelled into state and local law enforcement agencies may have amounted to the equivalent of pouring money down the proverbial drain.

We have seen what happens to the criminal justice system in the streets. But what happens in the courts? The courts represent two social goals that

---

[44]Quoted in Thomas B. Cronin, "The War on Crime and Unsafe Streets, 1960–1976: Policymaking for a Just and Safe Society." In *America in the '70s: Problems, Policies, and Politics*, Allen P. Sindler, ed. (Boston: Little, Brown, 1977), p. 240.

[45]*Ibid.*, p. 247.

[46]As quoted in *ibid.*, p. 252.

must be kept in tension with each other: protecting the rights of the accused and protecting the rights of society. This tension is normally called "justice."

THE COURTS: PROTECTING THE ACCUSED

Certainly an overriding problem in protecting the rights of the accused is that of overloaded courts. The nation's courts have more criminals than they can adequately process. By way of example, the New York City blackout of 1977, which resulted in the arrest of about 3,500 people on looting charges, also caused a massive overload in the city's court systems. Many of the accused were freed simply because the city's courts and jails did not have facilities for fairly trying the accused, and the police, judges, district attorney, and public defenders would not cooperate with one another to expedite the process.

THE OVERLOADED COURTS

Although the New York example is a dramatic one, it is not unique. In some sections of the country the overload problem is almost as severe on an everyday basis as it was in New York after the 1977 blackout. In the Cook County Circuit Court (Chicago), for example, in 1970 the average waiting time in a personal injury trial from the first step that involved the court to the trial's termination was almost sixty months (nearly five years), and in the New York Supreme Court of Bronx County, the average waiting time was almost fifty-nine months.[47]

Because many of the people held for trial are poor, they cannot make bail and must stay in jail. A survey of prisoners found that court delays resulted in prisoners' being held without trial for an average of ninety-one days; some had been waiting six months or a year in jail. One prisoner in the survey, who had been charged with murder, had been waiting for his trial for three years.[48]

When these kinds of delays occur, and they all too frequently do, the constitutional rights of the accused to a speedy trial are violated. And the accused are seldom granted a quick trial.

FOUR FAMOUS CASES

Other items relating to the protection of the accused are the rights guaranteed under the Constitution. With a series of rulings by the U.S. Supreme Court in the early 1960s, the poor (and for that matter, all citizens)

---

[47]Congressional Quarterly, *Crime and the Law.* (Washington, D.C.: Congressional Quarterly, Inc., 1971), p. 36, and Mark W. Cannon, "Administrative Change and the Supreme Court." *Judicature: The Journal of the American Judicature Society* 57 (March, 1974) 1–6.

[48]Henry Robert Glick and Kenneth N. Vines, *State Court Systems.* (Englewood Cliffs, N.J.: Prentice-Hall, 1973), p. 26.

have had their rights protected in court more than they might have otherwise. In 1961 the case of *Mapp* v. *Ohio* barred the use of illegally seized evidence under the Fourth Amendment, thus guaranteeing against unreasonable search and seizures. In 1963 the Court ruled in the case of *Gideon* v. *Wainwright* (an important decision) that the Fourteenth Amendment required that free legal counsel be appointed to all poor defendants in all criminal cases. In *Escobedo* v. *Illinois*, decided in 1964, the Court further ruled that a suspect was entitled to confer with his or her counsel as soon the police investigation changed its focus from "investigatory to accusatory." A final important decision, decided in 1966, was the famous case of *Miranda* v. *Arizona*, which required police to inform a suspect of all constitutional rights before questioning. These controversial decisions probably have gone further than any other legal development in twentieth-century America to protect the rights of defendants in the courts, in the precinct houses, and in the streets.

HOW GRAND IS THE GRAND JURY?

A third major component of the court system designed to protect the rights of the accused is the device known as the grand jury. Recently, the grand jury has been publicly called into question as a proper judicial device, notably by the former governor of Texas and former secretary of the treasury, "Big John" Connally.

The grand jury decides whether evidence presented to it by the public prosecutor is adequate to warrant placing a person on trial in a felony case. In theory the grand jury protects the accused from an overly zealous district attorney who may be more motivated by political ambition than by a sense of justice; it also serves as a protection for citizens against harassment by the public prosecutor.

How well the grand juries actually provide this protection is another question. One study found that a typical grand jury spent only five to ten minutes of deliberation per case, and that most of this time was devoted to listening to the prosecutor's recommendations on how the case should be decided. In more than 80 percent of the cases, the grand jury made a decision on the first ballot, without even discussion among jurors, and the votes were virtually always unanimous. An even more significant finding was that the grand juries followed the recommendation of the prosecutors in more than 90 percent of the cases presented to them.[49]

Why are the grand jurors the sheep to the prosecutor's shepherd (or some might say wolf)? Apparently it is because the district attorney controls the information submitted to grand juries; he or she assumes the role of teacher as opposed to prosecutor with jurors. In short, the use of the grand jury as a protection for the accused is at best questionable.

---

[49]Robert A. Carp, "The Behavior of Grand Juries: Acquiescence or Justice?" *Social Science Quarterly* 55 (March, 1975) 853–870.

THE COURTS: PROTECTING SOCIETY

America is founded on the unique idea that the individual is supreme and that his or her rights must be protected. Nevertheless, protection cannot be extended merely to the accused in a crime; it also must be extended to the victims of the crime and to those citizens who are potentially susceptible to future crimes. Thus, even in America, something called "society" must also be protected.

THE INJUSTICE OF PLEA BARGAINING

How well are the courts protecting society? Their record is not outstanding, and one reason is because the overloaded dockets of the judiciary, particularly at the state and local levels, have resulted in the widespread practice of plea bargaining. *Plea bargaining* is the negotiating that takes place between the accused's lawyer and the public prosecutor. The defense lawyer argues for a reduced charge while the prosecutor pushes for a conviction. Massive case overloads and resultant delays in local courts make it expeditious for all sides that the defendant plead guilty (usually to a lesser crime) since, in this manner, precious court time is not consumed, the defendant receives a minimal sentence, and the district attorney gets his sought-after conviction.

While expeditious, the almost total reliance on plea bargaining in state and local courts is hardly just. Considerable pressure is placed on the accused to plead guilty, and many observers feel that judges tend to hand out harsher sentences to guilty defendants who have demanded their constitutional right to a trial; the all-too-frequent, exceptionally long waiting period before a defendant's trial provides additional pressure on the accused to plead guilty so that he or she may at least be released from jail.

It is not surprising, therefore, that most defendants plead guilty. Some educated estimates calculate that at least 90 percent of all convicted defendants in state and local courts were never proven guilty because they never went to trial. Table 17–1, which shows the prevalence of guilty pleas in trial courts in selected states, seems to indicate that this estimate is accurate.

Plea bargaining undermines popular respect for the criminal justice system in two ways. If the accused really is guilty, then the victim of the crime watches the criminal "get off" with an extraordinarily light sentence; thus the victim does not receive justice. Recall, in this regard, the controversy surrounding the dramatically minimized sentence granted to former Vice President Spiro T. Agnew relative to the bribery and corruption charges against him, or the total pardon of all crimes, past and future, given out by President Gerald Ford to former President Richard Nixon after he resigned the presidency. Many Americans—the effective "victims" of both politicians—wanted far more severe punishments meted to both the vice president and the president, and felt that the Justice Department and President Ford, through some remarkable plea bargaining, had "let off" a couple of crooks. Conversely, if the accused is not guilty, but succumbs to the pressures brought to bear upon him to plead guilty—including pressure from his own

TABLE 17–1 PREVALENCE OF GUILTY PLEAS IN TRIAL COURTS OF GENERAL JURISDICTION IN SELECTED STATES

STATE (1964 UNLESS OTHERWISE NOTED)	TOTAL CONVICTIONS	% GUILTY PLEAS
California (1965)	30,840	74.0
Connecticut	1,596	93.9
Hawaii	393	91.5
Illinois	5,591	85.2
Kansas	3,025	90.2
Massachusetts (1963)	7,790	85.2
Minnesota (1965)	1,567	91.7
New York	17,249	95.5
Pennsylvania (1960)	25,632	66.8
Average		86.0

Source: President's Commission on Law Enforcement and Administration of Justice, *Task Force Report: The Courts* (Washington, D.C.: U.S. Government Printing Office, 1967), p. 9.

defense lawyer if he is appointed by the court—then the innocent citizen is saddled with a criminal record for the remainder of his or her life; thus, the accused does not receive justice.

SENTENCING WHIMSICALLY AND FIXEDLY

A second problem that the courts face in protecting society against criminals concerns the judges themselves. It is well known that some judges are extremely lenient in the sentences that they give to convicted felons; others are excessively harsh. In his 1970 State of the Federal Judiciary address, Chief Justice Warren E. Burger called to account the problem of wide variation in sentencing, noting, "Some judges let defendants off on probation for crimes that would draw five- or ten-year sentences by other judges. While flexibility in sentencing is essential in dealing justly with individuals, perceived inconsistencies damage the image of the courts in the public mind."[50]

How consistent are the courts? Consider some examples.[51] A businessman was convicted of embezzling $100,000 and given a suspended sentence, while a slum dweller was sent to prison for stealing a cheap watch. During one recent year one federal court in New York dealt bank robbers sentences that averaged 39 months; another federal court in the same state meted out prison terms averaging 130 months! In 1977 fifty federal judges in the Northeast were given a hypothetical profile of fictitious criminal defendants

---

[50]Warren E. Burger, Address on the State of the Federal Judiciary to the American Bar Association, August 10, 1970.

[51]The following examples are drawn from: "Stepped Up Drive to Make Punishment Fit Crime." *U.S. News & World Report* (September 5, 1977), p. 47.

377

Policies for
the
underclass:
crime in the
streets

by the Federal Judicial Center and were asked what sentences they would give; the sentences were alarmingly varied, with one judge giving one hypothetical defendant seven and one-half years in the "big house," and another giving the same defendant four years—on probation!

In response to the variation in sentencing a number of states have been experimenting recently with "fixed sentencing." *Fixed sentencing* means that, if a person is convicted of a particular type of crime, the law allows the judge no flexibility in determining the felon's sentence. Maine enacted the first fixed sentencing law in 1975 and Indiana followed in 1976; also in 1976 California passed its Uniform Determinant Sentencing Act, and a number of other states are considering similar legislation.

Fixed sentencing also calls into question the traditional penal concept of parole since, under the law, paroles simply are not permitted. In Maine, for example, a person convicted of robbery or rape must be sentenced for at least ten years and must actually serve slightly more than six years. Under Maine's former indeterminate sentencing law a judge could impose any sentence he wished for either crime. But the median sentence for armed robbery in Maine in recent years had been five years, and the average time actually served before parole was somewhat more than three years. For rape, the median sentence was seven years and the average time served was slightly more than four and one-half years.[52] California's new fixed sentencing law retains probation but limits it to one-and-a-half years; it also permits some reduction of sentences through proper behavior. But, unlike previous practices, these minimum times are written into the law and are not subject to the whimsey of parole boards or judges.

In some ways fixed sentencing is a return to "the good old days"—fixed sentencing was "standard operating procedure" in all the states until the turn of the century. By the 1920s reformist thinking in penology circles had brought about a complete conversion to indeterminate sentencing and to the parole board system. The reasoning was that once a prisoner was "rehabilitated," he or she should be released from prison and that this rehabilitation could be determined only by parole boards or penal officials. Society seems no longer to trust such judgments made by judges or prison officials, particularly in light of the failure of prisons to "rehabilitate" criminals and their corresponding recidivism rates (*recidivism rates* are the number of people who are sent back to prison for additional crimes they commit once they are out). Even so, there are those who are critical of the fixed sentence trend. They argue that considerably more prisons will be needed to house all the people forced into them. Others argue that in some cases (notably in California), too much latitude in sentencing is still permitted to judges even under fixed sentencing.

---

[52]Joseph Tybor, "New Trend Favors Fixed Prisons Sentences over Indeterminate Terms." Associated Press (September 26, 1976), syndicated nationally.

LOCKING UP THE FEW

A final area of protecting society involves the percentage of people found guilty who are actually incarcerated. The proportion of imprisonments to crimes committed in society is dismally small. In 1970 an actual arrest was made in only 20 percent of the reported crimes. In only 17 percent of the crimes was a person charged after the arrest was made. Only 5 percent pleaded guilty as charged. Of the offenses known, in only 2 percent of the cases was a convicted felon sent to jail. If we use as a base the findings of various victim surveys, in which "real" crimes are estimated to be two-and-a-half times the number of reported crimes, the percentages would be less than half of these figures; consequently, the number of people jailed as a percentage of real crime probably is less than 1 percent.[53]

In summary, the state and local criminal justice system may be understood as one which reconciles the inclination of society to protect itself by "coming down hard"—and occasionally unjustly—on those who have violated its laws, and the constitutional right of the citizen to full and equal protection under the law. How successful the courts have been in reconciling these two social realities is up to the reader to decide.

PRISONS: "FACTORIES OF CRIME"

Perhaps the single most vexing problem of the criminal justice system is the prisons. More than two million Americans are prisoners in some jail, penitentiary, or similar institution in any given year, and the great majority of them are released within that year. There are about 250,000 prisoners in state and federal prisons, of whom roughly 225,000 are in state prisons. These prisoners have been incarcerated for serious crimes, and approximately 90 percent of them had a record of crime (though not necessarily a past prison record) before they landed in the "big house."

PRISONS ARE LESS THAN PLEASANT

Prisons, both federal and state, are not pleasant; as a general rule they are substantially overcrowded and often seem to be run more by the kept than by the keepers. Some are so bad that a number of lawyers have begun questioning whether or not prisons in America today constitute "cruel and unusual punishment," in violation of the Eighth Amendment to the Constitution. The courts have become actively engaged in alleviating prison conditions, requiring state and city officials to spend more money and hire better personnel. Though the courts may order away to their hearts' content, however, the states and localities must provide the money. Nevertheless, the judiciary clearly has brought about change in some states and

---

[53]U.S. Bureau of the Census, Department of Commerce, *Statistical Abstract of the United States, 1970.* (Washington, D.C.: U.S. Government Printing Office, 1970), p. 146.

379

Policies for
the
underclass:
crime in the
streets

cities. In the Arkansas prison system, for example, which had been described as a "self-supporting slave camp industry" prior to court-ordered reform, the budget of the Arkansas system was raised from $1 million to $6 million by the courts, and the harshest conditions in the state penitentiary were eliminated. In New Orleans rulings by the court had the effect of permitting every inmate to have his or her own bed, indicating the serious degree of overcrowding in that jailhouse.

THE "REHABILITATION" MYTH

Despite their conditions prisons and jails in America are meant to "rehabilitate" their inmates; that is, they are supposed to turn criminals into law-abiding citizens. Regrettably there is absolutely no evidence whatever that prisons rehabilitate prisoners; in fact there is every reason to believe that they accomplish just the reverse. Approximately 80 percent of the nation's prisoners have been in prison at least once before—a recidivism rate that indicates prisons are hardly rehabilitating their inmates.

Whether or not prisons are equipped to rehabilitate is another matter; in spite of relatively low budgets, prison officials are expected to make inmates acceptable in a highly educated and skilled society. Yet, inmates as a group are extraordinarily undereducated and undertrained. Less than 5 percent of federal prisoners, for example, perform at the twelfth grade level or higher, and 85 percent lack any marketable skill.[54]

THE PROBLEM OF PAROLE

This population of the prisons is often sent back to society through a parole system of at least questionable effectiveness. Only 5 percent of the nation's prisoners will stay in prison for life, and two-thirds of those released come through parole rather than serving the duration of the sentence. The parole rate, however, varies widely among the states, ranging from 90 percent of prisoners released through parole to less than 30 percent; the industrialized states tend to favor release through parole more than the agrarian, rural states.[55] Parole seems to make no particular difference in whether or not a prisoner is likely to commit another crime. Careful studies of paroled prisoners versus nonparoled prisoners indicate "the almost total absence of linkage between correction variables and recidivism."[56]

In short, prisons have failed to rehabilitate their inmates. Former U.S. Attorney General Ramsey Clark has called American correctional institutions "factories of crime"; the former director of the Federal Bureau of Prisons stated that "anyone not a criminal will be one when he gets out of jail."[57]

---

[54]Congressional Quarterly, *Crime and the Law*, p. 11.

[55]Thomas R. Dye, *Politics in States and Communities*. (Englewood Cliffs, N.J.: Prentice-Hall, 1977), p. 215.

[56]Frank K. Gibson, *et al.*, "A Path Analytic Treatment of Corrections Output." *Social Science Quarterly* 54 (September, 1973) 291.

[57]Quoted in Congressional Quarterly, *Crime and the Law*, p. 11.

Thus far, we have examined the criminal justice system in state and local governments and have come close to concluding that it does not work; or, if it does work, it does not work very well. This is a serious matter. As Chief Justice Burger observed, "A sense of confidence in the courts is essential to maintain the fabric of ordered liberty for a free people." He listed three conditions that could destroy that confidence: "That people will come to believe that inefficiency and delay will drain even a just judgment of its value; That people who have long been exploited in the smaller transactions of daily life come to believe that courts cannot vindicate their legal rights from fraud . . .. That people come to believe the law . . . cannot fulfill its primary function to protect them and their families . . .."[58] Yet, neither the police, nor the courts, nor the prisons seem to be doing their jobs in terms of reducing crime, arresting suspects, convicting criminals, and rehabilitating prisoners.

Consequently, we must ask what does work. Or at least we should ask what is more likely to work in protecting both the rights of the individual citizen and the rights of society to be free from fear. Most people who have studied the question of what prevents crime are agreed that the most effective deterrence is the *certainty* of punishment, while severity of punishment does not seem to be much of a factor.[59]

DEATH ROW: ONE FORM OF PUNISHMENT

Of course, a major question in terms of the severity of potential punishment revolves around the death penalty in America. In the 1970s an argument was voiced that the death penalty constitutes "cruel and unusual punishment," and thus is in violation of the Eighth Amendment. Until 1972 the death penalty was the law in thirty states, and only fifteen had actually abolished capital punishment. In that year the U.S. Supreme Court ruled in *Furman* v. *Georgia* that capital punishment violated both the Eighth and Fourteenth Amendments, which prohibit cruel and unusual punishment and insure due process of law. But there was a catch in this ruling. The Court stated that the death penalty, only as currently imposed in the states which employed it, was in violation of the Constitution. For four years after the ruling there was a spate of rewriting of state legislation regarding the death penalty, and in 1976 the Supreme Court upheld state laws that were written to insure equity and due process, remarking that death itself was not cruel or unusual in the meaning of the Eighth Amendment. So the death penalty still is with us in most states and has been sanctioned by the U.S. Supreme Court.

---

[58]Burger, Address.

[59]Maynard L. Erikson and Jack P. Gibbs, "The Deterrence Question." *Social Science Quarterly* 54 (December, 1973) 534–551.

Source: Reprinted by permission of United Feature Syndicate, Inc.

Whether or not the prospect of the electric chair, gallows, gas chamber, firing squad, or hypodermic needle deters crime in the thirty-six states that use them is quite another question and, as noted, the evidence indicates that it probably does not. But the findings of academic research can be swept aside when it comes to such emotion-charged issues as the death penalty. Consider the instance of a New York State Senator, who objected before the Mohawk Valley Council of Churches (which opposed the death penalty "as a matter of faith") that Christianity would not exist if, instead of crucifixion, "Jesus got eight to fifteen years, with time off for good behavior."[60] It is by such reasoning that the death penalty becomes the cornerstone of Christiandom.

COMPENSATING VICTIMS

A related and even more basic reconsideration of criminal justice policy deals not with deterrence but with what to do once a crime happens. Since 1964, two dozen states have adopted the policy of compensating the victims of crime. Most of these states have set up crime compensation boards, composed of lawyers appointed by the governor. The boards' staffs investigate claims and, if the victim can demonstrate financial hardship (Hawaii is an exception; there no such hardship must be demonstrated), the victim becomes eligible to receive a usually modest award as compen-

---

[60]Zodiac New Service, as published in *New Times Weekly*, April 26, 1978.

sation. Apprehension of the criminal is not a condition for receipt of the award. The logic behind this approach is that the victim deserves at least as much attention as the offender, and financial compensation can cover some of the cost of medical treatment for injury that may have been sustained because of the crime and pay for bills that accumulate as a result of being out of work while recuperating.[61]

Crime compensation boards are a genuinely innovative policy that probably have helped the poor more than any other social group in society, since the poor are not only the more frequent victims of crime, but are also less likely to have any kind of insurance to protect them from the results of crime.

JUSTICE, VENGEANCE, AND THE "REHABILITATION OF PUNISHMENT"

Another major reconsideration concerning the problem of crime is extremely fundamental and deals with the role of vengeance in American society. Part of this reconsideration concerns the role of parole and indeterminate sentencing, which we already have discussed, but the crux of the reappraisal is the "rehabilitation of punishment." It is now being argued that rehabilitation as a policy against crime has been a failure and that we should face that failure and respond appropriately.

The challenge to the concept of rehabilitation has emerged from both the liberal and conservative political camps. Traditionally, the conservatives had always argued that rehabilitation "coddled criminals" and therefore was not only ineffective, but almost amounted to a reward for deviant behavior. Liberals traditionally had argued that rehabilitation was a humane way of "treating" people who were criminals largely because of past deprivations, and that crime was a "sickness" in society subject to "cure" by penal experts and behavioral scientists.

Jessica Mitford's controversial work, *Kind and Usual Punishment*, was the first liberal critique of rehabilitation. Mitford argued that the prison is a weapon of class oppression: "For the prison administrator, whether he be warden, sociologist, or psychologist, individualized treatment is primarily a device for breaking the convict's will to resist and hounding him into compliance with institution demands, and is thus a means of exerting a maximum control over the convict population. The care will be deemed effective to the degree that the poor/young/brown/black captive appears to have capitulated to his middle class/white/middle aged captor, and to have adopted the virtues of subservience to authority, industry, cleanliness, docility."[62] In support of her thesis, Mitford cites the situation in the

---

[61]See: Gilbert Geis and Herbert Sigurdson, "State Aid to Victims of Violent Crimes." *State Government* 50 (Winter, 1970) 16–20. Herbert Edelhertz and Gilbert Geis, *Public Compensation to Victims of Crime.* (New York: Praeger, 1974), and Barbra McClure, *Crime Compensation for Victims,* Issue Brief IB 74014. Congressional Research Service, Library of Congress, 1977.

[62]Jessica Mitford, *Kind and Usual Punishment: The Prison Business.* (New York: Knopf, 1973) p. 73.

Patuxent Institution of Maryland, in which all inmates were committed for indeterminate sentences subject to release only when the staff determined they had been "cured." Mitford found that 46 percent of Patuxent's inmates paroled from 1955 through 1965 had been confined *beyond the maximum sentence* imposed by state law for the crime they had committed![63]

On the conservative side of the issue is Ernest Van den Haag, who, in his book, *Punishing Criminals*, takes the position that felons are by no means "sick" people who somehow are not morally responsible for their crimes. He argues against the liberal notion that criminals are a kind of political rebel, struggling against an oppressive class structure.[64] Van den Haag contends that criminals are people who have broken the law and deserve to be punished; moreover, they should be punished almost on an eye-for-an-eye basis.

In any event the current thinking, both liberal and conservative, clearly is that rehabilitation has not worked and that only the certainty of punishment is likely to deter crime.[65]

In this and the preceding chapter we have discussed two major policies that apply to the forgotten fifth of American society, the poor. While policies for welfare and criminal justice apply to people other than the poor, they tend to focus more on the poor than other classes in American society, simply because more poor people are on welfare rolls and more poor people are in prisons. In the next three chapters we consider some major policies for the middle class: education, planning, land use, transportation, and housing.

---

[63]Mitford. *Kind and Usual Punishment.*

[64]Ernest Van den Haag, *Punishing Criminals.* (New York: Basic Books, 1976).

[65]For a more thorough discussion of the problem see Marc F. Plattner, "The Rehabilitation of Punishment." *The Public Interest* 44 (Summer, 1976) 104–114.

CHAPTER

18

POLICIES FOR THE MIDDLE CLASS: THE EDUCATION ESTABLISHMENT

Education in America is big business.[1] There are 43 million pupils enrolled in the nation's 86,174 grade schools, junior high schools, and high schools, and there are more than 11 million students enrolled in the country's 2,500 technical schools, colleges, and universities. In the mid-1970s the American taxpayers spent more than $61 billion for education at the elementary and secondary levels alone; more than $12.5 billion were appropriated in state tax funds for higher education, a sum which includes state grants to private institutions as well as allocated budgets for public ones. Education accounts for the largest single share of state and local expenditures and amounts to roughly 4 percent of the Gross National Product.

Given the colossal sums that Americans spend on educating their children and themselves, what do these institutions of learning actually do? As Stephen K. Bailey has stated, schools do more than teach the "three R's" (Reading, Writing, and Arithmetic). Now it is the "four R's," and they stand for Race, Resources, Relationships, and Rule—or, as Bailey prefers to call them the four B's: Bonds, Budgets, Buses, and Buildings. Bailey further notes that "some people prefer the letter C: Color, Coffers, Coordination, and Control; or even P: Prejudice, Pocketbooks, Partnerships, and Power."[2] These are major political issues by anyone's standard and we shall rely on Bailey's list in structuring this chapter. First let us consider the problem of budgets, bonds, and school finance.

PAYING FOR SCHOOLS: WHO DOES AND WHO SHOULD?

As with virtually all facets of public finance, paying for schools is inherently an intergovernmental process. Unlike many state and local financial situations, however, the federal government plays a relatively smaller role. About 92 percent of the $61 billion used to support secondary and elementary education is borne by state and local governments and, given the impact that the federal government has had on school boards and school districts during the last two decades, the 8 percent that the feds shell out is not particularly impressive.

---

[1] The figures in this paragraph are drawn from "Education." In *The Book of the States, 1976–77* Lexington Ky.: (Council of State Governments, 1976), pp. 318–339, and National Center for Education Statistics, as quoted in Associated Press, September 1, 1978, syndicated nationally.

[2] Stephen K. Bailey, "New Dimensions in School Board Leadership." *Journal of the New York State School Board Association* (September, 1969) p. 12.

Federal aid to local schools is conducted through some major pieces of legislation, notably the Elementary and Secondary Education Act (ESEA) of 1965, designed primarily for schools in poverty areas; the National Defense Education Act of 1958 (later amended in 1963), designed to improve curricula in a number of specific fields, but particularly in the sciences; the Federally Impacted Areas Aid Program, inaugurated in 1950, which assists areas in which federal property exempt from local taxes creates a financial crunch for the school; the National School Lunch and Milk Programs, initiated in 1946; and the Smith-Hughes Vocational Education Act of 1917, which is still providing federal grants and assistance for training in the trades.

Of these federal policies perhaps the legislation that has had the greatest political impact on local schools is the Elementary and Secondary Education Act. ESEA "has, contrary to some popular assumptions, markedly strengthened the role and influence of state education departments" by forcing school districts to turn to state agencies for approval of their proposals and for assistance in meeting their problems,[3] and local school districts have been forced to expand their involvement with other local groups; Title I of ESEA, for example, mandates that public school officials must consult with local Community Action Agencies in the development of their programs for the poor.

Although federal support for local elementary and secondary schools remains nominal, it has been growing. In 1962, the federal contribution to local school districts was slightly more than 4 percent; today it is twice that figure.

Although national assistance to schools is expanding, many educators, particularly those associated with big city schools where some of the nation's major educational problems are festering, feel it is still not adequate. In 1976 the heads of the nation's twenty-seven largest school districts called for billions of dollars more in federal aid to public schools. Nearly 5 million pupils, or 10 percent of the public school population, attend schools in big cities. Yet, as a national news magazine pointed out, "the education these children receive amounts to a national scandal."[4] Whether or not more money will actually help big city schools resolve the clear crisis they face is a moot point. A Rand Corporation study, which analyzed eleven New York ghetto schools that had received approximately $40 million in federal assistance during a four-year period, concluded that there had been "no improvement at all in the low academic levels and high truancy rates that the federal money was supposed to fight."[5]

---

[3]Michael B. Usdan, "The Future Viability of the School Board." In *Understanding School Boards,* Peter J. Cistone, ed. (Lexington, Mass.: D.C. Heath, 1971) p. 269.

[4]Merrill Sheils, *et al.,* "City Schools in Crisis." *Newsweek* (September 12, 1977) p. 62.

[5]*Ibid.,* p. 63.

Schools in small, rural districts do not have the problems of the big city schools and are less dependent on federal aid. Consider the example of the one-room schoolhouse with eleven students in the Walnut Grove Elementary District of Yavapai County, Arizona. In 1977, federal civil rights officials threatened to cut off Walnut Grove's federal aid because the district had failed to complete required paper work showing compliance with sex discrimination guidelines, an error that evidently was an oversight on the part of Walnut Grove officials. Washington officials snarled that they would turn off Walnut Grove's federal assistance but lost interest when school officials showed civil rights officers that federal aid had comprised a total of $16.57 of Walnut Grove's school budget during the preceding year.[6] Although the federal financial role in secondary and elementary education is relatively light, the impact of federal officials can be very heavy. We consider this impact later in our discussion of race and discrimination in schools.

THE STATE AND LOCAL BURDEN

Fiscally speaking, the states have a much larger say in how neighborhood schools conduct their affairs. In the 1970s, the states' share of the local education budget hovered between 40 and 45 percent and has been growing steadily over the years. In 1900 states contributed only 17 percent to the budgets of local schools. Indeed, both federal and state aid have been growing to the point that in 1973–1974, for the first time, the average local contribution to education budgets dipped below 50 percent because of steadily growing contributions from both the state and federal sectors. The sole exception to this arrangement is Hawaii, where the state government pays for all educational programs (aside from federal assistance) and the local governments bear none of the costs. Generally, however, local governments assume the largest portion of the educational budgetary burden, and normally this burden is around 50 percent.[7]

THE PRICE OF LEARNING

With an annual cost of elementary and secondary education alone exceeding $61 billion, the average taxpayer is well aware of education's price tag. The cost of schooling has risen dramatically in the last decade. Between 1965 and 1975 per-pupil costs averaged a 150 percent increase across the nation; in 1977 they exceeded $1,200.[8] Hikes in education's price tag have been felt in every state. According to HEW's National Institute of Education, schooling's costs rose from a low of 16 percent in Hawaii to a high of 95

[6]Cecelia Goodnow, "School Freed from Redtape." *Arizona Republic,* May 24, 1977.
[7]"Education," *Book of the States,* p. 314.
[8]*Ibid.*

percent in Alabama between 1971 and 1976, and average expenses went up by nearly 50 percent in forty-three states.[9] Some of the reasons behind these disconcerting increases were: the rising teacher militancy, which is at least partially responsible for the 86 percent hike in teachers' salaries between 1965 and 1975;[10] an alarming and growing vandalism in big city schools that cost the nation's elementary and high schools an estimated $600 million in 1977; soaring administrative costs (by indication, an analysis of New York City's education expenditures found that only 41 percent of New York's $2.9 billion annual education budget was spent on classroom instruction for the city's one million school children; the rest of the money went to school administrators);[11] and rising capital outlays for such items as buildings and playgrounds, the cost of which handily exceeds $5 billion a year.

THE DOUBLE IRONY OF EDUCATIONAL FINANCE

Ironically, the costs of schooling have been soaring while fewer students are being schooled. Enrollments have been declining in thirty-seven states since 1971, and in 1974, for the first time, all states recorded a dip in student enrollments. Between 1971 and 1976 the average cost of educating youth from kindergarten through high school shot up 56 percent, even though the nation's average enrollments declined by 2.3 percent during the same five years. It is projected by the National Institute of Education that enrollments will continue to fall off throughout the 1980s because of America's decreasing birth rate.[12]

The double irony is that, as a direct consequence of declining enrollments, the "formula" budgets used by states to fund education now seem to be backfiring insofar as teachers are concerned. During education's halcyon days of the 1960s when student enrollments went up nearly 23 percent, educators convinced their legislators that schools should be funded on a formula basis—that is, for every student taught, a certain amount of money would be provided. Legislators in all the states agreed with the concept, but now that enrollments are dwindling, many legislators are demanding that education's formula funding should work both ways—as enrollments shrink, so should budgets. Professional education interests, however, are suddenly not so sure.

THE CONSOLIDATION MOVEMENT

Because of dwindling enrollments and burgeoning costs and because school-ing consumes roughly half of the local tax dollar (a fact not lost on many taxpayers), educational policy makers have attempted to reduce costs where

---

[9] National Institute of Education, Department of Health, Education and Welfare, as quoted by United Press International, May 24, 1978, syndicated nationally.

[10] "Education," *Book of the States*, p. 314.

[11] Sheils, "City Schools in Crisis," pp. 63–64.

[12] National Institute of Education, *op. cit.* and Bureau of the Census, *1977 Census of Governments.* (Washington D.C.: U.S. Government Printing Office, 1978) pp. 7–9.

feasible. Certainly the major method that educators have used to cut school costs has been to drastically reduce the number of school districts across the nation. While the number of schools has been slashed, a centralization and enlarging of the neighborhood school also has occurred. In 1977, the latest year for which official figures are available, there were 15,174 independent school districts. (Actually, there were 16,548 school systems in 1977, of which 15,174 were autonomous districts. The remaining systems functioned as dependent arms of other governments, such as states or counties.) Such a number may seem like a lot, but consider that some thirty years earlier there were more than 108,000 local public school systems, and even in 1962 there were approximately 38,000.[13] Figure 18–1 illustrates the dramatic consolidation of school districts since 1952.

The rationale behind this reduction and centralization in school districts has been that of economy. Although the costs of education have certainly not declined with the number of school districts, it has been argued that the costs would be considerably higher if such consolidation had not occurred during the past generation.

Still, the theory that consolidation saves money has been questioned. A study sponsored by the National Institute of Education found that the big, new regional schools cost as much or more to run as the old, decentralized rural school ever did. In 1930 there were 149,000 single-teacher elementary schools in the country; by 1972 there were only 1,475 such schools. During that period more than 70 percent of all elementary schools were abolished and the number of four-year high schools was cut in half; at the same time student enrollments in junior high schools and high schools actually tripled. Although there were some savings from improved administrative efficiency, other cost increases may have offset these savings. Most significant were the

---

[13]John O. Behrens, "Financing Public Elementary and Secondary Education." In *Municipal Yearbook, 1974.* (Washington, D.C.: International City Management Association, 1974), p. 24.

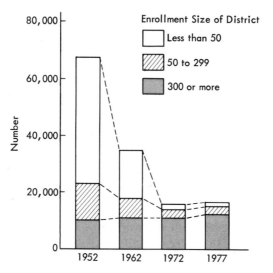

FIGURE 18–1 SCHOOL DISTRICTS, BY ENROLLMENT SIZE: SELECTED YEARS 1952 TO 1977

Source: U.S. Bureau of the Census, *1977 Census of Governments*.

higher transportation costs of busing students to centrally located regional schools and the increased demand for more specialized teaching skills, which bring with them increased salaries for the teacher. Finally, there was no evidence that consolidation had in any way improved the quality of education.[14]

THE TAXPAYERS' REBELLION

Regardless of whether or not the consolidation movement has succeeded, educational costs have risen steeply. One reaction to the rising costs has been the taxpayers' revolt that has been occurring sporadically, but with growing intensity, since the mid-1960s. Between 1960 and 1965 more than 70 percent of the school bonds proposed to local voters across the country succeeded. But during the next ten years this percentage dipped precipitously; between 1965 and 1975 only half of the school bonds offered were approved by the voters, and during the nation's Bicentennial year more than 90 percent of the school bond dollars put before the voters were defeated.[15] In Oregon and Ohio, schools were closed for part of that year because voters refused to appropriate bond issues.

In their seminal work on the subject, Philip K. Piele and John Stuart Hall found, as expected, that the person most likely to vote both in school finance elections and for greater school funding was relatively wealthy, relatively well-educated, middle-aged, the parent of school-aged children, a homeowner, and with a high interest in schools. More unsettling was the discovery that the larger the voter turnout, the smaller the percentage of favorable votes cast in school financial elections; in other words, the more democratic participation there is in school finance elections the more likely it is that school children will suffer.[16] This finding is particularly significant for education officials, who, one presumes, should be wary of launching "get-out-the-vote" drives in school finance elections.

REFORMING SCHOOL FINANCE

Even more significant than incipient taxpayers' revolts is the movement toward property tax reform, which is being felt across the country. Sparked in 1971 in the famous case of *Serrano* v. *Priest*, which was heard by the

---

[14]Jonathon P. Sher and Rachel B. Tomkins, National Institute of Education, as quoted by Associated Press, April 14, 1977, syndicated nationally.

[15]U.S. Department of Health, Education and Welfare, *Bond Sales for Public School Purposes, 1957–8 through 1973–4.* (Washington, D.C.: Department of Health, Education and Welfare, National Center for Education Statistics, U.S. Government Printing Office, 1975); and Lucia Mouat, "Voters Turning Down More School Bond Issues." *The Christian Science Monitor* (October 20, 1976), p. 5.

[16]Philip K. Piele and John Stuart Hall, *Budgets, Bonds and Ballots.* (Lexington, Mass.: D.C. Heath, 1973), pp. 152 and 169.

California Supreme Court, the school finance reform movement is now making a major impact across the nation.

The *Serrano* case was a class action brought by people who argued that the California system of financing public schools violated the equal protection clause of the Fourteenth Amendment of the Constitution. The suit stated that, under traditional educational financing, children in poorer districts were given educations that were inferior to the educations offered children in other, wealthier districts in California. The plaintiff contended that parents in poor areas of the state were victims of discrimination because they had to be taxed at a higher rate than residents in richer districts, simply to obtain equal or even inferior educations for their children. The example was brought up by the plaintiffs of two school districts within Los Angeles County. The per-pupil expenditure in the wealthy district of Beverly Hills, with a comparatively low tax rate, was $1,232 a year; the per-pupil expenditures in the poor district of Baldwin Park, despite a high tax rate, amounted to only $577 each year. Both the lower trial court and the appellate court rejected this argument, but the state supreme court overturned those decisions in a six-to-one decision. The court agreed that the California school financing system—a system typical throughout the country—discriminated on the basis of wealth and consequently was in violation of the Fourteenth Amendment. This was a major decision for all the states. Courts in Minnesota, Texas, New Jersey, Arizona, New York, Indiana, and Michigan soon reaffirmed the California decision, all finding that the school finance structures in their states were in violation of the U.S. Constitution.

In 1973, the United States Supreme Court heard the case of *Rodriguez* v. *San Antonio Independent School District* and overturned the decision of the Texas court, which had ruled that Texas's school finance structure, like those in other states, was in violation of the Fourteenth Amendment. The Supreme Court's reversal was not as serious a blow to the school finance reform movement as was first thought, since the Court indicated that school finance litigation could proceed on the basis of the state constitutions and statutes, but that school district inequities were not necessarily in violation of the national Constitution. Thus, courts in New Jersey, California, and Connecticut all found that the traditonal system of school finance was in violation of their *state* constitutions, but not all state courts have found this to be the case; courts in Idaho, Oregon, and Washington all have ruled that traditional structures of school finance are compatible with their own state constitutions. Thus the result of the *Rodriguez* decision has been to shift the focus of school finance litigation to the state level, where decisions now are being made on a state-by-state basis.

State legislatures have followed the judiciary's lead. Between 1970 and 1976, twenty-five states enacted educational finance reform laws; thirteen of these could be considered major reforms.[17] Most of the successful reforms

---

[17]Frederick M. Wirt, "Education Politics and Policies." In *Politics in the American States,* 3rd ed. Herbert Jacob and Kenneth N. Vines, eds. (Boston: Little, Brown, 1976), p. 337.

can be attributed to legislators who have shown political courage in reforming school finance; statewide referenda on finance reform measures, for example, consistently failed in the 1970s.[18] A number of legislatures (notably in California, Florida, Minnesota, Utah, Colorado, Kansas, Maine, and Michigan) have adopted measures that, in effect, guarantee each school district in their states a minimum level of per-pupil expenditures. Some states have gone further than merely underwriting a mimimum level of per-pupil expenditure; Maine, Montana, Utah, and Wisconsin, for example, have enacted measures that use "excess" revenue generated in the very wealthy districts to finance the poor school districts. These policies, known as "recapture provisions," are not politically popular, but they are being adopted by increasing numbers of states in a grassroots effort to equalize school finance.

Still, states are not pushing each other aside in their enthusiasm to pour money into their public schools. Rising educational costs and revenue constraints are a fact of budgetary life in most states, and a number of legislatures have enacted absolute limits on the amount of money that can be spent for education. Florida, Kansas, Maine, and New Mexico have set maximum school tax rates which, in effect, place limits on total school expenditures. Other states have limited educational expenditures to a fixed percentage of their revenue, but scale limits to the relative wealth of the local school district. This policy protects the state treasury, but still permits poor school districts to catch up with the higher spending areas.[19] It appears, however, that the trend in all the actions being taken by state legislatures concerning school finance is the gradual takeover by the states of all school finance in the interests of assuring an equitable distribution of revenues for financing schools.

WHO RUNS THE SCHOOLS?

If the states gradually are taking over school finance, running the schools still remains largely a local operation. Who runs the schools?

YES! SCHOOL BOARDS ARE BORED OF EDUCATION!

Throughout the country, the fate of local schools is determined by the nation's more than 15,000 school boards, and school boards have a political process that is uniquely their own. Mark Twain once described fools as God's practice before he created school boards, and perhaps the Lord's wisdom accounts for the oddities of school board politics.[20]

---

[18]Donna Shalala and Mary F. Williams, "State Tax Politics, the Voters, and School Finance Reform." *Phi Delta Kappan* 56 (September, 1974) 10–13.

[19]"Education," *Book of the States*, pp. 314–315.

[20]Mark Twain, quoted in Usdan, "Future Viability of School Board," p. 265.

School boards are an ancient and venerable tradition in this country. They originated with the Massachusetts school ordinance of 1647, which instructed every town to choose men to manage the "prudential affairs" of the schools,[21] but perhaps a more legitimate beginning was the law passed by the Massachusetts legislature in 1789, which amounted to the first comprehensive system of public schools in any American state.[22] Since then, of course, school systems have proliferated, and Figure 18–2 indicates their distribution among the states.

School districts are created by the states but, until two decades ago they were controlled largely by locally elected boards of education. Since 1960, school boards increasingly have been subjected to national regulation, particularly in the area of racial integration and busing, and since the turn of the century, school board officials have increasingly deferred their power to the professionals, notably the superintendents and the teachers.[23]

SCHOOL BOARD POLITICS: A VERY PRIVATE AFFAIR

School boards, which account for approximately one-sixth of all units of American government, are perhaps the least known and the least understood of any governmental type in America. A Gallup Poll found that the general public was largely ignorant of the functions of school boards and school board members.[24] This is not surprising in light of the fact that school boards are perhaps the most politically incestuous of any American institution. About 25 percent of all school boards are appointed rather than elected, and even on those school boards where members are elected by the public, 25 percent of the members had gained membership to the board as appointees to replace board members who had left with unexpired terms.[25]

As with most of the institutions of local government, incumbents rarely are defeated; two-thirds of the board members who leave office do so voluntarily and, adding to this overall appearance of political incest is the fact that, "board members have a lot of relatives in education; three-fifths have at least one. More than half of the board members have one or both parents or a spouse in education. While the great majority (88 percent) mention relatives who are teachers, 14 percent had relatives who were board members and 10 percent had school administrators among their kin . . .21 percent have held jobs in education . . ., it is apparent that the

[21]George R. LaNoue and Bruce L.R. Smith. *The Politics of School Decentralization.* (Lexington, Mass.: D.C. Heath, 1973), p. 12.

[22]Raymond E. Callahan, "The American Board of Education, 1789–1960." In Cistone, *Understanding School Boards,* p. 19.

[23]*Ibid.,* p. 20.

[24]National School Board Association, *The People Look at Their School Boards: Research Report 1975–1.* (Evanston, Ill.: National School Board Association, 1975.)

[25]Harmon Zeigler and M. Kent Jennings, with the assistance of G. Wayne Peak, *Governing American Schools: Political Interaction in Local School Districts.* (North Scituate, Mass.: Duxbury, 1974), p. 24.

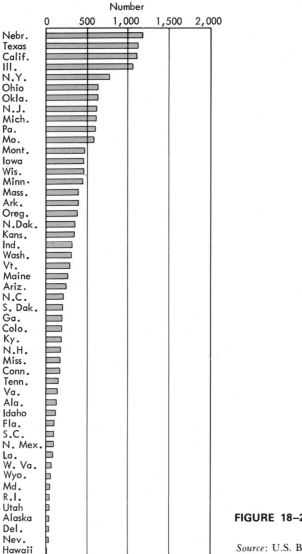

FIGURE 18–2 PUBLIC SCHOOL SYSTEMS, BY STATES: 1977

Source: U.S. Bureau of the Census.

occupational involvement of board members in education far exceeds the involvement of the general public."[26] In short, it should not be surprising that the relationship between teachers and school board members is a particularly cozy one characterized by low profile, a situation that has facilitated a lack of voter concern over school policy; only about one-third of a district's voters turn out for school board elections.

As a result of these conditions, school board members make school policy within an unobserved and isolated political environment. Ironically, how-

---

[26]*Ibid.*, p. 27.

ever, school boards generally do not govern but merely legitimate the policy recommendations of the professional educational staffs, and this holds true in the most political urban environments. Even in New York City, where interest group politics is extremely pervasive in city government, far-reaching educational decisions nonetheless are made within relatively autonomous professional school staffs.[27]

If a single person typically dominates decisions made about schools in this country, it is the school superintendent. "School governance has never completely fallen under the sway of the superintendent's office, but there is no question that the first half of the twentieth century saw enormous gains of power for the office."[28] Indeed, in comparison to city managers in council–manager governments, superintendents seem to exercise relatively more power over their boards than managers over their councils.[29]

Conversely, it should not be surprising that school board members are not particularly responsive to the demands of citizen groups, and most board members candidly admit to qualifying their wholehearted acceptance of requests brought by community groups concerning school board decisions. Oddly, appointed boards, in contrast to elected boards, tend to "overcompensate in their responsive behavior in the absence of being officially 'the peoples' choice'," and appointed boards actually seem to be more responsive to community requests than elected ones.[30]

Even so, all this must be cast in relative terms. Americans simply do not display much interest in school politics (other than property tax hikes related to school bond issues) and, while there are some notable exceptions, education politics tends to be a genteel form of good government—and a professionally inbred affair.

DO KIDS LEARN? NOT LATELY

It seems likely that the responsiveness—or unresponsiveness—of school boards to the public is going to be a matter of growing concern in the nation. Certainly there is a growing realization that schools are becoming increasingly less effective as institutions designed to teach reading, writing, and arithmetic. Among the evidence is the steady decline of the average scores on the Scholastic Aptitude Test (SAT) since 1963. The SAT is taken by roughly 1.5 million high school juniors and seniors every year. An investigation conducted by the College Entrance Examination Board found that the decline in scores measured a real decline in skills, not just a stiffening of the test itself. Why American students are learning less can be attributed to many factors (such as the increasing amount of time spent

[27]Wallace S. Sayre and Herbert Kaufman, *Governing New York City.* (New York: Russell Sage Foundation, 1960).

[28]Zeigler and Jennings, *Governing American Schools*, p. 27.

[29]*Ibid.*, p. 251.

[30]*Ibid.*, p. 87.

watching television as opposed to reading at home) that have little to do with what is happening in the classroom. Nevertheless, the report from the College Entrance Examination Board indicated that "our firmest conclusion is that the critical factors in the relationship between curricular change and the SAT scores are that less thoughtful and critical reading is now being demanded and done and that careful writing has apparently about gone out of style."[31]

In response to this distressing situation (along with suits being brought by parents who have discovered that their high school graduates could not read), thirty states had enacted "back-to-basics" policies by 1978, and a number of big city schools have signaled a return of "competency based education."[32] Chicago eliminated the assignment of students to grades (for example, seventh grade, ninth grade, etc.) in favor of permitting students to work at their own levels of competence until they met the standards for graduation set by the school board; these standards were the equivalent of the national average in reading and computational skills. In Boston, as a result of the entire school system being placed under the court's jurisdiction in 1974 (under an order in which the court decreed that all graduates of Boston's schools should have a "comprehensive education" by 1980), specific educational standards were set for all of Boston's students.[33]

THE THREE Vs: VIOLENCE, VANDALISM, AND VENALITY

Quite aside from the fact that schools seem to be teaching students less than ever before, parents and the public may wish to start exercising greater control over their schools for quite another reason: school violence. In 1976, the Gallup Poll identified the "lack of discipline" in America's schools as the "number one" issue in six out of the last seven years.[34]

This public concern is well founded. A survey of 757 school districts in 1975 found that violence and vandalism cost the American school as much as it spent on textbooks each year. Between 1970 and 1973 assaults on teachers went up almost 78 percent, assaults on students went up 85 percent, robberies in schools went up 37 percent, rapes and attempted rapes shot up 40 percent, murders went up 18 percent, and the number of weapons confiscated from students in schools increased by almost 55 percent.[35] The National Institute of Education reports that more than 5,000 teachers and nearly 300,000 students were attacked *each month*, and that

---

[31]College Entrance Examination Board, as quoted in David Broder, "Reading and Writing: The Principal Failings." Syndicated column, August 30, 1977.

[32]"Education," *Book of the States, 1978–79*, p. 331.

[33]Sheils, "City Schools in Crisis," pp. 67–70.

[34]"Education," *Book of the States, 1976–77*, p. 312.

[35]*Ibid.*

GRIN AND BEAR IT   by Lichty & Wagner

". . . And of the three R's, only one really starts with an R!"

Courtesy of Field Newspaper Syndicates

more than a fourth of all school buildings are vandalized in any given month.[36]

It is the taxpayers' money that is being destroyed by school vandalism, and it is costing an estimated $600 million a year, so it is little wonder that the ability of school boards to cope is being questioned. In 1976, the U.S. Law Enforcement Assistance Administration for the first time allocated funds to be used for fighting crime in school corridors and "playgrounds."

COLLECTIVIZING TEACHERS

It is clear from the statistics on declining student learning and growing student violence that, in the opinion of many, American schools are verging on failure. What the reaction of state and local governments will be to this failure has yet to be determined, but in view of the drying up of funding, rampant student violence, and a general public dissatisfaction with schools, it is perhaps to be expected that teachers have started trying to save what they have (and, indeed, to acquire a little more) in the face of what they perceive to be an increasingly hostile political environment.

---

[36]National Institute of Education, Department of Health, Education and Welfare, as reported by United Press International, January 7, 1978, syndicated nationally.

"HURRICANE AL" AND THE AFT

The most widely known teachers' union is the American Federation of Teachers (AFT), a national union affiliated with the AFL–CIO and boasting more than 450,000 members, mostly from the big northeastern cities. Originally headed by Albert ("Hurricane Al") Shanker, AFT has a reputation for being the most militant of the teachers' unions.

There was good reason, and there still may be, for Shanker's union to be as militant as it has been. Shanker, who taught in New York City until he moved up in union circles, recounts how the city's starting salary for teachers in 1960 was $4,800, although the then-mayor, Robert Wagner, consistently pleaded that the city had no money to raise salaries. During the year, a severe snowstorm and a hurricane forced the city to spend additional millions to clear the streets. Shanker queried how the city suddenly acquired the money and was informed that it was available only for disasters. Shanker has since stated, "That was when we decided to become a disaster."[37] It was also in 1960 that Shanker got his nickname of "Hurricane Al." Today, the salary in New York for teachers starts at $10,000, and they can make more than $20,000 within seven and a half years.

THE AWAKENING GIANT OF THE NEA

The most powerful teachers' union, but one which does not have a tradition of militancy, is the National Education Association (NEA). The NEA not only is the country's second largest union after the Teamsters, but also is the nation's fastest growing labor organization; it claims to average about 4,000 new members *each week*! NEA currently is engaged in, according to one observer, "a no-holds-barred, jurisdictional war with the AFL–CIO American Federation of Teachers."[38]

The NEA currently has 1.8 million teachers of the nation's total of 2.3 million elementary and secondary school teachers as members, indicating that America's teachers are approximately 80 percent unionized. Until recently, the NEA was a genteel—according to some, even a timid—organization. Between 1952 and 1963 the NEA was not involved in a single work stoppage of teachers. Then something happened. By 1966 the NEA was participating in one-third of all the educational work stoppages; in fact, 80 percent of the striking teachers in 1966 were members of the NEA. The NEA has initiated 70 percent of the 720 teachers' work stoppages and strikes since 1960, and all teacher unions accounted for 70 percent of the six million work days lost by teachers by 1975.[39] In that year alone more

---

[37]Thomas Redburn, "Government Unions: The New Bullies on the Block." *The Washington Monthly* (December, 1974) p. 21.

[38]Robert A. Dobkin, "NEA's Militancy Defies Inflation Spiral: They Want Theirs!" Associated Press, January 9, 1976, syndicated nationally.

[39]Ronald G. Corwin, "The Organizational Context of School Board-Teacher Conflict," in Ciston, *Understanding School Boards*, p. 131.

398

than one million students were given extended summer vacations because of teachers' strikes and, in the fall of 1978 strikes occurred in thirteen states, keeping more than a quarter million pupils out of elementary and high schools.[40]

POLITICIZING TEACHERS

Another facet of the NEA's new-found militancy is its growing political clout. In 1972 the NEA first entered the political arena by investing a comparatively modest $30,000 in political contributions. By 1974 NEA's contributions had increased to $250,000, and in 1976 it donated $579,000 to House and Senate candidates, plus an additional $2 million through its state and local affiliates to candidates for Congress and state offices. In 1972 the NEA sent only thirty-six delegates to the Democratic National Convention, but four years later, with organized labor sending a record 600 delegates, the NEA provided the biggest single block (135) of labor's delegates to the Democratic convention. The NEA endorsed 323 candidates for the U.S. House of Representatives in 1976, of whom 272 won. It endorsed 26 candidates for the Senate, of whom 19 won—not a bad record for any lobby.[41]

Both the AFT and NEA want a separate U.S. Department of Education and a collective bargaining bill for state and local employees at the national level. Such legislation would give public school teachers the same rights that workers have had in private industry since the passage of the Wagner Act in 1935. Organized teachers want an act that would mandate collective bargaining for all teachers in all states and localities, although currently only nineteen states do not have collective bargaining legislation.

Because of "formula funding" for education used by the states, declining enrollments are almost certain to cause fiscal hardships for a number of school districts, and teachers can obviously see the writing on the wall. In 1977, for example, almost half of the nation's school districts had cut back their personnel during the past two years.[42]

Because the message is grim, teachers have begun pressuring legislators in an increasingly well-organized way, but the legislative policies resulting from this pressure have been mixed. A sophisticated study of the education lobby conducted in a dozen states found that teachers, as opposed to administrators and school board members, were by far the most politically active. Teachers directed most of their efforts toward providing information

[40]"Education," *Book of the States, 1976–77*, p. 310, and United Press International, September 22, 1978, syndicated nationally.

[41]Dobkin, "NEA's Militancy Defies Inflation Spiral."

[42]"Education," *Book of the States, 1978–79*, p. 330.

TABLE 18–1 LEGISLATORS' ASSESSMENTS OF THE INFLUENCE OF THE EDUCATION LOBBY IN TWELVE STATES

STATE	TOP GROUPS	AMONG TOP GROUPS	AMONG LESS IMPORTANT GROUPS	NOT AT ALL INFLUENTIAL	TOTAL
California	4	10	3	0	17
Colorado	3	9	4	0	16
Florida	2	1	2	1	6
Georgia	5	6	1	1	13
Massachusetts	0	4	1	0	5
Michigan	7	5	3	0	15
Minnesota	6	6	3	0	15
Nebraska	1	4	2	0	7
New York	1	5	3	0	9
Tennessee	5	6	0	0	11
Texas	4	5	0	0	9
Wisconsin	2	10	3	0	15

Source: J. Alan Aufderheide, "Educational Interest Groups and the State Legislature." In Roald Campbell and Tim L. Mazzoni, Jr. (eds.), *State Policy Making for the Public Schools: A Comparative Analysis.* (Columbus, Ohio: Educational Governance Project, Ohio State University, 1974), 309. Reprinted by permission.

to legislators, although campaign money was also contributed.[43] Table 18–1 shows how legislators rated the political influence of their state's education lobby; in California, for instance, four legislators viewed education interests to be the most powerful lobbies in the state, ten felt education was among the top groups, and three believed education to be only moderately influential.

The level of political clout of educators in any given state appears to associate with the degree of urbanization and economic mix of a state; the education lobby was seen by legislators as having less influence in those states that had relatively advanced economies, were socially heterogenous, were more urbanized, and had a high level of legislative professionalism. Interestingly, the amount of money, staff, and membership that the education lobbies had in each state bore no particular relationship with how legislators ranked the power of the state's education lobby.[44]

RACE AND SCHOOLS

In our discussion of educational politics, we have not yet considered what Republicans in the White House once called, "the big enchilada," race and the schools. In terms of providing an equal education to all children irrespective of their race, state and local governments have a dreary record. As late as 1954, seventeen states mandated the racial segregation of public

---

[43]J. Alan Aufderheide, "Educational Interest Groups and the State Legislature." In *State Policy Making for the Public Schools: A Comparative Analysis,* Ronald Campbell and Tim L. Mazzoni, Jr., eds. (Columbus, Ohio: Educational Governance Project, Ohio State University, 1974).

[44]Wirt, "Education Politics and Policies," pp. 309–310.

schools. All were in the Old Confederacy, but there also were some surprising examples (given today's outlook), such as Delaware, Maryland, Missouri, Oklahoma, and West Virginia. Congress required racial segregation of the schools in Washington, D.C., and four additional states—Arizona, Kansas, New Mexico, and Wyoming—permitted local school boards to segregate or not segregate as they saw fit.

THE LIFE AND TIMES OF JIM CROW

Racial segregation in the Deep South, of course, went far beyond the schools as a public policy. Blacks and whites, as a matter of law, were not permitted to use each other's elevators, drinking fountains, restaurants, waiting rooms, libraries, restrooms, and even some stores; southern public policy at mid-century had created a society very similar to what Americans now decry in Rhodesia and South Africa. The U.S. Supreme Court had tried to alleviate this situation as far back as 1896 in the case of *Plessy* v. *Ferguson,* in which the Court stated that separating the races as such was not necessarily discrimination, provided that equal accommodations were furnished for all. This rationale became known as the famous "separate-but-equal" doctrine, and soon was used as an excuse for implementing racial segregation policies throughout the nation.

Unfortunately, and as everyone knows, blacks and whites were given separate but not equal facilities. In 1950, for example, in the seventeen segregated states there were fourteen medical schools for whites, but not one such school for blacks; there were sixteen law schools for whites and only five for blacks; there were fifteen engineering schools for whites, but there were no engineering schools for blacks; there were five schools of dentistry for whites and none for blacks.[45]

In 1954, the Supreme Court committed a very rare act and reversed a previous decision. In the case of *Brown* v. *the Board of Education of Topeka, Kansas,* the Court reversed its 1896 *Plessy* ruling as it applied to public schools and stated that segregation *in and of itself* constituted discrimination. A year later, the Court ordered local school boards to move with "all deliberate speed" to integrate public schools.

THE PRINCIPLES OF SCHOOL DESEGREGATION

The Court's decision in 1954, along with the gradual dawning that the federal government intended to enforce that decision, caused bitterness among southern whites, hope for the nation's blacks, and violence between whites and blacks throughout the South in the years that followed. During

---

[45]James MacGregor Burns, J.W. Peltason, and Thomas E. Cronin, *Government By the People.* 9th ed., National, State, and Local Edition. (Englewood Cliffs, N.J.: Prentice-Hall, 1975), p. 187.

those years, the Supreme Court heard a plethora of cases on school desegregation and, in the process, developed the following five basic principles:[46]

1. School segregation is unconstitutional if it results from intentional actions of state and local governments. This principle prevents schools from being constructed on sites that effectively exclude by their locations one race or the other from being taught in them.
2. Busing is an acceptable and, on occasion, necessary solution for attaining desegregated schools. This is a point to which we shall return later.
3. Desegregation may not normally be required across jurisdictional boundaries (for example, between cities and their suburbs), but busing can be ordered across jurisdictional lines in special cases—if, for instance, city limits appeared to further segregation by design.
4. Entire school districts must be desegregated if proof can be found of intentional segregation in just a part of a district.
5. Once a school district is desegregated, school officials do not need to take any additional action, even if the schools become resegregated because of changes in housing patterns.

YANKEE RACISM

What have been the results of desegregating the races in the public schools? Despite racial riots and an occasional need to send in federal troops to desegregate the schools, the South has achieved a truly admirable record of integrating the races in its schools. Although much remains to be done, it is a genuine feat of democracy that school desegregation in the South has outstripped that of the North. In 1964, only 8 percent of black pupils in the South attended integrated schools; by 1972, 92 percent of black pupils were attending desegregated schools. In most of these cases, desegregation had been accomplished by busing children away from their neighborhood schools.

By contrast, considerably more than half of the black children outside the South attend schools that are at least 90 percent black, and this is particularly true in the big cities of the North. According to 1977 statistics, the public schools in New York City are 67 percent nonwhite; in Chicago, they are 70 percent nonwhite; in Philadelphia, the figure is 62 percent; in Detroit, 81 percent; in Baltimore, 75 percent; and in Washington D.C., 96 percent.[47] Indeed, public schools in the Midwest and Northeast are the most segregated schools in the nation, and those in the South are the least segregated. Approximately 60 percent of black students in the Northeast, Midwest, and the border states are attending what amount to segregated schools; in the South, only 10 percent of black children are attending "intensely segregated" schools in which only a token integration has taken

---

[46]David E. Rosenbaum, "New Rights Drive Perplexes Nation," *New York Times* (July 7, 1977), p. 28.
[47]*Ibid.*

place (in other words, a school that has more than 90 percent minority enrollment). Figure 18–3 illustrates the lack of progress made in Yankeeland relative to the Old Confederacy.

It is often forgotten when discussing school desegregation that there are other minorities besides blacks. The segregation of children from Spanish-speaking cultures—the Latinos—is even more pronounced than that of blacks, and Latinos are segregated from white schools most effectively in Texas and New York. In contrast to the figures for black pupils, which show a general decrease in segregation in all areas of the country except the Northeast, segregation of Spanish-speaking children is actually increasing. In 1970, according to a 1976 study conducted by the Department of Health, Education and Welfare, 64.2 percent of Latino pupils were attending predominantly minority schools, and 29 percent were attending "intensely segregated" schools. By the 1974–1975 academic year, these levels had increased to 67.4 percent and 30 percent respectively.[48] Figure 18–4 shows the degree to which Hispanics are segregated in American schools.

THE BUSING BUNGLE

In light of the discouraging indications that racial segregation in some quarters of the country may actually be increasing rather than decreasing, how is the nation to assure equality of education between the races? The tentative answer thus far has been: Bus them.

---

[48]Department of Health, Education and Welfare, as quoted by Associated Press, June 20, 1976, syndicated nationally.

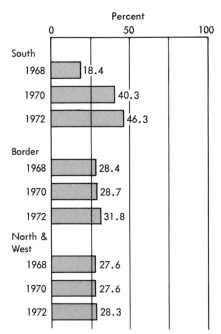

FIGURE 18–3 THE TOKENISM MEASURE: REGIONAL DESEGREGATION, 1968–72. BLACKS ATTENDING SCHOOLS WITH 50–99.9 PERCENT WHITE ENROLLMENT

Source: Office for Civil Rights, Department of Health, Education and Welfare.

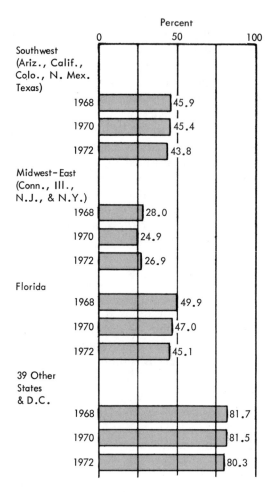

Percent

FIGURE 18–4 THE TOKENISM MEASURE: REGIONAL DESEGRE-GATION, 1968–72.
SPANISH-SURNAMED AMERI-CANS ATTENDING SCHOOLS WITH 50–99.9 PERCENT ANGLO ENROLLMENT

Source: Office for Civil Rights, U.S. Department of Health, Education and Welfare.

Few political issues have been as controversial as the busing issue. Busing began when a sociologist from the University of Chicago, James S. Coleman (whom *Time* Magazine has called a "sort of godfather to busing"),[49] issued a major study that found that black students attending predominantly black schools had lower achievement scores and lower levels of ambition than blacks from similar social and economic backgrounds who attended predominantly white schools. Indeed, comparisons indicated that the differences in achievement amounted to more than two grade levels.[50] Although Coleman has since questioned his own research, this finding appalled many people in government and angered blacks.

---

[49]"Coleman on the Griddle." *Time* (April 12, 1976), p. 79.
[50]James S. Coleman, *Equality of Educational Opportunity*. (Washington, D.C.: U.S. Government Printing Office, 1966.)

In 1971, the U.S. Supreme Court heard the now-famous case of *Swann* v. *The Charlotte-Mecklenberg Board of Education,* in which the Court stated that southern school districts must eliminate all vestiges of dual school systems and that such a responsibility could require the busing of students to and from various schools that were located away from their neighborhoods in an effort to desegregate schools that were segregated because of residential patterns. In 1974 the Supreme Court modified its *Swann* decision and ruled in the case of *Milligan* v. *Bradley* that the Fourteenth Amendment did not require busing across city and suburban school district boundaries to achieve integration. The reasoning underlying this decision was that it was more difficult to prove that northern governments had purposely established segregated school systems than it was to prove that southern governments had. While the effect of this decision has been to help keep whites in the suburbs and blacks in the central cities, it did not preclude the Court-ordered desegregation of white and black school districts that are located *within* the same city. Because such intracity desegregation attempts were not precluded, in 1974 and 1975 Judge W. Arthur Garrity, Jr., was able to issue his famous orders in Boston calling for wide-spread busing, which subsequently caused wide-spread rioting by Irish-Americans—"the Southies"—in South Boston.

Traditionally, the Department of Health, Education and Welfare (HEW) has been able to keep the pressure on urban governments to desegregate their school systems through busing with the threat of withholding federal funds, but in 1977 Congress removed HEW's authority to withhold federal funds from school districts that refused to desegregate by employing busing. This decision, in effect, threw the issue back to the courts, which now must rule on busing plans on a case by case basis.

The American people generally do not like busing, apparently because of personal inconvenience and racism. On the one hand, white Americans have largely changed their attitudes toward racial issues in schools over the years, and there is a clear and growing acceptance of racial desegregation by whites. According to a Gallup Poll of 1975,[51] a majority of white parents in both the South and North would not object to sending their children to a school where as many as half of the students were black. In the South 38 percent of white parents objected to this proposal in the 1975 poll, but by contrast 78 percent had objected to the same proposal in 1963. Outside the South, 24 percent responded that they would not object in 1975, compared to 33 percent in 1963.

On the other hand, such figures do not apply to busing. Indeed, a 1978 Harris poll found that 85 percent of whites and 43 percent of blacks oppose busing to achieve racial desegregation. Even so, 56 percent of white parents whose children were bused found the experience "very satisfactory," and

---

[51]George Gallup, syndicated column, October 12, 1975.

nearly half of the white parents believed that black children would be better off in desegregated schools; significantly, more than two-thirds of the white parents denied that their children would suffer in integrated schools.[52]

The excuses made by parents and others who are unwilling to permit their children to be bused to a school usually involve a desire for children to attend a "neighborhood school" and concerns over the high cost of busing; but these excuses are not founded on fact. Nearly 44 percent of all school children in the nation ride a bus to school. Local governments spend $1.7 billion annually for busing, and this sum has been declining over the years. In 1953 busing cost the American taxpayer 4.5 percent of the total school budget, but in 1967, with more than twice as many children being bused, the cost amounted to 3.7 percent of the school budget. Children also are safer in a school bus; according to the National Safety Council, busing is safer than walking to school or riding in a private vehicle.[53]

Desegregating schools and using a bus to do so has disrupted communities across the country. Has it been worth the effort? The answer is unquestionably, "Yes!" School desegregation does work, according to the U.S. Commission on Civil Rights, but it works best in those cities where community support is the highest.[54] Despite violence in Boston, Chicago, Little Rock, Birmingham, New Orleans, Louisville, Prince George's County, and other places where it has occurred over the years since *Brown* v. *Topeka Board of Education,* state and local governments have achieved one of the world's great accomplishments in the desegregation of their schools. While much remains to be done, particularly in the Snowbelt states, few other nations have been able to give minority kids an equal educational chance—or even to admit they have a problem. Busing may not be the best way of achieving desegregation; integrating neighborhoods would be. But the Supreme Court has not put its prestige behind that option, and the fact remains that state and local governments have made a major effort—and have achieved a fair degree of success—in bringing black, brown, and white children together in the same educational system. The progress made toward desegregating schools has been a major accomplishment.

HIGHER EDUCATION: CRACKS IN THE IVORY TOWER

Let us now move from the violence, racism, and general tawdriness of elementary and secondary education and climb the ivory tower of higher learning. If you believe the implications of that sentence, then you should

---

[52]Harris Poll, as cited in: Dennis A. Williams, *et al.*, "A New Racial Poll," *Newsweek* (February 26, 1979), p. 48.

[53]George Mair, "School Busing Is Phony Issue, Integrated Housing Is Not." Syndicated column, March 13, 1977.

[54]United States Commission on Civil Rights, *Twenty Years After Brown.* (Washington, D.C.: U.S. Government Printing Office, 1975).

find the remaining portions of this chapter most illuminating, as violence, racism, and tawdriness pervade academe's halls, too.

THE RADICALISM OF AMERICAN HIGHER EDUCATION

American higher education is unique. Indeed, one could argue that it is a genuinely radical form of education; only in America has the ideal that all citizens should have an opportunity to go to college been attempted as a matter of public policy. Every country in the world (with the on-again, off-again exception of the People's Republic of China) has predicated its advanced educational system on the notion that higher education is a program reserved for the intellectual and social elites of the nation. (In China, the basic precept has been, on occasion, that education is reserved for the politically trustworthy.)

As a policy meant for "the masses," American higher education, therefore, is a policy of some magnitude.[55] More than $50 billion are spent on it, more than 1.25 million academic degrees are conferred by it, more than 11 million students are educated in it, and approximately 700,000 professors are teaching in it in any given year. Not all these dollars expended, degrees conferred, students taught, and teachers teaching are done in institutions that are supported by public funds; about 25 percent of the nation's college and university students are enrolled in private institutions. Even so, state governments have an impact even in this area; in the mid 1970s forty-two states appropriated approximately $800 million in direct or indirect aid to private institutions for such items as student aid, equalization of tuition, and contracts.

THE STATE AND CITY PATRONS: A LESSER LARGESSE

Americans always have had a high level of interest in higher education. The first colleges were founded privately in Massachusetts and Virginia in the seventeenth century, and the first public university to be chartered by a state legislature was in Georgia in 1794. Nevertheless, state involvement in higher education really began with the passage by Congress of the Morrill Land Grant Act of 1862. The Morrill Act encouraged states to set up practically oriented universities emphasizing agricultural education. The West and Midwest were the most affected by the legislation, as students in the South and East continued to attend, by and large, private institutions. Only in the 1960s did the Northeast become truly interested in fostering its own public higher education programs.

Concurrent with state activity has been a more limited activity at the local level. City governments either have founded or taken over colleges and

---

[55]The following statistics are drawn from "Education," *Book of the States, 1978–79,* p. 352.

universities in Charleston, New York, Akron, Cincinnati, Toledo, Louisville, and Omaha among others. In recent years, a number of these city-run institutions have fallen on hard times and state assistance is increasingly necessary. Perhaps the most spectacular example of this development is the City University of New York, the third largest higher educational system in the country (only California's and New York State's University systems are larger). In 1976 the university was temporarily closed down, shutting out some 250,000 students, 16,000 faculty, and 11,000 other employees, because of its inability to meet payrolls. In that year, the university, for the first time since its founding in 1847, began charging students tuition—and a stiff tuition at that.

State institutions of higher education are also suffering under fiscal constraints in the 1970s, and austerity budgets are increasingly the rule. Decreasing state expenditures often means that the money will be drawn from students and faculty. Between 1970 and 1975, the total cost to a student at a public, four-year institution rose by nearly 50 percent. Even so, students at public four-year institutions were getting an education for dramatically less money than students at comparable private institutions, where the costs of fees and tuition were almost four times that at public universities.[56] Similarly, professors' salaries have declined in terms of real purchasing power since 1974, with inflation outstripping by substantial margins the increases in faculty salaries allocated by legislatures.[57]

Ironically, and unlike enrollments in elementary and secondary schools, registration in public colleges and universities is increasing, although the rate of increase declined in the 1970s relative to the 1960s; the largest enrollment increases are occurring in two-year institutions. Still, the overall fiscal picture appears to be bleak. A study of forty-one representative public and private universities found that more than half of this sample either were in financial difficulty or could be in financial difficulty in the near future.[58]

GOVERNING THOSE IVIED HALLS

States govern their institutions of higher education in different ways, but most states appoint a board of regents or similar body of distinguished citizens to look after the affairs of the major state institutions. Increasingly, the states have become interested in forming system-wide governing bodies and only three states—Delaware, Nebraska, and Vermont—have no statutory central planning or coordination agency for higher education. The federal government recently has taken a major interest in encouraging statewide planning for higher education through the education amendments

---

[56]"Education," *Book of the States, 1976–77*, p. 333.
[57]Chart in *The Chronicle of Higher Education*, 15 (October 3, 1977) 2.
[58]Earl F. Cheit, *The New Depression in Higher Education.* (New York: McGraw-Hill, 1971).

of 1972. These amendments redefined the range of state and federal concern for higher education, stipulating that planning should encompass all areas of post-secondary education, including private institutions as well as public ones. The amendments also authorize the states to establish post-secondary planning commissions, and these have been set up in nearly all states.

The main concern of both post-secondary commissions and state boards of regents has been how to deal with a shrinking revenue base for higher education. Increasingly, boards of regents have taken to eliminating whole academic programs from state institutions, and the slashes have been particularly severe in such states as California, Kansas, New York, Oregon, and Washington.

UNIONIZING UNIVERSITIES

Partly as a result of this retrenchment process underway in most states, faculties have become increasingly interested in unionizing as a means of resistance. By 1975, 267 colleges and universities with 432 campuses were involved in collective bargaining with university administrators. Of these campuses, 373 were public. Most were community or junior colleges, but 157 of them were full four-year or better institutions.

Unionizing professors is a new trend in university life, and it appears to be a result of a deepening pessimism on the part of professors concerning their slipping status and their uncertain economic futures. The 1977 Ladd-Lipset annual survey of college faculty found that by an "overwhelming margin, professors are now of the opinion that their own economic status is eroding in comparison with people employed in nonacademic professions" and that there is a feeling among America's college faculty that "they are being singled out for special income discrimination."[59]

Twenty-two states have legislation requiring collective bargaining for institutions of higher learning. The major representatives of the organized professoriate are the American Association of University Professors, the National Education Association, and the American Federation of Teachers. Strikes by professors occurred in the mid-1970s in New Jersey, Rhode Island, and Illinois, among other states, and in 1978 some 170,000 college students were kept out of classes because of faculty strikes.

Just as the unionization of public employees in other fields affects the general citizenry to the point that taxpayers' representatives actually have been brought into the bargaining process in some localities, the unionization of professors affects the students who both pay for and consume their services. As a result, students increasingly are getting involved in the collective bargaining process. Montana and Oregon, for example, require

---

[59]Everett Carl Ladd, Jr. and Seymour Martin Lipsett, "The Faculty Mood: Pessimism Is Predominant." *The Chronicle of Higher Education* 15 (October 3, 1977) 14.

that students be involved in such negotiations by law, and this has occurred in practice in Massachusetts.

PROFESSORS IN THE PUBLIC SERVICE

Another trend occurring in American higher education is the effort by the professoriate to be of greater use to state and local governments. Although legislators occasionally have disdained "intellectuals," public administrators in the states have often made use of the expertise that resides on their campuses. This expertise frequently comes at a far cheaper price than that charged by private consultants, and both students and faculty have shown a remarkable willingness to be of use to their state and local governments. A survey of college students indicated that 67 percent of them believed that colleges should have a responsibility for helping solve the social problems of society, and not just through research.[60] The same view was held by 42 percent of 53,000 college faculty members surveyed who engaged in public service professional consulting without pay, and by another 38 percent who consulted off-campus for pay.[61]

A unique study of colleges and universities in fourteen southern states found that the eighty-four institutions surveyed controlled a public service budget of more than $200 million and that the region's higher education institutions held contracts and grants with state agencies amounting to almost $33 million, or 16 percent of their overall budgets. A remarkable 95 percent of the state officials surveyed had used or were using the services of the academic community occasionally or often.[62]

In short, public universities are attempting to pay back their state governments for their tax dollars by supplying them with the knowledge that their campuses hold in relevant and useful ways. Of course, education, regardless of the level at which it is conducted, pays back society many times. An educated citizenry is a democratic cornerstone—such, at least, is the belief of the American middle class and, as a consequence of that belief, the institutions of education affect the lives of more citizens than in perhaps any other country.

The American middle class also is interested in other state and local public policies, notably local planning, land use, transportation, and housing. We consider these next.

---

[60]Carnegie Commission on Higher Education, *Reform on Campus: Changing Students, Changing Academic Programs.* (New York: McGraw-Hill, 1972.)

[61]American Council on Education, *ACE Faculty and Staff Survey Newsletter* (August, 1973) p. 1.

[62]Nicholas Henry, "State Agencies and Academia." *State Government* 49 (Spring, 1976) 99–104.

CHAPTER

POLICIES
FOR THE
MIDDLE CLASS:
THE
PLANNING ETHIC

As with the preceding chapter on education, it is not entirely unfair to posit planning as a uniquely middle-class policy. Planning, like education, affects all classes of society but it is the middle class that has traditionally chosen the neat rows of picket-fenced houses, tidy boulevards free from pushcarts and litter, and the comfort of knowing that one's residential neighborhood always will be just that—a residential neighborhood. Although the planning profession in recent years has broadened its traditional concerns, it is nonetheless such middle-class values that gave urban planning in particular its beginning. In this chapter, we shall examine the origins of the planning ethic and the evolution of professional planners from ineffectual "do-gooders" to increasingly powerful urban and regional policy makers, focusing especially on the impact that planners are having in forming public policies for land use and transportation.

THE ROOTS OF URBAN PLANNING

Early urban planning was part and parcel of what was known around the turn of the century as the "city beautiful movement," and central to this movement was the concept of physical design of cities. Hence, urban planning was related to the architecture profession, but it was also closely associated with the "good government" reform movement: "A better city (the city beautiful movement), an honestly and ably run city government (municipal reform), and efficient local government (early public administration) were ends to be advanced by city planning. In this sense, early city planning had a moralistic flavor to it, and it was viewed as the means of promoting the good life."[1] Indeed, it was precisely this early moralistic flavor that has led us to base this chapter on the concept that planning is essentially a policy for the middle class.

Nevertheless, planning did bring about some notable early achievements on the American urban scene. It was planners who were responsible for the creation of Pullman in South Chicago, and the design and execution of Garden City in Long Island, and Shaker Heights in Ohio.[2] More recently two complete communities—Columbia, Maryland, and Reston, Virginia—have been developed directly from the pens of planners rather than from the avarice of developers.

---

[1] Don Allensworth, *Public Administration: The Execution of Public Policy.* (Philadelphia: Lippincott, 1973), p. 32.

[2] National Research Council, *Towards an Understanding of Metropolitan America.* (San Francisco: Canfield, 1974), p.59.

THE STRUCTURE OF LOCAL PLANNING

Approximately three-quarters of all American communities with more than five thousand people have some sort of published plan.[3] Almost eleven thousand municipalities have planning boards (a figure representing more than half of the local governments that might be expected to have such boards), and virtually all the large cities, those with fifty thousand or more people, have planning boards. Ninety percent of cities and towns in the five thousand to fifty thousand population range have planning boards, and all state governments have planning agencies and programs.[4]

Although planning boards are being integrated into the standing city bureaucracy at an increasingly rapid rate, they nonetheless operate somewhat autonomously as governmental units. Members of planning boards are usually appointed or elected for specific terms on a staggered basis. Staggering the terms contributes to the independence of the local planning commission's members since their terms of office do not necessarily coincide with that of the mayor or council members. Boards have an average size of eight to nine members. A highly educated planning staff generally serves the board, and political reality is such that board members usually follow the advice of the professional staff. (Recall, in this light, our discussion of school boards and superintendents in the last chapter.)

Community planning commissions are generally responsible for revising and updating the comprehensive plan, making rezoning decisions, drawing a zoning map, administering community subdivision regulations, and suggesting changes of the laws in these areas. Planning commissions have particular power in formulating the comprehensive plan and developing land-use controls, the most notable authority here being zoning. Local planning commissions rarely have programs of their own, but they are involved in the programs of a number of other agencies, especially such federally sponsored programs as urban renewal, model cities, community development, and mass transit, and they also are involved in local building and housing code programs.

The actual amount of clout that local planning commissions have in these programs varies. Don Allensworth points out, for example, that the staff director of Philadelphia's Planning Commission was a "crucial participant in the urban renewal process for years,"[5] while Scott Greer found that the local planning commissions functioned as a "rubber stamp of approval" in urban renewal programs in many communities.[6]

---

[3] Allen D. Manvel, *Local Land and Building Regulations*. (Washington, D.C.: U.S. Government Printing Office, 1968), p. 31.

[4] Allensworth, *Public Administration*, p. 33.

[5] Allensworth, *Public Administration*, p. 38.

[6] Scott Greer, *Urban Renewal in American Cities*. (Indianapolis: Bobbs-Merrill, 1965), p. 76.

413

THE USES OF THE URBAN PLAN

Although the official plan of a community does not have any legal weight as such, professional planners nonetheless have a variety of tools at their disposal with which to implement their plans. Among these tools are zoning ordinances (perhaps the most significant single tool), regulations concerning subdivisions, the power to draw official maps of the area, building and construction codes, decision-making authority regarding the location of public facilities and buildings, and devising a capital improvement program. Communities increasingly are developing *comprehensive plans,* by which is meant a land-use plan for an urban area that includes all relevant aspects of the system. More commonly used is the *functional plan,* which refers to the specialized planning done by such agencies as urban renewal authorities, health departments, highway departments, and recreation agencies. In this chapter we concentrate on the comprehensive aspect of planning, since comprehensive plans are being used increasingly by local policy makers.

A survey of all cities with more than 150,000 people found that comprehensive planning documents were "frequently" used by city governments to set priorities in the budget process—54 percent of the responding cities reported such a use. On the other hand, about a third of the cities reported that they use their planning document only "to qualify for federal grants." This was particularly true of economic development plans and, to a lesser degree, land-use plans. Such a finding is not too surprising when we recall the attitudes of local policy makers concerning the federal government, discussed in Chapter 15.[7]

THE STRUCTURE OF STATE PLANNING

Some of the more exciting developments in planning have been occurring at the state level. Traditionally, the states did little other than permit their local governments to establish planning commissions. In the 1970s however, states became increasingly active in planning, and California, Massachusetts, and Michigan are leading the way in shaping planning policies for their own urban areas. Eighteen states have interagency coordinating councils of some kind and forty-five states have in-state regional planning organizations. Virtually all these regional organizations relate to the A-95 clearinghouse procedures in some fashion (soon to be discussed), and most function in the areas of specialized planning, such as health, manpower, aging, land use, housing, economic development, criminal justice, and transportation. Two-thirds of the states in 1979 had policy planning commissions which ranged from "alternative futures" to planning public investments.

---

[7] Thomas Thorwood, "The Planning and Management Process in City Government." In *Municipal Yearbook, 1973.* (Washington, D.C.: International City Management Association, 1973), pp. 28–38.

States have also shown a greater inclination to cooperate with each other on a regional basis and, while the states contribute funds, these regional commissions receive their principal support from the federal government. Currently, there are eight such federally sponsored economic development groups and another half-dozen river basin commissions in the country.

THE FEDERAL GOVERNMENT AND THE POWER TO PLAN

As the preceding discussions of local and state planning have implied, planning is an intensely intergovernmental process. There are more than six hundred regional councils of all types, and all are involved in some form of comprehensive or functional planning. About 70 percent are policy councils of various kinds, such as Economic Development Districts (managed through the U.S. Department of Commerce) and Rural Area Development Committees (administered through the U.S. Department of Agriculture), both of which are controlled almost entirely by the federal government, with only relatively minor concessions to state and local governments. Forty-six percent of these policy councils are regional planning councils, and 30 percent of regional councils of all types are Councils of Governments.[8] The key difference between a Council of Government and a regional planning council is that Councils of Government are voluntary associations of governments while regional planning commissions are generally set up by state legislation, often as a result of pressure from Washington, and they are primarily responsible for comprehensive planning.

National pressure, in fact, is a major aspect of developing rational planning among America's plethora of governments. It can be traced back at least to 1928 with the enactment of the U.S. Department of Commerce's Model Planning Act, known as the Standard City Planning Enabling Act. This act was designed to serve as a guide to state legislatures in permitting their localities to engage in planning, and it was this act that encouraged the establishment of independent planning commissions at the local level.[9]

Since that time, a number of federal laws have encouraged (or even forced) states and localities to engage in more comprehensive and rational public planning. Among the more significant of these acts is the Urban Planning Assistance Act of 1954. Under its section 701, federal grants were allocated to regional, state, and local planning agencies to promote coordinated planning. Now known as the "701" program, these funds are administered by the Department of Housing and Urban Development (HUD), and HUD has granted almost $200 million to subnational planning agencies under its auspices. Later the Demonstration Cities and Metropoli-

---

[8] David B. Walker and Albert J. Richter, "Regionalism and the Counties." In *The County Yearbook, 1975.* (Washington, D.C.: National Association of Counties and International City Management Association, 1975), p. 15.

[9] Allensworth, *Public Administration*, p. 33.

tan Development Act of 1966 (model cities), the Intergovernmental Cooperation Act of 1968, and the National Environmental Policy Act of 1969
were enacted. All encouraged the development of Councils of Governments
and regional planning agencies. In 1974 the Housing and Community
Development Act was passed; Title IV of this act authorizes grants to local
and regional governments for planning purposes. Also in 1974 eligibility
for "701" comprehensive planning assistance was expanded to include
activities leading to the development and carrying out of comprehensive
plans, improving management skills to implement such plans, and developing policy planning and evaluation capacities. It is hoped that these
changes will permit local governments to use "701" grants for the purpose
of improving planning management.[10]

While the federal government definitely has encouraged state and local
planning efforts through its "701" program and related legislation, it also
is evident that both federal and state policies have contributed to the
decentralization of metropolitan areas. The interstate highway system,
federal mortgage policies, national and state tax incentives, and other factors
have had a decentralizing influence on the nation's megalopolises. In that
light, President Carter has stated that his administration favors a national
urban policy that would take into heavy account the value of discouraging
metropolitan decentralization and urban sprawl.

Money, planning, and bureaucracy are essentially intertwined in this
country, and it is difficult to treat these components as cleanly separate
entities. The overall effect of federal legislation has been to make local,
state, and regional planning boards increasingly dependent on the federal
government for both policy guidance and financial assistance. But if such
federal legislation has, to a degree, limited the traditional prerogatives of
local governments, it has done just the reverse for the planning profession.

PLANNERS, POWER, AND POLITICS

Traditionally, planners have had an extraordinarily limited role in government. They were there to advise city hall and, more often than not, city hall
ignored such advice. This pattern slowly is changing, primarily because
professional planners are now needed to get federal funds. No doubt
Circular A–95 of the Office of Management and Budget (OMB) was as
crucial to changing traditional patterns as any other federal policy. First
released in 1969 and later expanded in 1971, Circular A-95, as we noted in
the chapter on federalism, encourages a process of "review and comment"
on all intergovernmental projects submitted to the federal government for
funding by establishing planning clearinghouses. Usually these clearing-

---

[10] Mavis Mann Reeves and Paris N. Glendening, "Congressional Action Affecting Local
Government." In *The Municipal Yearbook, 1976.* (Washington, D.C.: International City Management Association, 1976), p. 55.

417

Policies for
the middle
class: the
planning
ethic

houses have evolved into Councils of Government or regional planning commissions that must be recognized by the Office of Management and Budget to qualify for funds.

PLANNERS AND THE PEOPLE

While such national policies as that represented by OMB Circular A–95 have given new powers to local planners, perhaps an even more significant development has been what appears to be a change of attitude by the public on the role of planning. As Samuel Kaplan has astutely observed, in the past it has been easy to

> . . . put down good government group efforts in support of rational land use by joining with special interests in waving the red flag. Master planning "socialism," and the reputations of some well-intentioned residents were smeared at local hearings by thinly veiled red baiting. The motto of America's suburbs was well stated in the inscription on a wall in the meeting hall of the county supervisors of Los Angeles: "This county is founded on free enterprise. Cherish and preserve it."[11]

And, as Kaplan notes, look what has happened in Los Angeles!

Perhaps because of Los Angeles's example—an example, some contend, of the world's worst case of urban sprawl—planning may be gaining popular acceptance. Studies indicate that the satisfaction of a community's residents correlates with increasing levels of planning and the legal power of local officials to plan. One study of ten communities found that where urban planning was the most extensive, the residents were the most satisfied with the areas in which they lived. Although there was not a one hundred percent match, the tendency was that the greater degree of planning, the higher the people's satisfaction.[12]

WHO ARE THE PLANNERS?

While planning has traditionally been quintessentially middle class in both outlook and action, the preceding discussion at least implies that the planning profession is growing increasingly political and in the process is recognizing the needs of other kinds of people. Planners as professionals are beginning to learn that to get along they must go along. Still, the field's acceptance of politics as legitimate is by no means total, as no professional planner wishes to "prostitute" his or her values for the sake of politics. A survey taken in 1971 confirmed that planners are very professionally oriented. More than one-third of the planning directors in big cities come

---

[11] From *The Dream Deferred* by Samuel Kaplan. Copyright © 1976 by Samuel Kaplan. Used by permission of The Seabury Press, Inc.

[12] J. B. Lansing, R. W. Marans, and R. B. Zehner, *Planned Residential Environments.* (Ann Arbor, Mich.: University of Michigan, Institute for Social Research, 1970).

directly from an educational background in planning; most of the remaining two-thirds have educations in engineering, landscape architecture, and public administration, respectively. Seventy percent of all planning directors have planning as their chief work background; of the remainder most have backgrounds in enforcing zoning and code ordinances, engineering, and public administration. Planning directors are extremely well educated, considerably more so than the typical city council member, with 39 percent holding master's degrees and another 48 percent having bachelor's degrees.[13]

THE POLITICIZATION OF PLANNERS

Given these kinds of educational and professional backgrounds, it is not surprising that some planners elect not to participate in the political process to get their plans implemented. A number of studies have shown that planners adopt three distinctly different professional roles. Francine Rabinowitz has categorized these roles on a professional–political continuum. They range from the *technician,* who develops plans purely on the basis of professional values and who does not get involved in whether or not the plan is accepted by the local government; to the *broker,* who plays the role of a confidential advisor to local officials and is concerned over whether or not a plan is "marketable"; to the *mobilizer* who goes out and seeks support in the community for the comprehensive plan and solicits the backing of various local interest groups.[14] Corresponding roles are posited by David C. Ranney, who used the same concepts but dubbed them *political agnostic, confidential advisor,* and *political activist.*[15]

In the 1960s the planning profession itself began to recognize that politics did play a role in urban planning. An example of this recognition was the rise of "advocacy planning," by which was meant that planners legitimately could be overtly political in getting their plans accepted by the community. Most "advocate planners," as they call themselves, were and are consciously in favor of achieving the goals of the poor, the black, and the dispossessed— advocacy planning clearly was a departure from the normal, staid, middle-class perspective of professional planning.[16]

Although the concept of advocacy planning has declined in recent years, nonetheless, the planning profession is becoming increasingly political in its viewpoints and is accepting politics as a legitimate component of the planning process. Increasingly, planning agencies themselves are becoming

---

[13] B. Douglas Harman, "City Planning Agencies: Organization, Staffing, and Functions." In *The Municipal Yearbook, 1972.* (Washington, D.C.: International City Management Association, 1972), p. 63.

[14] Francine Rabinowitz, *City Politics and Planning.* (New York: Atherton, 1969).

[15] David C. Ranney, *Planning and Politics in the Metropolis.* (Columbus, Ohio: Charles E. Merrill, 1969), pp. 147–150.

[16] See, for example, Paul Davidoff, "Advocacy and Pluralism in Planning." *Journal of the American Institute of Planners* 31 (December, 1965) 331–338.

419

Policies for
the middle
class: the
planning
ethic

integrated into the political workings of city hall and the state capital. Moreover, such a trend long has been advocated by scholars of urban affairs. Herbert J. Gans, for example, has urged that planners see themselves as—and become—policy makers, arguing that to remain "technicians" or "political agnostics" will keep planners in ineffectual positions at a time when they are sorely needed if metropolitan growth is to be intelligently managed.[17] As Allensworth has observed, "The planning bureaucracy is immeshed in politics, and planning policy can normally be traced to a political base. The planning administrator cannot escape this reality."[18]

THE POLITICS OF THE PLANNING PROCESS: LAND USE

Political and popular realities may be giving more power to planners, but economic reality is not. The suburban tract developer, in the view of many, remains the antithesis of rationally planning the more intelligent use of land since, in essence, comprehensive regional and urban planning is the determination of how land will be used to best benefit people—all people. A fact of politics is that most people see their own special interests as being in the interests of all the people ("What's good for General Motors is good for the country!"). Some states and cities, however, have made conscious efforts to build citizen participation into the planning process in a way that genuinely reflects the interests of all the citizens.

THE LOCAL LOBBIES OF LAND USE PLANNING

Nevertheless, state, regional, and local planning agencies must deal with different interest groups and citizens' associations.[19] The real estate community demands plans that will facilitate development. Builders favor growth, physical revitalization of the downtown, and zoning recommendations that bring more profits for new land uses; they tend to favor increased population density. Construction interests also prefer "flexible" subdivision administration policies. Professional planners (who themselves can be seen as an interest group) generally like seeing their somewhat abstruse models transferred to the world of political and economic realities—a wish that, on occasion, is less than realistic. Then too, the professional planners are public employees, and as such often have their jobs at stake when the planning process gets rough.

Political executives, such as the mayor or city manager, display a desire to control the planning process as a means of building their political bases.

---

[17] Herber J. Gans, "The Need for Planners Trained in Policy Formulation." *Urban Planning in Transition,* Earnest Erder, ed. (New York: Grossman, 1970), pp. 239–245.

[18] Allensworth, *Public Administration*, p. 52.

[19] The following discussion on interest groups is drawn from *ibid,* pp. 46–47.

Businesspersons obviously tend to favor plans that encourage commerce and that do not introduce new competitors into the community. Commercial interests also favor painting as roseate pictures of their towns as is humanly possible, as in the typical Chamber of Commerce brochures. The state judiciary can be viewed as an interest group in that it may provide standards to which community decision makers must adhere, particularly in the areas of subdivision regulation, administration, and zoning. Other state bureaucracies often act as lobbyists in the planning process. Perhaps the most notorious of these are the state highway commissions. Highway interests can be extremely effective in assuring that the community plan is compatible with their plans for future roads and highways, despite the fact that planning commissions and highways commissions often act separately of each other. Similarly, sewer and water districts, public works agencies, school districts, and public housing authorities may have their own uses for comprehensive plans. Of course, citizens' associations are themselves interest groups and usually call for a plan that preserves the status quo and stops land from being developed. In contrast to real estate interests, they favor low residential densities and maintaining the "integrity" of existing neighborhoods.[20]

When planning agencies call public hearings, which often are required by federal law if an agency wishes to keep on getting federal dollars, citizen groups can stage a political drama of the highest order. Consider the following quotation from one such participant:

> Public hearings are unique events, with many bordering on mass hysteria. I have seen at hearings mature professionals transformed into raving demagogues, liberal politicians into fascists, modest laymen into nitpicking self-appointed experts, and loving mothers into shrews. I have heard at hearings clergymen curse, atheists call on God with conviction, and more threats than I care to remember. School auditoriums built and maintained with hard-to-come-by taxpayers' dollars have been wrecked, not by vandals or juvenile delinquents, but by law-abiding parents out of anger when confronted simply by multi-colored charts and maps of a plan presented "for discussion purposes only." I have witnessed at hearings bloody fights and, despite my bulk, have been pushed and shoved and had my clothes ripped. To stand before a packed auditorium and sense the fear of an audience over a particular plan turn into hate is a frightening feeling.[21]

In other words, citizens can be interest groups, too.

THE ZONING ZANINESS

Perhaps the single greatest—and most fear-inducing—power that local planners have is the power to zone. Few areas of public policy make suburban homeowners and the Junior Chamber of Commerce angrier than proposed changes in zoning. Zoning policies, believe it or not, are as close

---

[20] *Ibid,*, p. 46.

[21] Kaplan, *The Dream Deferred,* pp. 67–68.

421

Policies for
the middle
class: the
planning
ethic

as America comes to a comprehensive land-use policy. At root, zoning simply is a plan of how certain sections of the community may be used—for stores, residences, recreation, or whatever. Virtually all American communities have zoning regulations, although Houston stands alone as a major city that not only does not have but has never had zoning. There are sections of Houston where expensive townhouses are located next to topless-bottomless bars, but neither residents or businesses in that city seem to mind. Such a combination may not be acceptable in other cities, however.

Those urbanists who are for the abolition of zoning in the style of Houston argue that zoning inflates housing costs by limiting the amount of land available for residential building. Moreover, simply by restricting the supply of land on which homes can be built, and then further limiting the number of houses that can be built per acre, zoning forces the construction of dull and dreary housing developments by requiring (as zoning regulations often require) uniform building heights and specifications on what houses and apartments may look like. They also argue that zoning contributes to sprawl and a waste of energy since it makes it difficult to convert low-density residential areas in old inner cities into apartments. It fosters the bureaucratization of housing development and thus encourages graft because so much money is at stake in urban development. Finally, they argue, zoning encourages prejudice against the poor and minorities, a point to which we shall return later.[22]

Cities, of course, may enact land-use controls in addition to those that are permitted by traditional zoning ordinances. In a survey of all municipalities with ten thousand people and more, it was found that of nine possible types of land-use controls, only 17 percent of the cities had not enacted any of them.[23] The single most popular land use control was that of requiring developers to install public facilities (such as sewer lines); 83 percent of the cities responding had enacted such ordinances. Roughly a quarter of all the responding cities had passed ordinances regarding architectural appearance, growth limitations, and historical preservation; from one-third to one-half of the cities had ordinances that zoned for flood plains, open spaces, and natural resources; 12 percent had marsh land controls.

TDR: ALTERNATIVE TO ZONING

An innovative new concept in local land use control policies is known as "Transferrable Development Rights," or TDR, which is gaining popularity in the Northeast as well as in Colorado and Alaska.[24] TDR is a compromise

[22] The arguments against zoning are drawn from: Neal R. Pierce, "Municipal Zoning, Dinosaur of the 1970s." Syndicated column, June 3, 1977.

[23] Steve Carter, Lyle Sumek, and Murray Frost, "Local Environmental Management." In *Municipal Yearbook, 1974.* (Washington, D.C.: International City Management Association, 1974), p. 259.

[24] The discussion of Transferrable Development Rights is drawn from: Gladwin Hill, "New Community Planning Tool Potential Boon." *New York Times,* October 12, 1977.

between the values of the zoners and the antizoners and, in many ways, is as satisfactory an approach to the problem of urban land use as any. TDR separates the right to improve property from the right to own property, much in the same sense that the right of prospectors to exploit minerals and oil that may be found under the ground can be separated from ownership of the land's surface. Under a TDR program a community can directly give or withhold development rights in order to restrict development in one area and to encourage development in another. Thus, owners of property in an area where development is banned, such as a street of historic value, are permitted to develop someone else's property in another section, where development is needed. In the event that property owners do not wish to develop property in another portion of the city, they can sell their development rights to another party and thus be compensated. An example is the case of New York's Grand Central Station, where the courts committed the city to preserving the building as a cultural landmark, rather than permitting it to be replaced by a skyscraper, and compensated its owner, the Penn Central Railroad, by granting it rights to develop other portions of the city.

TDR may appear to be a violation of the traditional property right, but it is in many ways more equitable than zoning. Under zoning the property owner is not compensated at all if new restrictions are imposed on how he or she may use his or her land. Similarly, when property is condemned for public purposes (such as urban renewal), property owners may be compensated, but urban funds that are available for doing so are often limited. Thus, TDR permits historic and cultural monuments to be preserved while still permitting investment to flourish in a community.

ZONING FOR NO-GROWTH

In recent years, zoning has been used to encourage policies of nongrowth in communities.[25] From an environmental perspective, at least in some cases, restricting growth through zoning can be advantageous, but from the perspective of social equity such use of zoning becomes extremely controversial.

The movement to limit municipal growth through zoning can be traced to the town of Ramapo, a suburb of New York City. Between 1960 and 1970 Ramapo grew from 38,000 to 78,000 people, and the land being used by those additional Ramapoans was destroying what many felt was the character of the village. Consequently, Ramapo developed an unusual eighteen-year, "delayed-growth" model. This permitted the phased development of various service facilities such as water, power lines, and sewers and had the effect of rationing building permits to developers. Ramapo's

---

[25] The following discussions of Ramapo and Petaluma are drawn from Kaplan, *The Dream Deferred*, pp. 77–79.

423

Policies for
the middle
class: the
planning
ethic

policy quickly was challenged in the courts (*Golden* v. *Planning Board of Ramapo*); Ramapo lost the first round, but then won in the New York court of appeals. In 1972 the United States Supreme Court refused to review the decision, thus upholding the position of Ramapo.

Ramapo was an indirect inspiration to the citizens of Petaluma, a village near San Francisco. Petaluma had grown from 14,000 people in 1960 to 25,000 in 1970 and to 30,000 by the end of 1971. Petaluma was more straight-forward in its policy to limit growth than Ramapo and flatly rationed the community's growth to five hundred new residential units a year for the next five years. The city council's policy was ratified by Petaluma's voters in 1973. The city's ordinance soon was challenged in the courts (*Construction Industry Association of Sonoma County* v. *City of Petaluma*). Petaluma's lawyers contended that adding more Petalumans would over-burden the city's sanitation and school facilities, thus forcing the citizens to vote for increased taxes. The U.S. district court held against Petaluma, ruling that "neither Petaluma's city officials nor the local electorate may use their power to disapprove bonds at the polls as a weapon to define or destroy fundamental constitutional rights," notably the rights of people to travel and settle.

By this time Petaluma was becoming a symbol, with environmental and urban interests taking the side of the city, and civil rights groups and construction interests banding against Petaluma. Petaluma took its case to the federal appeals court which reversed the decision of the lower court, stating that Petaluma had a right to use its zoning power "in its own self interest" by employing zoning as "lawfully delegated to it by the state." The judges observed that "the federal court is not a superzoning board" and "should not be called on to mark the point at which legitimate local interests are outweighed by legitimate regional interests."

Since *Petaluma,* a number of local governments have wrangled over civil rights and status quo. In part, this controversy is racial and economic since, by restricting new housing, local governments are limiting the number of new residents that may join their communities and often these policies can amount to *de facto* segregation of whites and blacks, rich and poor. Never-theless, zoning for no-growth, or for controlled growth, is not the same as "exclusionary zoning," which often amounts to a flat ban on low-income housing (but not on higher grade housing) in an effort to keep out minorities; we consider exclusionary zoning practices in the next chapter.

TOWARD STATEWIDE ZONING

The states are increasingly turning to comprehensive land-use plans, and many states have established creative working relationships with their towns and cities in evolving comprehensive land-use programs.

By the mid–1970s twenty-seven of the states had a total of thirty-eight general land-use programs, and five of these states had created ground-breaking comprehensive state programs permitting state officials to deal directly with local developers. In addition, all of the thirty eligible states participate in the federal coastal zone management program, and five of these states have enacted special laws to protect their shore lines. Forty-two states have passed preferential tax policies that encourage farmers and other owners of large parcels of land to retain their holdings, and thus resist selling out to real estate developers. Thirty-four states have legislation that deals with the siting of power plants, and thirty-eight states regulate strip mining.[26]

While the states have not been shy in their desire to encourage the planning of land use, enacting measures that grant governments regulatory authority to control land use is another matter, and most states have ceded a large portion of that authority to their local governments. Indeed, the local government is normally given the flexibility to plan for particular state objectives as well as particular local goals; the state develops the comprehensive plan and leaves the enforcement, by and large, to the local government.

California may become an exception to this rule. In 1977 Governor Jerry Brown proposed a sweeping reform of California's laws concerning urban growth, amounting to what some have called the most comprehensive proposal for land-use management in the nation. Brown rejected the development of new towns, noting that his state had become "the symbol of urban sprawl throughout the world," and instead concentrated on reviving existing cities and suburbs, protecting prime farmland, distributing industry and other commerce more equitably, and providing housing, employment, and public services to the 4 to 8 million new residents expected to migrate to California—already the nation's most populous state—over the next twenty years. Richer communities would be required to share revenues from their sales and property taxes with poorer communities on a regional basis; cities and counties would be ordered to adopt five-year rehabilitation programs; slum lords would be replaced by court-appointed "receivers" to manage rehabilitation; and other comparatively "radical" strategies also were proposed. California, the symbol of sprawl and perhaps the most urbanized state in the country with 90 percent of its 22 million people teeming in a mere half-dozen metropolitan areas, will be watched carefully to see whether or not it adopts or rejects such a plan, and whether or not it implements it.[27]

THE POLITICS OF THE PLANNING PROCESS: TRANSPORTATION

Thus far, we have examined the public planning process as it relates to urban areas and land use. But there is at least one other major field of importance to state and local governments where planners are having a

---

[26] Council on Environmental Quality, *Environmental Quality.* Seventh Annual Report of the Council on Environmental Quality. (Washington, D.C.: U.S. Government Printing Office, 1976), p. 67.

[27] Gladwin Hill, "California Growth: Sprawl Control Suggested." *New York Times,* June 12, 1977.

425

Policies for
the middle
class: the
planning
ethic

renewed impact, and that is transportation. Planning for transportation has its own peculiar politics. For better or worse, the politics of transportation planning can be summarized in a single word: highways.

In the mid-1970s the federal, state, and local governments spent more than $21 billion for their 3.8 million miles of roads and highways. Expenditures by state and local governments just for highways, excluding such other kinds of transportation expenditures (such as aviation, waterways, and mass transit), are the third largest consumer of local funds after education and public welfare.[28]

FINANCING HIGHWAYS

Highways in America are financed from five major sources of revenues: toll roads, property taxes, special assessments, user taxes, and federal aid. The most important are user taxes and federal aid, and significant among the former are the state taxes on gasoline and motor vehicle licenses. Approximately half of all state and local highway revenues are derived from user taxes levied on vehicle owners. The federal government also collects gasoline taxes to the tune of four cents per gallon, generating almost $6 billion a year, and these revenues are deposited in the Federal Highway Trust Fund. The Federal Highway Trust Fund, known to some as the "ever-normal trough," is a device set up under the Federal Highway Act of 1956 that absorbs the lion's share of all federal gasoline taxes. The fund is earmarked specifically for paying for the interstate highway system. Currently, the federal government pays 90 percent of interstate highway construction costs across the country; the states chip in a nominal 10 percent.

THE STATES ORGANIZE FOR TRANSIT

Highway policy in this country represents a partnership between the states and the national government, although with the passage of the Federal Highway Act of 1956 the partnership became considerably more the responsibility of the federal government than the state governments. Still, the states in the 1970s made notable efforts to upgrade their role not only in the area of highways and roads (the states are solely responsible for some 790,000 miles of the nation's roads), but in all types of transportation. In 1977 thirty-one states had departments of transportation, in contrast to the more traditional bureau of public roads, although each department of transportation had varying levels of responsibility and authority. Like the Federal Highway Trust Fund, state departments of transportation rely on an ever-normal trough of earmarked user taxes as a means of financing highways and other types of transportation construction.[29]

---

[28] James F. Runke and Charles G. Whitmire, "Transportation." In *Book of the States, 1976–77.* (Lexington, Ky.: Council of State Governments, 1976), p. 348, and James F. Runke, "Transportation," *Book of the States, 1978-79,* p. 368.

[29] Runke and Whitmire, "Transportation," p. 350.

THE FEDS AND HIGHWAYS

The federal government long has had an impact on the state and local system of roads, but especially in the area of interstate highways. At first the federal role in transportation policy was primarily rural, as expressed by the Federal Aid Road Act of 1916, which provided the first regular funding for public highway construction. A departure from this rural orientation was signalled in 1944 when the Federal Highway Act was passed. This act helped develop roads designed to help farmers get to markets, but it also provided for the extension of primary roads in urban areas. This latter innovation, known as "ABC funds," still is continued today, and federal funds are given to the states on a matching basis.

The Federal Highway Act of 1944 also promoted the development of the national system of interstate highways, under the logic that such highways were necessary for national defense, but it was only in 1956 that a new Federal Highway Act authorized enormous amounts of money to develop the interstate highway system. It was this new act which stipulated that highways could be developed with 90 percent federal funding and 10 percent state funding, an opportunity that the states could not resist. While the act called for the completion of the interstate highway system by 1972, only 87 percent of the goal was reached by that year. Thus, Congress in 1973 enacted the Federal Aid Highway Act. As amended in 1974 the act continued the 42,500 miles of the interstate highway system with authorizations of $3 billion and more for each year through 1979. The rationale behind the legislation is that official projections indicate that motor vehicle travel may increase by nearly 50 percent above 1975 levels by the year 1990.

THE CAR AND THE POLICY OF IMBALANCE

An incredible 143 million motor vehicles travel on America's nearly 4 million miles of tarmac. Highway travel dominates the nation's transportation by a ratio of more than ten to one. In fact, approximately 94 percent of all "person-miles" of travel in the United States is accomplished exclusively by highway vehicles (both automobiles and buses) and, within cities, the proportion is even higher—98 percent. Only 4 percent of this figure represents travel by bus as opposed to car. In the large urban areas where rail travel, such as subways and trains, is available, the combined travel on these two transportation modes amounts to only 11 percent of all daily trips; the remaining 89 percent is done by car.[30]

Four-fifths of all households in America have at least one car and 30 percent have two or more. Americans spend about twice as much each year just to register their cars as they do to ride buses or subways. Consumers

---

[30] *1974 National Transportation Report,* quoted in *ibid.,* p. 350, and Runke, "Transportation," p. 368.

427

Policies for
the middle
class: the
planning
ethic

paid more than $103 billion to buy and maintain cars in 1973; in comparison they spent $1.6 billion for public transit.[31]

One reason behind this clear preference for cars is the fact that automobiles are very convenient. Car drivers who travel ten miles to work average twenty-four minutes in commuting time; public transportation riders average fifty minutes to cover the same distance. The average time for trips to work is twenty-one minutes for the car driver and thirty-seven minutes for the transit rider. Moreover, the cost difference between rapid transit systems and private car is not that great. In 1973 the full economic cost of urban driving was calculated at slightly more than twenty-six cents per mile; using rapid transit cost twenty-five cents per mile. On the other hand, riding a bus costs the consumer only eight to nine cents per mile.

In the big cities, however, the reliance on urban transit is considerably greater. In New York 61 percent of the city's residents use public transit to and from work; in Boston the figure is 38 percent; in Philadelphia 37 percent; and in Chicago 36 percent. Fourteen major metropolitan areas account for 70 percent of *all* the nation's public transit passengers, and New York City alone accounts for 38 percent.

NATIONAL POLICIES FOR MASS TRANSIT

That America's urban transit policy is out of balance and favors the car is so obvious that even Congress has begun to notice. Through 1963 the federal government spent no money whatever on public transit, and in 1964 total federal support was a nominal $30 million; by contrast, total federal support for urban mass transit is now approaching $5 billion a year.[32]

Although the Federal Aid Highway Act of 1973 extended the controversial Highway Trust Fund, the act also permitted, for the first time, funds traditionally earmarked exclusively for highways to be used for urban mass transportation. This victory for the friends of mass transit was not a particularly financially significant one, but it was a qualitative change. Under the act, $780 million from the Federal Highway Trust Fund for fiscal 1974 and some $200 million for each of the years thereafter are allocated to cities and towns for developing public transit systems, including buses, railroads, and highways. These projects are to be selected by appropriate local officials in concert with state governments. The act also established a ratio of 80 percent federal funds and 20 percent local funds for urban mass transportation administration grants.

In 1974 the National Mass Transportation Assistance Act was passed. This act expanded state and local opportunities for developing public transit

---

[31] The data in this and the following two paragraphs are drawn from: Wilfred Owen, *Transportation for Cities.* (Washington, D.C.: Brookings Institution, 1976), pp. 5–6 and 10.
[32] *Ibid.*, p. 1.

systems, providing $11.8 billion over a six-year period from 1975 through 1980.[33]

The legislation, while not entirely adequate, is needed to develop mass transportation facilities. For the past thirty years, the number of people carried by public transportation has declined from 23 billion passengers a year in 1945 to less than 7 billion in 1974. The public clearly prefers the automobile, but this may be due to the unavailability of alternative transportation. In the 1940s and the 1950s big cities (Los Angeles is a representative example), bowing to pressure from organized interest groups such as automobile manufacturers and oil companies, tore up trolley car tracks and discarded bus lines. It also seems clear that state and local transportation officials still prefer the automobile. During the first year that the Federal Aid Highway Act was operative, only two cities, New York and East St. Louis, Illinois, actually applied for and received funds; both used the funds to purchase additional buses.[34] Moreover, a survey concluded that transportation officials in a number of states were heavily biased in favor of more road construction and did not cotton to the idea of developing public transportation facilities.[35] Perhaps because of these attitudes held by state and local officials, plus a funding ratio that is less advantageous than the ratio for highway construction, only fifteen cities in the mid-1970s had rapid transit systems that either were operable or under construction.

"PARA-TRANSIT" AND THE SMALL-IS-BEAUTIFUL MOVEMENT

Another possible reason why state and local administrators are reluctant to embrace rapid transit may be that they recognize that such systems are not the proper solution to the problems of urban mobility. An interesting new approach to transportation policy is the adoption of the "small-is-beautiful" philosophy, which is beginning to make an impact on the thinking of transportation planners. The approach is called *para-transit,* and it refers to independent car pools, van pools, jitnies, and taxis, rather than big-time mass transit such as subways, trains, and buses.[36] The Twin Cities (Minneapolis and St. Paul) are among the leading municipalities in the development of para-transit. Local officials discovered that only 17 percent of the jobs in the Twin Cities area were located in downtown Minneapolis and St. Paul, and transportation planners concluded that to push increased busing and rail service to the downtown made little sense. In 1977 the Minnesota legislature appropriated $5.5 million to experiment with para-transit in

---

[33] Runke and Whitmire, "Transportation," p. 353.

[34] Ralph Blumenthal, "Mass Transit Use of Fund Lags." *New York Times,* April 21, 1975.

[35] "Transit Funds Weaken Review." *New York Times,* April 27, 1975.

[36] The discussion of para-transit is drawn from: Neal R. Pierce, "Transportation Planners Thinking Smaller." Syndicated column, June 17, 1977.

429

Policies for
the middle
class: the
planning
ethic

both urban and rural areas. One barrier to para-transit systems is the number of legalisms that often discourage or prohibit para-transit operations, notably restrictions that are the result of pressure from big labor, which perceives such efforts as a threat to union employment. Indeed, it has been estimated that regulatory obstacles prohibit 99.7 percent of drivers and 99.8 percent of vehicles on the road from providing transportation services for a fee to others. Yet, given the fact that rapid transit systems cost the consumer almost as much as a private automobile (buses, as noted, are the exception), para-transit could be an attractive alternative—provided that public policy permits it to flourish.

PUBLIC TRANSIT AS SOCIAL JUSTICE

Public transportation, whether small or large in scale, is needed for reasons other than simple convenience and economy. (Projections indicate that raising the average number of occupants in cars going to and from jobs from its present 1.2 people per car to 2 people can save more than one million barrels of oil a day.)[37] Public transit also is a matter of social justice. The old, the young, the poor, and the deprived stand out as groups that have been denied the necessary right of physical mobility because of lack of access to a car. In 1968, 32 percent of all households in the central cities did not have a car; only 13 percent of the households in the suburbs did not have one. Forty-four percent of Americans over 65 years of age had no car. In riot-torn Watts in Los Angeles only 38 percent of 538 males interviewed in 1967 had access to useable automobiles; the remainder had to rely on mass transit services, such as they were, or car pools.[38] Currently, nearly 55 percent of all households with incomes of $3,000 to $5,000 a year have no cars.[39] Without cars, the people who need jobs most cannot get to places of employment unless there are mass transit systems in urban areas. Thus, a balanced transportation policy becomes a matter of social justice.

THE GREAT GAME OF TRANSPORTATION POLITICS

A major reason why we have an unbalanced transportation policy can be found in the nature of the political transportation game. At the national level some of the most powerful interest groups in the United States have done battle over the continuation of the Highway Trust Fund. Arguing that

---

[37] Runke and Whitmire, "Transportation," p. 351.

[38] Melvin M. Webber and Shlomo Angel, "The Social Context for Transport Policy." In *Science and Technology in the Cities.* A compilation of papers prepared for the Tenth Meeting of the Panel on Science and Technology, Committee on Science and Astronautics, U.S. House of Representatives. (Washington, D.C.: U.S. Government Printing Office, 1969), pp. 57–72.

[39] Runke and Whitmire, "Transportation," p. 350.

it be continued and used solely for highway construction are the oil industry, the automobile interests, the rubber industry, the road construction interests, the trucking industry, and the American Association of State Highway Officials. Opposing the fund are less powerful interest groups (with the exception of the railroad industry), notably the environmental interests, busing interests, and such general urban lobbies as the United States Conference of Mayors and the National League of Cities. Thus, perhaps it is not too surprising that the real impetus for rectifying the policy of imbalance in transportation politics has come from the big cities rather than from Congress.

THE CITIES AS TRANSIT INNOVATORS

Although studies indicate that federal policies are a major influence on local transportation policy making, it also is increasingly clear that the central cities are taking the lead in developing mass transit systems rather than additional highways. Robert S. Friedman, for example, has found that there is "little evidence of a relation between the wealth or industrialization level of the states and their emphasis on highway expenditure. There is, however, a significant relation between highway expenditure and metropolitanism in which the states with the highest proportion of their population living in standard metropolitan statistical areas devote the smallest proportion of state and local expenditure to highways."[40] Similarly, a significant analysis of the politics of transportation in eight big cities concluded that there was some reason to believe that local policy making for urban transit was becoming increasingly democratic, systematic, and rational, although the structure and process for local transportation needs remain fragmented and characterized by disparities.[41] One problem is a lack of any local leaders, public or private, who are concerned with the whole urban area; most leaders are incline to confront transit issues only when they reach crisis proportions. Two other concerns are competition among various municipal units and an inordinate suspicion of the city held by the suburbs.[42]

THE "LOGICS" OF TRANSIT PLANNING

More critical, perhaps, as impediments to cohesive public planning of urban transportation policy are the relationships among the various "logics" of transportation politics in metropolitan areas. Despite the fact that urban

[40] Robert S. Friedman, "State Politics and Highways." *Politics in the American States*, 2nd ed., Herbert Jacob and Kenneth N. Vines, eds. (Boston: Little, Brown, 1971), p. 518.

[41] Allen Lupo, Frank Colcord, and Edward P. Fowler, *Rites of Way: The Politics of Transportation in Boston and the U.S. City.* (Boston: Little, Brown, 1971).

[42] Frank C. Colcord, Jr., "Decision Making in Transportation Policy: A Comparative Analysis." *Southwestern Social Science Quarterly* 28 (December, 1967). Reprinted in *Politics in the Metropolis*, Thomas R. Dye and Brett W. Hawkins, eds. (Englewood Cliffs, N.J.: Prentice-Hall, 1971), pp. 205–222.

431

Policies for
the middle
class: the
planning
ethic

transportation planning undoubtedly is the cities' single most powerful tool for attaining land use goals, Frank Colcord has identified at least three conflicting logics of transportation policy making which represent competing professional and political values: the logic of the technician, the logic of the planner, and the logic of the politician.[43]

The *techician's logic* continues to dominate the decision-making process in transportation at all levels of government, and it guides the thinking behind the present highway program. The technician assumes that his field, the highway, offers a "final solution" to a narrowly defined technical problem, that of transporting people and products from point A to point B with optimal efficiency. Unfortunately, the technician's logic fails to take into account such values as torn up neighborhoods, razed homes, marred urban landscapes, displaced people, environmental degradation, and a politically alienated urban citizenry. These variables do not enter the calculations of an engineering mentality and are irrelevant to the logic of the technician.

The *planner's logic* is broader in scope but, while the planner has the potential for considering the larger mission for the metropolitan community, this mission is nearly always unexpressed. This is not to imply that community goals larger than that of getting efficiently from one point to another are not present. In fact, it is the current preeminence of the technician's logic in transportation planning circles that has unwittingly encouraged the gradual emergence of the planner's logic as a means of achieving broader community objectives.

Finally, the *politician's logic* parallels the planner's logic of fostering the broader values of the community, but the politician also is susceptible to the short-range objectives of the technician. To the politician, temporarily relieving downtown traffic congestion by building a new freeway may be a most appealing alternative in the absence of expressed objections from various citizen groups or alternative policy choices offered by other planning groups. The logic of the politician, in brief, is supremely one of staying in power and this is achieved by responding to the pressures of the moment as they relate to the politician's idea of building a "good record" over time.

These distinctive logics of transportation planning coexist in metropolises and each has its uses. The planner must express the community's goals, present and future, and offer creative solutions. The politician must cooperate with and beneficially influence the planning process, provide leadership, and yield legitimacy. The technician must find efficient, novel, and effective means for implementing community goals as identified by the planner and the politician. According to Colcord, there may be a renewed trend in establishing a harmonious relationship among these traditionally discordant transportation logics in urban areas.

---

[43] Frank C. Colcord, "The Nation," in Lupo, Colcord, and Fowler, *Rites of Way*, pp. 204–237.

CHAPTER

POLICIES
FOR THE
MIDDLE CLASS:
HOME, HEARTH,
AND RACISM

Housing policy in America is geared almost entirely toward the needs of the middle class; far more governmental subsidies are designed to help middle-class homeowners than any other economic group. In this chapter we investigate how political pressure brought by the middle class has assisted in the degeneration of housing policy into the politics of racism, and we examine the role of American governments in providing housing—and to whom.

HOUSING: AMERICA'S MOST RACIST POLICY

It is important in understanding the nation's housing dilemma to know that a family's financial condition and the quality of its housing do not necessarily bear the relationship that one would expect. The poor do not necessarily live in slums nor the relatively wealthy in suburban ranchettes. In 1966 only 34 percent of the poor lived in dilapidated housing, while 41 percent of the deteriorating housing was inhabited by families with incomes of more than $15,000 a year, a substantial sum in 1966.[1]

Why are these middle-income families in deteriorating housing living under their means? A major reason appears to be that they are not white. True, more poor people than rich people live in slums, but even more black and brown people live in slums than white people. Race is much more clearly associated with dilapidated housing than any other variable, including the ability to pay for better housing.

We read in Chapter 2 how race correlated with suburbs and inner cities (the whiter—and richer—suburbs ring the blacker—and poorer—inner cities). More significantly, even within central cities and within suburbs, blacks and browns live in more dilapidated houses than whites. In 1973 8.4 percent of all people in poor white families lived in low-income areas of central cities; by contrast, 40.4 percent of all people in black families lived in the same kinds of areas. Similar patterns were found for people of Spanish-speaking origin.[2]

These patterns are reflected in the black ghettoes, with which we are all familiar. In the forty-seven cities with black populations of more than fifty thousand, the great majority of blacks live in predominately black census tracts; blacks comprise only 5 percent of the suburban population. Projections indicate that by the year 2000 the ratio of whites living in central cities

---

[1] Henry J. Aaron, *Shelter and Subsidies: Who Benefits from Federal Housing Policies?* (Washington, D.C.: Brookings Institution, 1972), pp. 23–24.

[2] U.S. Commission on Civil Rights, *Twenty Years After Brown: Equal Opportunity in Housing.* (Washington, D.C.: U.S. Commission on Civil Rights, 1975), pp. 9–11.

will drop from about 40 percent (as of 1970) to 25 percent; the proportion of blacks will decrease from 79 percent to only slightly less than 75 percent.[3] It has been estimated that 83 percent of all black families living in the nation's central cities would have to move from an all-black block to a white one if a genuinely random pattern of housing were to be achieved in the country.[4]

The U.S. Commission on Civil Rights attributes these patterns to simple racial discrimination, and supporting data indicate that such is the case. Blacks are more poorly housed than whites at *any* rent level or home value.[5]

Tables 20–1 and 20–2 speak to the racism of American housing policy as eloquently as any data could. They show that nearly a quarter of all black families live in tenements, compared with less than 6 percent of the rest of the population. More than three times as many urban blacks as whites have no plumbing; almost six times as many Mexican-Americans as whites are living in overcrowded conditions in cities.

Within this framework of bigotry are still more convoluted patterns of housing discrimination—racist circles within racist circles. Tables 20–3 and 20–4 fill out these patterns more amply. Table 20–3 estimates how many blacks in representative cities logically should own their own homes if income (as opposed to race) were the only determinant of home ownership, and contrasts those estimates with how many blacks really do own their own homes in those cities. Overall, there are anywhere from a third to a half less

---

[3] *Ibid.*

[4] David E. Rosenbaum, "A New Rights Drive Perplexes Nation." *New York Times* (July 7, 1977), p. 28.

[5] Aaron, *Shelter and Subsidies*, pp. 33–34.

TABLE 20–1 HOUSEHOLDS LIVING IN SUBSTANDARD UNITS BY INCOME AND RACE, 1970

FAMILY INCOME	ALL RACES	WHITE & OTHER	BLACK
All households	7.4%	5.7%	23.0%
Less than $2,000	23.8	19.4	45.6
$2,000 to $2,999	15.8	12.1	34.1
$3,000 to $3,999	12.5	9.4	29.5
$4,000 to $4,999	12.3	10.7	21.5
$5,000 to $5,999	9.1	7.3	19.0
$6,000 to $6,999	7.1	6.0	15.4
$7,000 to $9,999	4.5	3.6	13.7
$10,000 to $14,999	2.1	1.8	8.6
$15,000 and over	0.9	0.9	2.0

Note: Income is estimated family income. Table is based on Bureau of the Census, 1970 Components of Inventory Change Survey, unpublished data.

Source: Executive Office of the President: Office of Management and Budget, *Social Indicators,* 1973, table 6/6.

TABLE 20–2 SELECTED CHARACTERISTICS OF URBAN HOUSING BY RACE, 1970

	Total population	White	Black	Mexican Amer.	SPANISH ORIGIN Puerto Rican	Cuban	Indian	Other races[2]
Overcrowded units[1] Percent of all units occ. by racial groups in urban areas	7.5%	5.3%	17.5%	31%	22%	24.5%	18.6%	18.4%
Units lacking some or all plumbing facilities Percent of all units occ. by racial group in urban areas	3.6%	2.7%	8.4%	6.8%	3%	2.4%	7.3%	4.3%
Median value owner-occupied units	$18,100	—	$11,600	$12,600	$18,200	$18,400	$13,500	$25,880
Median contract rent	$92	—	$73	$74	$84	$110	$81	$105.40
Percent of all urban units occ. by racial group owned	58.4%	61.8%	38.8%	49.7%	9.9%	23.4%	38.6%	40.5%

[1]Overcrowded is defined as 1.01 persons or more per room.
[2]"Other races" includes Japanese, Chinese, Filipino, Korean, and all other races (Malayan, Polynesian, Thai, etc.).

Source: U.S. Department of Commerce, Bureau of the Census, Census of Housing: 1970, Vol. 1, Part 1 *United States Summary,* tables 10, 11, 12, 13, 14; *Housing of Selected Racial Groups,* series HC(7)–9, tables A–1, A–2, A–3; *American Indians,* series PC(2)1F, table 10; *Persons of Spanish Origin,* series PC(2)–1C, table 12.

TABLE 20-3 ACTUAL AND EXPECTED PROPORTIONS OF BLACK FAMILIES WHO ARE HOMEOWNERS BY SMSA, 1960

SMSA	ACTUAL	EXPECTED
Atlanta	31%	52%
Boston	21	43
Chicago	18	47
Cleveland	30	58
Dallas	39	54
Detroit	41	67
Los Angeles/Long Beach	41	51
Newark	24	50
Philadelphia	45	66
St. Louis	34	55
Baltimore	36	61
Birmingham	44	56
Houston	46	56
Indianapolis	45	58
Memphis	37	50
New Orleans	28	40
Pittsburgh	35	59
San Francisco-Oakland	37	51

Source: John F. Kain and John M. Quigley, "Housing Market Discrimination, Homeownership, and Savings Behavior," *American Economic Review*, June 1972, table 3.

black homeowners than there ought to be if income were the only factor; apparently, blacks are discouraged from purchasing a home because of their race.[6]

When blacks are able to buy a home, they pay for it more dearly than whites. One survey found that blacks paid 2 percent to 5 percent more than whites for housing of any given quality. Another study found that the median price of owner-occupied houses was more than $2,500 higher in all-black than in all-white neighborhoods, even after adjusting for other property and neighborhood characteristics.[7]

Similarly, black renters pay more than white renters. Table 20–4 indicates the estimated "race tax" for black and brown renters in selected cities; in Chicago, for example, the typical black or brown renter pays a rent that is higher by a fifth than the white renter's payment for the same apartment.

After reviewing such data it is not surprising to learn that blacks, whether they rent or own their own homes, pay more for the roofs over their heads

---

[6] Richard F. Muth, *Cities and Housing: The Spatial Problem of Urban Residential Land Use.* (Chicago: University of Chicago Press, 1969), pp. 238–239.

[7] Ronald G. Ridker and John A. Henning, "The Determinants of Residential Property Values with Special Reference to Air Pollution." *Review of Economics and Statistics* 49 (May, 1967) 256.

437

Policies for
the middle
class: home,
hearth, and
racism

than whites. It has been calculated that the median rent paid by black renters amounts to 24 percent of their incomes, whereas white renters and renters of other races pay only 20 percent of their incomes for rent. Similarly, black homeowners devote a median of 18 percent of their incomes to shelter, while whites and others allocate only 16 percent.[8] Another study arrived at a similar conclusion from a different perspective. It found that in all-white neighborhoods renters paid about 8 percent less and homeowners paid 5 percent less than renters and homeowners in all-black areas, even allowing for such factors as comparable public services and structural soundness.[9]

In sum, from any statistical standpoint and from any empirical investigation, housing policy in America is a policy of prejudice.

THE REASONS FOR RACISM

If our contention that housing is America's most racist policy in the 1980s is accurate, then what are the reasons for this racism? Although no one can answer that question entirely, we shall review here some of the more obvious

---

[8] U.S. Commission on Civil Rights, *Twenty Years after Brown*, p. 159.

[9] John F. Kain and John M. Quigley, "Measuring the Value of Housing Quality." *Journal of the American Statistical Association* 65 (June, 1970) 540.

TABLE 20–4 ESTIMATED MARKUPS FOR
NONWHITE RENTERS, 1960–61

CITY	PERCENT
Chicago	20.4
Los Angeles	9.5
Detroit	9.6
Boston	3.1
Pittsburgh	16.9
Cleveland	12.6
Washington, D.C.	3.0
Baltimore	17.4
St. Louis	13.4
San Francisco-Oakland	0.1

Source: Robert F. Gillingham, "Place to Place Rent Comparisons Using Hedonic Quality Adjustment Techniques Research" (Washington, D.C.: U.S. Department of Labor, Bureau of Labor Statistics, Office of Prices and Living Conditions, Discussion Paper No. 7, March 1973), p. 60. These percentages represent a combined estimate of 17.6 percent for nonwhite households residing in mixed blocks (20 to 39 percent nonwhite); 22.9 percent for nonwhite households residing in predominantly nonwhite blocks (more than 40 percent nonwhite).

factors that underlie and promote racist housing policies, focusing on public
opinion, "exclusionary zoning" practices by local governments, "racial steering" by real estate brokers, and "redlining" by banks.

THE PASSING PARADE OF AMERICAN PREJUDICE

Opinion polls indicate that white bigotry is a major factor in how housing
is distributed among the races, but that prejudice may be declining significantly. In 1978, only 14 percent of whites in a major national poll said they
would be very upset if blacks moved into their neighborhoods, compared
to 33 percent fifteen years earlier; 54 percent stated they could care less if
blacks moved in.[10]

Ironically, whites recognize that blacks are discriminated against in
housing; two-thirds of urban northern respondents state that they realize
some blacks "miss out" on good housing because of discrimination. Real
estate companies are the *only* American institution recognized by a majority
of whites as "keeping Negroes down" rather than "helping Negroes." Half
of America's whites believe black protests against housing discrimination are
entirely justified. A similarly optimistic note is that white attitudes appear to
be changing. The younger the white respondent is, the more likely he or
she is to favor blacks moving into their neighborhoods. Blacks feel the same
way: "When presented with a meaningful choice between an all-black
neighborhood and a mixed neighborhood, black respondents overwhelm-
ingly favored the latter . . . .those who favored mixed areas made it clear
that they did so for positive reasons of racial harmony even more than for
the obvious advantage of good neighborhoods."[11]

Black attitudes favoring interracial housing appear to be increasing,
although there is by no means any widespread desire among blacks to live
in mostly white areas. Somewhat surprisingly, blacks (with the exceptions of
blacks in Detroit and New York City) appear to have relatively conservative
attitudes toward private property rights; majorities of urban blacks indicate
that, "an owner of property should not have to sell to Negroes,"[12] a finding
that is all the more remarkable when we realize that roughly half of the
nation's blacks are clearly dissatisfied with their own housing conditions,
and that black resentment over housing appears to be increasing. Such
conservative attitudes by blacks are even more startling when we realize that
a majority of all American blacks are fully aware of the "race tax" that they
must pay in higher rents.[13]

---

[10]Harris Poll, as cited in: Dennis A. Williams, *et al.*, "A New Racial Poll," *Newsweek* (February
26, 1979), p. 48.

[11] Thomas F. Pettigrew, "Black and White Attitudes Toward Race and Housing." In *Racial
Discrimination in the United States,* Thomas F. Pettigrew, ed. (New York: Harper and Row,
1975), pp. 100–105.

[12] *Ibid.*, p. 118.

[13] *Ibid.*, p. 119. In 1978, 58 percent of blacks said they felt discriminated against in obtaining
decent housing. See Williams, *et al.*, "A New Racial Poll," p. 53.

To assure that whites, blacks, and browns do not live beside each other, some cities and suburbs have adopted the practice of "exclusionary zoning," which is an attempt to effectively zone out low-income housing by allowing only relatively expensive housing to be built. Although some would disagree, exclusionary zoning is not quite the same as zoning for controlled growth, which we reviewed in the last chapter. In contrast to no-growth zoning, exclusionary zoning is aimed at discouraging new housing for poor people. This is accomplished by restricting the kinds of residences permitted, by tacking on unreasonable construction requirements to deliberately raise the costs, and through a variety of administrative decisions that effectively restrict development, such as minimum floor space requirements for houses, large lot sizes, and so on.[14]

The device of exclusionary zoning has been recognized by a broad spectrum of scholars and legal experts as one that is clearly segregationist. In 1978 a massive, three-year study released by the American Bar Associa-

[14] Paul Davidoff and Mary E. Brooks, "Zoning Out the Poor." In *Suburbia,* Philip C. Dolce, ed. (Garden City: Anchor, 1976), pp. 145–147.

THE TREADWELLS

"THE POOR NEEDN'T ALWAYS BE WITH US, TREADWELL...IT'S BASICALLY A MATTER OF ZONING."

BOB BUGG. Courtesy of Chicago Tribune—New York News Syndicate, Inc.

tion stated that the practice has helped make new housing prohibitively costly for more than half of all Americans.[15]

Perhaps the most significant court test of exclusionary zoning involved Mount Laurel, New Jersey, a mostly white township that borders Camden, a community that is largely black and Puerto Rican. In 1975 Mount Laurel's long-standing zoning ordinances were overturned by the New Jersey Supreme Court on the grounds that, "every such municipality must, by its land use regulations, presumptively make realistically possible an appropriate variety and choice of housing."[16] Mount Laurel's zoning practices had excluded all dwellings except single-family detached houses and had included restrictions on minimum lot sizes, bedrooms, building sizes, and a few other items. The *Mount Laurel* decision has been hailed as "the most encouraging sign to date that exclusionary suburban zoning practices are being recognized as discriminatory."[17]

REALTORS, RACISM, AND "RACIAL STEERING"

Despite some encouraging signs of change, many whites do not want to live next to blacks, and real estate brokers have reacted accordingly. Indeed, real estate agents may have overreacted in their apparent zeal to keep the races separate and unequal. For example, a thorough investigation of about one hundred real estate agents in Detroit revealed "subtle" but nevertheless widespread discrimination against blacks seeking to buy suburban homes.[18]

The most widespread form of racial discrimination as practiced by real estate brokers is called *racial steering*. Both whites and blacks (but more commonly blacks) are encouraged to rent or buy a home in a neighborhood of their own race. Racial steering is against the Civil Rights Act of 1968, but identifying it and proving it in court is seldom easy.

In 1978 the most extensive study on racial steering ever conducted was completed. Sponsored by the Department of Housing and Urban Development, the survey made 3,300 checks with real estate firms in forty cities and found that blacks faced a 75 percent chance of being discriminated against by realtors when searching for an apartment to rent, and a 60 percent chance when looking for a house to buy. The researchers found that 20 to 30 percent of the real estate agencies engaged in discriminatory practices, and this was especially true in thirteen midwestern cities.[19]

---

[15] Richard P. Fishman, ed., *Housing for All Under Law: New Directions in Housing, Land Use, and Planning Law.* A Report of the American Bar Association Advisory Commission on Housing and Urban Growth. (Cambridge, Mass.: Ballinger, 1978).

[16] *Southern Burlington County NAACP, et al.* v. *Township of Mount Laurel*, quoted in Davidoff and Brooks, "Zoning Out the Poor," p. 156.

[17] *Ibid.*, p. 161.

[18] United Press International, February 21, 1977, syndicated nationally.

[19] National Committee Against Discrimination in Housing, as quoted by United Press International, April 17, 1978, syndicated nationally.

One reason why racial steering by realtors is relatively common relates to the role of the friendly American banker. In financing new homes for black and brown people, banks practice what is known as *redlining*. Although bankers generally deny that they redline, it is common knowledge that banking institutions can and do make it very difficult for a home buyer to purchase a house in a black, brown, or even integrated neighborhood. Indeed, a survey by the Federal Home Loan Bank Board found that 30 percent of the responding mortgage lenders admitted to disqualifying whole neighborhoods for home loans because of their "residential composition."[20] Some mortgage lenders responding to the poll openly admitted that the race of an applicant was a factor in determining whether he or she would be given a loan or the terms under which the loan would be made. Surprisingly, it was only in 1973 that the Federal Home Loan Bank Board for the first time specifically prohibited lenders from posing questions concerning race.

In 1975 Congress reluctantly passed the Mortgage Disclosure Act, under which some eighty-five hundred mortgage lenders were obliged to disclose data on their lending practices. Information obtained under the law found that about fifty such institutions in twenty-five cities indicated they curtailed their investments in older neighborhoods, in areas with large numbers of working-class families, and in sections of town with significant numbers of minority residents. Conversely, the institutions surveyed invested more than $109.8 million in a single year in neighborhoods that were not redlined.[21]

In contrast to the federal government, some states and cities have been notably aggressive in attempting to eliminate redlining policies. Boston, Chicago, Cleveland, Cincinnati, Philadelphia, and Rochester, for example, all have adopted ordinances that mandate city funds be deposited only in banks and lending institutions that disclose their lending policies for central cities. Illinois first adopted legislation in 1975 that required banks to disclose their mortgage loan patterns, and eight additional states followed suit during the next year.[22]

THE FEDERAL ROLE: MAKING HOMES FOR MIDDLE AMERICA

Housing people is essentially a state and local matter but the federal government has long been involved in planning housing policy. In 1934 the Federal Housing Administration (FHA) was created; it provides federal insurance and low down payments on long-term home mortgage loans. In

---

[20] Samuel Kaplan, *The Dream Deferred.* (New York: Seabury, 1976), p. 100.

[21] United Press International, November 8, 1976, syndicated nationally.

[22] Anne D. Stubbs, "Community Development and Housing." *Book of the States, 1978–79.* (Lexington, Ky.: Council of State Governments, 1978), p. 477.

the same year the first national housing act was passed; it authorized the formation of private secondary mortgage markets. These two legislative actions marked the entrance of the federal government into state and local housing policy in a big way. In 1938 the Federal and National Mortgage Association (nicknamed Fannie Mae) was set up as a conduit between idle savings and people who needed to borrow funds for new construction. The Housing Act of 1937, however, created the first permanent and direct subsidy program for low-income families. Under the act, the federal government pays the annual principal and interest on long-term, tax-exempt bonds used to finance the construction of new housing by local housing authorities set up by state law. In 1949 Congress passed another Housing Act that represented the first comprehensive housing and community development law. It provided substantial increases in funding for low-rent public housing and was the basis of the urban renewal program. In 1954 yet another Housing Act was enacted; it expanded earlier programs and was aimed at fostering total community development. This act mandated for the first time the preservation of existing structures, relocating families that were displaced by urban renewal projects, and some community-wide citizen participation in the planning of urban renewal.

The 1960s witnessed a spate of federally initiated activities in the area of planning for new housing. The Housing Act of 1961 was aimed toward finding new and rehabilitated housing for low-income families and the elderly. In 1965 Congress wrote a variation into the public housing program that allowed local housing authorities to lease dwellings in privately owned buildings and to make them available to families that were eligible for regular public housing. In 1965 Congress also created the Department of Housing and Urban Development. In 1967 two major presidential commissions on housing were established, the National Commission on Urban Problems and the President's Commission on Urban Housing. In response to the recommendations of both commissions, Congress passed the Housing and Urban Development Act of 1968. It called for the production or rehabilitation of 26 million housing units within ten years, including 6 million units for low- and moderate-income families. The act marked the first time that Congress had specified a housing goal in terms of real housing units within an established time frame.

In 1974 Congress passed the first Housing and Community Development Act. Under the act the secretary of HUD was authorized to make assistance payments on behalf of lower-income families who were living in new or substantially rehabilitated rental units. It did not, however, provide assistance for new construction or rehabilitation; the cost of these projects were borne by the developer or owner. The 1974 act (and its 1977 extension) also reflected a desire on a part of federal officials to begin a foundation for a national housing allowance plan; thus, the rental subsidy is tied to the *family* rather than to the *housing unit*. This innovation represents a real departure from past federal housing policies, although in a more traditional

443

Policies for
the middle
class: home,
hearth, and
racism

mode the act called for the construction or rehabilitation of 400,000 units annually for the next two years.

In 1977 Congress passed a second Housing and Community Development Act and substantially increased the funding of the 1974 act by signing into law a $14.7 billion program. The rent subsidies, together with additional financial aid to cities, assisted 345,000 more families to find housing at rents they could afford.

Though the federal role in housing may appear to be aimed at helping the poor, national policy has actually helped the middle class far more than any other economic group. The creation of the FHA and "Fannie Mae" in the 1930s were major boons to middle-class home purchasers, and the urban renewal programs consistently were oriented toward middle-class business interests located in the downtown metropolises. For example, the Housing Act of 1949, which initiated urban renewal, specified that any new developments replacing slums in cities must be "predominantly residential." Yet the Housing Act of 1954 added a 10 percent exception to this requirement; in 1959 the exception was increased to 20 percent; in 1961 the exception went to 30 percent; and in 1965 it was hiked to 35 percent. In short, businesspersons were and are the main concern in urban renewal.

Federal income tax policy also favors middle-class housing through the tax deductions on mortgage interest. Thus, in 1962 the federal government spent an estimated $280 million to subsidize housing for the poor, an amount that included savings resulting from income tax deductions as well as public housing and other forms of public assistance. But during the same year the federal government spent an estimated $2.9 *billion* to subsidize housing for those with middle-class incomes, when savings from income tax deductions are included.[23] And an analysis of the 1976 federal budget indicated that the highest 1 percent of the top income earners in the nation received 10 percent of all housing subsidies (including tax breaks), while the lower *half* of all income earners received only 25 percent of all housing subsidies; more than two-thirds of housing subsidy recipients have incomes above $10,000. In 1973, only 8 percent of new housing was available to the 29 percent of all American families with incomes below $8,000.[24]

THE STATE AND LOCAL ROLE:
PLANNING PUBLIC HOUSING FOR POOR PEOPLE

Although housing policy in America essentially is designed for the middle class, an effort has been made to encourage the development of housing for the poor, and this attempt has occurred primarily at the grassroots.

---

[23] U.S. Commission on Civil Rights, *Twenty Years After Brown*, p. 24.
[24] Cushing Dolbeare, "Let's Correct the Inequities." *ABA World* 30 (April–May, 1975) 9 and 35.

Even so, the effort has not been easy, and the political brawls over public housing have taken their toll of state and local officials.

PUBLIC HOUSING: PLANNERS AGAINST PEOPLE?

Public housing in this country generally is associated with unmitigated disaster. Many people think of public housing as "monolithic high-rise buildings filled with fatherless black welfare families, some of the most savage and dangerous spots on this continent—places like Providence's Chad Brown, Chicago's Robert Taylor Homes, New York's Fort Greene, and St. Louis's infamous Pruitt-Igoe."[25]

The examples are indeed depressing. Consider, for instance, the highrise of Cedar-Riverside in downtown Minneapolis. Built in 1971, it was part of the U.S. Department of Housing and Urban Development's "new-town in-town" program and was hailed by architects and urban planners as a major contribution to the community cityscape; in fact, Cedar-Riverside won a major architectural design award. In three years Cedar-Riverside was broke and HUD had been brought into a landmark suit to desist from funding the project's second stage.[26]

An even more serious failure of public housing was the Pruitt-Igoe complex in St. Louis, which also once was considered a national example of the best in public housing. Today it is sixty acres of rubble and weeds surrounded by a chain-link fence, and is evocative of Berlin after World War II. The thirty-three buildings of Pruitt-Igoe cost more than $35 million to build in 1954 and housed almost 12,000 poor people. In 1973 federal and local officials agreed that the project was a flop and ordered it razed simply to save the city's housing authority $12 million in annual operating costs. Many of the residents displaced by the destruction of Pruitt-Igoe were forced to move into nearby tenements.[27]

There are exceptions to such dismal stories as Pruitt-Igoe and Cedar-Riverside, and these exceptions seem to revolve around the notion of "small-is-beautiful." Public housing projects such as Valley View Homes, occupying eleven acres in Providence, LaClede houses in St. Louis, West Bluff in Kansas City, New York's Wise Houses and Twin Towers West, and San Francisco's North Beach are among those successful housing projects that seem to share certain common themes, such as being relatively small, staying clear of areas that patently cannot be rehabilitated, putting a strong manager in charge with considerable authority, promoting an effective tenant council, and providing adequate maintenance funds on a regular basis.[28]

---

[25] Neal R. Peirce, "Public Housing Projects Need Not Be Jungles." Syndicated column, November 2, 1977.

[26] Paul Goldberger, New York Times News Service, November 17, 1976, syndicated nationally.

[27] United Press International, October 10, 1976, syndicated nationally.

[28] Peirce, "Public Housing Projects."

PLACING PUBLIC HOUSING:
THE SUBURBAN WAR OF RESISTANCE

If urban analysts are correct in their perception that a number of inner-city ghettos cannot be rehabilitated by even the most advanced public housing, then policy makers must start looking elsewhere for public housing sites. This search has resulted in some of the most bitter community controversies in recent years. Middle-class suburbanites have shown themselves willing to fight to the last tax dollar in their effort to preserve the status quo of their neighborhoods by keeping out public housing. Poor blacks, browns—and whites—are less than welcome in many white middle-class and working-class suburbs.

Consider, for example, the case of Warren,[29] on the outskirts of Detroit. This is a working-class town predominantly peopled by residents of Polish, German, and Irish descent. In the late 1960s Warren decided to cut itself in for a slice of the federal pie. It applied for and received $13 million in urban renewal funds that could be used to upgrade a badly deteriorated sewer system in a portion of the city. To the surprise of Warren's city fathers, the Department of Housing and Urban Development required that Warren enact a fair housing ordinance and establish a human relations board to enforce it—a standard affirmative action proviso in all urban renewal grants.

HUD at that time was very interested in transferring blacks from the central city to the white suburbs, and the Detroit area was and is among the prime examples of residential segregation in the large northern cities. Officials in HUD wrote private memos to each other stating that, with the leverage of urban renewal funds, Warren presented a prime target for achieving some racial equity in housing. The confidential memos were leaked to the *Detroit News,* which published them in a series of front page articles in 1970. The subsequent blow-up in Warren was enormous, complete with picket lines and demonstrators. HUD's resultant backpedaling was fast and furious, but the citizens of Warren were so angered by that time that, in a special referendum, they rejected the whole urban renewal program for the city by repealing the moderate fair housing ordinance that the city council had passed in order to be eligible for federal funding. By its own choice Warren became the first town in the country to reject federal funds out of hand because of racial bigotry.

As a result, perhaps, of such political fiascoes the federal government has played an on-again, off-again role in the locating of public housing. Until 1968, federal regulations required that all federally subsidized housing receive approval by the appropriate local government before being built, and the effect of this requirement was to assure that public housing was kept out of the suburbs. With the passage of the Housing and Urban

---

[29] The following discussion of Warren is drawn from: Kaplan, *The Dream Deferred,* pp. 119–125.

Development Act of 1968, however, the requirement of gaining local approval for public housing projects was effectively abandoned.

With direct control of where public housing could be built wrested from their hands by federal legislation, localities responded with more subtle forms of resistance. In Cleveland, for example, the city fathers in effect cancelled plans to build a major public housing project when they found out that, for the first time, the housing would be situated in a predominantly white area; in the past, Cleveland had permitted the construction of such projects only in the minority areas of the city. In *Cuyahoga Metropolitan Housing Authority* v. *City of Cleveland*, the district court ruled in 1972 against the city, stating that the policy smacked of racism.[30]

In a significant case that took ten years of litigation, the U.S. Supreme Court ruled in 1976 that the Chicago Housing Authority was guilty of racial discrimination by selecting sites for public housing largely in minority areas and by assigning minority tenants to apartments located in minority areas. The Court noted in its decision on *Hills* v. *Gautreaux* that Chicago's public housing policies appeared to be based on race rather than income and therefore were in violation of the Constitution.[31]

This was an important distinction, because only five years earlier the Court had ruled in *James* v. *Valtierra* that a California law requiring approval by the local voters before low-rent public housing could be built was not in violation of the Fourteenth Amendment. The logic used by the Court was that economic, not racial, discrimination was allowed by the Constitution, even though minorities often make up the larger number of applicants for public housing.[32]

These and other court cases reflect the grimness of the war over public housing that is occurring in American cities. And as noted, the federal government likely has confused the issue even further with its vacillating posture on where to locate public housing. For example, the Nixon administration, whose political base was largely suburban, backed away from any kind of enforcement of fair housing requirements, and in 1973 the Nixon administration officially terminated all federal public housing programs. Moreover, it was clear from the behavior of HUD officials under Nixon that the affirmative action requirements for localities that were attached to such federal programs as urban renewal and model cities were going to be enforced less than rigorously.

Since Nixon's departure from Washington, federal public housing policy has changed. In 1976 the Carter administration announced plans to finance some thirty thousand additional housing units for the country's poorest families at a cost of almost $4 billion;[33] the plan represented a resurrection

---

[30] U.S. Commission on Civil Rights, *Twenty Years After Brown*, p. 135.

[31] Fishman, *Housing for All Under Law*, Appendix to Chapter 3.

[32] U.S. Commission on Civil Rights, *Twenty Years After Brown*, p. 138.

[33] "U.S. Planning Thirty Thousand Housing Units for Four Billion Dollars." *The Washington Post*, November 20, 1976.

447

Policies for
the middle
class: home,
hearth, and
racism

of the federal government's public housing programs. Nevertheless, it remains to be seen if a commitment by Washington to public housing also means a commitment to breaking up racial segregation in neighborhoods, and the odds are that the federal government, as always, will tread very carefully—and in different directions—when decisions are needed on where housing for poor people will be built.

THE STATES AS URBAN INNOVATORS?
YES, AT LEAST IN PUBLIC HOUSING

The states have been showing an increasing interest in entering the field of building housing for families with low and moderate incomes; in fact, it can be argued that the states have displayed more initiative in this area than perhaps any other level of government. By 1978, forty states had formed their own housing finance agencies and had financed more than 110,000 units of single family and multifamily housing.[34] The states have been encouraged by the Housing and Community Development Act of 1974 to finance low-income housing, since Section 8 sets aside special funds for state housing finance agencies, an offer many states have found extremely attractive.

Some state housing finance agencies have gone well beyond their original mission of building low-cost housing and have assumed the power to acquire land through eminent domain and to develop and recycle not only housing but industrial, community, civic, and commercial facilities as well. Indeed, housing agencies in eighteen states have the authority to acquire and develop land in these ways, and in Hawaii the housing authority has the right to override local zoning ordinances, making it among the most powerful of all the state housing finance agencies.

The Housing Development Commission in Missouri and the New York Urban Development Corporation both are deeply involved in "new-town in-town" redevelopment programs. The new-town in-town movement represents an effort to rehabilitate housing in the core cities by encouraging all families, but especially the poor and families of moderate incomes, to move back to the downtown areas.

URBAN HOMESTEADING

An aspect of the new-town in-town movement is the "urban homesteading" drive, which is among the more exciting of urban housing programs. The states, particularly California, Connecticut, Minnesota, and Rhode Island, have taken a major role in urban homesteading, although cities initially took the lead, notably Wilmington, Baltimore, and Philadelphia.

---

[34] Stubbs, "Community Development and Housing," pp. 475, 478: and U.S. Commission on Civil Rights, *Twenty Years After Brown,* p. 117.

In 1975, the federal government got into urban homesteading by providing low-interest loans to homesteaders to renovate their purchases. The loan program is important because, while a homesteader may buy a run-down townhouse from the city for a dollar, it costs several thousand dollars more to renovate it. By the late 1970s, about forty communities had federally sponsored urban homesteading programs involving nearly 2,000 homes, and a number of additional cities were running homesteading efforts without help from the federal government.[35] Urban homesteading is often used to preserve cultural areas and to revitalize downtown commerce by attracting young middle-class professionals to the core cities.

HOME IS WHERE THE HOUSE IS:
THE FUTURE OF AMERICAN HOUSING

AMERICA'S SHELTER SUPPLY

Housing statistics are readily available, but "the numbers tell a confusing story."[36] In 1950, new dwellings (including apartments but not mobile homes) were being produced at an average rate of about 1.5 million units a year; during the same period the population grew at an average rate of one million households a year. This growth, along with the increase in mobile homes, essentially represented the replacement of dwellings lost from the nation's housing pool, many of which were considered to be substandard. (*Substandard* is a Census Bureau term that means structurally dilapidated or without plumbing.) After 1966, however, there was considerable variation in this pattern of 1.5 million dwellings being built per year, with the number of new units dipping well below that figure during several years, apparently as a result of inflationary pressure.[37] In 1970 the president set as a national housing goal the construction or rehabilitation of six million dwellings with federal assistance, and another twenty million housing units without federal assistance; this goal was based on an analysis of substandard housing and projections of population growth.[38]

HOUSING: AMERICA'S NEW CLASS WAR

Virtually every projection indicates that housing—both public and private—will be one of the major domestic problems facing America's state and local governments in the future. There is reason to believe that housing will

---

[35] Ward Morehouse, "Urban Homesteading." Christian Science Monitor News Service, May 28, 1978.

[36] Aaron, *Shelter and Subsidies,* p. 23.

[37] Morton L. Isler, *Thinking about Housing.* (Washington, D.C.: The Urban Institute, 1970), p. 19.

[38] *Second Annual Report on National Housing Goals,* Message from the President of the United States. House Document 91–292. (Washington, D.C.: U.S. Government Printing Office, 1970), pp. 23–24, 44, and 53.

449

Policies for
the middle
class: home,
hearth, and
racism

become to America in the 1980s what Vietnam was in the 1960s: a major cause of increasing class consciousness and social division among Americans.

Consider some facts. Both the rents that Americans pay for apartments and rented houses and the mortgage payments that Americans dole to the banks have gone up dramatically as a percentage of family income during the past several years. In 1977 the Census Bureau and the Department of Housing and Urban Development reported that the ratio of American renters who must allocate 25 percent or more of their incomes to housing increased from less than 37 percent in 1970 to more than 42 percent in 1975. Among poor families, devoting this proportion of the family's income to housing greatly decreases the amount that can be spent on such basics as food, clothing, and health. In 1975 more than 18 million renter households had an annual income of less than $5,000, and the median proportion of income devoted to paying the rent was 35 percent; among the 3.2 million Americans who rented and who had an income of between $5,000 and $7,000, the proportion was 30 percent.[39]

Similarly, the middle class is also finding itself increasingly caught in a vicious squeeze play when financing their homes. If a house in the suburbs is an important value of the middle class (and national surveys indicate that between 90 and 95 percent of American consumers prefer a home of their own on a lot of their own), current economic trends indicate that they will be disappointed. A study conducted by Harvard University's and Massachusetts Institute of Technology's Joint Center for Urban Studies found that only 17 percent of the new homes sold in 1976 were purchased by families earning less than $15,000; ten years earlier, that same percentage of homes was purchased by families earning less than $5,000 per year. Moreover, the percentage of Americans who own their own homes—about 65 percent of all households—appears to be levelling off for the first time.[40] Between 1967 and 1976 the cost of new homes literally doubled—a fact that was attributed largely to increasing land costs and suburban governments that were zoning out moderate- and low-income home buyers. In 1976 only 27 percent of American families could afford the median new home price of $44,200; yet only six years earlier 47 percent of the nation's families could have afforded the median new home price of $23,400. The center has projected that the average new home price of the 1980s will exceed $78,000 and, according to its analysis, "Only the most affluent groups would be able to afford them."[41]

In brief, the soaring cost of shelter is going to affect all Americans, some more severely than others. Ironically, the increasing cost of owning a home is going to affect the middle class as well as the poor, and few objects are more dear to the middle-American heart than a home in the suburbs. If and when it becomes sufficiently clear to the average American that a home

---

[39] U.S. Census Bureau, as quoted by Associated Press, April 11, 1977, syndicated nationally.

[40] Joint Center for Urban Studies, as quoted by United Press International, March 4, 1977, syndicated nationally.

[41] *Ibid.*

in the suburbs is a fantasy rather than a realistic objective, we may witness a rebellion of American taxpayers that will parallel the revolt that the middle class precipitated during the 1960s and 1970s over the Vietnam War. As the president of the National Association of Home Builders observed, "Some young people are going to wonder how father could afford to own a single family house when they are making twice as much as papa and they can't afford one. That's going to shake them."[42]

---

[42] Lewis Cenker, as quoted in Kaplan, *The Dream Deferred,* p. 209.

CHAPTER

POLICIES
FOR THE
UPPER CLASS:
CORRUPTION
AND THE
COSA NOSTRA

CORRUPTION, THE HIGH ROLLER OF POLITICS

There are many kinds of corruption, and graft is by no means the exclusive preserve of the wealthy. But when corrupt politicans and the top dons of organized crime meet and deal, the amounts of money involved are often so enormous that, by any economic indicator, the domain of corrupt politics is controlled by the rich. An example is provided by the experience of Richard Hatcher, the mayor of Gary, Indiana, who was offered $100,000 by gambling interests to withdraw from the Democratic primary. He declined the proposition but it was renewed when it became apparent that Hatcher would win the race; the second time around, however, the gambling interests in Gary offered the bribe in hopes of reaching an an "understanding" with Hatcher. They were again refused.[1] Merely because of the high levels of "kumshaw," big-time corruption is largely a playground of the wealthy.

In this chapter we review the role of corruption in grassroots politics with the objective of explaining how organized crime is transforming the traditional meaning of governmental corruption. We shall discuss first some examples of corrupt politics in the traditional sense, the so-called "honest graft," then examine the phenomenon of honest graft degenerating into "systemic corruption" (using as examples surburban zoning practices and the Medicaid scandals), and finally consider what "systemic corruption" really means to the body politic. As we shall see, the Mafia can corrupt democracy far more pervasively than the simple graft of yesteryear. We must, by necessity, rely chiefly on the case studies in our review of state and local political corruption because systematic research on a phenomenon so obviously clandestine is difficult to come by. The chapter concludes with a discussion of how citizens can make their governments more resistant to corrupting influences and a summary of what the grassroots governments have done to protect themselves against graft.

KINDS OF CORRUPTION

Some political scientists defend what they call honest graft on the basis that it "makes the system work." To a degree, this is true. The person who best explained what honest graft means was George Washington Plunkitt, the undisputed boss of New York's Tammany Hall in the late 1800s. "There's

---

[1]Ralph Salerno and John S. Tompkins, *The Crime Confederation: Cosa Nostra and Allied Operations in Organized Crime.* (New York: Doubleday, 1969), as reprinted in: John A. Gardiner and David J. Olson, *Theft of the City: Readings on Corruption in Urban America.* (Bloomington, Ind.: Indiana University Press, 1974), p. 148.

453

Policies for
the upper
class:
corruption
and the cosa
nostra

an honest graft, and I'm an example of how it works. I might sum up the whole thing by sayin': 'I seen my opportunities and I took 'em.'"[2]

Perhaps a more accurate description of Plunkitt's so-called honest graft would be individual graft. *Individual corruption* is conducted in the tradition of Plunkitt's seeing his opportunities and taking them. *Systemic corruption* is different; it is graft that "does not disappear when it becomes entrenched and accepted: rather it assumes a different form, that of *systemic* as opposed to *individual* corruption."[3]

"HONEST GRAFT": AN AMERICAN TRADITION

Individual corruption, or honest graft, for better or worse, has always been a part of the American political panoply. As early as 1776 John Adams noted that a gun powder supplier had been granted an "exorbitant" contract by the Continental Congress and would, "without any risk at all," make a "clear profit of 12,000 pounds, at least." The firm was the trading house of Willing, Morse, and Company, and both these gentlemen happened to be members of the Secret Committee of the Congress, which had devised the contract.[4]

Adams was outraged over the shenanigans of some corrupt congressmen, and properly so. What, one wonders, would this founder of the Republic have thought about the kinds of pervasive corruption introduced by organized crime?

THE NEW BOYS IN TOWN

When organized crime enters the picture, the nature of political corruption changes and this change is new because it undermines the political system *as* a system. As Ralph Salerno and John S. Tompkins point out:

> The target of organized crime is always the district, ward, or county political leader who governs not as an elected officeholder, but as king of the clubhouse. Young men, entering public life, usually start out at the clubhouse level, under the tutelage and control of the local leader. The friends they make and the political debts they incur at that time follow them through their careers. It is for this reason that many a syndicate member can brag of a senator, a judge, or a mayor, that "I've known him for thirty years."[5]

---

[2] William L. Riordan, *Plunkitt of Tammany Hall.* (New York: Dutton, 1963), as reprinted in Gardiner and Olson, *Theft of the City,* p. 7.

[3] Gerald E. Caiden and Naomi J. Caiden, "Administrative Corruption." *Public Administration Review* 37 (May–June, 1977) 306.

[4] Cited in: George Amick, *The American Way of Graft.* (Princeton, N.J.: Center For Analysis of Public Issues, 1976), p. 4.

[5] Salerno and Tompkins, *The Crime Confederation,* p. 148.

With this kind of relationship between politicians and criminals as the base, high level criminals can be given virtually free access to the public trough.

The political access of organized crime is the most effective when it is the least noticeable. Indeed, to keep that relationship inconspicuous, organized crime has been known to pack up and move away from the cities that it controls to small towns, in order to avoid embarrassing the urban politicians it "owns." The most famous such transfer was the move of the Al "Scarface" Capone organization from Chicago to Cicero, Illinois. Scarface immediately established his control in Cicero, as the following quotation from the Illinois Crime Survey of 1929 notes:

> On the Monday night preceding the election, gunmen invaded the office of the Democratic candidate for clerk, beat him, and shot up the place. Automobiles, filled with gunmen, paraded the streets, slugging and kidnapping the election workers. Polling places were raided by armed thugs, and ballots were taken at the point of a gun from the hands of voters waiting to drop them into the box. Voters and workers were kidnapped, brought to Chicago, and held prisoners until the polls closed.[6]

It is this kind of activity that makes political corruption in the twentieth century rather different from political corruption in John Adams's eighteenth century. Recently the head of a major national firm that specializes in detecting white-collar crime commented, "Never have kickbacks, bribes and conflicts of interest been such a dominating factor in U. S. society."[7]

"HONEST GRAFT": EXAMPLES OF INDIVIDUAL CORRUPTION

Some examples of individual corruption, or honest graft (which, it should be noted, is not honest at all), clarify the concept. In 1973, the late Otto Kerner, former Illinois governor, author of the famous "Kerner Commission's" *Report on the Causes and Prevention of Violence*, and a federal judge, was sentenced to three years at a federal prison. He was found guilty of paying $50,000 for race track stock worth $300,000 as part of a deal to assure that certain racing groups would receive favorable race meeting dates during his tenure as governor. In 1977, one Allen G. Hochberg, the former chairman of the New York State Assembly's Ethics Committee, became the first sitting member of the assembly in New York's history to be sent to prison because he was found guilty for attempting to bribe a potential opponent not to run against him.[8]

---

[6]Illinois Crime Survey, 1929. Cited in Salerno and Tompkins, *The Crime Confederation*, p. 150.

[7]*U.S. News & World Report*, October 29, 1973, as quoted in Amick, *The American Way of Graft*, p. 5.

[8]National Municipal League, "Legislative Ethics Chairman Convicted." *Public Officials and The Public Trust*, No. 5 (February, 1977) 5–6.

FROM HONEST GRAFT TO SYSTEMIC CORRUPTION:
TWO CASES OF TRANSITION

While such examples of individual corruption are depressing, the direct impact of these acts on the political system is relatively limited; the influence of the corruption is, for the most part, restricted to the corrupt individual and his or her immediate cronies. In other instances, however, a large enough number of people are participating in corrupt politics so that the corruption no longer can be properly categorized as "individual corruption" or "honest graft." These kinds of corrupt politics are not so widespread that they can be accurately typed as "systemic corruption." These kinds of corruption are in a state of transition from an individual mode to a systemic one. To convey the flavor of transitional corruption, two examples follow; suburban zoning and Medicaid.

THE VERY RICH GETTING RICHER:
ZONING FOR HIGH STAKES

Consider the example of North Hills, a village in the town of North Hempstead. One of the wealthiest suburbs in the nation, it is situated just outside New York City. In 1970, North Hills had 1,757 acres, 318 residents, three private country clubs, and zoning that required two-acre minimum lots; the Chairman of the Board of CBS, the owner of the New York Mets, the owner of the Grace Shipping Line, and similar residents live in North Hills. Since 1929, when the village was incorporated, North Hills has been run by a five-member Board of Trustees which, according to Samuel Kaplan:

> . . .conducted many of their meetings by telephone, meeting irregularly at one another's homes, and even in the Manhattan offices of one of its members. The scheduling and siting of the meetings did not encourage, to say the least, other residents to attend. . . .North Hills was a fiefdom of five privileged persons, protecting their personal interest with the guise of home rule, which supposedly is the foundation of participatory democracy. In the case of North Hills, it was the foundation of greed.[9]

In 1966 there were signs of change in North Hills. The Board of Trustees authorized a comprehensive land-use study to be undertaken by a private firm. In contrast to its past performance for other small communities, the firm submitted a plan to the trustees of North Hills in remarkably short order. The plan called for, among other items, the elimination of all two-acre residential zoning; the trustees were reported to be pleased with the plan. The village planning board, however, had not been consulted nor had the residents of North Hills. William S. Paley, one of the largest land owners

---

[9]Samual Kaplan, *The Dream Deferred.* (New York: Seabury, 1976), p. 47.

in North Hills and Chairman of the Board of the Columbia Broadcasting System, had reservations over the plan and hired his own planner, who came up with a plan which, not surprisingly, incorporated most of Paley's suggestions. Again, the local planning board was not consulted. As a member of the planning board said, "The Trustees frankly were in this for personal gain. They just wanted to make sure their piece of the pie was protected, and the fewer residents putting their finger into it the better. Mr. Paley, of course, was the exception, because he had clout."[10]

In 1970 the people of North Hills voted to permit four residential units per acre, which represented a zoning increase of 800 percent, thus confirming the wishes of the board of trustees. The zoning change was opposed strenuously by the Council of the Greater Manhasset Civic Association, which represented a neighboring community. The council argued that an estimated ten thousand new residents moving into North Hills as a result of the zoning changes would overcrowd their schools and shopping areas and would place additional strains on Manhasset residents in the provision of water, garbage disposal, sewer, police, and fire protection—none of which were being provided by the 318 residents of North Hills.[11]

By this time, most of the residents of North Hills were trying to cut themselves in for a piece of the action. It was estimated by real estate experts that land worth $20,000 an acre under the two-acre zoning ordinances immediately went up in value to as much as $200,000 an acre. Soon virgin woods were being sold by private owners for condominiums, and for fat profits. The greed of already-rich suburbanites in North Hills provides an example of individual avarice degenerating into systemic corruption.

THE VERY RICH GETTING RICHER: HOW DOCTORS CASH IN ON YOUR HEALTH

A similar, but far more nation-wide, example of a corrupt political system is furnished by health care professionals and their defrauding of Medicaid and Medicare. The worst violations occur in the Medicaid program, which in the mid-1970s paid out $5.5 billion in assistance to approximately 28 million Americans who were eligible to have 50 to 78 percent of the cost of their health care paid through the program. Many of these dollars went to druggists and medical technicians, some of whom clearly were on the take. According to the Senate Committee on Aging, "The evidence is overwhelming that many pharmacists are required to pay kickbacks to nursing home operators as a precondition for obtaining a nursing home's business" under

---

[10]Quoted in *ibid.*, p. 48.
[11]George Vecsey, "Land Boom in North Hills Vexes Nassau." *New York Times*, March 18, 1977, pp. B1, B4.

457

Policies for
the upper
class:
corruption
and the cosa
nostra

Medicaid.[12] Moreover, clinical laboratories that wish to do business with certain nursing homes are required to make "special" payments and, since only the richer laboratories can afford to pay this kumshaw, they are rewarded disproportionately. Thus, in New York State sixteen clinical laboratories controlled 70 percent of the state's entire Medicaid business in 1977; in New Jersey, a dozen laboratories controlled 60 percent of the state's business; and in Illinois twelve laboratories controlled 65 percent of the business.

Such graft is difficult to prevent because not all the kickbacks are conducted by cash transactions; gifts of new cars, boats, paid vacations, medical supplies, and so forth number among the methods of payment.[13] A special investigation conducted by the Senate Committee on Aging of twenty-one laboratories in fifteen medical clinics in Illinois concluded that kickbacks were prevalent to the point that one dollar out of every five paid for lab services was wasted in the mid-1970s. Moreover, a reasonable case could be made that half of all such payments were at least inappropriate; and payments could be reduced by half without any loss of service.[14]

Physicians, who as a profession are even wealthier than pharmacists, seem just as inclined to fatten their wallets at the expense of the ill, the old, the poor, and the taxpayer. It is estimated that American doctors are stealing more than $300 million a year from the Medicare program alone by padding bills, playing kickback games with druggists, and simply lying on their claim forms. Investigations by Congress and the Department of Health, Education and Welfare (HEW) in the mid-1970s discovered one innovative surgeon who billed Medicaid for six tonsillectomies on the same patient and a New York chiropractor who submitted bills to Medicaid for eleven visits by a patient who had seen him only once. It also is becoming increasingly clear that physicians are performing unnecessary operations— even potentially dangerous ones—simply to earn more money by charging Medicaid. HEW officials have stated that the overall rate of surgery in the nation increased 23 percent between 1970 and 1975, with especially high rates for operations that often are of questionable utility, such as tonsillectomies and hysterectomies, and the Department has urged the public to get second opinions for elective surgery.[15] It is estimated that only 4 to 6 percent of the 250,000 physicians who participate in Medicaid and Medicare are perpetrators of fraud, but their activity alone accounts for 10 percent of the $3 billion that is paid to them under both programs. In 1977, the Department of Health, Education and Welfare issued a list of 405 physicians who

---

[12]U.S. Senate Committee On Aging, as quoted by: Associated Press, July 17, 1977, syndicated nationally.

[13]*Ibid.*

[14]M. Stanton Evans, "Strange Things Discovered in Medicaid Probe." Syndicated column, April 17, 1976.

[15]Associated Press, November 2, 1977, syndicated nationally.

had handled $100,000 or more in Medicare business in 1975, an indication of the high stakes involved in the Medicare program.

Admittedly it is extremely difficult to prosecute corrupt physicans, pharmacists, and other professionals for graft because of the nature of the fraud, which can be very covert and is often untraceable. Nevertheless, it is alarming to learn that, when doctors and others are brought to trial for health care fraud, they are generally let off lightly and most serve little if any time in prison. According to the Senate Subcommittee on Long-Term Care, only fourteen of 150 doctors convicted of defrauding Medicare and Medicaid between 1970 and 1975 were ever sent to jail, although one in every three defendants convicted in other federal fraud cases were imprisoned. Moreover, of those few physicians actually jailed for fraud, only five were sentenced to more than one year; generally, the swindling doctors received a suspended sentence and no fine.[16]

Partly because of these figures and also because of the enormous amounts of money that are being lost to crooked physicians, pharmacists, and nursing home operators, HEW launched "Project 500" in 1977 to ferret out some 500 doctors and pharmacists who had gyped the Medicaid system. It was estimated that the project potentially could save Medicaid $1 billion every year. Also in that year, President Carter substantially stiffened the penalty for fraud by signing into law a maximum $25,000 fine and five years in prison for persons found guilty of cheating the Medicare and Medicaid programs.[17]

Medicaid and Medicare are examples not only of the phenomenon of the very rich stealing from society for their own ends, but also of individual corruption inching dangerously close to becoming systemic corruption. While the Medicaid–Medicare scandals of the 1970s represent the venality of a small minority of health professionals, it nonetheless is clear that in certain parts of the programs (for example, the kickbacks that pharmacists were required to pay to nursing home operators) corruption had come close to attaining systemic proportions. Nor is it by any means assured that the efforts by HEW and Congress to clean up the health care mess will succeed.

SYSTEMIC CORRUPTION: THE IMPACT OF ORGANIZED CRIME

Although they appear to come close, the Medicaid scandals do not constitute corruption on a massive, pervasive scale in the sense of "systemic corruption," essentially because they are limited to a relatively small proportion of a group of closely related health professions. Political corruption becomes systemic when it takes over an entire state, city, or town and the most effective agent in taking over a government against the will of its people in

[16]"Doctors Medicare Fraud put at $300,000." *New York Times,* July 29, 1976.
[17]United Press International, November 26, 1977, syndicated nationally.

459

Policies for
the upper
class:
corruption
and the cosa
nostra

recent years has been organized crime, also known as the Mob, the Mafia, the Cosa Nostra (a Sicilian term for "our thing"), or the Syndicate.

In this section we describe the extent and the social price tag of the Mafia and review some illustrative cases of organized crime totally taking over political systems. The first example is that of a state, and its inclusion is more for the sake of demonstrating how governmental structure can make criminal penetration easier or more difficult, rather than as an example of a state government being totally controlled by Mafiosi (which, in this case, it is not). The second instance is of a city, and it is included precisely because it was a political system entirely under the thumb of organized crime. The final case considers the difficulties of reforming a polity that has been under the domination of systemic corruption, even after the rascals have been thrown out. The inevitable question is, are some governments incapable of reform? Regrettably, it is a query that can only be asked, not answered.

THE SUBSTANCE OF THE SYNDICATE

The Syndicate deals with politicians mostly at the state and local levels, and investigations have found that there is a national organized crime network of twenty-four to twenty-six "families." Each has jurisdiction over a single city, with the exception of New York, where five families have divided that territory among them. It is estimated that the total membership in the Mafia ranges from three thousand to five thousand people, but the mob's connections can extend this number to several hundred thousand operatives.[18]

Of course, not all organized crime is connected with the Mafia. In Hawaii, for example, the Cosa Nostra has been kept out by a strong local criminal organization comprised mostly of Orientals called "the Company." So strong is the Company that, when two Mafiosi were sent from Las Vegas to "rough up" a local leader, the Company murdered them and returned their bodies to the mainland in a trunk with a note attached reading, "Delicious, send more."[19] The Mafia declined.

THE COSTS OF THE COSA NOSTRA

It is estimated that the gross receipts of organized crime exceed $40 billion every year, chiefly from gambling, narcotics, and loan sharking.[20] One reason why organized crime has been permitted to flourish so profitably is the reluctance of national law enforcement agencies to combat it. The late

---

[18]Congressional Quarterly, *Crime and the Law.* (Washington, D.C.: Congressional Quarterly, 1971), p. 17.

[19]"Hawaii Mobsters Are Ranking In Millions." *Los Angeles Times,* June 5, 1977.

[20]Congressional Quarterly, *Crime and the Law,* p. 17.

J. Edgar Hoover, as chief of the Federal Bureau of Investigation, consistently took the position that large crime syndicates did not exist, and that if they did, they were state and local law enforcement problems. It was only in 1969 that the FBI began working with other agencies against organized crime.[21]

There can be no question, moreover, that organized crime takes its toll far beyond the $40 billion that American citizens unknowingly shell out to it. It has been estimated, for instance, that as many as half the street hold-ups in America are committed by drug addicts whose supply is controlled by organized crime. And perhaps the most victimized of all by the mob are the poor of the inner city, where drug usage is highest, loans most usurious, and prostitution cheapest.

THE GLAMOR OF THE GODFATHER

While most people have some inkling that the Mafia hurts them economically, some believe that, as a political alternative to inept government, it does not sound so bad: Justice is swift and sure, the organization guarantees that those who are loyal to it will not go wanting, and its "soldiers" are able to attain a sense of human dignity ("pursuit of happiness?") within its ranks. The most lucid exposition of this view is contained in Mario Puzo's novel, *The Godfather*.

Facts belie this view. "Soldiers" often are sacrificed for the gain of the capo dons, and life in the Syndicate is more in the style depicted by the movie, *Crazy Joey*, than by Puzo. The Mafia does not offer an option to government. Instead, the Syndicate inevitably must try to destroy government. To quote the President's Commission on Law Enforcement and Administration of Justice, "The purpose of organized crime is not competition with visible, legal government but nullification of it."[22]

We consider this nullification of—or at least attempts to nullify—grassroots governments by the Cosa Nostra next.

"THE OUTFIT" IN ARIZONA

Not enough is known about organized crime in Arizona to be able to compile a history of its evolution. It is clear, however, that the Syndicate exists in Arizona and that it has made inroads into the political hierarchy. The mob's influence was exposed in 1976 when an investigative reporter on the state's major newspaper was killed by a bomb planted in his car, evidently as the result of his investigations of criminal activities in Arizona.

---

[21]*Ibid.*, p. 16.

[22]President's Commission on Law Enforcement and Administration of Justice, *Task Force Report: Organized Crime.* (Washington D.C.: U.S. Government Printing Office, 1967), pp. 1–5, as reprinted in Gardiner and Olson, *Theft of the City,* p. 356.

461

Policies for
the upper
class:
corruption
and the cosa
nostra

As a victim of Syndicate penetration, Arizona is not alone in the West. San Francisco, Los Angeles, and Las Vegas are all cities that have felt the impact of the "the Outfit," as the Mafia family originating in Chicago is named; experts on crime agree that the Outfit is expanding its business into the West.[23] In Arizona, Chicago-based Syndicate figures have been joined by major dons from Detroit and New York, and some estimate that more that two hundred major Mafiosi reside in the state.[24]

In Arizona the Syndicate makes its greatest profits from land frauds and related swindles. In late 1977 a convicted federal prisoner claimed before the Arizona Legislature that organized crime preferred Arizona for their land fraud operations because the state was well known throughout the nation in these circles for its corrupt public officials. He went on to say that he himself had bribed state, county, and federal employees within Arizona. The confidence game most favored by Arizona Mafiosi is to set up a phony land company that from the beginning is designed to go bankrupt within a few years.It is claimed that state officials are bribed to sign forms indicating that the state or locality intends to lay sewer lines, erect power lines, and so forth, thus fraudulently increasing the value of the land, the better to bilk investors.[25] The assistant attorney general for Arizona has noted that state officials permitted a "Mafia-connected" company to operate almost four years *after* learning that the firm was completely bankrupt, noting further that "incompetence and bribe-taking were common among public officials." He also observed that Arizona was a "haven for fraudulent insurance companies, making it one of the two 'easiest states' in which insurance companies could be formed."[26]

The Arizona House Task Force on Organized Crime concluded that defrauded land purchasers might have been better served if Arizona had never had a state real estate department, noting that "a Real Estate Department without the tools and resources to do a complete job ought not to be in business at all. At least the public would not be lulled into a false sense of security." By way of indication, the task force noted that fraudulent land promoters in the state had fleeced the public of at least half a *billion* dollars during the last ten years, and that the state's real estate department, which was responsible for assuring honesty in property transactions, was grossly underequipped to deal with highly skilled land fraud swindles conducted by organized crime. In the 1970s, for example, the department had only three auditors and six investigators; they were responsible for handling more than 6,000 applications for real estate licenses every year,

[23]David Smothers, "Chicago Mafia Creating Empire in the West." United Press International, July 17, 1977, syndicated nationally.

[24]James Yuenger, "IRE: A Noble Experiment That Turned Out a Disaster." *Chicago Tribune,* April 20, 1977.

[25]Albert J. Sitter, "State's Infamy for Corruption Draws Fraud, Con-Man Claims." *Arizona Republic,* November 10, 1977.

[26]Arizona Assistant Attorney General, quoted in: Albert J. Sitter, "Expert on Crime Says Mob Directs Swindles at State." *Arizona Republic,* November 20, 1977.

for monitoring the activities of more than 17,000 licensed salespersons plus an additional 6,000 licensed real estate brokers, and for following through on more than 2,000 complaints about land promoters, salespersons, subdivision frauds, and similar reports.[27]

In 1977, partly in response to a rising recognition that organized crime was a political force in the state, Arizona adopted a completely new and comprehensive criminal code. The new code was a product of a four-year review and represented the first revision of Arizona criminal law since 1910. As one legislator noted, "Arizona law is still in boots and spurs in many respects. We've looked at criminals involved in gambling and prostitution and said, 'Let's let them have their fun,' often failing to realize that money they are using came from violence."[28] So loose, in fact, were Arizona's statutes concerning white-collar and organized crime that crooked land companies had been allowed to operate in the state for generations simply because fraudulent land companies literally were not illegal until 1976. Under such circumstances, it is not difficult for land fraud swindles to flourish, and flourish in Arizona it did.

In enacting its new criminal code, Arizona fell short of passing the strongest possible antimob legislation. A few Arizona legislators, as well as the state attorney general, advocated passage of the Racketeering Influence and Corrupt Organizations Act, the model law adopted by Congress as part of the federal Organized Crime Control Act of 1970. The model legislation is controversial and can be a cause of injustice to innocent citizens. Arizona elected not to pass such legislation, which is perhaps unfortunate in light of the fact that in 1977 the U.S. Department of Justice officially warned the state of Arizona that the Chicago Outfit was setting up the city of Phoenix as another target city for the money laundering racket and for establishing highly questionable corporations, notably in the areas of insurance and land speculation.

The new state code does make loan-sharking and usury crimes illegal, which they were not prior to adoption of the Arizona revised criminal code, and crooked land companies also are illegal for the first time in Arizona. But, while Arizona's new criminal code is very tough on crime, it is rather weak on the organized part of crime. To quote one investigator, "The law that provides the tools to find Mr. Big, break his organization financially, repay his victims, and convince a jury that a syndicate does indeed exist—that law went down to defeat in Arizona."[29]

While the full extent of the Cosa Nostra's activities in Arizona is unknown, it is clear that the state's political structure is such that Arizona has become a prime target for penetration by organized crime and the corruption of

---

[27]Arizona House Task Force on Organized Crime, as quoted by: Albert J. Sitter, "Land Agency Is a Liability, Panel Claims." *Arizona Republic,* November 14, 1977.

[28]As quoted by: Marc Adams, "Code Misses Mark in Effort to Control Mob." *Arizona Republic,* December 12, 1977.

[29]*Ibid.*

463

Policies for
the upper
class:
corruption
and the cosa
nostra

local officials. Arizona became the forty-eighth state in 1912, at the height of the populist movement, and its constitution reflected the views of a rural people who distrusted a strong executive. Thus, commissions and boards were created that were "responsible to the statute" rather than to the chief executive. Although the governor has the authority to appoint commissioners and boards (with legislative approval), he exercises no legal control over virtually any of them once the appointment is made. Whatever control the governor can maintain is done through the personal loyalty of the appointees and his own persuasive powers. Since 1912 Arizona's legislatures continued to create boards, commissions, and agencies, and a proliferation of commissions and boards resulted over the years. When the state was created, Arizona had only thirty-one government agencies. By 1971 the number of independent agencies reached a high of 176, which has since been decreased to less than 150. This decrease was due largely to a change in legislative philosophy. Working in concert with the governor, the legislature undertook to consolidate agencies of state government and to place the resultant "superagencies" under the control of the executive; eleven agencies since have been reorganized, consolidated, and placed under the direct control of the governor, including most of the major ones.[30] It was only in 1975, however, that the Arizona Real Estate Commission, which had been accused of gross corruption and bribe-taking by the assistant attorney general for Arizona in earlier years, was retitled the Arizona Real Estate Department and was placed under the control of the governor.

The point is that when an agency "reports to the statute," no one is in control. Thus, agency staff members, who often make the real policy (which then is "rubber stamped" by their board members), are extremely susceptible to pressures brought on by sophisticated and tough Mafiosi.

Of course, the opposite organizational structure of government can be corrupted, too. In a highly centralized government, in which all agency heads report to a chief executive, only the chief executive needs to be bribed or corrupted for criminal elements to gain a free hand. The most typical example of this occurrence is the average municipal police department, which usually is organized along hierarchical, military lines.

Normally, the more decentralized a government is, the more potentially susceptible it is to corruption—particularly if that government has been targeted by a highly centralized criminal organization. Certainly a paramount example of organized crime taking over a disorganized government is Newark, New Jersey. During the period when the Syndicate first moved in (the 1920s), Newark had a commission form of government—possibly the most decentralized and ineffectual form of urban governance ever devised.

---

[30]Nicholas Henry, "The Burgeoning Bureaucracy." *Of, By, and For the People.* Research report prepared by the State Universities of Arizona, Nicholas Henry, ed. and coordinater. (Phoenix: Arizona Academy of Public Affairs, 1977), pp. 10–12.

Newark, with more than 380,000 people, of whom more than half are black and more than 7 percent are Latinos, is among New Jersey's largest municipalities and is conveniently close to New York City. During most of the Prohibition Era a no-holds-barred gangland war raged in New York City, and out of it emerged New York's first Godfather, one Abner "Longie" Zwillman, who happened to be Jewish, not Italian, and who claimed Newark as his home town. Soon Zwillman had set up a regular ferry schedule on the New Jersey coastline designed to supply New York with illegal liquor. It was by far the most extensive bootlegging operation on the East Coast, reaping an estimated $50 million between 1926 and 1931 and accounting for approximately 40 percent of the entire bootleg liquor supply being transported across the nation's borders. With this fortune, Zwillman established himself as the Democratic boss of Newark's third ward, using his bootlegged money to finance the gubernatorial campaigns of all candidates—on the understanding that he would be allowed to approve the winner's nominee for attorney general.

As Zwillman gained power in Newark's third ward, one Ruggiero "Richie the Boot" Boiardo garnered control of the first ward. After considerable competition between the two dons, Zwillman and Boiardo supposedly had a reconciliation in 1930 and staged a two-day party to celebrate. Shortly after the close of the party, Boiardo was shot sixteen times in true gangland style, but somehow survived; evidently his life was saved when a bullet struck the Boot's $5,000 diamond belt buckle. After Boiardo recovered, he was sent to prison for two and a half years for carrying a gun when he was shot, but served only twenty months, sixteen of which were in a minimum security facility. He returned to his first ward and negotiated a division of turf in Newark with Zwillman while the law stood quietly aside.

Longie Zwillman committed suicide in 1959 and was succeeded by Gerardo "Jerry" Catena, who controlled the entire Jersey wing of the Vito Genovese family, and Boiardo became a part of the Catena operation. The Mafia's grip on Newark, and particularly the grasp of Richie the Boot, tightened with time. The Boot eventually, was succeeded by Anthony "Tony Boy" Boiardo, his son, who soon gained control of the city.

In 1962 Newark elected one Hugh Addonizio, known to all as Hughie, who had served as a U.S. congressman from Newark for the past fourteen years. Why did Hughie run for mayor? To quote Hughie, "There is no money in being a congressman but you can make a million bucks as mayor of Newark." Organized crime contributed heavily to Addonizio's campaign for mayor, with Tony Boy Boiardo himself setting a fine example by contributing $10,000. Addonizio, backed by Boiardo, soon started robbing the public till with such a vengeance that one Mafia chieftain complained, "The guy's [Addonizio] taking $400, $500 for little jobs!"[31]

---

[31]Ron Porambo, *No Cause for Indictment: An Autopsy of Newark.* (New York: Holt, Rinehart and Winston, 1971), as reprinted in Gardiner and Olson, *Theft of the City,* p. 87.

465

Policies for
the upper
class:
corruption
and the cosa
nostra

Shortly after his election, Hughie quickly secured his position by appointing one Dominic Spina, one of his campaign workers, as director of police and Spina appointed Police Captain Rocco Ferrante to head the intelligence division of Newark's finest. It was the division's job to investigate gambling and vice in the city, and Ferrante also served as Addonizio's official personal bodyguard. Meanwhile, Ralph Villani, a former mayor of Newark who had been indicted for corruption but never convicted (mainly because the statute of limitations had run out), still served as an elected member of the city council, and in 1962 and 1966 Villani was elected by his fellow councilmembers as president of the council.

While Addonizio and company were taking over the political structure of Newark, Tony Boy Boiardo founded the Valentine Electric Company which, within ten years, became the largest electrical contractor in the region, receiving half the contracts awarded by the Newark Housing Authority and doing $5 million worth of business a year. Boiardo was the real boss of Newark.

The basic mechanism for stripping Newark was a model of managerial efficiency—unlike anything else in Newark—and was based on Boiardo's ability to shake down contractors doing business with the city, demanding 10 percent of their contracts. Phony bills written by a phony supply company (the address of which was actually a vacant lot) were sent to the contractors, who dutifully paid into a phony bank account; the money eventually was withdrawn and turned over to Boiardo, although sizable portions of this money went directly to the mayor and eight of the nine members of the Newark City Council. It was estimated that Boiardo, Addonizio, and their accomplices eventually bilked the city of more than $1.4 million in kickbacks alone, a sum that is by no means inclusive of all the money lost though their systematic corruption.

With Spina and Ferrante in charge of Newark's police, shakedowns by cops in the city's black slums became commonplace, and in 1967 one of the worst race riots in American urban history exploded in Newark, killing twenty-three people and resulting in property damage estimated at $10.4 million. New Jersey Governor Richard J. Hughes quickly appointed a blue ribbon commission to determine the cause behind Newark's violence of that year, and it found that the chief reason was "a pervasive feeling of corruption" throughout the city, continuing that "A former state official, a former city official and an incumbent city official all used the same phrase: 'There is a price on everything at city hall'."[32]

A year after Newark's riots, the Nixon administration appointed a new U.S. Attorney for New Jersey, one Frederick Lacey, a distinguished lawyer who zeroed in on Newark's rampant corruption like a sharpshooter. Within a year, the mayor of Newark and a number of other city officials were indicted by a federal grand jury on charges of extortion and income tax

[32]As quoted in: Fred J. Cook, "The People versus the Mob, or Who Rules New Jersey?" *New York Times Magazine*, February 1, 1970, as reprinted in Gardiner and Olson, *Theft of the City*, p. 80.

evasion and, flouting precedent in such cases, actually were convicted—a rare, indeed almost unique, occurrence in New Jersey courtrooms when top Mafia dons and high political figures were involved. Addonizio was sentenced to ten years in jail, but Tony Boy Boiardo managed to avoid a trial until his death in 1978 on the basis that, because of a heart condition, his life would be in jeopardy as the result of the stress incurred by a courtroom proceeding.

JERSEY CITY: THE LEGACY OF REFORM?

What happens after a town is cleaned up politically and a new, reform-oriented administration is swept into office? Obviously, it depends on the town, but consider the example of another New Jersey municipality, Jersey City, a metropolis that some analysts still consider to be the most corrupt town in America.[33] Jersey City was controlled for a number of years by the famous political boss Frank Hague, who ruled with an iron hand. So rapacious was Hague that he amassed a fortune of $8 million purely on the basis of his political position. So open in his avarice was Boss Hague that, when he died, an elderly woman attended his funeral holding a hand-lettered sign that stated, "God have mercy on his sinful greedy soul!" One John B. Kinny, a lieutenant in the Hague organization, succeeded Hague as boss of the Jersey City machine, and his handpicked mayor, Thomas J. Whelan, soon was sent off to jail in 1972 for extorting millions in kickbacks from city contractors. Whelan was succeeded in a special election by a young public health physician, Paul T. Jordan, who was a vigorous reformist candidate. On winning the election Jordan proclaimed, "We are free at last!" Jordan chose not to run for office in the next election, but picked a like-minded successor who lost by a landslide to a close associate of the imprisoned Mayor Whelan; soon the loan sharks and the gamblers were back in town.

Why did Jordan's reform candidate lose to a man of the classic machine mold? Reformer Jordan had abolished the kickback system on city contracts (which added anywhere from 8 to 15 percent on all items bought by the city); he had cleaned up the police department, created a Mayor's Action Bureau which acted on some 15,000 to 20,000 citizen complaints every year, and initiated a number of similar reforms. Yet, 51 percent of Jersey City residents, according to a poll conducted at the end of Jordan's term, stated they would leave Jersey City if they possibly could, and another poll taken at the same time found that only 5 percent of the people of Jersey City thought that the reformist Jordan had done a good job; 50 percent rated his performance as poor. According to one observer, the relatively unsophisticated, less educated, and elderly citizenry who populated Jersey

---

[33]The discussion of Jersey City is drawn from: Neal R. Pierce, "Saga of Reform Lost in Jersey City." Syndicated column, July 29, 1977.

467

Policies for
the upper
class:
corruption
and the cosa
nostra

City longed for the return to the "good ol' days," which they defined essentially as less crime. The sad fact of the matter is that this perception bore little relationship to reality, since Jersey City's crime rate (that is, street crime as opposed to political corruption) is actually lower than that of other cities of comparable size. Moreover, Jordan himself appeared to project a somewhat aloof image and had lost the common touch, of which Boss Hague was a master. Thus, after six decades of openly corrupt politics, Jersey City granted itself a respite of five years, but it was soon back to its old ways. Apparently there is among some citizens a certain comfort to be derived from the corruption of others.

GRAFT AND THE GRASSROOTS

Regardless of how the good citizens of Jersey City, and possibly other communities, behave, it is reasonably apparent that the average American is deeply concerned about political corruption and the role of organized crime. A 1974 poll by Louis Harris conducted in 200 communities found that state and local government leaders ranked far below garbage collectors in public esteem and that "corrupt politicians" and "lack of confidence in government" were issues second in importance only to that of inflation. Overall, public opinion polls indicate that roughly 70 percent of all Americans believe that there is dishonesty in their state and local governments.[34]

In a sophisticated analysis of an unidentified, mid-sized city that was in the pocket of organized crime, an in-depth survey was taken of a representative sample of the city's citizens concerning their "tolerance of corruption." It was found that the residents of the city had very little interest in local politics, were aware that their government was a poor one, and were extremely suspicious of local officials. It was also found that high social status, high level of education, youth, and a relatively long residence in the city correlated with a low tolerance of political corruption.[35] In sum, then, it appears that while corrupt politicians and high-level criminals in some cities may be working hand-in-glove, the public neither likes nor approves of it; they merely feel powerless to change it.

WHAT MUST BE DONE?

It is perhaps easy to become despondent after reading the sorry tale of political graft, the Cosa Nostra, corrupt politicians, and capo dons. Can those relationships be broken and, if so, how?[36]

---

[34]Louis Harris Poll, as quoted in Amick, *The American Way of Graft*, pp. 9–10.

[35]John A. Gardiner, *The Politics of Corruption: Organized Crime in an American City.* (New York: Russell Sage Foundation, 1970), as reprinted in Gardiner and Olson, *Theft of the City,* pp. 347–348, 393–394.

[36]The following discussion of recommendations on how to make governments more graft resistant is drawn from Amick, *The American Way of Graft,* pp. 160–230.

Certainly the most obvious of policies that can be instituted to assure better government is the development of sound management. *Sound management* in this sense means (1) establishing centralized purchasing procedures; (2) auditing to be conducted by truly independent auditors; (3) enacting a single code concerning land-use development administered by a single agency and following prescribed rules of procedure; (4) establishing tax assessment districts, each headed by a full-time and professionally-qualified assessor; and (5) the institutionalization of an absolutely open licensing and franchising procedure for such industries as cable television, liquor businesses, race tracks, and so forth.

Arbitrary governmental decision making also should be eliminated. Steps in this direction include qualifying bidders for construction jobs at the state level and improving the government's bidding system. They would require ending one-man rule in public purchasing policies, training public purchasing officials in the rudiments of construction management, and establishing state licensing agencies with the power to set criteria for issuing licenses.

Clear avenues of appeal should be established to permit private enterprises dealing with state and local governments to appeal decisions made at lower levels; such areas include appeals on contracts, zoning decisions, and building codes. State agencies should be created to advise businesspersons wishing to locate or expand in the state and to intercede in their behalf with government agencies when necessary.

Compromising relationships between public officials and private citizens should be prohibited. Each state should adopt a conflict-of-interest law and full-time boards to enforce such laws. Professionals such as those in medicine and law should also be prohibited from engaging in conflict-of-interest situations. Prohibitions should be set on campaign contributions, and bipartisan commissions should be created by the states to oversee elections and administer and enforce campaign and election legislation.

"Sunshine laws" and legislation that require the fullest possible public disclosure of personal finances by public officials, both elected and appointed, should be enacted; government agencies also should be required to publicize the names of all firms with which they do business. Complete financial disclosure should be mandated for all owners of real estate whenever the government is involved in the purchase or sale of their property. Political campaign funding should be fully reported, and "right-to-know-laws" should be passed so that meetings of public agencies and legislative committees are virtually always open to the public.

Finally, citizens should adopt "the honesty ethic in public life," which encourages exemplary behavior by public officials and the enhancement of ethical standards among relevant professional societies. Significant in this effort is the attempt to judge whether or not police organizations are adequate to cope with political corruption.

WHAT IS BEING DONE?

ETHICS LEGISLATION IN THE STATES

While the list of the policies needed to help make public officials more resistant to graft is a good one, it obviously has not yet been fully adopted by America's state and local governments. Nevertheless, progress has been made, especially in the burgeoning enactment of conflict-of-interest legislation and financial disclosure laws. Still, the particulars of such policies frequently are controversial and, with some 52,000 elected officials and 13 million state and local government employees, it is not surprising that it is often difficult for legislators to determine who should and who should not be covered by such laws. Forty-two states have major ethics legislation; of these, thirty-seven apply the law to their own legislators. All forty-two states apply conflict-of-interest and financial disclosure policies to major public executives, usually covering administrators who have judicial and regulatory duties, or who spend significant amounts of public money, or who form policy. Only twenty-two of the forty-two states that have ethics legislation apply those laws to all or part of the judiciary and, in a few cases, to judicial employees. Nineteen states extend their ethics laws to officials of counties or municipalities, including, in some cases, members of school boards, special districts, and local commissions.[37]

Open meeting laws and related "sunshine" legislation also are increasingly popular in the states, and state governments in recent years have enacted more such reform measures than ever before. To quote the U.S. Advisory Commission on Intergovernmental Relations, recently enacted reform legislation has set up "a record unmatched since the turn-of-the-century Populist Era."[38] All fifty states have open meeting laws that apply to both state and local governments, and thirty-three of these passed such laws or strengthened them significantly in the 1970s. Seven states require advance public notice of meetings and thirty-four states have enacted legislation that punishes officials who violate sunshine laws. Most states also require lobbyists to register, and forty-three require lobbyists to report their expenses. Table 21–1 indicates the rise in state ethics legislation.

THE CITY MANAGER: THE RECORD OF REFORM

Similarly, important strides also have been made toward instituting sound management, particularly at the local level with the growing adoption of

---

[37]Council of State Governments, *Ethics: State Conflict of Interest/Financial Disclosure Legislation, 1972–1975.* (Lexington Ky.: Council of State Governments, 1975), pp. 1–7.

[38]Advisory Commission on Intergovernmental Relations, *State Actions in 1976* (M-109). (Washington: ACIR, 1977), p. 61.

TABLE 21–1 STATE ACCOUNTABILITY

STATE	FINANCIAL DISCLOSURE	LOBBYIST DISCLOSURE	CAMPAIGN FINANCING	OPEN MEETINGS	INDEPENDENT ENFORCEMENT BODY
			(NOVEMBER 1972–NOVEMBER 1976)		
Alabama	√	√			√
Alaska	√*	√+	√		√
Arizona	√	√	√	√	√
Arkansas	√*		√		
California	√*	√*	√*	√*	√*
Colorado	√*	√*	√	√*	√
Connecticut		√	√+	√	√
Delaware		√+	√	√+	
Florida	√+		√		√
Georgia			√		√
Hawaii		√	√+	√+	√
Idaho		√*	√*	√	
Illinois	√		√		√
Indiana	√		√+		√
Iowa		√	√+		√
Kansas	√*	√	√	√	√
Kentucky	√+		√+	√	
Louisiana	√		√	√	
Maine	√	√+	√	√+	√
Maryland	√		√		√
Massachusetts		√+	√*		√
Michigan			√	√+	
Minnesota	√	√	√	√	√
Mississippi				√	
Missouri	√*	√	√*	√	√*

470

Montana	✓+	✓+		✓	✓
Nebraska		✓	✓+	✓+	✓
Nevada			✓	✓	✓
New Hampshire					
New Jersey	✓	✓	✓	✓	✓
New Mexico	✓		✓	✓	
New York		✓+	✓+	✓+	✓
North Carolina	✓	✓	✓		
North Dakota	✓		✓*	✓*	
Ohio	✓+	✓+	✓	✓	✓
Oklahoma	✓	✓+	✓+	✓	✓
Oregon	✓*	✓	✓	✓	✓
Pennsylvania	✓	✓+	✓+	✓	✓
Rhode Island	✓+	✓	✓	✓+	✓
South Carolina	✓	✓	✓	✓	
South Dakota	✓	✓+	✓+		✓
Tennessee		✓	✓+	✓	
Texas	✓		✓	✓	
Utah		✓	✓		
Vermont	✓+	✓	✓+	✓	
Virginia	✓	✓+	✓	✓+	
Washington	✓*	✓	✓	✓	✓
West Virginia	✓	✓+	✓+		
Wisconsin	✓		✓+	✓+	
Wyoming			✓	✓	✓

*Voter initiative.
+1976 enactment or major revision.
NOTE: In some instances states have not acted because they had excellent laws prior to 1972.

Source: Advisory Commission on Intergovernmental Relations, *State Actions in 1976.* (Washington, D.C.: U.S. Government Printing Office, 1977), p. 62.

the council–manager plan. Contrary to conventional wisdom, being an honest city manager is not easy. Merely because the manager cherishes political anonymity (at least in most cases), it does not follow that he is removed from the pressures of politics. Consider the experiences of one LeRoy F. Harlow, a professional city manager with a wide background in urban administration. The following passage, written by a former member of his staff, indicates the reality of local political pressure:

> One week after I went to work as City Manager Harlow's principal assistant, a businessman telephoned to inform me that he was one of a group organizing to drive Harlow out of town. He suggested I quietly leave town before I was run out. As inducement, he said his group would secure for me a higher paying position in Minneapolis. This would reflect an advancement opportunity too good to ignore, and would look good on my record. A few weeks later, the police chief called me to his office to say he was securing legal counsel on how to separate me from my job. Both of these initial incidents were in response to major assignments given me by Harlow—to help establish a city merit system and centralized purchasing.[39]

While such "administrative" decisions as setting up a merit-based civil service and competitive bidding practices may not appear to be political at first glance, such professionalism can be intensely political. As the author of the preceding passage notes, city management "can be a rugged and vicious environment, not recommended for the faint-hearted."[40]

It is all the more surprising in light of these pressures that the city management profession has been able to resist political corruption as effectively as it has. As Paul N. Ylvisaker of Harvard University has noted:

> It is a remarkable profession, indeed, when you realize that for two generations, the pressures of America growing up and becoming too fat have not stalled you in your effort to perfect the [city managers'] code of ethics and to increase your power to enforce it. The small number of city managers who have been a discredit to that code is one of the remarkable tributes still remaining on the American political landscape, and . . .that kind of integrity is now the quality that this country most needs.[41]

In short, though organized crime and corrupt politicians always will be with us, the 1970s witnessed a spate of "good government" reforms at the state and local levels. Sunshine laws, professional ethics codes, governmental reorganizations, watchdog boards, conflict-of-interest legislation, and financial disclosure policies all work toward the reduction of graft at the

---

[39]Dwight Ink, "Foreword." In LeRoy F. Harlow, *Without Fear or Favor: Odyssey of a City Manager.* (Provo, Utah: Brigham Young University Press, 1977), p. ix.

[40]*Ibid.*

[41]Paul N. Ylvisaker, "Keynote Address." 1973 Annual Conference of the International City Management Association, quoted in John M. Patriarche, "Ethical Questions Which Administrators Face." *Public Management* (June, 1975) 19.

473

Policies for
the upper
class:
corruption
and the cosa
nostra

grassroots. Nevertheless (and trite as the cliché may be), it is the people who must ultimately be responsible for keeping government honest and efficient. While there are exceptions (such as when organized crime takes over an entire municipality by bribery or terrorism), it still is generally a fact that the people have the supreme power and may use it as they see fit.

There is no more fitting thought on which to close a book about democracy at the grassroots than that of the people's power.

GLOSSARY

Jargon is regrettably rife in any academic field, and political science is no exception. The following list is designed to explain certain terms used by political science, specifically as they pertain to state and local government. The list of words and terms provided below is in alphabetical order.

Advocacy planning. An ideological point of view espoused by members of the planning profession which holds that professional planners should promote the interests of the poor and minority groups more consciously in their planning.

Affirmative action. A government policy encouraging the hiring of members of disadvantaged groups on the grounds that government positions should be open to as many people as possible.

Aid to families with dependent children. A federal public assistance program designed to help poor families with children.

Annexation. The absorption of outlying areas by a municipality.

Appelate court. A court which reviews the decisions of lower courts.

Apportionment. Deciding on the basis of population how many representatives to a legislature that a district will be accorded.

At-large election. Elections in which candidates do not campaign in precincts or wards, but rather are elected by the voters as a whole.

Bicameral legislature. A legislature with two separate houses.

Biennial session. The practice of convening a state legislature every two years.

Blanket primary. *See* Open primary.

Block grant. Money granted by one government to another which is tied to a general area of concern but which permits relatively greater latitude by the receiving government on how the funds may be used. Community development is an example.

Board of Commissioners. The governing body for a county; usually the commissioners are elected at-large.

Board of supervisors. The governing body of a county; usually the supervisors are elected from wards rather than at-large.

"*Bona fide* occupational qualification." A term appearing in Title VII of the Civil Rights Act of 1964 and which has been a major issue in sex discrimination suits.

Bond. A certificate of indebtedness given by a borrower to a lender. A bond obliges the borrower to repay the debt with interest. The most common bonds are municipal bonds which are issued by local governments to pay for needs that cannot be financed from tax and other revenues.

Bureaucracy. The executive side of government, characterized by specialization of functions, adherence to rules, and hierarchy of authority.

Categorical assistance programs. Grants for particular welfare programs such as aid to the disabled, the elderly, and the blind.

Categorical grant. Money granted by one government to another which is highly specific in its purpose. Also called project grant. Urban renewal is an example.

Caucus. A meeting of politicians usually held for purposes of nominating candidates.

Central committee. The policymaking committees of a political party. *Also called* the Executive Committee.

Charter. The basic law of a local governmental body, such as a county or city; charters are granted by the states.

Chief administrative officer. The top appointed manager in either a city or county government. Unlike the city manager, the chief administrative officer reports directly to the mayor or the chief elected official of the county.

Circuit breaker. A device intended to render the property tax more equitable by reducing or eliminating the property tax when it exceeds a predetermined percentage of the personal income of the property owner.

City-county consolidation. The merger of a major urban area with its surrounding county for purposes of administrative and economic efficiency.

City manager. The chief administrative official of a city. The city manager is appointed by and reports directly to the city council.

Civil case. A court case of a noncriminal nature.

Civil service. The administrative service of the government exclusive of the armed forces.

Civilian review boards. Groups of private citizens who review accusations of misconduct by the police.

Class action suit. A legal action undertaken by one or more plaintiffs on behalf of themselves and all other persons having identical interest in the alleged wrong.

Closed primary. A primary election in which only members of a given political party may vote in that party's primary elections. *Also called* a closed partisan primary.

Collective bargaining. Joint decision making between representative of employees and employers on such subjects as salaries, hours, and working conditions.

Commission plan. A weak executive form of government in which city commissioners generally are elected at-large and each member of the city council is both a legislator and administrator. In the counties, the commission plan is known as the plural executive plan.

Community. The economic, social, and political interdependence among people who fall into broad social categories.

Community development. The effort by governments and private citizens to improve the physical environment, social aspects, and performance of municipal governmental institutions, and to increase participation by local citizens in the policy making process.

Comprehensive plan. A plan of development for a community that touches all facets of community development. Usually a comprehensive plan focuses on land-use issues.

Conference committee. A special joint committee of members from both legislative houses who are selected to iron out differences when a bill passes both houses, but in different forms.

Constituency. The citizens residing in an elected office holder's district.

Constitution. A document establishing the mode in which a state is organized and the way in which power is distributed.

Constitutional commission. A variant of the constitutional convention in which the legislature generally appoints commissioners to study or prepare basic constitutional changes on an ongoing basis.

Constitutional convention. An assembly of representatives convened to draft or revise substantially a state's constitution.

Convention. A meeting of politicians and political party representatives generally held for purposes of nominating candidates. Conventions usually are more broadly representative than caucuses.

Conversion theory. The notion that when an inner city resident moves to suburbia, his or her voting behavior becomes more conservative.

Corruption. The buying and selling of political favors or improper behavior in political and governmental circles. *See also:* "Honest graft," Individual corruption, and Systemic corruption.

Cosa Nostra. A Sicilian term for "our thing." The Cosa Nostra refers to organized crime. Other terms for organized crime are: The Mob, The Mafia, and The Syndicate.

Council-administrator government. The county version of the council-manager form of urban government.

Council elected executive plan. A form of county government in which the executive branch is headed by a strong elected administrator who is comparable in power to a governor. An administrative officer reports directly to the county executive rather than to the county council.

Council–manager government. A form of urban government in which legislative and executive powers are separated as much as possible, with executive powers being vested in the city manager and legislative powers in the city council. In the counties, the council–manager form is known as the council-administrator form.

Councils of Governments. Voluntary associations of local governments that are designed to coordinate intergovernmental planning and policy. COGs have been encouraged to develop by the Demonstration Cities and Metropolitan Development Act of 1966, the Intergovernmental Act of 1968, the National Environmental Policy Act of 1969, and OMB Circular A–95.

County. The largest territorial division of local government within a state.

County manager. The chief administrative officer of the county. The county manager is appointed by and reports directly to the county board of supervisors.

Court administrator. A relatively new official, now used in all the states, who manages state court systems.

Court order. A directive issued by a court that requires a person to do or abstain from doing a specified act.

"Creatures of the states." A statement attributed to one Judge John F. Dillon in 1868 and which refers to the judicial interpretation that local units of governments have autonomy only as granted by their state governments.

Criminal justice. The system of police, courts, and prisons designed to control crime and provide justice to the citizenry.

De facto. A condition that exists in fact if not in law, such as *de facto* racial segregation in northern school systems.

De jure. A condition that exists in law if not in fact.

Demography. The study of population shifts and characteristics.

"Dillon's Rule." *See:* Creatures of the states.

Direct federalism. The relationships between local governments and the national governments which often involve the by-passing of state governments.

Discrimination. The act of discriminating against a person on the basis of race, creed, or sex.

Double-filing. A mechanism that permits a candidate to seek the nomination for the same office in two or more parties during the same primary election.

Due process of law. The concept of limiting government by granting citizens protection against the arbitrary deprivation of life, liberty, or property.

Earmark. The practice of setting aside certain revenues for specific uses through legislation; for example, federal gasoline taxes are "earmarked" for the Federal Highway Trust Fund and are used to build more highways.

EEOC. Equal Employment Opportunity Commission.

Electorate. The voters in a given political system.

Elitism. A point of view concerning political power which argues that power is concentrated in a ruling elite.

Equal Employment Opportunity Commission. A federal body created by the Civil Rights Act of 1964 designed to investigate discrimination complaints in both private and public sectors. In 1972, the Commission was given the power to sue private employers over civil rights issues.

Equal Rights Amendment. Approved by Congress in 1972, the ERA is a proposed amendment to the Constitution that, if ratified, will guarantee equal rights for women.

Event analysis. A research methodology that attempts to ascertain who has power in communities by tracing patterns of interaction among policy makers.

Exclusionary zoning. Zoning practices that are designed to restrict or discourage new housing for poor people and minorities.

Extradition. The return by one state to another

of a person accused of committing a crime by the second state.

"Fannie Mae." Federal and National Mortgage Association.

Federalism. The relations among governments, specifically, the series of legal, political, and administrative relationships established among units of government and which possess varying degrees of authority and jurisdictional autonomy.

Felony. A serious crime, in contrast to a misdemeanor.

FHA. Federal Housing Administration.

Fiscal federalism. The financial relationships between American governments.

Fixed sentencing. A recent trend in many states which legally requires a judge to give a particular sentence to persons found guilty of particular crimes. Under fixed sentencing, the law gives judges little or no latitude in determining the nature of the guilty person's sentence.

Food Stamp Program. A federal public assistance program administered through the U.S. Department of Agriculture in conjunction with state and local welfare agencies designed to improve nutrition for the needy.

Formula funding. The method used by states to fund education on the basis of numbers of students enrolled.

Formula grant. Money granted by one government to another in which money is distributed among all eligible recipients on the basis of some prearranged method. An example is Supplemental Security Income Assistance.

Freedom of information. A public policy, as expressed in the federal Freedom of Information Act of 1967 and subsequent freedom of information acts at the state and local levels, which yields access to government documents and records to private citizens.

Functional plan. Specialized planning done by such agencies as urban and rural authorities, health departments, etc.

"Gargantua." An argument advocating the cen-tralization of governmental authority over large metropolitan areas.

General assistance programs. Welfare programs for those who do not qualify for categorical assistance programs and which usually refer to state-initiated welfare policies in contrast to nationally initiated welfare policies.

Gerrymandering. To divide a territory into election districts for the purpose of giving one political party an electoral majority in a large number of districts while concentrating the voting strength of the opposition in as few districts as possible.

Government. The continuous exercise of authority and the performance of functions for a political unit.

Governor. The chief political executive of a state.

Grand jury. A body of twelve to twenty-three members that hears evidence presented by the prosecuting attorney against people accused of a serious crime. The grand jury may indict the accused and send the accused to a formal trial if it believes the evidence justifies such a trial.

Grant-in-Aid. Program under which the federal government awards funds to state and local governments. *See also*: Block grant, Categorical grant, and Formula grant.

Gross National Product (GNP). The total value of all goods and services in the nation produced in a single year.

HEW. Department of Health, Education and Welfare.

Home rule. Home rule occurs when a charter gives a local unit of government a high level of independence relative to the state government.

"Honest graft." *See* Individual corruption.

HUD. Department of Housing and Urban Development.

Impeachment. A formal accusation by the lower house of a legislature that brings a public official (such as a governor or judge) to trial in the upper house.

Implied powers. The authority of the federal government that is based on the inference of certain powers specifically delegated to the federal government in the Constitution. Through the doctrine of implied powers, the national government has broadened its authority relative to the states.

Income tax. A tax on personal income; favored by states and the national government.

Incorporation. The creation of a legal entity, such as a city, at the request of the area's inhabitants. Incorporated jurisdictions usually have a large measure of self-government.

Incumbent. An elected officeholder.

Indeterminate sentencing. The traditional method of sentencing persons convicted of crimes in which a parole board is granted authority to decrease a prisoner's term of sentence within broad parameters.

Individual corruption. The phenomenon of an individual, by dint of being in a particular situation, committing a corrupt political act.

Initiative petition. A document permitting a specified percentage of the voters to propose a constitutional amendment or similar basic change for purposes of putting it to a referendum vote.

Interest group. A collection of people with a specified policy that they would like to see enacted.

Intergovernmental relations. *See* Federalism.

Interlocal agreements. Cooperative agreements entered into by local governments.

Interparty competition. The degree to which political parties are competitive in elections.

Interstate compacts. Agreements between states that require congressional approval.

Item veto. A form of veto power in which a chief executive officer may delete sections or items of a bill, usually an appropriations bill, while signing the remainder of the bill into law.

Judicial court. A form of special courts used in some states to decide on the removal or retention of judges.

Judicial review. The power of the courts to declare laws and executive orders null and void because they are contrary to the constitution of the state or nation.

Judicial tenure commission. Organizations in the state that make recommendations on the removal or retention of lower court judges.

Lakewood Plan. An extensive network of contract service agreements between thirty-two municipalities in Los Angeles County.

Legislative council. A permanent professional staff that provides research on legislation on a continuing basis. Legislative councils are less *ad hoc* in nature than Legislative Reference Services.

Legislative reference service. A professional staff that provides research on upcoming legislation and often drafts bills for state legislatures.

Legislature. A body of peoples' representatives who make laws for a society. Legislatures normally refer to the lawmaking bodies of the states.

Legitimacy. The degree to which the people trust their political institutions.

Lobby. *See* Interest group.

Local government. Government as it is found in counties, cities, towns, and townships. Local government is distinguished from both state government and national government.

Long ballot. Elections in which the people vote for virtually every official, as opposed to minor officials being appointed by a few elected officials.

Machine politics. A tightly organized political entity that controls state or local elections and policy making. The political "machine" is dominated by a political "boss" who may or may not hold political office.

Majority. More than half of the votes cast in any one election.

"Matthew effect." An electoral situation, usually associated with the single member plurality vote system, in which the political party that accumulates the largest portion of a district's votes will garner even larger proportions of the district's legislative seats, while parties with relatively smaller percentages of the vote tend to acquire even less legislative seats.

Mayor and Council government. A form of municipal government in which councilmembers and the mayor are elected.

Medicaid. A federal public assistance program designed to provide health care to the needy and which is financed jointly between federal and state governments.

Medicare. A federal social insurance program that provides comprehensive medical care for people over 65.

Merit system. A system of public personnel administration in which hiring, promotion, demotion, and firing of public employees is determined by their ability to complete a task efficiently and effectively.

Metropolitan districts. A type of special district covering an entire metropolitan area.

Misdemeanor. A minor crime.

Missouri plan. A method of selecting judges in which the governor appoints the more important judges and, after an interim in office, the judges are put up for popular election.

Mobility. Mobility can be both demographic and social. *Demographic mobility* refers to the movement of people across the country. *Social mobility* refers to people going up and down the economic ladder in society.

Model Cities. A program initiated by federal legislation in 1964 designed to assist in community development. In 1974, it was subsumed under the Housing and Community Development Block Grant program.

Modified one-party Democratic systems. States in which the Democratic Party has general predominance but can be effectively challenged on occasion.

Modified one-party Republican systems. States in which the Republican Party has predominance but may be effectively challenged on occasion.

Multimember district. An electoral district from which several legislators are chosen on a proportional vote.

Multimember district system. An electoral formula in which the number of votes won by any particular political party is proportioned out accordingly to that party in terms of seats in the legislature.

Multipurpose district. A special function district that conducts more than one function of government.

Municipal bonds. *See* Bond.

Municipality. A city or town.

Mutual aid pact. A type of interlocal agreement that becomes operative only when some disturbance, such as a fire or riot, occurs.

Neighborhood corporations. Nonprofit organizations chartered by the state and managed for the public benefit in specified urban areas by that area's residents.

"New Towns-In Town." The movement by state and local governments to redevelop decaying urban areas through such programs as Urban Renewal and Model Cities.

Nonpartisan election. An election in which the candidate's party is not listed on the ballot.

OEO. Office of Economic Opportunity, *now* the Community Services Administration.

OMB. Office of Management and Budget.

One-party Democratic systems. States whose politics are dominated completely by the Democratic Party.

Open primary. A primary election in which all voters may vote regardless of party affilation. *Also called* a blanket primary.

Override. The ability of the legislature to enact legislation regardless of the veto by a governor or mayor. Usually an override requires at least two-thirds of the legislature.

"Para-transit." The enactment of public policies which promote the use of independent car pools, van pools, jitnies, and taxis, in contrast to mass-transit concepts such as subways, trains, and buses, as a major method of resolving the urban transportation crisis.

Parole. The conditional release of a prisoner

who has served part but not all of a prison sentence.

Party. A collection of people with an overarching political program.

Patronage. Awarding public office on the basis of political loyalty as opposed to professional merit.

Periodic registration. A system of registration in which voters must register periodically, such as every year.

Permanent registration. Registering as a voter on a permanent basis.

Planning boards. Local agencies designed to devise a comprehensive community plan, make re–zoning decisions, administer community subdivision regulations, and make policy in related areas. Usually, but not always, the members of local planning boards are elected. Local planning boards also are known as local planning commissions.

Planning commissions. *See* Planning boards.

Plea bargaining. The negotiations that occur between the lawyer of a person accused of a crime and the public prosecutor. The objective on the part of the accused's lawyer is to reduce the charge, while the objective of the public prosecutor is to gain a conviction.

Plural executive plan. The county version of the commission form of government used in some municipalities.

Pluralism. A point of view on political power which argues that power is dispersed among many competing groups and individuals.

Plurality. The most votes cast in a given election. A plurality can be less than half the votes cast but still be the most votes cast for any one candidate or issue.

Political culture. The basic beliefs of a group of people regarding political activity, the role that citizens play in the political process, and the nature of that process.

Polity. The political system.

Poll tax. An obsolete and unconstitutional tax in which voters had to pay a tax in order to vote.

Postcard registration. Registering to vote by mail. The method is used by about one-third of the states.

"Poverty line." A measure devised in 1955 by the federal government as a definition of poverty. The official poverty line is a point slightly more than three times the average annual cost of what nutrition experts determine to be an adequate diet.

"Power shift." Kirkpatrick Sales' notion that political power is shifting from the Snowbelt to the Sunbelt in this country.

Precinct. Neighborhood political units that comprise, in their totality, a ward.

President *pro tempore*. The presiding officer of a state senate. State senates usually elect a president *pro tempore* when the state has no Lieutenant Governor.

Pressure group. *See* Interest group.

Primary election. Nominating party candidates by means of direct popular election. *See also* Closed primary, Open primary, and Run-off primary.

Probation. The suspension of a prison sentence by the court, but with conditions set for a period of time.

Progressive tax. Taxes are progressive when the ratio of tax to income rises as income rises.

Project grant. *See* Categorical grant.

Property tax. A tax levied on property owners and which is set according to the value of the property. Property may be real, such as land or buildings, or personal, such as cars, stocks and bonds. *See also* Circuit breaker.

Proportional tax. Taxes are proportional when the ratio of taxes to income is the same for all classes of income.

Public assistance. A federal benefit program funded out of general tax revenues. Public assistance includes Medicaid, Supplemental Security

Income Assistance, Aid to Families with Dependent Children, and Food Stamps.

Public choice theory. A school of thought in political science and public administration that advocates an economic approach to policy issues.

Public housing. The efforts by state and local governments, often using funds provided by the federal government, to build improved housing for poor people.

"Public technology." The effort by state and local governments to use scientific and technical advances in creative ways that benefit the broad range of citizens.

Quorum. A particular proportion of the total membership of a legislature that must be present for any official action to be taken. Usually this proportion refers to at least a majority of the membership.

Quotas. As used in public personnel administration, quotas refer to the argument that the traditional entry and promotion qualifications of Civil Service should be reduced or waived until the number of women and minority group members working in government at all ranks at least equals their proportion in the population at large.

"Race tax." A term used to connote the fact that black and brown people often must pay a higher rent or a higher price for a home than white people.

"Racial steering." The practice by some real estate brokers of "steering" minorities away from housing in largely white neighborhoods.

Ratification. Voter approval of action taken by state legislators or by members of a constitutional commission who have proposed amendments to the state constitution.

Reapportionment. *See* Apportionment.

Recall. A procedure that enables voters to remove an elected official from office.

Recidivism. The number of persons who are sent back to prison for additional crimes that they perpetrated once they are out of prison.

"Redlining." The practice by some American banks of making it difficult for home buyers to purchase a house in a minority neighborhood by not granting them mortgages and similar kinds of loans.

Referendum. A vote by the citizens of a political system on a particular issue, such as Proposition 13 in California.

Reform politics. The traditional American response to machine politics, which stresses that educated and well-informed citizens should establish policy without regard to partisan or machine considerations.

Regional planning council. Primarily responsible for comprehensive planning in intrastate regions. Regional Planning Councils are established through state legislation with federal encouragement. Examples of Regional Planning Councils are Economic Development Districts and Rural Area Development Committees, most of which are controlled entirely by federal administrators. Regional Planning Councils are not the same as Councils of Government, which are voluntary associations of state and local officials.

Regressive tax. Taxes are regressive when the ratio of tax to income falls as income rises.

Residence requirement. The stipulation that a potential voter must have resided in his or her community for a specified period of time before he or she is eligible to vote.

Reputational analysis. A research methodology that analyzes community power by attempting to ascertain members who have reputations for being powerful.

Revenue sharing. A policy initiated in 1972 by Congress that distributes federal funds to state and local governments on the basis of federal personal income tax funds provided by state and local jurisdictions.

"Reverse discrimination." The act of discriminating against white males as the result of attempting to comply with affirmative action requirements.

Revision. Basic change in a state constitution.

Right-to-know laws. Legislation which requires that meetings of public agencies and legislative committees are virtually always open to the public.

Roles. In sociology the term "roles" refers to the behavior of individuals and groups in particular situations.

Run-off primary. A second primary election held to choose a candidate when no candidate has received a majority of the primary votes. The run-off primary is favored in the South and other one-party states.

Sales tax. A tax on goods, such as gasoline or liquor; favored by state governments.

School board. The policy-making body of school districts in most states. Usually, but not always, the members of school boards are elected.

School district. The autonomous unit of government that makes school policy in all the states except Hawaii.

Shared tax. A tax that state and local governments divide between themselves.

Short ballot. Elections in which the people may vote only for a limited spectrum of highest level candidates.

Single member district. An electoral district that sends one representative to a legislative body.

Single member plurality vote system. An electoral formula under which each electoral district in the state may elect one representative to the legislature by plurality (in contrast to majority) vote.

SMSA. Standard Metropolitan Statistical Area.

Snowbelt. The states in the Midwest and Northeast. *Also known* as the Frostbelt or the Graybelt.

Social insurance. Benefits paid to individuals by the federal government, which are funded by compulsory payroll taxes. Social insurance usually is called "Social Security" and includes Old Age, Survivor's Disability, and Health Insurance (OAS-DHI), Medicare, unemployment benefits, and general health care.

Speaker of the House. The presiding official of the House of Representatives in the states.

Special district. A governmental type with authority to perform a particular governmental function, such as fire protection or water supply.

Specialized local trial court. A court of relatively limited jurisdiction which deals primarily with minor cases.

Standard Metropolitan Statistical Area. Urban areas of 50,000 people or more.

Stare decisis. Judicial precedent, or the reliance by the judiciary on past cases in making decisions.

Status categories. A Census Bureau term that bases certain social and economic measures on occupational type, level of education, and amount of income.

Substandard housing. A Census Bureau term that means structurally dilapidated or without plumbing.

Suburbanization. The movement of people from the inner cities to the surrounding surburbs.

Suffrage. The right to vote.

Sunbelt. The states located in the Southeastern and Southwestern portions of the country. *Also known* as the Southern Rim.

Sunset laws. Legislation that requires a periodic legislative review of agencies for purposes of determining whether or not those agencies should be continued.

Sunshine laws. Legislation that requires the fullest possible public disclosure of personal finances by public officials, both elected and appointed.

Supplemental Security Income Assistance. A federal public assistance program that, in 1974, combined Old Age Assistance, Aid to the Blind, and Aid to the Permanently and Totally Disabled and which displaced the states' role in these programs.

Supreme Court. The final court of appeals in the states. *Also called* Superior Court.

Systemic corruption. Corruption that is entrenched and accepted by the political system and goes far beyond the commitment of an individual act of graft.

Tax. A charge levied by government for purposes of generating revenues. *See also:* Income tax, Poll tax, Progressive tax, Property tax, Proportional tax, Regressive tax, Sales tax, Shared tax, and Use tax.

TDR. Transferrable Development Rights, which amounts to a variation on traditional zoning by separating the right to improve property from the right to own property. Under TDR, a community can directly give or withhold development rights from a private developer in order to restrict development in one area and to encourage development in another.

Town. A unit of local government.

Township. A unit of local government favored in the Northeast and North Central states.

Transplantation theory. The notion that voters moving to the suburbs always have been conservative, but only start voting conservative when they leave the inner city.

Trial court. A court which has general jurisdiction and the broadest authority in the state court systems.

Trial court of general jurisdiction. A court which deals with criminal felonies and civil cases.

Trial court of limited jurisdiction. *See* Specialized local trial court.

Two-party systems. States which are genuinely competitive between the Republicans and Democrats.

"Ultralocalism." A prevalent ideology that advocates a fragmenting of governmental authority.

Unicameral legislature. A legislature with only one house. Only Nebraska has a unicameral legislature.

"Urban hardship." A term developed by the Brookings Institution which compares inner cities with their outer suburbs and, from that comparison, derives a measure of how badly off or better off a city is relative to its surrounding area.

Urban homesteading. An aspect of the "new town-in town" movement in which public policies are enacted designed to encourage the movement of young professionals back to the inner cities through such devices as selling abandoned houses for virtually nothing.

Urban renewal. The attempt to improve the physical environment of cities through federal programs with local cooperation. In 1974, federal Urban Renewal was subsumed under the Housing and Community Development Block Grants Program.

Urbanization. The movement of people from the countryside to the cities.

Use tax. A tax on the use of particular amenities, such as a toll on highway use.

Veto. The ability of a chief executive to cancel legislation that has been passed by the legislature. *See also* Item veto.

Victimless crime. A violation in which it is difficult to prove there was ever a victim. An example would be public drunkenness.

Voting registration. Recording oneself as a voter in the community in which one resides. *See also:* Periodic registration, Permanent registration, and Postcard registration.

Ward. The division of a city for the purposes of electing members to the city council.

Welfare. *See* Public assistance.

"White flight." The phenomenon of white people leaving urban areas for the suburbs.

Women's Liberation. The movement by women to have equal rights with men.

Zoning. A local land-use plan concerning how certain sections of the community may be used. *See also:* Exclusionary zoning and TDR.

RESEARCH RESOURCES IN STATE AND LOCAL GOVERNMENT AND POLITICS

Writing a term paper on state and local politics can be considerably easier and faster, and the results probably better, if you know what to look for in your library. The following information sources not only will give you a head start in writing that paper but will give some familiarity with how to use your university's library as well. The sources are listed in alphabetical order and a short description accompanies each title.

ABC POL SCI: Advance Bibliography of Contents: Political Science and Government. Santa Barbara, Calif.: American Bibliographical Center–Clio Press, 1969–. Published eight times a year, it reproduces the tables of contents of about 260 journals in political science, public administration, law, and related fields. An annual subject index and an author index appear in each issue and are cumulated twice a year.

ABS Guide to Recent Publications in the Social and Behavioral Sciences. Beverly Hills, Calif.: Sage Publications, 1965–. This is a cumulation of abstracts appearing in the "New Studies" section of the *American Behavioral Scientist.* The first volume contains the abstracts that appear from 1957 through 1964. Annual cumulative volumes have been issued since 1966. The abstracts are listed alphabetically by author, with a subject and methodological index.

American Behavioral Scientist. Beverly Hills, Calif.: Sage Publications 1957–. Each monthly issue contains an insertion section entitled "New Studies: A Guide to Recent Publications in the Social and Behavioral Sciences," which contains brief abstracts of articles selected from over 300 journals, plus significant new books.

Book of the States. Chicago: Council of State Governments, 1935–. Published biennially and "designed to provide an authoritative source of information on the structures, working methods, financing and functional activities of the state governments."

County Yearbook. Washington, D.C.: National Association of Counties and International City Management Association, 1975–. Patterned after the *Municipal Yearbook,* the county version contains some excellent analyses of county government with an emphasis on intergovernmental relations. Has a bibliographical section for additional sources.

Current Contents: Behavioral, Social and Management Sciences. Philadelphia: Institute for Scientific Information, 1969–. Published weekly, it reproduces the tables of contents to about 700 journals in various social science disciplines, along with an author index.

ERIC (Educational Resources Information Center). Washington, D.C.: U.S. Office of Education. An extraordinarily comprehensive information system for all aspects of education, including the political. More than 35,000 abstracts of reports and 20,000 abstracts of articles appear each year and are keyed to more than 6,800 terms in the *Thesaurus of ERIC Descriptors.*

Holler, Frederick L. *The Information Sources of Political Science.* Santa Barbara, Calif.: American Bibliographical Center–Clio Press, 1971. A useful compendium covering information sources in the discipline by subfield and by type of source (e.g., guidebooks, dictionaries, book review indices, etc.).

International Political Science Abstracts. Oxford: Basil Blackwell, 1951–. Prepared quarterly, each volume contains about 350 abstracts, including 150 abstracted journals. In the first volume, a very broad subject group is arranged with an author and subject index. Subsequently, the arrangement is alphabetical by author, with cumulated subject and author indices in the fourth issue of each year.

Metropolitan Area Annual. Albany, N.Y.: Graduate School of Public Affairs, State University of New York at Albany, 1966–. An annual reference volume. Section entitled "Metropolitan Area Bibliography" lists recent books, articles, and pamphlets. "Metropolitan Surveys" section lists studies in progress or recently completed on metropolitan problems.

Metropolitan Area Problems: News and Digest. New York: Conference on Metropolitan Area Problems, 1957–. Each bimonthly issue has a section entitled "Recent Publications on Metropolitan Area Problems," which contains a selective listing of books and articles.

Monthly Checklist of State Publications. Washington, D.C.: U.S. Government Printing Office, 1910–. There is no complete list of all state documents, but this is the most extensive listing available. About 20,000 publications are listed each year, arranged alphabetically by state, with an annual index. Publications issued by regional organizations and associations of state officials are listed in a special edition.

Municipal Yearbook. Washington, D.C.: International City Management Association, 1934–. Provides "information on current activities and practices of cities throughout the United States." Contains extensive data on Governmental Units, Personnel, Finance, and Municipal Actities. Includes directories of city officials. Has bibliographical sections which refer to additional sources.

Public Affairs Information Service Index. New York: Public Affairs Information Service, 1915–. This index, with annual cumulations, unifies a wide variety of sources concerned with public affairs. It lists books, pamphlets, periodicals, and government documents. Most articles include brief explanatory items.

Sage Yearbooks in Politics and Public Policy. Beverly Hills, Calif.: Sage, 1975–. Published in conjunction with the Policy Studies Organization, the *Yearbooks* are edited on a thematic concept (e.g., federalism) and contain original essays.

Sage Public Administration Abstracts. Beverly Hills, Calif.: Sage, 1974–. A quarterly publication that lists and abstracts more than 1000 publications in the field annually. Abstracts are indexed by author, title, and subject, and a year-end cumulative index is published.

Sills, David, ed. *International Encyclopedia of the Social Sciences.* 15 volumes. New York: Macmillan and Free Press, 1968. Supplements the old *Encyclopedia of the Social Sciences,* published in the early 1930s. A synthesis and summary of the "state of the art" in all the social sciences.

Universal Reference System. Edited by Alfred de Grazia. New York: Metron, Inc., 1967–. A superb series of computer-produced bibliography indexes covering ten sub-fields of political science. URS publishes basic bibliographical volumes, called Codexes, which cover the significant literature—including periodical articles, books, and documents—of each subfield. The Codexes are supplemented by "Quarterly Gazettes" bringing coverage up-to-date, with an annual cumulation for each gazette at the end of the year. The Universal Reference System issues Codexes and "Quarterly Gazettes" in the following subject areas (asterisks indicate those volumes of particular interest to state and local researchers):

International Affairs
*Legislative Process, Deliberation, and Decision Making
*Administrative Management: Public and Private Bureaucracy
*Current Events and Problems of Modern Society
*Public Opinion, Mass Behavior, and Political Psychology
*Law, Jurisprudence, and Judicial Process
Economic Regulation, Business, and Government
Public Policy and the Management of Science
Comparative Government and Cultures
*Bibliography of Bibliographies in Political Science, Government, Public Policy.

Urban Affairs Annual Reviews. Beverly Hills, Calif.: Sage Publications, 1967–. A series of "annual reference volumes designed to present critical analyses" in various fields of urban studies.

U.S. Bureau of the Census. Washington: U.S. Government Printing Office. *Census of Governments, 1967, 1972, and 1977.* Probably the most authoritative source of information on governmental trends in the United States.

U.S. Bureau of the Census. *County and City Data Book.* Contains selected statistical series, based on census data, for each county in the U.S., Standard Metropolitan Statistical Areas, and cities with more than 25,000 population. More than 140 items are presented for each unit.

U.S. Bureau of the Census. *Directory of Federal Statistics for Local Areas, 1966.* A finding guide to sources of federal statistics for metropolitan areas, counties, and urban areas.

U.S. Bureau of the Census. *Directory of Federal Statistics for States: A Guide to Sources, 1967.* A subject listing of sources containing data on the state level.

U.S. Political Science Documents. Pittsburgh: University of Pittsburgh Center for International Studies, 1975–. An annual, annotated series of volumes covering about 120 American journals relating to political science.

MAJOR JOURNALS AND PERIODICALS ON STATE AND LOCAL GOVERNMENT AND POLITICS AND RELATED POLICY AREAS

Some of the more significant synopses and annotated bibliographies of research on state and local government and politics and related areas are listed and described in Appendix A. In this Appendix, we list and briefly describe the more important journals on the same topics. The list is necessarily selective, but an effort has been made to include those journals published by state and regional political science associations as well as national periodicals of a relevant but nonacademic nature.

Many states and cities publish magazines that, though more entertaining and culturally oriented than publications listed here, occasionally have articles of political value. Local newspapers are also a major source of information, and your own university may have an Institute of Government or similar unit that sponsors its own publications program focusing on state and local issues. These can be helpful in researching a term paper that concerns politics in your own state or town.

Selected journals and periodicals with national circulation are listed in alphabetical order, together with a brief description.

American County Government. Published monthly by the National Association of Counties, each issue focuses on a theme, such as county home rule.

American Journal of Political Science. Published by the Midwest Political Science Association, *AJPS* has a decidedly behavioral orientation.

American Political Science Review. Published by the American Political Science Association, *APSR* is the leading national political science journal. Excellent book review section.

Annals of the American Academy of Political and Social Science. Each issue concentrates on a specific area in the social sciences and produces an extensive book-review and notes section covering the social sciences.

Governmental Finance. Quarterly journal published by the Municipal Finance Officers Association, it focuses on urban fiscal issues.

GPSA Journal. Published by the Georgia Political Science Association, the *Journal* tends to stress national more than statewide politics.

Idaho Journal of Politics. A state-oriented journal published by the Idaho Political Science Association.

Journal of Criminal Law, Criminology and Police Science. Devoted to policy and administration of law enforcement.

Journal of the American Institute of Planners. Devoted to public planning.

Journal of Political Science. Published by the South Carolina Political Science Association.

Journal of Politics. A quality journal published by the Southern Political Science Association.

National Civic Review. A very informative periodical on urban affairs published monthly by the National Municipal League. Articles are policy-oriented.

National Tax Journal. Perhaps the best single journal on state and local taxation policies.

Nation's Cities. Monthly publication of the National League of Cities, it often focuses on federal/urban relations.

Perspectives on Minnesota Government and Politics. Published by the Minnesota Political Science Association, *Perspectives* zeroes in on that state's politics.

Policy Studies Journal. Published quarterly by the Policy Studies Organizaton.

Polity. A quarterly journal with a philosophic bent published by the Northeastern Political Science Association.

Proceedings. The Political Science Associations of Oklahoma, Tennessee, and West Virginia each publish annual *Proceedings* of their statewide meetings.

Public Administration Review. The most significant American journal concerned with public administration. Published bimonthly by the American Society for Public Administration.

Public Administration Times. (formerly **P.A. News & Views**) State and local governments run "help wanted" ads in the *Times.* Published biweekly by the American Society for Public Administration; the newsletter also carries articles on state and local government.

Public Affairs. A public affairs, public policy journal.

Public Choice. A policy journal with a political economy orientation; published by the Public Choice Society.

Public Finance Quarterly. A journal emphasizing economic approaches to budgeting in the United States.

Public Interest, The. High-quality articles on public policy issues.

Public Management. Short articles devoted to urban administration. Published monthly by the International City Management Association.

Public Personnel Review. Short articles devoted to public personnel administration. Published quarterly by the International Personnel Management Association.

Public Policy. Excellent articles on public policy and public affairs.

Public Welfare. Devoted to policy and administration of public welfare in the United States.

Publius. A journal devoted to intergovernmental relations and federalism.

Review of Public Data Use. A quarterly journal designed "to encourage the use of publicly available data for research or analysis applied to local, regional, or national problems."

Sage Professional Papers in Administrative and Policy Studies. Twelve academic papers are published annually in three issues, devoted to the policy sciences.

Sage Professional Papers in American Politics. Twelve academic papers are published annually, each with a distinctly theoretical cast.

Short Essays in Political Science. Compilation of papers presented at the Spring Conference of the National Capitol Area Political Science Association.

Social Science Quarterly. Policy-oriented articles of interest to political scientists. Published jointly by the Southerwestern Social Science Association and the Southwestern Political Science Association.

State and Local Government Review. A quarterly journal on theoretical and substantive topics.

State Government. Devoted to state government problems. Published quarterly by the Council of State Governments.

State Government Administration. Conversational articles that concern public administration in the states.

State Government News. A useful monthly publication that reviews current state legislation and policy. Published by the Council of State Governments.

Urban Affairs Quarterly. Devoted primarily to sociological and political treatments of urban areas.

Urban Research News. A biweekly newsletter for the urban specialist. "Reports on current developments—personnel, meetings, research projects, publications, etc.— at the over 200 centers engaged in urban research."

Washington Monthly. A liberal-journalistic publication of high quality. It focuses on the injustices of the public bureaucracy as well as on policy issues.

Western City. Published monthly by the League of California Cities, the magazine has an urban administration focus; all western cities are featured.

Western Political Science Quarterly. Published jointly by the Western Political Science Association, the Pacific Northwest Political Science Association, and the Southern California Political Science Association, *WPSQ* features articles of both national and western relevance.

SELECTED ACADEMIC, PROFESSIONAL, AND PUBLIC INTEREST ORGANIZATIONS, WITH ADDRESSES

The following national groups all have a direct relevance to state and local government and politics. Virtually all publish journals and newsletters on topics of interest, and you may wish to contact some of them for their materials. The organizations are listed in alphabetical order, together with a brief description and their addresses.

Academy for Contemporary Problems. 1501 Neil Avenue, Columbus, OH 43201. A "think tank" specifically oriented toward state and local governmental problems.

Advisory Commission on Intergovernmental Relations. Washington, DC 20575. Founded in 1959, the ACIR is publishing increasingly significant studies of the federal system.

American Academy of Political and Social Science. 3937 Chestnut Street, Philadelphia, PA 19104. Publishes the *Annals* of the American Academy of Political and Social Science.

American Association of State Highway and Transportation Officials. 444 North Capitol Street, Washington, DC 20001. The major association of state transit officials.

American Civil Liberties Union. 22 East 40th Street, New York, NY 10016. The major legal association that takes on cases relating to individual freedom.

American Institute of Planners. 1776 Massachusetts Avenue, N.W., Washington, DC 20036. The major association of public planning officials.

American Political Science Association. 1527 New Hampsire Avenue, N.W., Washington, DC 20036. The chief academic association of political scientists.

American Public Welfare Association. 1155 Sixteenth Street, N.W., Washington, DC 20036. The major organization of public welfare officials.

American Society for Public Administration. 1225 Connecticut Avenue, N.W., Washington, DC 20036. The major organization of academics and professionals in public administration at all levels of government.

American Public Transit Association. 1100 Seventeenth Street, Washington, DC 20036. The major association of public officials interested in mass transit.

Brookings Institution. 1775 Massachusetts Avenue, N.W., Washington, DC 20036. A major academic think-tank with important concerns in state and local public affairs.

Center for the Study of Democratic Institutions. P.O. Box 4068, Santa Barbara, CA 93103. A high-level study group devoted to advancing democratic theory.

Committee for Economic Development. 477 Madison Avenue, New York, NY 10022. A private group that studies issues relating to business and public policy.

Common Cause. 2030 M Street, N.W., Washington, DC 20036. An organization of more than 300,000 members dedicated to political reform.

Council of State Community Affairs Agencies. 1612 K Street, N.W., Washington, DC 20006. The major association of state community affairs officers.

Council of State Governments. Ironworks Pike, P.O. Box 11910, Lexington, KY 40511. Publishers of *The Book of the States* and other publications relating directly to state governments.

Freedom of Information Center. School of Journalism, University of Missouri, P.O. Box 858, Columbia, MO 65201. Conducts studies on the public's uses of federal, state, and local Freedom of Information Acts.

International Association of Chiefs of Police. 11 First Field Road, Gaithersburg, MD 20760. The major organization of police chiefs.

International City Management Association. 1140 Connecticut Avenue, N.W., Washington. DC 20036. The major organization of city managers and other individuals interested in city management.

International Personnel Management Association. 1313 East Sixtieth Street, Chicago, IL 60637. The major organization of public personnel administrators at all levels of government.

Movement for Economic Justice. 1609 Connecticut Avenue, N.W., Washington, DC 20009. An organization concerned with utility rate increases, real estate practices, and property taxation.

Municipal Finance Officers Association. 1313 East Sixtieth Street, Chicago, IL 60637. The major organization of budgetary and taxation officers in local governments.

National Association for the Advancement of Colored People. 733 Fifteenth Street, N.W., Washington, DC 20005. The most prestigious political organization of blacks.

National Association of Counties. 1735 New York Avenue, N.W., Washington, DC 20036. The major organization of county officials, publishers of research on county government.

National Association of Housing and Redevelopment Officials. 2600 Virginia Avenue, N.W., Washington, DC 20037. The major association of state and local officials concerned with community development.

National Association of Regional Councils. 1700 K Street, N.W., Washington, DC 20036. The major organization of Councils of Governments and related organizations.

National Conference of State Legislatures. 1405 Curtis Street, Denver, CO 80202. The major association of state legislatures.

National Committee Against Discrimination in Housing. 1425 H Street, N.W., Washington, DC 20005. A national organization dedicated to ending racial discrimination in housing.

National Governors Association (*formerly the* **National Governors Conference**). 444 North Capitol Street, Washington, DC 20001. The organization of American governors.

National League of Cities. 1620 Eye Street, N.W., Washington, DC 20006. One of the major associations of urban governments.

National Municipal League. 47 East 68th Street, New York, NY 10021. A private reform-orientated organization that focuses on local governments.

National School Boards Association. 1055 Thomas Jefferson Street, Washington, DC 20007. The major organization of local school board officials.

National Welfare Rights Organization. 1420 N Street, N.W., Washington, DC 20005. Works to improve and expand welfare policy.

Tax Foundation, Inc. 50 Rockefeller Plaza, New York, NY 10020. A private association concerned with tax issues.

Urban Environment Conference. 1609 Connecticut Avenue N.W., Washington, DC 20009. Coordinates civil rights groups and labor organizations on land-use issues.

Urban Institute. 2100 M Street, N.W., Washington, DC 20037. A research organization devoted to urban issues.

United States Conference of Mayors. 1620 Eye Street, Washington, DC 20006. The major association of American mayors.

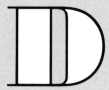

HOW TO ADDRESS PUBLIC OFFICIALS

Information, like money, is one of those things of which there is never enough. When you need information on a public issue that is not publicly available, it often is a good idea to write and ask someone who knows. A correct form of address can add to the effectiveness of your request to a public official, so this final appendix lists the proper ways of addressing public officials. By all means, write them!

PUBLIC OFFICIAL	FORM OF ADDRESS	SALUTATION
alderman	The Honorable John Green	Dear Mr. Green:
assemblyman	—*see representative, state*	
associate justice, Supreme Court	Mr. Justice Green The Supreme Court of the United States	Dear Mr. Justice:
cabinet officers (as the secretary of state and the attorney general)	The Honorable John (or Joan) Green Secretary of State The Honorable John Smith Attorney General of the United States	Dear Sir: (or Dear Madam:)
chief justice, Supreme Court	The Chief Justice of the United States	Dear Mr. Chief Justice:
commissioner	The Honorable John Green	Dear Mr. Smith:
councilmember	The Honorable John Green	Dear Mr. Green:
former U.S. president	The Honorable John Green	Dear Mr. Green:
governor	The Honorable John Green Governor of —	Dear Governor Green:
judge, federal	The Honorable John Green United States District Judge	Dear Judge Green:
judge, state or local	The Honorable John Green Chief Judge of the Court of Appeals	Dear Judge Green:
lieutenant governor	The Honorable John Green Lieutenant Governor of —	Dear Mr. Green:
mayor	The Honorable John Green Mayor of —	Dear Mayor Green:
president, U.S.	The President	Dear Mr. President:
representative, state (same format for assemblyman)	The Honorable John Green House of Representatives State Capitol	Dear Mr. Green:
representative, U.S.	The Honorable John Green The United States House of Representatives	Dear Mr. Green:
senator, state	The Honorable John Green The State Senate State Capitol	Dear Senator Green:
senator, U.S.	The Honorable John Green United States Senate	Dear Senator Green:
speaker, U.S. House of Representatives	The Honorable John Green Speaker of the House of Representatives	Dear Mr. Speaker:
vice-president, U.S.	The Vice-President United States Senate	Dear Mr. Vice-President:

INDEX

Aaron, Henry J., 315
ABC funds, 426
Action Grant Program, 209
Adams, John, 41, 453
Addonizio, Hugh, 464–65, 466
Advisory Commission on Intergovernmental Relations (ACIR), U.S., 177, 196, 197, 255, 300, 327, 370, 469
Affirmative action, civil service, 267–74. *See also* Merit system, civil service.
  quota systems, 268–69
Aging, Committee on, Senate, U.S., 456, 457
Agnew, Spiro T., 375
Agriculture, Department of (U.S.), 415
Aid to the Blind, 340
Aid to Families with Dependent Children (AFDC), 336, 337, 341, 343, 345, 346–47, 349, 351, 352, 353, 355. *See also* Poverty
Aid to Permanently and Totally Disabled, 340
Air pollution control, 177, 233
Alabama, 39, 52, 69, 110, 149
Alaska, 39, 43, 50, 58, 78, 119, 311
Albritton, Robert, 337, 346, 349
Alienation, political: local government and, 188–89 nonvoting and, 60–61 of the young, 59–60
Alioto, Joseph, 282
Allensworth, Don, 413, 419
American Association of State Highway Officials, 176
American Association of University Professors, 409
American Bar Association, 149, 439
AFL-CIO, 13, 398
American Federation of State, County, and Municipal Employees (AFSCME), 274, 275, 278
American Federation of Teachers (AFT), 274, 275, 398, 400, 409
American Judicator Society, 149
Ames, Albert A., 225
Anaconda Company, 68–69
Apportionment, legislative, 82–88
Arizona, organized crime in, 460–63
Arkansas, 39, 52, 116, 149
Aronson, J. Richard, 286

Baer, Michael A., 73, 74, 98
Bailey, Stephen K., 385
Baker v. Carr, 84, 85
Bakke, Allan, 269–70
Ballot, secret, 42
Banfield, Edward, 181, 202
Barber, James David, 105
Bay Area Rapid Transit (BART) District, 194
Beame, Abraham, 325
Berg, Paul, 14
Berry, Fred, 4
Bicameralism vs. unicameralism, 78

Bill drafting service, 108
Blacks: crime and, 364, 365 education of, 400–406 enfranchisement of, 50–53 housing for, 433–41, 445–47 migration of, 347 office-holding by, 235–36, 362 police and, 367–68 poverty and, 334–36, 347–48 in public employment, 267–74 in state legislatures, 103–4 unemployment and, 334 unrest of, 360–63 urbanization of, 20–21 voting behavior of, 56
Bloc grants, 196, 296, 301–2
Blue Earth County, Minnesota, 190
Boiardo, Anthony, 464, 465, 466
Boiardo, Ruggiero, 464
Bollens, John C., 199
Boss and machine, political, 225–27
Boundaries, political disputes over, 187–95
Bradley, Tom, 235–36
Brookings Institution, 22, 299, 301, 372
Brown, Edmund G., Jr., 124–25
Brown, Edmund G. (Pat), Sr., 124, 235
Brown, Jerry, 424
Brown v. The Board of Education of Topeka, Kansas, 401–2, 406
Bryan City, California, 173
Bureaucracy: governors and, 120–23 policy-making and, 246–48 size and composition of, 247–48 technology and, 248–55
Burger, Warren E., 376, 379
Burke, Edmund, 101

California, 5, 12, 37, 39, 70–71, 86, 87, 110, 139, 145, 149, 173, 376, 377, 424
  Proposition 13, 317–19
  Supreme Court, 143–44
Capital punishment, 380
Capone, Al "Scarface," 454
Carter, Jimmy, 42, 117, 355, 359, 362, 416, 446, 458
Categorical grants, 296, 297, 300, 338
Catena, Gerardo, 464
Census, Bureau of the, U.S., 9, 21, 31, 58, 59, 277, 448, 449
Chambers, William Nisbet, 38
Charters: municipal, 181–82 types of, 181
Chavez, César, 125
Chief administrative officer form of municipal government, 157
Child Support Enforcement Program, 353
Circuit breaker, 315
Circular A-95, 416
Citizens' Conference on State Legislatures, 110
City Bosses in the United States (Zink), 225
City council(s): membership of, 218–21 pressure groups and,

221–23 Roles of, 221,223
City manager, 237–41, 273. *See also* Mayor political corruption and, 469, 472–73
City University of New York, 408
Civil Rights, Commission of, U.S., 406
Civil Rights Act: of 1964, 12, 51, 52, 53, 56, 267, 269, 270 of 1968, 440
Civil Service, state and local: administration of, 258–59 affirmative action and, 267–74 federal government and, 257–58, 264–65, 267–71 grwoth of, 271 merit system and, 257–64, 283–84 political action and, 264–66 unionism and, 274–84
Civil Service Act (1883), 257
Civil Service Commission, 265
Civil Service Reform Act (1978), 257
Clark, Peter B., 202
Clark, Ramsey, 379
Closed partisan primary, 42
Colcord, Frank, 431
Coleman, James S., 404
Collective bargaining, in public employment, 277, 278–79
College Entrance Examination Board, 395, 396
Colorado, 183
Commerce, Department of (U.S.), 415
Commission on Civil Rights, U.S., 272, 434
Commission on Crime, President's 365
Commission form of municipal government, 155
Commission on Law Enforcement and Administration of Justice, President's, 359, 365, 460
Commission plan of county government, 160–62
Commission on Urban Housing, President's, 442
Committee for the American Electorate, 57
Committee for Economic Development, 190
Committees, legislative, 79–82
Community(ies): defined, 199–200 event analysis of, 201 neighborhood as, 200 power, 201–23 reputational analysis of, 201
Community Action Groups and City Government (Steggert), 206
Community development, federal government and, 206–10
Community Development Programs, 301
Community planning commissions, 413
Community Services Administration, U.S., 208
Comprehensive Employment and Training Act (1973) (CETA), 339, 355

Comprehensive plans, 414
Comprehensive urban county plan, 194–95
Computers and government, 250–52
Conference of Chief Justices, 149
Conference committees, 81
Conference of Mayors, 177, 430
Congress, U.S., 81
Congressional Budget Office, 326
Connally, John, 374
Connecticut, 41, 81, 108, 159, 183, 310
Consolidation, as approach to metropolitan government, 190–93
Constituency: legislative process and, 101–3
Constitution, U.S., 36 Amendments: Fourth, 373 Eighth, 380 Tenth, 174 Fourteenth, 84, 269, 373, 380, 391, 405 Fifteenth, 51 Sixteenth, 304 Nineteenth, 52 Twenty-fourth, 52 Twenty-sixth, 50, 53, 59. federal-state relations and, 173–75 voting qualifications and, 50, 51–53
Constitutional commission (State), 37
Constitution convention (State), 37
Construction Industry Association of Sonoma County v. City of Petaluma, 423
Conventions, 41
Coolidge, Calvin, 281
Corporate income tax, 308
Corruption in government, 7–8
Cosa Nostra, 459–64. *See also* Mafia
Council-administrator plan of county government, 162–63
Council-elected executive plan of county government, 163–64
Council-manager form of municipal government, 156
Council-manager plan, 469
Council of State Governments, 58
Councils of Governments (COGs), 177–79, 415, 417
County government, 158–60, types of: commission plan, 160–62 council-administrator plan, 162–63 council-elected executive plan, 163–64. urban, 164–65
County sheriff, 365–66
Courts. *See also* Crime; Police; Prison. civil rights and, 373 grand juries and, 373–74 plea bargaining and, 374–76 sentencing practices of, 376–78 work load of, 372–73
Courts, state. *See also* Judges; Judiciary. access to, 135–36 financing of, 131 jurisdiction of, 131–35 organization of, 131–35 as policy innovators, 143–44 procedures in, 136 reform of, 144–50 role in, 135–36
Cox, George B., 225
Creative accounting, 323
Crime. *See also* Courts; Cosa Nostra; Mafia; Police; Political corruption; Prison. by age, 365 control of, 365–78 drug abuse and, 363 fear of, 363–64 federal government and, 371–72 lower class, 359–63 organized, 452, 543–54, 458–67 poverty and, 359–60 punishment of, 379–83 by race, 365 rate of,

364–65 riots, 360–63 victims of, compensating, 381
Criminal code, 148
Cross-filing, 70, 71
Cuyahoga Metropolitan Housing Authority v. City of Cleveland, 446

Dahl, Robert, 201
Daley, Richard, 154–55, 228–29, 232, 262
Death and gift taxes, 308
Deckard, Barbara, 11
Decriminalization, 148–49
Delaware, 39, 41, 69
Democratic Party, 39, 60, 69, 86
Demonstration Cities and Metropolitan Development Act (1966), 178, 208, 415–16
Desegregation: schools, 400–406
Dill, Robert, 214
Dillon, John F., 181
Dillon's rule, 181, 182
Double-filing, 42–43
Double standard, 11
Drug abuse, 363
Durham, Israel W., 225
Dye, Thomas R., 45, 51, 87, 97, 110, 118, 123, 205

Economic Opportunity Act (1964), 189, 207, 208, 209
Economic Opportunity, Office of (OEO), U.S., 207
Education, 293–94, 295 cost of, 385, 387–88 desegregation issue in, 400–406 evaluation of, 395–96 federal aid to, 386–87 finance of, 385–92 governance of, 392–95 higher, 406–10 politics of, 392–95, 399–400 taxes and, 390
Elazar, Daniel J., 27, 31, 40
Election campaign, 43–44
Elections. *See also* Nominations nonpartisan vs. partisan, 211–14 off-year, 54. participation in, 53–61 regional differences and, 54
Election-day registration, 59
Elementary and Secondary Act (ESEA) (1965), 386
Environmental impact statements, 178
Environmental Protective Agency, U.S., 296
Equal Employment Opportunity Act (1972), 268
Equal Employment Opportunity Commission (EEOC), U.S., 12, 368
Equal Pay Act (1963), 12
Equal Rights Amendment (ERA), 13
Escobedo v. Illinois, 373
Ethics legislation in the states, 469
Exclusionary zoning, 423, 439, 440

Fair Labor Standards Act (1938), 12
Family Court, New York (State), 11
Federal Aid Highway Act (1973), 426, 427, 428
Federal Aid Road Act (1916), 426
Federal Bureau of Investigation, U.S., 371, 460 Uniform Crime Reports, 364
Federal Bureau of Prisons, U.S., 379
Federal Election Campaign Act, Amendments of 1974, 265
Federal Highway Act: (1944), 426 (1956), 425, 426
Federal Highway Trust Fund, 425, 427, 429

Federal Home Loan Bank Board, U.S., 441
Federal Housing Administration (FHA), U.S., 441
Federal Insurance Contributions Act (FICA), 338, 340
Federal Judicial Center, 376
Federal and National Mortgage Association, 442
Federalism. *See* Intergovernmental relations.
Federalist, The (Madison), 63, 174
Federally Impacted Areas Aid Program, 386
Federal Reserve System, 326
Feminism, 10–13. *See also* Sexism; Women
Fenton, John, 40
Ferrante, Rocco, 465
Finance, public: federal government role in, 388–97 grants-in-aid, 290, 294, 296, 297–98 revenue-sharing, 298–302 growth of, 286–88 indebtedness and, 219–27 intergovernmental relationships in, 288–302 regionalism and, 302–4 taxes and, 304–19 state judiciary system, 131
Fixed sentencing, 376–77
Florida, 11, 86, 87, 108, 238, 356–57
Flournoy, Houston, 125
Food and Nutrition Service, U.S., 341
Food Stamp Act (1964), 341
Food stamps, 341–42, 350, 352, 353–54, 355
Ford, Gerald, 125, 265, 321, 375
Ford Foundation, 253
Formula grant, 296–98
Friedman, Robert S., 430
Furman v. Georgia, 380

Gallup poll, 58, 59, 102, 270, 298, 363, 393, 396, 405
Gans, Herbert J., 419
Gardner, John, 78
Garn, Jake, 177
Garrity, W. Arthur, Jr., 405
General Accounting Office, U.S., 354, 372
General act charters, 181–82
Genovese, Vito, 464
Georgia, 4, 39, 50, 86
Gerrymandering, 85–86
Gideon v. Wainright, 373
Gilbert, Claire, 205
Gladwin, Thomas, 336
Godfather, The (Puzo), 460
Golden v. Planning Board of Ramapo, 423
Goldwater, Barry 232
Gompers, Samuel, 281
Government: corruption in, 7–8 public opinion and, 7–9 state and local, 10–16
Governor, 43, 116–29 career paths toward office of, 116 legislature and, 119–20 office of, 118 party affiliation and, 119 post-gubernatorial careers of, 117–18 powers of, 119–24 style of, 124–29 term of office of, 116–17 veto power of, 119
Graft, 452–58
Grand jury, 373–74
Grant, Daniel R., 183
Grant, Edward D., 37–38

Grants-in-aid system, 290, 297–98
block grants, 296, 301–2
categorical grants, 296 formula
grants, 296–98 goals of, 294, 296
problems of, 297–98 project
grants, 297
Green Edith, 208
Greer, Scott, 413
Griswold, "Fast Lucy," 5
Gun control, 369–70

Habeus corpus, 174
Hague, Frank, 466, 467
Hall, John Stuart, 390
Hamilton Alexander, 175
Harlow, LeRoy F., 472
Harper v. *Virginia State Board of Elections*, 50
Harris poll, 9, 21, 367, 369–70, 405, 467
Harvard University, 13–16
Hatch Act. *See* Political Activities Act (1939)
Hatcher, Richard, 452
Hawaii, 43, 124, 311
Hayakawa, S. I., 5
Hayes, Wayne, 91
Health, Education and Welfare (HEW) Department of, U.S., 352, 353, 354, 405, 457, 458
Health insurance, 339–40, 354. *See also* Medicaid; Medicare
Heinz, John, 246
Henry Patrick, 174
Higher education: cost of, 385, 407 faculty unionism in, 409–10 governance of, 403–9 public financing of, 407–408 public service and, 410
Hills v. *Gautreaux*, 446
Hispanics: education of, 403 poverty and, 335–36 unemployment and,335
Hochbert, Allen G., 454
Hofferbert, Richard, 45, 87
Home rule charters, 182
Hooks, Benjamin L., 361, 363
Hoover, J. Edgar, 371, 460
Housing: federal government and, 441–42, 445–47 future of, 448–50 middle-income, 441–43 for the poor, 433–48 public, 443–47 race discrimination, 433–41 state and local government and, 443–48 supply of, 448 zoning for, 439–41
Housing Act: (1937), 442 (1949), 207, 390, 442, 443 (1954), 442, 443 (1961), 442
Housing and Community Development Act: (1974), 209, 210, 290, 301, 442, 447 (1977), 209, 290, 443
Housing and Urban Development Act (1968), 442
Housing and Urban Development (HUD) Department of, U.S., 178, 179, 184, 209, 249, 302, 336, 415, 440, 442, 444, 445–46, 447, 449
Hughes, Richard J., 465
Hunter, Floyd, 201, 202
Hustle, Larimore, 6

Idaho, 181
Illinois, 39, 40, 124, 149
Income tax, 304–7
Indebtedness and public finance, 319–27
Indiana, 40, 131, 183, 376
Individual corruption, 453, 454, 458
Initiative petition, 37

Institution for Judicial Administration, 149
Intergovernmental Cooperation Act (1968), 178, 184
Intergovernmental relations, 170–97 Advisory Commission on, 177, 196, 197 between cities, 185–95 between states, 180–81 county-city, 193, 194, 195, 196, 197 federal-local, 176–77, 184–85, 199–223, 290 federal-state, 173–76, 195–97, 290 financial aspects of, 288–302 state-local, 181–83, 196, 290, 292–94
Intergovernmental Relations, Office of, 177
Interim committees, 81
International Association of Fire Fighters, 275
Iowa, 45, 97, 105
Item veto, 119

Jackson, Jessie, 362
James v. *Valtierra*, 446
Jefferson, Thomas, 41
Jewell, Malcolm, 87
Johnson, Lyndon Baines, 91, 207
Joint Center for Urban Studies, 449
Jones, E. Terrance, 369
Jones, Victor, 183
Jordan, Paul T., 466, 467
Judges. *See also* Courts, state; Judiciary.
administration of, 148 characteristics of, 138 party affiliation and, decisions of, 140–41 political ideologies and decisions of, 141–42 public policy and, 136–40 race and religious affiliation of and decisions of, 141 removal of, 146–48 roles of, 142–48 selection of, 145–46 terms of, 146–47
Judicial courts, 147
Judiciary, in state government, 131–36. *See also* Courts, state; Judges
Justice, Department of, U.S., 8, 185, 268, 375, 462
Justices of the peace, 132

Kansas, 45
Kaplan, Samuel, 184, 417, 455
Katzenbach, Nicholas, 176
Kaufman, Herbert, 204
Kelley, John, 225
Kelly, Red, 5
Kemeny, John, 250
Kennedy, Edward, 372
Kennedy, Robert F., 253
Kentucky, 50, 174
Kerner, Otto, 454
Key, V. O., Jr., 39, 44
King, Martin Luther, Jr., 228
Kinny, John B., 466
Koch, Edward, 325

Labor Statistics, U.S. Bureau of, 279, 367
Labor Unions and government. *See* Unionism in public employment
Lacey, Federick, 465
LaGuardia, Fiorello, 232
Lakewood Plan, 164–65, 186
Land use: control, 173 planning: pressure groups and 419–20 zoning and, 420–24

Law Enforcement Assistance Act (1965), 371
Law Enforcement Assistance Administration (LEAA), U.S., 371–72, 297
Lawyers in state and local government, 131
Lazy Lakes, Florida, 298
League of Cities, 177
Legislative council, 108
Legislative reference service, 108
Legislature: apportionment of, 82–88 bicameral vs. unicameral, 78 budget and, 122–23 committees of, 79–82 evaluation of, 109–14 functions of, 79 members of, 103–7 organization and procedures of, 79–82 powers of, 79, 90–91 professionalization of, 107–9 relationship with governors, 119–20 representation in, 83–84 rules of, 90–97 sessions of, 79 structure of, 78–79
Lieutenant governor, 43, 79
Lile, Stephen E., 310
Lindsay, John V., 232–34, 237, 282
Literacy test, 50–51, 52
Lobbies. *See* Pressure groups
Lobbying, 63, 72–75, 97–101 municipal governments and, 176–77 state governments and, 175–76
Local governments. *See also* County government; Municipal government; Regional councils; School districts; Special districts. consolidation of, 190–93 growth of, 170–73 jurisdictional disputes and, 187–95 planning by, 413 political alienation and, 188–89 public welfare and, 339, 342, 343, 356–57
Lockard, Duane, 67, 90, 91
Logue, Edward J., 253
Lomasney, "Czar" Martin, 225
Long, Huey P., Jr., 126–29, 142
Long-Term Care, Subcommittee on, Senate (U.S.), 458
Los Angeles county, 164–65
Lotteries, public, 310
Louisiana, 37
Lowi, Theodore J., 170, 246
Lundin, Frederick, 225
Lynd, Helen, 203
Lynd, Robert, 203

McCulloch v. *Maryland*, 175
McGovern, George, 235
McLaughlin, Hugh, 225
McManes, James, 225
Maddox, Lester G. 4, 262–63
Madison, James, 63, 174
Mafia, 452. *See also* Cosa Nostra. membership of, 459, 464–66
Mahan v. *Howell*, 85
Maine, 43, 45, 59, 66–68, 69, 81, 376
Management and Budget (OMB), Office of, 178, 416–17
Mapp v. *Ohio*, 373
Margiotta, Joseph M., 226–27
Marshall, John, 175
Marshall, Thurgood, 270
Maryland, 58, 412
Marx, Karl, 332
Mass transit, 427–31
Massachusetts, 73, 81, 98, 149
Massachusetts Institute of Technology, 13–16
Matthew effect, 83, 86
Mattis, Carl, 6

Maxwell, James A., 286
Mayor. *See also* City manager. powers of, 227 tenure of, 227, 229 veto power of, 227–38, 230–31
Mayor—council form of municipal government, 154–55, 156
Medicaid, 340, 343, 349, 350, 352, 354, 456–58
Medicare, 338, 354, 456–58
Merit system, civil service, 259–64, 283–84. *See also* Affirmative action, civil service; Unionism in public employment.
    definition of, 257 growth of, 257–58 performance standards and, 260–62
Metropolitan areas, 24–27, 168, 177–79 government of, 187–95 planning for, 415–16
Metropolitan district, 194
Michigan, 40, 69, 139, 149
Middle-income housing, 441–43
Milligan v. *Bradley*, 405
Millspaugh, Alfred, 366
Minnesota, 40, 58, 59, 78, 95, 183
Minorities, in state legislatures, 103–105
Minority groups: education of, 400–406 housing for, 433–41, 445–47 police and, 367–68 poverty and, 334–36 in public employment, 367–74
Miranda v. *Arizona*, 373
Mississippi, 52, 124, 149, 307
Missouri, 59, 71, 145, 182
Missouri Plan, 145, 146
Mobile, Alabama, 326
Model Cities program, 189, 208, 301
Mogulof, M. B., 179
Montana, 68–69, 181, 311
Morehouse, Sarah McCally, 118, 119, 124
Morrill Land Grant Act (1862), 407
Mortgage Disclosure Act (1975), 441
Moynihan, Daniel P., 347–48
Multimember district system, 83
Multipurpose districts, 166–67
Munger, Frank J., 110, 203–204
Municipal government, 13–16 consolidation of, 190–93 lobbying by, 176–77 political corruption and, 469, 472–73 science and technology in, 253–55 types of, 154–57
Murray, Douglas R., 370
Muskie, Edmond, 67

Nagel, Stuart, 141
National Academy of Public Administration, 356
National Advisory Commission on Civil Disorders, 237, 361
National Advisory Council on Criminal Justice Standards and Goals, 366
National Association for the Advancement of Colored People (NAACP), 64
National Association of Attorneys General, 176
National Association of Counties, 301
National Association of Home Builders, 450
National Association of Housing and Redevelopment Officials, 176
National Association of State Budget Officials, 176
National Center for State Courts, 149

National Commission on Urban Problems, 188, 190, 442
National Committee for an Effective Congress (NCEC), 44
National Conference of State Legislators, 301
National Defense Education Act (1958), 386
National Education Association (NEA), 274, 398–99, 400, 409
National Environmental Policy Act (1969), 178
National Governor's Association (NGA), 176, 301, 355
National Governor's Conference. *See* National Governor's Association (NGA)
National Housing Conference, 176
National Institute of Education, 387, 388, 389, 396
National Institutes of Health (NIH) U.S., 14, 15
National Labor Relations Act (1935), 281
National League of Cities, 176, 236, 301, 430
National Mass Transportation Assistance Act (1974), 427
National Municipal League, 156
National Organization of Women (NOW), 13
National Rehabilitation Association, 357
National Research Council, 24, 164, 168, 200
National Safety Council, 406
National School Lunch and Milk Program, 286
National Urban League, 335
National Women's Political Caucus (NWPC), 13
Nebraska, 36, 78, 95
Neighborhood, as community, 200
Neighborhood corporations, 189
Nevada, 4, 39, 78
New Hampshire 37, 43, 45, 78, 116, 310, 311
New Jersey, 43, 70, 82, 149
New Mexico, 60
New-town-in town redevelopment programs, 447
New York State, 43, 58, 79, 86, 87, 109, 124, 139, 310
Nie, Norman, 213
Nixon, Richard M., 177, 207, 337, 375, 446
No-growth zoning, 422–23
Nominations, 41. *See also* Elections
Nonpartisan elections, 211, 214
Nonvoters, 56–57
North Carolina, 98, 119
North Dakota, 45
Northeast-Midwest Economic Advancement Coalition, 302

Off-year elections, 54, 56, 57
Ohio, 40, 70, 97, 139
Oklahoma, 73
Old Age, Survivors, Disability, and Health Insurance (OASDHI), 338
Old Age Assistance, 340
Omnibus Crime Control and Safe Streets Act (1968), 371
"One-person, one-vote" principle, 83, 84
Open primary, 42
Oppenheimer, Robert, 14
Optional charter laws, 182
Oregon, 37, 59, 73, 98, 181, 307, 310, 311

Organized Crime Control Act (1970), 462
Oriental Exclusion Act, 5
Ostrom, Vincent, 170, 187

Paley, William, 455
Para-transit, 428–29
Parole, 376, 379
Partisan gerrymandering, 86
Party affiliation, 60 influence of, on governors, 119 judicial decisions and, 140–41 legislative process and, 95–97
Party finance, 39
Party organization, 29–40 control of, 40–41
Patronage, 122, 149
Patronage system, civil service, 262–64 definition of, 257
Patterson, Samuel C., 86, 87, 92
Peak, G. Wayne, 63
Pei, I. M., 253
Pendleton Act. *See* Civil Service Act (1883)
Pennsylvania, 108, 139
Pensions, 278
Periodic registration, 49
Permanent registration, 49
Perry, Williams, 147
Piele, Philip K., 390
Planners: education and experience of, 417–18 roles of, 418–19
Planning: federal government and, 415–16 housing, 433–49 land use, 419–24 politics of, 416–19 by state and local government, 412–15 transportation, 424–31
Planning boards, 413
Plea bargaining, 374–76
Plessy v. *Ferguson*, 401
Plunkitt, George Washington, 452–53
Plural executive plan. *See* Commission plan of county government
Plurality vote, 82, 86
Police, 365–72. *See also* Courts; Crime; Prison.
    alternatives to, 369–72 citizen attitudes toward, 367–68 civilian review boards and, 371 community relations, 367–68, 370–71 county sheriff, 365–66 effectiveness of, 368–69 salaries of, 367 selection and training of, 366–67
Police Foundation, 369
Political action and civil service, 264–65
Political Activities Act (1939), 208, 264–65
Political bosses. *See* Boss and machine, political
Political corruption. *See also* Crime. eradication of, 467–78 graft and, 452–58 kinds of, 452–54 organized crime and, 452, 453–54, 458–67
Political parties, states and, 38–47
Politics: humor in, 4–7 regionalism and, 27, 31
Poll taxes, 50, 52
Poor, the, 332, 333–34, 337 housing for, 433, 443–48 legal services for, 360 public welfare and, 351
Population: mobility of, 9 shift, 28–29 urban vs. suburban, 20–24
Port Authority of New York and New Jersey, 180, 194

Postcard registration, 58–59
Poverty. *See also* Aid to Families with
Dependent Children.
    crime and 359–60 definition of,
    332–33 race discrimination
    and, 334–36 unemployment
    and, 334, 335, 338–39
Powell, Lewis, Jr., 269, 270
Power structure, local, 201–223 in
    big cities, 202, 203–4 citizen
    participation in, 206–18 federal
    government and, 206–10 pluralist
    vs. elitist, 201–6 in small towns,
    203, 204
Presidential elections, 54, 56, 57
Presidential nominations, 42
Pressure groups, 63–76 alliances of,
    66–68 conflicting, 69–70 land use
    planning and, 419–20 legislative
    process and, 97–101 lobbying by,
    72–75 public interest and, 75–76,
    216–18 single-interest, 68–69
    sources of, 63–64, 66 types of,
    66–71
Primary system, direct, 39, 41–43
    closed, 42–43 open, 42
Prison. *See also* Courts; Crime;
Police.
    conditions in, 378 parole and,
    379 rehabilitation of criminals
    and, 378–79
Privacy and computers, 251–52
Progressive Reform Movement, 145
Progressive taxation, 310
Project 500, 453
Project grants, 297
Project Match 353, 356
Property tax, 207–8
Public administration: in standards
    of performance in, 358–64 in state
    government, 120–23 technology
    and, 246–55
Public assistance, 340–42
Public Choice Society, 187
Public housing, 443–47
Public interest groups, 216–18
Public opinion: crime and crime
    control, 363–64, 367–68, 369–70
    government and, 7–9 housing
    and, 438 New York City's
    indebtedness and, 326 state
    legislature and, 110, 113 taxes
    and, 316–19
Public opinion polls. *See also* Gallup
    polls; Harris poll, *et al.*
Public personnel administration,
    258–64
Public Services Job Program, 355
Public Technology, Inc. 253
Puzo, Mario, 460

Quill, Michael, 281–82
Quinn, Sally, 7
Quorum calls, 91
Quota systems in public
    employment, 268–69

Rabinowitz, Francine, 418
Race discrimination, 50–53, 85 in
    civil service, 267–74 education
    and, 400–406 housing and,
    433–41, 445–47 police and 367–68
    poverty and, 334–36 reverse,
    269–71 in urban politics, 235–36
    zoning and, 423
Race riots, 360–63
Racial gerrymandering, 86
Racial steering, 440
Rand Corporation, 184, 386
Ranney, David D., 47, 418

Rayburn, Sam, 91
Reagan, Ronald, 42, 235, 236
Reapportionment, 83–88
Recidivism rates, 377
Redistricting, 83–84
Redlining, 441
Referendum vote, 37
Regents of the University of California v.
    Bakke, 269
Regionalism, 27, 31, 90, 177–79
    elections and, 54 public finance
    and, 302–4
Regressive taxation, 310
Rehabilitation of criminals, 378–79,
    382–83
Reich, Charles, 332
Republican party, 60, 69, 86, 214–16
Revenues, public, 287, 288, 290,
    292–93 taxes, 304–19
Revenue sharing, 195–96, 298–302
    definition of, 298 use of, 299
Revenue Sharing, Office of, U.S.,
    298
Reverse discrimination, 269–71
Reynolds v. *Sims,* 84, 85
Rhode Island, 39, 116, 159, 340, 366
Ribicoff, Abraham, 100, 228
Ripley, Randall B., 246
Rockefeller, Nelson, 262–64
Rodriguez v. *San Antonio Independent*
    School District, 391
Roosevelt, Franklin Delano, 117,
    127, 177, 207
Roosevelt, Theodore, 176, 207
Rosenfeld v. *Southern Pacific Company,*
    12
Rural Area Development
    Committees, 415

Sale, Kirkpatrick, 28
Salerno, Ralph, 453
Sales tax, 306–7
Salisbury, Robert, 246
Samish, Artie, 70–71
Sayre, Wallace B., 204
Schick, Allen, 122
Schlesinger, Joseph, 117, 124
Schmandt, Henry J., 199
School(s). consolidation of, 388–90
    control of, 392–95 cost of, 387–88
    enrollment, 385, 388 finance,
    388–92
School boards, 392–95.
School busing, 402, 403–6
School districts, 167, 173, 193, 195,
    388–92
Schooler, Dean, Jr., 246
Schultze, Robert O., 203
Science (magazine), 14, 15
Science and technology, public policy
    and, 248–55
Secret ballot, 42
Securities and Exchange Commission
    (SEC), 325
Serrano v. *Priest,* 143, 390–91
Shade, William, L., 110
Shanker, Albert, 398
Shared tax, 290, 292
Sharkansky, Ira, 45, 118
Simonson, Archie, 148
Sindler, Alan P., 126
Single member district, plurality vote
    system, 83, 86
Smith, T. V., 114
Smith v. *Allwright,* 42
Smith-Hughes Vocational Education
    Act (1917), 386
Social insurance, 338–40
Social Security: cost of, 342–45
    public assistance and, 340–42

social insurance and, 338–40
Social Security Act (1935), 338, 349,
    353
Sorauf, Frank, 106
South Carolina, 39, 49, 105, 108, 124
Southern Pacific Railroad, 70
Southern Regional Council, 56
Special act charters, 181
Special courts, 135
Special districts, 167, 168, 173
Specialized local trial courts, 132
Special or select committees, 81
Spina, Dominic, 465
Standard City Planning Enabling Act
    (1928), 415
Standard Metropolitan Statistical
    Areas (SMSAs), 24, 154, 167, 194, 430
Standard State Zoning Enabling Act
    (1924), 173
Standing committees, 81
Stare decisis, 136
State appellate courts, 131–32
State government, 36–47
    constitutional change and, 36–38
    judiciary and, 131–50 lobbying by,
    175–76 political parties and, 38–47
    public administration and, 120–23
    public corruption and, 469, 470–71
    public housing and, 447 public
    welfare and, 339, 342, 343, 344,
    352–53, 356–57 science and
    technology in, 252 sexism and,
    10–13 structure of, 36 voting
    regulation by, 49–61
State and Local Fiscal Assistance Act
    (1972), 298
State political parties, 38–47
    competition among, 44–47
    functions of, 38, 41–44
    organization of, 39–40 regulation
    of, 39–40
State trial courts, 132
Staunton, Virginia, 156
Steggert, Frank X., 206, 223
Stephens, G. Ross, 196
Strikes, in public employment,
    279–83
Students. educational status of,
    395–96 violence and vandalism of,
    396–97
Suburbanization, 20–27, 359
Suburbs: growth of, 20–24 housing
    in, 439–40, 445–47 political
    bossism in, 226–27
Suffrage, 49–53. *See also* Voting
Sullivan, "Big Tim," 225
"Sunshine" laws, 469
Supplementary security income
    (SSI), assistance, 340–41, 345, 350,
    355
Supreme Court (State), 135, 136,
    139–40, 143–44
Supreme Court, U.S., 12, 50, 53,
    143, 181, 373, 380, 401, 423, 446
Swann v. *The Charlotte-Mecklenberg*
    Board of Education, 405
Systemic corruption, 453, 455,
    458–67

Taxes: coportate income, 308 death
    and gift, 308 education and, 390
    fairness and, 310, 311, 314–15
    general property, 307–8, 311,
    314–15 income, 304–6, 312–13
    progressive, 310 public opinion
    and, 316–19 regressive, 310 sales,
    306–7, 311 shared, 290, 292 use,
    308, 310

Task force on Land Use and Urban Growth, 173
Teachers. political action by 299–400 student violence against, 396 unionism and, 397–99
Technology. *See* Science and technology
Tennessee, 4, 43, 50, 70, 91
Texas, 42, 52, 58, 69, 82, 124, 183
Thompson, Frank J., 258, 260, 271, 272
Tiebout, Charles M., 187
Tompkins, John S., 453
Topeka v. *Brown*, 136
Towns and Townships, 165–66
Transferrable Development Rights (TDR), 421–22
Transportation, Department of, U.S., 184
Transportation planning, 424–31 federal government and, 425, 426, 427–28 highways, 424–27 mass transit, 427–29 policy, 430–31 politics of, 429–30
Trial courts: of general jurisdiction, 135 of limited jurisdiction, 132
Tunney, John V., 5
Tweed, William M., 225
Two-party system, 45

Unemployment, 334, 335, 338–39
Unemployment insurance, 338–39
Unicameralism vs. bicameralism, 78
Unionism in public employment, 274–84. *See also* Merit system, Civil service.
  collective bargaining, 277, 278–79 growth of, 274–77 strikes, 279–83 teachers, 397–400
United Automobile Workers, 69
United Farm Workers Association, 125
United Mine Workers Union, 54
United Nations Fund for Drug Abuse, 363
United Public Workers of America (CIO) v. *Mitchell*, 265
United States Bank, 175
U.S. Civil Service Commission v. *Letter Carriers*, 265
United States Conference of Mayors, 176, 301, 302
Unruk, Jesse, 119

Urban areas, growth and decline of, 20–24
Urban Coalition, 176
Urban county, 164–65
Urban Development Action Grant Program, 209
Urban homesteading, 447–48
Urban League, 207
Urban planning. *See* Planning
Urban Planning Assistance Act (1954), 178, 415
Urban Renewal program, 207
Urban/rural split, 88–90
Urban/suburban split, 88
Use of Land, 173
Use taxes, 308
Utah, 54, 98, 108

VanDalen, Hendrik, 66, 72
Van den Haag, Ernest, 382
Vare, Edwin H., 225
Vellucci, Al, 15
Verba, Sidney, 213
Vermont, 45, 116
Veto power, 119
Villani, Ralph, 465
Virginia, 39, 43, 52, 412
Voting. *See also* Suffrage. eligibility for, 50–51 federal government and 50, 51–53 in local elections, 210–16 participation in, 53–61 registration for, 49–51, 57–60 right of, 49–53 state regulation of, 49–61 the young and, 59–60
Voting Rights Act, 51 (1965), 53, 56 (1970), 51, 53, 59 (1975), 185

Wagner, Robert, 281–82, 325
Wagner Act (1935), 400
Wahlke, John C., 63, 64, 70, 92, 95, 98, 100, 101, 106
Walker, Jimmy, 234
Wallace, George, 42
Warren, Earl, 84
Warren, Michigan, 445
Warren, Robert, 187
Washington, D.C., 327, 402
Washington (State), 5, 181, 310
Water policies, public, 180–81
Weeks v. *Southern Bell Telephone and Telegraph Company*, 12

Welfare, public, 294, 295, 302. *See also specific programs.* controversial aspects of, 346–47, 352–53 cost of, 342–45 evaluation of, 351–54 federal government and, 349 growth of, 342–49 policy, 332 programs of, 338–42 recipients of, 332, 333–34, 337 reform of, 354–57 state and local governments and, 339, 342, 343, 344, 349–51
West Virginia, 54
Westberry v. *Sanders*, 84
Whelan, Thomas J., 466
White flight, 20–21, 173
White primary, 42
Who Governs (Dahl), 201
Wildavsky, Aaron, 204
Wilson, James Q., 181
Wisconsin, 39, 40, 41, 59, 108, 277, 308
Women. *See also* Feminism discrimination against, 10–13 in local government, 220 in state legislatures, 104 in public employment, 271, 273 status of, 11–12
Women's liberation movement. *See* Feminism
Wood, Robert C., 189, 215
Wyoming, 45

Ylvisaker, Paul N., 472
Yorty, Sam, 235–36
Youth Employment and Demonstration Projects Act (1977), 339

Zeigler, Harmon, 63, 64, 66, 72, 73, 74, 75, 98
Zimmerman, Joseph, 182
Zink, Harold, 225, 228
Zisk, Betty A., 218, 223
Zoning, 420–24 exclusionary, 439–40 no growth, 422–23 political corruption in, 455–56 racial segregation and, 423, 439–40 statewide, 423–24 transferrable development rights and 421–22
Zwillman, Abner, 464